THEOLOGICALLY ENGAGED ANTHROPOLOGY

Theologically Engaged Anthropology

Edited by
J. DERRICK LEMONS

OXFORD
UNIVERSITY PRESS

OXFORD
UNIVERSITY PRESS

Great Clarendon Street, Oxford, OX2 6DP,
United Kingdom

Oxford University Press is a department of the University of Oxford.
It furthers the University's objective of excellence in research, scholarship,
and education by publishing worldwide. Oxford is a registered trade mark of
Oxford University Press in the UK and in certain other countries

Published in the United States of America by Oxford University Press
198 Madison Avenue, New York, NY 10016, United States of America

British Library Cataloguing in Publication Data

Data available

Library of Congress Control Number: 2018932143

ISBN 978-0-19-879785-2

Contents

List of Contributors

Nicholas Adams is Professor of Philosophical Theology at the University of Birmingham.

Jon Bialecki is Honorary Fellow of Social Anthropology at the University of Edinburgh.

James S. Bielo is Assistant Professor of Anthropology at Miami University, Ohio.

Fenella Cannell is Lecturer in Anthropology at the London School of Economics.

Francis X. Clooney, SJ is Parkman Professor of Divinity and Professor of Comparative Theology at Harvard University.

Sarah Coakley is Norris-Hulse Professor of Divinity and Fellow of Murray Edwards College, Cambridge.

Douglas J. Davies is Professor in the Study of Religion at the University of Durham.

Khaled Furani is Associate Professor at Tel Aviv University.

Naomi Haynes is Chancellor's Fellow in Social Anthropology at the University of Edinburgh.

Brian M. Howell is Professor of Anthropology at Wheaton College.

Timothy Jenkins is Reader in Anthropology and Religion at Jesus College, Cambridge.

Daniel J. King is a Faculty Member at Clapham School, Wheaton, IL.

Paul Kollman is Associate Professor of Theology and Executive Director of the Center for Social Concerns at the University of Notre Dame.

Timothy Larsen is McManis Professor of Christian Thought at Wheaton College.

J. Derrick Lemons is Assistant Professor of Religion at the University of Georgia.

Alister E. McGrath is Andreas Idreos Professor of Science and Religion at Harris Manchester College, Oxford.

Martyn Percy is Dean of Christ Church, Oxford.

Joel Robbins is Sigrid Rausing Professor of Social Anthropology at Trinity College, Cambridge.

Michael A. Rynkiewich is Professor of Anthropology at Asbury Theological Seminary.

Don Seeman is Associate Professor at Emory University.

Joseph Webster is Lecturer in Anthropology at Queen's University Belfast.

Introduction

Theologically Engaged Anthropology

J. Derrick Lemons

Joel Robbins suggests that the relationship between theology and anthropology is awkward. This awkwardness has led most anthropologists to ignore engaging theology as a discipline. Anthropologists have studied religion through the lenses of anthropological theories such as structural functionalism, interpretivism, and structuralism. However, many anthropologists are reluctant to theorize using theology and to consider theology's impact on religion. Robbins calls anthropologists to move beyond treating theology with suspicion and suggests that theology can give anthropologists a deeper understanding of religion.[1] There is a critical need for theologians and anthropologists to work together to create materials that anthropologists can use to enhance their understanding of how theology is done and how it can be used to develop a deeper understanding of human religion. This book seeks to answer the central question, "What can theology contribute to cultural anthropology?" without forgetting the equally important question, "What can anthropology contribute to theology?"

My interest in engaging theology grows out of my research of a church renewal movement within Protestant American churches: the missional church movement. The missional church movement pivots on the statement that a church in mission is being sent out and called beyond to interact with the outside culture, share Christ, and serve the community.[2] In the ethnographic process, I interact with Karl Barth's theology of the *Missio Dei*

---

[1] Joel Robbins, "Anthropology and Theology: An Awkward Relationship?" *Anthropological Quarterly* 79/2 (2006): 286, 292–3.

[2] Lois Barrett et al., *Treasure in Clay Jars: Patterns of Missional Faithfulness* (Grand Rapids, MI: Eerdmans, 2004), x; Stephen B. Bevans and Roger P. Schroeder, *Constants in Context: A Theology of Mission for Today* (New York: Orbis Books, 2004), 8–9.

and Lesslie Newbigin's theology of the gospel within pluralistic societies. These theologies were developed by academic and practical theologians, implemented by local church pastors, and eventually embraced by several Protestant denominations—all of which were dispersed around the world. Using these theological perspectives, I discovered that people within the missional church movement were heavily influenced by a theological call to evangelize outside the walls of the church. The challenge for me was to decide what to do analytically with the importance of these theologies to the people I studied.

While my questions about what to do with theology in my own fieldwork may be considered the genesis of this project, the project became a reality because of several interactions that took place at the 2013 annual meeting of the American Anthropological Association in Chicago, Illinois. First, I organized a panel that introduced me to other scholars who were interested in the role of religious identity in fieldwork and questions of how anthropologists should approach the divergence between belief and disbelief in research. For that panel, I wrote a paper that described how theology helped me to understand better another anthropological study of mine focused on understanding the actions of American Pentecostal emergency room doctors who worked in Haiti during the relief efforts following Haiti's 2010 earthquake. These doctors volunteered to use their professional skills as physicians and their spiritual gift of exorcising demons, and I analyzed their efforts through the lens of the theology of their home church. After the panel concluded, I hurried to the business meeting of the Society for the Anthropology of Religion, so I could meet Joel Robbins in person for the first time. Joel was very gracious and surprised me by asking what I was working on. Because I just had walked over from my panel where I discussed theology and anthropology, my first thought was to share about my paper. Joel surprised me again when he handed me his business card and asked me to email my paper to him because he was very interested in the awkward relationship between theology and anthropology. After the Society for the Anthropology of Religion's business meeting, I attended a gathering of Christian anthropologists led by Brian Howell. During the time designated for introductions and announcements, Paul Wason, the Vice President for Life Sciences and Genetics at the John Templeton Foundation, mentioned that he would like to talk to anyone who was interested in developing a grant considering anthropology and theology. Inspired by my own research interests and my conversation with Robbins, I decided to talk with Paul after the meeting.

Ultimately, the project was awarded funding from the John Templeton Foundation to develop frameworks for a theologically engaged anthropology. To develop these frameworks, theologians and anthropologists were gathered for two mini-conferences in Atlanta, Georgia, in September 2015 and in

Cambridge, England, in February 2016. For the better part of six days, the following scholars presented essays, debated, and enjoyed meals together: Alister McGrath, University of Oxford; Francis X. Clooney, SJ, Harvard University; Joel Robbins, University of Cambridge; Derrick Lemons, University of Georgia; Don Seeman, Emory University; Brian Howell, Wheaton College; Paul Kollman, University of Notre Dame; Jon Bialecki, University of Edinburgh; Timothy Larsen, Wheaton College; Michael Rynkiewich, Asbury Theological Seminary; James Bielo, Miami University, Ohio; Khaled Furani, Tel Aviv University; Sarah Coakley, University of Cambridge; Fenella Cannell, London School of Economics and Political Science; Naomi Haynes, University of Edinburgh; Martyn Percy, University of Oxford; Tim Jenkins, University of Cambridge; Nicholas Adams, University of Birmingham; and Joe Webster, Queen's University Belfast. In an attempt to summarize the meetings, Frances X. Clooney said, "This conversation attempts to rectify a historical split between theology and anthropology and take advantage of the obvious commonalties, in a sense rectifying an old divorce that seems now to be ready to be overcome." Joel Robbins summarized the conferences in the following way: "We were mapping uncharted territory, and we did a good job of tracing the key routes through it. We realized how hard it is to define theology from an anthropological point of view. We also learned how anthropologists can approach theology and theologians from a lot of different directions: as a topic whose role in society they can study anthropologically, as fellow academics with whom they can debate, and as a form of thought that can transform their own theoretical thinking." These meetings started a long overdue conversation about the relationship between theology and cultural anthropology.

*   *   *

In an effort to connect broadly the essays from this book with future research, I chose the title "theologically engaged anthropology" to bracket the topic. My hope is that, under this name, scholars will push the boundaries of anthropology and theology and attempt to connect them. In the following, I will consider individually the terms *theology*, *engagement*, and *anthropology* and conclude with ethnographic examples produced from the synergistic combination of *theologically engaged anthropology* to provide an overview of the essays and a starting point for future research.

THEOLOGY

Defining theology is a challenging task. Describing theology as "faith seeking understanding" provides a basic definition, but many theologians view this definition as too simplistic.[3] Even so, it offers a good starting place for anthropologists who are novices at theology. The term *faith* suggests theology is developed from within a religious community of the faithful to provide an emic understanding of the cosmos, the ultimate meaning of things and their God. The term *seeking* suggests that theology is not a static body of knowledge but an area of study that changes over time and space. Timothy Jenkins underscores in this volume the corrective nature of theology by reminding anthropologists that "theological texts are not description, but acts of repair."[4] In other words, anthropologists should understand that "theological critique is not usually written for the pleasure of philosophers, but to rectify specific forms of practical life."[5] Finally, the term *understanding* means that the faithful believe that there is more to know and experience than is known and experienced at present. Viewing theology as faith seeking understanding provides anthropologists an opportunity to learn from an emic perspective about religious beliefs that change over time and space.

The work of theologians Sarah Coakley and Kathryn Tanner emphasizes that theology is best defined and understood within the culture that produces it. Stephen Bevans views all theology as contextual and says, "Theology that is contextual realizes that culture, history, contemporary thought forms, and so forth are to be considered, along with scripture and tradition, as valid sources for theological expression."[6] Understanding theology as rooted in humanity's quest to seek a contextual understanding about God provides common ground for anthropologists and theologians to begin a dialogue. Naomi Haynes offers a promising definition of theology in this volume to begin this dialogue. She defines theology "as a particular kind of reflexive action, aimed at understanding who God is, how he works in the world, how people ought to relate to God, and what they can expect from him."[7] Her definition is very accessible to anthropologists, but it also pushes theologians to consider the dynamic cultural contestation within all theological discourse.

Brian Howell argues in this volume that forms of theology most closely rooted in a specific confessing community are most helpful to anthropologists because of the interest of many anthropologists in connecting ethnography with a local culture.[8] Martyn Percy and Fenella Cannell support Howell's claims by reminding us that implicit forms of theology found in religious communities are often neglected but tremendously helpful to understand the spectrum between belief and practice and the building blocks for religion.[9] On the other hand, Nicholas Adams reminds us that theology is most easily

---

[3] Daniel L. Migliore, *Faith Seeking Understanding: An Introduction to Christian Theology*, 3rd edn (Grand Rapids, MI: Eerdmans, 2014), 2.
[4] Timothy Jenkins, Chapter 6, 106.   [5] Jenkins, Chapter 6, 119.
[6] Stephen Bevans, *Models of Contextual Theology* (New York: Orbis Books, 1992), 4.
[7] Naomi Haynes, Chapter 15, 267.   [8] Brian M. Howell, Chapter 2.
[9] Martyn Percy, Chapter 17; Fenella Cannell, Chapter 14.

concerned with the vast or cosmological.[10] While anthropologists can most easily engage with implicit theology, Robbins pushes anthropologists to seek theological opportunities that force them to consider the whole spectrum between the implicit and the cosmological.

ENGAGEMENT

Authors in this book agree that theologians and anthropologists benefit from working together. The proposals for how they should work together, by and large, fall under two frameworks of engagement—stratified and transformational. The stratified framework encourages anthropologists and theologians to dialogue around common religious topics or problems with the understanding that "a complex reality, such as religion, will have multiple layers or strata, each of which demands to be investigated by a research method appropriate for that stratum."[11] Alister McGrath thinks that "theology and anthropology can engage in a principled, informed, and respectful dialogue, in which neither discipline is required to surrender its integrity or distinctiveness, while the same time recognizing its limits and being open to the possibility of being enriched by disciplines that transcend those boundaries."[12] While all of my collaborators would agree that a theologically engaged anthropology expands the partial perspectives of each discipline, some of my collaborators believe "an important caveat should be heeded, theology should not seek to become anthropology and anthropology should not seek to become theology in terms of either method or content.... Neither anthropology nor theology should become less itself but, rather, more itself in a dynamic interchange. Each discipline retains its own autonomy and language and yet draws knowledge and insight from the other."[13] The advantage of a stratified framework is that a thicker ethnographic description emerges and illuminates previously shadowed motivations for Christians to live in a certain way. This stratified type of engagement is very popular for scholars involved in the religion and science debate and is an excellent example for theologians and anthropologists who are beginning to explore the fruitfulness of a theologically engaged anthropology. Furthermore, this is the least controversial way to move forward.

The second type of engagement between anthropology and theology is transformational and is defined as a deep engagement in which theological

---

[10] Nicholas Adams, Chapter 10.   [11] Alister E. McGrath, Chapter 7, 131.
[12] McGrath, Chapter 7, 124.
[13] Todd Salzman and Michael Lawler, "Theology, Science and Sexual Anthropologies: An Investigation," *Louvain Studies* 35/1–2 (2011): 71–2.

and anthropological questions, problems, issues, or topics pass through a process of mutual collaboration and new insights emerge. This transformative type of engagement is more radical but offers real opportunities for productive exchange. In fact, as Robbins says, "the time is right for anthropologists, more and more interested in rendering frank judgments, to come into dialogue with theologians about the role of judgment in their tradition and the ways its practice is best cultivated and carried out."[14] Furthermore, Robbins suggests that anthropologists "can learn from theology about responsible ways of making any kind of judgments" and "theologians might also learn from anthropologists about the depth and complexity of the kinds of cultural expressions they are often called upon to judge."[15] Robbins' observations result in a transformed anthropology and theology in that the boundaries between each discipline are not so neatly maintained. This freedom is exemplified by Furani's, Jenkins', and Robbins' essays in this book. Of course, this type of engagement runs the risk that anthropologists and theologians feel out of step with their peers because the boundaries between the two disciplines are so entrenched. That being said, a moment just shy of a collective effervescence was experienced at a meeting of my collaborators at Trinity College, University of Cambridge, when Jenkins pronounced that a transformative engagement holds the most interesting possibilities.

ANTHROPOLOGY

Like theology, the term *anthropology* is challenging to define. Defining anthropology as the study of humankind is doing little more than translating the word. On the whole, the essays generated by this project did little to define anthropology directly. One reason for this omission is the wording of our central question: "What can theology contribute to anthropology?" The question seems only to emphasize the need to justify the use of theology. However, we need to consider ways in which we justify the use of anthropology, too. To refocus our efforts, perhaps the central question should be asked in a different way: "What can anthropology contribute to theology?" Asking both questions together will help anthropologists overcome many of the inherent idols within anthropology that Khaled Furani critiques in his essay.

The one direct definition came from McGrath: "identify patterns of human behavior through empirical methods, which it seeks to group and, secondarily, to explain or predict."[16] While direct definitions of anthropology are largely

---

[14] Joel Robbins, Chapter 13, 241.   [15] Robbins, Chapter 13, 242.
[16] McGrath, Chapter 7, 126.

missing, indirectly several of the essays discuss anthropology. For example, Robbins writes, "anthropology at its best looks at how the different parts of a cultural formation are tied together in knots that often are in fact quite intricate, and anthropologists insist that when one does so none of the parts will appear to be freakish or bluntly irrational, nor will they evidence the simple ignorance of those who live in light of them."[17] Another observation about the implied definition of anthropology from the essays and the discussions at the mini-conferences is that the foundational tenet for anthropologists of cultural relativism is rarely questioned. In fact, a reflexive relativism was encouraged by most of the authors in order to question the secular underpinnings of anthropology and the marginalization of theology. More specifically, the authors question the type of secular anthropology that would deem theology as an unfit collaborative discipline. In substance, anthropologists should be open to engagement with a committed discipline such as theology. In the end, anthropology should be defined as an academic discipline that analyzes cultures and uses all resources available, including theology, to do more thorough analysis.

THEOLOGICALLY ENGAGED ANTHROPOLOGY

A theologically engaged anthropology is a synergistic combination filled with tensions. You will notice tensions among essays, a few suggested frameworks on which to build a theologically engaged anthropology, and a heavy focus on theologies of Christianity. An example of tension would be that Jon Bialecki, Timothy Larsen, Daniel J. King, and Khaled Furani are at odds about the usefulness of aligning theology and anthropology through origins-based genealogical accounts. However, the creative tensions among the essays are very important to recognize and provide clues to important areas for future research. In reference to the focus on Christian theology, the reason for this focus is that most of the scholars involved in this project work directly with Christianity. In the planning, some thought was given to the need for this first project to work in a religion with a perceived demand for interaction at this time—partly fostered by the recent rise of the anthropology of Christianity[18]— and to gather scholars around one religion to provide common ground for discussion. However, Clooney makes clear that solely equating theology with

---

[17] Robbins, Chapter 13, 235.
[18] For background read Joel Robbins and Naomi Haynes (eds), *The Anthropology of Christianity: Unity, Diversity, New Directions*, Special Issue of *Current Anthropology* 55/S10 (2014): S155–S366.

Christian theology needlessly limits the opportunities for theological engagement across religious traditions.

Generally speaking, the essays are ordered from the more theoretical to the more ethnographic. Chapters 14 through 19 are especially helpful in that they provide ethnographic examples of various ways theologians and anthropologists are experimenting with a theologically engaged anthropology. Of note are the ways that theologians ground theology within lived experience and the ways anthropologists allowed theology to provide another lens through which to view their ethnographic research. In the end both examples provide a deeper understanding of religion. The following abstracts provide an overview of each chapter.

CHAPTER 1—NEW INSIGHTS FROM AN OLD DIALOGUE PARTNER

J. Derrick Lemons argues that a growing number of anthropologists are ready to engage theology but struggle to find a framework that supports this type of inquiry. His essay examines the creative tension and history between anthropology and theology and contends that generating a reflexive theologically engaged anthropology improves anthropological research. To support his thesis, he provides an example from his fieldwork involving American evangelicals who use missional church theology to inform their lived religious experience.

CHAPTER 2—WHICH THEOLOGY FOR ANTHROPOLOGY? TYPES OF THEOLOGY FOR ANTHROPOLOGICAL ENGAGEMENT

Brian M. Howell suggests that defining the concept of theology may seem more suited for the professional theologian rather than the anthropologist, yet it may be the anthropologist who is best positioned to investigate theology in order to discover what conversations can be profitably brought into the work of anthropology. His essay begins with a typology of theology first suggested by Hans Frei in the latter part of the twentieth century. The typology serves to compare the present project to one undertaken recently by anthropologists engaging philosophy. Finally, the essay presents an ethnographic vignette from fieldwork in the Philippines to illustrate how this particular understanding of philosophy–theology may serve to answer anthropological puzzles.

CHAPTER 3—THE DEPENDENCE OF SOCIOCULTURAL ANTHROPOLOGY ON THEOLOGICAL ANTHROPOLOGY

Timothy Larsen and Daniel J. King argue that classic Christian theological anthropology has emphasized that all human beings are part of the one human family descending from Adam and Eve, created in the image of God, yet fallen and sinful. These beliefs have been traditionally expounded with reference to Genesis 1–3. Sociocultural anthropologists, in contrast, have often prided themselves on shedding Christian beliefs. The Genesis narrative, in particular, has been the object of attacks. Nevertheless, when some nineteenth-century freethinking anthropologists took this way of thinking to the next step and argued that belief in the monogenesis of the human race was just the result of the influence of an erroneous Judeo-Christian myth, the discipline weeded such thinking out of its midst. Thus, even as it sidelined Christianity, orthodox anthropology from the founding of the discipline to the present has affirmed the doctrine of the psychic unity of humankind. This essay argues that this foundational conviction of anthropology is informed by Christian thought.

CHAPTER 4—THEOLOGY REVEALING THE HĀJIBS OF ANTHROPOLOGY

Khaled Furani proposes ways in which theology could promote a critique of idolatries in modern anthropology. It culls resources for this undertaking by scouring Nietzsche's arguments against modernity. Nietzsche enables a vision of modern anthropology as symptomatic of God's death in the West, thus inducing questions about the ways its adoration of idols may inhibit a truer inquiry. He finds examples to this effect in anthropology's engagement with the nation state, humanism, and the constitutive concept of culture. He then speculates as to how a theological repudiation of anthropology's idols could support a conceptual and institutional renewal going far beyond enhancing its study of religion. For instance, anthropology awakened by theistic rationality could adequately engage with the concept of tradition. It could also forge a new grammar of connectivity within the discipline as well as within the disciplinary arrangements of the modern university.

CHAPTER 5—WHAT CAN THEOLOGY CONTRIBUTE TO CULTURAL ANTHROPOLOGY?

Paul Kollman, after considering his personal history engaging theology and anthropology, examines the consequences of Robbins' influential 2006 article on the disciplines' relationship. Paul thinks that Robbins' decision to focus on theologian John Milbank to make the case unintentionally discouraged consideration of other theologians who draw upon anthropological theory. Inspired by his own research on missionary activity in Africa and how theological understanding yielded insights into it, he turns to two frameworks that consider the outcomes of Christian missionary practices: anthropological writings by Kenelm Burridge and the theological essays of Andrew Walls. Both consider the dialectical relationship between the Christian message that missionaries bring and the reception of that message by those evangelized. He explores the similarities and differences between their two approaches and then considers what this comparison reveals about the potential mutual fruitfulness of bringing theology to bear on anthropological study.

CHAPTER 6—THEOLOGY'S CONTRIBUTION TO ANTHROPOLOGICAL UNDERSTANDING IN T. M. LUHRMANN'S *WHEN GOD TALKS BACK*

Timothy Jenkins offers a particular example of the contribution theology might make to anthropology by taking T. M. Luhrmann's ethnography of evangelical Christian prayer practices, *When God Talks Back* (2012), as its focus. The argument has two aspects: first that theological criticism of notions of religious experience need to be taken seriously and will contribute to the anthropological description and, second, that something is missing from the anthropological description offered because certain theological ideas—in this case, principally, the direction of travel of the soul with respect to God—are underplayed. The case study illustrates the complexities we may expect from a project of the kind pursued in this volume.

CHAPTER 7—NARRATIVES OF SIGNIFICANCE: REFLECTIONS ON THE ENGAGEMENT OF ANTHROPOLOGY AND CHRISTIAN THEOLOGY

Alister E. McGrath explains that narratives are important both to anthropology and theology. His chapter initially considers the general role that narratives play in an anthropological account of the construction of meaning and social identity before moving on to consider how certain narratives acquire a sacred status. This cultural analysis is then interpreted theologically as a first step in developing a theologically engaged anthropology of narrative.

Although he interacts with leading voices in contemporary theological reflection, many of the more interesting theological engagements with the importance of narrative originate from literary circles, and he proposes to incorporate these in his reflections, considering how narratives can generate and sustain a sense of the sacred, provide an imaginative resource for theological reflection, and develop a framework of meaning. Finally, the manner in which such a theological framing of the role and significance of narratives may illuminate anthropological approaches is considered.

CHAPTER 8—AN ANTHROPOLOGIST IS LISTENING: A REPLY TO ETHNOGRAPHIC THEOLOGY

James S. Bielo focuses on a commitment that has been gaining force among practical theologians and Christian ethicists since the early 2000s. The commitment is that ethnographic fieldwork can be used to generate theological reflection and knowledge. He hopes to encourage a substantive shift—from a one-way engagement into an actual and generative dialogue between ethnographic theologians and anthropological ethnographers. The animating question is this: What does each dialogue partner—anthropology and theology—stand to gain from such an open exchange about ethnography? To address this question, he argues that ethnographic theologians can work with a more diverse conception of ethnography while anthropological ethnographers can learn how theologians engage normativity in their work. He concludes by reflecting on genres of ethnographic writing as an opportunity for dialogue.

CHAPTER 9—ANTHROPOLOGY, THEOLOGY, AND THE PROBLEM OF INCOMMENSURABILITY

Jon Bialecki argues that anthropologists and theologians cannot speak about the contributions that theology could make to anthropology without first discussing the relationship between the two disciplines. Rejecting both genealogical accounts and universalist narratives that deny the historical and institutional specificity of either discipline, he sees theology, anthropology, and the people about whom they write as all being engaged in the same work. They are all struggling with immanent and virtual problems in the sense of the word used by Gilles Deleuze. This means rejecting understandings of anthropology and theology as second-order accounts, however, and seeing theological and anthropological thought as just other ways of thinking the problem through, albeit ways that often more clearly index the underlying problem. Finally, he illustrates this argument by showing similarities in anthropological, theological, new atheist, and Mormon attempts to grasp what may be the twenty-first century's greatest challenge: an incipient technical possibility of transcending our humanity.

CHAPTER 10—SUPERSTITION AND ENLIGHTENMENT: ENGAGEMENTS BETWEEN THEOLOGY AND ANTHROPOLOGY

Nicholas Adams first engages two cases where anthropologists draw on the work of theologians and then develops a normative account of the relation between the two disciplines via a third—philosophy—by drawing attention to questions of scale in these engagements. The second part considers, briefly, the distinctive approach to time that theological work often articulates in its concern with the past for the sake of the future. This construct can be presented as an ideal scheme. The past is a resource for reparative thinking; the present is an abundance of signs of suffering calling for repair; the future is imagined as a life where suffering has been healed. He interprets Robbins' and Jenkins' interest in theologians' work in the light of this approach to time, suggesting that both are concerned with change but in different ways.

CHAPTER 11—ANTHROPOLOGY AND THEOLOGY: FUGUES OF THOUGHT AND ACTION

Douglas J. Davies writes a tripartite chapter in the hope that attention will be fixed on human creativity as it engages diverse themes while striving for satisfying resolutions of disciplinary tensions between anthropology and theology even if these are not achieved. The first part, entitled "Intrapersonal and Interpersonal Dialogue," is heavily autobiographical, and he trusts that readers will accept his offering as its own kind of case study of reflexivity, excusing its indulgence in biographical reflection on account of its intention to pinpoint the very particular and contextual nature of idea development. The second part, headed "Further Conversation Pieces," picks up just such ideas open to anthropological–theological conversation, including a cautionary gloss on the over-easy use of *anthropology* and *theology* as discrete terms. The third and final part, described as "Disciplinary Quandaries," takes some of these formal classifications of disciplines further and also brings together some personal and institutional factors surrounding both anthropological and theological practice.

CHAPTER 12—ATHENS ENGAGING JERUSALEM

Michael A. Rynkiewich presents a case in which the emergence of the individual is often credited to theological anthropology filtered through the Enlightenment. This concept has been reshaped with secular meaning, yet critical theological thinking continues to enhance our understanding of the person. Pannenberg's *exocentricism* situates the formation of the person in relationship to the Other. Moltmann's work on the fragmented self confirms the possibility of change, offering hope to a discipline where it is sadly lacking. The embodiment of the soul in a non-dualistic, non-reductionist theology recovers the Eastern Church Fathers, particularly Maximus the Confessor, in their understanding of the goal of participation in God through participation in the Other.

CHAPTER 13—WORLD CHRISTIANITY AND THE REORGANIZATION OF DISCIPLINES: ON THE EMERGING DIALOGUE BETWEEN ANTHROPOLOGY AND THEOLOGY

Joel Robbins reviews recent changes in anthropology and theology to suggest that these changes bring them to a point where, in fact, their paths are ready to cross. The change in anthropology he considers is the unexpectedly rapid rise of what is called the anthropology of Christianity. More specifically, he examines the prosperity gospel, in which believers are convinced that God wants health and wealth for them in this world and overwhelmingly stress these themes in their worship. Scholars in the Western academy, at least, tend to find this kind of Christianity hard to assimilate to their more general understandings of the faith, or at least to their favorite understandings. Robbins believes a closer look at how this kind of Christianity trips up both theologians and anthropologists reveals places where both disciplines would be open to help from each other, the provision of which might lay the basis for a new kind of transformative dialogue.

CHAPTER 14—LATTER-DAY SAINTS AND THE PROBLEM OF THEOLOGY

Fenella Cannell's research reveals that contemporary American Latter-Day Saints lead lives shaped by a conscious and often partially conflicted relationship to the authoritative teachings of their church hierarchy. This doctrine represents the power of present-day revelation channeled through the current Prophet; however, many Latter-Day Saints believe that prophets may also make human mistakes. For an important minority, including some feminist intellectuals, these tensions have been experienced as an attempt to prohibit the development of theology. The problematic status of "Mormon theology" may be one reason why many church members seek to reconcile doctrine with personal experience through the means of narrative and auto-biography, producing a culture of Mormon stories. This chapter considers how some Mormon feminist excommunicates attempted to project religious authenticity against the grain of the institution. Mormon ethnography thus provides an instance of the anthropological approach to theology as a lived category, including the contestation of the space for theology itself.

CHAPTER 15—THEOLOGY ON THE GROUND

Naomi Haynes provides an ethnographic exploration of theology *on the ground*, focusing on Pentecostal Christians on the Zambian Copperbelt. For Copperbelt Pentecostals, theology means drawing analogies between their experience and the stories recorded in the Bible. Through these analogies, believers insert themselves into the narrative of Scripture in an effort to change their personal circumstances. This analogical work has visible social effects because it positions people on different sides of the biblical narrative. While interpreting these effects simply in political terms would be easy, she argues that Pentecostal theology is more than just a struggle for power because the theological efforts of her informants represent conduits for divine action. The ethnographic study of Pentecostal theology, therefore, addresses one of the most vexing problems in the anthropology of religion—namely, how to write God into our analysis.

CHAPTER 16—COMPARATIVE THEOLOGY: WRITING BETWEEN WORLDS OF MEANING

Francis X. Clooney, SJ, focuses on comparative theology, a form of tradition-grounded theological practice that learns deeply and effectively from another religious tradition or traditions. Even solidly textual work—translations, the study of scholastic systems, the tracing of lines of thought in commentaries, the decipherment of ritual and moral codes—proceeds as transformative learning indebted to the religious Other. It is a matter of engaged, empathetic learning that allows one to see inside that other tradition, even while the learning, its fruits, and the person of the comparativist remain grounded in a home tradition. For this complex interreligious learning to flourish, certain essential virtues are valued: humility, conviction, interconnection, empathy, generosity, imagination, risk-taking, and patience with ambiguity. This comparative theological learning exists in the liminal space between traditions, yet the comparative theologian still intends to return home, even if irrevocably changed by the journey abroad. Comparative theology thus cultivates virtues operative in anthropological research distinguished by empathetic dwelling in and with the Other.

CHAPTER 17—PASSIONATE COOLNESS: EXPLORING MOOD AND CHARACTER IN ECCLESIAL POLITY

Martyn Percy explores and analyzes the ecclesial identity of a local parish church in a rural context. Deploying the concept of implicit theology, a subgenre of ethnographic theology, he argues that the character of the church is composed through core and cherished values that are seldom explicitly articulated. What emerges from the study is that the character of rural Anglicanism in the Church of England can be understood as primarily but not exclusively temperate, mild, aesthetic, and rational. Moreover, there may be a link between the grammar and timbre of worship and the kind of God individuals and congregations subsequently believe they experience. Percy also notes a broader sociological significance of selecting to study a rural church. That said, this study pointedly avoids reductionism, but it does recognize the formation of an alloy in need of attention in the emergent social and theological construction of reality.

CHAPTER 18—THE EXCLUSIVE BRETHREN "DOCTRINE OF SEPARATION": AN ANTHROPOLOGY OF THEOLOGY

Joseph Webster draws inspiration from Webb Keane's (2014) suggestion that "we shouldn't decide in advance what ethics will look like,"[19] and seeks to

---

[19] Webb Keane, "Freedom, Reflexivity, and the Sheer Everydayness of Ethics," *HAU: Journal of Ethnographic Theory* 4/1 (2014): 443–57 (here 444).

contribute critically to new scholarship within the anthropology of morality and detachment by constructing, in a very literal sense, an anthropology of theology via an analysis of the Exclusive Brethren doctrine of separation. Specifically, he seeks to answer two questions: (1) How do the Exclusive Brethren try to live good lives? and (2) What can we learn anthropologically from these models of *the good* and from the objections they provoke? He concludes by arguing that detachment and disconnection, as well as the negative statements of non-belonging that accompany them, can be found in spheres of thought and practice not normally regarded as religious.

CHAPTER 19—DIVINITY INHABITS THE SOCIAL: ETHNOGRAPHY IN A PHENOMENOLOGICAL KEY

Don Seeman argues that theologians and anthropologists should consider themselves *natural* (if sometimes conflictual) conversation partners because "divinity inhabits the social," which means that neither field can avoid dealing with central themes theorized by the other. From a phenomenological anthropology viewpoint, theological languages contribute to new and more adequate accounts of lived experience. Based on women's accounts of divine blessing at an Atlanta homeless shelter, this essay maintains that a continuum exists between academic theology and vernacular religion roughly analogous to the one between biomedical and vernacular accounts of suffering. Theologically engaged anthropology should emulate the analytic program of medical anthropology in probing the relation between these. Ways must also be found to broaden the kinds of expert knowledge that count as theology, especially in non-Christian traditions. The goal should be a theoretically robust program that contributes to more than just the anthropology of religion.

CHAPTER 20—ANTHROPOLOGICAL AND THEOLOGICAL RESPONSES TO THEOLOGICALLY ENGAGED ANTHROPOLOGY

Sarah Coakley and Joel Robbins provide insightful responses to the essays included in this book, informed by their respective disciplines—anthropology and theology. Together, they give serious consideration to the foundation of a theologically engaged anthropology while at the same time forging a pathway to propel theologians and anthropologists forward. Their responses reveal the exciting possibilities and cautionary pitfalls that this emerging field of study offers to both anthropologists and theologians. Overall, they suggest that the conversation between anthropology and theology has only begun. As this collaboration continues, theologically engaged anthropology is well positioned to aid anthropologists and theologians in their search for a deeper understanding of religion.

*   *   *

In closing, the essays in this book should be viewed as preliminary words about theologically engaged anthropology and not the last word. Furthermore, this book does not offer simple solutions for how anthropologists and theologians should engage with each other's disciplines. If there were simple solutions, this topic would have been adequately dealt with long ago. Instead, this book offers the opportunity for the reader to join the conversation that will continue for years to come. I look forward to seeing scholars take substantial steps toward answering the question, "What can theology contribute to anthropology?" without forgetting the sibling question, "What can anthropology contribute to theology?"

J. Derrick Lemons

University of Georgia

1

New Insights from an Old Dialogue Partner

J. Derrick Lemons

Anthropology and Christian theology have a complicated history that ultimately led to anthropologists marginalizing the use of theology in anthropological research. While marginalizing theology has been the accepted practice, a growing number of anthropologists think theology is worth engaging. During my research of the missional church movement in America, which began in 2006, I discovered that theology was central to its understanding. However, I was unsure what to do with theology and could not find guidance in the anthropological literature about how to engage with missional church theology in a way that respected its importance.

Roy Rappaport provided the traditional guidance about how to marginalize theology. In his book, entitled *Ritual and Religion in the Making of Humanity*, Rappaport provides an anthropological approach to exploring religion. He connects religion with language and ritual to examine human evolution over time and space.[1] Influenced by Emile Durkheim, Rappaport brings a functionalist approach to the anthropology of religion and qualifies his work:

> This book is not a theological treatise but a work in anthropology. As such, its ambitions are more general than those of any particular theology. As an anthropological inquiry, its assumptions are, of course, exclusively naturalistic, but it respects the concepts it seeks to understand, attempting not only to grasp what is true of all religions but what is true in all religions, that is, the special character of the truths that it is in the nature of all religions to claim.[2]

Rappaport's assertion that his book is not a work of theology supports a long-standing boundary within anthropology between theological and naturalistic explanations for human origins. However, Rappaport's boundary is not easily

---

[1] Ellen Messer and Michael Lambek (eds), *Ecology and the Sacred: Engaging the Anthropology of Roy A. Rappaport* (Ann Arbor: University of Michigan Press, 2001), 244.
[2] Roy A. Rappaport, *Ritual and Religion in the Making of Humanity* (New York: Cambridge University Press, 1999), 2.

maintained throughout the book. He uses theological terms, such as *logos*, *salvation*, and *holy*, for his analysis of culture and freely quotes theologians such as Paul Tillich, Rudolf Otto, Rudolf Bultmann, and Hans Küng. Unwittingly, Rappaport demonstrates that the anthropology of religion is difficult to divorce from theology and that a productive tension exists between anthropology and theology.

Joel Robbins' 2006 article "Anthropology and Theology: An Awkward Relationship?" would have been helpful, but this article was just being published as I was searching for answers about how to deal with missional church theology and would not be well-known for several years. In this article, he questions the marginalization of theology by anthropologists and suggests anthropologists need to engage with theology. Specifically, he outlines three ways in which anthropologists can engage theology. First, anthropologists can discover and understand the influence of theology on anthropological thought. Second, anthropologists can use theological discourse to reveal clues about important cultural shifts in religion. Third, anthropologists can use theology, which is an example of a committed discipline that articulates a life worth living, as an inspiration to find "hope for real change" in the world.[3]

As I sensed intuitively, Rappaport demonstrated unintentionally, and Robbins suggested explicitly, anthropologists must engage with theology to deepen and expand the scholarship of the anthropology of religion. This chapter examines the creative tension and history between anthropology and theology and argues that generating a reflexive theologically engaged anthropology improves anthropological research. Furthermore, this chapter concludes with an illustration of how engaging with missional church theology helped me produce a more informed anthropological account of the missional church movement within the Wesleyan Church.

✳ ✳ ✳

To develop a useful theologically engaged framework for anthropological research, reflexivity is an excellent place to begin. The concept of reflexivity is grounded in the work of the renowned anthropologist Pierre Bourdieu. Reflexivity, the discipline of considering the ethnographer's own perspective and presence as part of the research setting, causes us to analyze our research findings from alternative perspectives, in particular the perspectives of those who are participants in research. Without it, he argues, the quest for scientific knowledge may make the humans we seek to understand tangential to the anthropological research. Bourdieu was greatly concerned by researchers' tendency to attribute "to the object of their observations characteristics that are inherently theirs."[4] In

---

[3] Joel Robbins, "Anthropology and Theology: An Awkward Relationship?" *Anthropological Quarterly* 79/2 (2006): 286, 292–3.

[4] Michael Grenfell, *Pierre Bourdieu: Key Concepts* (Stocksfield, UK: Acumen Publishing, 2008), 201.

other words, the scholarly contributions of anthropologists often reveal more about their projected worldview than the worldview of their participants. Bourdieu worked passionately to secure the underpinnings of social scientific knowledge by insisting on a rigorous reflexivity.

To reinforce his reflexive focus, Bourdieu often talks about the need for the anthropology of anthropology. This play on words reflects his desire for anthropologists to submit their research to scientific scrutiny and acknowledge their biases. Specifically, Bourdieu highlights three potential biases for anthropologists to consider. First, the ethnicity, class, gender, and religion, or a professed lack of religion, of anthropologists can influence their interactions with the participants in their research. Second, anthropologists stand to gain a position of power within their academic field of study by supporting the work of opinion leaders in their area of academic inquiry, which may put researchers at odds with the interests of the participants in their research. For example, many participants in anthropological research believe in a spiritual world that can be accessed, manipulated, or placated, but most anthropologists do not share similar beliefs. Third, anthropology has protected domains of knowledge that often limit the possibilities of categories for consideration in analyzing data from an anthropologist's field research.[5] Theology is a prime example of a domain of knowledge that is most often excluded for the reasons previously stated.

Bourdieu utilizes the term *participant objectivation* to remind researchers to work past their biases and trust the scientific method to control for biases.[6] Bourdieu suggests that collaborating with multiple people with emic and etic points of view helped researchers overcome their worldview limitations. Therefore, Bourdieu invites collaborators to view his data, collect their own data, and then compare the two datasets to increase rigor in the research. In addition, he thinks that researchers should utilize multiple fields of study through collaborative research and publishing across academic disciplines to overcome biases intrinsic within a particular academic field. For example, Bourdieu published his research in multiple disciplines, including philosophy, anthropology, sociology, and psychology. In sum, Bourdieu's reflexive approach supports the use of theology within anthropology by helping anthropologists better understand how theology influences religious cultures of a globalized world.

*   *   *

To consider how anthropologists can reflexively engage with theology, a basic definition of theology is needed. Theology, literally translated *the study of God*, is often connected with the definition attributed to Anselm—faith seeking

---

[5] Pierre Bourdieu and Loic J. D. Wacquant, *An Invitation to Reflexive Sociology* (Chicago: University of Chicago Press, 1992).

[6] Bourdieu and Wacquant, *An Invitation*, 259.

understanding.[7] Paul Tillich describes theology as the "*logos of theos*, the rational word about God."[8] Both definitions contain metaphysical and existential claims in that they both assume a "rational inquiry into the structure of being" and a divinely given "universal claim for truth."[9] Abelard, who is credited with first promoting the term *theology*, saw it as an opportunity to develop questions that lead to better understanding, resulting in a more informed faith.[10] With a focus on faith, church bodies develop official dogma. With a focus on understanding, the truth of dogma can be tested through systematic theology with the goal of supporting or refuting the dogma.

Pannenberg makes the case that systematic theology should be known as the science of God because of a shared systematic methodological approach with anthropology.[11] Specifically, he argues that a comparative anthropological study of religion is foundational to theology. This type of study tests the dogma of a religious tradition across time and space against the lived experience of that dogma. In other words, Pannenberg uses an anthropological methodology to compare emic (i.e., religious insider) beliefs and behaviors with dogma in an effort to gain a more complete understanding of faith.[12]

Scholars inside and outside of theology mistakenly disconnect theology from human cultures. Kathryn Tanner offers a helpful corrective by pointing out that theology is not solely a tradition bound by dogma. She says, "Theology is something that human beings produce. Like all human activities, it is historically and socially conditioned; it cannot be understood in isolation from the rest of human sociocultural practices."[13] If anthropologists see theology as a sociocultural product of the time in which that theological framework emerged, they can use theology to understand human activities in a particular time and space. Furthermore, theological engagement can lead to metaphysical and existential insights that often elude anthropologists. In the end, anthropologists are offered an opportunity to make deep connections with real otherness in the world.

Engagement with theology does not mean that anthropologists must ignore the social scientific nature of anthropology. In fact, anthropology can be a

---

[7] Daniel L. Migliore, *Faith Seeking Understanding: An Introduction to Christian Theology*, 3rd edn (Grand Rapids, MI: Eerdmans, 2014), 2.

[8] Paul Tillich, "Relation of Metaphysics and Theology," *The Review of Metaphysics* 10/1 (1956): 58.

[9] Tillich, "Relation," 57–8.

[10] Ralph Norman, "Abelard's Legacy: Why Theology Is Not Faith Seeking Understanding," *Australian eJournal of Theology* 10/1 (2007): 2–3, <http://aejt.com.au/__data/assets/pdf_file/0011/378074/AEJT_10.3_Norman_Abelard.pdf>.

[11] Gunther Wenz, *Introduction to Wolfhart Pannenberg's Systematic Theology* (Bristol, UK: Vandenhoeck & Ruprecht, 2013), 28–9.

[12] Wenz, *Introduction*, 35.

[13] Kathryn Tanner, *Theories of Culture: A New Agenda for Theology* (Minneapolis, MN: Fortress Press, 1997), 63.

constructive and critical dialogue partner for theology. In his call for scientific
theology, Alister McGrath argues that when theology is tested against human
experience, a refined theological understanding of God results.[14] Thomas
Torrance anchors theology within the human pursuit to understand God:
"[Theology is] a human enterprise operating with revisable formulations in
a manner similar in significant respects to that of a science operating with
fluid axioms, but always under the constraint of the objective realities being
explored."[15] This connection with human culture means that theology is properly understood within the culture in which the ideas about God emerged and
that anthropological methodology provides another way to understand theology.
The basic anthropological method includes (1) moving into the community,
(2) learning the language, (3) asking questions, (4) collecting data, (5) making
records, (6) analyzing data, and (7) interpreting native perspectives. In sum,
anthropologists are encouraged to use their depth of perception and methods to
connect human cultures with the study of theology.[16]

*   *   *

While Rappaport separates theological and naturalistic understandings of
human origins, the two disciplines are historically connected. Anthropology
is the holistic study of humanity. The word *anthropology* as the study of
humanity is a term derived from the Greek language, first used by Magnus
Hundt (1501) in *Antropologium de hominis dignitate*. Hundt in his text was
interested in "der ganze Mensch," or the whole person, by which he meant the
physiological, psychological, spiritual, and philosophical nature of humanity.
As a practicing physician with a doctorate in theology, Hundt was dissatisfied
with a purely anatomical and physiological approach to anthropology. Hundt
thus outlined the holistic approach to the study of humans that is central to
contemporary anthropology. As the field of anthropology matured after the
Enlightenment, Hundt's call to study the theological basis of human spirituality was largely lost.[17]

While theology lost a primary influence in anthropology, theology continued
to influence indirectly the development and practice of anthropology. Michael
Rynkiewich argues that the entanglement of anthropologists and missionaries
in the late nineteenth and early twentieth centuries greatly influenced the
early development of the field of anthropology. For example, anthropologists,
including E. B. Tylor, relied heavily on well-known missionary ethnographers

---

[14] Alister E. McGrath, *A Scientific Theology*, vol. 3: *Theory* (Grand Rapids, MI: Eerdmans,
2003), 29.

[15] Thomas F. Torrance, *Reality and Scientific Theology* (Eugene, OR: Wipf and Stock, 1985), viii.

[16] Peter Connolly (ed.), *Approaches to the Study of Religion* (London: Cassell, 1999), 229.

[17] National Library of Medicine, "Hundt, Magnus. *Antropologium de hominis dignitate, natura
et proprietatibus, de elementis, partibus et membris humani corporis*," US National Library of
Medicine, <www.nlm.nih.gov/exhibition/historicalanatomies/hundt_bio.html>.

because missionaries were living with, learning from, and writing about the people anthropologists wanted to research. In some cases, the roles of anthropologists and missionaries were combined. Maurice Leenhardt, a missionary and anthropologist, held the same chair of the fifth section of religious sciences at École Pratique des Hautes Études as did Emile Durkheim, Marcel Mauss, and Claude Levi-Strauss.[18] In a compelling history of the role of Christianity within anthropology, Timothy Larsen provides examples of the collision of "doubt and faith" with "anthropological theory and evidence."[19] Larsen reveals how E. B. Tylor's and James Frazer's abandonment of Christian faith and the faithful practice of Christianity of E. E. Evans-Pritchard, Mary Douglas, Victor Turner, and Edith Turner influenced the development of anthropology as a discipline of study. These examples of Christian and anthropological entanglements suggest that while theology is not at the center of anthropology, theological concerns never totally disappeared.

I have already noted that Hundt assumed that theological concerns were a necessary part of understanding anthropology. However, enlightenment assumptions and influential anthropologists (e.g., Frazer, Radcliffe-Brown, and Malinowski) saw religious belief as "erroneous and untenable," which led to a form of anthropology that cast aside theology.[20] This closed approach to collaborative areas of research, including theology, limits the potential of anthropology to illuminate an understanding of humanity across time and space.

∗   ∗   ∗

The time is right for anthropologists to engage with theology to deepen and expand the scholarship of the anthropology of religion. A theologically engaged anthropology is needed to rediscover the connection between humanity and humanity's quest to understand the spiritual side of life. Moreover, overlooked or ignored fields of study can renew anthropological inquiry and become highly productive areas of research. Indeed, the astute observation of Robbins to view Christianity no longer as an "inessential feature" of modern societies and an evil partner of colonialism led to new insights about how Christianity influenced the Urapmin of Papua New Guinea. Ultimately, Robbins, Fenella Cannell, Webb Keane, and others argue that anthropologists have been "insufficiently self-critical," which led to important categories of research being deliberately avoided.[21] Their openness to a new field of research led to the formation of the field of the anthropology of Christianity, which is now one of the most productive within the larger field of the anthropology of religion.

---

[18] Timothy Jenkins, "The Anthropology of Christianity: Situation and Critique," *Ethnos: Journal of Anthropology* 77/4 (2012): 15; Michael A. Rynkiewich, "Do We Need a Postmodern Anthropology for Mission in a Postcolonial World?" *Mission Studies* 28 (2011): 154, 158.

[19] Timothy Larsen, *The Slain God: Anthropologists and the Christian Faith* (Oxford: Oxford University Press, 2014), 10.

[20] Ibid., 10.   [21] Jenkins, "The Anthropology of Christianity," 462.

As a scholar who works within the anthropology of Christianity, theology is a vital partner in my ethnographic research. My research focuses on how the missional church movement has influenced the Wesleyan Church in the United States of America. I use ethnographic methods, anthropological theories, historical approaches, and theology to discover how the development of missional church theology is informing the missional church movement within the Wesleyan Church.

Let me begin with a brief history of the missional church movement by connecting key figures in the movement.[22] The modern missional church movement began in 1932 with a paper given by Karl Barth at the Brandenburg Mission Conference:

> The congregation, the so-called homeland church, the community of heathen Christians should recognize themselves and actively engage themselves as what they essentially are: a missionary community! They are not a mission association or society, not a group that formed itself with *the firm intention* to do mission, but a human community *called* to the act of mission.[23] (italics added)

From Barth's paper Karl Hartenstein in 1934 coined the term *Missio Dei* to make the point that churches do not exist for themselves. They exist to participate in God's mission to the world. After World War II, the missional church movement reemerged at a meeting in 1952 in Willingen, Germany. One of the historically significant parts of the Willingen meeting was that Lesslie Newbigin, who at the time was bishop in Madura and Ramnad for the Church of South India, began to help guide the discussion about the missional church movement.[24] The missional church model of ministry continued to build momentum in 1958 at Achimota, Ghana, at the International Missions Council meeting. After this meeting, Newbigin published a pamphlet that summarized his understanding of a missional church. The following quote highlights the heart of Newbigin's message: "(1) 'The church is the mission,' which means that it is illegitimate to talk about the one without at the same time talking about the other; (2) 'the home base is everywhere,' which means that every Christian community is in a missionary situation; and (3) 'mission in partnership,' which means the end of every form of guardianship of one church over another."[25] Newbigin's understanding of these issues grew and

---

[22] J. Derrick Lemons, *The Pastor as Missional Church Architect* (Ann Arbor: ProQuest Information and Learning, 2009), 15, 16.

[23] Karl Barth, "Die Theologie und die Mission in der Gegenwart," *Theologische Fragen und Antworten* (Zollikon, Switzerland: Theologischer Verlag Zürich, 1957), 115, quoted and translated in Darrell Likens Guder, "From Mission and Theology to Missional Theology," *The Princeton Seminary Bulletin* 24/1 (2003): 42.

[24] H. Dan Beeby, "Lesslie Newbigin: Biography," [obituary], <http://gospel-culture.org.uk/newbio.htm>; Stephen B. Bevans and Roger P. Schroeder, *Constants in Context: A Theology of Mission for Today* (New York: Orbis Books, 2004), 290.

[25] Bevans and Schroeder, *Constants in Context*, 370.

culminated in his seminal work, *The Gospel in a Pluralist Society*, published in 1989. By appealing to the social scientific theories of Michael Polanyi's tacit knowledge and Peter Berger's plausibility structures, Newbigin articulates a theology that challenges the ideas that truth can only be discerned through the modern scientific method and that religious pluralism necessarily invalidates Christian claims of truth.[26]

As a self-described practical theologian, Newbigin emphasizes the importance of telling the story of Christianity as the valid religious story among a multitude of options.[27] He then highlights six characteristics of a missional church that assume the church's missional nature. He wrote that missional churches praise God, stand on Christian truth, engage with secular community, empower to disperse, model an exemplary community, and are grounded in Christian hope and focused on the eschaton.[28] Today, the missional church movement continues to expand its influence as churches that previously flourished within cultures where Christianity was the *de facto* religion attempt to rediscover meaning within pluralistic and secular cultures where Christianity is one option among many religious options.[29]

With this background, I want to consider how culture and theology influence each other. The prevalent cultural issues during the 1980s and 1990s of secularism and pluralism greatly influenced what were viewed as theological and ecclesial concerns. For example, in 1989, the same year that Newbigin published *The Gospel in a Pluralist Society*, Francis X. Clooney published an article in *Religious Studies Review* where he distilled from six important books the salient issues facing Christian theology. Clooney discovered that pluralism and secularism were of primary concern. Clooney writes the following: "1) Christians cannot realistically ignore the many religions flourishing in today's world, and indeed there is no reason to want to do so; 2) respect for these religions and a willingness to learn from them are essential to viable dialogue; 3) faithfulness to the Christian heritage remains essential; 4) the Christian tradition must therefore be read anew in the light of today's situation, so that Christians can responsibly account for the new while remaining faithful to their heritage."[30] During this same time period, John Milbank's book *Theology and Social Theory: Beyond Secular Reason* served as another example of a Christian theologian articulating a way to overcome the challenges of pluralism and secularism.[31] In short, Milbank offers a theological critique of the secular underpinnings of the social sciences and suggests the

---

[26] Lesslie Newbigin, *The Gospel in a Pluralist Society* (Grand Rapids, MI: Eerdmans, 1989), 5, 25.
[27] Ibid., 117.   [28] Ibid., 227–33.   [29] Ibid., 7.
[30] Francis. X. Clooney, "Christianity and World Religions: Religion, Reason and Pluralism," *Religious Studies Review* 15/3 (1989): 199.
[31] John Milbank, *Theology and Social Theory: Beyond Secular Reason* (Oxford: Blackwell Publishing, 2006).

social sciences undermined theological enquiry. Influenced by the salient issues in theology during that same time period, the emergence, development, and growth of the missional church movement took place.

Given this history, let me return to my ethnographic research on the Wesleyan Church to illustrate how the use of missional church theology, which as I have shown was influenced by the cultural issues of a particular time and space, allowed me to interpret the decisions by the Wesleyan Church denomination to become missional. The Wesleyan Church is an evangelical, Protestant denomination based in the United States and rooted in the holiness tradition inspired by John Wesley's Methodism.

Wesleyan churches have a longstanding view that Christians should limit interaction with the secular world due to a focus on living a life of holiness. When I did fieldwork among members of a rural Wesleyan congregation in the southeastern United States, I often heard this biblical phrase used by the opinion leaders in the congregation: "We are to be in the world but not of the world." This statement reflects an assumption of Wesleyans more broadly that once a person becomes a Christian, she or he must disengage from non-Christians in order not to be hindered spiritually. One demonstration that I viewed from a Wesleyan Church youth group exemplifies this point. A youth group leader will ask one person to stand on a chair and ask another to stand on the floor. The person on the floor clasps hands with the person standing on the chair and tries to pull the person off the chair. Inevitably, the person on the chair ends up on the floor with the person who started there. The leader then explains that the person standing on the chair represents a Christian and the person standing on the floor represents a non-Christian. If the Christian interacts with the non-Christian, the Christian will be pulled down to the ways of the non-Christian. The moral of the illustration is that Christians should disengage from secular people in order to maintain Christian purity and to keep from being *pulled down* spiritually.

In November 2009, the General Board of the Wesleyan Church mandated that their general superintendents make recommendations to reinvent "The Wesleyan Church as an intentionally missional denomination for the 21st Century."[32] The heart of the Wesleyan Church's missional directive was to develop "a mindset that regards the Church as the people of God who are sent out into the world to join Him in His mission of reconciling others to Himself through Christ. This perspective, if embraced, supersedes all others on a congregation or denomination's agenda, calling for its transformation into a mission force, rather than its own self-contained, self-focused, self-serving mission field."[33] Eventually this recommendation was brought before the

---

[32] General Board Meeting of the Wesleyan Church, "Wesleyan Church Reinvention," white paper, Indianapolis, IN, May 4–5, 2010.
[33] Ibid., 1.

General Conference of the Wesleyan Church in Lexington, Kentucky, in June 2012. The recommendation was ratified when the Wesleyan Church General Conference voted to become a missional denomination. Of course, as a result, the Wesleyan Church will no longer emphasize disengagement from a secular pluralistic society.

Since voting to become missional in 2012, the July 2015 ruling of the United States Supreme Court legalizing same-sex marriage has been the most significant challenge to this missional affirmation. This ruling tests the missional motivation to stay connected with secular society, and the leadership of the Wesleyan Church responded. The official response of the Wesleyan Church was to continue to affirm heterosexual marriage as the only valid Christian marriage—no surprise there. More surprising was the encouragement to continue engagement with those who embrace same-sex marriage. Specifically, leaders of the Wesleyan Church stated in the official response, "The church is compelled by the love of Christ to care about all people.... When our stance becomes less popular in a society that is, in some ways, moving farther from God, love does not let us withdraw."[34] Here we see that the missional church movement's theological influence allowed the Wesleyan Church to navigate the redefinition of the union of marriage by the United States government by providing a framework for the denomination to stand on Christian truth and continue to engage with secular community.

An understanding of the dynamic relationship between culture and theology allowed me to discover new insights into the Wesleyan Church, which would have been missed if I had avoided theological engagement. In this case, missional church theology provided the Wesleyan Church an approach to ministry that fits a secular and pluralistic world and helps them navigate the legalization of same-sex marriage. Furthermore, the structure of theology was central to the Wesleyan Church redefining the mission of the denomination. In sum, a knowledge of the theology of the missional church movement provided me with vital information to explain how the Wesleyan Church has changed over recent time and space.

*   *   *

At the beginning of this chapter, I suggested that the time is right for anthropologists to engage with theology to deepen and expand the scholarship of the anthropology of religion. In fact, some examples exist of anthropologists who are already engaging with theology as an important counterpart—the major example being the December 2013 special issue of the *Australian Journal of Anthropology*, which was titled *Anthropological Theologies: Engagements and*

---

[34] The Wesleyan Church, "Response to 2015 Supreme Court Ruling on Same-Sex Marriage," June 26, 2015, <www.wesleyan.org/3753/response-to-2015-supreme-court-ruling-on-same-sex-marriage>.

Encounters.[35] In this special edition of the journal, the editors and contributors argued that theology must be taken seriously to uncover new anthropological insights. Additionally, an article entitled "Engaging the Religiously Committed Other: Anthropologists and Theologians in Dialogue" appeared in the February 2014 issue of *Current Anthropology.*[36] This article uses the problem of violence to illustrate the need for a space for Christian anthropologists to speak within scholarly circles. More generally, theologians and ethnographers are developing a rigorous research collaboration between the social sciences and theology as evidenced by two issues of *Practical Matters* dedicated to ethnography and religion.[37]

An engaged theology adds another theoretical framework for anthropologists of Christianity but could also offer a theoretical framework for any field of anthropological religious inquiry because the home tradition need not necessarily be Christian.[38] Benefits of engaging with theology for anthropologists include a reflexive understanding of the creative tension between theology and anthropology, a deeper knowledge of the influence of theology within religion, and discovery of a real otherness in the world and with the hope for real change. Engaging theology may be challenging for anthropologists, but the challenge is worth taking. Anthropologists who embrace theology might find that adopting a theologically engaged anthropological framework within which to examine religions opens up new lines of inquiry into understanding humanity across time and space.

---

[35] Fountain, Philip and Sin Wen Lau, "Anthropological Theologies: Engagements and Encounters," *Australian Journal of Anthropology* 24/3 (2013): 227–34.

[36] Eloise Meneses, Lindy Backues, David Bronkema, Eric Flett, and Benjamin L. Hartley, "Engaging the Religiously Committed Other: Anthropologists and Theologians in Dialogue," *Current Anthropology* 55/1 (2014): 82–104.

[37] Don E. Saliers, Joyce Burkhalter Flueckiger, Dianne Stewart Diakité, and Don E. Seeman, "Ethnography and Theology: A Critical Roundtable Discussion," *Practical Matters Journal* 3 (March 1, 2010), <https://wp.me/p6QAmj-j3>; *Engaging Religious Experience: A Return to Ethnography and Theology, Practical Matters Journal* 6 (March 13, 2013), <http://practicalmattersjournal.org/category/issue-6/>.

[38] Francis X. Clooney, *Comparative Theology* (Chichester, UK and Malden, MA: Wiley-Blackwell, 2010), 11.

2

Which Theology for Anthropology?

Types of Theology for Anthropological Engagement

Brian M. Howell

> When we became Christians, everything changed. We did not fight. We did not want to kill. We want[ed] to praise God and live in peace.... He will protect the Ikalahan.... It was very hard [to forgive], but we must. We forgive, and we praise God, because He forgives. We are all one now.... It is not just Ikalahan. We are brothers with them and we love each other.
>
> —Omis Balinhawag[1]

Living in the thick forests and rugged terrain of the Gran Cordillera Mountains of North Central Luzon, the Ikalahan (or Kalingoya) people successfully resisted Spanish colonialism for centuries. Like their neighbors, the Ifugao and Ilongot, they were subsistence cultivators and hunters who protected their territories through traditions of violence, including the taking of human heads.[2] With the arrival of US colonialism in 1898, Protestant missions and educational projects moved into the mountains but with relatively less of the political domination upland groups had successfully resisted during Spanish rule. As with many other Southeast Asian upland areas, Protestant Christianity became a means of establishing connections with global movements and power without adopting the main lowland religions and jeopardizing ethnic distinctiveness.[3]

---

[1] Pseudonyms are used for participants in my ethnographic research.

[2] Filomeno V. Aguilar, *Social Forestry for Upland Development: Lessons from Four Case Studies* (Quezon City: Institute of Philippine Culture, Ateneo de Manila University, 1982); Roy Franklin Barton, *The Religion of the Ifugaos* (Menasha, WI: American Anthropological Association, 1946); Felix M. Keesing and Marie Keesing, *Taming Philippine Headhunters: A Study of Government and of Cultural Change in Northern Luzon* (New York: AMS Press, 1934); Renato Rosaldo, *Ilongot Headhunting, 1883–1974: A Study in Society and History* (Stanford: Stanford University Press, 1980).

[3] Charles F. Keyes, "Christianity as an Indigenous Religion in Southeast Asia," *Social Compass* 38/2 (1991): 177–85; see also Cornelia Ann Kammerer, "Customs and Christian Conversion

While still an undergraduate student, I first visited an Ikalahan community in 1990. Lacking training, method, and experience, I arrived for a ten-week summer stay to understand the relationship between missionary methods, conversion, and social change. I stumbled along, gathering data that is now more than twenty-five years old. My data-gathering techniques were haphazard, and the technology less friendly. Mini-tape cassettes, several that have yet to be transcribed, still exist in my home office if only I could find a recorder on which they could be played. I did write an undergraduate thesis from the material and managed to keep notes of various kinds around. Looking back through this data and reconstructing the work through memory and my own previous writing, I can now see how the generosity of this community to an anthropological innocent opened up more than I could see at the time.

The project grew out of a seminar on Christian missions taken at Wesleyan University in 1990 in which I encountered a narrative of missions that complicated the colonializing, hegemonic account dominating much of the literature in history, economics, and anthropology. I wanted to understand mission in terms of the responses of local populations and the ways in which methods and theology of missions could influence these responses. The only missionary of whom I was aware was a man named Delbert Rice, supported by my childhood United Methodist church in Washington State. Calling him up out of the blue (i.e., reversing the time zone and waking him in the middle of the night), I asked to come visit his community. He graciously agreed.

Armed with a semester's worth of reading on colonial and church history in the Philippines, a dash of Philippine culture studies, and a lot of youthful enthusiasm, I traveled to Imugan. This small regional *barangay*[4] in the southern end of the Cordillera mountain range of Northern Luzon had a population of approximately 120 families, not including the many outlying farms and homesteads. The majority of the population was Christian and, according to both the leaders of the community and as evidenced by the attendance on Sunday morning, the vast majority of those were Protestant members of the local United Church of Christ of the Philippines.

Rice, who had lived with his wife and three sons in the community since 1958, spoke the local language (Ikalahan/Kalangoya), along with the regional language (Ilokano) and the national language (Tagalog), seemingly with equal fluency. He occupied a position of considerable influence in the community although he had not served as pastor of the local congregation since the

---

among Akha Highlanders of Burma and Thailand," *American Ethnologist* 17/2 (1990): 277–91; Nicholas Tapp, "The Impact of Missionary Christianity upon Marginalized Ethnic Minorities: The Case of the Hmong," *Journal of Southeast Asian Studies* 20/1 (1989): 70–95.

[4] A *barangay* is a sociopolitical unit with a governmental *captain* and defined borders within a larger municipality. In a rural area such as Imugan, the *barangay* limits may encompass a fairly large geographic area around a small population center to bring in outlying farms and homesteads in the forest.

mid-1960s. He was still a US citizen, meaning he could not hold any Filipino government position, yet he had cultivated many connections throughout the Protestant Christian communities of the Philippines, the development community, as he was an enormously entrepreneurial man who had helped to establish multiple economic and educational institutions in Imugan and surrounding areas, and internationally in the United States and Europe.

My research interest was, to be honest, undercooked as I ventured into the community to take up residence in the Rice home. I spent most of my days following Rice, talking with his wife, meeting local church leaders, or spending time with the dozen or so students who were living in the Rices' home while they attended school in the community. Over the course of the few months I was in the community, and even more so as I wrote up the data in the following year, I came to focus on the ways Rice's particular missionary methods, what I called *vernacular Christian missions*, shaped the response of converted church members toward a particular view of their own ethnic identity and cultural history.[5]

What I did not develop to a great extent were the theological emphases most at work in Imugan. I considered their views mostly in political terms. I argued, following Lamin O. Sanneh,[6] that Rice's use of local languages contributed to an understanding among the people of Imugan that their cultural particularity and identity were worthy of respect and of equal value to those of lowland majority groups. This practice provided symbolic capital for the creation of educational, economic, and political institutions that served as resources against the hegemony of lowland cultural and political interests. I interpreted their actions and history primarily in terms of the economic and political struggles they identified as most afflicting their community.

While I can still look at these efforts as legitimate sound analysis as far as they went, reviewing the data again reveals clear religious—specifically Christian—dimensions to their lives that I oddly and somewhat ironically missed. In a context where much of their conflict was framed in upland–lowland terms, they also shared with many of these lowland groups a Christian faith, even within the same denomination, that gave them an ability to understand the conflict not simply in political terms but in distinctly Christian, theologically informed ways. Considering how they were framing their own efforts to relate to political and economic conflicts in Christian terms sheds light on their world in ways political economic analyses lack. What Omis Balinhawang, the Ikalahan elder quoted at the beginning of this chapter, was saying to me was not first and foremost a political statement about cooperation but a theological

[5] Brian M. Howell, "Unto All the World: Vernacular Christian Missions and the Protection of Minority Cultures," undergraduate honors thesis (Wesleyan University, 1991).

[6] Lamin O. Sanneh, *Translating the Message: The Missionary Impact on Culture* (Maryknoll, NY: Orbis Books, 1989).

commitment to love. Understanding this community and their changing relations with the wider Philippines required not simply an anthropological analysis but a theological one as well.

                                        *   *   *

Connections between theology and anthropology are not new. From the earliest years of British social anthropology, scholars have used theological categories not only as data but also as formative concepts. William Robertson Smith drew on German biblical criticism in his theories of ritual.[7] James Prichard drew on an orthodox doctrine of creation to defend anthropological understandings of human unity.[8] Prominent twentieth-century anthropologists such as E. E. Evans-Pritchard and Mary Douglas, both confessing Catholics, explicitly included theological categories in their anthropological analysis.[9] Moreover, the use of theology has not been limited to anthropologists claiming a Christian identity or even Christian concepts. In more recent work, Talal Asad draws on the theological notion of *grace* to argue his now widely accepted thesis that secularism is a social and cultural formation that has created, rather than merely recognized, the modernist category of *religion*.[10] Charles Hirshkind cites Fahmi Howeidy's use of *shari'a* as a social concept for the interrogation of Islamic political culture.[11] Thus, the current project to bring theology into conversation with anthropology is not so much about starting this effort as it is about formalizing or recognizing what is already happening in a more piecemeal fashion and, indeed, what is arguably inescapable in anthropological theory.[12] As Mary Douglas once argued, theology will surface in any conversation in which ultimate meanings, values, and morality are implicated.[13] Given that virtually all social anthropologists find themselves intersecting with these questions, a more deliberate focus on theological thinking should aid in the work of developing conceptual and theoretical frames for considering how anthropologists imagine the ultimate meanings, values, and morality in the social lives of others.

---

[7] William Robertson Smith, *Lectures on the Religion of the Semites* (London: Sheffield Academic Press, 1995).

[8] James C. Prichard, *Researches into the Physical History of Mankind* (London: Sherwood, Gilbert, & Piper, 1847).

[9] E. E. Evans-Pritchard, *Theories of Primitive Religion* (Oxford: Clarendon Press, 1965); Mary Douglas, *Natural Symbols* (London: Barrie & Rockliff, 1970).

[10] Talal Asad, *Formations of the Secular: Christianity, Islam, Modernity* (Palo Alto, CA: Stanford University Press, 2003), 35.

[11] Charles Hirschkind, "Beyond Secular and Religious: An Intellectual Genealogy of Tahrir Square," *American Ethnologist* 39/1 (2012): 49–53.

[12] For more background on the theology–anthropology conversation, see Philip Fountain, *Anthropological Theologies: Engagements and Encounters*, Special Issue of the *Australian Journal of Anthropology* 24/3 (2013); Joel Robbins and Matthew Engelke, "Introduction," *South Atlantic Quarterly* 109/4 (2010): 623–31.

[13] Timothy Larsen, *The Slain God: Anthropologists and the Christian Faith* (New York: Oxford University Press, 2014), 170.

For my part, I hope to add to the discussion a closer look at theology as a discipline to suggest how, or—more to the point—*what kind of* theology can best contribute to anthropological thinking. Theology, like every discipline, is comprised of various, and often competing, schools of thought and method. While I do not intend to suggest that only one sort of theology is relevant for anthropology, by looking more closely at the contours of the discipline, I suggest fruitful directions for anthropologists seeking to investigate theological thinking. By considering the fields of anthropology and theology with some specificity, I hope to help frame this project and create bridges between disciplinary vocabularies and conceptualizations.

To work through this discussion, I start by exploring five types of theology as described by a theologian well-known for his engagement with anthropological frameworks—postliberal theologian Hans W. Frei. A key work of his exploring theology as differentiated into identifiable forms was one of the final projects of his distinguished career and one that developed very particular arguments he sought to make at the time.[14] Nevertheless, as a number of commentators noted subsequently, his typologies present a helpful discussion of theology as a discipline and serve as a good resource for those seeking to link Christian theology with new projects.[15]

Reading his work as an anthropologist, I engage his typologies to suggest how they speak to anthropological concerns. I build on this concept by looking at a recently published, and somewhat parallel, project involving anthropology and philosophy. Philosophy, so often a conversation partner with, and sometimes virtually indistinguishable from, theology gives a particular insight into the ways anthropology can benefit from, and interact with, a discipline such as theology. Connecting this work on philosophy with Frei's typologies, I argue that some sorts of theological work are better suited for contemporary anthropological engagement. Finally, I conclude by returning to the Philippine data collected years ago.

*   *   *

Theology is not an inherently Christian word, as other large-scale religions such as Hinduism and Islam have venerable and important uses of the idea of theology in their own contexts and comparatively.[16] At the same time, to speak of *theology* in the abstract is to invite category confusion between these various traditions and even within a tradition such as Christianity. Likewise, within

---

[14] Hans W. Frei, *Types of Christian Theology*, ed. George Hunsinger and William C. Placher (New Haven, CT: Yale University Press, 1992).

[15] Yasir S. Ibrahim, "Hans Frei's Typology of Christian Theology: A Comparative Look at the Islamic Tradition," *Journal of Ecumenical Studies* 44/4 (2009): 642; Fergus Kerr, "Frei's Types," *New Blackfriars* 75/881 (1994): 184–93; Jason A. Springs, "Between Barth and Wittgenstein: On the Availability of Hans Frei's Later Theology," *Modern Theology* 23/3 (2007): 393–413.

[16] For example, see in this volume Khaled Furani, Chapter 4, 66–82 and Francis X. Clooney, Chapter 16, 280–95.

Hindu or Islamic contexts, the questions around how one practices theology and what counts as theology are rather different. To simply speak of *theology* as a neutral category is problematic, just as *religion* is not a simple or singular category.[17]

Considering what sort of theological work can contribute to anthropology requires an understanding of the different sorts of theology at work. This proposition is complex in any discipline and infinitely contestable. However, eminent twentieth-century theologian Frei has provided a strong basis for the work in his collection of essays and published lectures, *Types of Christian Theology*, edited by two of his most prominent students and posthumously published in 1992. Based primarily on his Shaffer lectures delivered at Yale in 1983 but including others as well, the book was conceived to provide, in Frei's own words, a "useful humanistic study,...a richer guide to the varieties of thinking internal to [Christianity]."[18] With five typological versions of theology, Frei presents distinct, some might say idiosyncratic, accounts of how Christian theology has proceeded in organizing itself. Differentiating first-order statements about the nature and structure of philosophical and transcendental structures from second-order appraisal of its own "language and actions under a norm or norms internal to the community itself," Frei's typologies serve as a particular form of intellectual organization.[19]

Typologies in general pose problems, of course, in that they invariably fix particular ideas and thinkers in bounded sets, where there is a great deal more fluidity and complexity than the types allow. Moreover, by the editors' own admission, the original context of these typologies as public presentations made them somewhat more polemical and informal than was typical in Frei's published work.[20] Finally, typologies are rarely neutral categories merely describing analogous ideas and thinkers but are presented to advance an argument. These typologies are certainly no different, as Frei remained committed to advancing the work of Karl Barth, a theologian with whose ideas he began his scholarly career. Frei favors types 4 and 5 with Barth being in the former as a way to advance his argument against the possibilities of a systematic or foundationalist theology outside of Christian ontology.[21]

Nevertheless, even given the somewhat polemic, specific, and even temporally fixed nature of Frei's typologies, his work can be helpful for this project. Picking up the question of the relationship of theology to philosophy and

---

[17] Bruno Latour, *On the Modern Cult of the Factish Gods* (Durham, NC and London: Duke University Press, 2010); see also Talal Asad, *Genealogies of Religion: Discipline and Reasons of Power in Christianity and Islam* (Baltimore, MD: Johns Hopkins University Press, 1993).

[18] Hans W. Frei, *Types of Christian Theology*, ed. George Hunsinger and William C. Placher (New Haven, CT: Yale University Press, 1992), 1.

[19] Ibid., 2.   [20] Ibid., xi.

[21] John Allan Knight, *Liberalism versus Postliberalism: The Great Divide in Twentieth-Century Theology* (New York: Oxford University Press, 2013), 126–7.

viewing them, even loosely, in these five modes can facilitate our interpretation of how this present work is (or should be) like a recent project focused on philosophy and suggest what sorts of theological thinking are helpful in concrete ethnographic application.

* * *

Frei begins his typologies noting that the "naturally cognate discipline to theology is philosophy" in terms of transcendental analysis as well as positive procedure in epistemology, ontology, and so forth.[22] Unsurprisingly, then, one form of theology is, essentially, *a philosophical discipline* in which philosophy is the conversation partner and the goal is to find universal coherence within formal rules of logic. Frei points to Immanuel Kant as the architect of this theology. In this, "distinctions between external and internal description tend to disappear."[23] In other words, for this philosophical theology, self-description is irrelevant to the enterprise. The experience, language, or "private or idiosyncratic norms" of particular communities "must come before the bar of the gradually emerging common discipline of theology" (Kaufman, as cited in Frei).[24] The work of theologians, then, is to look for the formal universal categories on which to build particular theological statements.

This elevation of formal categories and concepts over the experience of communities and traditions poses obvious problems for the anthropologist. Social theory certainly has expressions of universalistic *religion*, particularly in terms of those structuralist, psychological, or evolutionary explanations of religion that universalize the varied expressions of morality and transcendence found throughout the ethnographic record (e.g., Durkheim, Freud, Jung, Boyer). When considering how theology *qua* theology, as opposed to theology expressing social order, psychological state, or evolutionary strategy, may be useful to anthropology, such abstracted universal notions of theological expression require a kind of comparative anthropological project that does not dwell in the fine-grained analysis of ethnographical particularity but rises to the meta-level of analysis and the human condition, posing particular problems for anthropology. Although Frei does not use this term in describing this form of theology, this is a modernist, foundationalist approach that searches for the universal categories. This is like Asad's well-known critique of Geertz's definition of religion in which Asad argues that in creating a universal definition of religion, Geertz relies on "modern, privatized, Christian" understandings of religion, culture, and the self.[25]

---

[22] Frei, *Types of Christian Theology*, 2.   [23] Ibid., 3.
[24] Gordon Kaufmann, *An Essay on Theological Method* (Chico, CA: Scholars Press, 1975), 67; Frei, *Types of Christian Theology*, 29.
[25] Talal Asad, "Anthropological Conceptions of Religion: Reflections on Geertz," *Man* 18/2 (1983): 247.

Frei's second type of theology is likewise subsumed under philosophical categories, but rather than philosophical concepts ostensibly drawn from universal, transcendent categories, these philosophies are drawn from human experience to find those underlying universal principles. In this mode of theology, the particular tradition in which theology is undertaken is fore-grounded in a way that is not for the type 1 theologian. Thus, for Christian theology, Christian distinctiveness becomes the object of contemplation and analysis (whereas it is a gateway for the type 1 theologian), but in its distinct-iveness, it should be understood as articulating a common human experience. Holding up Paul Ricoeur as the philosophical founder, Frei understands this work as a *phenomenological theology* in which Christianity is one mode of consciousness under the auspices of philosophical anthropology.

Of course, to invoke phenomenology is to raise another set of complexities, as phenomenology has multiple varieties[26] and innumerable discussions about how phenomenology should be understood and applied.[27] In invoking Ricoeur, Frei means to invoke a phenomenology that "supposes constant kinds of experience, even if their positive contents have to be articulated in all varying cultural terms."[28] These constant kinds of experience provide a stability to text and meaning that transcends the contingencies of culture and tradition. In this way, types 1 and 2 theologies come to the same conclusion about the final relevance of experience to the theological task: Both are seeking "formal and universally applicable, context-invariant criteria by which [the-ology] is governed," as the transcendental or metaphysical grounds on which the human religious experience rests.[29]

This particular linkage of theology and a particular discipline of philosophy again poses particular problems for the anthropologist. First, as Asad points out in his critique of Geertz, such a quest for universal underpinnings of human experience rests on modernist assumptions of humanity as able to stand at some remove from the institutions, structures, and power relation-ships that are deeply central to contemporary views of culture and society.[30] Second, even in type 2 theology, the particularities of ethnographic and historical context are not of primary interest and become so much background noise to the fundamental work of finding universal principles. As many anthropologists, particularly anthropologists of Christianity, have long noted,

---

[26] Regarding the varieties of phenomenology, and a concise discussion of the development of phenomenological analysis in philosophy, see *Encyclopedia of Phenomenology*, ed. Lester Embree et al. (Dordrecht, Netherlands and Boston, MA: Springer, 1996), s.v. "phenomenology/#4."

[27] For a recent example in anthropology, see Sarah S. Willen and Don Seeman, "Introduction: Experience and Inquiétude," *Ethos* 40/1 (2012): 1–23. In theology, see Patrick Masterson, *Approaching God: Between Phenomenology and Theology* (London: Bloomsbury Academic, 2013).

[28] Frei, *Types of Christian Theology*, 32.   [29] Ibid., 33.

[30] Asad, "Anthropological Conceptions of Religion."

this approach undermines much of what makes anthropology relevant in contemporary social analysis. Type 2 theology opens itself up to a critique similar to that of structuralism—namely, that it is rooted in an asocial formalism that can take little account of present social–material realities.[31] In order for theology to engage contemporary anthropology, local context cannot be a means to an analytical end but must be centrally important in the analysis itself.

* * *

Type 3 theology, along with types 4 and 5, begins to move theology as a discipline away from philosophy and toward ethics, making particularity, context, tradition, and history more central to the work of the theologian. It becomes less possible to speak of theology in the abstract and necessary to speak of Christian (or Hindu or Islamic) theology(ies) in the particular. In this type, theology is a second-order didactic language in which particular self-description and academic theological description are *correlated* but not hierarchically arranged nor reaching for a universal principle of description. Using Schleiermacher as the example of this theology, in type 3 Frei sees a theology in which philosophy is not at the base, but phenomenology, ethics, and self-description are correlated with external description of Christianity as religion. Schleiermacher, as the exemplar of this type, is not always sure how much or even *if* Christianity, or any specific tradition, can be effectively correlated to external descriptions. The possibility of such a correlation, however, provides a link between the specific community in which a religious tradition is developed and disciplines such as philosophy. The language of the church, in this type of theology, can never be dissolved into a more general cultural or philosophical–technical vocabulary. It is always community-specific. As one commentator on Schleiermacher writes, "Theology is, thus, the science of God in a particular sense; it communicates a way of being conscious of God as given in Christianity. Similarly, it is reflection upon the religious faith of human beings as expressed by Christianity. Theology presupposes the historical and empirical given-ness of the Christian religion. It is the form in which reflection upon the Christian religion takes shape, and that happens in different ways."[32] This emphasis on particularity corresponds to the call by some anthropologists[33] to attend to the specificity of particular Christianities rather than assume a uniform essence of the religion. As Fenella Cannell notes in her Malinowski lecture, Christians in diverse contexts (re)construe their doctrines of the faith and their resulting identities as Christians in strikingly distinct

---

[31] See, for example, Simon Clarke, *The Foundations of Structuralism: A Critique of Levi-Strauss and the Structuralist Movement* (Sussex, UK: Harvester Press, 1981).

[32] Willhelm Gräb, "Practical Theology as Theology of Religion: Schleiermacher's Understanding of Practical Theology as a Discipline," *International Journal of Practical Theology* 9/2 (2005): 185.

[33] For example, see Fenella Cannell, "The Christianity of Anthropology," *Journal of the Royal Anthropological Institute* 11/2 (2005): 335–56.

ways, even in regards to such seemingly essential doctrines as transcendence, resurrection, and salvation. Anthropologists, who join Schleiermacher in approaching Christianity (or any religious tradition) phenomenologically, could likewise endorse his view that the meaningfulness of religious concepts (e.g., *sin* and *grace* in the Christian tradition) comes from their correlation with a general or universal human experience of self-consciousness.

At the same time, anthropologists in the past several decades have often moved away from the general or universal aspects of human life to drill down to specificity and particularity as the only locus of anthropological investigation. In these modes, anthropology would find even type 3 theology insufficiently related to the nature of meaning as historical, temporally, and culturally contingent.

*   *   *

As with H. Richard Niebuhr's famous typologies of Christ and culture, Frei leads from his early types, which he does not favor, to his preferred vision. For type 4, Frei turns to the theology of Barth as an exemplar of the type of theology that moves even further toward particularity and the internal language of Christianity as the site of theological method and meaning. This *dogmatic theology* places all theology within a tradition. Regarding Barth's theology, Frei writes, "The situation of the Church, or Christian life in our culture in our day, is such that Christian subjectivity, or how to become a Christian, must be—not existentially, but theologically—subordinate to the *what* of Christianity."[34] Theology, in this view, has no universal first principles on which it can stand, moving theology even further from any grounding in philosophy.

As David Martin observed about the relationship of the religious and the secular, the concept of the religious presupposes that of the secular and vice versa.[35] On the other hand, Barthian dogmatic theology resolutely held that Christian theology was not defined in contradistinction to other, non-Christian theologies, or secularism, or as a religion among others. Instead, Barth argued that Christian theology properly served as a *critique* of religion and secularism in which God, speaking through the Church, governed the work of the theologian to produce a second-order discourse subordinated to the life of the Church in God.

This Wittgensteinian appeal to internal grammars and logics does not eschew rules or guiding interpretive frameworks completely but does contextualize them to particular communities of interpretation. The application of

---

[34] Frei, *Types of Christian Theology*, 43. Barth has been subject to a great deal of discussion regarding his relationship to philosophy, particularly in his rejection of liberal theology in the years after World War I. For an in-depth discussion, see Kenneth Oakes, *Karl Barth on Theology and Philosophy* (Oxford: Oxford University Press, 2012), <http://search.ebscohost.com/login.aspx?direct=true&scope=site&db=nlebk&db=nlabk&AN=551487>.

[35] Daniel Jenkins, "*The Religious and the Secular*: David Martin," *The Journal of Religion*, 51/4 (October 1971): 295–300.

philosophical schemes becomes an ad hoc affair rather than a foundation for universal theorizing. In relating this approach to the puzzles of anthropologists, this fourth type moves further from any sort of definitive grounding of social life in universal categories. While not every anthropologist would be happy to embrace such moves, many of those entangled with the questions of morality, values, and the creation of meanings, which is to say a lot of us, would find more analytical freedom to account for the fluidity and variety of social encounters as truer to the plurality of actual worlds in which we find ourselves over those forms of theological inquiry that continue to drive toward universals.

For example, in their article posing the question "Who is a Christian?" anthropologists William Garriott and Kevin O'Neill pick up the idea raised earlier in the anthropology of Christianity about the nature of Christianity as an anthropological object, the possibilities for meaningful comparison, and the relationship of Christianity to another key anthropological problematic—religion. They argue that the concept of Christianity, for Christians and anthropologists, emerges through a dialogic process, much as the concept of culture emerges in anthropological circles. Anthropologists, such as Barthian theologians, must then look for the definitions of key concepts within the dialogic practice of particular communities instead of working to connect them to philosophical or anthropological universals: "Rather than debate Christianity's 'cultural content' (Robbins, 2004a)—Is Christianity essentially other-worldly? Is Christianity essentially individualistic? Is Christianity essentially a-political?—anthropologists should turn their eye towards the kinds of problems Christian communities themselves seem to be preoccupied with."[36] Only in this way, they argue, will anthropologists be able to realize the goal of allowing Christians to "make sense in their own terms."[37] Type 4 seems to bring theology into focus much as some anthropologists of Christianity see their own discipline best engaging Christianity as a kind of anthropological object.

Type 5 places theology as wholly internal to religion. This theology says, along with Peter Winch, "One cannot apply criteria of logic to modes of social life as such. For instance, science is one such mode and religion is another; and each has criteria of intelligibility peculiar to itself."[38] Thus, only in the confession of faith, a particular faith, combined with the meaningfulness that comes with living out these confessions in context can theological reflection and proclamation take place. Citing D. Z. Phillips as an exemplar of this position, Frei argues that such a theological approach leans resolutely on Wittgenstein

---

[36] William Garriott and Kevin Lewis O'Neill, "Who Is a Christian? Toward a Dialogic Approach in the Anthropology of Christianity," *Anthropological Theory* 8/4 (2008): 388.

[37] Joel Robbins, "What Is a Christian? Notes toward an Anthropology of Christianity," *Religion* 33/3 (2003): 193.

[38] Peter Winch, *The Idea of a Social Science and Its Relation to Philosophy* (London: Routledge, 2008), 94.

to emphasize the internal grammar of any religious language, such that any language of belief and faith is "incommensurable" with philosophical language of rational or empirical foundationalism. While Frei never tips his hand as to which sort of theology he favors in these last two typologies, Phillips frequently, and favorably, refers to one of Frei's most eminent students, George Lindbeck.[39]

Lindbeck is best known for *postliberal theology*. Postliberalism, of which Frei is often considered a founder, offers a *cultural–linguistic* approach to theology, drawing on the semiotics of Clifford Geertz, along with the philosophy of Wittgenstein, among others. Like languages, says Lindbeck, religions are grammatical systems, having internal consistency and meaning but not making *truth claims* properly understood. Theology, they would argue, consists of second-order statements about religion. Theology is like the particular grammatical features of a language, while the religion is a language unto itself. Theology, then, is not properly making truth claims but elucidating the system of thought and life at work.[40]

Such a method has clear resonance with many anthropologists' work on religions. They stop short of trying to determine truth claims but similarly work out what the doctrines (values, beliefs) of adherents mean in relation to the system of understandings that constitute the tradition as a whole. What any particular theology should do, argue the postliberals, is to conform the believer to the overall system of the tradition's narrative rather than reconstruct the narrative either to a cultural formation or a kind of extra-narrative or philosophical adjudication of truth. This form of theology goes the furthest in privileging the internal and *local* in defining what theology is and what it does in any particular instance. Similarly, what many anthropologists of religion, particularly Christianity, seek to do in their own work is develop a deep understanding of specific Christianities without requiring a venture into claims of universal conceptual frameworks.

This type of theology leans toward the sort of radical emphasis on cultural specificity that has defined the so-called ontological turn in anthropology. The ontological turn, rooted in the work of Amazonianists who have long grappled with radical cultural alterity, not only argues against the imposition of universal categories or philosophical foundationalism in anthropological analysis but goes further to push against a universal ontology in the nature of reality.[41]

---

[39] Although Phillips is critical of Lindbeck, his engagement with Lindbeck is substantial and sustained. He acknowledges the affinity of their thought. See D. Z. Phillips, "Lindbeck's Audience," *Modern Theology* 4/2 (1980): 133–54; also, D. Z. Phillips, *Faith after Foundationalism* (Oxford: Routledge, 1988).

[40] George Lindbeck, *The Nature of Doctrine: Religion and Theology in a Postliberal Age* (Louisville, KY: Westminster John Knox Press, 1984).

[41] See, for example, Eduardo Viveiros de Castro, "Cosmological Deixis and Amerindian Perspectivism," *Journal of the Royal Anthropological Institute* 4/3 (1998): 469–88.

Whether *ontology* is simply another name for culture is an issue for debate,[42] but no doubt this discussion is a further push in anthropology to put the specific life worlds and experiences of specific people at the center of all anthropological thinking. Like theology as confession, culture as locally specific ontology makes any statements about truth or reality representations of experience rather than phenomenologically accessible objects in themselves. Some anthropologists of Christianity have argued that this approach is a problem, side-stepping the very basic question of what object an anthropology of Christianity is trying to study,[43] but such a critique is only warranted because so much anthropology of Christianity has gone forward without an overarching definition of Christianity in place. One of the earlier and most prominent voices in the anthropology of Christianity, Joel Robbins, made the following argument in 2003:

> Fearful of resting their efforts on groundless essentialisms, anthropologists are not these days inclined to accept that there is a single thing called Christianity that they might make the object of comparative investigation. There are many kinds of Christianity, and when the number of different kinds is multiplied by the number of different situations in which they have been spread and the number of different cultures to which people have adopted them, it is hard to escape the conclusion that at best we are dealing with Christianities rather than with Christianity, and that at worst these Christianities really have rather little in common with one another.[44]

Approaching Christianity as a plural object in many locally specific guises poses challenges to the comparative project many anthropologists of Christianity seek. Yet, rooted in prevailing views of cultural specificity, anthropologists generally remain strongly inclined to engage the particular local shape of Christian life as opposed to moving quickly, if at all, to an overarching category of Christianity.[45]

* * *

In presenting these five types of theology, I have made no secret that the trend moves from type 1 to type 5 in terms of which sort of theology appears most compatible with anthropology. Types 1, 2, and 3, with their stronger ties to foundationalist philosophy, modernity, and philosophical universals, suggest

---

[42] Michael Carrithers, Matei Candea, Karen Sykes, Martin Holbraad, and Soumhya Venkatesan, "Ontology Is Just Another Word for Culture Motion Tables at the 2008 Meeting of the Group for Debates in Anthropological Theory, University of Manchester," *Critique of Anthropology* 30/2 (2010): 152–200.

[43] See, for example, Jon Bialecki, "Virtual Christianity in an Age of Nominalist Anthropology," *Anthropological Theory* 12/3 (2012): 295–319.

[44] Robbins, "What Is a Christian?" 193.

[45] Bialecki argues that this position is untenable within the anthropology of Christianity and proposes a philosophical solution through the concept of the *virtual* as articulated by Deleuze and Guittari. Bialecki, "Virtual Christianity," 296.

less compatibility with much current work in anthropology generally, and the anthropology of Christianity in particular, in terms of their ability to engage the locally contingent and contextually specific forms of life most interesting to social anthropologists.

The purpose of arguing for the application of these typologies is not to restrict the theologies or theologians available to anthropologists. As Kollman notes in his chapter, Evans-Pritchard drew "neo-Thomistic categories redolent with overt and implicit references to Aristotle" in his work on the Nuer.[46] Though to the point here, Kollman further notes that later anthropology tended to displace, if not reject, these sorts of theological and philosophical groundings.

Similarly, this discussion is not meant to be an opportunity to wrestle over what type 4 or type 5 theology really is. Instead, these typologies and this discussion are meant to interrogate the relationship between theology and philosophy and understand the various categories some theologians recognize. Of course, with the presenting issue being that of the relationship between theology and philosophy, and potential problems with the overt reliance of particular types of theology on philosophical concepts, these typologies call for the question of anthropology's relationship to philosophy as well. However, as is clear from the types of theology, all anthropologists and theologians work with the insights of philosophers, though of different sorts. Types 1, 2, and 3 fall into what might be classed as analytical philosophy, while 4 and 5 draw on the work of continental philosophy. Types 1, 2, and 3 turn to metaphysics, while 4 and 5 invoke philosophies of language, post-structuralism, and, in the case of Deleuze, "transcendental empiricism."[47] By exploring how contemporary anthropologists engage the range of philosophy, we can begin to move closer to a sense of how, and what kind of, theologies might best be used by anthropologists in the puzzles that present themselves in ethnography.

*   *   *

For those familiar with anthropology, the notion that philosophy is an unsuitable conversation partner would seem absurd. Anthropology has long been in conversation with philosophy to the point that the disciplines can seem inextricably bound together. British social anthropologist Tim Ingold once quipped that anthropology is a kind of completed philosophy, saying, "Anthropology is philosophy with the people in."[48] However, in spite of the long history of philosophy informing social anthropology, only recently did a number of prominent anthropologists produce an edited volume in which they asked scholars working in diverse theoretical and geographic areas to reflect on their own

---

[46] Paul Kollman, Chapter 5, 86.
[47] Gilles Deleuze, *Difference and Repetition* (New York: Columbia University Press, 1994).
[48] Tim Ingold, "Editorial," *Man* 27/4 (1992): 695.

mode of engagement with philosophy.[49] Specifically, the editors asked contributors to address questions about the ethnographic and theoretical issues that have pushed them to engage specific philosophers or philosophical traditions.

Their project has strong resonance with the project at hand—anthropologists engaging theology—in several ways. First, philosophy and theology, like philosophy and anthropology, have been conversation partners for as long as both have existed. In many ways, theology and philosophy are indistinguishable as projects in seeking truth and meaning often through abstract and conceptual processes.[50] Second, as the different types of theology that were previously elucidated indicate, many theologians make the manner and kind of philosophy they engage a key feature of their theological work. In other cases, they argue for the sublimation or exclusion of philosophy generally.[51] Exploring the relationship of philosophy to anthropology as it is explicitly modeled in this work may clarify some of the issues at play for those in anthropology seeking to engage theology.

As Frei argues, the types of philosophy deployed in theologies emphasizing context and contingency tend toward antirealism and linguistic limits such as seen in the work of Wittgenstein and Deleuze. The anthropologists engaging philosophy also profess the importance of submitting philosophy to the ethnographic encounters in which it can be called forth: "The turn to philosophy may be compared with the turn to analogy, whereby we grasp the familiar by way of the strange, or with narrative conventions of framing an account of reality by invoking a place and time distant from our own."[52] Of the twelve chapters in *The Ground Between: Anthropologists Engage Philosophy*, several look toward Deleuze, or Deleuze and Guttarri, as key interlocutors for grappling with the "play of forces in the world"[53] or the desire to confront "the in-between, plastic, and ever-unfinished nature of *a* life."[54] Others lean on the

---

[49] Veena Das, Michael Jackson, Arthur Kleinman, and Bhrigupati Singh (eds), "Introduction," in *The Ground Between: Anthropologists Engage Philosophy* (Durham, NC: Duke University Press, 2014), 1–26.

[50] Oliver Crisp and Rowan Williams, *Theology and Philosophy: Faith and Reason* (London: T&T Clark International, 2012); see also Knight, *Liberalism versus Postliberalism*.

[51] Antony Flew, *God & Philosophy* (London: Hutchinson, 1966).

[52] Michael Jackson, "Ajala's Heads: Reflections on Anthropology and Philosophy in a West African Setting," in *The Ground Between: Anthropologists Engage Philosophy*, ed. Veena Das, Arthur Kleinman, Singh Bhrigupati, and Michael Jackson (Durham, NC: Duke University Press, 2014), 28.

[53] Bhrigupati Singh, "How Concepts Make the World Look Different: Affirmative and Negative Genealogies of Thought," in *The Ground Between: Anthropologists Engage Philosophy*, ed. Veena Das, Arthur Kleinman, Bhrigupati Singh, and Michael Jackson (Durham, NC: Duke University Press, 2014), 160.

[54] João Biehl, "Ethnography in the Way of Theory," in *The Ground Between: Anthropologists Engage Philosophy*, ed. Veena Das, Arthur Kleinman, Bhrigupati Singh, and Michael Jackson (Durham, NC: Duke University Press, 2014), 104.

work of Agamben (particularly the notion of *bare life*), or Hannah Arendt and her contextualization of biological life as social, political, and qualified.[55] Similarly prominent are Bourdieu's emphases on the social production of (philosophical) knowledge as the "homing and building" of the world in which people deploy social capital.[56]

Undoubtedly, a different selection of anthropologists would refer to a different corpus of philosophers, but the themes are consistent and unsurprising. What does not appear is the work of Descartes, Kant, or Aristotle except as foils to the philosophy these anthropologists cite. Even more contemporary thinkers such as Rawls, Russell, or Ryle provide little purchase for these anthropologists puzzling with the messy social realities from places as diverse as the slums of Brazil and Delhi, the cities of Qum and Taipai, the highlands of Yemen, and the shanties of Morocco. Although these anthropologists do not use the term, each has a nonfoundationalist philosophy as a primary interlocutor. As Das, Jackson, Kleinman, and Singh write in their introduction, "While all the authors of the chapters that follow are in implicit or explicit agreement that the social is not the ground of all being, the state of the human is seen in that of a 'being-with,' of a thrownness together; there is no originary moment or foundational contract from which human relationships (including those between the anthropologist and his or her respondents) emerge."[57] As with Frei's theology types 4 and 5, the sort of philosophy that resonates with anthropology is that which has the task of bringing ethnography and reality closer together by "generating concepts from life" rather than attempting to explain life through abstract discussions and thought experiments.

This is not to say that the anthropologists of this work, or anthropologists generally, are restricted to a narrow corpus of philosophical thought. Even in the twelve chapters presented, creative explorations of Heidegger, William James, and Henri Bergson appear to speak into the complexities of ethnographic account, moral uncertainty, and "the hunt for wisdom."[58] Still, all have the common theme of finding relevance and explanatory power in philosophies that operate in the intrasubjective narratives of real life, in real places, and with real people. In the same way for theology, anthropologists will likely

---

[55] Didier Fassin, "The Parallel Lives of Philosophy and Anthropology," in *The Ground Between: Anthropologists Engage Philosophy*, ed. Veena Das, Arthur Kleinman, Bhrigupati Singh, and Michael Jackson (Durham, NC: Duke University Press, 2014), 59ff.

[56] Ghassan Hage, "Eavesdropping on Bourdieu's Philosophers," in *The Ground Between: Anthropologists Engage Philosophy*, ed. Veena Das, Arthur Kleinman, Bhrigupati Singh, and Michael Jackson (Durham, NC: Duke University Press, 2014), 152.

[57] Das et al. (eds), "Introduction," 5.

[58] Arthur Kleinman, "The Search for Wisdom: Why William James Still Matters," in *The Ground Between: Anthropologists Engage Philosophy*, ed. Veena Das, Arthur Kleinman, Bhrigupati Singh, and Michael Jackson (Durham, NC: Duke University Press, 2014), 125.

find their most fruitful interlocutors in specific theological traditions and faith communities.

Theologians who have turned to anthropology in their work have acknowledged this debt clearly enough. Christian Scharen and Aana Marie Vigen, a Christian theologian and ethicist respectively, argue for the centrality of ethnography as theological method. Leaning into the anthropology of theorists such as Bourdieu, Wocquant, and Rabinow, Scharen and Vigen describe a theology that is "always particularly incarnate with the life of this or that Christian community."[59] Similarly, theologian Michael Banner has recently drawn on anthropology to produce a moral theology that does not merely address the hard cases but can speak to an ethics of the unfathomable choices by people in the face of daily pressures and constant moral decision making. He has done so by putting anthropology into conversation with theologians such as Barth who seek to place theology in the context of the confessing community.[60]

In this final section, I want to bring the discussion to anthropological concerns by revisiting my earliest fieldwork as previously mentioned. Had this conversation been extant when I first began anthropological fieldwork, aspects of the context could have opened in ways anthropological theory or philosophical principles alone did not provide.

* * *

The upland–lowland conflict of the Philippines bears many similarities to those throughout Southeast Asia. Lowland populations tend to view the upland tribal groups as backward, primitive, wild, and uncivilized. Government policy in the 1950s and 1960s tended towards objectives of civilizing and pacifying upland communities. Political representation tended to be inequitable, and upland communities had few opportunities to represent themselves to lowland authorities. Upland communities, for their part, were distrustful of lowland communities and resentful of the preferential treatment they so clearly received. Though faced with few choices for where to send their children for high school or university, personal and political relations between upland, tribal Filipinos and their lowland compatriots were difficult at best.

By the time Delbert Rice and his family arrived in Imugan in 1958, their primary political concerns were mostly focused on insecure land tenure, a lack of local educational institutions that could teach something other than the ethnocentric attitudes of lowlanders, and economic relationships that exploited the upland communities. US Americans such as Rice and his family were viewed relatively positively, as the US legacy in the mountain regions was often

---

[59] Christian Scharen and Aana Marie Vigen (eds), *Ethnography as Christian Theology and Ethics* (London and New York: Continuum, 2011), 56.

[60] Michael C. Banner, *The Ethics of Everyday Life: Moral Theology, Social Anthropology, and the Imagination of the Human* (Oxford: Oxford University Press, 2014).

understood as one of development and political respect as opposed to the exploitation and violence of Spanish and lowland rule.

In 1990, when taking in the story of Imugan, it was easy to view their efforts to promote and protect their community as ethnically distinct and culturally valuable exclusively through these lenses of political and economic struggle. Framed in terms of how their view of God and newfound faith affirmed their value relative to messages of subservience and backwardness they often received from lowland communities, I argued that Rice's missionary methods, valorizing local cultural forms and language, supported local goals of political and economic power.

I could see even then, however, that a central part of the story involved the ways the Ikalahan of Imugan reimagined their relationship to lowland people, particularly fellow Christians, in particularly Christian ways. The development of institutions and political strategies to manage exploitation of lowland people did not stem merely from the coalescence of people with a common enemy. According to Rice, as the local church grew and local leadership came into positions of influence, the doctrine of Christian brotherhood and sisterhood had begun to heal the animosity the mountain people had developed towards the lowlanders. He noted, in particular, that the local Ikalahan term *gait*, meaning *citizen* or *neighbor*, had begun to be extended to refer to lowland Christians who belonged to the United Church of Christ of the Philippines. This term was normally reserved only for other Ikalahan, non-Ikalahan living in the community, or, occasionally, other mountain people. According to Rice, and several other community members present as he noted this change, this development was significant and indicated a radical shift in the understanding of the nature of community among these formerly antagonistic groups.

Whatever positive feelings may have been reflected in the expansion of the notion of the *gait*, what supported the general optimism of the Ikalahan was their conviction that God was sovereign over their future and the future of their relationships with lowlanders. Omis Balinhawang, a local elder, told me of his trust in God to "protect the Ikalahan" and that he had made them "brothers with [the lowlanders]." This conviction did not reassure him that lowland communities and authorities would never try to take advantage of the Ikalahan again, but he argued, "You cannot just cheat a brother. Your brother can say, 'This is not the way.' God is our Father, so they are our brother. We can tell our brother and he must listen."

This understanding of having a common father, brotherhood, and the necessary social relationships that would result speaks to a deep reordering of being a person in relation to other people, specifically other Christian people. Several of those in the community with whom I spoke brought up similar ideas, though not necessarily framed in kinship terms, about their reason to be optimistic for their future, that God had created a new relationship with lowland Christians that would reorder the relationships towards mutuality, if not equality. Though they viewed the new order as having positive economic and social consequences, and often spoke in those terms, the underlying logic was Christian: United in God through Christ, brothers and sisters could make claims for justice and fairness on one another.

This theological understanding of social life was sectarian and specific, understood as existing throughout the Ikalahan church, among other Christians, and as a normative statement of human life. To view this idea only in terms of the political consequences or in terms of the changes in a socio-economic order misses the subjective motivations at work. Barth argues in his theological anthropology that humans can only know themselves and others through the "real man" of God's self-revelation in Christ.[61] Letitia Baluyan, an ethnic Ilokana from a lowland province who married an Ikalahan man and moved to Imugan as a teacher in the high school, viewed the unity of upland and lowland people as being in Christ, in which exploitation could be addressed through spiritual bonds of faith. When discussing why she believed that relations would continue to improve, she said that as fellow Christians, common bonds to Christ would, eventually, reshape these human relationships. "How can we [continue to cheat one another]?" she rhetorically asked me, declaring that we cannot "cheat Christ, cheat God."[62] She went on to say that "as Christians," the Ikalahan were "born again" and were now in a true relationship with lowland Christians aspiring to Christ-like-ness and mutuality. In other words, Baluyan, like Barth, appears to hold to a Christological position in the "one true man" of Jesus Christ. Only in relationship with Christ, Baluyan suggests, do human beings find their true selves, and understand their true relationships to one another.[63]

On one level, this analysis falls into what Robbins notes as an extant use of theology in the anthropological literature, theology as ethnographic data.[64] However, I would agree with Kollman that to leave this use of theology as *only* a datum in the ethnographic record "narrows the potential impacts of theology on anthropology in unnecessary ways."[65] In this particular case, I suggest that the expression of Christian unity is not an abstract reality of individual equality and common citizenship merely expressed in Christian terms. Such an assertion would veer into the sort of

---

[61] See Karl Barth, *Church Dogmatics*, III/2: *The Doctrine of God*, ed. G. W. Bromiley and T. F. Torrance, trans. H. Knight et al. (Edinburgh: T&T Clark, 1960), 197–8.

[62] Like too many of my notes from this work, I captured these comments only roughly. The larger context of this conversation is lost, but my notes clearly state that she used these terms to refer to her views of what these upland–lowland conflicts would or *should* look like in the future.

[63] Most Protestant Christians in the Philippines understand Catholics as having a fundamentally different relationship with and understanding of Christ. This thinking may be the reason Catholics are not included in the broader brotherhood/sisterhood.

[64] Joel Robbins, "Anthropology and Theology: An Awkward Relationship?" *Anthropological Quarterly* 79/2 (2006), 285–94.

[65] Kollman, Chapter 5, 90.

political–economic reduction I embraced earlier but now as a kind of philosophical reduction. What seems more helpful in taking the Ikalahan seriously
as Christians is to take seriously their dogmatic confessions of Christ, God,
and the Holy Spirit as an ontological shift. Many of the Ikalahan have a sense
that their claims on the lowlanders to treat them justly come from their own
decision to reject their pagan past and be born again in Christ, which has
reconfigured the nature of their relationships. Once in this relationship with
lowland Christians, they have become, in the sense the spiritual–ontological
change that is conversion suggests, part of a theologically defined community
with a specific center. Though I never heard local Ikalahan people develop
this concept as a reflection of Trinitarian theology, their emphasis is on how
God has put the Ikalahan into a new relational dynamic with the lowland
Christians. These ethnic minority Christians were coming to understand and
experience their relationship with other Christians in terms of personhood, as
that idea has been elaborated in Christian theology, rather than moving too
quickly from their theological commitments to universal claims of human
rights, equality, and citizenship.[66]

To relate this short example to the original conversation about the type of
theology that is potentially most helpful, this theology is rooted in a confessing
community, from that community and for that community. It is, *pace* Haynes
in her chapter,[67] theology as a verb, not rooted in Scripture per se, but worked
out in light of being born again, remade in terms of the Body of Christ. It is not
theology seeking universal principles grounded in philosophical universals or
seeking transcendent grounding. This sort of theology, this second-order
thinking about the nature of humanity and God in particularity, can emerge
as a potentially potent source of thought about the things that puzzle anthropologists as much as they also puzzle theologians.

*   *   *

This brief ethnographic illustration cannot exactly build the sort of case to
which I am alluding if only because of the poor quality and limited duration of
the fieldwork. Nevertheless, by thinking in terms of the specificity of the
theological concepts at work through the dogmatic theology of a scholar
such as Barth, aspects of their experience become clearer. In taking the
world of these Christians seriously, it becomes unhelpful to remain in an
analytical frame of universal categories such as equality, citizenship, or even
religiosity.

---

[66] For only a few of the many examples of theology connecting Trinitarianism and Christian
life and selfhood, see Catherine Mowry LaCugna, *God for Us: The Trinity and Christian Life* (San
Francisco: HarperCollins, 1991). See also Stanley Grenz and John Franke, *Beyond Foundationalism: Shaping Theology in a Postmodern Context* (Louisville, KY: Westminster John Knox Press,
2001), 192–202.

[67] Naomi Haynes, Chapter 15, 266–79.

Beyond the specifics of this case, what I suggest is the importance of recognizing how some forms of theology illuminate the contexts in ways that resonate with contemporary anthropology, rather than relocating the place of interpretation away from the community toward universals and generalities. While a number of anthropologists have critiqued the nominalism of contemporary anthropology, I do not mean that anthropologists should cease comparative projects. Rather, I want to emphasize the ways in which theological concepts intrinsically rooted in specific traditions rather than incidentally rooted in those traditions can speak into the particularities of the worlds from which they come. Instead of rendering all these cases hopelessly idiographic, I argue such thinking opens up the emic categories in ways that allow for them to be brought to theologically and anthropologically comparative projects.

This position is not meant to exclude theologians or theologies from the conversation. Certainly, more insightful minds than mine can see ways philosophical theologies intersect with ethnographic realities, particularly as those ethnographic realities range into transnational, fluid, and dynamic contexts—the very places where the universal is often explicitly sought by people themselves though often in particularistic ways. Seeking out the ways theology can aid anthropology in life's puzzles may prove more advantageous when starting with those types of theology that most powerfully support the emphases on the local, cultural, and contingent aspects of life that ground our anthropological work. At the very least, we better serve anthropology to recognize the ways in which theology, as a discipline, confronts some of the very issues that have worried anthropologists as well. In this commonality, we may find common ground.

3

The Dependence of Sociocultural Anthropology on Theological Anthropology

Timothy Larsen and Daniel J. King

Classic Christian theological anthropology has emphasized that all people are part of the one human family descending from Adam and Eve, created in the image of God, yet fallen and sinful. From the beginning of Christian thought, Genesis chapters 1–3 have thus been foundational for a doctrinal understanding of the nature of the human race. For example, Pauline theology emphasized that all human beings share the same plight because everyone is "in Adam" (1 Cor. 15:22). This theological conviction has direct application for thinking about issues of human diversity, not the least of which are race and ethnicity. To wit, the Acts of the Apostles records that in his famous sermon in Athens the apostle Paul taught that God "hath made of one blood all the nations of men" (Acts 17:26). This text had a prominent role to play in establishing the discipline of social anthropology in the nineteenth century. The King James Version will, therefore, be used throughout this chapter as it was quoted in those foundational debates. Because all the diverse peoples of the world share a common origin and a common current condition and are all part of the one human family, they also all share in a common destiny as God's redeemed family—a family that is declared in the Revelation of St John the Divine to be systematically inclusive of all the racial and ethnic groups of the entire world: "After this I beheld, and, lo, a great multitude which no man could number, of all nations, and kindreds, and people, and tongues, stood before the throne, and before the Lamb, clothed with white robes" (Rev. 7:9). Again, orthodox Christian thought has always recognized the import of these theological convictions in responding to ethnic and racial diversity across the continents. For example, the most influential theologian in the Western tradition, St Augustine of Hippo, explicitly pronounced on this issue in his magnum opus, *The City of God*. The question he posed there is whether, in exploring the globe, one might encounter racial diversity so great as to make untenable this theological assumption of human unity:

There are accounts in pagan history of certain monstrous races of men.... Some of those monsters are said to have only one eye, in the middle of their forehead.... There is also a story of a race who have a single leg attached to their feet; they cannot bend their knee, and yet have a remarkable turn of speed.... Now we are not bound to believe in the existence of all the types of men which are described. But no faithful Christian should doubt that anyone who is born anywhere as a man—that is, a rational and mortal being—derives from that one first-created human being. And this is true, however extraordinary such a creature may appear to our senses in bodily shape, in colour, or motion, or utterance, or in any natural endowment, or part, or quality.... If these races are included in the definition of "human", that is, if they are rational and mortal animals, it must be admitted that they trace their lineage from the same one man, the first father of all mankind.... The accounts of some of these races may be completely worthless; but if such people exist, then either they are not human; or, if human, they are descended from Adam.[1]

Classic Christian theology has emphatically emphasized the unity of the human race.

Social and cultural anthropologists, by contrast, have often been people who shed the faith of their fathers and mothers for a secular outlook. Edward Burnett Tylor (1832–1917), who was the first person to hold a faculty appointment in anthropology (at the University of Oxford), is generally considered to be the founder of the discipline of anthropology. He was raised in the Society of Friends and was a pious Christian in early adulthood, but he lost his faith once he began his ethnological studies and, therefore, resigned his church membership in 1864. The most famous anthropologist of the next generation was James George Frazer (1854–1941), the author of the highly influential *The Golden Bough*. Despite his devout Presbyterian childhood, Frazer likewise rejected Christianity and religious belief altogether as an adult. Tylor, Frazer, and many other anthropologists of their era and subsequent generations saw religious beliefs as just misguided, irrational answers to questions correctly answered by science.[2] The historian Henrika Kuklick's judgment on anthropologists in the late nineteenth and early twentieth century was: "In the aggregate ... their attitude to religion was hostile."[3] The theories of the French sociologist Émile Durkheim (1858–1917) became deeply influential in the discipline of anthropology. Many social scientists found it telling that Durkheim, even though he was born into a family of rabbis, adopted a secular identity. Likewise, Bronislaw Malinowski (1884–1942), who is credited with pioneering intensive participant–observer fieldwork, shed the Catholicism

---

[1] St Augustine, *The City of God*, trans. Henry Bettenson (London: Penguin Books, 1984), 661–4 (from book XVI, ch. 8).

[2] Timothy Larsen, *The Slain God: Anthropologists and the Christian Faith* (Oxford: Oxford University Press, 2014).

[3] Henrika Kuklick, *The Savage Within: The Social History of British Anthropology, 1885–1945* (Cambridge: Cambridge University Press, 1991), 79.

of his childhood for an agnostic stance. Franz Boas (1858–1942), commonly known as the father of American anthropology, abandoned the Judaism of his ancestors for a rationalistic humanism. Moreover, in keeping with Tylor and Frazer, many sociocultural anthropologists continued to view social science as a kind of substitute for religious thought. In short, they assumed that theology and anthropology were incompatible, competing modes of thought rather than potentially complementary or mutually enriching ones. As Jean La Fontaine, Lecturer in Social Anthropology at the London School of Economics, noted succinctly in 1977 in a splendid example of the human tendency toward binary thinking, "Once you stop religious thought, you start thinking anthropologically."[4] As another random example, Elmer S. Miller, Professor of Anthropology at Temple University, wrote an entire book published in 1995 that was a how-to de-conversion narrative, "depicting the move from theological to anthropological discourse."[5]

In such a climate, Genesis 1–3 has been a particularly tempting target for anthropologists. The following are just a few examples given in chronological order. T. H. Huxley (1825–95) is usually thought of today as a biologist, but, in those early days when no one was a full-time anthropologist, he was so committed to anthropology that he rose to be the president of the leading British scientific organization for the study of anthropology—the Ethnological Society of London—and was instrumental in the creation of what is now called the Royal Anthropological Institute. Therefore, the highest honor that the Royal Anthropologist Institute has to confer is the Huxley Memorial Medal. Huxley went out of his way to argue at length that the Genesis narrative was only a myth and was impossible to harmonize with modern scientific thinking. As a result, it must simply be eliminated from all scholarly discourse. Nothing annoyed him more than a brilliant, learned individual who thought that some fragment from Genesis, rightly interpreted, had an illuminating or constructive role to play in contemporary scientific discussions.[6] In *Folklore in the Old Testament* (1918), Frazer strove to show that the accounts of Genesis 1–3 were just the absurd and erroneous thinking of savages, as intellectually worthless as parallel accounts by such degraded, irrational creatures as "Hottentots" and "Bushmen."[7] The eminent Cambridge anthropologist Edmund Leach published *Genesis as Myth* in 1969. In it, he carried on the assumption that theological and anthropological thinking were incompatible. After presenting

---

[4] Sheila Hale, "Closely Observed Brains," *Harper's Bazaar and Queen* (January 1977), 70–3, 244 (here 71).
[5] Elmer S. Miller, *Nurturing Doubt: From Mennonite Missionary to Anthropologist in the Argentine Chaco* (Urbana: University of Illinois Press, 1995).
[6] T. H. Huxley, *Essays upon Some Controverted Questions* (London: Macmillan, 1892), 75–130 ("The Interpreters of Genesis and the Interpreters of Nature" and "Mr Gladstone and Genesis").
[7] James George Frazer, *Folk-Lore in the Old Testament* (London: Macmillan, 1918), 3–77.

the view of "the believer," Leach averred by way of contrast: "The anthropologist's viewpoint is different. He rejects the idea of a supernatural sender."[8] The social scientist not only writes from a perspective that does not assume divine revelation, but to be a true anthropologist, according to Leach, he or she must actively reject that idea as false. As to the contents of the Genesis narrative, Leach explained that Christian believers value these accounts precisely because of their extravagant nonrationality, as claiming to believe the unbelievable is a kind of extreme sport among the faithful.[9]

Indeed, the Christian claim that all people are part of the one human family had already been widely challenged in learned circles well before the founding of the discipline of anthropology. By the time of the Enlightenment, freethinking philosophers and scientists were no longer willing to accept an idea because it was an article of religious faith. Those intellectuals who did not accept the authority of orthodox Christianity held the dominant view that racial differences were so great that the idea of a fundamental familial unity that could hold together all that diversity was not reasonable. Already in the eighteenth century, Deists, freed from the constraints of the authority of Scripture, gravitated to polygenesis—the assumption that Europeans and Africans cannot be part of the same human family but must be distinct in origin. Voltaire abandoned old-fashioned, orthodox Christian ideas regarding the universal brotherhood of humanity and replaced them with enlightened racism. Likewise, the religious skeptic David Hume was eager to lead the way to a more reasonable age:

> I am apt to suspect the negroes, and in general all the other species of men (for there are four or five different kinds) to be naturally inferior to whites. There was never a civilized nation of any other complexion than white, nor even any individual eminent either in action or speculation.... Such a uniform and constant difference could not happen, in so many countries and ages, if nature had not made an original distinction betwixt these breeds of men.[10]

One influential text was *Sketches of the History of Man* (1774) by Lord Kames (1696–1782), a central figure in the Scottish Enlightenment. "The colour of the Negroes," he averred, "affords a strong presumption of their being a different species from the Whites."[11] Having laid out the evidence for polygenesis at length, Kames concluded that science has no way to suppose that all the races are part of the same species. He then pressed the point that the only reason why anyone would imagine such a thing is out of deference for religion: "But this opinion [polygenesis], however plausible, we are not permitted to adopt;

---

[8] Edmund Leach, *Genesis as Myth* (London: Jonathan Cape, 1969), 9.   [9] Ibid., 7.

[10] David Hume, *Essays and Treatises on Several Subjects*, 4th edn (London: A. Millar, 1753), 1: 291.

[11] Lord Henry Home Kames, *Sketches of the History of Man*, ed. James A. Harris (1788; repr. Indianapolis: Liberty Fund, 2007), 1: 41.

being taught a different lesson by revelation—namely, That God created but a single pair of the human species. Though we cannot doubt the authority of Moses, yet his account of the creation of man is not a little puzzling, as it seems to contradict every one of the facts mentioned above."[12] To reiterate, this thought became the standard, majority view for men and women of science who were not also willing to defer to the authority of the teachings of Christianity. Moreover, polygenetic freethinkers wrote most of the books that dealt with the question of polygenesis versus monogenesis as well as most of the ones that were generally accepted to be scientifically convincing.

*   *   *

The story to tell in this setting is how in nineteenth-century Britain certain learned Christians resisted this assumption of polygenesis and sought to rebuild scientific thinking about humanity once again upon the foundation of orthodox theological anthropology, how an account of that effort is also the story of the founding of social anthropology as a scholarly discipline, and how theological anthropology successfully defeated freethinking, polygenetic anthropology to become foundational in the discipline.[13] This story is primarily institutional, but it begins with an individual—the pioneering ethnologist James Cowles Prichard (1786–1848). Tylor is generally acknowledged to be the father of anthropology but, as ethnologists know, most everything has a prehistory, and Tylor himself claimed that Prichard "merits the title of the founder of modern anthropology."[14] Prichard was raised as a devout Quaker and, in adulthood, became a zealous, earnest, evangelical Anglican. He made an influential, scientifically current case for monogenesis in his *Researches into the Physical History of Man*, the first edition of which was published in 1813. In a splendid example of an author identifying his own situatedness, Prichard wrote in the preface:

> My attention was strongly excited to this inquiry many years ago by happening to hear the truth of the Mosaic records implicated in it and denied on the alleged impossibility of reconciling the history contained in them with the phaenomena of Nature, and particularly with the diversified characters of the several races of men. The arguments of those who assert that these races constitute distinct species appeared to me at first irresistible, and I found no satisfactory proof in

---

[12] Kames, *Sketches*, 47.

[13] Key scholarly accounts of aspects of this story are given in George W. Stocking, Jr, "What's in a Name? The Origins of the Royal Anthropological Institute (1837–71)," *Journal of the Royal Anthropological Institute* 6/3 (September 1971): 369–90; George W. Stocking, Jr, *Victorian Anthropology* (New York: The Free Press, 1987); Efram Sera-Shriar, *The Making of British Anthropology, 1813–1871* (London: Pickering & Chatto, 2013).

[14] George W. Stocking, Jr, "From Chronology to Ethnology: James Cowles Prichard and British Anthropology, 1800–1850," in James Cowles Prichard, *Researches into the Physical History of Man*, ed. George W. Stocking, Jr (Chicago: University of Chicago Press, 1973), x.

the vague and conjectural reasonings by which the opposite opinion has generally been defended.[15]

In other words, as a believer, he was rattled to hear the theology of the Genesis account rejected on the grounds of insurmountable human diversity, but, when he looked into it, he was forced to admit that the polygenetic case was more convincingly presented in the current scientific literature. However, he hoped that the massive book he was introducing would make a scientifically convincing case for monogenesis. Having admitted his theological bias, Prichard went on to declare that in the book itself, "I have made no reference to the writings of Moses," as some readers would not accept the authority of divine revelation and even those who did still wished to know how far the teachings of Christianity about the human race accord with what can be discovered independently.[16] Not the least fascinating part of Prichard's book was the section entitled, "Primitive stock of men Negroes," in which he argued that whites were descendants of black people.[17] In a pre-Darwinian context, this thought was deeply offensive to many Britons at the time. While such a view could be read in a progressive frame in which white people represent the pinnacle of evolutionary perfection, Prichard was a pre-Darwinian defender of orthodox Christianity—as were many of his readers. In such a theological frame, the implication was that when Genesis 1 says that God first created human beings in his very own image and pronounced the result to be "very good," these statements are being made about "negroes."[18]

Moving on to an institutional story—a history, this setting must be kept in mind throughout, which is the direct lineage of the Royal Anthropological Institute. This genealogy begins with the Aborigines Protection Society (APS), which was founded in 1837. The APS was a classic evangelical effort to do good in the world. It was a logical next step from the evangelical effort to abolish slavery. Indeed, William Wilberforce's close colleague and chosen successor in the political opposition to slavery, the evangelical Anglican T. Fowell Buxton (1786–1845), was the APS's first president. The Quaker Dr Thomas Hodgkin (1798–1866) was officially recognized as "the Father and Founder of the Aborigines Protection Society."[19] The APS's committee was packed with leading evangelical Anglicans, Quakers, and Congregationalists. In fact, its committee looks strikingly like that of even such a thoroughly religious organization as the British and Foreign Bible Society, and, in truth, many of the same people served both organizations. The APS even met in Exeter Hall, London, a venue whose very name was used in popular discourse as a synonym for evangelical activism. The APS had so many eminent divines

---

[15] Prichard, *Researches*, ii.   [16] Ibid., iii.   [17] Ibid., 233–9.   [18] Ibid.
[19] *First Annual Report of the Aborigines Protection Society* (London: Aborigines Protection Society, 1838), 11.

involved that its annual meeting commonly conducted business by having its motions both resolved and seconded by a minister of religion. The APS was explicit that it was a Christian organization motivated by "the genius of that holy and eminently benevolent religion which we profess."[20] As to theological anthropology, its official motto was *ab uno sanguine* (of one blood), a direct quotation from Acts 17:26, the import of which was to declare that Almighty God had revealed that all the peoples of the world are blood relations and, therefore, must be treated with brotherly love. To underline the true nature of the APS, the following article from the *Zoologist* in 1868 provides a description of the society in order to go on to criticize what the author saw as misguided philanthropy: "In the year 1836 a number of these philanthropists associated themselves in a body which they called the Aborigines' Protection Society: they took for a motto the words 'Ab uno sanguine'; and their avowed object was to protect those savages whom they found in the possession of the soil, on the ground that all the races or varieties of the genus Homo were descended from one stock. They even objected to the word 'savage' as applied to men...."[21] From the very beginning, the APS pursued scholarly and scientific interests. It even declared that its "first object" was to collect "authentic information" regarding the "character, habits, and wants" of indigenous peoples.[22] Therefore, the APS quickly established itself as the only organization in existence that furthered the aims of those interested in the study of anthropology. After a few years, members recognized the advantage and sensibility of having a separate organization dedicated to the purely scholarly side of the APS's mission. Thomas Hodgkin has the honor of being the founder of the Ethnological Society of London (ESL), which came into existence in 1843 and initially even met in his home. He continued, of course, to give leadership in the APS; thus, the two organizations had overlapping lists of supporters, including, most notably, Richard King and Henry Christy, who were office holders in both organizations, and, to return to an earlier discussion, Prichard. The ESL was also evangelical in ethos. It continued to adhere to the APS's commitment to the monogenesis of the human race. The full title of the ESL expounded that it was "for the study of the human race in all its varieties."[23] While that mission could still serve rather well for an anthropological society today, it was rather pointed at the time in its insistence that the varieties all belonged to a singular entity called *the* human race. Prichard became the ESL's second president and was serving in his second term when he died in 1848. Finally, the ESL was quite willing to evoke Scripture and theology as relevant sources of authority but not, of course, as a substitute

---

[20] Ibid., 9.
[21] Edward Newman, "The Death of Species," *Zoologist* (second series) 3 (October 1868): 1385–95 (here 1386).
[22] Stocking, "What's in a Name?" 370.
[23] *Transactions of the Ethnological Society of London* n.s. 1 (1869): [xvi].

for scientific findings. For example, Robert Dunn was a vice president of the ESL and a contributor to *Transactions of the Ethnological Society of London*. In an 1861 article entitled "On the Physiological and Psychological Evidence in Support of the Unity of the Human Species," after the presentation of recent findings, Dunn went on to aver:

> I cannot dismiss the consideration of the physiological evidence without advert-ing to the confirmation which the revelations of the microscope have given to the dicta of Holy Writ—that *God has made of one blood all the nations of the earth, to dwell upon all the face of the earth*; for these prove to demonstration that human blood, whether from Caucasian, Mongolian, Ethiopian, or half-caste, presents the same identical corpuscles, and contains the same elementary constituents—in other words, that the blood is precisely the same in all the races of man.[24]

The evangelical-orientated ESL was the champion of the unity of the human race in social scientific thought.

Of course, polygenetic thinking had not simply gone away. Notably, the ethnologist Robert Knox (1793–1862) was a religious skeptic who was apt to annoy people with his anti-Christian quips, and he made the case against the universal brotherhood view in *The Races of Men* (1850). In the very first paragraph he warned that his book would be unsettlingly anti-orthodox: "the views it contains being so wholly at variance with long received doc-trines, . . . as old at least as the Hebrew record."[25] His judgment on "the black man" was that his color was just the beginning of what made him fundamentally different: "He is no more a white man than an ass is a horse or a zebra."[26] In a recent study, Efram Sera-Shriar categorizes Knox as "a staunch polygenist."[27] The ESL found Knox's work and its author so unacceptable that when he applied to join the society in 1855 the vote of the existing fellows went against him, and his application was rejected. This act, in turn, was seen as scandalously unacceptable—that a leading figure in British anthropology would be barred from the one organization dedicated to that field of study, so a workaround compromise was finally arranged in 1858 and he was named an honorary fellow. A freethinker who was deeply influenced by Knox's work was James Hunt (1833–69). Hunt became co-secretary of the ESL in 1860, but he increas-ingly chafed against its evangelical, monogenetic ethos.

Tellingly, the break came over a plan to reproduce in the society's journal some drawings of the people of Sierra Leone. Sierra Leone, of course, was an abolitionist experiment in a free black society, which again underlines the

---

[24] Robert Dunn, "On the Physiological and Psychological Evidence in Support of the Unity of the Human Species," *Transactions of the Ethnological Society of London* 1 (1861): 186–202 (here 191–2).

[25] Robert Knox, *The Races of Men: A Fragment* (Philadelphia: Lea & Blanchard, 1850), 7.

[26] Ibid., 163.   [27] Sera-Shriar, *Making of British Anthropology*, 82.

strong ties between the ESL and APS. The drawings presented these black men and women as beautiful, elegant, dignified, and civilized.[28] Hunt was livid. When he failed in his attempts to prevent their publication, he resigned from the ESL and in 1863 founded his own rival organization, the Anthropological Society of London (ASL), which, in direct contrast to the ESL, was anti-orthodox Christianity and polygenetic in ethos. Hunt, as president of the new society, insisted that the ESL's commitment to religious thought made it unscholarly, whereas the ASL would not flinch at defying orthodoxy: "This Society is formed with the object of promoting the study of Anthropology in a strictly scientific manner. . . . No Society existing in this country has proposed to itself these aims."[29] In *On the Negro's Place in Nature* (1863), Hunt argued that the unbiased, scientific view clearly supported polygenesis. Echoing Knox, his general deduction from the evidence he presented was as follows: "That there is as good reason for classifying the Negro as a distinct species from the European, as there is for making the ass a distinct species from the zebra; and if, in classification, we take intelligence into consideration, there is a far greater difference between the Negro and European than between the gorilla and chimpanzee."[30] In a direct challenge to the Acts 17:26 proof text so beloved by the opposite camp, Hunt triumphantly appealed to evidence from "a lady who assisted in the microscopical investigations of some scientific men in the Confederate States of America," which, according to his informant, revealed that "the blood is vastly dissimilar."[31] According to Hunt, the anthropologists of the ESL insisted that all members of the genus *homo* were one species for only one reason: Theologically, they were "wedded to the theory of a single pair for the origin of man."[32]

In order to grasp the next twist in this story, it is necessary to overturn a popular misconception—namely, that evangelicals by and large rejected Darwinism as a horrifying and unchristian theory. This assumption comes from backdating the views of twentieth-century fundamentalists to nineteenth-century evangelicals. In fact, many leading evangelicals actually promptly welcomed Darwinism. The evangelist Henry Drummond (1851–97), for example, a close colleague of the leading revivalist D. L. Moody, made a career out of writing highly popular devotional books that drew spiritual lessons

---

[28] For reproductions of some of these images, see Sera-Shriar, *Making of British Anthropology*, 122–4.

[29] James Hunt, *On the Negro's Place in Nature* (published for the Anthropological Society; London: Trübner and Co., 1863), 55.

[30] Ibid., 51–2.

[31] Ibid., vii–viii. For a recent study that demonstrates how often Christian thought was a roadblock to racist theories and how often anti-orthodox freethinking led to more aggressively racist stances, see Colin Kidd, *The Forging of Races: Race and Scripture in the Protestant Atlantic World, 1600–2000* (Cambridge: Cambridge University Press, 2006).

[32] Hunt, *On the Negro's Place in Nature*, 26.

from the truth of evolution by natural selection.[33] The ESL, therefore, became the institutional home for the evangelical–evolutionary alliance. Even Darwinists who were personally religious freethinkers emphatically chose the ESL over the ASL. Huxley, who has been called "Darwin's bulldog" and who coined the word *agnosticism* to describe his own lack of religious convictions, nevertheless called the ASL "that nest of imposters" and, when they tried to soften him with an honorary recognition, sent it back.[34] The evangelicals at the ESL so welcomed Darwinism that Huxley was soon on its council and, by 1868, was president. The ASL, by contrast, although it marketed itself as standing for pure science and unfettered free thought, vehemently rejected Darwinism. Hunt declared that there was no real difference between being "a disciple of Darwin and a disciple of Moses."[35] Evolution through natural selection, of course, fully explained how white people could have descended from black people and thus strengthened the case for monogenesis which, indeed, was the chosen view of the Darwinists. Hunt fumed against Huxley's "dogmatic assertions," loading his rejection of Darwinism with words that insisted it was just a disguised reassertion of ortho-dox Christian theological anthropology:

> We are asked indeed as men of science to have faith, because on some curious process of reasoning it must have been as they teach. We entirely fail to see a particle of foundation either in reason or analogy for the unity hypothesis on Darwinian principles. We are called on to believe with those disciples in the unity of origin of mankind simply as an article of faith. There is no more foundation for a dogma promulgated on such evidence than for that taught by the majority of theologians in the present day.[36]

An American equivalent was Josiah C. Nott of Alabama, author of *Types of Mankind* (1854), whom the ASL declared to be "the greatest living anthro-pologist in America."[37] Nott was also a polygenetic thinker, an ultra-racist, a religious unbeliever who enjoyed rattling Christians, and an opponent of evolution by natural selection right to his death in 1873.[38]

Here is the point to grasp: The wider anthropological community was determined to excommunicate and eradicate the ASL and its polygenetic

---

[33] David N. Livingstone, *Darwin's Forgotten Defenders: The Encounter between Evangelical Theology and Evolutionary Thought* (Edinburgh: Scottish Academic Press, 1987).

[34] Stocking, "What's in a Name?" 377.

[35] Ibid., 378. For recent studies exploring this aspect of the Darwinists, see Adrian Desmond and James Moore, *Darwin's Sacred Cause: How a Hatred of Slavery Shaped Darwin's Views on Human Evolution* (Boston: Houghton Mifflin Harcourt, 2009); B. Ricardo Brown, *Until Darwin: Science, Human Variety and the Origins of Race* (London: Pickering & Chatto, 2010).

[36] James Hunt, "On the Application of the Principle of Natural Selection to Anthropology," *Anthropological Review* 4/15 (October 1866): 320–40 (here 330–1).

[37] Desmond and Moore, *Darwin's Sacred Cause*, 332.

[38] Terence D. Keel, "Religion, Polygenism and the Early Science of Human Origins," *History of the Human Sciences* 26/2 (2013): 3–32.

anthropology. When Hunt gave a paper at the British Association for the Advancement of Science, he was greeted with "loud hisses."[39] Huxley and the others thought it was scandalous that the discipline of anthropology should be ostensibly represented by this rival organization. They schemed to destroy the ASL. After Hunt was dead, they planned a merger, which was really a takeover. In 1871, the ESL and the ASL came together as the Anthropological Institute of Great Britain and Ireland. The evangelicals and evolutionists then changed their policies so as effectively to eliminate former members of the ASL from leadership positions in the new organization. The freethinking, anti-evolution, polygenetic anthropologists realized they had been defeated and broke away again to form what they called the London Anthropological Society, but their faction had been too effectively routed and this new organization quickly dissolved. As Adrian Desmond and James Moore have recently written, the ESL captured and decapitated the ASL.[40] In 1907, the renamed ESL was granted patronage from the crown and thus became the Royal Anthropological Institute.

Like the Vatican retrospectively pronouncing on who were the true popes and who were the antipopes during the Western Schism, so in the official, collective memory, the early figures in British anthropology have become the Prichard–Huxley line and not the Knox–Hunt one. Tylor first became interested in the subject when Henry Christy (1810–65), a leading light of both the APS and the ESL, befriended him. Tylor shed his Christian faith, accepting the binary of moving from thinking theologically to thinking anthropologically, but he was careful to maintain a commitment to monogenesis. In the first ever textbook for the nascent academic discipline, *Anthropology: An Introduction to the Study of Man and Civilization* (1881), he insisted that "all tribes of men, from the blackest to the whitest...descended from a common ancestry."[41] Tylor had been a devout Quaker, as was Christy who remained so, and his post-Christian self still thought like a Quaker in many ways, most obviously in his visceral antiwar stance. In short, to use a Tylorian category, it seems reasonable to suggest that his commitment to monogenesis can at least partially be seen as a survival from Christian theological anthropology. Albeit one would need to amend the theoretical perspective with the Malinowskian insight that this orthodox conviction continued to have an ongoing function.

*   *   *

The primary way that classic Christian theological anthropology has always funded, and continues to fund, sociocultural anthropology is through the "doctrine of the psychic unity of mankind," now made gender-inclusive as

---

[39] Hunt, *On the Negro's Place in Nature*, v.

[40] Desmond and Moore, *Darwin's Sacred Cause*, 366.

[41] Edward B. Tylor, *Anthropology: An Introduction to the Study of Man and Civilization* (London: Macmillan, 1881), 5–6. For Tylor and religion, see Larsen, *Slain God*, 13–36.

humankind. This doctrine assumes the basic biological unity of all people (i.e., there is only one living species in the genus *homo*) and adds to it the stronger claim that all people also share a basic psychological and intellectual unity, that, at the very least, the various racial and ethnic groups are all endowed with the same rational capacities. The German anthropologist Adolf Bastian (1826–1905) is credited with being the main theorist to formulate this view.[42] He did so in a series of works published in the period 1881–95. Nevertheless, the basic idea of this doctrine had been asserted and denied much earlier. Already in the first half of the nineteenth century, Prichard argued that all people, irrespective of race or ethnicity, have "the same mental endowments, similar natural prejudices and impressions, the same consciousness, sentiments, sympathies, propensities, in short a common psychical nature or a common mind."[43] Furthermore, to tie the loop back to Bastian, nineteenth-century German anthropology was deeply influenced by Prichard. Stocking observed: "Prichard felt that his work was 'ever more favorably estimated' in Germany than among his 'own utilitarian countrymen'... Many of the arguments Boas was to use against racism can also be found in Prichard."[44] Hunt, by way of contrast, argued not only for fundamental biological differences between Europeans and Africans but found even more telling "the psychological inequalities of human races."[45] Hunt's position, however, was condemned as heretical and became literally intolerable in the discipline of anthropology. Boas served as Bastian's assistant at the Berlin Museum of Ethnology precisely in those years when he was formulating the doctrine of the psychic unity of humankind.[46] Boas, having imbibed the convictions of his mentor, went on to make opposing racist views part of the core ethos of his school of anthropology. In his classic work, *The Mind of Primitive Man* (1911), he confidently insisted, "It appears, therefore, that modern anthropologists not only proceed on the assumption of the generic unity of the mind of man, but tacitly disregard quantitative differences which may very well occur. We may therefore base our further considerations on the theory of the similarity of mental functions in all races."[47] Boas, in turn, mentored A. L. Kroeber (1876–1960) who spent two pages in his textbook, *Anthropology: Race, Language, Culture, Psychology, Prehistory* (1923), which was widely used for decades, teaching the "the famous 'psychic unity of man.'"[48] Clifford Geertz (1926–2006), in his classic work, *The Interpretations of Cultures* (1973),

[42] Klaus-Peter Koepping, *Adolf Bastian and the Psychic Unity of Mankind: The Foundations of Anthropology in Nineteenth-Century Germany* (St Lucia: University of Queensland Press, 1983).

[43] Prichard, *Researches*, lxxxiii.   [44] Stocking, "From Chronology to Ethnology," cix.

[45] Hunt, *On the Negro's Place in Nature*, 10.

[46] Douglas Cole, *Franz Boas: The Early Years, 1858–1906* (Seattle: University of Washington Press, 1999), 90.

[47] Franz Boas, *The Mind of Primitive Man* (1911; repr. New York: Macmillan, 1929), 155.

[48] A. L. Kroeber, *Anthropology: Race, Language, Culture, Psychology, Prehistory*, rev. edn (1923; New York: Harcourt, Brace and Company, 1948), 572–3.

spoke of "the doctrine of the psychic unity of mankind, which so far as I am aware, is today not seriously questioned by any reputable anthropologist.... It asserts that there are no essential differences in the fundamental nature of the thought process among the various living races of man."[49] Brad Shore, professor of anthropology at Emory University, declared confidently in 2000 that Bastian's "notion of psychic unity has become something of an article of faith for modern anthropologists, reaffirming as it does the fundamental unity of the species, and the common psychological capacities of all humans."[50] The *Encyclopedia of Anthropology*, published in 2006, has a four-page entry for "Humankind, Psychic Unity of." It declares that "the idea arguably remains at the very heart of the anthropological enterprise."[51]

As an uncontested, fundamental, theoretical presupposition of the entire discipline of social and cultural anthropology, it is, of course, not evoked when the results of fieldwork are written up but only occasionally becomes explicit when a special effort is made to spell out what can normally be taken for granted, such as in these examples of textbooks and works of reference. Some might concede that the psychic unity of humankind is indeed foundational to the discipline but resist the claim that it is derived from, and dependent upon, Christian theological anthropology. This claim, however, has evidence even in the very phrase itself. It is the *doctrine* of the psychic unity of humankind; everyone agrees on that premise. Kroeber, Geertz, Shore, and the *Encyclopedia of Anthropology* all refer to it as a *doctrine*. Natural sciences and other social sciences have laws, theories, hypotheses, paradigms, and principles, but none of them have doctrines. The exception that proves the rule is the Monroe Doctrine, the Bush Doctrine, and so on, which refer to the policy of a politician rather than a principle of the discipline of political science. This language of a *doctrine* is, of course, partially the result of the fact that psychic unity was formulated in the nineteenth century, but that is not a sufficient explanation. Many things were called doctrines in the nineteenth century that have been retained without that term. For example, evolution by natural selection was spoken of as a doctrine by the Victorians, but it is now standardly denominated a theory.

The psychic unity of humankind is still typically referred to as a doctrine because that best describes what it is. As has already been said, to reject it would not just mean that one was in error; it would be to become unorthodox, a heretic. Other possible words seem ill-suited because either they make it sound like it could be a legitimate, scientific enterprise to try to overturn them

---

[49] Clifford Geertz, *The Interpretation of Cultures* (New York: Basic Books, 1973), 62.

[50] Brad Shore, "Human Diversity and Human Nature. The Life and Times of a False Dichotomy," in *Being Humans: Anthropological Universality and Particularity in Transdisciplinary Perspectives*, ed. Neil Roughley (Berlin: Walter de Gruyter, 2000), 81–103 (here 91).

[51] Sebastian Job, "Humankind, Psychic Unity of," in *Encyclopedia of Anthropology*, ed. H. James Birx (Thousand Oaks, CA: Sage Publications, 2006), 3: 1252–5.

(as is the case, for example, for a hypothesis or a paradigm) or that it is the result of the collection and analysis of data (as is, for example, a law or a theory). The psychic unity of humankind is not so much a finding of anthropological research, however, as a presupposition of it. As Kroeber candidly explained, "This cannot be considered to be either a proved fact or an axiomatic principle....The anthropologist...proceeds *as if* the principle were proved."[52] Likewise, the leading authority on the thought of Bastian has explained that the way the German anthropologist organized his work can appear confusing unless one understands that the psychic unity of humankind was actually something that he "assumed a priori."[53] Shore no less revealingly described it as "an article of faith."[54] Geertz reassuringly argued, "The doctrine of the psychic unity of mankind has found increasing empirical substantiation as anthropological research has proceeded,"[55] but that formulation is strikingly reminiscent of Robert Dunn asserting that the findings of the microscope have confirmed what people already believed on the basis of theological conviction.

In his delightful, seminal chapter in this volume, Jon Bialecki has cautioned against attempting to align theology and anthropology through origins-based genealogical accounts. The chapter, however, is certainly not falling into the genetic fallacy as it is very much about understanding what sociocultural anthropologists believe today rather than arguing that what others believed in the past should somehow curtail their freedom in the present. Moreover, Bialecki rejects a specific type of genealogical account—namely, one that becomes controlling—and our argument and presentation certainly do not fall within that category. Far from arguing that sociocultural anthropology must be a certain way because of its origins, this chapter demonstrates that sociocultural anthropology *is* a certain way today: As "an autonomous secular discipline" it is perfectly free right now to follow the Knox–Hunt path of demonstrating its disdain for theological anthropology by rejecting the psychic unity of humankind.[56] The discipline of anthropology seems markedly unwilling to go in that direction, however. On the contrary, one might argue somewhat mischievously that, if forced to choose, rather than follow Knox and Hunt into polygenesis, most sociocultural anthropologists would rather follow one of Naomi Haynes's Zambian Pentecostal preachers as she expounded on the motherhood of the biblical Eve in a way that called everyone imaginatively to see themselves and every other member of the genus *homo* living in this expansive present.

*   *   *

---

[52] Kroeber, *Anthropology*, 573.
[53] Koepping, *Adolf Bastian and the Psychic Unity of Mankind*, 33.
[54] Shore, "Human Diversity," 91.   [55] Geertz, *The Interpretation of Cultures*, 62.
[56] Jon Bialecki, Chapter 9 in this volume.

In this chapter, we have argued that the unity of the human race was outed by unorthodox scholars in the eighteenth and nineteenth centuries as derived from Christian thought, but the discipline of anthropology decided that this presupposition was essential to its work; therefore, it excommunicated the unbelievers and made this theological doctrine serve as an anthropological one as well. In this revisionist account, far from rejecting Christian orthodoxy for free thought, anthropology emphatically chose the evangelical ESL over the freethinking ASL and made the Christian-inflected doctrine of the psychic unity of humankind fundamental to the discipline. Sociocultural anthropology is revealed to be dependent on theological anthropology because an attempt was made to try to do without it, which was vehemently rejected as untenable. Nevertheless, even if one accepts the claim that a certain amount of theological anthropology has been smuggled into cultural anthropology, one might still argue that, in any event, the passageways have since been decisively blocked so that no such Christian contraband could now find its way into the discipline. As a kind of concluding unscientific postscript, therefore, we would like to wonder aloud about whether there still might be a viable route left for God's smugglers to pursue.

As philosophers observe, first principles cannot be proven, which is partially why the word *doctrine* has such utility. Moreover, it is quite possible to learn from, and find insightful, a study that is based on presuppositions or a theoretical commitment or first principles or doctrines that one does not share. The reader might even reject a foundational commitment of the author as scientifically false but nevertheless still appreciate the way that it manages to serve as a fruitful heuristic device. A lot of twentieth-century anthropology, for example, was written from a Marxist perspective, and another stream of studies presupposed the validity of Freudian theories. Some of this work was, and still is, celebrated as illuminating the human condition even by those who formally reject Marxist and Freudian doctrine. Indeed, anthropologists commonly draw on convictions that they have developed prior to or outside of their discipline—feminism, human rights, environmentalism, for example—or the work of theorists outside of the discipline of anthropology, such as Darwin, Freud, Marx, Foucault, Said, and Butler, and import these into their anthropological studies. Furthermore, another anthropologist who rejects this conviction or theory still might find admirable and insightful an anthropological work that made sympathetic use of it. Therefore, we are putting forward the possibility that theological convictions and theologians can serve in this same way. In other words, twenty-first-century anthropologists could bring their theological convictions or the work of a theologian to bear on their study, and even anthropologists who rejected these theological convictions might still value the resulting anthropological work. Why should theologians be the one group of theorists and theological beliefs the one set of convictions that are barred from this otherwise common practice?

For example, to return to Genesis, it is argued theologically that murdering another human being is wrong because, even if they are from a different racial or ethnic group, they are still equally created in the image of God (Gen. 9:6). In other words, Christian thought has a way of warranting and discussing why all human beings should have the same fundamental rights. Belief in universal human rights is likewise a kind of *doctrine* rather than a finding or a hypothesis and, while one can argue for it in secular ways, it is an idea that can be readily grounded by Christian thought. One of the greatest anthropologists of the twentieth century, Mary Douglas, once observed the difficulty of keeping theology out of any discussion that is pursued long enough to lead in the direction of ultimate values, warrant, and meaning.[57] Even when the American Declaration of Independence deftly dodged the issue by stating that it would consider human equality a "self-evident" truth, it found theology so difficult to dispense with entirely that it immediately fell back into it by expounding that people "are endowed by their Creator with certain unalienable rights." An anthropological monograph drawing on the claim that all people are made in the image of God or a theologian expounding this doctrine might be discerned to have inherent worth and beauty even by scholars who self-identify as atheists. To recapitulate, anthropologists who did not accept the truthfulness of Christian claims could nevertheless welcome reflections framed in theological terms (such as all people being created in the image of God) as having heuristic value, illuminating eloquence, and insight into the human condition. At the very least, we can hope that future discourse will move beyond the old, tired binary of theological versus anthropological ways of thinking.

---

[57] Larsen, *Slain God*, 170.

4

Theology Revealing the Hājibs of Anthropology

Khaled Furani

In much contemporary usage the world over, and in Muslim ethics, the word *hijab* has come to denote a woman's headscarf, traditionally worn in response to precepts of piety. However, in Arabic, the root h.j.b., from which *hijab* emanates, emits other senses eluded by the modern prevailing sartorial reference. In various conjugations, it also means screen, block, obstruction, partition, and, of course, veil. Thus, a Qur'anic expounding of the distance between divine and human speech states, "And it is not to any human that God speaks except through revelation or from behind a *hijab* [here meaning *partition*]" (42:51). Relatedly, God's voice, light, or signs are likely obstructed (*mahjoub*) by any act entailing forgetting God's oneness.[1] Moreover, those searching for protection from demons may turn to items or rituals that can evoke mediating powers, which furnish a *hjabaat*, *hujub*, or *ahjiba*—a shield from the work of jinns.[2] From the courtly lexicon in the history of Muslim rule, the office of *hājib* was invariably charged with managing security arrangements, including screening off subjects from the sovereign. In anatomy the eyebrow is called hājib, for it functions as a protective screen for the eyes. Thus, in this chapter, hājib must not be confused with hijab as in headscarf.

This detour into hājib's supple semantics is intended to foreground my usage in connoting an act of partitioning. I evoke a verbal form of hājib in order to examine ways in which the modern discipline of anthropology has come to wear a series of partitions, whereby such donning constitutes a certain

---

[1] See, for example, "Verily, from the light of their Lord, that day, will they be veiled [*la-mahjuboon*]" (Quran 83:15). See also the notion of *hajb al-shirk* (polytheism's obstructions) in Ibn-Qayyim al-Jawziyyah, *BuMadarij al-Salaikeen* (Damascus, Syria: Dar al-Kitab al-Arabi, 1980).

[2] See Taufik Canaan, "The Decipherment of Arabic Talismans," *Berytus Archeological Studies* 4 (1937): 69–110 and Taufik Canaan, *Mohammadan Saints and Sanctuaries in Palestine* (London: Luzac, 1927), ch. 2.

idolatry. More specifically, assuming that anthropology—the science of humanity—has been constituted by secular reason, I argue that a theological critique could reveal how this reason has impelled it into modern idolatries composed of a series of attendant hājibs (i.e., partitions), affecting its vision and vitality.

Retaining the semantic ambiguity the term *theology* bore prior to the thirteenth century as, at once, the word *of* God as well as words *about* God,[3] I employ the term to signal dispositions of rationalities that surmount modern humanism, itself understood as a deification or at least a securing of the sovereignty of humankind.[4] Theology, perforce an inquiry into the ultimate Other, here refers to all that was regarded as excess on the way to "exclusive humanism's" ascent in modernity,[5] entailing precepts about the sovereignty of human reason, the autonomy of humankind, and a regnant immanence of a world whose realities are accordingly construed. That theology and modern anthropology, awkward as the relation between them may be,[6] share stakes in the question of the Other can be gleaned from Wittgenstein's exegesis:

> I wish to understand how the other now bears the weight of God, shows me that I am not alone in the universe. This requires understanding the philosophical problem of the other as the trace or scar of the departure of God. This descent, or ascent, of the problem of the other is the key way I can grasp the alternative process of secularization, called romanticism. And it may explain why the process of humanization can become a monstrous undertaking, placing infinite demands upon finite sources.[7]

This exploration also has an enabling premise running throughout that before difference became cultural it long (long as in the *Egyptian Book of the Dead* or the Mesopotamian epic of *Gilgamesh*) stood for that which exceeds the finite or the humanly knowable (e.g., death).

While the nexus between the modern discipline of anthropology and theology is complex, surmounting the mere suppression of the latter by the former, anthropology also continues theology by other means, such as through ethnographic immersion. Although the question of theological preservation in

---

[3] Amos Funkenstein, *Theology and the Scientific Imagination: From the Middle Ages to the Seventeenth Century* (Princeton: Princeton University Press, 1986), 4.

[4] Seeing that every form of humanism bears a metaphysics, Heidegger intimates as much in holding: "Expelled from the truth of being, the human being everywhere now circles around himself.... Humanism now means... that the essence of the human being is essential for the truth of being." Martin Heidegger, *Pathmarks*, ed. W. McNeill (Cambridge: Cambridge University Press, 1998), 260–3.

[5] Charles Taylor, *A Secular Age* (Cambridge, MA: Harvard University Press, 2007).

[6] Joel Robbins, "Anthropology and Theology: An Awkward Relationship?" *Anthropological Quarterly* 79/2 (2006): 285–94.

[7] Cited in Stanley Cavell, *The Claim of Reason: Wittgenstein, Skepticism, Morality, and Tragedy* (New York: Oxford University Press, 1999), 470.

anthropology merits its own investigation, in this chapter I want to explore ways whereby theology could mount a potentially revitalizing critique of anthropology. This approach, I submit, responds to the impetus guiding this collection as to what theology can contribute to cultural anthropology and how it can formulate challenges to understandings of the human.

Rather than a notable—and to my mind, potentially salutary—propensity of recent writing aimed at finding a *modus vivendi* or *via media* for redressing a slanted relation and enabling coexistence between theology and anthropology,[8] this chapter proposes that theology can offer far more than to (1) ameliorate the anthropology of religion, (2) show the insufficiency of the secular and conversely demonstrate the theological within the discipline, and (3) refine anthropology insofar as it inquires into human differences. Theology mobilized as a repudiation of modern anthropology's ideology could perhaps attend to the discipline's religiosity—whether appropriate or not, admitted or denied, absent or present—despite its mistaken self-identity as theology's inherently other. In sum, while in much recent writing the anthropology–theology nexus tips towards the ends (i.e., that a relation between the two fields is of value in and of itself), I here approach this nexus as a means (i.e., that it offers a strategy or strategies for a critique of anthropology).

While not speaking of a critique per se but rather contribution of theology to anthropology, Bialecki similarly seeks in this book to explore the conceptual renewal the former offers the latter.[9] With a Deleuzian tenor, Bialecki searches for ways in which theology could help anthropology *work back* to its problems (e.g., incommensurability), grasping them as though they were mathematical forms—that is, as specific realizations of relations underpinned by structuring through an indeterminate constellation of forces. While Bialecki posits anthropology and theology as possibly joint ventures for working on common problems, theology interests me insofar as it posits anthropology as itself a problem, and a generative one at that. This chapter, therefore, mobilizes theology in order to (1) examine anthropological idols as epistemic hājibs in the discipline's purview, and (2) reveal possibilities for disciplinary conceptual and institutional revitalizing when these obstructions are indeed recognized as such.

With these two objectives for anthropology, the modern discipline that studies human difference, I want to turn now, although not without risks, to a modern thinker who excavated difference all the way back to Heraclitus, Dionysius, and even Zarathustra. I am referring to Friedrich Nietzsche. His attention to difference is but one of a number of reasons I find his work useful for purposes of criticizing modern anthropology from a theological standpoint. My other reasons relate to his devastating attentiveness to theology, his

---

[8] See, for example, Philip Fountain and Sin Wen Lau, "Anthropological Theologies: Engagements and Encounters," *Australian Journal of Anthropology* 24/3 (2013): 227–34.

[9] Jon Bialecki, Chapter 9, 156–78.

genealogical method, and, above all for the purpose of this chapter, his diag-
nostic abilities vis-à-vis the modern condition. I want to assay what kind of
resources Nietzsche—not in actuality a theologian but a student of theology who
garnered its tools to re-evaluate values—supplies for a diagnosis of anthropology's modern idolatries.

I open by exploring ways in which Nietzsche could offer tools for a
theological critique of the discipline. More specifically, I focus on his notion
of divine death for understanding anthropology's entailment of idolatry. Next,
I illustrate anthropology's partaking in idolatry via three foundational concepts and conditions: humanism, culture concept, and the state—all of which,
I suggest, have the power of hājib over the discipline. I conclude by speculating
as to how recognition of anthropology's idols can renew its inquiry conceptually and institutionally. By way of example, I look at the concept of tradition
and the organization of knowledge in the modern university.

*   *   *

I find it useful, even if dangerous, to turn to Nietzsche's diagnosis of the
Divine's modern death as an entry to exploring the possibilities offered by a
theological critique.[10] It is useful because of Nietzsche's standing on the critical
edge of much that is at stake in the crisis of the modern intellect—the same
intellect from whose modern life and conditions emerged the academic
discipline of anthropology. It may be dangerous because an argument so
triggered cannot be securely immune from becoming a victim, as Nietzsche
himself was, of its own villainies.[11] As a preventive measure, I will apply
Nietzsche's own medicine to his writing—that is, asceticism.

For the purposes of my argument, I essentially draw on Nietzsche's radical
perceptions into the modern condition and disregard his Teutonic prescrip-
tions (e.g., *ubermensch*). In addition to facing danger, I must also work
through counter-intuition. I regard this effort as worthwhile because it behoves
the discipline that has made its career from studying difference to learn from
this singular modern thinker about difference,[12] who exalted life comprised of

---

[10] On the indebtedness of Nietzsche's proposition of the death of God to an established
tradition of German religious thought, see Luft who urges us to regard it as "an intricate and
dynamic metaphor." Eric Von Der Luft, "Sources of Nietzsche's 'God Is Dead' and Its Meaning
for Heidegger," *Journal of the History of Ideas* 45/2 (1984): 263–76.

[11] See Alasdair MacIntyre, *After Virtue: A Study in Moral Theory* (Notre Dame: University of
Notre Dame Press, 1984), esp. ch. 18, for a brilliant discussion of Nietzsche's entrapments in
some of the very basic flaws he saw himself fleeing in the modern age. More recently, John
Milbank, *Theology and Social Theory: Beyond Secular Reason* (Oxford: Blackwell Publishing,
2006), 268, questions the primacy of the category of power in social theory, contending that
Nietzsche could not avoid colluding with what he sought to expose.

[12] Gilles Deleuze points out that in his radical thinking about difference, Nietzsche ceaselessly
assaulted equalizing and the erasing of multiplicity in the fields of atoms, numbers, values, and
logic. Gilles Deleuze, *Nietzsche & Philosophy*, trans. H. Tomlinson (New York: Columbia University Press, 2006), 45.

a self's becoming as opposed to its being, up to the point, quite ironically, of deification, such as in his notion of "eternal return."

To illustrate what I mean by my counter-intuitive turn to Nietzsche for resources for a theological critique, I wish to recall his contempt for theologians: "Whoever has theologian's blood in his veins sees all things in a distorted and dishonest perspective to begin with."[13] He even went so far as to declare war on their dispositions: "Against this theologians' instinct I wage war."[14] Perhaps ironically, Nietzsche's contempt led him to excavate theological sensibilities relentlessly wherever they might be hidden: "I have dug up the theologian's instinct everywhere."[15] So relentlessly did Nietzsche unearth theology lurking within modern reason that he recommended turning to the leading German institution of theological learning, Tübingen Seminary, to "understand what German philosophy is at bottom: an insidious theology."[16] Nietzsche unearthed theology to the extent that it surpassed its role as a target of his animus—and this is a crucial point for my argument—to furnish his arsenal for assaulting Western enslavements.

Nietzsche thus at times sounds like a theologian, or even like one of the ancient criticizers, for he resorts to a seemingly Abrahamic act. He aims to "philosophize with a hammer," entitling his final section of *Twilight of the Idols*, "The Hammer Speaks."[17] He also declares in *Ecce Homo*, "No new ideals are created by me ... overthrowing idols (my word for ideals) comes closer to being part of my craft."[18] Thus, idolatry, a category of criticism in monotheistic traditions, stands as a prime weapon in Nietzsche's arsenal for the repudiation of ideals–idols—that is, for regulating principles of human rationalities. Relatedly, consider what I call an Abrahamic act in Foucault's words on genealogy whose "knowledge is not made for understanding, it is made for cutting."[19] More pronounced still, this Abraham-like idol-smashing as a name for the labor of criticism is evident in Wittgenstein's stating, "All that philosophy can do is to destroy idols. And that means not making any new ones—say out of the 'absence of idols.'"[20] Moreover, during a time when modern reason triumphantly declared its purge of theology, Nietzsche reminded others of its persistence into modern time (as a genealogist) and its endemic prevalence (as a physiologist).

---

[13] Friedrich Nietzsche, *The Portable Nietzsche*, trans. W. Kauffman (New York: Viking Press, 1968), 575.

[14] Ibid.   [15] Ibid.   [16] Ibid., 576.   [17] Nietzsche, *Portable Nietzsche*, 563.

[18] Friedrich Nietzsche, *Genealogy of Morals and Ecce Homo*, trans. W. Kauffman (New York: Vintage Books, 1989), 217–20 (here 217–18).

[19] Cited in Gary Gutting, *Thinking the Impossible: French Philosophy since 1960* (Oxford: Oxford University Press, 2013), 94.

[20] Cited in Moshe Halbertal and Avishai Margalit, *Idolatry* (Cambridge, MA: Harvard University Press, 1992), 244.

In *Twilight of the Idols*, Nietzsche builds and names this model of thought to distinguish the real from the unreal, the true from the false, a concern endemic to religion, especially to monotheism: "There are more idols than realities in the world."[21] Thus, for all his animus towards the priesthood, Christianity, and Judaism, idols continued to evoke for Nietzsche what they evoked in monotheism: obstructions of realities and truth, erectors of hājibs. Whereas others saw modernity as prevailing over false beliefs, Nietzsche saw it as reconstituting them in new guises. His radical honesty was such that he was willing to admit theology's existence—as much as he despised it—when a pandemic pretense to either its extinction or insulation prevailed in modernity's self-image.

*   *   *

While, quite predictably, theology in Nietzsche's hands could and has, in fact, promoted a genealogical vision of academic disciplines (such as in Foucault's *Les Mots et les Choses*[22]), theology in his hands—and this is the point that matters here—can also enhance a symptomatic vision. Pursuing a genealogical vision, theology can signal anthropology's unstable, wanting, and discontinuous secular identity in a discipline bent on perceiving the theistic as its exteriority. Against a pretense to stability of the discipline's secular identity, a genealogically driven critique of anthropology with eyes towards throttled theologies would accomplish what Foucault exhorts: "To make visible all of those discontinuities that cross us, ... its intention is to reveal the heterogeneous systems which, masked by the self, inhibit the formations of any form of identity"[23] In pursuing a symptomatic vision, theology can offer a hallmark category—namely, idolatry—for diagnosing anthropology as itself a symptom of modern forms of domination that obstruct an enlarged inquiry into our human vision. In sum, while a theological critique driven by Nietzsche's genealogical method could show how theology never extricated itself from anthropology with the ascent of secular reason, Nietzsche's physiology could reveal how in modern anthropology idolatry proliferates.

In a symptomatic viewing, theology becomes no less than Nietzsche's means for defining and diagnosing the modern condition: "This modernity was our sickness."[24] With the advent of modernity, while other seminal philosophers have adored the birth of modern state powers (Hobbes), individual autonomy (Rousseau), reason's sovereignty (Kant), and history (Hegel and Vico), ironically Nietzsche, whose contempt for theology was probably

---

[21] Nietzsche, *Portable Nietzsche*, 465.

[22] Michel Foucault, *Les Mots et Les Choses: Une Archéologie des Sciences Humaines* (Paris: Gallimard, 1966).

[23] Michel Foucault, "Nietzsche: Genealogy, History," in *Foucault Reader* (New York: Pantheon Books, 1984), 76–100 (here 95).

[24] Nietzsche, *Portable Nietzsche*, 569.

the greatest among them, found refuge in theology's words to announce openly "the reduction of the divine"[25] as essentially constituting the modern condition. In other words, for all his animus towards theology, Nietzsche insisted that a theistic event constitutes the modern condition.

*   *   *

I further wish to propose that Nietzsche's proclamations about the death of God ever so faintly intimated the consequent and symptomatic birth of anthropology, as well. In regarding this event as anthropology's *ursprung*, I have in mind Heidegger's means of naming a historically originating decision or founding event providing a "destiny" or "truths" from which a tradition learns to distinguish the great from the base, the meaningful from the meaningless. Heidegger too intimates the possibility that anthropology— insofar as it is an enterprise whose object is difference and whose method is representation—is a symptom of the modern killing of God. He comments:

> The killing means the act of doing away with the supersensory world that is in itself—an act accomplished through man. It speaks of the event wherein that which is as such does not simply come to nothing, but does indeed become different in its Being. But above all, in this event man also becomes different.... The uprising of man into subjectivity transforms that which is into object. But that which is objective is that which brought to a stand through representing.[26]

Some of Nietzsche's depictions of this event and its consequences are as follows:

- "The greatest recent event [is] that 'God is dead....' The belief in the Christian God has become unbelievable [and] is already starting to cast its first shadows over Europe."[27]
- "God is dead; but given the way people are, there may still for millennia be caves in which they show his shadow."[28]
- "We will no longer take anything to heart. We will choose the masks as supreme divinity and as a redeemer."[29]
- "What holy games will we have to invent for ourselves.... There was never a greater death; this tremendous event is still on its way."[30]

---

[25] Ibid., 584.

[26] Martin Heidegger, "The Word of Nietzsche 'God Is Dead,'" in *The Question Concerning Technology and Other Essays* (New York: Harper Torchbooks, 1977), 53–114 (here 107).

[27] Nietzsche, *Portable Nietzsche*, 447.

[28] Friedrich Nietzsche, *The Gay Science*, ed. Bernard Williams, trans. Josefine Nauckhoff (Cambridge: Cambridge University Press, 2001), 109.

[29] Cited in Michael Haar, "Nietzsche and the Metamorphosis of the Divine," in *Post-Secular Philosophy: Between Philosophy and Theology*, ed. P. Blond (New York: Routledge, 1998), 82–92 (here 87).

[30] Nietzsche, *Gay Science*, 120.

Coming from arguably "the most radical thinker of difference,"[31] I choose to view these statements as imploring us to attune to the crisis and possibilities of critique they identify. They invite us to consider anthropology as a fever, as a symptom of that divine death, or perhaps as some kind of *Aufhebung*, as Hegel would say, in the sense that anthropology both *surpasses* and *preserves*, transcends and fulfills theology. Anthropology reformulates theology in re-placing God with humans as its object of study and preserves it by continuing, albeit not without perversion, the study of difference.

Attention to this diagnosis, I submit, is especially demanded by anthro-pology's existential stake in studying difference constituted as *cultural* rather than as Absolute, as in the language of philosophy, or as about God, as in the language of theology. The Nietzschean diagnosis induces questions about anthropology's complicated relation with forms of domination other than capitalist, colonial, Orientalist, or imperial—indeed also with the domination of modern secular transcendence whose triumph is based on the premise, in Marx's words, that "theology itself has failed."[32] Perhaps most significantly, it is useful for better understanding the secular reason that forms this academic discipline, which, in turn, disciplines and thereby inhibits the study of the enduring subject of difference, erecting hājibs that obscure difference's fullness.[33]

Here is secular reason when safely but not always usefully presumed as constituting the rational and the real. In the words of American poet Robert Duncan, "The term 'God' is not fitting where the reality of things is to be considered.... The modern mind [has] chickened out on God."[34] Philosopher Charles Taylor, although a severe critic of Nietzsche, evoked a version of the divine death for secularism's dominion through his notion of "experience-far," wherein concepts such as God are marginalized and undermined, in a secular age denoting belief in the divine as an attenuated personal preference within a market of choices for human fulfillment.[35]

Taking note of this death or displacement of the divine as an "enabling experience"[36] for the discipline's emergence, perhaps anthropology may be a kind of idolatrous shadow in a cave—Nietzsche's metaphor for the contracted

---

[31] Milbank, *Theology and Social Theory*, xiv.

[32] Karl Marx, "Towards a Critique of Hegel's Philosophy of Right: Introduction," in *Karl Marx: Selected Writings*, ed. D. McLellan (Oxford: Oxford University Press, 1977), 63–74 (here 69).

[33] Discussing a variety of "anthropocentric theologies" or "atheistic theologies" whose begin-nings trace back to the seventeenth century with figures such as Libnetz, Vico, Newton, Galileo, and Descartes, prior to the antireligious savants of the eighteenth century, which stressed the self-sufficiency of the world and the autonomy of humankind. Funkenstein evokes the question of them as modern anthropology's forbears (Funkenstein, *Theology*).

[34] Robert Duncan, "Man's Fulfillment in Order and Strife," *Fictive Certainties: Essays* (1969; New York: New Directions, 1985), 111–41 (here 121).

[35] Taylor, *Secular Age*, 143.

[36] Edward Said, *Orientalism* (New York: Vintage Books, 1979), 122.

human condition in modernity.[37] Given anthropology's allurement that practitioners notably associate with the sense of release they can attain via ethnographic emersion when and if it exposes them to other ways of being in the world, we may ask in what ways fieldwork practices or cultural concepts might serve as masks or perhaps idols mimicking redemption and divinity. Perhaps the constitutive practice of fieldwork and regnant, though contested, ideal–idol of culture stand as *holy games* for secular modern anthropologists.[38]

In proposing a theological Nietzschean-enabled critique of the discipline,[39] *idols* stand for those ideals that orient the discipline in ways that, in addition to directing inquiry fruitfully, function as hājibs. A close reading may reveal that the discipline's ultimate truths are not ultimate, its "final vocabulary"[40] not all that final, and its absolute values requiring absolute re-evaluation, both ethically and epistemically. The notion of idolatry I wish to advance here is faithful neither to theological discourse nor to its nemeses, as with Nietzsche's, in any strict sense. Instead, I take idolatry to be a "category of criticism,"[41] aiming it at a number of forms of false worship: misplacing fidelity; conflating things finite with the infinite; confining thought by hājibs set up for bounding rational faculties; ignoring or demeaning anything that defies human reason, will, or cognition; and deifying that which is transient.[42] In short, while different models of thought animate the notion of idolatry in both modern and pre-modern languages, that most fitting my exploration arises when "any non-absolute value . . . is made absolute and demands to be the center of a dedicated life."[43] Conversely, to repudiate idolatry is to strive against compromised, shrunken, conceited forms of worship or lifelong devotion. Considering idolatry in anthropology thereby implies interrogating the false and flawed aspects of the devotion it demands of lives committed to it.

---

[37] Lexido, "Friedrich Nietzsche, The Gay Science. Die fröhliche Wissenschaft," <www.lexido. com/EBOOK_TEXTS/THE_GAY_SCIENCE_THIRD_BOOK_.aspx?S=108>.

[38] One may think here of anthropological works that contest the concept of culture and even declare it defunct (e.g., Lila Abu Lughod, "Writing against Culture," in *Recapturing Anthropology: Working in the Present*, ed. R. Fox (Santa Fe, NM: School of American Research Press, 1991), 137–54; Fredrik Barth, "Overview: Sixty Years in Anthropology," *Annual Review of Anthropology* 36 (2007): 1–16) by offering alternatives such as "halvies" processes, critique of power, and human diversity. Yet all such attempts seem nevertheless to perpetuate an ingrained romantic impulse in the discipline's *humanism* as our ethical and political salvations or at least their amelioration.

[39] See the discussion in Halbertal and Margalit, *Idolatry*, of thinkers who before Nietzsche recruited the category of "idolatry" to critique modern morality—namely, to criticize "idols of the mind" (e.g., Bacon) and "commodity fetishism" and "money as the jealous god of Israel" (e.g., Marx).

[40] Richard Rorty, *Contingency, Irony, and Solidarity* (Cambridge: Cambridge University Press, 1989), 73.

[41] Halbertal and Margalit, *Idolatry*, 250.

[42] Amos Funkenstein notes, "Ideals of sciences . . . express the ultimate criteria of rationality of their time" (Funkenstein, *Theology*, 18).

[43] Halbertal and Margalit, *Idolatry*, 246.

Idolatry is useful in this exploration to the extent that it can be reasonably claimed that a traditional devotion to the category of the other (and its affinal signs of difference, diversity, and culture) has been foundational although never absolute and uncontested in anthropology. Even anthropology's very foundation can at the very least be argued as relevant to idolatry's modern history. In his reflection on the French anthropological tradition known as *ethnology*, Derrida notes its genesis out of the demotion of a prescientific, theistic center: "In fact one can assume that ethnology could have been born as a science only at a moment when decentering had come about: at the moment when European culture—and in consequence, the history of metaphysics, and its concepts—had been *dislocated....*"[44] The category of *idolatry* can help us examine the ways in which anthropologists' commitment to *the cultural* constitutes an idolatry that conflates the finite with the infinite, whereby this category's transcendence coincides with and conforms to transcendent categories sanctioned by the modern nation state and its attendant forces.[45] I wish now to turn to the concept of culture, to humanism, and to the modern state as examples of idolatrous objects to consider in a putative theistic critique of anthropology.

* * *

Anthropology's prized differences must accordingly align with those differences the modern state condones, manages, polices, or encourages in its administration of populations within and without its regimes of inclusion and exclusion. If the state is a "new idol," as Nietzsche contends, "where the slow suicide of all is called 'life,'"[46] in a theistic critique, anthropology's commitment to *life* within that state must be measured for the extent of its contribution to or amelioration of that *slow suicide*. Indeed, with Nietzschean eyes on idolatry, culture as a god of anthropology appears far from an achievement. Where others may see in the concept and phenomenon of culture a redeeming ideal,[47] Nietzsche interprets culture as "theft—and everything becomes sickness and troubles...."[48] Thus, while endorsers identify culture within and outside

---

[44] Jacques Derrida, "Structure, Sign, and Play in the Discourse of the Human Sciences," in *Writing and Difference*, trans. Alan Bass. (London: Routledge), 278–94; see <http://hydra.humanities.uci.edu/derrida/sign-play.html>.

[45] Asad argues that rather than assume the absence of "transcendence" in modernity one should recognize and critically examine the way certain secular formations are themselves transcendent forces; e.g., "humanity," "free speech," "the state," and "the market." Hasan Azad, "Do Muslims Belong in the West? An Interview with Talal Asad," *Jadaliyya*, 2015, <www.jadaliyya.com/Details/31747/Do-Muslims-Belong-in-the-West-An-Interview-with-Talal-Asad>.

[46] Friedrich Nietzsche, *Thus Spake Zarathustra* (Hertfordshire, UK: Wordsworth Classics, 1997), 46.

[47] For a view of the culture concept performing a constantly transmuting form of critique—say of civilization, biological determinism, or power—see Marshall Sahlins, "What Is Anthropological Enlightenment? Some Lessons of the Twentieth Century," *Annual Review of Anthropology* 28 (1999): i–xxiii.

[48] Nietzsche, *Thus Spake Zarathustra*, 46.

anthropology as a secularized version of spiritual attainment,[49] by adopting a symptomatic vision, diagnosing the discipline itself as a cultural event, we may be able to identify the hājibs preventing us from recognizing the concept of culture, and the related phenomena modernity categorizes as *cultural*, as idolatry.

One final example of an *idol* that a theistic critique of anthropology could address is *humanity*, which "installs each of its violences in a system of rules and thus proceeds from domination to domination."[50] Again, a critique of modern anthropology's idolatries demands an account of the discipline's ceding to the modern domination otherwise known as humanism. If the violences of *man*—humanity's transcendent object, if the theft that is *culture*, and if the idol that is *the state* are all sites wherein anthropology's idolatrous practices take place, and if as idols they operate as hājibs, then we need to uncover what they have been obstructing.

In an attempt to raise hājibs, I thereby wish to experiment with applying the Nietzschean-inspired critique I previously outlined to the kinds of statements that anthropologists make about the concepts and practices of their discipline. More specifically, I want to essay it on some of anthropology's epistemic entrapments inhabiting modern forms of domination. To begin recognizing the discipline's idolatries, that is, to begin understanding the complicity anthropology may have, at least in foundational phases, with conditions it seeks to criticize, the following two testimonies by leading anthropologists evince faith in humanism. I find valuable in these testimonies the sense of triumph or accomplishment that guides their authors and likely represents the perspectives of their fellow disciplinary disciples. Here, renowned anthropologist Elisabeth Colson reflects on her attraction to anthropology: "It is difficult to remember, however, what it was that made us love anthropology other than the fact that it seemed to provide a powerful critique of the world as we knew it—particularly of the social rules that confined us. But we could also believe that anthropology had an important role in encouraging difference and in combating racial and ethnic differences."[51] Clearly, for Colson anthropology is a project of ethical becoming, discovering ways of being in the world. Anthropology thus is not only a practice for knowing but also for renewal of being (encouraging difference) and for acting in the world (powerful critique and combating prejudices).

---

[49] The German etymology of the term *culture* (*Kultur*) more clearly reveals it as a secularized version of spiritual attainment. See Eric Wolf, *Envisioning Power: Ideologies of Dominance and Crisis* (Berkeley: University of California, 1999), 28–9; Raymond Williams, *Marxism and Literature* (Oxford: Oxford University Press, 1977), 14–15.

[50] Foucault, "Nietzsche," 85. Note, for example, in opposing humanism Heidegger evokes its *lowering* effect: "Humanism is opposed because it does not set the humanitas of the human being high enough" (Heidegger, *Pathmarks*, 251).

[51] Elizabeth Colson, "Overview," *Annual Review of Anthropology* 18 (1989): 1–16 (here 5–6).

These abilities to critique, to transform, and to combat prejudice constitute anthropology's ethical triumph. This sense of triumph, as Webster contends in his chapter, may constitute a dogma of the discipline, so far as it serves as a functional equivalent to Christian theology in elevating exclusion of anti-pluralism to a "cardinal virtue."[52] This anthropological *dogma*—namely, cultural difference—signals celebration. There is no disquiet from the fact that the only differences that arrive on anthropology's radar coincide with differences crucial to secular modern state knowledge and population management: race and ethnicity. Nor does disquiet arise from the implicit assumption consonant with liberal humanism that what threatens to diminish the autonomy, read humanity, of the individual are only external social norms. If we can consider the possibility that these differences and this social critique are *freedom toys* thrown in for building sedative and comforting norms in the iron cage of secular reason, then perhaps we can observe anthropology's secular entrapments in modern state projects.

The concept of culture, itself an idol, plays a particular role in this secular entrapment. As a concept, it has undoubtedly had and continues to have numerous careers, ranging from say Michel de Montaigne's cannibals to Michel Foucault's discourse. Eric Wolf offers a particularly apt description of its enduring effect: "The concept of unlimited human variability...gave many people the feeling that their own lives could be recut upon other patterns, that new different possibilities were in the air."[53] The optimism that Wolf's observation exudes simultaneously suffocates a healthy skepticism towards anthropological celebrations of cultural diversity. Diagnosing idolatries and hājibs demands that we retain the possibility that cultural diversity represents only a certain kind of diversity and with it a certain vision of the world, more specifically a vision emanating from loss and not accomplishment. Stanley Diamond reflects, "We study men...because we must, because man in civilization is the problem. Primitive people do not study man, it is not necessary."[54]

The necessity of studying "man" as stemming from a problem and not necessarily a noble achievement can permit us to consider the culture concept as an idol congruent with, not dissonant from, that transcendence the state has authorized. Culture is the state-condoned god that anthropology is permitted to adopt for constituting its activities and charting its goals. Walter Benjamin

---

[52] Joseph Webster, Chapter 18, 333. However, Webster's argument that disconnections make up society is only possible by his conceptually decoupling the disconnecting act from its inherent twin: the connecting one. More specifically, in his case of the Brethren's theology of separation, every disconnect from the external world to which they are committed constitutes the very connections that make up their society, detached as it may be.

[53] Eric Wolf, *Anthropology* (1964; New York: W. W. Norton, 1974), 23.

[54] Stanley Diamond, "Anthropology in Question," in *Reinventing Anthropology*, ed. D. Hymes (New York: Random House, 1972), 401–29 (here 408).

cautions, "Mankind, which in Homer's time was an object of contemplation for the Olympian gods, now is one for itself. Its self-alienation has reached such a degree that it can experience its own destruction as an aesthetic pleasure of the first order."[55] The culture concept has been modern anthropologists' aesthetic, ethical, and epistemic experience of, not to say participation in, that idolatrous destruction.

Accordingly, the constrictive concept of culture is always changing in relation to the battles of anthropology and the state's power in whose epistemic configuration it strictly operates. Culture has come to redeem anthropologists from a slew of ill thoughts having to do with evolution, nature, racism, historicism, patriarchy, and, most recently in our age, so-called post-ideological power as such. The hardly theistic, evidently annoyed words of Sahlins furnish an example: "So nowadays all culture is power. It used to be that everything maintained the social solidarity. Then for a while everything was economic or adaptively advantageous. We seem to be on a great spiritual quest for the purpose of cultural things."[56]

Sahlin's evocation of a spiritual quest highlights an apt route for pushing our thinking about revitalizing anthropology by repudiating its idolatries. Insofar as culture has been and remains the good and the god, marking differences in the finite realm without connecting with God, First Principles, the Absolute Being, "the ground of all possibilities," or whatever signifies the incalculable, the unknowable, the infinite, the grounding for all grounds, it may function as a hājib-inducing idol that hinders measure-taking of the distance between anthropology's reasoning and that of the modern state.[57]

* * *

I want now to move from identifying anthropology's idols to considering what their recognition as such could reveal. I will speculate, albeit only preliminarily, what an anthropology, intent on revealing its idols with their accompanying hājibs, could become. I contend that a theological critique of modern anthropology so pursued could proceed in directions both conceptual and institutional. In what follows I will sketch an example of each, speculating on the ways anthropology could develop a serious and attenuated engagement with overlooked concepts and pursue a repudiation—discursive

---

[55] Walter Benjamin, "The Work of Art in the Age of Mechanical Reproduction," in *Illuminations: Essays and Reflections*, ed. H. Arendt (New York: Schocken Books, 1968), 217–52 (here 242).

[56] Sahlins, "What Is Anthropological Enlightenment?" 6.

[57] I take the occasion here to wonder if recent concepts advanced by post-structural philosophers (e.g., Derrida's difference, Deleuze's abyss, Agamben's "the open," or Levinas's Other) are, in a sense, idiosyncratic strategies for breaking out of finite discourses they find imprisoning. Levinas's attempt indicates such when he holds that "alterity is mystery and future, with what is never there, can't be there." Emmanuel Levinas, *Time and Other* (Pittsburg: Duquesne University Press, 1987), 88.

and organizational—of the existing and insular distributions of the disciplines (i.e., gated communities) interested in the human condition within the modern university. Alasdaire MacIntyre testifies to particular manifestations of this assault: "In the contemporary research university neither philosophy nor theology find their due place. Theology has for the most part been expelled altogether from the research university."[58]

I wish here to pursue the example of tradition as an overlooked concept. A serious and critically revived engagement with this notion could take as a starting point its immolation from the secular project of modernity with its Lutheran roots, whose prevailing self-image includes a triumph over tradition. With tradition's problematic positioning in the modern world[59] and collapse of its epistemic and political authority, we can hardly expect it to survive modern bureaucratic and scholarly languages. Viewing the concepts of tradition and authority as "interconnected," Hannah Arendt notes:

> Practically as well as theoretically, we are no longer in a position to know what authority really is. . . . Historically, we may say that this loss of authority is merely the final though decisive phase of a development which for centuries undermined primarily religion and tradition.[60]

Thus, a theistic critique of anthropology's idolatry could inquire into what ways the discipline's promotion of culture as its foundational concept demotes *tradition* as a figure of thought, albeit paradoxically, as well as constitutes its epistemic survival. With the discipline's proclivities ranging from the evolutionary to the discursive, one could argue that with its culture idol anthropology avails tradition's conceptual endurance, wherein anthropologists have been de facto studying traditions as that of which cultures are made, even if they are not always and everywhere explicitly recognized, theoretically or empirically, as such.

A less charitable reading of modern anthropology would view it as participating in the conceptual demotion of tradition and in more than one way. Consider, for example, the economy of indexical terms in a recent program of the American Anthropology Association Meeting and how the entry *tradition* fares in terms of frequency in relation to other entries in the normalized—and vastly liberal—moral economy of the discipline, such as individual, power, agency, resistance, and sovereignty. Consider also anthropology's relative under-theorization of tradition or the scarcity of courses taught on the concept.[61] The disciplining

---

[58] Alasdair MacIntyre, *God, Philosophy and Universities: A Selective History of the Catholic Philosophical Tradition* (Lanham, MD: Rowman & Littlefield, 2011), 175.

[59] Richard H. Roberts, *Religion, Theology and the Human Sciences* (Cambridge: Cambridge University Press, 2002), 192.

[60] Hannah Arendt, *Between Past and Future* (1968; New York: Penguin Classics, 2006), 92.

[61] It is beyond the scope of this essay to explore in what ways the relative under-theorization of the concept of *tradition* helps explain the contention that "cultural change itself is not a well

of our silence or forgetfulness towards tradition precisely functions as a hājib in our costly dedication to the ideal/idol of culture.

If my account is correct that the concept of culture as a regulative principle has had idolatrous effects on the discipline, a critique of this idolatry cannot remain confined to forging a restorative (in distinction from disinterested or outright dismissive) relation with tradition and other ignoble concepts. Where, for example, is an anthropology that challenges the hājibs of modern disciplines and values fear and anxiety, as Kierkegaard did in refusing to see them as privative modes of human being?

However, beyond or prior to promoting a rehabilitation of the discipline's relation to this or that concept currently regarded as assaulting liberal reason, anthropology could undertake a theologically driven self-critique by comprehending what is at stake in the death of its own organizing principle.[62] I am referring, of course, to humanism, whose power once gave the discipline its very name—the science of man.

To state that culture and kindred terms (e.g., man, humankind) have been and continue to be the logic—disputed and faltering it may be—of the discipline's aspiration to unity is almost to engage in banality. However, it is a banality which it is helpful not to pass over and from which to start considering what anthropology could do in the modern university, if and when ready to renew its grammar for an integrative inquiry. Wolf's words supply a prelude to such renewal: "The unity of man is due neither to an ultimate biological homunculus inherent in each, nor to a unitary process located in the mind of God. It is a process of the involvement of man with man, through the mediation of human culture."[63]

In the search for a comprehensive vision of humankind and affine species, the concept of culture (or humanity) can be said to be the good around which anthropologists unite—though do not necessarily agree—and towards which the professional layers of their lives are dedicated. Yet what is probably less banal or less considered in anthropology is that its principle of unity is invalidated by the day. I am referring to humanity, that quiddity of the anthropological concept of culture. Insofar as humanity resides in the nucleus of this culture, anthropology draws its resources today from a cadaver, as the now well-known pronouncement about the "death of man" should remind us. Incidentally, one might say that Nietzsche anticipated the death of man as a consequence of the death of God. With the "true world" referencing the

---

theorized notion in anthropology." Joel Robbins, "Between Reproduction and Freedom: Morality, Value, and Radical Cultural Change," *Ethnos* 72/3 (2007): 293–314 (here 301).

[62] The reference here is to the "death of Man" thesis. For a review of positions in twentieth-century philosophy that this thesis entailed, see Stefanos Geroulanuos, *An Atheism That Is Not Humanist Emerges in French Thought* (Stanford: Stanford University Press, 2010).

[63] Wolf, *Anthropology*, 95.

place of God in Western intellect, in *Twilight* Nietzsche observes, "We have abolished the true world. What has remained: The apparent one. Oh no, with the true world we have also abolished the apparent one."[64] Moreover, an anthropology truly committed to reducing its losses with the help of theological means must contend with another loss, aside from the philosophical collapse of humanism, on which it rests as a science of culture—the loss of human diversity.

Anthropology must also contend with the absence of an integrative vision of inquiry in the modern university,[65] which is bent on an unending fissuring into distinct areas of expertise, riveting as they may be, in which theology operates as a "nature preserve,"[66] if not as the vestigial field that occasionally appears as no more than an item in the natural history museum of extinct faculty at the university. Again, one might argue that anthropology has operated like a pseudo-theology in that it has sought to furnish a unity, wholeness, or oneness of ultimate truth around human diversity. It has sought to do what traditionally theology has done, that is, offer an integrative vision of things, albeit supplanting God with humanity.

An anthropology bent on re-examining its dedication to holism would do well to decry the hājibs in its midst. An anthropology committed to looking or hearing beyond its idols demands that it contend adequately with the fact that its regulative principle of culture has long been pronounced dead and its pretions to study it increasingly occur within corporate-assaulted institutions bent on generating unaware, partitioned, and inconsequential coroners. Anthropology attuned to theology's othering in the modern secular university would remind it to restore corporation as its original vitality over its contemporary vitiation.[67]

Whether it burrows underneath (with Nietzsche's genealogy) or views from its exterior (with theology), the modern discipline of anthropology bears the potential for finding a way towards dismantling the hājibs its idols erect. In other words, it can forge new ways of organizing knowledge, truths, and values that transcend modern distinctions. It could unsettle capitulations to Kant's settlement of the struggle among the faculties, begun in Europe since leaving the Middle Ages, whereby revelation (or religion broadly speaking) was pit against reason, and reinstate humans' ability for rational inquiry into what exceeds their own rationality.

---

[64] Cited in Hannah Arendt, *Responsibility and Judgment* (New York: Schocken Books, 2003), 159–92 (here 162).

[65] MacIntyre, *God, Philosophy and Universities.*   [66] Roberts, *Religion*, 194.

[67] Recall that *university* in Roman law referred to *corporation* in the sense that the university incorporates universal knowledge, pursuing all its branches, theology included. John Henry Newman, *The Idea of a University Defined and Illustrated* (New York: Holt, Rinehart & Winston, 1968), 15.

In a similar vein, questioning the adequacy of the Renaissance humanist model of "struggle of faculties" for understanding all intellectual strategies and resources of medieval philosophy, Alain de Libera objects to "tutelles narratives," which (1) trample a vision of plurality of forms of rationalities and (2) enact a partition between theology and reason. An intellectual rehabilitation dismantling this divide for anthropology and other secular disciplines would demand inquiring into the paradoxes revelation poses to reason.[68]

Anthropology well attuned to theology should additionally articulate a better vision of the university and explore a new grammar for integrative inquiry. A university, whose prevailing rationality obstinately reduces God into, as Kant taught, a "methodological assumption,"[69] will as an institution likely serve and service the idols' market. A good student of theology refusing the rivalry between reason as sovereign and faith as its subject, anthropology could participate in charting a new *Gänze* (i.e., integrated vision) for the age.

Fearing for the sovereignty of reason, as it immures the anthropological discipline along with those others making up the modern university, suspecting an assault on our secular sense of intellect and criticism, we have unnecessarily learned the irrelevance or menace of excesses and either demoted them or rejected them outright. This secularizing hājib awaits a quintessential anthropological task: investigating anthropology itself as a secular effect whose freedom as a discipline and for unwarranted reasons has required its alienation, as well as that of the institution hosting it, from theistic rationality. By further recognizing who anthropologists are and what we could still become when committed to studying difference to the fullest, untrammeled by a discourse of finitude, not succumbing to our rationalities' fears in the face of what surpasses our frailty, an anthropology could emerge that strives beyond rather than succumbs to idols, Mammon or any other.

---

[68] Alain de Libera, *Penser au Moyen Age* (Paris: Editions du Seuil, 1996), 150.
[69] Funkenstein, *Theology*, 356.

5

What Can Theology Contribute to Cultural Anthropology?

Paul Kollman

"This is the worst news I've ever heard, Vic," Max Gluckman reputedly admitted to Victor Turner when his former student and younger colleague had, with his wife Edith, become Catholic.[1] One wonders what fed the sense of betrayal that Gluckman expressed: the embrace of religious faith in general, Catholicism in particular, or something else. One wonders, too, if Gluckman reconsidered this judgment before his death in 1975, eight years before Turner's own, given the way that Turner's later very influential analyses of ritual theory arguably drew upon his Christian faith. More certain is that Turner's earlier close attention to ritual among the Ndembu led to his conversion. As Timothy Larsen writes of the Turners, "What happened in Africa refused to stay in Africa. Witnessing and participating in Ndembu rituals changed them."[2] That change, however, has not been universally celebrated and not only by the Turners' Manchester School colleagues. Indeed, some contend that Turner's conversion distorted his anthropological writing afterwards. Such critics—perhaps Gluckman was among them—find his earlier work about the Ndembu more compelling than his later, less ethnographically specific, and more eclectic anthropological theorizing.[3]

This work, like the conferences before it, addresses how anthropology and theology ought to relate to one another and presumes a more fruitful potential in that relationship than Gluckman's instinctive disappointment suggests.[4]

---

[1] I heard this from a former professor who claimed to have heard it from Turner himself. Timothy Larsen does not recount it, though he does describe the consternation at the Turners' conversion among other Manchester School colleagues like Gluckman. Timothy Larsen, *The Slain God: Anthropologists and the Christian Faith* (Oxford: Oxford University Press, 2014), 182–3.

[2] Ibid., 183.

[3] Mathieu Deflem, "Ritual, Anti-Structure, and Religion: A Discussion of Victor Turner's Processual Symbolic Analysis," *Journal for the Scientific Study of Religion* 30 (1991): 1–25.

[4] See Brian M. Howell, Chapter 2, 29–49.

I accept both sociocultural anthropology and theology as broad fields that can encompass each other from within their disciplinary perspectives. In principle, theology is arguably broader insofar as it seeks to understand the implications of faith—thus to see all things in light of faith. At the same time, in practice anthropology often seems broader, since, though it remains at least agnostic about the bases of faith in revelation, the range of the vast scope of its subject— the human—leads anthropologists to cover subjects that theologians, who usually work from within particular traditions of faith, rarely touch upon. My own remarks will have three parts, oriented by the following guiding question: What might theology contribute to anthropology?

I will begin with an autobiographical sketch of my journey between these two disciplines, and among theology and the social sciences more broadly, to explain how I seek to work among them and why the anthropology of Christianity has appealed to me. Second, I will consider Joel Robbins' seminal 2006 article, "Anthropology and Theology: An Awkward Relationship?"[5] as a piece that has set a certain orientation for this discussion. I will argue that some of Robbins' assumptions can, perhaps quite unwittingly, potentially foreclose mutually enriching conversations that might proceed between the two disciplines. I thus appreciate a more recent article in which he discusses other opportunities in the awkward potential of the interrelationship between these two disciplines.[6]

I will conclude by comparing the work of two scholars—one scholar from each discipline—who discuss a similar issue from within their fields in ana-logical but distinctive ways. Both the anthropologist Kenelm Burridge and the theologian and church historian Andrew Walls analyze the dialectical rela-tionship between Christianity as at once both a localized reality and a univer-sal religion. Their competing yet compatible modes of analysis, I will argue, show how theology might contribute to anthropology, giving a potentially illuminating example for future interdisciplinary engagement. This compari-son and contrast also embodies what I think Robbins seeks in his recent piece on the relationship between anthropology and theology.

*   *   *

In thinking of the relationship between anthropology and theology, my personal engagement has changed over time. Two stages are worth delimiting.

First, I was first trained in Catholic theology as an undergraduate and then as a graduate-level seminarian in a US-based, firmly post-Vatican II Catholic mode. Like other academic disciplines, theology has a variety of subfields, their precise number and interrelationships being understood differently. In

---

[5] Joel Robbins, "Anthropology and Theology: An Awkward Relationship?" *Anthropological Quarterly* 79/2 (2006): 285–94.
[6] Joel Robbins, "Afterword: Let's Keep It Awkward: Anthropology, Theology, and Otherness," *Australian Journal of Anthropology* 24 (2013): 329–37.

addition to the disciplinary subfields, I learned about the different approaches to theology that orient a given theologian's interests, approach to theological sources, and methodology.

During a stretch of seminary study in Kenya and exposure to a new "ecclesial climate," to use Martyn Percy's term in this work,[7] I first read academic anthropology in order to understand better the structuring nature of African cultural features on African Christianity and theology. I found anthropology thrilling and illuminating and recall a paper in which I explored how African cultural realities shaped the practice and theology of the Eucharist, Christianity's normal mode of remembering Christ's last meal before his death. To this point, I found anthropology useful for theology, the directional arrow of instrument to application being clear: I was not an anthropologist and looked to the field of anthropology as a tool for better theological reflection.

In so doing, I was, in this first stage of my life as a scholar, without being aware of it, following a theological method analogous to that of many before me. After all, we think with the categories available to us, and theological thinking is no different, drawing on anthropology—understood less as an academic discipline and more broadly as explicit and implicit assumptions about human nature—regnant when and where it is carried out. Implicitly, two giants in western Christian theology, Augustine and Thomas Aquinas, both drew upon what they saw as the best anthropology of their day—for Augustine, neo-Platonic, and for Aquinas, Aristotelian assumptions about human nature in their theological explications. More recently, Friedrich Schleiermacher's thought has obvious roots in German Romanticism, while Karl Rahner and Edward Schillebeeckx, both twentieth-century Catholic theologians, drew upon Heideggerian approaches to interpersonal encounter, among many other things. The tendency continues. Liberation theologian Gustavo Gutiérrez relies upon the Frankfurt School Marxism of his own academic formation in post-war Europe, and Paul Tillich, H. Richard Niebuhr, Kathryn Tanner, and Gerald Arbuckle, in their own ways, have engaged categories from discipline-bound cultural anthropology in pursuit of theological elaboration on the nature of God, Christ, theological ethics, and Christian discipleship. Thus stage one, for me, in an implicit, unschooled way, drew anthropology and theology together to consider how anthropology and, by extension, social science or its philosophical precursors shape theology. Many, I believe, have produced theology in similar ways.

Stage two for me began as I studied anthropology more formally on its own in my own doctoral work. After being a Catholic priest active in ministry a few years, I wanted to pursue advanced study of African religions that would

---

[7] Martyn Percy, Chapter 17, 307.

combine anthropology and theology in some way and prepare me to teach at a university. I eventually landed in the History of Religions program at the Divinity School of the University of Chicago, which was alongside Haskell Hall, home of the anthropology department. I learned of the various subfields of anthropology, which like theology's subfields are described in varying ways, though my obvious interest was sociocultural anthropology. I learned too of the orientations that guided different anthropologists in their work, producing different approaches to sources and different methods. There, in addition to the Divinity School's theologians and historians of religion, I met John and Jean Comaroff, whose work on missionary Christianity in southern Africa had become influential.[8] I also worked closely with the late Martin Riesebrodt, a Weberian sociologist of religion.[9]

In studying with them and their colleagues, I began to see that not only did theology draw upon anthropology, but that certain anthropologists—some in their theory, others in their practice—drew upon theological assumptions. In a directed readings course on African religions, for example, I was reading Evans-Pritchard's *Nuer Religion*, then Godfrey Lienhardt's *Divinity and Experience*, about the Dinka.[10] I did not know the biographies of either, but in reading them, I noted all sorts of obvious—to this Catholic priest's instincts—theological assumptions and framings in how they depicted the religions of the Nuer and Dinka of southern Sudan. John Comaroff remarked to me that both eminent anthropologists were, in fact, Catholics. The deployment by Evans-Pritchard in particular of neo-Thomistic categories redolent with overt and implicit references to Aristotle became clear to me as he described Nuer religion's practices and religious specialists. He adduced Aristotelian categories of matter and form to describe the sacrificial ritual work of the Nuer leopard-skin priests, whose roles resembled those of Catholic clergy in presiding over the sacraments. I later learned that Mary Douglas and Victor Turner, portrayed in Larsen's recent work, were also Catholic.

Anthropology in its broader practice, however, and in the post-structuralist mode that it was often being taught then, as well as in the neo-modern/neo-Marxist mode of the Comaroffs, tended to be different from what was practiced by Evans-Pritchard, Lienhardt, and the others in Larsen's book. Foundational assumptions were supposedly masked, modes of description

---

[8] Their two volumes on the appearance of Christianity among the Tswana have become classics with large influence in social anthropology and related fields. A third has been promised. Jean Comaroff and John Comaroff, *Christianity, Colonialism, and Consciousness in South Africa*, 2 vols (Chicago: University of Chicago Press, 1991–7).

[9] Among Riesebrodt's work, see especially the following, written before his untimely death: *The Promise of Salvation: A Theory of Religion* (Chicago: University of Chicago Press, 2010).

[10] E. E. Evans-Pritchard, *Nuer Religion* (Oxford: Clarendon Press, 1956); Godfrey Lienhardt, *Divinity and Experience: The Religion of the Dinka* (Oxford: Clarendon Press, 1961).

seemed more purely phenomenological, even while certain arguably totalizing ideological orientations—in John Milbank's terms, attempts to "police the sublime"[11]—were obvious. Much of the mode was deconstructionist, since uncovering the biases of past approaches was important in making sense of new insights—for example, into the constructed history of naturalized identities subsumed under the problematic term *tribe*, similarly once solid-looking assumptions about gendered and age-structured social authority, and other categories of social analysis whose unquestioned status dissolved under critical inspection.

In the end, I, too, studied missionary Christianity, shaped in important ways by the historical anthropology that the Comaroffs, Marshall Sahlins, Bernard Cohn, and others practiced, along with certain orientations in historical sociology. I looked closely at missionary practices and responses to them by Africans as discernible through archival research and other types of critical study.

I realized rather quickly that my theological knowledge, though not especially substantial, was quite useful for appreciating aspects of this historical process that others overlooked. The value of theological awareness was obvious in the case of the practices undertaken by the Catholic missionaries on whom I focused, for their theology operated to shape their behavior. Theological assumptions coexisted with other concerns deriving, for example, from nineteenth-century French social and colonial history that also oriented their actions. I considered the ecclesiological assumptions regarding the near-unquestionable perfection of the Catholic Church and all its structures that guided nineteenth-century Catholic missionary practice, the spirituality that shaped the seminary formation in which the missionaries in question had been formed, the complex relationships between the Catholic Church and the French nation state they carried with them upon arriving in eastern Africa, and ways their missionary practices reflected both overtly theological influences and developing social theories dependent on nineteenth-century European urban planning and penitentiary practices, especially those connected with juveniles.

Deeper awareness of the missionaries' orientations in turn allowed me to interpret the historical written record describing their evangelizing, most of which they produced. It also allowed me to see African responses more clearly, since awareness of the missionaries as actors and producers of historical record allowed me to interpret better what they wrote. Over time, I gleaned a way to think about African responses to the missionaries' practices that also drew on certain categories and frameworks, some of them theological or at least theologically inclined as well. After all, the one-time slaves on whom

[11] John Milbank, *Theology and Social Theory: Beyond Secular Reason* (Oxford: Blackwell Publishing, 1990), 3, 101ff.

I focused were subjected to years of missionary evangelization, and their multiple responses drew upon myriad structuring assumptions, including those linked to their (at times) evolving Christian faith.[12] Not only were they seeking as much freedom as they could pursue given their vulnerable state—escaping, organizing, protesting—but they also drew upon Catholic assumptions about their human dignity as they defended and advanced their interests.

Here in phase two, the arrow of service had reversed itself. Instead of anthropology being at the service of theology as in stage one, now theology was generally in the service of anthropology, especially in the service of an anthropological understanding of distinct historical processes such as those I studied. Much of the theology at work in these episodes was implicit, the value of which I, like Martyn Percy, Brian Howell, and others in this volume, appreciated.

I have now been a faculty member in a theology department at a Catholic university for nearly two decades. Many of my departmental colleagues engage the social sciences in their work, though only a few do so in the service of historical understandings of Christianity-in-practice, for in our department, the dominant mode for historical study is what might be called historical theology rather than the history of Christianity. Thus, I have often felt out of place around my colleagues, few of whom have my training or read the things I read. I knew of theologians who took the discipline of anthropology (and other social sciences) very seriously—Gordon Kaufman, David Tracy, Kathryn Tanner, Gerald Arbuckle—yet they were not my colleagues.[13] I have not had extensive anthropological training nor carried out ethnographic fieldwork of much depth and thereby lack the experiences that typically qualify one as an anthropologist.

This lack of a secure disciplinary niche in which to place myself helps situate and explain the personal delight I took when the anthropology of Christianity first came to my attention. I found myself reading thoughtful expositions of self-aware scholarly practice that described—much better than I could have—something that resembled what I had rather instinctively and uncritically been doing for about a decade in my own professional academic work. Even if few of the anthropologists of Christianity whose work I admired—among them Fenella Cannell, Webb Keane, Matthew Engelke, Naomi Haynes, Birgit Meyer, and Joel Robbins—had theological training like mine (as far as I know), they

[12] Paul Kollman, *The Evangelization of Slaves and Catholic Origins in Eastern Africa* (Maryknoll, NY: Orbis Books, 2005).

[13] The important scholarship advancing ethnography as a tool in theology and ethics, embodied by my Notre Dame colleague Todd Whitmore, is also inspiring, though my work has been more historical and less constructive, generally speaking, than such work. Todd Whitmore, "Whiteness Made Visible: A Theo-critical Ethnography in Acoliland," in *Ethnography as Christian Theology and Ethics*, ed. Christian Scharen and Aana Marie Vigen (London and New York: Continuum, 2011), 184–206.

considered theology important and sought to make themselves conversant with scholarship in the field as they wrote and researched.

I find myself these days moving in my academic writing and my teaching between theological and nontheological approaches to religious phenomena all the time. I find myself enacting an informal flexibility of approach that, without sitting firmly within a single disciplinary orientation and training, believes that insights into past and present human action can come from various disciplines even when a single one—anthropology or theology, for instance, or sociology or the discipline of history—serves as the organizing discipline in a particular analysis. The Eucharist is what Catholics believe it to be, as well as human ritual action shaped by historically discernible decisions made in time and space. Funerary rites in African people groups repair the social whole rent by death yet also speak to a spiritual desire for transcendence that God possibly has placed within us. Human behavior is shaped by many things, and insights from evolutionary biology and the doctrine of original sin need not be mutually contradictory in grasping that behavior.

The oscillation that occurs through discipline-bound redescriptions of similar phenomena now feels almost instinctive—my default mode—and I am grateful when I find anthropologists and theologians describing the same sorts of things from different vantage points deriving from their disciplinary perspectives. Often, mutual illumination occurs as the roads taken by different scholars who follow their own paths occasionally run parallel and even come together or illuminate contrasts with helpful distinctions.[14] Certainly theologians can, in practice, unhelpfully mystify processes considered by anthropologists, and certainly anthropologists can, in practice, unhelpfully reduce processes considered by theologians. However, accusations of each toward the other need not always be fair, and I find that in such accusations of, for example, mystification or reduction, insight can still be gained. Such efforts, like those of so many in this volume, promote an advance beyond mutual misunderstandings and unhelpful generalizations.

Before turning to one such example close to my own work, I want to spend some time thinking about how the anthropology of Christianity has been positioned to engage theology. In particular, I worry that anthropologists of Christianity are moving away from formal engagement with the work of theologians rather than toward it, despite this volume and the conferences prior to it. To elaborate on this assertion, I turn to Robbins' article on "the awkward relationship" between the two disciplines, which has shaped the conversation, and to his more recent article where he admits earlier limitations. Previously an anthropologist at the University of California at San Diego and now at Cambridge, Robbins wrote an important monograph on the

---

[14] I find inspiring in this regard Douglas J. Davies, *Anthropology and Theology* (Oxford: Berg Publishers, 2002), and much of what I describe is inspired by my impressions of his work.

Christianization of the Urapmin of New Guinea, seen as a seminal work in the anthropology of Christianity,[15] and he has also authored a number of articles that have shaped the emergent subdiscipline.[16]

*   *   *

In 2006, Robbins wrote on the awkward relationship between anthropology and theology an article rightly seen as a seminal introduction to the interdisciplinary discussion regarding the relationship between the two disciplines that hovers around the anthropology of Christianity, helpfully diagnosing some of the difficulties that arise. Evidence for the 2006 article's importance includes its role in prompting the 2013 forum in the *Australian Journal of Anthropology* (*TAJA*) invoked in the convening of our conferences. Nearly all the *TAJA* articles cite Robbins' 2006 article, who himself offers an "Afterword" that plays on the title of his earlier piece—and to which we shall return. References to the 2006 Robbins article also appear in a February 2014 article in *Current Anthropology* by five Christian anthropologists who push the value of theological thought for anthropology and in some of the responses in the forum that followed.[17]

In the 2006 piece, Robbins organizes his argument around three ways in which theology might contribute to anthropology. First, theology can help anthropology discover its own disciplinary origins. Second, theology can shed light on cultures that are shaped by theological presuppositions. Third, theology can cause anthropologists to "revise their core projects."[18] Robbins is quick to identify the limits of the first two options and spends most of the article elaborating the third.

Two aspects of Robbins' approach, I believe, have potentially problematic consequences for subsequent discussions of anthropology's engagement with theology. First, by sidelining the first two options, he limits rather significant possibilities arising in the second option, in which theology can inform ethnographic understanding by deepening awareness of human actors and what they do. Second, the way he discusses his third option narrows the potential impacts of theology on anthropology in unnecessary ways.

Arguing that Robbins shortchanges the possibilities in the second of his options represents an admittedly self-interested assertion, since my academic work has aligned with this option. In seeking to understand certain Christian practices and processes, my own work exemplifies this second option. I often

---

[15] Joel Robbins, *Becoming Sinners: Christianity and Moral Torment in a Papua New Guinea Society* (Berkeley: University of California Press, 2004).

[16] For a list of these publications, see <www.socanth.cam.ac.uk/open-access-documents/oa-online-publications/robbinspublications.pdf>.

[17] Eloise Meneses, Lindy Backues, David Bronkema, Eric Flett, and Benjamin L. Hartley, "Engaging the Religiously Committed Other: Anthropologists and Theologians in Dialogue," *Current Anthropology* 55/1 (2014): 82–104.

[18] Robbins, "Anthropology and Theology," 287.

approach "[A]ny given piece of theology...as data that can inform us about the particular Christian culture that produced it."[19] I had drawn upon my awareness of Christian theology to understand the motivations and actions of Christian actors, firstly missionaries, and by extension had sought to understand the theological motivations of others whom I was studying to appreciate their actions. Thus their theology—whether actually operative or simply professed, conscious or unconscious—was certainly not the only thing I tried to understand, but I did seek to understand how theological discourses and related practices affected them.

Robbins depicts this second option, like the first he identifies, as quite limited. Such options "expect theological ideas to contribute to already established anthropological projects but not transform them."[20] He continues that thus in the second option, "theology is at bottom simply another kind of ethnographic data anthropologists can draw on in developing their analyses of specific cultures."[21] In short, theology is perceived as limited to one window on its producers.

I remember thinking the first time I read Robbins' piece soon after its appearance, "Well, yes, I suppose theology does constitute 'only ethnographic data' for me, but this is a strange sort of dismissal, since theology is not simply 'another kind of ethnographic data.' After all, for many of those whom anthropologists study and have studied, theology in its broadest sense represents implicit or explicit reflection on what they claim to be the most important truths in the world."[22]

Robbins contrasts his first two options—whose limits he identifies clearly—with invocations of theology of a third sort that, unlike the first two, fundamentally challenge anthropology as a discipline. This third option raises the stakes, so that anthropologists "would have to imagine that theologians might either [first] produce theories that get some things right about the world they currently get wrong or [second] model a kind of action in the world that is in some or other way more effective or ethically adequate than their own."[23] Certainly my invocations of theology in most of my academic writing have not either challenged anthropology's descriptive or ethical achievements. As a historian of African Christianity, my interests are in thinking about theology less as a foundational discipline that contests assumptions in other disciplines such as anthropology and more as a human practice that sheds light on other human practices.

---

[19] Ibid., 286.   [20] Ibid., 287.   [21] Ibid., 286.

[22] Robbins' dismissal of option two has resonated and been repeated. Meneses et al., "Engaging the Religiously Committed Other," mention it briefly on page 85, as does Haynes in her response to their piece. See Naomi Haynes, "Repairing an 'Awkward Relationship'?" *Current Anthropology* 55/1 (2014): 93–4. Even more explicitly, Fountain and Lau speak of the first two options Robbins identifies as follows: "Neither allows for anything more than a limited anaemic encounter with theology." See Philip Fountain and Sin Wen Lau, "Anthropological Theologies: Engagements and Encounters," *Australian Journal of Anthropology* 24/3 (2013): 227–34 (here 228).

[23] Robbins, "Anthropology and Theology," 286.

Again, the first time I read Robbins' article, I remember my instinctive response to his identification of the two possible ways that theology can fundamentally challenge anthropology. To the first, in which theology prompts theoretical reconsideration by anthropologists, I wondered if an anthropologist can truly accept a theologian's theory about something without accepting the assumptions that guide the theologian to his or her conclusions. The anthropologist then might actually be leaving anthropology for theology, perhaps in an imaginary way that tries to inhabit the thought-worlds of others as fully as possible. To the second—that is, finding ethical resources in theology unavailable in anthropology—I asked if the anthropologist was thereby joining the community in relation to whose faith the theologian was practicing the discipline or at least embracing that community's ethical ideals. In short, I saw Robbins—and he reiterates this longing clearly if somewhat obliquely in his conclusion—seeming to want anthropology-inflected-by-theology to grant something like the hope-providing security of mutually supportive believing, belonging, and behaving that religious adherents enjoy. He closes his article by lamenting anthropologists' "inability to anymore show the world how to find hope for real change without [God]."[24] He wonders, in short, if theology can supply what anthropology has failed to give.

Robbins explains the promise in this third option by describing as just such a work—one that can lead anthropologists to revise their core projects and maybe also provide hope for real change—John Milbank's *Theology and Social Theory*, first published in 1990. Milbank influentially presents a concerted defense of theological reasoning against that carried out in the social sciences, showing the contradictory ontological assumptions that, he believes, underpin each. Milbank sees social science reasoning as subtly undermining theological assumptions; thus, he argues that it ought to be treated carefully in Christian theology, which has its own social theory. Robbins deploys Milbank's book ostensibly to show that theology can, unlike anthropology, not only display otherness but also presume the compelling nature of otherness in ways that anthropology, with the aloofness of cultural relativism, usually cannot. The implications for Robbins are that Milbank's argument does not simply inform anthropology. It ought to lead anthropologists to consider the presumptions operative in their own discipline.

Robbins' discussion of theology's potential for anthropology through this third option, I believe, has resulted in a rather narrow view of theology as a discipline and in three ways. First, theology, though never defined, is presumed by the example chosen as its representative—Milbank's book—to be the written practice of elites. This restriction overlooks the multiple ways theology operates in human life without being written, something Howell and Percy

---

[24] Ibid., 293.

note in their chapters.[25] If theology is broadened to be a reflection upon religious faith more generally, then its role in shaping human action—at least the actions of the vast majority of human persons who have claimed to have had religious faith—is much more extensive than Robbins' discussion implies.

Second, theology is presumed to be what theologians sometimes call systematic,[26] which again is a narrowing, this time to a specific subfield within a larger discipline. The field of theology apprehends more than systematic reflection on first principles, which is Milbank's focus as he criticizes appropriations by theologians of unhelpful assumptions contained in the social scientific tools they borrow in their theological analysis, since those assumptions undermine theology's first principles. Many have described the theological task, beginning early in Christian history, and it found an important systematization in the work of Schleiermacher, as well as another influential formulation by Bernard Lonergan in his *Method in Theology*.[27] For all practitioners, theology takes many forms, as James Bielo, Francis Clooney, and Brian Howell remind us in their chapters in this book.[28] My own historical research into theology as shaping the practices and reception of evangelization engages missiology, usually seen as a branch of practical theology, which Bielo supports as anthropologically fruitful.

Third, by isolating Milbank among systematic theologians and focusing on his early work only, a further narrowing occurs, since the founder of radical orthodoxy is far from representative of systematic theology or even a representative of how theologians normally engage anthropology and other social sciences. The largely deconstructive task of *Theology and Social Theory* means that by taking it as representing theology, Robbins has done something analogous to choosing Talal Asad's early essay on the problematic assumptions embedded in Clifford Geertz's theory of religion as representative of the discipline of anthropology,[29] except that Milbank is probably more polarizing in academic theology than Asad in academic anthropology.[30]

---

[25] Howell, Chapter 2, 29–49; Percy, Chapter 17, 296–314.

[26] Theology is divided up in various ways, so that sometimes what is called in one arena systematic theology resembles something elsewhere called fundamental or philosophical theology. And sometimes each of these is seen to be a subheading under the larger umbrella of the other.

[27] Bernard Lonergan, *Method in Theology* (New York: Seabury Press, 1979).

[28] Howell, Chapter 2, 29–49; Bielo, Chapter 8, 140–55; Clooney, Chapter 16, 280–95.

[29] Talal Asad, "The Construction of Religion as an Anthropological Category," in *Genealogies of Religion* (Baltimore, MD: Johns Hopkins University Press, 1993), 27–54.

[30] For one criticism of Milbank's method, see Neil Ormerod "It's Easy to See: The Footnotes of John Milbank," *Philosophy and Theology* 11/2 (1999): 257–64. This article describes the sweeping generalizations, vague argumentation, and problematic attributions that Ormerod believes characterize much of Milbank's writing. Though rather awestruck by his range and often dazzled by his rhetoric, I find Milbank's assessments of many social theorists in the 1990 work quite problematic, and likewise his portrayals of the theologians whose work is allegedly deformed by reliance on them—these constitute his real target.

I think the consequences of Robbins' article have been problematic for self-conscious discussions of academic theology within anthropology. The 2013 *TAJA* issue that focused on Robbins' "Anthropology and Theology" article was valuable, but, in fact, precious few theologians' work is even cited in the issue, and none is discussed at length.[31] The February 2014 article by Christian anthropologists in *Current Anthropology* who urged more thorough engagement with theology by anthropologists discusses theology more fully, but none of the authors is someone squarely within the anthropology of Christianity.[32] More ominously, the even more recent December 2014 issue of *Current Anthropology* dedicated to the anthropology of Christianity had only one of its numerous contributors refer to Robbins' 2006 piece at all,[33] though much of Robbins' other work is cited and discussed extensively. Though theologians' works are cited more than in the *TAJA* issue, engagement with their ideas is usually very slight.[34]

That said, if theology is seen to be broader than the narrow confines assumed in the early Robbins article, then theology has been engaged very regularly, even when anthropologists do not name it as such. A great many of the articles in the *TAJA* volume consider theology in an informal mode, beyond the confines of systematic theology, and without reference to academic theologians. The issues engaged range widely into discussions of theological perspectives and practices operative in Islam, agnosticism, paganism, and Hare Krishna devotion, as well as in Melanesian religiosity. In the issue as a whole, as one contributor notes, "Theology is seen variously as a social science, a lay discourse, an intellectual framework and a kind of reflexive practice."[35] The same is true of the articles in the 2014 issue of *Current Anthropology*, which range even more widely across forms of religiosity. In addition to citing living or recently deceased theologians such as Kwame Bediako, Sara Butler, Mary Daly, Catherine Keller, Donald McGavran, Jaroslav Pelikan, Rosemary Radford Ruether, David Tracy, and Robert Wilken, the pieces also consider the living theology embodied in a number of times and places, including contemporary secular humanism. More overtly religious settings explored include Cao Dai in Vietnam, eastern Orthodox Christianity past and present,

---

[31] Robbins, "Anthropology and Theology"; "Afterword." My quick perusal of the citations noted the following: Milbank, Rudolph Otto, Paul Tillich, Starhawk (in the article on paganism), Desmond Tutu, and Graham Ward. None of these people is a living theologian whom most other Christian theologians would define as representative. Milbank and Ward would be closest, both closely linked to radical orthodoxy.

[32] Meneses et al., "Engaging the Religiously Committed Other."

[33] I refer to the December 2014 special issue of *Current Anthropology* 55/S10, entitled "The Anthropology of Christianity: Unity, Diversity, New Directions."

[34] One book in the anthropology of Christianity that does engage contemporary theology is Matthew Engelke's *A Problem of Presence: Beyond Scripture in an African Church* (Berkeley: University of California Press, 2007).

[35] Fountain and Lau, "Anthropological Theologies," 230.

Christian communities in Papua New Guinea, contemporary urban China, Damascus, and Zambia.

Robbins himself in his "Afterword" admits that his "Anthropology and Theology" article was problematic.[36] He accepts that his earlier article presented theology too narrowly, as intellectualized, written, and often semi-official discourse by intellectuals, when, in fact, theology, understood anthropologically at least, ought to be seen as a much more capacious human undertaking. He appreciates the move toward finding theology in believers' practices rather than only in written reflection that many of the authors undertake, and recognizes that he has only rarely done so in relation to the Urapmin Christians of New Guinea whom he studied closely as a basis for many of his own anthropological insights. After accepting that his own "Anthropology and Theology" article represents "further testament to the existence of general impediments to taking theology seriously within anthropology,"[37] Robbins concludes by embracing the awkward yet productive nature of the interaction between the disciplines: "[T]he dialogue between anthropology and theology likely works best when it is preoccupied not with seeking agreement, but with registering what the differences between the two fields have to teach both sides."[38] He wants to keep the relationship between them alive, even if inevitably awkward.

Howell in this work notes that examples of such mutually fruitful exchanges are not impossible. He argues, however, that they do require scholarly effort to place different disciplines in relationship to one another and mindfulness about which options in each discipline can be most beneficial in mutual conversations.[39]

*   *   *

I would like to share an example in order to illustrate how theology might contribute to anthropology in the back-and-forth manner reminiscent of my own journey—and in somewhat of a fulfillment of Robbins' more recent suggestion—by describing two different perspectives, one anthropological and one theological, on a similar topic—namely, the dynamics at work in the manifestation of Christianity among people who come anew to the faith. The first comes from anthropologist Kenelm Burridge's book *In the Way: A Study of Christian Missionary Endeavours*. Burridge tries "to expose and explicate the contradictions and ambiguities involved in missionary endeavors and to establish a theory about the apparently inevitable processes that arise out of the nature of Christianity and the building of a Christian community."[40] The second is a widely cited essay by Andrew Walls, first published in 1982, where

---

[36] Robbins, "Afterword," 332–3.   [37] Ibid., 333.   [38] Ibid., 336.
[39] Howell, Chapter 2, 29–49.
[40] Kenelm Burridge, *In the Way: A Study of Christian Missionary Endeavours* (Vancouver: UBC Press, 1991), frontispiece.

Walls seeks to offer a framework to think about Christianity's capacity for remarkable diversity in its manifestations across time, space, and culture, all the while maintaining its unity as a single recognizable religion.[41]

These are very different pieces of writing. Burridge's monograph claims to offer not quite an anthropology of missionaries but more "a conceptualized and reflective portrait of missionary endeavors."[42] Building on his Melanesian fieldwork beginning in the 1950s, which not only produced important books in the field[43] but also put him in contact with many missionaries, Burridge discerns an unavoidable conflict faced by missionaries. This conflict arises between the call to unconditional love of others that lies at the heart of Christianity and the task of bringing the Christian message to people who do not know it, a task predicated on the assumption that something could still be better for those among whom the missionary works—a task that calls into question the unconditionality of the love in the first place. Burridge labels the two opposed, yet always present tendencies in what he calls "the Christian systemic"—by which he means a common, repeatable, and observable social regularity—as the "Devotional" and "Affirmative." The "Affirmative" refers to the aspect of love that, in its unconditional nature, accepts a culture and those who share it, while the former refers to the impulse to bring the values of Christianity understood as a metaculture—a term he uses to express Christianity's continuities across cultural variation so that it is *above* individual cultures—more fully to bear on those evangelized. He writes, "Centered in the message of the gospels, Christianity, here termed a metaculture, emerges into culture to involve complementarities that, in their systemic, become moral dialectics." Burridge continues, "Every missionary is caught in movement between God or the Divine and the human or culture, conviction and skepticism, quietism and universalism, rejecting and embracing culture, the faith and/or social work, stability and change."[44] Burridge sees an inevitable dialectic in Christianity's social appearances.

In building the depiction of this *systemic*, the book sometimes avers directly to Burridge's observations of missionaries in the field and other times refers to episodes in Christian history more broadly. He also deploys the philosophical anthropology articulated in his book, *Someone, No One: An Essay on Individuality,*

---

[41] Andrew F. Walls, "The Gospel as Prisoner and Liberator of Culture," in *The Missionary Movement in Christian History: Studies in the Transmission of Faith* (Maryknoll, NY: Orbis Books, 1996), 3–15 (here 15).

[42] Burridge, *In the Way,* ix.

[43] Burridge's works in Melanesian anthropology include *Mambu: A Melanesian Millennium* (Princeton: Princeton University Press, 1960); *Tangu Traditions. A Study in the Way of Life, Mythology and Developing Experience of a New Guinea People* (Oxford: Clarendon Press, 1969); *New Heaven, New Earth: A Study of Millenarian Activities* (Oxford: Basil Blackwell, 1969); *Encountering Aborigines: A Case Study: Anthropology and the Australian Aboriginal* (Elmsford, NY: Pergamon Press, 1973).

[44] Burridge, *In the Way,* xiv.

which develops a theory of personal identity emerging out of social order, as undifferentiated but socially located *persons* who exist as *someone* due to their secure identity, become through self-assertion truer *individuals* by resisting social conformity, thus becoming (within their default social order) *no one*.[45] Here, however, my focus lies in the Devotional and the Affirmative as twin principles that Burridge identifies in the Christian systemic, the reason being their analogical similarity to principles identified by Walls in his article.

Walls' essay begins with a thought experiment, in which an interplanetary, time-traveling observer drops in on earth and observes Christians in a series of episodes from shortly after the crucifixion of Christ in Jerusalem to an early ecumenical council, to an Irish monastery in the sixth or seventh century, to a Christian meeting of fervent nineteenth-century Victorian gentlemen in London, to a raucous African independent church in Nigeria—all rather normal Christian scenes from the date and time of the putative visit. However, their variety challenges whether they are really the same religion, for amid the abiding references to Jesus and the Bible, "these continuities are cloaked with such heavy veils belonging to their environment that Christians of different times and places must often be unrecognizable to others, or indeed even to themselves, as manifestations of a single phenomenon."[46] Such diversity raises the question about whether Christianity is in fact a single thing in any real way.

The profound divergences and even dissonance among these scenarios, along with the less obvious but still recognizable continuities, lead Walls to identify two principles or tendencies he sees always at work in church history. First there is the "indigenizing principle," based on the fact that "God accepts us as we are, on the ground of Christ's work alone, not on the ground of what we have become or are trying to become."[47] This principle means some at least conditional acceptance not only of individuals but also the social realities in which they live. At the same time, the gospel and thus church history have also a second tendency that Walls calls the "pilgrim principle," by which God takes people not simply to affirm their present circumstances but "in order to transform them into what He wants them to be."[48] Walls continues, "Just as the indigenizing principle...associates Christians with the *particulars* of their culture,...the pilgrim principle,...by associating them with things and people outside the culture,...is in some respects a *universalizing* factor."[49] Walls then draws upon these principles to consider the inevitable tensions moving forward within Christian communities arising from the spread of the faith to new peoples, with an attention especially to African Christian

---

[45] Kenelm Burridge, *Someone, No One: An Essay on Individuality* (Princeton: Princeton University Press, 1979).
[46] Walls, "The Gospel," 7.　　　[47] Ibid., 7.　　　[48] Ibid., 8.　　　[49] Ibid., 9.

theology that struggles to assert itself in the face of opposition in older theological circles.[50]

These two works have had different fates within their respective disciplines, or so I believe. Walls' "The Gospel as Prisoner and Liberator of Culture" article has come to be seen as a classic in discussions of world Christianity and continues to be widely read in mission studies circles and classes that look at the diversity of the world Christian movement. Burridge's *In the Way* has been subject to criticisms from other anthropologists, some of them quite dismissive, and my sense is that his fate has resembled that of Victor Turner among his peers.[51] Still, few anthropologists have shown as sensitive an appreciation for or attention to the missionary task, and I have heard missionaries praise his empathy for their circumstances.

The two pairs of tendencies that Walls and Burridge identify as they consider the diversity of Christian forms across time, space, and culture have striking similarities. Both the Devotional–Affirmative pair and the twin indigenizing and pilgrim principles represent tendencies in tension that are always operative in Christian history. In explaining them, both Burridge and Walls adduce numerous historical episodes in Christianity's history, beginning in the Acts of the Apostles, to illustrate their paired tendencies at work. Both authors also accept that Christianity is a single thing, yet has a nearly infinite range of possible instantiations in human communities, with the principles operating to explain both the continuity and the variations.

The key difference between them surrounds the nature of the agency that allows the two to operate in a productive tension in each case, and this discrepancy locates their disciplinary orientation within theology and anthropology. Walls finds his two principles operative in church history because each "has its origin in the Gospel itself."[52] The agent at work in enacting the principles in Walls' account is primarily God, acting in Jesus and the Holy Spirit through the life of the church shaped by the Bible. Burridge, however, places the agency squarely on missionaries themselves—human agents who,

---

[50] The brief accounts of these two works overlooks much; there are important differences between them: one a heavily researched and footnoted monograph of nearly 300 pages, the other a reflective, musing article of thirteen pages; one reliant on impressions from decades of close observation of missionaries in action and a rather dense philosophical anthropology, the other using a thought experiment and unapologetically employing theological language.

[51] For criticisms of Burridge's later works, see Thomas Beidelman's devastating review of *In the Way* in *American Ethnologist* 21/3 (1994), 660–1, and also an article by Robert Tonkinson entitled "*Homo Anthropologicus* in Aboriginal Australia: 'Secular Missionaries,' Christians and Morality in the Field," in *Anthropology of Morality in Melanesia and Beyond*, ed. John Barker (Burlington, VT: Ashgate, 2007), 171–89. Burridge's earlier works such as *Mambu* and *New Heaven, New Earth* are more broadly appreciated than his later works, which delve into philosophical anthropology and broader theorizing instead of remaining grounded in ethnographic observation.

[52] Walls, "The Gospel," 7.

shaped by the constant demands of Christian love as laid out in the New Testament especially, have an irresolvable tension at the heart of their undertaking. Though he sees them as inevitably motivated by theological assumptions, Burridge locates the agency in the dialectical play of the two principles within practices carried out by human persons, not God.

The varying notions of the agency at work in each case leads to other differences between Walls' and Burridge's approaches to Christian continuity and differentiation. Elsewhere, Walls fills out the ways divine agency enacts this "diversity and coherence,"[53] identifying especially the notion of the Incarnation of God in the person of Jesus of Nazareth and the subsequent translations of that message—both literally, in terms of the Scriptures rendered in new languages, and the life of faith "translated" into new cultural settings.[54] God or God's Spirit is at work through missionaries and new Christians in cooperating in the unfolding of the pilgrim principle and the indigenizing principle, yet "both are the direct result of that incarnational and translational process whereby God redeems us through the life, death, and resurrection of Christ."[55] Divine power drives the unfolding of Christianity.

Burridge's notion of the missionary agency that drives the Devotional–Affirmative dialectic draws upon his depiction of the totality of Christianity as a metaculture that inevitably appears as a particular Christian culture in response to local circumstances. The metaculture normally operates as the Devotional impulse, always driving the Christian manifestation-in-process toward more universal and less parochial embodiment, while the Affirmative impulse situates the emergent and dynamic Christian community within a particular time and space and within distinct languages and customs.[56]

Despite the similarity between Walls' and Burridge's approaches, it matters which one of their pairs one thinks actually is a better description of how Christianity evolves over time—that is, where the agency ought best be identified or expected, as well as described and analyzed. Anthropologists are not theologians, and vice versa. Many anthropologists and not a few theologians would have trouble with these respective formulations as well, finding them incomplete, misleading, or ill-considered. The similarity of these two ways of addressing the problem, however, suggest to me that in thinking about regularly witnessed social patterns such as those observable when Christianity spreads, anthropologists have things to learn from theologians, and vice versa. Missionaries can be agents in the working out of Walls' pilgrim and indigenizing principles, so that Burridge's insights into their work fill in how those principles operate in practice. In turn, the missionary

---

[53] Ibid., 23–4.
[54] Ibid., 26–42, 53–4. This theme is taken up in the influential work of Lamin Sanneh.
[55] Ibid., 54.   [56] See the discussion in Burridge, *In the Way*, 36–42.

contradictions that Burridge discerns might well be appreciated more fully by considering the compulsively localizing and universalizing factors always at work in Christianity's unfolding.

Still, one does feel the impasse between the two. Though similar, each adopts a perspective that partially omits the other. Theologians such as Walls presume foundational assumptions that anthropologists cannot, in their analytical work, accept, and anthropologists like Burridge seek to ground all analysis in the non-divine without reference to operative causes linked to divine revelation that many theologians assume. Even more challenging, the more difficult assumptions for anthropologists to accept are regularly those closest to the heart of what theologians assume to do their work: the truths of faith—for Christians, for example, the Incarnation and other core doctrines.

*   *   *

Despite the inevitable impasse, however, the back and forth can itself be illuminating, and in this process the anthropology of Christianity can help. It does so by providing critically researched ethnographic cases and comparatively derived theoretical frameworks through which to think about Christianity's manifestations in new ways that generate insight across such inevitable disciplinary gulfs. It is the kind of approach to Christianity that fosters the back and forth among disciplinary perspectives that shed light in unexpected and mutually illuminating ways. As Robbins suggests in his "Afterword" to the 2013 *TAJA* issue, the most productive interactions might take place when differences between the two fields are considered along with the similarities.

The possibilities certainly entice in this instance. For example, the notion of affordances, referred to by three of the articles in the December 2014 *Current Anthropology* special issue on the anthropology of Christianity, seems one promising way to advance the discussion of always–already simultaneous Christianity's universality and local embeddedness.[57] The term *affordance* comes from psychology and, more recently, discussions of human–computer interfaces to describe the relationship between an organism or object and the environment in which it exists, especially the relationship that makes the object or organism available for human manipulation or use. The psychologist who coined the term likens affordances to *action–possibilities* that depend on both certain conditions in a setting and also latent potentials in what exists in

---

[57] See the articles by Webb Keane ("Rotting Bodies: The Clash of Stances toward Materiality and its Ethical Avoidances," S312–S321), Naomi Haynes ("Affordances and Audiences: Finding the Difference Christianity Makes," S357–S365), as well as by Julia Cassaniti and T. M. Luhrmann ("The Cultural Kindling of Spiritual Experiences," S333–S343), all in *Current Anthropology* 55/S10 (2014). In the present volume, Brian M. Howell makes a similar point about the value of theological scholarship close to actual practices—that is, as he puts it, theology attentive to "the locally contingent and contextually specific forms of life most interesting to social anthropologists" (Howell, Chapter 2, 29–49).

the given setting.[58] Another possible redescription of the two pairs identified by Walls and Burridge, therefore, lies in thinking about Christianity's affordances—that is, a variety of potentialities in what Burridge might describe as the metaculture which get enacted in a distinct culture, or, to use Walls' terms, as the indigenizing and pilgrim principles work themselves out in historical practice. As these undergo cultural kindling—that is, the collective discursive development that makes something discernible in a given place and time, a term invoked by Julia Cassaniti and T. M. Luhrmann's article[59]—Christianity's abiding possibilities appear in contingent form.

It remains true, however, that few anthropologists of Christianity engage at length in discussing the work of theologians. This inattention seems to me unfortunate, for both disciplines. Theologians need the kinds of criticisms that anthropologists can bring and the creative redescriptions that their disciplinary conventions and methods can provide. The best theology has always been informed by the best anthropology, broadly speaking.

To answer directly the question guiding this chapter, for anthropologists, the benefits might also be great, of engaging formal theology more directly—first into an anthropological understanding of religions such as Christianity in which theology, informal and formal, is always ongoing. As the anthropology of Christianity continues to advance, perhaps this gulf is another frontier to be crossed, so that Christian actions carried out every week—the reading of the Bible in study groups, the gathering for Eucharistic and other liturgical celebrations, retreats and service trips, preaching and hymn-singing—are studied both through the participants' perspectives, seemingly an anthropological necessity, but also with closer attention to the official explanations of such practices provided by sponsors, interpreters, and apologists for them—that is, by theologians.

Whether or not anthropology as a discipline can provide hope for humanity, as Robbins seems to imagine, and can do so from engaging theology, I am not so certain, nor am I sure it should aspire to such a role, which seems to ask much of academic work. Theologians themselves—at least Christian ones—are wary of the consequences of intellectual work on religious truths, even theological study, absent practiced engagement with the implications of such truths. Perhaps it is enough that in studying believers and their communities—and their theologians—inspiration of a less exalted sort might come from understanding them better.

---

[58] In psychology, James Gibson first used the term, and others have taken it up in design, notably Donald Norman. For discussions of affordances, see the following seminal works: James J. Gibson, "The Theory of Affordances," in *Perceiving, Acting, and Knowing: Towards an Ecological Psychology*, ed. Robert Shaw and John Bransford (Hillsdale, NJ: Lawrence Erlbaum Associates, 1977), 67–82; Donald Norman, *The Design of Everyday Things* (New York: Basic Books, 1988).

[59] See note 57.

6

Theology's Contribution to Anthropological Understanding in T. M. Luhrmann's *When God Talks Back*

Timothy Jenkins

In order to see what theology might contribute to cultural anthropology and ethnography, it is worth looking at an example. In her recent book, *When God Talks Back: Understanding the American Evangelical Relationship with God*, T. M. Luhrmann puts theological writings to work in developing an anthropological description of the motivations and worldview of contemporary evangelical Christians.[1]

While this work forms part of an increasing concern among anthropologists with gaining insight into and understanding of North American Christianity,[2] and may be set in the broader context of the anthropology of Christianity worldwide,[3] Luhrmann's study stands out from this anthropological background

---

[1] This section incorporates material published in the online journal *HAU* in 2014; see <www.haujournal.org/index.php/hau/article/view/hau3.3.018>.

[2] Jon Bialecki, "Disjuncture, Continental Philosophy's New 'Political Paul,' and the Question of Progressive Christianity in a Southern California Third Wave Church," *American Ethnologist* 36/1 (2009): 35–48; James S. Bielo, *Words upon the Word: An Ethnography of Evangelical Group Bible Study* (New York: New York University Press, 2009); James S. Bielo, *Emerging Evangelicals: Faith, Modernity, and the Desire for Authenticity* (New York: New York University Press, 2011); Susan Friend Harding, *The Book of Jerry Falwell: Fundamentalist Language and Politics* (Princeton: Princeton University Press, 2000).

[3] Fenella Cannell (ed.), *The Anthropology of Christianity* (Durham, NC: Duke University Press, 2006); Matthew Engelke, *A Problem of Presence: Beyond Scripture in an African Church* (Berkeley: University of California Press, 2007); Joel Robbins, "What Is a Christian? Notes toward an Anthropology of Christianity," *Religion* 33 (2003): 191–9; Joel Robbins, "Continuity Thinking and the Problem of Christian Culture," *Current Anthropology* 48/1 (2007): 5–38; Webb Keane, *Christian Moderns: Freedom and Fetish in the Mission Encounter* (Berkeley: University of California Press, 2007); see also Chris Hann, "The Anthropology of Christianity *per se*," *Archives européennes de sociologie* 48/3 (2007): 383–410; Timothy Jenkins, "The Anthropology of Christianity: Situation and Critique," *Ethnos* 77/4 (2012): 459–76. For a detailed recent bibliography,

for two reasons: because of its detailed focus on the category of religious experience, on the one hand, and due to its identification of specific theological texts concerned with experience of God and employment of them as significant anthropological sources, on the other. To my knowledge, Luhrmann brings the two disciplines into a closer relation than has previously been attempted.

She tells the reader how she came to this research topic: The daughter of a former Christian Scientist and of a Baptist minister, with cousins who remained deeply conservative Christians, she has personal understanding of the incomprehension that separates believers from more liberal minds around the issue of the reality of God. This insight lends energy to her research and her wish to explore the issues on behalf of the ordinary reader, and may explain her serious engagement with both disciplines.

Luhrmann offers an account of the Vineyard Church's understanding of prayer, with its focus on experience and creation of the self. Her focus is on one variety of religious experience, to echo William James's title. She asks, "How does God become real for people?"[4] pointing to the problems of the invisibility of God, the skepticism of outsiders, and the lack of evidence to support belief. She portrays herself as brokering the relationship between skeptic and believer, suggesting that contemporary cognitive science misses the point: The question is not how is religious belief possible, but rather, how does God remain real for believers? Skeptics and believers share the same psychological world; the issue is how do believers maintain their belief despite their own skepticism and doubt?

In the course of this exploration of religious experience, Luhrmann introduces sources that are usually neglected by anthropologists reading theological writings on prayer practices. She not only employs the contemporary literature that is read by church members, but also explores the Christian traditions that lie behind these practices and investigates their rationale, in this fashion both expanding the resources normally available to anthropologists and making the case for the inclusion of historical theological materials in an anthropological description.

This material is found in particular in chapter 6, which is the fulcrum of the argument, making the transition between the section concerned with formation (chapters 2–5) and the one that explores religious experience (chapters 7–9). The first and last chapters (1 and 10) contribute to the historical framing of, but are not as crucial to, the argument. The recourse to Christian theology lies at the heart of Luhrmann's approach.

see Joel Robbins and Naomi Haynes (eds), *The Anthropology of Christianity: Unity, Diversity, New Directions, Current Anthropology* 55/S10 (December 2014).

[4] T. M. Luhrmann, *When God Talks Back: Understanding the American Evangelical Relationship with God* (New York: Alfred A. Knopf, 2012), xi.

That being so, my approach is clearly set out: focusing on chapter 6, I shall look first at the topic of religious experience and then at the uses made there of theological writings. Before starting out on this work largely of exposition and critique, let me sketch out my underlying argument.

It draws on the tension between psychological and anthropological approaches, a tension present in the text. The concept of religious experience is complicated because it is never simply "present," but is always constructed through anticipation and retrospective revision. Luhrmann is aware of this problem; she has a long-term interest in small groups and how in them people collectively learn to create the possibility of experiencing certain kinds of phenomena. This interest began with her work on witch covens,[5] and she expresses this process of formation as "learning to do rather than learning to think,"[6] the topic of the first part of the recent book. Nonetheless, the second half of the book concerns the detailed production of a certain kind of mental state that can be identified with directly "religious" experiences. This is a refinement of, and is in tension with, the first concern, and is carried out through an empirical study. The principal mental state is identified as absorption/self-hypnosis/sensory override, and she distinguishes its expressions from other, pathological forms. In this concern with mental states, processes of social construction tend to be lost sight of, and there is a certain flattening of the temporal structure of experience, so that it has principally a present focus.

As we shall see, this tension is negotiated through the "theological" chapter which separates the two parts. Part of my argument is that the same tension—between experience as always deferred, either to come or in the past, and "direct" experience, present and real to the experiencing self—is to be found in the various religious and theological texts appealed to. Luhrmann tends to read over this tension, and so misses some of the historical interest of the twentieth-century documents on which she draws, as well as something of what is at stake in the earlier debates she outlines.

Despite this, she offers a historical framing. Having identified her object—the development of experience-focused evangelical worship—she traces a genealogy of the form in the first chapter, linking this kind of expression to California in the 1960s and the Jesus People. And in the last chapter, she sketches in the place of this kind of religious experience within the wider history of American evangelical religion, and offers an account of it as a response to certain historical problems.

In presenting the history in these terms, Luhrmann has taken over something of the theological categories of her informants, tracing the forms of direct religious experience in twentieth-century American religious history, rather than noting continuities and changes in the social forms and practices

---

[5] T. M. Luhrmann, *Persuasions of the Witch's Craft* (Oxford: Basil Blackwell, 1989).
[6] Luhrmann, *When God Talks Back*, xxi.

of discipline, self-formation, control, and so forth in a spectrum of groups. For, in constructing a quasi-naturalistic account (about which she is quite frank), Luhrmann not only follows certain familiar social scientific protocols but also replicates the consciously articulated categories of the group she is studying. Indeed, one way of reading the final chapter is as suggesting that religious groups in the twentieth century have self-consciously created the notion of "religious experience," a category that has then been imported into a good deal of the academic study of religion, forming what might be called a Protestant sociology or psychology. Bender gives an account of this process of mutual implication.[7]

While Luhrmann could argue that she is simply investigating these indigenous categories, matching method to object, it is also possible to claim that she takes on the indigenous concerns without sufficient critical distance, reproducing these categories in her analytical approach, supported in so doing by wider tendencies in the contemporary social sciences which focus on the social productivity of individual mental activities.

In this chapter, I want to look at the role Luhrmann's account of the Christian discipline of prayer plays in her overall description of these recent forms of evangelical Christianity, with their focus on religious experience. There are two stages to the argument, or two faces. In the first place, I sound a general note of caution about the notion of "experience" as a category for investigation. This is not a simple matter, for, as Luhrmann emphasizes, recent forms of Christianity have placed a premium upon "religious" experience as a desired and valued part of the life of faith, and have claimed to be in continuity with Christian tradition in so doing.

In the second place, I want to explore the historical theological materials Luhrmann introduces in chapter 6 in particular. For the social scientific debate that I wish to raise around experience and its usefulness as an analytic category is also replicated within Christian theology: there is a debate between, on the one hand, a theology with a focus on direct experience and, on the other hand, a theology that is critical of experience as a foundational category. Luhrmann introduces elements from both sides of this theological debate but, I will suggest, she has flattened out the critique of experience that is found in her sources, in this, once again, following the practice of her informants.

What is the pay-off of this discussion? We may find two things. First, that something has been left out from the theological debates Luhrmann looks at; in essence, that the debates are over approaches—or categories—rather than descriptions. And second, something may also be missing from the ethnography; again, there are hints in some of the descriptions offered. In short, to signal the significance of Luhrmann's contribution, theology may contribute

---

[7] Courtney Bender, *The New Metaphysicals* (Chicago: University of Chicago Press, 2010).

to anthropological description (and this may be the first clear example); the theology unsurprisingly could do with more examination (which is true of any pioneering effort); and better anthropological description may follow this examination.

Why should a better anthropological description follow from refining the theological account? It is a common enough trap offered to anthropologists engaged in this kind of work to imagine that theology books contain transcriptions of the practices and beliefs of believers. In fact, educated theological reflection bears at best an oblique relation to these practices and beliefs. That oblique relation is in many instances a function of a pastoral relationship— that is, an embodied relationship that seeks to identify the limitations and even insufficiencies of certain local practices and to repair them. Luhrmann has identified a crucial source for anthropological insight in this kind of work: These works represent situated reflection on how practices are learned in specialized social settings, on the patterns of development (and attendant crises) that accompany this learning, and on the surrounding practices and institutional supports which are needed to carry a focus on experience, with its limits and lacunae. In short, theological texts are not description, but acts of repair—and in the chosen texts, the crux is a debate about the nature of experience.

My proposal is then twofold. First, in paying too much attention to the categories of direct experience, a good deal of what is going on in these churches and the lives of practitioners may be ignored or underplayed, just as the indigenous categories in prayer manuals and other sources emphasize certain practices and neglect others. And second, by excavating certain theological critiques of experience we may gain resources for a more nuanced anthropology of Christianity, one that enters even closer into a nonreductive understanding of the lives being studied. Luhrmann's book represents a case study where theological materials make a contribution to an anthropological understanding.

*   *   *

My first proposal, which is scarcely an original one, is that "experience" is a difficult concept to employ in an anthropological argument, and this is particularly the case with the notion of "religious experience" conceived as a distinct kind of exceptional sensory input. Before considering Luhrmann's approach to religious experience in chapter 6, I want to identify the broad issues concerning "experience" as a social scientific concept.

The problem is not so much that experience is unreliable as that it is constructed, and that its construction involves a complex relation to time, so that there is never a single moment when "experience" is present to the individual, constituting raw data that can then be the object of the psychologist's investigation. Rather than following Derrida's critique of these matters, a visual example may be helpful.

In Max Ophül's film 'Madame de . . .' there is a famous scene in which a man and a woman fall in love: He is in a customs shed, waiting for a woman whom he has noticed on the train; we see from his point of view the woman and her maid enter and cross the room, pass in front of him, and go through passport control; then, from her point of view, we see her look up momentarily and notice him, and we are shown over her shoulder what she sees: the man standing, gazing at her; then she turns and passes through the barrier, and the man is frustrated from speaking to her by the officials. We would appear to have here a complete psychological moment caught on camera, the igniting of mutual desire, and Ophüls boasts that "the camera exists . . . to show what can't be seen elsewhere." We might imagine a psychological study isolating and measuring such moments as a class of experience.

And yet this moment, even within the logic of the film, is a fiction; it is only because of two subsequent chance encounters (and a host of other socially determined factors) that a love affair develops and this first encounter takes on the significance it then can be given: love at first sight. Indeed, Ophül's claim in full is this: that "the camera exists to create a new art—to show what can't be seen elsewhere, either in theatre or in life." The task of the anthropologist or the historian is comparable: to appraise critically these kind of events, and the measurement of raw experience is practically irrelevant to it; we do not know, for example, how many men or women each character noticed in the course of the journey, nor even in how many cases eye contact was established without any later outcome. Monitoring the moment of individuation in the customs shed would eliminate more or less everything of importance germane to understanding the situation. And "religious experiences" as a class must bear many similarities to this kind of event, for they have a similar complex temporal construction.

In chapter 6 Luhrmann gives us more of an insight into her analytic framework. She offers us a summary of sorts of the previous four chapters of empirical material, which focused on psychological techniques involved in the formation of the praying self, and she now expands the context through engaging in a wider discussion of the Christian tradition of prayer. She does so by introducing an account of her instruction in Ignatian prayer, or builds around and up to such an account, always bearing in mind the comparisons that can be made between secular psychotherapy and religious practices; for this reason, she can also introduce some comparative material on contemplative practices in other traditions.

My argument here is twofold. The first aspect, as I have suggested in the introductory section, is that by concentrating on mental techniques and the production of individual experience, Luhrmann consistently underplays what I would call the "rhetorical" or collective nature of the practices she describes. Her work is insufficiently anthropological to produce a thorough account of the motivations and intelligibility of the lives with which she is concerned. The second is that she repeats this focus and occlusion in her account of Christian traditions of prayer and, in so doing, repeats a reduction that is present in her materials. Twentieth-century Christian practices promote ideas that concentrate on individual experience and psychological techniques, and so does she. In this way, she offers a modern, liberal Protestant sociology.

Exploiting this overlap, Luhrmann can work in a comparative way, introducing first Catholic and then non-Christian traditions into a discussion of contemporary Protestant prayer practices because she focuses on psychological techniques that bring together the mind and the world, inside of the head and outside it. She sums up the chapter in this way: "The surprising lesson from this excursion into the spiritual disciplines is that inner sense cultivation—the deliberate, repeated use of inner visual representation and other inner sensory experience, with interaction, interweaving, and sensory enhancement—has been central to the tradition of Christian prayer. It is central to evangelical prayer."[8]

At the same time, because she focuses on the work of the individual to gain this experience—although she mentions the role of monasteries and the place of instruction in prayer groups—she effectively ignores the role that collective practices play, and takes their contribution for granted. Her object remains, as it has become in earlier chapters, "the mental muscles developed in prayer work on the boundary between thought and perception, between what is attributed to the mind . . . and what exists in the world. They focus attention on the words and images on one side of the boundary, and they treat those words and images as if they belonged on the other."[9]

Now this focus and omission has its consequences in her reading of the Christian tradition of prayer, and she adopts a coherent modern position that has been identified by theologians. One might point to her belief that there is a class of person—"experts" in her terms, "saints" or "mystics" in others—who have achieved exceptional experiences, experiences that are then open to explanation in terms either of psychological mechanism or in terms of discipline and gifts of divine grace as symptomatic. This is Ann Taves' territory: identifying "experience" that can be treated either in an outsider, "materialist" fashion or in an insider, "intuitionist" fashion.[10] Once one has created a class of experts and experiences, questions of definitions and criteria emerge, together with the distinguishing of stages of spiritual expertise, and histories of attaining such stages, and also the business of distinguishing false claims from true. Although Luhrmann does not touch on this last problem, she occupies a recognizable position with regard to saints and religious experience.

---

[8] Luhrmann, *When God Talks Back*, 184.   [9] Ibid.

[10] See Ann Taves, *Fits, Trances and Visions: Experiencing Religion and Explaining Experience from Wesley to James* (Princeton: Princeton University Press, 1999).

I want to review how she presents this position in her chapter and to point out some reservations one might have from a theological point of view. This is not in order to suggest she should have read more theology, because her range of reading and sensitivity to the issues is impressive and, indeed, exceptional among anthropologists, but because the reservations point to the sort of anthropological questions I wish to raise with regard to her account concerning what might have been omitted or underplayed in the ethnographic description. We might suggest that she has made a mistake typical of interdisciplinary work, in that she has taken certain theological categories as positive achievements, to be transferred to and used in another context, rather than treating them as the provisionally achieved products of situated critical thinking.

For there is a second possible contemporary stance with regard to the disciplines of prayer and their object—one that is also held within theology, although at first sight it will sound like a secular attack on the object in question. I shall put it in skeptical terms for the moment: It may be that prayer is not concerned with exceptional and exotic mental states, gained after a long and arduous training in which ordinary experiences are set aside, a training to be compensated for by successive stages of ever more extraordinary experiences—experiences which are, by their nature, a challenge for the writer to convey to the common reader and which are for this reason marked by elevated and vague language. More positively, we might notice that this second kind of theology focuses more on issues of language and the appropriate categories to use in speaking of the conditions of the possibility of faith in the world, taking faith to be an ordinary anthropological condition and not an exceptional mental state. The second purpose of this chapter is to explore how theological debate of this kind might enrich anthropological description.

* * *

Luhrmann begins by distinguishing between two kinds of prayer practice. The one she calls negative prayer practice, or apophatic prayer; the other she terms active prayer practice, or cataphatic prayer.[11] One is a practice of denial, of rejecting human attempts to describe God, while the other is a practice of affirmation, of using human inwardness and the imagination to go beyond the human to reach God.[12] She cites a recent authority on the Christian mystical tradition, Denys Turner, on whom I shall repose a good deal of trust, too, but it is worth noting that Turner, defending the older tradition, says it is improper to distinguish between apophatic and cataphatic *spiritualities*, and that they are "more properly understood as expressive of different . . . styles available within a common, overarching discourse and practice."[13]

---

[11] I have followed Turner's spelling of *cataphatic* rather than Luhrmann's *kataphatic*.
[12] Luhrmann, *When God Talks Back*, 161.
[13] Denys Turner, *The Darkness of God: Negativity in Christian Mysticism* (Cambridge: Cambridge University Press, 1995), 257.

Luhrmann however has her own authorities, and she cites Cardinal Ratzinger in support of her move to set aside apophatic theology and concentrate instead on a cataphatic theology of action, which can be interpreted in psychological terms.[14] She indeed opposes the two as a more elitist to a more popular form of Christian prayer, and possibly as male to female, the one a warrior initiation, the other learning to get in touch with your emotions. She sets the one aside, turning instead to the other which allows her to focus on Ignatian prayer and its likeness to evangelical practices. Let us trace this procedure.

Her initial step is to identify the core activity of evangelical prayer. One can give an insider's account, she suggests, recognizing it as a series of activities and giving it a content ("Adoration, Confession, Thanksgiving, and Supplication").[15] One could also give an anthropological account, describing a series of behaviors, bodily postures, tones of voice, and verbal forms and formulas. But Luhrmann is concerned to return to the question of technique, or what she calls a technology of prayer (drawing on Foucault), for "prayer changes the way the person uses his or her mind by changing the way that person pays attention."[16] This point was established in her previous chapter.

These techniques, she claims, are taught obliquely, through the example of others in services, prayer ministry, and house groups, together with manuals and occasional classes or courses. But explicit teaching is usually confined, in these circles, to the content (ACTS); the mental techniques are learned implicitly.

Yet "the central act of prayer is paying attention to internal experience— thoughts, images, and the awareness of your body—and treating these sensations as important in themselves rather than as distractions from the real business of your life."[17] And further, these sensations are to be regarded as "in some sense public and externally real speech," for God is present and active in these sensations. There are then two moments in the technique of evangelical prayer: "The person praying has to learn to use the imagination to experience God as present, and then to treat what has been imagined as more than 'mere' imagination."[18] Attention is first shifted towards the internal, and then takes this object discovered to be external.

Luhrmann traces the technique producing this double movement through a series of evangelical manuals: learning to hear what God's voice sounds like, from reading the Bible; going to a quiet place and stilling one's thoughts and emotions; paying mindful attention to spontaneous images and thoughts and dreams; and writing out the ensuing "dialogue" between self and God, so that it becomes real. She concludes that "The central but often implicit

---

[14] Luhrmann, *When God Talks Back*, 167. [15] Ibid., 157. [16] Ibid., 158.
[17] Ibid. [18] Ibid. 159

technology of evangelical prayer is an intense focus on mental imagery and other inner sensory experience."[19]

At this point, Luhrmann displaces the focus of attention, for she has learned the articulated model of this practice elsewhere, in pursuing Ignatian forms of prayer.[20] She approaches an account of her fieldwork experience in this regard (a course of Ignatian prayer) through a recapitulation of the history of prayer and, in particular, the kind of prayer that focuses on the imagination, and this account of the tradition comes to a focus in the figure of Ignatius Loyola (born 1491).[21] I want to make two points: First, Ignatian spirituality is a particular form of religious practice, one that focuses on the imagination, experience, and recall; and second, Luhrmann's account loses sight of many of the dimensions and subtlety of this kind of practice.

Let us address the second point first. Ignatius' concern centered on discernment of the heart. It builds on Augustine's observation that the human heart is restless until it finds its rest in God. As Luhrmann notes, during a convalescence, Ignatius had two kinds of mental occupation: chivalric and romantic daydreaming, and reading a life of Jesus and lives of the saints. He enjoyed both kinds of activities, but came to remark their after-effects in himself: secular dreams of noble deeds "left him restless and unsatisfied," but religious imagination of imitating the saints "left him happy."[22] So far, so good. But she leaves out his crucial observation that his responses were a function of the movement of his soul: Had his soul been moving away from God—which it might well have been, for he was an ambitious man and a soldier—the chivalric tales might have left him satisfied and the gospels displeased or bored him. And this omission in fact conceals a second: The interpretation of mental images is held, in Ignatius's case, within a much wider intellectual framework, one that includes the doctrines of the Church, including complex social categories of the body and soul. This framework is created by collective work and has to be taught to the individual through apprenticeship. Although Ignatius appeared to learn by paying attention to his own experience, this may be a myth, and certainly normal practice is to interact with a spiritual director, an experienced person who helps the novice better to discern the movements of his or her heart, in part by passing on the wider framework of interpretation. If the novice simply followed experience without such discernment, and exercised the power over self and others such inner-directed attention can give, the practice might well lead to disaster. These sorts of problems are the other side of such mental disciplines. In short, this method is not primarily experience-focused, but instead focuses

---

[19] Ibid., 161.

[20] Ibid., 176ff. The basic text is Ignatius Loyola, *The Spiritual Exercises*, trans. George Ganss (Chicago: Loyola, 1992).

[21] Luhrmann, *When God Talks Back*, 172ff.   [22] Ibid., 172.

on experience interpreted within a complex perspectival framework of insti-
tutionalized categories and persons.

Luhrmann's use of Ignatius as a model for prayer is itself distorted, possibly
as a result of her membership of evangelical circles. For these focus on the
personal experience of God without much attention to or respect for the
human institutional forms of mediation, forms which Ignatius saw as essential, and which could be summed up as the doctrines, practices, liturgies, and
other disciplines of the Church (which would have been Ratzinger's interest).
It is not that modern evangelical forms discard these Christian categories, but
that they take them for granted, without reflection.

What are we to make of the first point—that Ignatian spirituality appears to
make certain choices with respect to prayer in this account? As we have seen,
Luhrmann identifies two named styles of spiritual discipline: apophatic and
cataphatic prayer. She suggests these may be the dominant forms of mental
spiritual discipline in any faith (and in later pages brings in inner sense
cultivation in Tibetan Buddhism and Jewish Kabbalah).[23] Apophatic prayer
is in this account a way of denial: "a cluster of techniques through which
attention is shifted away from internal and external sensation . . . Any mental
event . . . is treated as meaningless in the search for God, because God is the
unknowable. . . . The apophatic rejects the human to find the divine."[24] Cataphatic prayer takes the opposite path of positive affirmation, treating "thought
as more important than an ordinary mental event. . . . its techniques help to
intensify the imaginative act. They engage the senses, they evoke vivid memories, and they generate powerful emotions, . . . us[ing] the human capacity to
go beyond itself."[25]

We have seen how Luhrmann focuses on the experiential element in
cataphatic prayer while ignoring the framing presuppositions that allow it
to work. What is her account of the way of denial? I believe that she mistakes
the task of apophatic theology, which, rather than teaching a form of (non)
experience, is a social apprenticeship that recasts the categories used to
interpret experience, and even, in this apprenticeship, adjusts the distinction
between categories and experience; it is both a social practice and, shall we say,
philosophical: a job of repair and adjustment of tools. She however concen-
trates on experience or, in this case, the irrelevance of experience to apophatic
prayer. Its central concern, she notes, is that "God is the unknowable, the
unimaginable, the not-this."[26] Yet we might express the core of negative
theology in the following terms. On the one hand, God (as Creator) is not
"like" anything, nor is any kind of thing: He cannot, therefore, be mapped in
language, experience, thought, or by comparison of any kind. If all existing
forms are created out of nothing, creatures can know nothing of the Creator by

---

[23] Ibid., 186–7.   [24] Ibid., 161.   [25] Ibid.   [26] Ibid.

the exercise of their creaturely faculties such as reason; their only clues are provided by the faith put in them by the Creator. The initial work of faith is then to deny every comparison, every key offered to understanding God as misleading, so that human desire can be freed from wanting idols—that is, goods of human creation, firstly worldly goods and secondly religious goods—for all our imaginings must be erroneous. On the other hand, this negative work is only preparatory, for in weaning desire from inessentials, space is created within the believer for God's initiative and movement, which is always present even if unrecognized. The believer in this second kind of work is returned to the world, but this time not moved by his or her own desire but by that of God. Apophatic prayer is then a process of attention to categories and a purification of desire, decentering the self so that it participates in divine processes and desire in the world, rather than assuming itself (and the human) as the origin and center of all activity.[27]

These two stages are not consecutive in a person's history but simultaneous, and the second described may correspond with cataphatic prayer. In both kinds of prayer there is a theory of desire for God at the heart of the account, together with an assumed apparatus of Scripture and ecclesial discipline, expressed in the need for spiritual direction. There are also characteristic patterns of apprenticeship over time. Neither form of prayer depends on a universal psychology and a naturalistic account of experience as something that can be trained, but on a theological and institutional construction of a desiring person as part of God's purposes, shaped and instructed by the Church and the traditions it carries. Luhrmann, however, sums up her account of the two disciplines as follows: "Yin and yang, these two disciplines share the same goal: . . . 'to centre the attention of the body, the emotions, the mind and the spirit' upon God, and to diminish attention to the everyday."[28] The Foucauldian focus on technique is inadequate not only because it eliminates the social but also because it obscures the motivations and means at work, for which another, naturalistic account is substituted.

* * *

Luhrmann gives a brief historical account of the two disciplines—centering prayer and imaginative prayer, in her terms—beginning with the desert fathers and their withdrawal from society to pray,[29] and then invoking the fourteenth-century *The Cloud of Unknowing* as the "classic expression of the apophatic method."[30] She attributes the disappearance of contemplation as a widespread

---

[27] See Alain Cugno, *St. John of the Cross: The Life and Thought of a Christian Mystic* (1979; London: Burns and Oates, 1982).

[28] Luhrmann, *When God Talks Back*, 161.

[29] She draws on Peter Brown, *The Body and Society* (New York: Columbia University Press, 1988).

[30] Luhrmann, *When God Talks Back*, 162.

"method" to the Reformation,[31] and its rediscovery in the twentieth century to Thomas Merton, whose work lies behind the development of the concept of centering prayer in the 1970s.[32] This recent approach employs techniques of halting thoughts and focusing the mind, taught through instruction and silent retreats, techniques that produce effects that can be mapped in bodily expression and brain traces.[33] Luhrmann discards these practices as too specialized and too elitist. She compares participants who have taken these retreats with "Sioux warriors returning from a vision quest," and the techniques employed with Buddhist and Hindu practices. These latter comparisons are common currency in the milieu and can give rise to controversy, for evangelical religion tends to distrust other faiths and also to distrust the "idea that humans should reach out for God without language."[34] This is also the point at which she notes Ratzinger's critique of inwardness, to wit, that all we find by looking within is ourselves; humans cannot know God, in Ratzinger's account, and "that is why . . . we were given Christ, and that is why Christ and the words are crucial, for they enable the twofold movement through which humans can reach God and God can reach back to humans."[35]

Luhrmann therefore turns to imaginative prayer, "rich in the images and stories of Christ." The difficulty perhaps is that, in splitting the two "techniques" or "methods" of prayer and choosing the more democratic path, her account reproduces the simplifications of the neo-evangelical theology she is studying. As I have suggested, her account of the history of each approach neglects the complex intellectual and institutional framework of presuppositions and practices that the classical forms at least assume. It may well be that Merton's contribution has been to create a psychological (individualistic and decontextualized) version of apophatic prayer for the mid-twentieth century (Turner hints at this; see the next section), and it is characteristic of this approach that Luhrmann cites Saint Theresa but makes no reference to the more austere John of the Cross. And at the same time, she imports the somewhat unfocused neo-evangelical account of positive prayer, which slides easily in talking between the persons of the Trinity, so that we start with "stories of Christ" but quickly turn to "daydreams of God."[36] Once more, her focus is on the "loose accumulation of different imaginative practices [drawn from the history of the Christian cataphatic tradition], which techniques seem to be selected again and again because they work."[37] This focus allows her to

---

[31] Following the Introduction to William Johnston (ed.), *The Cloud of Unknowing* (New York: Doubleday, 1973).

[32] Thomas Merton, *Contemplative Prayer* (New York: Herder & Herder, 1969); see Basil Pennington, *Centring Prayer: Renewing an Ancient Christian Prayer Form* (New York: Doubleday, 1980).

[33] Luhrmann, *When God Talks Back*, 166.   [34] Ibid., 167.   [35] Ibid., 168.

[36] Ibid.   [37] Ibid.

make comparisons and to draw conclusions, but she misses the intellectual and moral framework, the world of meanings, which generates these effects.

We then are offered a sketched genealogy of cataphatic prayer comparable to the earlier one for apophatic prayer, beginning with Dionysus the Areopagite's use of images to reach beyond language, and then considering the development of monastic practices of memorizing images from Scripture and visualizing the life of Christ as a part of religious formation. Luhrmann notes the logical development of these methods in the creation of complex symbolic systems that were intended to act on the world through the manipulation of symbols, touching on Renaissance magic and the proto-sciences of alchemy, astrology, and Kabbalah.[38] These are early modern systems, and the Ignatian method of prayer emerged in the same period, which she describes as a "prayer practice . . . so elaborate and systematic that it lays out the structure of evangelical prayer practice like a dissection."[39]

Luhrmann has been instructed in the modern Ignatian method, and her brief history comes from the introductions to these publications (though she must have added Renaissance magic on her own account). As I have noted, the focus is light on the institutional and theological setting and strong on practices/techniques and experience. Again, she remarks that there are strong Protestant reservations about the use of the *Spiritual Exercises*, reservations that link with broader concerns about the role of images, which can "intervene between a human and his maker."[40] But she is able to write about her experience in a group of evangelical women as they are taught these exercises. She comments on the structure of the exercises, as they work with passages of Scripture through God's saving work and, in particular, through the life, death, and resurrection of Christ, and the employment of the practice of participation in the chosen biblical scenes through visualization. She also went on a Catholic-led retreat, and notes the contrast between the practice of the exercises in the two groups: the one (Catholic) focusing on the person of Jesus, the other (evangelical) on the direct experience of God and his presence in the participant's life.[41] And she gives testimony from the group members as to the vivid and emotional nature of the experiences gained through the exercises, a form of knowing God with the senses.

Luhrmann suggests that the emotions felt and the connections made are taken to be God, the "movement of God in the lives of the practitioners."[42] The language of contact with God is familiar and psychological, starting with

---

[38] Luhrmann cites Francis Yates, *The Rosicrucian Enlightenment* (London: RKP, 1972); Claire Fanger (ed.), *Conjuring Spirits* (University Park: Penn State University Press, 1998).

[39] Luhrmann, *When God Talks Back*, 172.   [40] Ibid., 174.   [41] Ibid., 177.

[42] A contemporary introduction to the exercises suggests, however, that the practitioner, while noting feelings and emotions, should set them aside because of the perspectival approach being adopted. Feelings indicate different spiritual conditions according to the direction in which the soul is traveling, towards or away from God. See Gerard Hughes, *God of Surprises* (London: DLT, 1985).

notions of dark and light, and mood descriptions, and moving to identifying these emotional states with God's actions and leading. She qualifies this account of "language of emotion-as-God"[43] by saying that, for the practitioners, "God was the cause of emotion, not the substance," but then she pursues the question of why the experience is so emotion-focused by examining in further detail the structure of the exercises and how the "way they direct the imagination generates intense feeling."

She identifies "three explicit features" of the prayer practices of the *Exercises*, which she labels "interaction, interweaving, and sensory enhancement."[44] Concerning the first, the practitioner interacts with what he or she imagines, the object of imagination being, in this instance, a function of talking to God. Luhrmann notes that Ignatius speaks of "consolation" and "desolation," which she takes to mean the practitioner's feeling good or feeling bad, but she links one to the experience of God and the other to distance from God.[45] This account misses the perspectival element whereby an approach to God (or God's nearness) may be experienced as desolation or abandonment. She maintains a static account of interaction, as if God were an object or a place.

Concerning the second feature, she talks of the process of interweaving specific prayers and passages from Scripture with private, personal reflection, as the practitioner tacks back and forth between the text and experience, first comparing current experience to the passage and then the text to one's life, reinterpreting secular experience. This process, Luhrmann claims, "blurs the boundary between what is external and what is within,"[46] and goes beyond the normal processes of using language to think with by "using past personal memories to create the details of the scriptural story." In this fashion, the practitioner participates in the story being read both as modern self and as one of the biblical actors.[47]

Concerning the third feature, "sensory enhancement," she writes that the "exercises use sensory detail to intensify that [participatory] process and make the abstract personal and near."[48] This practice is called "application of the senses" and Luhrmann draws on the example of visualizing the torments of hell. She suggests that this kind of practice in fantasy has its counterpart in real

---

[43] Luhrmann, *When God Talks Back*, 180.   [44] Ibid.   [45] Ibid., 180–1.
[46] Ibid., 181.
[47] In a note, she suggests that "linguistic anthropologists argue that this layering strategy guarantees the authenticity of the person praying, for God is heard to speak through that individual as recognizably both God and individual" (ibid., 347, note 45), citing Robin Shoaps, "Pray Earnestly," *Journal of Linguistic Anthropology* 12/1 (2002): 34–71, and Michael Silverstein and Greg Urban (eds), *Natural Histories of Discourse* (Chicago: Chicago University Press, 1996). Yet surely authenticity—as with also authority—is a function of collective representations not of psychology?
[48] Luhrmann, *When God Talks Back*, 182.

life in the reliving of past events, re-enacting and remembering our reactions, pleasures, pains, and so forth. Ignatius employs sensory memory to make Scripture real enough to respond to.

Luhrmann has run through her explanatory account at this point: These detailed devices of Ignatian prayer allow the mixing of thought and perception, the mind and the world. Her informants, she suggests, identify belief with experiences, sometimes spoken of as a sense of presence made vivid.

*   *   *

There is no doubt that Luhrmann has reproduced an account that is faithful to the accounts her informants have given her, particularly the writers. But in so doing, she has eliminated a good deal of the work the categories of contemplative prayer are capable of. Would paying attention to this capacity change the anthropological description? That is, is there more going on than is captured either in the native written accounts or in the anthropologist's description?

If we look to Turner, he makes the double suggestion, first, that mystical theology was originally concerned with neither experience nor the self and, second, that "mysticism" with an emphasis both on experience and the self is a recent invention, probably dating from the nineteenth century (though he does not try very hard to establish that history). Turner puts his thesis in this fashion: "whereas our employment of the metaphors of 'inwardness' and 'ascent' appears to be tied in with the achievement and the cultivation of a certain kind of experience—such as those recommended in the practice of what is called, nowadays, 'centring' or 'contemplative' prayer—the medieval employment of them was tied in with a 'critique' of such religious experiences and practices."[49] As the reference to "centering prayer" indicates, Luhrmann falls fully into this recent camp, which is fair enough; we might say that the categories and practices of mysticism have been turned on their heads, and Luhrmann's work—along with that of her informants and teachers, both Catholic and Protestant—reproduces this inversion.

Turner is concerned to draw our attention back to the original Neoplatonic epistemological context of apophaticism, which he represents as a dialectical critique of the common stock of imagery of light and dark, ascent of the soul, and so forth, both language and critique deriving from Platonism. This language, he suggests, is used "self-subvertingly" so that, in the commonest images, the divine light is so bright that it causes "darkness and unknowing to the soul."[50] For this reason, he continues, we have to distinguish between the contradictory language or images that are used at the cataphatic or first-order level, and the apophatic negation of those descriptions at the second-order

---

[49] Denys Turner, *The Darkness of God*, 4. Turner is cited by Luhrmann, *When God Talks Back*, 345, note 10.
[50] Turner, *The Darkness of God*, 252.

level. For negative imagery is used in two ways, both to try to describe the soul's ascent to God, with the denials and transformations implicit in that path, and also to bring out the impossibility of language and its distinctions being able to give such a description. Giving up such pairs of terms as interiority and exteriority, progression and slipping back, and even the distinction between the soul and the Creator, is part of the formation being alluded to. Hence Turner's remark cited earlier that you cannot separate out two kinds of spirituality: "They are more properly understood as . . . styles within a common, overarching discourse and practice."[51]

Moreover, this practice emphasizes the sacraments, liturgical worship, and the Church's teachings and authority: contemplation cannot be seen as a more advanced set of techniques and experiences than meditation provides, set aside for an elite of saints, but rather could be read, for example, liturgically, in terms of a move from public worship to the mysteries of the mass, a transformation that is shared by every believer.[52] The apophatic and the cataphatic speak of the same thing under two aspects: the action of grace. If you separate them out, as Luhrmann does, you denature them and lose sight of what they are trying to grasp and what permits the description they sketch; in short, they cease to do the work for which they were designed, and perform other tasks.

I suspect that, in practice, Turner too oversimplifies matters. He idealizes the medieval Christianity he is reading and, if we follow his description of the "ascent" in his authors, we end up with something like the created soul being immediately present to the Creator.[53] Although the focus on the impossibility of language ever grasping this moment or speaking of it—or indeed the co-presence ever quite being achieved in this life—saves the mystery, the absolute opposition of medieval Christendom to modernity still seems to share a potentially Protestant core of a notion of unmediated presence. So the supposed perversion of "mystical theology" into "mysticism" is not quite the break that Turner wishes to portray it as and, in particular, in Ignatius and in John of the Cross we are dealing in hinge figures who attempt to articulate precisely the kind of distinction with which we are concerned. Nevertheless, precautions of the kind outlined in the previous paragraph tend to be absent from the nineteenth-century (and later) phase of the interest in mysticism and the rediscovery of the earlier tradition.

The second part of Turner's argument is then that this dialectical or self-subverting approach is deformed in the recent period into what he calls "experientialism," with which we return to the starting point in this chapter. This "deformed" approach takes the second-order critique of the categories of experience and its possibility to be instead a form of first-order experience, to be describing a special kind of experience, called "mystical experience." This

---

[51] Ibid., 257.   [52] Ibid., 258.   [53] Ibid., 256.

kind of deformation was an issue in the end of the medieval/beginning of the early modern period; it is a particular topic for John of the Cross. One might say that it takes a moment of worship—one in which the worshipper recognizes reserve, denial, unknowing—and treats it "as if it were a rival practice which displaces that Christian ordinariness."[54] "Experientialism," Turner writes, is the "displacement of a sense of the negativity of all religious experience with the pursuit of some goal of achieving *negative experiences.*" It is, in short, the "positivism" of Christian spirituality: It cashes out what were reservations about the adequacy of categories of thought dealing with ordinary life in a currency of experienced inwardness and the techniques that can achieve this. This, we noted previously, is standing apophaticism on its head, in the sense of privileging instead of distrusting sensory experience: It offers what we might call a religion for Lockean sensationalists. This is a hint that could be taken up in considering chapter 10 of Lurhmann's book and its placing of Vineyard spirituality in the wider continuities of American religion.[55]

Turner sums up this shift in terms with which we are familiar. In the first place, we come to identify "mystics" as a special class of persons who have had "mystical experiences," experiences which permit the formation of a canon of "mystical writings" (with named authors), and definitions and criteria which allow mystical experiences to be distinguished from ordinary ones. This corresponds to Luhrmann's class of experts. Turner notes that such a concept may be a twentieth-century idea.[56] In the second place, this mysticism focuses on experience to the exclusion of other types of thought or mental activity. Turner points to the influence, in this respect, of Cuthbert Butler's work, which seeks to identify specific passages in Augustine as reporting "mystical experiences" as distinct from "speculation." By doing so, Butler conjures away any notion of the insufficiency both of experience as a basis for understanding human activity and of language as a tool for knowing God.[57]

* * *

Theological critique is not usually written for the pleasure of philosophers, but in order to rectify specific forms of practical life. Can we take Turner's critique

---

[54] Ibid., 259.

[55] It could also create a frame for evaluating the work of an exciting group of historians of American religious life with whose work Luhrmann's may be associated. See Ann Taves, *Fits, Trances and Visions: Religious Experience Reconsidered. A Building-Block Approach to the Study of Religion and Other Special Things* (Princeton: Princeton University Press, 2009); Ann Taves, *Religious experience reconsidered. A Building-Block Approach to the Study of Religion and Other Special Things* (Princeton: Princeton University Press, 2009); Leigh Schmidt, *Hearing Things: Religion, Illusion, and the American Enlightenment* (Cambridge, MA: Harvard University Press, 2000); Robert Orsi, *The Madonna of 115th Street: Faith and Community in Italian Harlem, 1880–1950* (New Haven, CT: Yale University Press, 2010).

[56] Turner draws on Bernard McGinn, *The Presence of God: A History of Western Christian Mysticism*, vol. 1 (New York: Crossroad, 1992).

[57] Cuthbert Butler, *Western Christian Mysticism* (New York: Dutton, 1923).

of "experientialism" and ask what are its implications for Luhrmann's work? Turner's argument in brief is that the work of prayer cannot be focused on direct experience, because experience of any kind has to be interpreted by the believer within a narrative framework that is controlled by the "direction of travel" of the person in question, and the direction of travel is determined by his or her relation to God and divine initiative. This narrative framing only makes sense within a shared set of categories, concepts, disciplines, and institutions. And a focus on raw experience—however it is produced— conjures away all this work of interpretation, flattens the social apparatus, and makes divine initiative a matter of what you can bring yourself to believe.

This conjuring away corresponds to the features I detect in Luhrmann's approach, and about which I therefore have reservations. By focusing on experience and the techniques and training required to gain a special kind of experience, Luhrmann ignores the more sociological aspects of the phenomena with which she is concerned. If we suggest that "mind" is largely to be found "outside the head," in the collective classes and categories shared by groups, and that language is, for the most part, used not descriptively but rhetorically, in attempts to persuade others and to achieve ends, we might offer a different description to the kind she presents us with. Her work does not ignore social products and collective activities, far from it, but in relying on the prayer manuals and the discourses that the churches produce, she replicates a form of thought that neglects many of the dimensions of the practices being transmitted, through a focus on the interior mind and the notion of individual experience. So the question becomes: What does this kind of approach leave out or obscure by the focus on the individual and the cultivation of experience?

I would identify three topics. First, it occludes a good deal of how the practices are learned. In chapters 2–5, Luhrmann both tends to downplay the social forms of apprenticeship the person learning to pray undergoes, the public prayer after services, the prayer-training groups, and so forth, and also leaves out of consideration what other forms of apprenticeship are going on in the church, among, for example, those who are not so "gifted" with experience, which might explain why they remain part of the church.

Second, it does not explore the typical patterns both of development and crisis that emerge as the "prayer expert" exploits the resources of this kind of approach and discovers the limits of experience as a religious category. Luhrmann looks only at the potential overlap with mental illness, yet there must be characteristic long-term trajectories to be identified, which lead through an engagement with experience to other forms of religious life.

And third, it neglects the resources that must be present, particularly in the leadership of the church, not least those needed to cope with the recurrent problems presented by an over-reliance or exclusive focus on religious experience. There will be forms of guidance and care that return the prayer expert to the concerns of everyday life and integrate his or her trajectory into wider patterns of activity.

In short, a fascination with experience as an unproblematic presence of sensory input is both a current concern within the church and is an insufficient basis to understand what is going on in the life of the church, conceived as a social practice.

Moreover, in its neglect, this form of thought matches the emphasis and focus of contemporary scientific approaches to human and, in particular, religious behavior, so there is a matching blindness in both the social scientific categories and those of the object under study. Evangelicals, we may suggest, do not readily have access to categories that allow them to articulate and explain all that they do, and this limitation is reproduced and reinforced by a psychological vocabulary. In sum, Luhrmann offers what I earlier called a liberal Protestant sociology.

For this kind of reason, Luhrmann cannot offer an account (any more than some modern theology can) of why reading the Scriptures, or praying, or acting charitably, or living a life of restraint and service, can have effects in the world. She can only offer an account which says that people convince themselves that they do. Yet the sources she has identified demand that we pay more attention to the possibilities transmitted in collective representations, and the nature of obligation, and the power (and scale) of the common mind, and claim that by doing so one could give a different account of the realities of human lives and the strange things they get up to.

We might note that the aspect of faith communities that is most difficult to grasp in an anthropological account is the power of initiative granted by these groups to non-human agencies. This aspect is brought out most vividly by the anthropology of Christian groups, because the social sciences have a long history of excluding—or transforming—their particular forms of non-human agencies, but the problem is present in any account of a group not sharing our own collective categories. Yet the unique feature of Christian groups may reside in the degree to which some members of these groups have reflected (for pastoral reasons) on this precise problem of how to grasp effects that cannot be readily controlled by human categories: there is a strong Christian tradition of engagement with the recognition of non-human agency, given that agency is not graspable in human terms, and nevertheless is attributed initiative in human affairs. The problematic relationship between belief, language, and experience identified by Needham is not a novelty to theologians.[58]

In particular, then, I would look for evidence of what I have called the "direction of travel" in the practice of the informants, indicating that they on

[58] Rodney Needham, *Belief, Language, and Experience* (Oxford: Basil Blackwell, 1972).

occasion situate their intentions with respect to God's initiatives, and also look for indications of an awareness of the inadequacy of language and precaution concerning the reliability of experience because of this theological insight. It is this dimension that is missing from many anthropological descriptions of Christian practices. This is the area to which Luhrmann points by identifying theological concepts as anthropological resources; the work she has initiated is incomplete, but it constitutes a major contribution to the field.

7

Narratives of Significance

Reflections on the Engagement of Anthropology and Christian Theology

Alister E. McGrath

Some see interdisciplinary boundaries as protecting disciplinary integrity; others as preventing dialogue and intellectual enrichment. A middle way between these concerns is clearly necessary. In a series of writings, Edward O. Wilson argues for the need for *consilience*—the ability to weave together multiple threads of knowledge in a synthesis that is able to disclose a more satisfying and empowering view of reality.[1] As a result, one wonders if an informed and intellectually hospitable conversation between anthropology and theology might lead not merely to a better working relationship between these disciplines but also to the development of new research programs and insights within them.

There is a growing realization that the serious academic engagement between the natural sciences and the humanities must amount to more than simply a pragmatic conversation, given the prominent place that both science and religion occupy in contemporary culture. The debate over the two cultures continues[2] within culture at large and is, indeed, an intramural discussion within the broad academic community interested in questions of anthropology. Anything that can be done to increase mutual understanding and the potential of significant conversations is clearly to be welcomed. At the same time, clearly those involved need to develop a more rigorous intellectual framework within which such discussions and correlations can take place. I do not mean a safe place in which disagreement and divergence is excluded

---

[1] Edward O. Wilson, *Consilience: The Unity of Knowledge* (New York: Vintage, 1999).
[2] C. P. Snow, *The Two Cultures* (Cambridge: Cambridge University Press, 1959).

or discouraged, reducing complexities to binaries,[3] but a collegial environment that allows radical disagreement as potentially illuminating and constructive, declining to evade such challenges precisely because it safeguards intellectual integrity.

I, and many others within the discipline of Christian theology, would certainly welcome such a conversation, believing that it has the potential to be both intellectually interesting and generative. Christian theology and the natural sciences may offer each other insights and approaches that might lead to an expansion of their vision of reality. The idea is fascinating and important, fraught with difficulty yet rich in imaginative and cognitive possibilities.[4] In this chapter, I propose to reflect on some ways in which theology and anthropology can engage in a principled, informed, and respectful dialogue, in which neither discipline is required to surrender its integrity or distinctiveness, while at the same time recognizing its limits and being open to the possibility of being enriched by disciplines that transcend those boundaries.

The anthropological community is also showing unmistakable signs of a growing interest in pursuing these conversations and in exploring the potential interfaces of the discipline—for example, in dialogue with philosophy.[5] This curiosity is now being extended to theology. For example, Philip Fountain, an anthropologist at Victoria University of Wellington, has recently called for the development of what he terms a "post-secular anthropology," which might emerge from a fruitful intellectual exchange between theology and anthropology.[6] The motivations for developing such conversations are complex, leading to some awkwardness and hesitations.[7] Some see these as motivated by a pragmatic recognition of the importance of interdisciplinary conversations, particularly those between the humanities and natural sciences.

My own interest in exploring the interface between theology and cultural anthropology emerged around the year 2010, as I began to appreciate the importance of narratives in shaping communal identities. In this chapter, I propose to explore the use of narratives in theology and anthropology in more detail, while setting this discussion against an informing context of the relationship of the natural sciences and Christian theology as a whole.

---

[3] Tom Greggs, *Theology against Religion: Constructive Dialogues with Bonhoeffer and Barth* (London: T&T Clark, 2011), 151–4.

[4] Alister E. McGrath, *The Big Picture: Why We Can't Stop Talking about Science, Faith and God* (New York: St Martin's Press, 2015).

[5] Veena Das, Michael D. Jackson, Arthur Kleinman, Bhrigupati Sing (eds), *The Ground Between: Anthropologists Engage Philosophy* (Durham, NC: Duke University Press, 2014); Sune Liisberg, Esther Oluffa Pedersen, and Anne Line Dalsgård (eds), *Anthropology and Philosophy: Dialogues on Trust and Hope* (Oxford: Berghahn, 2015).

[6] Philip Fountain, "Toward a Post-Secular Anthropology," *Australian Journal of Anthropology* 24/3 (2013): 310–28.

[7] Joel Robbins, "Anthropology and Theology: An Awkward Relationship?" *Anthropological Quarterly* 79/2 (2006): 285–94.

I concede from the outset that there are some difficulties with any assumption that anthropology can generally be treated as a natural science, not least on account of its historical and interpretative elements;[8] nevertheless, for the purposes of this work, we shall focus on the genuinely empirical aspects of certain approaches to anthropology and leave open the debate within the discipline itself over its relationship to the humanities, especially history, social science, and natural sciences.

The simple fact is that cultural and social anthropology, in particular, cannot avoid raising religious or theological issues even if many working within those disciplines feel reluctant or unable to engage these directly on the basis of their own working assumptions. Equally, theological debates regularly reflect and occasionally rest upon essentially anthropological issues. A good example is the theological dispute over the doctrine of grace between Augustine of Hippo and Julian of Eclanum, which is more fundamentally a debate about culturally regnant conceptions of human nature in late classical antiquity.[9] Theology here seems to be a placeholder for what is really a proxy conflict about what we today would consider to be anthropological issues.

While the discipline of the anthropology of religion is not without import-ance and intrinsic interest, my particular concern lies in developing a theo-logically informed anthropology, seeking to find if Christian theology provides a motivating and informing framework for anthropology and if anthropology contributes insights that illuminate and inform the work of theologians. However, it is unrealistic to speak of a theologically engaged anthropology or an anthropologically informed theology without recognizing and at least be-ginning to address the significant anxieties that such notions engender within both professional communities of discourse. We must, therefore, identify some of these core concerns and see what can be done to alleviate them.

* * *

Most academic communities are resistant to intrusions on their disciplinary space, raising important questions about what can be done to foster a properly informed interdisciplinarity that recognizes convergence while respecting difference.[10] A core concern within both the theological and anthropological academic communities is that a dialogue or engagement might directly or indirectly lead to a surrender of the methodological or intellectual autonomy

---

[8] David I. Kertzer, "Social Anthropology and Social Science History," *Social Science History* 33/1 (2009): 1–16.

[9] Andreas Urs Sommer, "Das Ende der antiken Anthropologie als Bewährungsfall kontex-tualistischer Philosophiegeschichtsschreibung: Julian von Eclanum und Augustin von Hippo," *Zeitschrift für Religions- und Geistesgeschichte* 57 (2005): 1–28.

[10] Katri Huutoniemi, Julie T. Klein, Hanne Bruun, and Jane Hukkinen, "Analyzing Inter-disciplinarity: Typology and Indicators," *Research Policy* 39/1 (2010): 79–88; Nancy Tuana, "Embedding Philosophers in the Practice of Science: Bringing Humanities to the Sciences," *Synthese* 190/11 (2013): 1955–73.

of an established discipline, so that intellectual sovereignty is reduced to what is, at best, a disciplinary suzerainty. The anthropologist will naturally, and rightly, want to raise concerns about the intrusion of nonempirical methods and outcomes into an essentially scientific discipline, committed to evidence-based reasoning and resistance to any form of ideological manipulation. Although fears of religious institutions interfering with scientific research have receded, the specter of past intrusions still lingers in contemporary reflections. Many will have some sympathy for Stephen Jay Gould's notion of "non-overlapping magisteria (NOMA)," which unfortunately secures intellectual independence for both the sciences and theology by insisting that they cannot have meaningful, and especially not challenging, conversations.[11]

Any such dialogue between theology and anthropology must take account of debates within the discipline of anthropology itself over its nature and scope and whether it is indeed an *empirical* discipline. Anthropology designates a diversity of methods, assumptions, and outcomes. Many questions remain open: (1) Does anthropology study material cultures using an implicit behaviorist paradigm from outside? (2) Does it describe symbolic cultures from within? or (3) What is the role of theory in observation? The recent critical assault on the presuppositions, methods, and conclusions of Margaret Mead's ethnographical bestseller *Coming of Age in Samoa*, which defined for many what anthropology was all about, does not discredit the discipline but does raise important questions about the status of external observers and their agendas.[12]

As a non-anthropologist, I must simply note such debates and plead that we avoid over-stipulative accounts of an imagined or idealized anthropology and instead focus on what anthropology seems to me to do very well—identify patterns of human behavior through empirical methods, which it seeks to group and, secondarily, to explain or predict.[13] It cannot, and does not seek to, verify or falsify any religious or metaphysical views that might be held to lie behind such patterns of behavior or use of symbols. It can, however, elicit the implicit or explicit assumptions within societies about their ultimate grounding. Individual anthropologists may have their own views about, for example, the nature of religion or the concept of the *transcendent*. They still, however, try to identify the assumptions that seem to undergird behavioral patterns within societies, whether they agree with them or not.

The theological community also has its anxieties wherein it might feel threatened by the alternative understandings of the nature of evidence and

---

[11] Stephen Jay Gould, "Nonoverlapping Magisteria," *Natural History* 106 (1997): 16–22.

[12] Derek Freeman, *The Fateful Hoaxing of Margaret Mead: A Historical Analysis of her Samoan Research* (Boulder, CO: Westview Press, 1999); *Margaret Mead and Samoa: The Making and Unmaking of an Anthropological Myth* (Cambridge, MA: Harvard University Press, 1983).

[13] Lawrence A. Kuznar, *Reclaiming a Scientific Anthropology*, 2nd edn (Lanham, MD: AltaMira Press, 2008).

authority, which are regnant within any empirical discipline, and the unspoken anxiety of some form of explanatory reductionism that, in effect, demonstrates that religion, in general, or theology, in particular, are epiphenomenal. To use Karl Marx's outdated but still helpful way of putting things, theology might turn out to be an *Überbau* that emerges in a scientifically explicable manner from a social or cultural basis. The fear of territorial encroachment remains potent in many sectors of the theological community, which has witnessed a radical contraction of the area in which theology can lay claim to intellectual authority since the dawn of the Scientific Revolution.[14] This, of course, is not a problem unique to theology. Many philosophers resent the seemingly irreversible intellectual encroachment of the empirical sciences into what was once seen as philosophical territory.[15] Many theologians, such as Stanley Hauerwas and John Milbank, are clearly concerned that such theological issues as ecclesiology could be dominated by, if not reduced to, an essentially anthropological analysis.[16]

Historically, this theological concern has been particularly associated with the Swiss Protestant theologian Karl Barth (1886–1968), most notably his concern that theology would be reduced to an understanding of human nature, which is determined on the basis of empirical means, thus denying or sidelining a specifically theological foundation for an understanding of human nature. Barth's anxieties, reflecting potential vulnerabilities in his theology, appear to have rendered him inattentive to the need to develop a distinctively Christian and theologically grounded understanding of human nature to counter rival understandings that were achieving cultural dominance in the 1930s—above all, those grounded on Marxist presuppositions. Friedrich Gogarten, a close colleague of Barth within the dialectical theology movement, argued for the necessity of such an approach,[17] encouraging Emil Brunner to produce what is arguably one of the finest such statements of a Christian anthropology.[18]

Despite his limited knowledge of the natural sciences, Barth correctly realized that the fundamental modernist assumption that a single research method could be deployed to investigate every aspect of reality was unsustainable. Theology, like every intellectual discipline, had its own norms and

---

[14] Peter Harrison, *The Territories of Science and Religion* (Chicago: University of Chicago Press, 2015).

[15] Neil Tennant, *Introducing Philosophy: God, Mind, World, and Logic* (New York: Routledge, Taylor & Francis, 2014), 20–1.

[16] Gale Heide, *System and Story: Narrative Critique and Construction in Theology* (Eugene, OR: Pickwick Publications, 2009).

[17] Friedrich Gogarten, "Das Problem einer theologischen Anthropologie," *Zwischen den Zeiten* 7 (1929): 493–511; Stefan Holtmann, *Karl Barth als Theologe der Neuzeit: Studien zur kritischen Deutung seiner Theologie* (Göttingen: Vandenhoeck & Ruprecht, 2007).

[18] Emil Brunner, *Der Mensch im Widerspruch: Die christliche Lehre vom Wahren und vom wirklichen Menschen* (Berlin: Furche-Verlag, 1937).

conventions shaped by the nature of the object under investigation.[19] There was no *mathesis universalis*; rather, science designated a multiplicity of approaches adapted to what was being approached. In marked contrast, Wolfhart Pannenberg's clear preference for Heinrich Scholz's modernist approach to criteria of theological verification sits very uneasily with contemporary understandings of the scientific method, raising troubling questions about whether Pannenberg has really understood the essence of empirical science.[20]

Happily, some theologians clearly have grasped some scientific fundamentals. One of the best examples remains Thomas F. Torrance, whose *Theological Science* continues to model the intellectual virtues of a scientifically informed exposition of the methods of Christian theology. Torrance rightly held that all intellectual disciplines or sciences are under an intrinsic obligation to give an account of reality "according to its distinct nature."[21] For Torrance, this means that both scientists and theologians are under an obligation to "think only in accordance with the nature of the given."[22] The distinctive characteristic of a *science*, whether theology or anthropology, is thus to give an accurate and objective account of things in a manner that is appropriate to the reality being investigated.

A further difficulty for theology is the challenge of integrative complexity—the need to position two very different disciplines with quite distinct methods, histories, and scholarly conventions in such a manner that a meaningful conversation is possible. Sadly, I can only report that most theologians seem unwilling and possibly unable to rise to this challenge. Their reflections are likely to be skewed by an inadequate understanding of the methods of the empirical sciences and the functioning of a scientific culture, which very often leads to a significant misreading of key scientific ideas and methods within a theological context. Pannenberg's problematic reading of the notion of a *field* is a case in point, apparently suggesting a worrying ignorance of quantum field theories. Although this fearful and suspicious misconstrual is perhaps most strikingly obvious in the case of the application of psychology to theological issues,[23] there is little doubt that this is a general difficulty in the broad field of science and religion. Sadly, this misreading of such ideas can only diminish the esteem in which this field is held within the scientific community. My own

---

[19] Alister E. McGrath, "Theologie als Mathesis Universalis? Heinrich Scholz, Karl Barth, und der wissenschaftliche Status der christlichen Theologie," *Theologische Zeitschrift* 62 (2007): 44–57.

[20] Nancey Murphy, *Theology in the Age of Scientific Reasoning* (Ithaca, NY: Cornell University Press, 1990), 19–50, 174–211; Daniel R. Alvarez, "A Critique of Wolfhart Pannenberg's Scientific Theology," *Theology and Science* 11/3 (2013): 224–50.

[21] Thomas F. Torrance, *Theological Science* (London: Oxford University Press, 1969), 10.

[22] Ibid., 9.

[23] Joanna Collicutt, "Bringing the Academic Discipline of Psychology to Bear on the Study of the Bible," *Journal of Theological Studies* 63/1 (2012): 1–48.

view, which is not popular in the theological community, is that research experience in both an empirical science and some field of Christian theology is essential for any credible attempt to undertake such a comparison.

In this chapter I propose to consider how such a significant and respectful conversation can lead to some potentially important and fruitful outcomes for both theology and anthropology, while at the same time recognizing such concerns and sensitivities. I shall be focusing on the category of narrative, which plays a distinct and significant role in both anthropology and Christian theology, and seems to me to open up some significant possibilities of mutual intellectual enrichment and the appropriate challenging of disciplinary boundaries.

The first stage in any such engagement is to offer some theoretical frameworks that allow us to position such an interaction, including the tensions and divergences that necessarily arise in such a conversation.[24] In what follows, I shall sketch two such frameworks, each of which gives a provisional and partial mental picture, revealing how anthropology and theology might, while looking at the same reality, offer distinct and potentially enriching insights. I offer these as heuristic frameworks, clearly capable of elaboration and expansion, which enable an engagement between theology and anthropology, which is not dependent on resolving issues of priority and privilege and thus facilitates open dialogue and discussion.

*   *   *

The first approach to be considered sees theology and anthropology as approaching their subjects from different angles, thus offering partial, and potentially complementary, accounts of a greater reality. As the philosopher Mary Midgley points out, we need "many maps, many windows" if we are to represent the complexity of reality, reflecting the fact that "there are many independent forms and sources of knowledge."[25] She suggests thinking of the world as a "huge aquarium," which has to be seen from different angles, yielding a cumulative account of a greater whole, which is only seen in part by any single research method or angle of approach: "We cannot see it as a whole from above, so we peer in at it through a number of small windows...We can eventually make quite a lot of sense of this habitat if we patiently put together the data from different angles. But if we insist that our own window is the only one worth looking through, we shall not get very far."[26] Midgley's basic principle of using multiple maps to represent a complex reality raises some challenges and some significant questions, such as the need to develop and deploy an appropriate interpretative framework to settle boundary disputes.

---

[24] Eloise Meneses, Lindy Backues, David Bronkema, Eric Flett, and Benjamin L. Hartley, "Engaging the Religiously Committed Other: Anthropologists and Theologians in Dialogue," *Current Anthropology* 55/1 (2014): 82–104.
[25] Mary Midgley, *The Myths We Live By* (London: Routledge, 2004), 26.   [26] Ibid., 27.

Another version of this framework is found in the writings of the theoretical chemist Charles A. Coulson, one of the most significant advocates of an integrated and mutually respectful engagement between science and faith in the 1950s.[27] Coulson was not prepared to countenance the notion of "some sort of hedge in the country of the mind" that separated these two domains.[28] He was highly critical of any view that held the possibility of allocating different intellectual domains to science and religion. It was, he declared, bad for science and bad for religion, and it was especially bad for any coherent human attempt to make sense of the universe that tried to weave these components together into an integrated whole.

Coulson, a keen mountaineer, used the Scottish mountain Ben Nevis as his visual aid in setting out his distinctive notion of "multiple perspectives" on reality. Seen from the south, Ben Nevis presents itself as a "huge grassy slope"; from the north, it is seen as "rugged rock buttresses."[29] Those who know the mountain well are familiar with these different perspectives. It is the same mountain, yet a full description requires these different perspectives to be brought together and integrated into a single coherent picture: "Different viewpoints yield different descriptions."[30] The scientist might thus stand at the north side of the mountain, the poet at the south, and so on. Each reports on what they find, using their own distinct language and imagery, adapted to what they see: "Each looks at the mountain; each sees certain things and each tries to describe his encounter with the mountain in terms that make sense. Each devises a language that is suitable for his particular purpose."[31] Where one observer might see grassy slopes, another might see a rocky mountain, yet both are representative and legitimate viewpoints. For Coulson, this makes the need for an overall, cumulative, and integrated picture of reality essential: "Different views of the same reality will appear different, yet both be valid."[32]

Coulson refuses to allow for demarcated *scientific* and *religious* worlds, which are each experienced in different manners. We experience one and the same world, and that experience is complex, requiring and mandating both scientific and religious approaches: "The two worlds are one, though seen and described in appropriate terms; and it is only the man who cannot, or will not, look at it from more than one viewpoint who claims an exclusive authority for his own description."[33]

This approach clearly raises some important questions. For example, are certain perspectives privileged, or are all to be regarded as equally valid and significant? Coulson does not resolve this question, probably because he did

---

[27] C. A Coulson, *Christianity in an Age of Science* (London: Oxford University Press, 1953); *Science and Christian Belief* (London: Oxford University Press, 1955).
[28] Coulson, *Science and Christian Belief*, 19.
[29] Coulson, *Christianity in an Age of Science*, 19.   [30] Ibid., 20.   [31] Ibid.
[32] Ibid., 21.   [33] Ibid.

not think it needed to be resolved. Nevertheless, the imaginative framework of multiple maps allows us to see theology and anthropology as illuminating different aspects of a complex reality. They fill in different aspects of a big picture. Without such collaboration or dialogue, only a partial glimpse of this big picture might be possible.

∗ ∗ ∗

A second approach recognizes the stratification of reality. In other words, we need to speak about different levels of reality and develop research methods that are appropriate to each of these levels. This understanding of scientific engagement is integral to the "critical realism" developed by the social philosopher Roy Bhaskar, who argued that the world must be regarded as differentiated and stratified. Each individual science deals with a different stratum of this reality, which, in turn, obliges it to develop and use methods of investigation adapted and appropriate to this stratum. These methods must be established a posteriori through an engagement with each of these strata of reality. Bhaskar's account of the relation of the natural and social sciences affirms their methodological commonalities while respecting their distinctions, particularly when these arise on account of their objects of investigation: "Naturalism holds that it is possible to give an account of science under which the proper and more or less specific methods of both the natural and social sciences can fall. But it does not deny that there are significant differences in these methods, grounded in real differences in their subject-matters and in the relationships in which these sciences stand to them.... It is the nature of the object that determines the form of its possible science."[34]

Bhaskar insists that each stratum of reality, whether physical, biological, or social, is to be seen as *real* and capable of investigation using means appropriate to its distinctive identity.[35] A complex reality, such as religion, will have multiple layers or strata, each of which demands to be investigated by a research method appropriate for that stratum. To apply a single research method to religion simply reduces religion to the level for which that research method was developed. Religion is indeed a social reality; it is, however, rather more than this. Equally, it could be seen as a "system of symbols."[36] Again, this designates only one level of a complex reality.

This approach suggests that anthropology and theology could be considered to engage human nature at different levels, reflecting the intrinsic complexity of human nature and the incompleteness of any single level of explanation.

---

[34] Roy Bhaskar, *The Possibility of Naturalism: A Philosophical Critique of the Contemporary Human Sciences*, 3rd edn (London: Routledge, 1998), 3.

[35] Alister E. McGrath, *A Scientific Theology*, vol. 2: *Reality* (London: T&T Clark, 2002), 195–244.

[36] Clifford Geertz, "Religion as a Cultural System," in *The Religious Situation*, ed. D. R. Cutler (Boston: Beacon Press, 1968), 639–88.

Inevitably, there are boundary disputes here, as in the case of Richard Dawkins' perhaps unwise attempt to offer a biological explanation of what many regarded as human properties that were more properly studied by social anthropology.[37] This difficulty does not invalidate the insight that humanity can be and, indeed, ought to be investigated at the physical, chemical, biological, and sociological levels, to mention a few of the possibilities. None of these multiple levels is to be regarded as normative or definitive but should be considered part, and only part, of the complex reality that we know as humanity. This way of thinking helpfully allows us to locate the fundamental flaw in Francis Crick's simplistic neurological overstatement: " 'You,' your joys and your sorrows, your memories and your ambitions, your sense of personal identity and free will, are in fact no more than the behaviour of a vast assembly of nerve cells and their associated molecules.... You're nothing but a pack of neurons."[38] The *multiple levels* approach affirms that we are indeed *made up of* neurons as well, of course, as many other constituents, too numerous to mention. This does not, however, mean that we *are* nothing but neurons. Crick confuses a component or level within a system with the system as a whole. We must instead consider human beings as complex totalities that cannot be defined or described in terms of any of their constituent parts.

Both these frameworks of multiple maps and multiple perspectives offer ways of conceiving, defending, and applying a theologically engaged anthropology. They affirm the possibility of complex accounts of human nature, attentive and respectful to the multiple layers and levels of human beings, whether as individuals or communities. An anthropological account of behavior, symbol systems, and rituals can be correlated with a religious system of ideas and values, not necessarily on the basis of the assumption that these are correct but on the assumption that these are presumed to be correct and meaningful by those who hold them. Although Douglas Davies does not deploy such frameworks of approach, his exploration of the correlation of theological and anthropological concepts, such as incarnation and embodiment, salvation and merit making, and sacrament and symbolism, reveal the real possibilities for mutual illumination here.[39]

The two frameworks I propose avoid any notion of intellectual privilege or precedence and lend intellectual rigor to mutual conversations of the kind that Davies and I clearly wish to encourage. No one need assume the priority of one discipline over the other; the two can be construed as having their own distinct integrities and points of focus. The dialogue of enrichment and expansion that

[37] Maurice Bloch, "A Well-Disposed Social Anthropologist's Problem with Memes," in *Darwinizing Culture: The Status of Memetics as a Science*, ed. Robert Aunger (Oxford: Oxford University Press, 2000), 189–203.

[38] Francis Crick, *The Astonishing Hypothesis: The Scientific Search for the Soul* (London: Simon & Schuster, 1994), 3.

[39] Douglas J. Davies, *Anthropology and Theology* (Oxford: Berg Publishers, 2002).

these two frameworks encourage and legitimate allows two quite distinct ways of considering life and experience to converse, even if they do not converge, yielding an outcome that is highly likely to be more than the sum of its parts. As in any interdisciplinary conversation, boundary issues clearly need more detailed consideration and elaboration[40] that, however, lie beyond the scope of this chapter.

*   *   *

To make anthropology and theology interact constructively and positively while maintaining a radical openness to their different approaches and distinct intellectual identities a manageable task, I will have to focus on a single theme that is significant within and for both disciplines, allowing interdisciplinary cross-fertilization and enrichment as well as raising some important issues for reflection. Happily, many issues of interest can be explored in this way. I have chosen to focus on the use of narratives to convey meaning and significance. Since about 1950, cultural anthropologists and others have noted how human beings use narratives as tools of interpretation of complex realities, including history and identity: "[We] are animals who must fundamentally understand what reality is, who we are, and how we ought to live by locating ourselves within the larger narratives and metanarratives that we hear and tell, and that constitute what is for us real and significant."[41]

Empirical study suggests that human beings regard the construction of meaning, often framed in terms of *grand narratives* or *big pictures*, as both significant and legitimate, enabling us to make sense of life and cope with its difficulties and ambiguities.[42] We tell stories to make sense of our individual and corporate experience, whether this sense making could be framed in religious or more general terms, and in order to transmit these ideas within culture.[43] Narratives provide a means of organizing, recalling, and interpreting experience, allowing the wisdom of the past to be passed on to the future.[44]

---

[40] Thomas F. Gieryn, "Boundary-Work and the Demarcation of Science from Non-Science: Strains and Interests in Professional Ideologies of Scientists," *American Sociological Review* 48 (1983): 781–95.

[41] Elinor Ochs and Lisa Capps, "Narrating the Self," *Annual Review of Anthropology* 25 (1996): 19–43 (here 19).

[42] Jonathan Gottschall, *The Storytelling Animal: How Stories Make Us Human* (Boston: Houghton Mifflin Harcourt, 2012); Joshua A. Hicks and Laura A. King, "Meaning in Life and Seeing the Big Picture: Positive Affect and Global Focus," *Cognition and Emotion* 21/7 (2007): 1577–84; Crystal L. Park, "Religion as a Meaning-Making Framework in Coping with Life Stress," *Journal of Social Issues* 61/4 (2005): 707–29.

[43] Michael Bamberg, "Who Am I? Narration and Its Contribution to Self and Identity," *Theory & Psychology* 21/1 (2011): 3–24; Jérôme Bruner, "La culture, l'esprit, les récit," *Enfance* 2/58 (2006): 118–25.

[44] Stephen Crites, "The Narrative Quality of Experience," *Journal of the American Academy of Religion* 39/3 (1971): 291–311; Lewis P. Hinchman and Sandra K. Hinchman (eds), *Memory, Identity, Community: The Idea of Narrative in the Human Sciences* (Albany: State University of New York Press, 1997).

Theorizing about the function of narrative is always secondary to its actual importance, as judged by empirical studies of the role of narratives in helping individuals and communities gain a subjective sense of social or religious identity and historical location.[45]

The use of narratives in theology is well attested. The Christian faith is arguably based upon a narrative, dealing with a God who chose to enter into and be disclosed within the historical process. It is perfectly acceptable to speak of the *story of God* in that the character of God can be seen as *rendered* or *performed* through defining narratives that both disclose the character of God and shape the identity of God's people.[46] The biblical account of the Exodus from Egypt can be seen as one such disclosing and defining narrative, but others can easily be noted, above all the story of Jesus of Nazareth. The complex and problematic notion of salvation history is a clear example of a narrative that is held to be intellectually illuminating while at the same time serving as the point of focus and marker of identity of a religious community.[47]

The Enlightenment's dislike of narrative, linked with its controlling assumption that history could not disclose the necessary and universal truths acceptable to reason, led it to marginalize biblical narratives, seeing them as, at best, contingent vehicles for a rational truth that could be more reliably obtained by other means.[48] Yet a shifting cultural mood has led to a realization of the value of narrative for articulating and safeguarding human meaning and identity within the flux of history, giving a new significance to the local and particular.[49] Christian theology is, therefore, to be seen as a form of discourse that arises from reflection on a narrative[50] whose core themes are recalled, interpreted, and enacted through the Eucharist, in which our own local and

[45] Bamberg, "Who Am I?"; Douglas Ezzy, "Theorizing Narrative Identity," *The Sociological Quarterly* 39/2 (1998): 239–52; Heinz Streib, "Erzählte Zeit als Ermöglichung von Identität. Paul Ricoeurs Begriff der narrativen Identität und seine Implikationen für die religionspädagogische Rede von Identität und Bildung," in *Religion und die Gestaltung der Zeit*, ed. D. Georgi and H.-G. Heimbrock (Kampen, The Netherlands: Kok, 1994), 181–98; Jean-Marc Tétaz, "L'identité narrative comme théorie de la subjectivité pratique: Un essai de reconstruction de la conception de Paul Ricœur," *Études théologiques et religieuses* 4/89 (2014): 463–94; Tony J. Watson and Diane H. Watson, "Narratives in Society, Organizations and Individual Identities: An Ethnographic Study of Pubs, Identity Work and the Pursuit of 'The Real,'" *Human Relations* 65/6 (2012): 683–704.

[46] Coleman A. Baker, "Early Christian Identity Formation: From Ethnicity and Theology to Socio-Narrative Criticism," *Currents in Biblical Research* 9/2 (2011): 228–37.

[47] Wolfhart Pannenberg, "Weltgeschichte und Heilsgeschichte," in *Probleme biblischer Theologie: Gerhard von Rad zum 70. Geburtstag*, ed. Hans Walter Wolff (Munich: Kaiser Verlag, 1971), 349–66.

[48] Hans W. Frei, *The Eclipse of Biblical Narrative: A Study in Eighteenth and Nineteenth Century Biblical Hermeneutics* (New Haven, CT: Yale University Press, 1977).

[49] James A. Holstein, *The Self We Live By: Narrative Identity in a Postmodern World* (New York: Oxford University Press, 1999).

[50] George W. Stroup, *The Promise of Narrative Theology: Recovering the Gospel in the Church* (Atlanta: John Knox Press, 1981).

particular existences are contextualized and given meaning through being located within a greater narrative. The Eucharistic narrative, linked with its attendant practice, can serve as both a marker and foundation of Christian ecclesial identity. Anthropology does not create such an identity; it can, however, illuminate how this is actualized through a comparison with cognate examples that help us grasp how group identity is established, articulated, and safeguarded.[51]

This understanding of the role of narratives in human culture has important implications for systematic theology. In contrast to natural narrative modes of discourse, systematic theology often uses highly abstract forms of thought, which, although arguably grounded in the narrative of Jesus of Nazareth, nevertheless represent a transposition from story to theory. Where the telling of stories is cognitively natural, the abstractions of systematic theology are not.[52] The resurgence of narrative theology since World War II may be seen, in part, as a recognition of the cognitive naturalness of storytelling in theology and, in part, as a reappropriation of an older way of doing theology, which was regarded as rationally deficient by the Enlightenment.[53] C. S. Lewis is one of many writers to emphasize the priority of the Christian story over its intellectualized interpretations, such as those found in the creeds. Christian beliefs are, according to Lewis, "translations into our concepts and ideas" of that which God has already expressed in a "more adequate" language—namely, the "grand narrative" underlying Christian faith.[54]

Individuals and communities tell stories for multiple purposes—for example, to recall events of importance, to articulate a sense of identity or uniqueness, to legitimate claims or grievances, and to give events a context or framework of meaning. Anthropologists who study narratives aim to document the narratives being told and to develop a good sense of at least some of the reasons why they are being told without being in a position to evaluate their validity. In effect, the anthropologist is called on to create a greater narrative to accommodate the ones that they hear told, while at the same time confronting questions of privilege, bias, and "historical placement" on their part as observers.[55]

---

[51] For a good example, see Atsuhiro Asano, *Community-Identity Construction in Galatians: Exegetical, Social-Anthropological, and Socio-Historical Studies* (London: T&T Clark International, 2005).

[52] Robert N. McCauley, *Why Religion Is Natural and Science Is Not* (New York: Oxford University Press, 2011).

[53] Frei, *The Eclipse of Biblical Narrative*.

[54] Alister E. McGrath, "A Gleam of Divine Truth: The Concept of Myth in Lewis's Thought," in *The Intellectual World of C. S. Lewis* (Oxford: Wiley-Blackwell, 2013), 55–82.

[55] Eleni Coundouriotis, "Writing Stories about Tales Told: Anthropology and the Short Story in African Literatures," *Narrative* 6/2 (1998): 140–56; Rodolfo Maggio, "The Anthropology of Storytelling and the Storytelling of Anthropology," *Journal of Comparative Research in Anthropology and Sociology* 5/2 (2014): 89–106.

These concerns do not in any way invalidate the exercise. They do, however, place it in an informing context, which alerts us to the risk of misreading narratives on account of prior assumptions about what narratives ought to be and what they ought to do. Anthropology is itself a form of storytelling, which inevitably blurs the boundaries between anthropology as storytelling and the anthropology of storytelling.

The question is what story might be told to make sense of our propensity to tell stories.[56] Given that human beings tell many stories, a system is needed to prioritize them. Perhaps there is a master narrative that exercises hermeneutical hegemony over its alternatives. If so, then one must find some way of determining whether one narrative is sacred and another is not. Perhaps more importantly, we should look at why people tell these stories and do not simply use reasoned argument from first principles, as some writers of the eighteenth-century Enlightenment believed to be the case. These are clearly issues of anthropological and theological interest with the potential for interdisciplinary reflection.

* * *

In his remarkable account of his period during the 1930s as an ideologically committed Marxist, Arthur Koestler recalled how he viewed history, politics, and nature through the prism of a single metanarrative, written in "the language of physical equations and social determinants."[57] As his faith in Marxism's explanatory capacities and political outcomes faded, he found that the world became a more complex place, incapable of being adequately explained by any single grand story.

Koestler's experience resonates with the empirical observation that most people use multiple narratives to make sense of the world around them and within them. Anthropologists have noted that no single metanarrative seems adequate to organize and correlate on its own the complexities of human existence and experience. Multiple stories need to be told to make sense of the multiple perspectives or levels of human existence. The evidence for this conclusion and its outcomes have been explored by sociologist Christian Smith who points out that we must, and, as a matter of observable fact, do, use multiple narratives to locate ourselves within our world and understand what we experience.[58] Smith identifies a number of narratives that provide frameworks of meaning in the twenty-first century. Examples of relevance to this chapter include the Christian narrative, the Scientific Enlightenment narrative, and the Chance and Purposeless Narrative. Smith notes that those who affirm the primacy of one master narrative still find themselves drawing

---

[56] Gottschall, *The Storytelling Animal*, 87–116.
[57] Arthur Koestler, *The Invisible Writing: An Autobiography* (Boston: Beacon Press, 1954), 13.
[58] Christian Smith, *Moral, Believing Animals: Human Personhood and Culture* (Oxford: Oxford University Press, 2009), 63–94.

on others to provide detail, texture, and color for their rendering of reality. Many today regard any totalizing narrative with suspicion, preferring to see such narratives as local and particular.

In one sense, Smith's conclusion is ultimately functional: We need multiple stories to illuminate, inform, and engage different aspects of our experience. His analysis does not prohibit us from asking this question: Given that human beings develop and use multiple narratives, is there a single narrative that provides a framework for understanding both the general human propensity to value and use stories and the general drift of those stories? This question can be explored using the framework developed by Eric Csapo, who used the term *myth* to designate an ideology expressed in narrative form. Noting that there "has been a general coalescence of the concept of myth with the concept of ideology" in more recent thinking, Csapo argued that the notion of myth is no longer limited to significant stories sourced from ancient or primal cultures but now extends to modern narratives of identity and value, including those of the Enlightenment itself.[59] Csapo's deft analysis both confirms the general anthropological endorsement of the importance and ubiquity of narratives of identity, while at the same time raising the possibility that one such narrative might prove to have such imaginative and explanatory potency that it is capable of accommodating to other such narratives, if not directly replicating their content.

How might theology engage with these considerations and, perhaps, give them a new direction? Curiously, some of the most interesting reflections on these themes come from the pens of writers who were amateur anthropologists and theologians, if they are to be judged by the professional standards of those academic guilds, yet nevertheless made important intellectual connections that need to be taken seriously, even if we might choose to develop them in dialogue with those who might be seen as more credible representatives of both guilds.

J. R. R. Tolkien's anthropological explorations, particularly in the field of Nordic culture and literature, persuaded him that *myths*—that is, a narrated account of reality, appealing primarily to the imagination and secondarily to the reason—were ubiquitous, and some theological explanation of this human propensity was required. Tolkien located this explanation in the theological notion of the "image of God," which he held to function as a narrative template with a fundamentally theistic teleological impetus. Since humanity was created in the image of God, the capacity to create stories that in some way reflects the divine rationality remained embedded within humanity, despite the Fall: "Fantasy remains a human right: we make in our measure and in our derivative mode, because we are made: and not only made, but made in the image and likeness of a Maker."[60] This theology of subcreation, set out especially in the 1931 poem "Mythopoeia," led Tolkien to develop a sophisticated yet subtle

[59] Eric Csapo, *Theories of Mythology* (Oxford: Blackwell Publishing, 2005), 292–3.
[60] J. R. R. Tolkien, *Tree and Leaf* (London: HarperCollins, 2001), 56.

theology of religion grounded in the Christian metanarrative's capacity to accommodate pagan myths, both in terms of their literary form and their existential yearnings. By offering "a far-off gleam or echo of evangelium in the real world,"[61] pagan myths elicit wonder and longing, creating both an appetite and an opening for the discovery of the deeper truth that underlies all truth, however fragmentary and veiled.[62]

For Tolkien, the Christian myth thus created intellectual and imaginative space for other stories. Tolkien's advocation of this idea proved critically important in persuading C. S. Lewis to move from a generalized theism to a specific embrace of Christianity, conceived not primarily as a set of doctrines or moral principles but as a controlling and informing grand narrative that generated and sustained such ideas and values.[63] Like Tolkien, Lewis came to hold that myths offered a real though unfocused gleam of divine truth falling on the human imagination. Christianity, rather than being one myth alongside many others, is thus to be seen as representing the fulfilment of all myths—the *true myth* towards which all other myths merely point. Christianity thus tells a true story about humanity, which makes sense of all the stories that humanity tells about itself.

Underlying this understanding of the divine creation of humanity with an intended capacity to tell stories of meaning lies a theological framework that is best articulated in terms of the notion of *mythos spermatikos*.[64] The patristic period made extensive use of the notion of *logos spermatikos*—a "seed-bearing reason" interpreted as God's implanting, through the act of creation, rational tendencies and intuitions that were capable of leading individuals to discover God.[65] This important notion, however, is framed in terms of a capacity to reason and is deficient imaginatively. In speaking of *mythos spermatikos*, we are emphasizing that this created capacity to intuit the divine is to be framed in terms of creating and telling stories, not simply in terms of arguments or rational concepts.

This analysis raises a question that is implicit in much of what has already been considered but has not received proper attention. The question of what determines when a narrative is perceived to be sacred is certainly of theoretical interest. In one sense, religious faith arises through a recognition that a certain narrative is of ultimate significance, which is sometimes held to entail an exclusive commitment to both the narrative itself as a sole medium of revelation or authority, as well as to ideas and values that are held to emerge from it.

---

[61] Ibid., 71.

[62] Verlyn Flieger, *Splintered Light: Logos and Language in Tolkien's World* (Kent, OH: Kent State University, 2002).

[63] McGrath, "A Gleam of Divine Truth."

[64] Fabienne Claire Caland, "Le mythos spermatikos," in *Horizons du mythe*, ed. Denise Brassard and Fabienne Claire Caland (Montréal: Cahiers du CELAT, 2007), 7–32.

[65] Mark J. Edwards, *Image, Word, and God in the Early Christian Centuries* (Farnham, UK: Ashgate, 2013).

However, providing an empirical definition of the *sacred* without importing decidedly non-empirical notions in its support is simply impossible. This is reflected in the difficulties in offering an anthropological account of *religion* when the concept and vocabulary are often absent within cultures, which, in effect, have to be accommodated or adapted to Western notions of religion. Religion may be a universal phenomenon, open to anthropological exploration, yet religion is not a universal concept. Certain secular ideologies, such as Nazism and Stalinism, which demanded total intellectual and social commitment, used religious language and imagery to lend imaginative and emotional appeal to their political narratives and thus legitimized violence against those perceived to oppose them.[66] *Sacred* is often reduced to functional categories, such as lying beyond criticism or challenge,[67] or eliciting a response of awe and wonder.[68] There is clearly scope for further research here on the social mechanisms by which certain narratives achieve the status of sacred stories.

* * *

This chapter has set out to affirm the importance of a respectful and informed dialogue between anthropology and theology, alert to the sensitivities and concerns within both disciplines. I have focused more on theological anxieties and how these might be alleviated, yet clearly these have their anthropological counterparts, which must also be respected and engaged. I have teased out some potential areas of research and possibilities for collaborative exploration by focusing on the single category of *narrative*, which is significant both to anthropology and theology and unquestionably opens up possibilities of mutual intellectual enrichment. The two heuristic models of *multiple perspectives* and *multiple levels* noted previously provide a framework for such lines of exploration. Anthropology can clarify the cultural appeal and prevalence of this form of discourse; theology can offer an account of why humanity thinks in this way and its own grand narrative that positions other stories and articulates its own distinctive vision of reality.

I believe that, when brought together in a critical yet positive manner, both theology and anthropology can help to create a big picture of reality, which transcends their individual limits. While this process of engagement is likely to be intellectually productive to both communities, it is also certainly interesting—a judgment that I believe applies to the entire spectrum of possible engagements and interactions between theology and anthropology and not simply to this single case study.

---

[66] Geoff Eley, *Nazism as Fascism: Violence, Ideology, and the Ground of Consent in Germany 1930–1945* (London: Routledge, 2013), 13–58, 156–97.

[67] Shigemi Inaga, "Crime, Literature, and Religious Mysticism: The Case of the Japanese Translator of Salman Rushdie's *Satanic Verses*," in *From Ritual to Romance and Beyond*, ed. Manfred Schmeling and Hans-Joachim Backe (Würzburg: Königshausen & Neumann, 2011), 45–58.

[68] Rudolf Otto, *Das Heilige: Über das Irrationale in der Idee des Göttlichen und dein Verhältnis zum Rationalen*, 16th edn (Gotha, Germany: Leopold Klotz, 1927).

8

An Anthropologist Is Listening

A Reply to Ethnographic Theology

James S. Bielo

The goal of this book is to foster a theologically engaged anthropology. We do this goal a favor when we recognize that theologians have been engaged with professional anthropology since at least the late 1980s. In this chapter, I focus on a commitment that has been brewing among practical theologians and Christian ethicists since the early 2000s. The commitment is that ethnographic fieldwork can be used to generate critical theological reflection. I hope to encourage a substantive shift from a one-way engagement into an actual and generative dialogue between ethnographic theologians and anthropological ethnographers. In doing so, I echo my graduate school mentor, Fredric Roberts, who once sought "to begin a serious dialogue between anthropologists and liturgists."[1] Inspired by Mikhail Bakhtin's conception of dialogic selves and societies, Roberts insisted that meaningful dialogue "requires open-endedness, vulnerability and a lack of finalization" and that dialogue partners "can, should and must be able to argue as well as agree."[2]

The animating question I pose is this: What does each dialogue partner—anthropology and theology—stand to gain from an open exchange about doing and writing ethnography? After introducing the field of ethnographic theology, this chapter is divided into two main sections. The first responds to the work being done by ethnographic theologians from the standpoint of anthropological ethnography. In particular, I highlight the promise of working with a more varied conception of what doing ethnographic fieldwork means.

---

[1] Fredric M. Roberts, "Are Anthropological Crises Contagious? Reflexivity, Representation, Alienation and Rites of Penance," in *Reconciling Embrace: Foundations for the Future of Sacramental Reconciliation*, ed. Robert J. Kennedy (Chicago: Liturgy Training Publications, 1998), 45–64.

[2] Ibid., 46.

The second section then outlines one way in which anthropologists might benefit from engaging with ethnographic theology, which is explored more fully by Webster's contribution to this book.[3] To conclude, I propose that reflecting on genres of ethnographic writing is yet another opportunity for future dialogue between the two fields.

Ethnographic theology emerged out of a turn among academic theologians toward social and cultural theory that began in the 1980s. A key instigator of this turn was the school of postliberal theology.[4] For example, Lutheran theologian George Lindbeck argued that doctrine is always formed and produced within the cultural–linguistic world of a particular religious tradition.[5] To understand, contribute to, or change doctrine requires an understanding of the tradition, which requires the tools to analyze cultural–linguistic worlds. In the 1990s theologians such as Don Browning and Kathryn Tanner further advanced the theological use of social science. Browning called for a more empirically grounded approach to practical theology, a field that focuses on maintaining and refining how Christians live as part of the church.[6] Tanner argued for an engagement with postmodern anthropological theories of culture and their ingrained equations of reflexivity > neutrality, power as pervasive and inescapable > power as isolated in a few particular social institutions, and sociality defined by conflict and struggle > coherent or harmonious unity.[7]

In the early 2000s, practical theologians and ethicists influenced by this cultural turn settled on the commitment that producing theological knowledge is not the sole reserve of the professional theologian and that doing theology is not limited to intellectual acts of literacy. These scholars called for a more dynamic exchange between the people in the pews and formally trained theological scholars. Following Browning and inspired by Tanner, these scholars adopted ethnographic fieldwork as a way to engage and explore the lived theologies of everyday Christians.[8]

An organizing principle for ethnographic theology is that fieldwork methodology is not "a mere tool in the doing of theology," but can actually be "an

---

[3] See Joseph Webster, Chapter 18, 315–36.   [4] See Brian M. Howell, Chapter 2, 29–49.

[5] George Lindbeck, *The Nature of Doctrine: Religion and Theology in a Postliberal Age* (Louisville, KY: Westminster John Knox Press, 1984).

[6] Don Browning, *A Fundamental Practical Theology: Descriptive and Strategic Proposals* (Minneapolis, MN: Fortress Press, 1991). For an early statement on the nature of practical theology see Friedrich Schleiermacher, *A Brief Outline of Theology as a Field of Study*, trans. Terrence N. Tice (1811; Louisville, KY: Westminster John Knox Press, 2011).

[7] Kathryn Tanner, *Theories of Culture: A New Agenda for Theology* (Minneapolis, MN: Fortress Press, 1997). Cf. Delwin Brown, Sheila Greeve Davaney, and Kathryn Tanner (eds), *Converging on Culture: Theologians in Dialogue with Cultural Analysis and Criticism* (New York: Oxford University Press, 2001).

[8] For an early feminist precursor to this more programmatic turn, see Ada Maria Isasi-Diaz, *En La Lucha/In the Struggle: A Hispanic Women's Liberation Theology* (New York: Orbis Books, 2004). Cf. Nicolas Healy, *Church, World, and the Christian Life: Practical–Prophetic Ecclesiology* (New York: Cambridge University Press, 2000).

expression of theology."[9] That is, the ethnographic theologian does not simply use anthropological resources to collect and analyze data *then* pivot to the task of theological reflection. Doing ethnographic theology is about generating theological reflection through the research process.[10] Peter Gathje, a contributor to a landmark volume in ethnographic theology, captures this empirical spirit well: "The creating of a countercultural Gospel vision of life within contemporary Christian virtue ethics is an exercise in what might be called 'cheap virtue' unless it attends to the practice of that vision in real life by real people in real communities."[11]

A refined and representative example of ethnographic theology is Natalie Wigg-Stevenson's book *Ethnographic Theology: An Inquiry into the Production of Theological Knowledge.*[12] Wigg-Stevenson explores the theological life of one small group in an urban Nashville Southern Baptist congregation. In her assessment, everyday and academic theology typically exist segregated from one another and she aims to bring them into a fruitful and lasting exchange. To do so, she used a year in the life of the group as they completed two Bible study curricula. As an ordained minister, Wigg-Stevenson designed the curricula and served as the course instructor. She models her ethnographic presence after Loïc Wacquant's "observant participation" outlined in *Body & Soul.*[13] Throughout the book, she uses the stories of individuals and relationships from the group to illustrate how spiritual struggle is central to how theological meaning and identity are constructed. Ultimately, she presents her ethnographic experience with the group as a model for bridging academic and everyday theology so that they produce theological knowledge collaboratively.

At this nascent stage, ethnographic theology is an approach with articulated foundations and a few thorough applications. Beyond the pages of books and journals, ethnographic theology has begun institutionalizing in the form of

---

[9] Christian B. Scharen and Aana Marie Vigen (eds), *Ethnography as Christian Theology and Ethics* (London and New York: Continuum, 2011).

[10] For formative statements on ethnographic theology, see Mary McClintock Fulkerson, *Places of Redemption: Theology for a Worldly Church* (Oxford: Oxford University Press, 2007); Christian B. Scharen, *Fieldwork in Theology: Exploring the Social Context of God's Work in the World* (Grand Rapids, MI: Baker Academic, 2015); "Judicious Narratives or Ethnography *as* Ecclesiology," *Scottish Journal of Theology* 58/2 (2005): 125–42; Scharen and Vigen, *Ethnography as Christian Theology and Ethics*; John Swinton and Harriett Mowat, *Practical Theology and Qualitative Research* (Suffolk, UK: SCM Press, 2006); Pete Ward (ed.), *Perspectives on Ecclesiology and Ethnography* (Grand Rapids, MI: Eerdmans, 2012); Todd Whitmore, "Crossing the Road: The Role of Ethnographic Fieldwork in Christian Ethics," *Journal of the Society of Christian Ethics* 27/2 (2007): 273–94; Natalie Wigg-Stevenson, *Ethnographic Theology: An Inquiry into the Production of Theological Knowledge* (New York: Palgrave, 2014).

[11] Peter R. Gathje, "The Cost of Virtue: What Power in the Open Door Might Speak to Virtue Ethics," in *Ethnography as Christian Theology and Ethics*, ed. Christian B. Scharen and Aana Marie Vigen (New York: Continuum, 2011), 207–26 (here 223).

[12] See note 10.

[13] Loïc Wacquant, *Body & Soul: Notebooks of an Apprentice Boxer* (New York: Oxford University Press, 2011). Cf. Scharen, *Fieldwork in Theology*.

academic programs in both North America and the United Kingdom.[14] As an anthropological ethnographer, it is more than refreshing to see one's vocation adopted with excitement, sincerity, and diligence. This sense is especially true in the post-2008 financial crisis age when anthropologists feel increasingly embattled amid decreases in federal funding and ill-informed attacks from politicians.[15] However, despite being more than a decade in development, ethnographic theologians have received no response from anthropologists.[16] While I am deeply appreciative of, and grateful for, ethnographic theology as a project, reading this literature as a professional anthropologist reveals some limitations in how they have chosen to engage ethnography. Humbly, I offer a few words of constructive critique to my colleagues in the field.

* * *

Ethnographic theology engages what might be called the classic model for doing ethnographic fieldwork.[17] Todd Whitmore, a leading practitioner in the field, uses descriptions by founding British social anthropologists W. H. R. Rivers and Bronislaw Malinowski to capture the nature of ethnography: doing extended fieldwork, learning the local language, being a participant observer, working inductively, and systematically using field notes and interviewing. The model of fieldwork employed by ethnographic theologians is akin to a description I recently used to present ethnography in a theoretical primer for the anthropology of religion: ethnography as equal parts science, art, and craft.[18]

As a science, we recognize how fieldwork is conceived and conducted systematically. We care about standards of reliability and accuracy, and we contribute to comparative areas of research in order to refine theoretical concepts. As a craft, we recognize that ethnographic fieldwork is the kind of practice one always gets better at doing but never perfects. Like the luthier or the winemaker, the only way for the ethnographer to improve is to hone his or her skills constantly through doing the craft. Laborious and often

---

[14] For a sampling of MA and PhD programs that explicitly teach ethnographic theology, see Durham University, University of Aberdeen, Vanderbilt University, Emory University, Boston University, and the University of Notre Dame.

[15] For example, see "Rick Scott, Florida Governor, Says of Anthropologists, 'We Don't Need Them Here,'" *The Huffington Post*, December 12, 2001, <www.huffingtonpost.com/2011/10/12/rick-scott-florida-govern_0_n_1006743.html>.

[16] The one exception of which I am aware is an invited essay contribution to a roundtable review of *Ethnography as Christian Theology and Ethics* (2011) by Joao Biehl, "The Right to a Nonprojected Future," *Practical Matters Journal* 6 (March 2013): 1–9, <https://wp.me/p6QAmj-lJ>.

[17] The single exception I have identified is one use of Michael Burawoy's extended case method: Luke Bretherton, "Generating Christian Political Theory and the Uses of Ethnography," in *Perspectives on Ecclesiology and Ethnography*, ed. Pete Ward (Grand Rapids, MI: William B. Eerdmans), 145–66.

[18] James S. Bielo, *Anthropology of Religion: The Basics* (New York: Routledge, 2015), 31–2.

tedious, crafts are also inherently creative: living traditions in which individual techniques become second nature but remain open to invention and adaptation. To see ethnography as art recognizes the human—the passionately, agonizingly human—ways in which fieldwork produces knowledge intersubjectively. Ethnographic success and failure hangs in the balance of how well we establish and nurture relationships with fellow humans, mend them when wounded, and restore them when broken. In *Mama Lola*, a widely praised spiritual biography of a voodoo priestess, anthropologist Karen McCarthy Brown described fieldwork as "a social art form."[19] This art form is tethered to trust, vulnerability, mutual responsibility, excitement, regret, curiosity, patience, passion, and other affective dynamics that define human relationality.

Ethnographic theologians also prize the power of intimate human relationships. Through relationships the spiritual goals of Christianity are to be sought and realized. Relationships redeem, restore, reconcile, and heal. Relationships are generative and primary, not resultant and secondary. Relationships are not a means to an end, not merely a useful strategy or helpful way to cope. They are what we ought to pursue. They are, very simply, good. Mary McClintock Fulkerson, whose ethnography of a diverse urban congregation in Durham, North Carolina, is widely cited in the field, writes, "Our social relations are not just secondary or optional in Christian traditions; the relation to the neighbor is a central litmus for the God-relation."[20]

The consistent use of a classic fieldwork model by ethnographic theologians put to rest an initial suspicion I harbored when first beginning to read this literature: that disciplinary interlopers would play fast and loose with the science/craft/art I have been in love with since my days as an undergraduate anthropology major cutting my teeth on ethnography. I would urge ethnographic theologians to write with more transparency about their process and decision making with respect to research design, methodology, and analysis, but clearly they are engaging ethnography with profound respect and increasingly deft skill.

However, for ethnographic theologians to confine their work to the classic model of fieldwork is a limitation. The primary constructive critique I have to offer is this: there are other ethnographic modes to consider, and they promise to open new opportunities regarding the central goal of producing critical theological reflection. As one example, I present an ethnographic mode that self-consciously works as an alternative to the classic model of fieldwork: studying up.[21]

---

[19] Karen McCarthy Brown, *Mama Lola: A Vodou Priestess in Brooklyn* (Berkeley: University of California Press, 1991), 2.

[20] Fulkerson, *Places of Redemption*, 238.

[21] I encourage ethnographic theologians to explore other ethnographic modes that anthropologists have developed—for example, the ethnography of communication, dialogical ethnography, and collaborative ethnography.

Studying up was first proposed by the anthropologist Laura Nader.[22] Her purpose was twofold. First, she sought to encourage more anthropological study of the United States in order to complement the wealth of anthropological research about small-scale, non-Western societies. Second, and related, she wanted to see future anthropologists not restrict their ethnographic ambitions to communities and groups that existed largely outside of power. To study up is to study those "who shape attitudes and control institutional structures."[23]

Nader justified her call on three grounds: (1) Her students believed that their moral indignation at abuses of power and the reproduction of inequalities was prohibited in the context of scholarship; (2) scientifically, it is more valuable to have reliable research about *both* those in *and* those outside of power; and (3) studying up promised to heighten the democratic relevance of anthropology by producing research that enabled a more informed citizenry. Nader's prophetic call was not an immediate game changer for anthropology, but since its publication four-and-a-half decades ago, it has persistently provoked fieldworkers to expand their ethnographic ambition. With no small thanks to Nader, we now have, to name a few, ethnographies of a nuclear weapons lab, investment bankers, global advertisement agencies, and mass media producers.[24]

I recommend studying up to ethnographic theologians among other alternative ethnographic modes for two interlaced reasons. The first is that ethnographic theology has cohered largely as the study of *everyday* Christians. They are described as *everyday* because they do theology and reflect theologically without the symbolic capital of graduate degrees and, more often than not, live social lives as working-class and poor citizens. The editors of *Ethnography as Christian Theology and Ethics* write that a fundamental purpose of ethnographic theology is "confronting and contesting sites of privilege."[25] The impetus here is important (i.e., to resist reproducing the worldly structures of inequality in our scholarship), and it capitalizes on a key strength of ethnography (i.e., to help those who typically lack a public voice to be heard more clearly). However, recalling Nader, understanding and addressing privilege is not only or always most effectively accomplished by doing ethnography among

---

[22] Laura Nader, "Up the Anthropologist—Perspectives Gained from Studying Up," in *Reinventing Anthropology*, ed. Dell Hymes (New York: Vintage Press, 1969), 284–311.

[23] Ibid., 284.

[24] Hugh Gusterson, *Nuclear Rites: A Weapons Laboratory at the End of the Cold War* (Berkeley: University of California Press, 1998); Karen Ho, *Liquidated: An Ethnography of Wall Street* (Durham, NC: Duke University Press, 2009); Shalini Shankar, *Advertising Diversity: Ad Agencies and the Creation of Asian American Consumers* (Durham, NC: Duke University Press, 2015); Barry Dornfield, *Producing Public Television, Producing Public Culture* (Princeton: Princeton University Press, 1998).

[25] Scharen and Vigen, *Ethnography as Christian Theology*, xx.

those who suffer due to lack of privilege. Sometimes fieldwork should take us into the very engines of power and privilege to see how they operate and who is laboring to keep the pistons firing.

Studying up might take any number of forms for ethnographic theologians, but a few possibilities come directly to mind. If interested in the theological exchange and production that happens through Christian popular culture, studying cultural consumers will not be enough. It requires seeking out sites of cultural production: the music studio, the Christian writers' guild, design studios, and corporate offices. If interested in how academic culture mediates theological exchange and production, it is imperative to study the culture of seminaries. If interested in how bureaucratic culture mediates theological exchange and production, one can study up to the elite echelons of denominations and parachurch organizations. Building a robust understanding of the lived faith of power brokers will shed significant light on how conditions for theological engagement are established at the everyday level.[26]

The second reason is that studying up will necessarily require ethnographic theologians to imagine fieldwork beyond the site to which they have gravitated most frequently and easily: the local congregation. Urban, suburban, exurban, rural, and multisite churches are undoubtedly vital centers of theological knowledge production and reflection. They are not, undoubtedly, the only sites. Depending on what you want to know about theological knowledge production and reflection, the local congregation may not be the most relevant location. Much like Nader, I am not suggesting an either/or stance, not for individual researches and certainly not for an entire field. This situation is a both/and. Ethnographic theologians should work with local congregations *and* seminaries, congregations *and* denominations, congregations *and* parachurch ministries, congregations *and* Christian mass media producers, congregations *and* transnational networks. Again, like Nader, my argument is that the project as a whole will be far better off if both are happening, and not simply the studying down and laterally that has thus far defined ethnographic theology.

Consider a brief example from my own fieldwork, which was designed, conducted, and written with strictly cultural interests and questions, not theological ones. Still, I hope it can inspire future ethnographic theologians to study up. The example comes from an ethnographic project I conducted on the Emerging Church movement from 2007 through 2011.[27] Local pastors and congregants were the ethnographic backbone of this project, but in the

---

[26] Ethnographic theologians compelled by this argument may be interested in two works of qualitative sociology that address these issues: Nancy Ammerman, *Baptist Battles: Social Change and Religious Conflict in the Southern Baptist Convention* (New Brunswick: Rutgers University Press, 1990); D. Michael Lindsay, *Faith in the Halls of Power: How Evangelicals Joined the American Elite* (New York and Oxford: Oxford University Press, 2007).

[27] James S. Bielo, *Emerging Evangelicals: Faith, Modernity, and the Desire for Authenticity* (New York: New York University Press, 2011).

summer of 2008 I did a series of interviews with Christian book publishing editors. Both of these publishers maintained book series targeting the Emerging movement, and I wanted to learn something about how this particular market niche of Christian readers was understood from the publishing side.[28]

One interview took me to a meeting with a self-described evangelical Anglican who handled the entire Emerging catalogue for one of the publishers. Our conversation focused primarily on his role in the process of acquisition and editing. As the interview progressed, he kept using the word *viable* to describe how potential book projects are assessed. After his use of this term became conspicuous, I had to ask what he meant:

JAMES: So, what makes a project viable?

EDITOR: We're a publishing house, so viability is always at the end of the day about sales.

JAMES: But what you think will sell is bound to be based on a set of ideas about what is viable, right?

EDITOR: That's true. The exception is if you're a big name. But, for unknown authors, yes, then it always comes down to good concepts and good writing.

JAMES: What makes a concept good? What makes writing good?

EDITOR: I don't think there's a formula for good writing or concepts. It can come in many forms. There are lots of different ways to be good.

JAMES: Certainly there is some criteria? Some rubric perhaps?

EDITOR: It's interesting you're asking this because I'll be doing two writing workshops in the fall where I'm supposed to have some of these ideas articulated. We do always tell our authors that on the continuum of theoretical to concrete, you should always be more concrete. Also, we try to stay away from writing that is too vitriolic. There is some tension around the issue of taking pot shots at sacred cows. There are certain things that are fundamentals of our faith, and if I get a manuscript that is treating one of those fundamentals in a way that's not appropriate, that needs to be changed. You know, we are who we publish and we publish who we are.

JAMES: That dynamic really makes your role pretty crucial.

EDITOR: Absolutely. If someone else were doing this job, someone with different theological or personal interests, there would be different books being published by [our] Press.

The progression in this excerpt moves from a distinctly market logic to a more biographical, human logic. His final remark is particularly worth attention. Given a change of cast—such as someone interested in protecting different sacred cows, someone convinced that the scriptural theme of idolatry deserves

---

[28] The following three vignettes are reconstructed from field notes.

more attention, someone hell-bent on critiquing rapture anticipations, someone suspicious of Christian Zionism, or someone fed up with megachurch growth—their contributions to home, church, and seminary libraries would be different. Of course, the issue is not simply that this publisher would be producing different books; the Christian public would encounter a different set of consumer choices as they sought books to read, give as gifts, and use in congregational small groups.

My next interview took me to meet a former Baptist, former pastor, current nondenominational evangelical editor who had worked for the second publisher since the early 1990s. He was not only the main acquirer for their Emerging catalogue; he had been embedded in the Emerging movement as a participant since its inception. During our interview, he highlighted a 2005 book as a milepost of contention because it pushed how open a Christian publisher could be. Personally, he disagreed with numerous arguments in the book, but he and the author fundamentally agreed on a few commitments: asking hard questions of the Establishment, highlighting the lunacy that Christianity's theological canon could ever be closed once and for all, and ensuring that open dialogue, especially around issues of theological controversy, is necessary. He then transitioned into a comparison with Jossey-Bass, a non-Christian publisher that he believed was increasingly attractive to Christian authors. His explanation for why Jossey-Bass was having success recruiting Christian authors was that they impose no theological guidelines or oversight to negotiate: "You can say whatever you want." Somewhere in the middle of this explanation, he stopped and summarized how he approached the role of being an editor: "I'm a big supporter of the broker of ideas model." His description portrayed a marketplace of ideas that allowed him some leeway and experimentation. Things that foster "Truth, capital T" will stick; all else will fall away. His job is to facilitate the sticking of as many promising ideas and directions as possible.

My third interview took me back to the academic division of the first publisher and a meeting with an editor for an Emerging-inspired book series.[29] We talked in his office—a relatively small, square room with reams of loose paper, hectically shelved books, and miscellaneous items on display (e.g., a Seinfeld bowl, a buddy Jesus, a sign reading "Sinners Only," and a framed portrait of John Calvin). The series' initial idea was "little books by big people": roughly 150-page essays by well-established theologians. He explained that the founding of this series marked a change in leadership at the publisher: "This would not have appeared ten years ago." As an example, he

---

[29] This series is the same one that Christian B. Scharen's book, *Fieldwork in Theology: Exploring the Social Context of God's Work in the World*, is published in. I do not know whether the same editor continues to work with the series.

fingered through books on a shelf to find the series' third book. He described the author as a "left-leaning Catholic," an identity the press would have systematically policed against in previous eras. He said there was much that is controversial in the book—for example, advocating that the Bible be read through the lens of deconstruction and continental philosophy. Whatever might be controversial about the author, his style, or his theology only reinforced for this editor the purpose of the series: to publish ideas for people to "chew on," not to monitor every sentence for "proper content," to move "the conversation" in a good direction, and to provide academic theologians room to "color outside the lines." Exact phrasing aside, this model is the same "broker of ideas" advocated by the second editor.

In retrospect, I would have devoted much more ethnographic labor to editors and other staff members in the Christian publishing industry. The data generated by these three interviews was fascinating and irreplaceable and convincing enough to me that a thorough anthropological ethnography of Christian publishing would be a major work.[30] My point here is that an ethnographic theology of Christian publishing holds its own distinct promise. Following Wigg-Stevenson's framing question, studying up in this way would enhance an understanding of everyday theological reading by exploring the conditions of academic and popular theological production. How do the theological commitments of editors help structure the publication of books? How is a theological message shaped by the conditions of publisher identity, marketing, and editorial guidance? Certainly, a studying-up project of this sort would inform ethnographic theology's guiding interests.

* * *

My hope for this chapter is not merely to bring the insight and experience of anthropological ethnography to bear on ethnographic theology but to encourage a mutually generative dialogue between the two fields. In that spirit, I will outline one possible benefit anthropologists stand to gain from listening to ethnographic theologians. The benefit I have in mind is the way in which ethnographic theologians engage normative concerns through fieldwork. This benefit has been named before by theologically engaged anthropologists. For example, Joel Robbins wrote, "[Theology] models a kind of action in the world that is in some or other way more effective or ethically adequate than [our] own."[31] Similarly, Joao Biehl writes, "Theological sensitivities and concerns might well help ethnographers be more mindful of the existential and ethical stakes of our [anthropological] engagements."[32]

---

[30] See cultural historian Daniel Vaca's forthcoming book on the evangelical book publishing industry.

[31] Joel Robbins, "Anthropology and Theology: An Awkward Relationship?" *Anthropological Quarterly* 79/2 (2006): 285–94 (287).

[32] Biehl, "The Right to a Nonprojected Future," 5.

Perhaps a useful place to begin is to reflect on a basic question: why do anthropological ethnographers conduct and publish research? There are nuances to unpack in each of these, but I see four general, though not mutually exclusive, answers to this question:

1. *Comparison*—to produce an accurate, reliable account that enhances cross-cultural knowledge and understanding. The impetus here is scientific, to contribute a defined case that builds on and/or speaks back to theorizing in the larger discipline.

2. *Particularism*—to document and showcase the particular experience of particular people living amid the particular conditions of a particular place and time. The impetus here is humanistic, to further illustrate the complexity of the human condition.

3. *Citizenship*—to inform the listening, viewing, and reading public about a certain set of anthropological issues. The impetus here is pedagogical, to shape the knowledge and perspective of the democratic public (e.g., to advance cultural relativism and fight against ethnocentrism).

4. *Activism*—to mobilize anthropological perspective, knowledge, and data to address a social–material problem. The impetus here is collaborative, to foster positive change in the world by working closely with a community.

Each of these goals should be celebrated, and I would advocate strongly for an anthropology that maintains ample room for all. The observation I want to raise is that none of these goals is without normative commitments. Most obviously, *activism* works from normative assumptions about what counts as a social–material problem, which problems are worth addressing, and what the end result of addressing a problem should be. *Citizenship*, too, has a clear normative element, as it advances certain perspectives as valuable (e.g., cultural relativism) while working against others (e.g., ethnocentrism). *Particularism* incorporates the normative decision of choosing to highlight one version of particularity over another, effectively saying which particular experience a researcher wants to prioritize as deserving attention. *Comparison* is the least overtly normative, but any introductory text that honestly covers anthropology's post-1970s critical turn will treat the premise that theories are value-laden as an epistemological given. Ethnographic theologians are deeply familiar with English Anglican theologian John Milbank's *Theology and Social Theory*, which argues much the same, contrasting a secular ontology of violence with a more theocentric ontology of peace.[33]

---

[33] John Milbank, *Theology and Social Theory: Beyond Secular Reason* (London: Wiley-Blackwell, 1990).

Despite the normative aspects of producing anthropological knowledge, many anthropologists remain uncomfortable with the suggestion that research be oriented toward normative ends. This discomfort is a significant point of contrast with ethnographic theology, which is designed, conducted, analyzed, and written always with normative purpose. Christian Scharen and Aana Marie Vigen, editors of *Ethnography as Christian Theology and Ethics*, advocate "pursuing knowledge for the sake of something—well-being, understanding, justice, or as we [Christians] would put it, 'to have life and to have it abundantly' (John 10:10)."[34] Put differently, and I find quite eloquently, Christian ethicist Elizabeth Phillips writes, "We are not scientists, and human beings are not our subjects. We are theologians, and we enter into the lives and struggles of fellow human beings because we need to hold them before God and for God to hold them before us so that we can see them as they are, and allow them to help us see ourselves anew for what we are."[35] I am not suggesting that all or, for that matter, any anthropologists start incorporating theological issues and questions into their research agendas. I am suggesting that anthropological ethnographers interested in using their research to engage normative issues and questions might learn from the way ethnographic theologians integrate descriptive empirical research with interpretive and explanatory cultural theory and normative visions for a good life, good community, good work, and good society.[36] Integrating these forms of inquiry is, at present, the central question with which the emerging field of ethnographic theology is wrestling.[37]

In reading the ethnographic theology literature, I have been consistently inspired by the way a normative vision is engaged through fieldwork. It is inspiring to see ethnographic material marshaled not just to illustrate or demonstrate theoretical concepts, as in much of anthropological ethnography, but to pursue a normative vision constructively for how some slice of human reality ought to be. Recalling Wigg-Stevenson's work, she used her interviews with group participants and her experiences leading the small group to demonstrate a kind of productive exchange that ought to occur between everyday and academic theology. She was not just documenting *how* their exchanges happened; she was pursuing a model for how those exchanges *could* and *should* happen.

I believe this is an especially rich area of potential because the normative visions of anthropological ethnographers and ethnographic theologians can overlap around shared problems.[38] One example is the problem of how to use

---

[34] Scharen and Vigen, *Ethnography as Christian Theology and Ethics*, xxv.

[35] Elizabeth Phillips, "Charting the 'Ethnographic Turn': Theologians and the Study of Christian Congregations," in *Perspectives on Ecclesiology and Ethnography*, ed. Pete Ward (Grand Rapids, MI: William B. Eerdmans, 2012), 95–106 (here 106).

[36] See Webster, Chapter 18, 315–36.   [37] Wigg-Stevenson, *Ethnographic Theology*, 167.

[38] See Jon Bialecki, Chapter 9, 156–78.

the experience of fieldwork to help form a normative vision for engaging the Other. The power of this question is heightened as we think about doing fieldwork among groups that challenge, or clash with, anthropologists' moral worlds.[39] In a 2007 article, anthropologists Peter Benson and Kevin Lewis O'Neill provide a model for how anthropological ethnographers might listen to ethnographic theology.[40] Benson and O'Neill argue strongly against the notion that the Other in ethnographic fieldwork is merely the source of empirical data or some necessary social resource. They draw on the work of Jewish philosopher Emmanuel Levinas to claim a much more ambitious responsibility for engaging the Other. Levinas wrote extensively on how Self–Other relations ought to be understood: "For Levinas, the self is infinitely responsible, which means that one is responsible not just for the other, a single individual, but indeed for all others, for all individuals."[41] And, extending this to a definitional element of being human: "Levinas does not think that ethical responsibility for the other is only a situational imperative, but rather the constituting force of the human condition."[42]

Benson and O'Neill argue that Levinas's ambitious approach to the Other provides a model for how ethnographers ought to understand their fieldwork engagements. As a thought experiment, consider this question: how might anthropology be different if every graduate program taught this approach as the normative standard? Benson and O'Neill's use of Levinas opens a space for dialogue with ethnographic theologians who also reflect intensively on the meaning of engaging the Other, how this normative vision structures the fieldwork encounter, and how we might use the fieldwork encounter to further this normative vision both within and beyond the field.

*   *   *

Another common problem that anthropological ethnographers and ethnographic theologians share is how to represent their ethnographic material through the medium of the written word. It is the problem of how to translate what is experienced and learned in the field into a narrative form that others can read, learn from, argue with, and use comparatively. For this reason, I conclude with some reflections on writing ethnography.

Reflexivity in and about the process and product of ethnographic writing became a disciplinary imperative among anthropologists with the publication of seminal works in the 1980s. For example, Clifford and Marcus's *Writing Culture*, a volume cited regularly by ethnographic theologians, explored how

---

[39] See Webster, Chapter 18, 156–78; Susan F. Harding, "Representing Fundamentalism: The Problem of the Repugnant Cultural Other," *Social Research* 58/2 (1991): 373–93.

[40] Peter Benson and Kevin Lewis O'Neill, "Facing Risk: Levinas, Ethnography, and Ethics," *Anthropology of Consciousness* 18/2 (2007): 29–55.

[41] Ibid., 40.   [42] Ibid., 44.

forging ethnographic texts is imbued with dynamics of power and epistemo-logical partiality and ideology.[43] In *Works and Lives*, Clifford Geertz approached the question of producing ethnographic texts from a different angle, that of the writing itself. Geertz focused on the rhetorical strategies used to construct ethnographic texts and endow them with authority: "[Anthropologists'] capacity to convince us that what they say is a result of their having actually penetrated (or, if you prefer, been penetrated by) another form of life . . . is where the writing comes in."[44] I focus here on the established genres of writing in anthropological ethnography, what opportunities exist for ethno-graphic theologians outside these genres, and what those opportunities may have to say back to anthropological ethnographers.

Geertz described a central challenge of ethnographic writing as one of wearing two hats at once: "how to sound like a pilgrim and a cartographer at the same time."[45] This challenge is about capturing both the experience of the fieldwork journey and mapping out in not entirely subjective terms what was discovered on this journey. John Van Maanen outlines three dominant genres of writing that anthropologists have used to confront and navigate this pilgrim-cartographer challenge: realist, confessional, and impressionistic, each of which is full of its own strategies and conventions.[46]

Realist ethnography assumes the voice "of a third-party scribe reporting directly on the life of the observed. . . . Authority rests largely on the unexpli-cated experience of the author in the setting and the 'feel' [he or she] has apparently developed for the time, place, and people."[47] Realist writing boasts a certain confidence that what is being reported and argued aligns closely with the way things really were and, through the rhetorical device of the ethno-graphic present, still are. Confessional ethnography "attempts to represent the fieldworker's participative presence in the studied scene. . . . It is necessarily a blurred account, combining a partial description of the culture alongside an equally partial description of the fieldwork experience itself."[48] Confessional writing invites the reader into the fieldwork process and the ethnographer's journey of discovery but ultimately pulls back in perspective to explain with the authority of having been there. For example, Geertz's essay, "Deep Play," widely cited by ethnographic theologians, all of whom seem devoted to the project of thick description,[49] begins in a confessional mode ("everything was

---

[43] James Clifford and George Marcus (eds), *Writing Culture: The Poetics and Politics of Ethnography* (Berkeley: University of California Press, 1986). Far more than the main chapters, Clifford's introduction is cited throughout the ethnographic theology literature.

[44] Clifford Geertz, *Works and Lives: The Anthropologist as Author* (Stanford: Stanford University Press, 1988), 4–5.

[45] Ibid., 10.

[46] John Van Maanen, *Tales of the Field: On Writing Ethnography* (Chicago: University of Chicago Press, 1988).

[47] Ibid., 64.   [48] Ibid., 91.   [49] See Martyn Percy, Chapter 17, 296–314.

dust and panic"). It then pivots sharply to a realist account of what the Balinese cockfight symbolizes and how its performance is a lived expression of shared meaning ("a story they tell themselves about themselves").[50] Finally, impressionist ethnography highlights "the episodic, complex, and ambivalent realities that are frozen and perhaps made too pat and ordered by realist or confessional conventions.... They attempt to be as hesitant and open to contingency and interpretation as the concrete social experiences on which they are based."[51] Use of the ethnographic representation as a mirror for the utterly complex, messy, contested, ambiguous, and uncertain nature of social life and cultural reality brings about the authenticity of the impressionist text.

Van Maanen observes that these three genres exist side by side in contemporary anthropology, each satisfying distinct purposes, and that they do not exhaust our representational possibilities. Establishing these genres as legitimate has been hard-won by many anthropologists over many years, and they serve the discipline well. The provocation I want to offer ethnographic theologians is that it would be a mistake to simply adopt these genres as delimiting the range of representational possibilities given their distinctive ends (as they have directly adopted particular methodological practices, such as Wacquant's observant participation and the classic model of fieldwork). As ethnographic theologians continue to translate their ethnographic material into essays, articles, books, and, perhaps soon, a documentary film, I urge them to confront the problem of representation using the ethical and semiotic resources that derive from their own deep well of tradition.

Realist, confessional, and impressionist ethnographic writing differ in their conventions, but they all face the same direction. They all aim to address social, cultural, and experiential truths. Anthropologists excel at disagreeing about the defining object of their discipline. For some it remains culture, though this focus splits in numerous directions, from Boasian historical particularism to Geertzian interpretive anthropology to materialist conceptions, and so on. For others, it is the power-laden dialectic of structural conditions and agentive action. For others, it is phenomenological experience.[52] Most recently, many anthropologists have become enthralled with the ontological turn. While ethnographic theologians may be deeply influenced by a cultural turn, their *telos* is not social theorizing. Their *telos* is the revelation of Truth, as it is experienced, negotiated, questioned, taught, learned, doubted, and lived in practice. Their authorial imagination should be calibrated to match.

As a non-theologian who has spent a fair bit of time listening to everyday and academic theologians, a few possibilities come to mind. What if ethnographic theology was written as a form of witnessing? How would a vignette

---

[50] Clifford Geertz, "Deep Play: Notes on the Balinese Cockfight," *Daedalus* 134/4 (1972): 56–86.
[51] Van Maanen, *Tales of the Field*, 119.   [52] See Don Seeman, Chapter 19, 336–54.

sound if it was pitched as a rebuke? What would be different about recounted field notes if they took the form of a Christian confession? How might the ethnographic theologian channel their prophetic voice as they analyze an interview or speech event transcript? What would be the performative force of writing ethnography as prayer? Witnessing, rebuke, confession, prophecy, prayer—how could these discursive genres become representational genres for ethnographic writing, and how would they shape the organization of a book, the pitch of an argument, the choice of which fieldwork story to share, which quote to use as illustrative data, and how to present the complexities of a life?

What is most striking to me about these writing possibilities and questions, as an anthropological ethnographer, is how they are off limits to me and those in my field (i.e., What *would* a flagship journal in anthropology say about an ethnographic manuscript submitted as a prayer?). This returns me to the observation about seeking a normative vision in anthropological ethnography. While these particular Christian genres may not instigate the next big wave in anthropological ethnography, perhaps their use by ethnographic theologians can inspire us to imagine new possibilities for being both pilgrim and cartographer. Perhaps through shared problems, such as engaging and representing Selves and Others, an ethnographic dialogue between anthropologists and theologians can blossom.

9

Anthropology, Theology, and the Problem of Incommensurability

Jon Bialecki

In this volume, we are tasked with a particular question: How can theology contribute to anthropology? The question seems ripe. Numerous people are asking various iterations of it. Examples include last decade's explosion of work engaging both *political theology* and Karl Schmitt, Joel Robbins' essay on the awkward relationship between theology and anthropology, Michael Banner's attempt to reconfigure the discipline of moral theology, the 2013 special issue of the *Australian Journal of Anthropology* focusing on anthropological theologies, and Meneses et al.'s article arguing for a theological voice within anthropological debates.[1] However, most of these works have an aspirational or subjunctive edge. Robbins has argued that anthropology and theology are most productive when they are "preoccupied not with seeking agreement, but with registering... the differences" between the two fields.[2] Similarly, Michael Lambek has suggested that there is a core "incommensurability" between the theological/religious and the anthropological,[3] and anthropologist Matthew Engelke has suggested that any achievement of commensurability between

---

[1] Karl Schmitt, *Political Theology: Four Chapters on the Concept of Sovereign* (Cambridge, MA: MIT Press, 1985); Joel Robbins, "Anthropology and Theology: An Awkward Relationship?" *Anthropological Quarterly* 79/2 (2005): 285–94; Michael C. Banner, *The Ethics of Everyday Life: Moral Theology, Social Anthropology, and the Imagination of the Human* (Oxford: Oxford University Press, 2014); Eloise Meneses, Lindy Backues, David Bronkema, Eric Flett, and Benjamin L. Hartley, "Engaging the Religiously Committed Other: Anthropologists and Theologians in Dialogue," *Current Anthropology* 55/1 (2014): 82–104; Philip Fountain and Sin Wen Lau, "Anthropological Theologies: Engagements and Encounters," *Australian Journal of Anthropology* 24/3 (2013): 227–34.

[2] Joel Robbins, "Afterword: Let's Keep It Awkward: Anthropology, Theology, and Otherness," *Australian Journal of Anthropology* 24/3 (2013): 329–37 (336 here).

[3] Michael Lambek, "Facing Religion, From Anthropology," *Anthropology of this Century* 4 (May 2012), <http://aotcpress.com/articles/facing-religion-anthropology/>.

the two fields would leave both of them the weaker for it.[4] This hesitancy comes from theology as well. While theologians such as Hans Frei see a similitude between anthropology and theology,[5] Milbank argues that a long-running unidirectional attempt by academic theology to forge a rapprochement with the social sciences has denatured and emaciated theology.[6] In anthropology as well, some complain that theology already has too much influence on anthropology; they would point to definitions that make *religion* a counting noun or definitions that are based on a voluntaristic mental assertion or propositional endorsement.[7] Both these concepts are, according to critics, too Christian already.

However, we should be careful to say that these are necessarily theological ideas. They may be Christian ideas, but Christianity is not the same as theology. After all, up until the thirteenth century, for the most part Christianity was happy enough to go without theology, seeing it as a pagan category.[8] I think a refusal to conflate Christianity with theology is important if we want to talk about the relation between theology and anthropology. If we are talking about the exertion of theological influence on anthropology, then we have to have some delineation of each field. Such delineations also help us make a *true* encounter with theology, as opposed to merely a misunderstanding. Absent a true encounter with theology (even if it is a true encounter that goes a different direction than theology would mandate on its own), this exercise is pointless; it would be no better than a cross-fertilization with any discipline, chosen just to produce randomizing effects.

A true encounter between the two disciplines can only occur if that encounter is mediated by some third term or field, but it cannot be a term or field that is ontologically constituted in the same way that anthropology or theology

---

[4] Matthew Engelke, "Exchanging Words: Anthropology and Theology," plenary talk, Anthropology and Enlightenment Association of Social Anthropologists of the UK and Commonwealth Decennial Conference, Edinburgh, UK, June 21, 2014.

[5] Hans W. Frei, *Types of Christian Theology* (New Haven, CT: Yale University Press, 1992).

[6] John Milbank, *Theology and Social Theory: Beyond Secular Reason*, 2nd edn (Oxford: Blackwell Publishing, 2006).

[7] Jonathan Z. Smith, *Map Is Not Territory: Studies in the History of Religions* (Leiden: Brill, 1978); Malcolm Ruel, "Christians as Believers," in *Religious Organization and Religious Experience*, ed. John Davis (London: Academic Press, 1982), 9–31; Benson Saler, "Religio and the Definition of Religion," *Cultural Anthropology* 2/3 (1987): 395–9; Talal Asad, *Genealogies of Religion: Discipline and Reasons of Power in Christianity and Islam* (Baltimore, MD: Johns Hopkins University Press, 1993); Jonathan Z. Smith, "Religion, Religions, Religious," in *Critical Terms for Religious Studies*, ed. M. Taylor (Chicago: University of Chicago Press, 1998), 269–84; Tomoko Masuzawa, *The Invention of World Religions: Or, How European Universalism Was Preserved in the Language of Pluralism* (Chicago: University of Chicago Press, 2005); Galina Lindquist and Simon Coleman, "Introduction: Against Belief?" *Social Analysis* 52/1 (2008): 1–18; Brent Nongbri, *Before Religion: A History of a Modern Concept* (New Haven, CT: Yale University Press, 2013).

[8] Peter Harrison, *The Territories of Science and Religion* (Chicago: University of Chicago Press, 2015), 17.

is constituted. The mediation has to occur by having each discipline work back to a problematic. Rather than an encounter with some extant and concrete tradition, institution, or discourse, I am advocating for an encounter with the virtual in the sense deployed by Gilles Deleuze,[9] defined as a real but not actual generative problem. Such a move would also mean a shift in conceiving the projects of both theology and anthropology. We would both have to put aside the idea that we ourselves are studying others. Instead of imagining that we are engaged in second-order analysis, observing at a distance others who wrestle with some problem, we would see ourselves standing beside them, grappling with the same problems, albeit it realizing those problems in much different ways and under much different material and institutional circumstances. This approach may be a challenge for both disciplines, but it may be a much more bitter pill for anthropology. The reason that anthropology may find it less palatable is because this argument will suggest that while anthropology's practice is still valuable, the gap between anthropology and anthropology's informants that does so much psychic work in the discipline is only perspectival and fictive. To concretize what I am saying, I will close this chapter by discussing my fieldwork with religious transhumanists. Here, I will suggest that the plethora of different substantive and academic positions are not best understood through using specific articulated anthropological or theological propositions in order to make veridical statements about transhumanism and religion. Rather, we need to work back to the contours of the problem and, by doing so, map out the possibility spaces implicit in the issue.

I will begin by pointing out two framings of the anthropological–theological relation that we should avoid: origins-based genealogical accounts and universalisms. Both of these accounts are predicated on a denial of change and, hence, are roundabout ways of stating that our work here is already for naught because the relationship between the two systems is already set. I am not claiming that I can rule out either of these accounts completely, of course, or that they have no analytic value, but these accounts inevitably lead to pictures of anthropology and theology as static fields and, therefore, do little to help us understand and engage with the actual state of play in these disciplines.

First, the origins-genealogical account is seen at times both in theological critiques of anthropology and in anthropological accounts of the origins of the discipline of anthropology, such as the ones put forward by Pamela Klassen and John Milbank.[10] I want to be clear that I am not speaking of all forms of

---

[9] Gilles Deleuze, "The Actual and the Virtual," in *Dialogues II*, rev. edn, trans. Eliot Ross Albert (New York: Columbia University Press, 2002), 148–52; *Difference and Repetition* (New York: Columbia University Press, 1994).

[10] Pamela Klassen, "Christianity as a Polemical Concept," in *A Companion to the Anthropology of Religion*, ed. Janice Boddy and Michael Lambek (New York: John Wiley & Sons, 2013), 344–62; Milbank, *Theology and Social Theory*.

genealogical thought. Genealogical thinking, at least in its Foucauldian incarnation,[11] is about repeated and historical discontinuities in what appears to be the same concept; through charting how ideas have shifted over time, or come from unlikely sources that bear little resemblance to contemporary forms, the force and insistence of these ideas are relativized. While I will not address the issue here, I think that genealogical approaches, while not entirely unproblematic, are more or less benign. But the Foucauldian version of this approach is not the only form of genealogical thinking out there.

The forms of which we should be wary are genealogical claims that state that knowing about different earlier theological constellations or surprising foundations of anthropology in some ways give us a grasp of the contours of anthropological thought today. The underlying claim is almost always that since anthropology had its origins in theological anthropology, its horizons of thought are, therefore, inescapably theological. The first problem with this reasoning is the assumption that origins control outcomes. If origins do control, then how does one account for the obvious shifts in the kind of questions a secular sociocultural anthropology asks? Here, we are not talking about the fact that anthropology has changed in relation to its supposed theological origins, since that is the very proposition that is being questioned. Rather, we are talking about the fact that anthropology has self-differed over its career as an autonomous secular discipline, with these differences situated both diachronically (i.e., disciplinary development over time) and synchronically (i.e., differences within the discipline). Such a range of variation suggests that no single historical moment can be completely controlling, since such control would result in a historically monologic discipline, in the Bakhtinian sense: a discipline where no debate or conversation can occur.[12] Monologic seems to be a poor descriptor for either discipline. Of course, I might suggest that theology and anthropology have moved in lockstep with each other. Such a suggestion would not account for the original divergence between theology and anthropology, though, but even more worrisome for this project is that absent some mechanisms that would allow for theological institutions and discourse to continue to control anthropological institutions and discourse, changes in both disciples are epiphenomenal, a function of or response to some other more expansive factor, such as secularism, capitalism, epistemes, or the world-spirit. If some other force or set of forces are controlling, though, then why are we monkeying around with anthropology and theology, which are mere effects?

---

[11] Michel Foucault, "Nietzsche, Genealogy, History," in *Essential Works*, vol. 2, ed. James Faubion (New York: The New Press, 1998), 369–91.

[12] M. M. Bakhtin and Michael Holquist, *The Dialogic Imagination: Four Essays* (Austin: University of Texas Press, 1981); Matt Tomlinson, *Ritual Textuality: Pattern and Motion in Performance* (New York: Oxford University Press, 2014).

We can see elements of some of the difficulties with genealogy in both Timothy Larsen and Daniel J. King's and Khaled Furani's otherwise excellent contributions to this book.[13] Furani's genealogical investigation of anthropology, for all its perspicuity, erases the fact that in its original early twentieth-century actualizations, culture was a polysemous, capacious, and disputed term,[14] which troubles any account that would see culture as a reified idol. Furani's account also obscures other modern anthropologies such as the structuralism of Claude Levi-Strauss. Levi-Strauss, of course, was famous for his statement that the goal of anthropology as a "Human Science [is] not to constitute, but dissolve man."[15] This quote hardly reads as a humanist manifesto. Furani's account, of course, does not stand or fall on these points, but we can see strands of the monological tendency in critical anthropological genealogy that is so concerning. We see something similar in Larsen and King's careful historical excavation of anthropology's forgotten polygenetic tendencies. The difference here is that the monologic force falls on evangelicalism and not anthropology. Evangelical theological dalliances with polygenesis are excluded.[16] Polygenesis was never the dominant evangelical account, and, of course, later generations of British and American evangelicals would come to see polygenesis as heretical even as it persisted in groups such as the British Israelite movement. However, this determination of heterodoxy was a subsequent normative judgment and not a map of the potential forms of evangelical thought on human origins that existed in a previous dispensation. The full range of evangelical thought is worthy of note because the ethical charge of Larsen and King's argument is a little different if one realizes that polygenesis is as much a historical evangelical conceptual possibility as it was an anthropological one.

The second suspect account is any narrative that allows for either or both a universal theological and/or anthropological faculty. This class of suspect narratives includes claims about implicit or ethno-theology. These claims are suspect because any such account either effectively says nothing, forecloses change, or is corrosive of theology and anthropology as distinct historically situated disciplines. It risks saying nothing in that, if it admits diversity and change, saying that everyone had a theology, it becomes what Geertz, following Krober, called an empty universal, a vapid statement along the lines of "everyone takes shelter" or "everyone has a kinship system."[17] These claims, even if true, tell us nothing

---

[13] Timothy Larsen and Daniel J. King, Chapter 3, 50–65; Khaled Furani, Chapter 4, 66–82.

[14] Robert Brightman, "Forget Culture: Replacement, Transcendence, Relexification," *Cultural Anthropology* 10/4 (1995): 509–46.

[15] Claude Lévi-Strauss, *The Savage Mind* (Chicago: University of Chicago Press, 1966).

[16] See Gideon Mailer, "Between Enlightenment and Evangelicalism: Presbyterian Diversity and American Slavery," in *Faith and Slavery in the Presbyterian Diaspora*, ed. William Harrison Taylor and Peter C. Messer (Bethlehem, PA: Lehigh University Press, 2016), 54.

[17] Clifford Geertz, *The Interpretation of Cultures: Selected Essays* (New York: Basic Books, 1973), 39.

inasmuch as shelter and kinship can vary to a wild degree, and so, presumably, granting everyone a theology and an anthropology would tell us nothing about any specific ethno-theology or ethno-anthropology.

Mandating substantive or formal universals also eviscerates the historical development of theology and anthropology. Such a move also makes it difficult to differentiate theology or anthropology as a discipline from lay attempts to think through difference, not just in other societies but in our society, as well. While I am not saying that one is inevitably superior to the other, there seem to be important differences between academic and non-academic modes of thought: I would like to say that my professionalized anthropological thought has capacities different from the lay anthropology of, say, Donald Trump. Meaningfully specific claims regarding ethno- or implicit theology, though, would make this claim untenable.

This difference in organization and capacities does not mean that there will not be instances where there is some relation between academic theology and what we would want to call ethno- or implicit theology—or what I would prefer to call simply *religion* or *thinking about religion*. In instances where we do see a logic of resemblance, we should not look to ideational systems but to other mechanisms, such as media distribution, denominational forms of power, or particular strategic and tactical reasons from people to accept theological statements as authoritative or, alternately, reasons why a theologian might want to speak authoritatively on the behalf of lay members and denominational bodies. This account of isomorphism between lay and academic understandings is, in a sense, the Foucauldian language of power, but we should not take this account to mean that we are discussing something sinister or necessarily done in bad faith. As recent work in the anthropology of religion and ethics has been arguing for almost a decade and a half now,[18] sincere religious motivations are a perfectly rational explanation for people to produce and submit to power relations that shape their subjectivity. We should understand such relations through causal lenses and not through lenses of representation or through an already given commonality of thought.

*   *   *

So how are we to think of these two fields, then? Two mutually exclusive possible framings are left to us, and I would like to argue for both of them. When making a choice between a particularism of pure difference and a commonality, though not a universalism, that joins them all, we should respond by saying yes to both.

---

[18] See, for example, Michael Lambek (ed.), *Ordinary Ethics: Anthropology, Language, and Action* (New York: Fordham University, 2010); James D. Faubin, *The Anthropology of Ethics* (Cambridge: Cambridge University Press, 2011); Saba Mahmood, *Politics of Piety: The Islamic Revival and the Feminist Subject* (Princeton: Princeton University Press, 2005); and Talal Asad, *Genealogies of Religion: Discipline and Reasons of Power in Christianity and Islam* (Baltimore, MD: Johns Hopkins University Press, 2009).

To see how this is possible, we should begin by describing each option, starting with pure particularism. Particularism follows from our discussion of the relation between academic theology and lay attempts at thinking about religion. If we are to be as particular as possible, we need to think of all the contingent specificities and have a robust sociology of knowledge. Specifically, I suggest we borrow the kind of hyper-empiricist techniques similar to actor–network theory. Such an approach would not consider theology as a practice in the abstract but ask what sort of different institutions are sites for the production of theology and further ask what effects funding, communication technologies, and nodes of intellectual and material redistribution have. Similar work can be done with anthropology. I think that making this claim about the nature of specific disciplines being an expression of a multiplicity of concrete arrangements should not be very controversial. A wide body of literature analyzing college and university-level education and scholarship production in just this mode already exists,[19] and the rather dull way that this literature reads should show us how unchallenging these statements are.

I would like to focus on what this picture of disciplines as being shaped entirely by specific difference means for the reception of theological material by anthropology. A particularist reading would necessitate questioning the concept of the transparent porting of ideational material from one discipline to the other, as the differences between specific assemblages of concrete material, institutional structures, and individuated subjects would mean that ideas from one domain would be received in very different ways in another and would be put to different uses. For Bruno Latour, who has given the most thought to accounts that focus on specific and particular networks of mixed forces, no such thing as transparent communication exists. Exchanges between one actor and another, human or otherwise, are always instances of translation because the specificity of context can never be recreated. This is translation in the "traduttore, traditore" sense of things.[20]

Given the broad epistemic, orientational, and material-organizational gulfs between theology and anthropology, we would never have any understanding of one term in another. We would only have misunderstandings, instances where the contours of ideational material operate to different effect because they are now resituated in a different ecology. Misunderstandings are not necessarily a bad thing; there is always the possibility of creative and productive misuses, and many might claim that I am engaged in a great deal of creative misreading here.

---

[19] See, for example, Tara Fenwick and Richard Edwards (eds), *Researching Education through Actor–Network Theory* (New York: John Wiley & Sons, 2012).

[20] Bruno Latour, "Reassembling the Social: An Introduction to Actor–Network Theory" (Oxford: Oxford University Press, 2005); *We Have Never Been Modern* (Cambridge, MA: Harvard University Press, 1993).

However, there is also the possibility of misunderstandings that are actually corrosive, resulting from moments when the gulf between theology and anthropology is too great. At this point, a concrete example might help. Meneses et al.'s groundbreaking but troubling article has both proximate and far-reaching goals. The ultimate goal is to demonstrate the anthropological value of theology, which is presented as having been foreclosed by a secular anthropology. The proximate goal, though, is simply to make space for theological thought. The chief complaint here is that theological ideational material is automatically precluded from consideration in anthropological discourse. They write, "We must be willing to engage in the project of understanding humanity by refraining from preemptively privileging any one perspective over the others,"[21] suggesting that every form of thought should be on the anthropological table.

If we presume a certain autonomy to theology and anthropology, and also presume that they are different activities engaged in different projects, as Robbins argues, then at the level of explicit content, complaints about a lack of engagement by anthropology are not unlike a botanist complaining that his or her explanations are not welcome in discussions of nuclear physics or literature. The question is not whether there is only one frame of reference. Rather, the question is whether theological framings are best suited for theology as an institution and anthropological framings best suited for anthropology.

This is not to say that attempts at importing theological material in anthropology are disallowed; I am not volunteering anyone for the role of border guard. The question is what risks of decoherence come from these attempts at importation and deterritorialization. Deterritorialization's effects are visible when we discuss Meneses et al.'s exemplar, which is what a theological turn could offer the anthropological study of violence. For Meneses et al., violence is understood theologically as occurring when humans have "fearfully, pridefully, and willfully abused [the] power [of their] dominion over the earth."[22] Meneses et al.'s etiology of violence suggests that social orders are human constructions and thus asks, "What then in human beings is the origin source of the problem?"[23] This question, of course, is a confusion of structural and temporal causation: Even if human collectivities presuppose the existence of individual humans, there were never humans outside of society initially instituting such an order. This conflation of structural and temporal causation results in a sundering of the self from social formation. Quoting the theologian Miroslav Volf, Meneses et al. indicate that the question is, "What kind of selves do we need?"[24] This approach forecloses our asking about other possibilities, such as inquiring about different social formations or articulation of justice.

---

[21] Meneses et al., *Engaging the Religiously Committed Other*, 85.   [22] Ibid., 87.
[23] Ibid.   [24] Ibid., 88.

This framing also leaves us with no explanation for regularities and patterns in the distribution of violence. We are told that the cure for violence is our "recover[ing] the image of God within us." Does this mean that there is a one-to-one correlation between a lack of recognition of an internal image of God and violence? What do we make of traditionally Christian populations where there were protracted periods of ethnic violence, such as Northern Ireland? Are we to say that they were not truly Christians? If so, should it be the ethnographer who makes this judgment? This approach also has the potential to come across as a bit of a card trick: Whenever anything negative occurs, it is labeled as not being Christian, while only positive events are acknowledged as Christian. This prevents any kind of Christian ownership of a legacy of what is, like every other legacy, a mixed inheritance. Further, what are we to make of non-Christian areas that have no history of the ethnic or genocidal violence discussed by Meneses et al.? It may be that Meneses et al. would say that a lack of the image of God results in some social pathology but not necessarily that of violence. If this is the case, then there must be some other controlling variable; therefore, we cannot see violence as a direct and unmediated expression of a lack of an internalized and recognized image of God.

We are left with a situation where a universal—humanity's fallen nature and rejection of the image of God—results in specific and situated acts of violence. Further, we have social processes such as collective violence falling to the level of responsible individuals. This claim may be right. It could be that there is a universal lack that can only be remedied by developing an affective and ethical acceptance of a particular historical superhuman figure who, even today, is not known worldwide, but this hypothetical universal lack tells us nothing on a case-by-case basis about the social relations that result from and control the expression of this supposed spiritual injury. We have no way to talk about the varieties and variance of violence, and all this is also putting aside the question of asking how an anthropologist is supposed to know the correct theological approaches to employ.

This is not a claim that there is no such thing as anthropology from a Christian vantage; there clearly can be anthropology that is informed by Christian sensibilities,[25] just as there can be Christian practice that is influenced or informed by anthropological sensibilities.[26] All that is being said here is that propositions

---

[25] Matthew Engelke, "The Problem of Belief: Evans-Pritchard and Victor Turner on the Inner Life," *Anthropology Today* 18/6 (2002): 3–8; Brian M. Howell, "The Repugnant Cultural Other Speaks Back: Christian Identity as Ethnographic 'Standpoint,'" *Anthropological Theory* 7/4 (2007): 371–91; Timothy Larsen, *The Slain God: Anthropology and the Christian Faith* (Oxford: Oxford University Press, 2014).

[26] Brian M. Howell, "Anthropology and the Making of Billy Graham: Evangelicalism and Anthropology in the 20th-Century United States," *American Anthropologist* 117/1 (2015): 59–73.

formed by particular and historically situated disciplines cannot translate freely. Meneses et al.'s claims regarding humanity's fallen nature are perfectly cogent propositions within theology, but translated into anthropological discourse, the intelligibility breaks down.

*   *   *

There are three ways forward. One is simply not to care about the incommensurability between the two fields. Here, theological and anthropological concepts would be in a double capture, which is the "misunderstanding" framework discussed previously. As that discussion suggests, misunderstanding is not always productive.

Another way would be for anthropology and theology to be so deeply engaged in an exchange that either one field mutates due to the injection of cognitive material from the other or theological and anthropological material passes through the process of mutual misunderstanding and an emergent sense of its own develops as a third system. It is hard to extrapolate from the present moment what such a new field would be like. Built upon mutual misunderstandings, neither the anthropological nor theological elements would function as they did in their source domains, and there would likely be many novel conceptual bridges and workarounds that would be informed by the crises and logics of this still-only-hypothetical third field. It is even not quite certain what its putative object would be, or what it would look like, though one might imagine that Michael Banner's recent book could be a step in that direction.[27] The (hypothetical) development of a third system is one of those experiments where the only way to have an understanding of what the result could be is to undergo the process itself, to participate in its collective unfolding over real time.

For those who prefer leaps to careful tinkering, there is a way to overcome the incommensurability between theology and anthropology: to use incommensurability productively. We do this by approaching both theology and anthropology through a third term with which they have a shared relation. The seemingly natural choice for a third term would be *people engaging in religion*. We could think of both theology and anthropology as sharing what we might call a second-order relation with things such as God, ritual, and ethics. The interest that they have, particularly in the case of anthropology, is not in a fully endorsing, participatory, and uncritical response to these issues; rather, anthropology and theology are in the business of presenting commentary and critique of some other group's activity.

If pressed, though, this framing is less solid than it seems. It assumes that critique and skepticism are things that follow religion, rather than being something that can co-occur or even precede it, and that the people doing

---

[27] Banner, *The Ethics of Everyday Life.*

religion are not themselves self-reflective about this process.[28] This seems untenable, as well as a back door to privileging a certain kind of modernist Protestant sincerity.[29] Here, there are those who really are doing the activity, and then there is us. The Protestant assumption, of course, is that *really doing* the activity is the essence of the activity, and that non-endorsement or participation without assent does not itself constitute having a meaningful and important relationship. This is not necessarily true. We could imagine a situation where participation, or even belief, is outsourced to some other party as a part of the division of labor in a society structured along the lines of organic solidarity. Some might even say that we have that very relationship in the anthropology of religion already: Secular anthropologists have others do religion for them so that they do not have to participate yet can still exist in a religious space.

If theology and anthropology are *about* some other first-order practice, then we return to many of the same issues we had when we were discussing the mutual incommensurability of anthropology and theology. There is the problem of resemblance. If the theological and anthropological projects are *about* some other shared object, then we can have differing degrees of fidelity to the project, which means that the same difficulty we have in judging anthropology and theology is now just carried over to judging how they relate to the third term. If we are to engage in that work, from what vantage point do we do it? If we do it from the space of peoples and practices that are the object of anthropology and theology, then we are assuming a complete self-transparency for this group and that they can understand themselves enough to state that other understandings also understand them, or do not. However, if there was a complete self-transparency, or at least sufficient self-transparency for carrying out this kind of judgment, again why are we mucking around with theology and anthropology, when we could just direct our questions to this group? Theology and anthropology, if they are about a people or a practice, presume that they can unveil knowledge that the people could not produce about themselves. This is not an absolute statement, as there will be many areas, and perhaps most areas, where the people who are the object of study know more about themselves than those who are interrogating them. Nevertheless, there will always be the possibility that anthropology or theology could, perhaps in some cases, produce knowledge about certain elements of the group that the group cannot. Therefore, the people cannot be the judge, or at least not the sole judge, of the sufficiency of the knowledge contained by the two disciplines.

[28] Matthew Engelke, "Secular Shadows: African, Immanent, Post-Colonial," *Critical Research on Religion* 3/1 (2015): 86–100.
[29] Webb Keane, *Christian Moderns: Freedom and Fetish in the Mission Encounter* (Berkeley: University of California Press, 2007).

At the same time, we cannot have anthropology be the judge either because one of two things will happen. Either it will simply endorse its own reasoning because it is its own reasoning, or, if its judgment favors theology, it will automatically endorse it, vitiating not just its own value but also the value of anthropology's determination that theology exceeds anthropology. If anthropology reasons that the reasoning of some other group is better, then the reasoning behind that very anthropological determination places anthropological reasoning into question. The option of turning to an exterior judge is no better, as we will then have one of two problems. Either the new judge is mutually incommensurable with both anthropology and theology, and then we have the same set of problems as when we were weighting anthropology and theology together but now with four players on the field, instead of simply one. Or alternately, the new judge will favor one term over the other by way of a preexisting intellectual similarity or kinship. That preexisting similarity or kinship would suggest the game is rigged.

The real difficulty underlying this challenge of adjudication is with the system of representation and identity as a framework. This difficulty is capable of being framed as either an epistemological or ontological problem. We can understand this challenge in a neo-Kantian way as being about an impossibility of having certain knowledge due to issues concerning discipline-derived heuristics, or we can see it as being about the impossibly of an absolute knowledge due to metaphysical causes. Either way, the result is the same. Whenever we try to adjudicate the differing degrees of identity that representations from the two different disciplines have with a third object, we lose our moorings.

This is only an issue, though, if we think of the third term as having definite contours. If we chose a third term that was not a fixed demographic set or a definable set of practices or preferences, not a particular ethnos, praxis, or (to mix Greek and Latin) religio, we could frame it as a generative problem that subsists under and occasions these things.

Focusing on a shared problematic would be a way of having some consistency. We can see a common, fixed, and determining object, but because a problem is by definition predicated on a certain incommensurability and engenders differential and incompatible resolutions, we should not expect all the responses to be the same. In other words, if we assume that the problem is not "the problem of adequately representing or decoding an ethnos/praxis/religio" but something else, some other problem, then we can put judgment aside. If the proper problem is not the problem of adequate representation, though, then one wonders what it is and how to maintain a tie to a particular population studied if it is also denied representation. Obviously, anthropology and ethnography are usually not concerned with a *whatever-anthropos* but with particular, definable groupings, and theology is not just about a *whatever-theos* but about particular traditions, rites, texts, divine personages, and religious polities. Such specific ties can be maintained if we say that, at least when properly articulated, the problem is not the problem of representing a human collectivity or object but is the same problem with which the particular human collectivity or object itself is wrestling or from which it comes, depending on the perspectival question of whether the object in a specific case seems to lead to or follow as a result of the problem. The problems of our informants, in all of their particularity, are our problems as well, and when our problems are well chosen, the reverse is also true.

What I am putting forward here may seem to be a difficult claim. Can we say that a scholarly essay or monograph is the same as, say, doing a ritual, engaging in a practice, or holding a belief? Even more to the point, what kind of knowledge is being produced by way of this academic production, if it is not a representation? The second issue helps us understand the first, but only if we focus on the temporality of the problem, or rather temporalities, because problems partake in two temporalities. The first temporality is the moment of its occurrence: It arises as a specific historical juncture where it insists to the degree that it is pressing for the people that hold it. If we see problems as a set of interlinking hypothetical relations, we can see that, in another sense, they are always already there, in the same way that abstract mathematical forms can be said to exist, even if no one is working with them, or if they have not even been conceived yet.[30] Like mathematical forms, we can be working with a problem and still not grasp its full contours.

Also like mathematical forms, these problems-as-relations are never encountered directly; we only see specific and particular instantiations of them. All realizations are equal in the sense that they are all expressions of the problem as compared to a mathematical equation with open variables where different values will result in different formations. However, this equality does not necessitate a similarity or identity of capacities of each realization of the problem. Some realizations will be such that they will be easier to use to work back to the underlying set of relations that constitutes the problem in the ahistorical sense of the term.

This lack of identity in the various realizations is the key to understanding the value of academic approaches to the problem. Academic approaches are actualizations of the problem carried out in restricted ontological strata: Rather than being full, embodied realizations of the problem, they are ideational and discursive realizations, even if certain material and institutional arrangements are necessary to produce work in this restricted key and if every realization of the problem will have certain *disciplinary* features as a result of specificity of these necessary supplements. Because of these historical–disciplinary effects, certain aspects in the realization of the problem will be

---

[30] See the discussion of Chronos and Aion in Gilles Deleuze, *The Logic of Sense* (New York: Columbia University Press, 1990).

hyper-cognized, and others will barely be expressed. But this should be expected. Any expression of the problem that is sensually encountered will not be complete but only a particular expression of the problem: It will always be a historically specific version because every expression of the problem is historically specific.[31] However, because of the restricted manner in which they are expressed, academic expressions of the problem can be closer to the underlying and underdetermined problematic. Therefore, it is easier to work back to the problem when it is articulated in a scholastic mode.

Problems never come alone. They have all sorts of potential lateral ties to other problems that are revealed by various actualizations, and problems themselves come with different degrees of resolution and can be taken up in ways that either dilate or contract them. Disciplinary conversations run from problem to problem, and some conversations may float suspended between two problems. This conflation or suspension might be so insistent in some cases that the contours of a single distinct problem may never come to the fore. Therefore, we would not expect that anthropology and theology would consistently share the same set of problems across the board or take them up at the same level of resolution. Even when talking about the same putative object, they may, in fact, be taking up different problems, as putative objects can be grappling with multiple challenges. When they are working on the same problem, it is possible to work back to the intersecting forces and relations that constitute the problem and that are actualized in different ways by anthropology and theology and also by those who are usually understood as being the object of analysis but who are actually colleagues, working through the problems in different media, in different manners and scales.

* * *

What does this look like in practice? I would like to close by briefly walking through an example: religion and transhumanism. This confluence is a productive exemplar to think through because it prismatically produces a host of different crystallized reactions, giving us an opportunity to see how various parties, academic and otherwise, react. And building from this example, it is even possible to take small steps to counter-effectuate the various reactions—that is, to work back to the structuring but indeterminate underlying constellation of forces or, in other words, to work back to the problem.

Transhumanism, along with a series of other concepts and identifiers, such as extropianism and the singularity, is a way of talking about what many perceive to be an immanent world-historical tipping point in the technical development of the species. The idea is that rapidly expanding technologies such as bioengineering, nanotech, genomics, cryonics, and information technology, particularly artificial intelligence, hold the prospect to transform our

---

[31] Asad, *Genealogies of Religion.*

nature effectively to an extent theretofore unheralded in the history and prehistory of humanity. It is mostly but not exclusively a white, male, and American concern and has proximate roots in the confluence of a series of unlikely groups: the 1960s counterculture, the US military's Defense Advanced Research Projects Agency, Oxford philosophers, science fiction authors, and Silicon Valley.

These roots are merely proximate because this current wave of transhumanism is just the last iteration of a larger idea. While we can find all sorts of historical moments that have resonances with transhumanism, such as Benjamin Franklin's desire to be pickled in Madeira wine so that he could be scientifically resurrected after sufficient advances in technology, the term transhumanism is generally traced to Julian Huxley, who is supposed to have first coined it sometime in the first half of the twentieth century.[32] But there are other instances of what we might call lexical prior art. For instance, the same term can also be found in an 1814 English translation of Dante's *Divine Comedy*. What is interesting here is that the section of Dante being translated was a portion of the "Paradiso" where Dante was referencing St Paul's discussion in 2 Corinthians 12 of being caught up to the third heaven.[33]

I mention these religious precursors because they point to a specific ambiguity in the transhumanist project: Is this technological surpassing of the human a religious concept? For most self-identified transhumanists, the answer appears to be no. The *singularity*, the name used for the transhumanist tipping point, is often referred to as "the rapture of the nerds," but among many of the people who are most invested in the concept, it is a resolutely secular concept and often one that has New Atheist resonances.[34] An example can be seen in Zoltan Istvan, an author, volcano surfer, self-proclaimed philosopher, and 2016 presidential candidate of the American Transhumanist Party. Istvan has repeatedly identified religion as an intolerable block to progress, and his fictional narrative/manifesto *The Transhumanist Wager* ends in what can only be called a cultural genocide, where all religious writing and religious material culture worldwide is purposefully and systematically destroyed.[35]

Most secular transhumanists have less extreme visions, but still, not unlike classical secularization theorists, they do not expect religion to be a part of the future. The usual reason given is that religion will inevitably be understood as a form of unreason and as an instigator of bias and violence, which brings a

---

[32] Nicholas Bostrom, "A History of Transhumanist Thought," *Journal of Evolution and Technology* 14/1 (2005): 1–25.

[33] Peter Harrison and Joseph Wolyniak, "The History of Transhumanism," *Notes and Queries* 62/3 (2015): 465–7, doi: 10.1093/notesj/gjv080.

[34] R. U. Sirius and Jay Cornell, *Transcendence: The Disinformation Encyclopedia of Transhumanism and the Singularity* (Newburyport: Red Wheel Weiser, 2015): 194–5; Cory Doctorow and Charles Stross, *Rapture of the Nerds* (New York: Tor, 2012).

[35] Zoltan Istvan, *The Transhumanist Wager* (Futurity Imagine Media, 2013).

twinge of irony to Istvan's account. The other major reason given is that religion is simply a less sophisticated analytic framework and, hence, will inevitably be abandoned for a more robust one as individuals find that transhumanist technologies can meet many of their needs, especially the need for some sort of immortality. Anthropological accounts see a definite gap between transhumanism and religion but understand this gap differently. Abou Farman is an anthropologist who has done serious and prolonged work with secular transhumanists. He sees this movement as a techno-scientific sublime that has been able to take up a space in the human imagination that has been traditionally ceded to religion. The withdrawal of religion's ability to make truth claims about cosmological events, in combination with the evacuation of the concept of the soul as the seat of the self, has allowed people to imagine themselves as plastic enough to transform themselves into technological entities that can eventually operate at a cosmological scale.[36]

Not everyone imagines the relation between transhumanism and religion as an overcoming or a succession. There is also a small but growing religious transhumanist community. The greatest expression of religious transhumanism is the almost decade-old, five-hundred-member-large Mormon Transhumanist Association (MTA), which stands at the center of my current research project. This group consists mostly of Mormons in good standing with the Latter Day Saints (LDS) but also includes a large number of ex-Mormons and Protestant Christians who share the group's interest in transhumanism and religion.

MTA conferences, meet-ups, and online discussion groups host numerous and sometimes contentious debates about the history, culture, politics, and leadership of the LDS. Despite this range of variance, there is a general feeling among MTA members that not only are transhumanism and religion compatible, but in some ways they necessitate each other. Many MTA members, in particular, see a close relationship between mainstream LDS doctrine and transhumanism. Lincoln Cannon, a founding member and former president of the LDS, has said on several occasions that not all transhumanists are Mormon but that all Mormons are transhumanists.[37]

---

[36] Abou Farman, "The Intelligent Universe," *Maisonneuve* 66 (2010): 36; "The Mode of Prediction," *Anthropology Now* 2/3 (2010): 89–94; "Re-Enchantment Cosmologies: Mastery and Obsolescence in an Intelligent Universe," *Anthropological Quarterly* 85/4 (2012): 1069–88; see also Ian Hacking, *Rewriting the Soul: Multiple Personality and the Sciences of Memory* (Princeton: Princeton University Press, 1995). Since writing this chapter, I have come across the work of Anya Bernstein on transhumanism and cosmism in Russia; I would have included her in this discussion had I known of her at the time I was composing this. See generally Anya Bernstein, "Freeze, Die, Come to Life: The Many Paths to Immortality in Post-Soviet Russia," *American Ethnologist* 42/4 (2015): 766–81; "Cyborgs, Weak Cosmists, and a Russian Planet," *NYU Jordan Center for the Advancement of Studying Russia* (2014), <http://jordanrussiacenter. org/news/cyborgs-weak-cosmists-russian-planet/#.V9b57ztWKHe>.
[37] Lincoln Cannon, "What is Mormon Transhumanism?" *Theology and Science* 13/2 (2015): 202–18 (here 213).

Statements such as this one can be made because Mormon religious thought and tradition contain many elements that are capable of being presented in what we might call a transhumanist key. Specific doctrines capable of trans-humanist rearticulation include the Mormon belief that *spirit* is simply a more refined form of nature, that natural laws precede rather than follow from God, and that miracles work through incredibly sophisticated divine technology rather than through breaks with the natural order. However, the concept of *theosis* is the idea that resonates most with Mormon transhumanism. It was central to nineteenth-century Mormonism, though its centrality has receded during the twentieth century as church leadership has engaged in an extended campaign to present itself being essentially in harmony with conservative Protestant theology.[38] This earlier idea of Godhead as a status that can be achieved through human effort, even if a righteous human effort guided by a divine hand, is often presented as the essential transhumanist idea. If miracles are technology that is unimaginably superior to current technology, then, according to Mormon transhumanists, incipient technological developments suggest that we are on the verge of performing miracles.

Among MTA members is a plasticity as to how these concepts are deployed. For some, these Mormon ideas are part of an apologetics or a speculative cosmology; these members tend to center their discussion on issues such as how God has used technology to create the current universe and the plan of salvation. For others, this is about Mormon values. For these believers, the MTA's center of gravity is how somewhat collectivist values harken back to nineteenth-century roots. These values would be used to mobilize society towards an ethical development of the sort of technical change imagined by transhumanism. Often this aspect of Mormon transhumanist thought is used to critique Silicon Valley and secular transhumanism, both of which are seen as libertarian and amoral. When Mormon transhumanism is deployed as mobilization or critique, it often stresses the inspirational and aspirational value of Mormon thought rather than its presumed veridical character. In conversation, MTA members leap between these frameworks, hopping quickly from techno-religious speculation to religion as shared aspirational ethical imperative. Importantly, a similar shifting pattern of emphasis can be identified in the much smaller and much more recent Christian Transhumanist Associ-ation (which is often referred to as the CTA).

These shifts from techno-religious speculation to ethical imperatives are as seemingly unconscious as they are common, though this shift is occasionally noticed and thematized by group members. One founding MTA member has tried to smooth over the disjuncture between a technical and inspirational

---

[38] Terryl Givens, *Wrestling the Angel: The Foundations of Mormon Thought: Cosmos, God, Humanity* (Oxford: Oxford University Press, 2015). O. Kendall White, Jr, *Mormon Neo-Orthodoxy: A Crisis Theology* (Salt Lake City, UT: Signature Books, 1987).

framework by referencing Paul Tillich's concept of "broken myths" in arguing for a purposeful interrogation and repurposing of the Mormon religious imagination.[39] Tillich has also been referenced in interviews with Christian transhumanists and is even occasionally referenced by secular transhumanists, though usually not those of the New Atheist strain. Other members of the CTA have loosely employed N. T. Wright in conversation, suggesting the open and processual aspects of his work can ground transhumanism as a theological concept. It is important to note two things about this invocation of theology. The theology being employed here is not theology as originally intended by the theologians. The technological resurrection being spoken of here is very different from the supernatural resurrection of the dead that Wright had in mind, and one theologically trained CTA member has suggested in conversation with me that transhumanist uses of Tillich "don't really understand him at all."[40] This is also not theology as an expression of lay belief; rather, this is a lay belief wrenching theology out of context to use it for different purposes in a different assemblage. This thought is not any worse for not being academic theology, but it is different.

If this body of thought is not theology, then it seems fair to ask what theology "proper" makes of transhumanism. With the MTA, at least, this question is complicated because it is not certain there is such a thing as Mormon theology. While the term *theology* was often used in nineteenth-century exegetical texts, such as Parley Pratt's *Key to the Science of Theology*,[41] what this word signifies in this context is not quite theology as it operates in Protestant or Roman Catholic institutional spaces. The importance of revelation, as well as the capacity for continuing authoritative revelation, limits the need for what might be called speculative Mormon theology, and even though the LDS is intensely hierarchical as far as governance goes, the fact that it operates under a system of the priesthood of all male believers to a large degree waters down the division of

---

[39] Carl Youngblood, "Demythologizing Mormonism," <www.scribd.com/document/211362143/Demythologizing-Mormonism>. Youngblood is drawing on Paul Tillich, *Dynamics of Faith* (New York: Harper & Row, 1958). It should be noted that while this paper was originally presented at an MTA annual conference, Youngblood's reading of Tillich has been discussed by Mormon public intellectuals without overly focusing on the transhumanist aspect of his argument. See Dan Wotherspoon, "The Positive Spiritual Effects of Disenchantment and Demythologizing," *Mormon Matters*, podcast audio, December 9, 2015, <www.mormonmatters.org/podcast-item/312-313-the-positive-spiritual-effects-of-disenchantment-and-demythologizing/>; James Patterson, "Carl Youngblood on Transhumanism and Mormon Myth-Breaking," *A Thoughtful Faith*, podcast audio, October 12, 2015, <www.athoughtfulfaith.org/carl-youngblood-on-transhumanism-and-mormon-myth-breaking/>.

[40] This assessment on the wider use of Tillich does not quite seem correct to me, but the fact that my judgment as an anthropologist is not in accord with the judgment of someone trained in academic theology merely serves to prove my overall point.

[41] Parley Pratt, *Key to the Science of Theology: Designed as an Introduction to the First Principles of Spiritual Philosophy, Religion, Law and Government, as Delivered by the Ancients, and as Restored in this Age, for the Final Development of Universal Peace, Truth and Knowledge* (Salt Lake City, UT: Deseret, 2015).

labor necessary for the production of a formal theology. As the Brigham Young University-endorsed *Mormon Encyclopedia* notes, much of what is called Mormon theology is actually better articulated as Mormon dogmatics.[42] That qualification of the term "theology" aside, though, influential and well-regarded LDS intellectuals who often write on subjects that one might understand as theological, such as Mormon religious intellectual history or the history of the early Mormon Church, do not dismiss the MTA. Both Terryl Givens and Richard Bushman have contributed to an edited volume presenting Mormon transhumanist thought,[43] and Adam Miller, another respected Mormon intellectual and apologist, has paid Mormon transhumanism the compliment of serious critique.[44]

Protestant and Catholic theological thinkers have taken different approaches. Roughly, they have four different reactions to transhumanism. In the first, theologians often propose Christian historical genealogies for transhumanism, referencing thinkers such as the Russian Orthodox Nikolai Fyodorovich Fyodorov or Pierre Teilhard de Chardin.[45] More ambitious genealogies also either reach further back to the Christian tradition in thinkers such as Francis Bacon, or, for the more recent but relatively obscure, they reference ideas such as the Jesuit theology of Karl Rahner.[46] The second reaction is to present a defense against the secular transhumanist/New Atheist critiques of religion. This move is often done not by claiming that religion is against transhumanism but that the divination of humanity as a consequence of the Incarnation is, in effect, transhumanism *avant le lettre* and, hence, suggests a structural instead of genealogical homology with religion.[47] These essays, which often conflate transhumanism with New Atheist thinkers such as Dawkins, are most often responses

---

[42] Daniel Ludlow (ed.), *Encyclopedia of Mormonism* (New York: Macmillan, 1992), 1475–6; see also Fenella Cannell, Chapter 14, 244–65.

[43] A. Scott Howe and Richard Bushman (eds), *Parallels and Convergences: Mormon Thought and Engineering Vision* (Salt Lake City, UT: Greg Kofford Books, 2012).

[44] Adam Miller, "Keynote: Why Suffering is Eternal and the Body is Forever," keynote address, Conference of the Mormon Transhumanist Association, Salt Lake City, UT, April 29, 2014, <www.youtube.com/watch?v=yVElI5FfcY8>.

[45] Michael Burdett, "Contextualizing a Christian Perspective on Transcendence and Human Enhancement: Francis Bacon, N. F. Fedorov, and Pierre Teilhard de Chardin," in *Transhumanism and Transcendence: Christian Hope in an Age of Technological Enhancement*, ed. Ronald Cole-Turner (Washington, DC: Georgetown University Press, 2011), 19–35; David Grummet, "Transformation and the End of Enhancement: Insights from Pierre Teilhard de Chardin," in *Transhumanism and Transcendence: Christian Hope in an Age of Technological Enhancement*, ed. Ronald Cole-Turner (Washington, DC: Georgetown University Press, 2011), 37–49.

[46] Burdett, "Contextualizing a Christian Perspective"; Ronald Cole-Turner, "Going beyond the Human: Christians and Other Transhumanists," *Theology and Science* 13/2 (2015): 150–61.

[47] Cole-Turner, "Going beyond the Human"; Brent Waters, *From Human to Posthuman: Christian Theology and Technology in a Postmodern World* (Aldershot, UK: Ashgate, 2006); see also Stephan Garner, "The Hopeful Cyborg," in *Transhumanism and Transcendence: Christian Hope in an Age of Technological Enhancement*, ed. Ronald Cole-Turner (Washington, DC: Georgetown University Press, 2011), 87–100, on Christianity as thematically hybrid/cyborg in nature.

to secular transhumanist claims that Christianity effectively endorses death, rebutting them by pointing to Christianity's healing mission and historical ties to the establishment of hospitals and other medical science institutions, or that Christianity's claim of current human finitude means that it is resolutely against individual or species betterment.[48] This second approach sometimes tacitly acknowledges value in transhumanist thought, even if it does not endorse it. This tendency to defend against or rebut secular transhumanist critique stands apart from a third approach, which is to, in turn, mount a robust critique of transhumanism. This critique is often centered on a supposed transhumanist indifference to the problem of evil, making the sorts of claims about finitude and mortality that other theologians refute in their engagements with transhumanism.[49] The final approach is to claim a current resonance or compatibility between Christianity and transhumanism by suggesting that transhumanism needs assistance from a Christian theological supplement or by arguing for a Christian transhumanism.[50]

[48] Todd Daly, "Chasing Methuselah: Transhumanism and Christian Theosis in Critical Perspective," in *Transhumanism and Transcendence: Christian Hope in an Age of Technological Enhancement*, ed. Ronald Cole-Turner (Washington, DC: Georgetown University Press, 2011), 131–4; Brian Patrick Green, "Transhumanism and Roman Catholicism: Imagined and Real Tensions," *Theology and Science* 13/2 (2015): 187–201; Nelson Kellogg, "Cybernetic Immortality and Its Discontents," *Theology and Science* 13/2 (2015): 162–74; Ted Peters, "Progress and Provolution: Will Transhumanism Leave Sin Behind?" in *Transhumanism and Transcendence: Christian Hope in an Age of Technological Enhancement*, ed. Ronald Cole-Turner (Washington, DC: Georgetown University Press, 2011), 63–86; "Theologians Testing Transhumanism," *Theology and Science* 13/2 (2015): 130–49; Brent Waters, *Christian Moral Theology in the Emerging Technoculture: From Posthuman Back to Human* (Aldershot, UK: Ashgate, 2014).

[49] Ronald Cole-Turner, "Going Beyond the Human: Christians and Other Transhumanists," *Theology and Science* 13/2 (2015): 150–61; Daly, "Chasing Methuselah"; Celia Deane-Drummond, "Taking Leave of the Animal? The Theological and Ethical Implications of Transhuman Projects," in *Transhumanism and Transcendence: Christian Hope in an Age of Technological Enhancement*, ed. Ronald Cole-Turner (Washington, DC: Georgetown University Press, 2011), 115–30; Green, "Transhumanism and Roman Catholicism"; Peters, "Progress and Provolution"; "Theologians Testing Transhumanism"; Waters, *From Human to Posthuman*; Brent Waters, "Whose Salvation? Which Eschatology? Transhumanism and Christianity as Contending Salvific Religions," in *Transhumanism and Transcendence: Christian Hope in an Age of Technological Enhancement*, ed. Ronald Cole-Turner (Washington, DC: Georgetown University Press, 2011), 163–75; see also J. Jeanine Thweatt-Bates, "Artificial Wombs and Cyborg Births: Postgenderism and Theology," in *Transhumanism and Transcendence: Christian Hope in an Age of Technological Enhancement*, ed. Ronald Cole-Turner (Washington, DC: Georgetown University Press, 2011), 101–14, critiquing transhumanism for a supposed dualism that runs against a claimed Christian primacy of embodiment.

[50] Karen Lebacqz, "Dignity and Enhancement in the Holy City," in *Transhumanism and Transcendence: Christian Hope in an Age of Technological Enhancement*, ed. Ronald Cole-Turner (Washington, DC: Georgetown University Press, 2011), 51–61; Calvin Mercer, "Whole Brain Emulation Requires Enhanced Theology, and a 'Handmaiden,'" *Theology and Science* 13/2 (2015): 175–86; Michael Spezio, "Human or Vulcan? Theological Consideration of Emotional Control Enhancement," in *Transhumanism and Transcendence: Christian Hope in an Age of Technological Enhancement*, ed. Ronald Cole-Turner (Washington, DC: Georgetown University Press, 2011), 145–62.

These approaches are modular. One can have a claim for a Christian genesis for transhumanism and use it as a springboard either to endorse or impeach transhumanism. Alternately, one can militate for a transhumanism based not on genealogy but on ahistorical readings of what is presented as the Bible's message or Christian truths and likewise see transhumanism as ally or rival. One can even have a defense of what is presumed to be secular transhumanist mischaracterizations of Christianity paired with a critique of secular transhumanism. There is, in essence, no single theological position on the question of the relationship between transhumanism and religion. The best we can do to summarize the theology of transhumanism is to sketch a rough possibility space,[51] a map of actual and imaginable theological positions. But this sketching of the combinatory possibilities and of the different imaginable paths forward, we should note, is exactly what we also did when interrogating transhumanists and transhumanism. Through this chapter, we have treated transhumanism as being comprised of two different types: secular and religious. However, if we consider transhumanism as an unfixed and open category, we can see transhumanism as potentially taking a variety of responses to religion and theology, just as theology has taken numerous approaches to transhumanism. And in the same way that theologians can accept or reject transhumanism, transhumanists can accept and reject theology, and this move is analytically distinguishable from the question of whether they will accept or reject religion, since occasionally secular transhumanists will reterritorialize and deploy theological thought such as Tillich, de Chardan, or Fyodorov.

What controls where specific theologians or transhumanists fall in this possibility space? At the level of the actual, their initial conditions do, but if we stay in the virtual–problematic, the resonances with other problems that exist at the moment of actualization control the form expression takes. We can see the effects of these virtual resonances most clearly in the MTA. The challenge for the MTA is how to take a foundational claim in Mormon thought that there is no tension between science and religion, while making that claim be at peace with a large segment of the LDS that is dead-set against evolution and other scientifically derived claims regarding general human capacities, histories, and futures. This tension is made all the more exquisite because despite this common anti-evolutionary stance in the LDS, LDS-associated educational institutions such as Brigham Young University have invested heavily in the evolutionary sciences; similarly, science-intensive high technology has also done quite well in some of the urban parts of the Mormon corridor, most likely because of the relatively higher levels of education in the wider Mormon community. Leaving the LDS is also a challenge. Kinship, and particularly kinship-infused capacities to engage in ceremonial life, business, and local

---

[51] Manuel DeLanda, *Philosophy and Simulation: The Emergence of Synthetic Reason* (New York: Continuum, 2011), 18–21.

politics, are often folded into LDS belonging.[52] This fact, working in combination with the lack of any real Mormon denominational system, means leaving the LDS has serious social costs.[53] One can imagine the hermeneutic challenges that this state of affairs poses to those who want to retain a degree of orthodoxy yet still foster a deep investment in some of the more radical possibilities being opened up by contemporary science and technology. This problem, while specific to MTA members, has particular resonances with the wider problem of whether transhumanism is anti-religious, areligious, or essentially religious. Others dealing with this question are driven by the resonances with different problems, including, in the case of theologians, disciplinary issues.

The disciplinary problems bring us back to the question of the anthropological approach. As stated, there is already a theoretically sophisticated and historically informed anthropological genealogy of transhumanism, which sees it at its core not as a religion or a crypto-religion but as a mode of thought made possible in the wake of religion's diminishment after secularisms and modernity. This anthropology of transhumanism could be seen to conflict with the presence of either a theological transhumanism or the actual transhumanists with whom I work, but I think that to presume such a conflict is to mistake a sketch of transhumanism's trajectory at a moment for a complete elaboration of all the mutations that transhumanism can undergo. A project such as transhumanism can only have its structuring problematic appear under specific historical conditions: The sundering of religion and science is necessary for them either to vie with one another over the same existential and cosmological questions or to work towards a rapprochement. Just because the past is fixed, though, it does not mean that the immanent and imminent future is not underdetermined and that the internal relations constituting transhumanism are sorted.

In short, there are multiple anthropological possibility spaces, and they have not necessarily yet to be all charted. This anthropological charting of the possibility space of transhumanism can only be done in the same way that

---

[52] See Fenella Cannell, "The Blood of Abraham: Mormon Redemptive Physicality and American Idioms of Kinship," *Journal of the Royal Anthropological Institute* 19/S1 (2013): S77–S94; Fenella Cannell, "The Re-Enchantment of Kinship," in *Vital Relations: Modernity and the Persistent Life of Kinship*, ed. Fenella Cannell and Susie Mckinnon (Santa Fe: SAR Press, 2013), 217–40. This imbrication of kinship with LDS social life and ritual practice is so deep that anthropologist Bradley Kramer has claimed that "Mormonism is, in the fullest sense, not so much a religion as it is a kinship system." Bradley Kramer, "Keeping the Sacred: Structured Silence in the Enactment of Priesthood Authority, Gendered Worship, and Sacramental Kinship in Mormonism," PhD dissertation (University of Michigan, 2014), 211.

[53] There are other groups that, like the LDS, trace their history back to Joseph Smith, such as the Community of Christ. There are also numerous Mormon fundamentalist groups. However, unlike the Protestant denominational system, where different denominations acknowledge each other as valid variants of Christianity, for the most part there is no systemic pattern of mutual recognition among these various Smith-descended movements.

the theological work can be done—by grasping the problem and working through its iterations and realizations. An anthropological account that sees transhumanism presently as essentially religious is as correct as one that denies any religiosity, as long as they both lead back to the underlying incommensurabilities. Both anthropological accounts are not necessarily equally useful for a larger transhumanist community. Utility for my inform-ants is future-facing; they must take the question of the relationship between transhumanism and religion and work forward with it in their day-to-day lives by acting in the world. Theology and anthropology, though, are best served by working back to the question and allowing us to see the multitude of possi-bilities inherent in it. This process may be the ideal contribution that theology could make to anthropology—a different tracing of the land by a different hand interested in different features. In combination they can be used by yet others to create a working map of the conceptual terrain.

10

Superstition and Enlightenment

Engagements between Theology and Anthropology

Nicholas Adams

This chapter explores some uncertainties arising from the question of what theology might contribute to social anthropology. It offers reflections on the proposal by Joel Robbins in "Theology and Anthropology: An Awkward Relationship"[1] and contrasts its approach with some recent work by Timothy Jenkins.[2] I read both anthropologists as bearers of the legacy of G. W. F. Hegel (1770–1831). Robbins and Jenkins are described here as reprising Hegel's account of the struggle of the Enlightenment against superstition, but in different ways.

Robbins in his essay is concerned with a normative account of the relationship between theology and anthropology. He suggests that each discipline mocks the other. In brief summary, theology addresses a community of readers with an expectation of transformation of life but struggles persuasively to show an alternative social ontology. Anthropology persuasively demonstrates alternative social ontologies but has no community of readers whose lives its descriptions might transform.

The focus of my remarks will be the parallelism between Marilyn Strathern's own awkward relationship essay and Robbins' extension of its scope to an engagement with theology. Each case has a disciplinary strength and a weakness on each side, with each discipline having the capacity to compensate for the weaknesses of the other.

---

[1] J. Robbins, "Anthropology and Theology: An Awkward Relationship?" *Anthropological Quarterly* 79/2 (2006): 285–94.

[2] T. Jenkins, "Anglicanism: The Only Answer to Modernity," in *An Experiment in Providence* (London: SPCK, 2006), 103–16; *The Life of Property: Family and Inheritance in Béarn, South-West France* (London: Berghahn, 2010).

Strathern's "An Awkward Relationship: The Case of Feminism and Anthropology" attempted to chart the ways in which the interests of feminist writing and those of anthropologists overlap and diverge from one another. Strathern's inquiry is motivated by the perceived failure of feminism to transform anthropology. She investigates the question of what counts as transformation, especially the terms of the then still fashionable idea of paradigm shifts and the requirement that a theoretical transformation means an identifiable change in the framework of inquiry, and considers what makes feminist inquiry distinctive with a familiar division between distinctive objects—namely, women's agency—and distinctive methods—namely, the researcher's relation of solidarity to those studied. Strathern suggests that because anthropologists already investigate women and because the discipline already has a proliferation of frameworks, it is difficult to identify any particular nameable theoretical transformation whose causes could readily be identified with feminism. Feminist anthropology can be "tolerated as a specialty that can be absorbed without challenge to the whole."[3] Strathern is more interested in the distinctive relation of solidarity between the anthropologist and the women who are the subject matter of feminist inquiry. For Strathern, both feminism and anthropology promote difference: for feminism it is between men's and women's interests; for anthropology it is between the researchers' and the informants' ways of making sense of things. Anthropology and feminism mock each other "because each so nearly achieves what the other aims for as an ideal relation with the world."[4] Anthropology sustains the otherness of the informants' world but desires that the evocation of this world be an enterprise shared by anthropologist and informant. Feminism mocks this pretension by drawing attention to the different interests of the two.[5] Feminism produces a shared enterprise (the interests of the researcher and of the subject of study converge) but desires to sustain the difference of a feminist viewpoint from that of the wider patriarchal society. Anthropology mocks this desire by drawing attention to the fact that any feminist construction of subjectivity is undertaken "within the sociocultural constraints of their own society" and is only meaningful because this is so.[6]

It is worth naming the fundamental categories in play in Strathern's claim about feminism's and anthropology's mutual mockery. The two to which Robbins draws attention in his interpretation of Strathern's essay are "real community of interest" (feminism) and "distance from their own society" (anthropology).[7] In Robbins' brief account of Strathern, feminism sustains

---

[3] M. Strathern, "An Awkward Relationship: The Case of Feminism and Anthropology," *Signs* 12/2 (1987): 276–92 (here 288).

[4] Ibid., 286.   [5] Ibid., 290.   [6] Ibid., 290–1.

[7] Robbins, "Anthropology and Theology."

community but struggles to achieve distance, while anthropology sustains distance but struggles to achieve community. It is a nice chiasmus.

This thesis, and almost exactly this same formulation, has a long history. To understand it, and thus to see why it has such force for Robbins, one can tell a little story about Hume and Hegel.

The most famous articulation of this chiasmus (community without distance, distance without community) is in Hegel's *Phenomenology of Spirit*, about 350 pages into the book in the late discussion of "Spirit." Its location in the text is significant because it falls into that part of the work philosophers tend not to read, given their much greater enthusiasm for the earlier parts that concern epistemology. Hegel's discussion is titled "the struggle of the Enlightenment against superstition."[8] Hegel takes up Hume's contrast, without attribution, between superstition and enthusiasm or, as they are more normally named, Catholicism and Protestantism in "Of Superstition and Enthusiasm" published in 1777.[9]

Hume describes superstition as a response to fear of the unknown manifested in "ceremonies, observances, mortifications, sacrifices, presents, or in any practice, however absurd or frivolous."[10] Enthusiasm, by contrast, is a product of the confidence and presumption that accompany prosperity: "The inspired person comes to regard himself as a distinguished favourite of the Divinity."[11] It is a rhetorically pleasing contrast.

Hume makes three succinct points. First, superstition elevates the authority of priestly institutions, whereas enthusiasm has "a contempt of forms, ceremonies and traditions."[12] Second, superstition starts out "gradually and insensibly" but then, when holding the balance of power, acts tyrannically and destructively to the extent of unleashing the violence of the Thirty Years' War to maintain that power. Enthusiasm takes the opposite path: it starts out violently in revolt, but then calms down and leads to a generation of free-thinkers. Third, "superstition is an enemy to civil liberty, and enthusiasm a friend to it."[13]

Hegel cannibalizes this account for his own purposes. In Hegel's much longer account, the feature upon which he seizes is the way in which faith inherits a habitable world. It is a domain of received certainties that structure ordinary and largely unreflective life: "In its certainty, faith stands in an unencumbered relation to its absolute object [i.e., God]. It is a pure knowledge of that object, and it never lets letters, paper, or copyists interfere with its

---

[8] G. W. F. Hegel, *Phänomenologie des Geistes*, ed. H. Clairmont and H. F. Wessels (Hamburg: Meiner, 1987), 357–79.

[9] D. Hume, "Of Superstition and Enthusiasm," in *Essays Moral, Political, and Literary*, ed. E. F. Miller (Indianapolis: Liberty Fund, 1987), 73–9.

[10] Ibid., 74.   [11] Ibid.   [12] Ibid.   [13] Ibid., 74–5.

consciousness of the absolute essence."[14] This is contrasted with the pure insight of the Enlightenment, which in its pursuit of truth is corrosive of tradition and which single-mindedly pursues freedom to the point of existential emptiness. In Strathern's idiom, faith mocks the Enlightenment with its real community; the Enlightenment mocks faith with its spirit of free inquiry.[15] Much more can be said about this fascinating discussion, and I have written on it elsewhere.[16] The main point here is Hegel's development of the chiasmus. Faith has community without free inquiry; the Enlightenment has free inquiry without community.

Hegel challenges the self-perceptions of both perspectives. Like Hume, who draws attention to enthusiasm's friendliness towards liberty, but developing the idea further, Hegel argues in some detail that the Enlightenment's freedom of inquiry is a historical development of certain impulses of the Reformation. For Hegel, the anti-institutionalism of the Reformers molds the intellectual habits and available shapes of thought found in more developed forms in the Enlightenment. The Reformers dared to think for themselves against received Catholic doctrine, and the Enlightenment champions dared to think for themselves against religion *tout court*. Both camps have a common root: Enthusiastic faith and Enlightenment are children of the Reformation, just as Reformation and Counter-Reformation are children of unstable late scholastic settlements.

On the face of things, and in Robbins' narration, it looks as though Strathern reproduces this chiasmus, which, in turn, facilitates Robbins' extension of it to the relation of theology and anthropology. There are obstacles that stand in the way of this perspective, however.

Strathern does not actually talk about real community: "real community of interest" is Robbins' gloss. Her own formulation is somewhat thinner. "Feminist scholars can claim substantial interests in common with the people they study. They may be speaking woman to woman, or else have a common ground in understanding systems of domination."[17] A "community of interest" (Robbins' term) is furthermore probably not what is typically meant, at least in theological writing, by community. The richer theological sense of community is, I suppose, precisely the kind that Robbins finds attractive in such writing. On the anthropological side, Strathern certainly talks of "breaking

---

[14] Hegel, *Phänomenologie des Geistes*, trans. Terry Pinkard, 366, <www.marxists.org/refer ence/archive/hegel/works/ph/pinkard-translation-of-phenomenology.pdf>.

[15] Hegel also has a much embellished and indeed darkly humorous version of Hume's account of superstition's gradually increasing hold upon the imagination and the unleashing of its violence. Space inhibits its inclusion here.

[16] N. Adams, "Faith and Reason," in *The Impact of Idealism: Religion*, ed. N. Adams (Cambridge: Cambridge University Press, 2013), 194–218.

[17] Strathern, "An Awkward Relationship," 290.

with the past"[18] as well as "distance and foreignness [that] are deliberately sustained."[19] These seem close enough to Hegel's characterization of Enlightenment impulses.

For Strathern the chiasmus is decidedly more uncertain, however. The feminist, not the anthropologist, has "the need to expose and thereby destroy the authority of other persons to determine feminine experience,"[20] and the anthropologist, although not to exclude the feminist, has the distinctive aspiration to make "an effort to remain open to people's emotional and personal lives."[21] In Hegel's account, it is, to the contrary, the Enlightenment that destroys while faith resources ordinary lives. This does not trouble Strathern's account of the mutual mockery, but it makes her account messier to map on to Hegel's.

Robbins' summary of Strathern's discussion achieves a neater map by smoothing that account somewhat. Having stabilized the relation between community and distance, this can then be put to work on the relation of theology to anthropology. These remarks need some careful elaboration.

Robbins' *homage* to Milbank is elegantly stated. He proposes a parallelism between the awkward relationship of feminism to anthropology and that of theology to anthropology. We can focus on what theology offers anthropology, given the terms of our discussion. Feminists "find it easy to create a real community of interest between themselves and their subjects, something that is extremely difficult for anthropologists to accomplish."[22] Theologians, in a comparable fashion, display more confidence in their claims that different ways of conceiving and living life are so fundamental and compelling that their readers should change their lives.[23] Milbank's *Theology and Social Theory* is offered by Robbins to his readers as a model of such confident and compelling writing.[24]

We can readily discern Hegel's chiasmus. Theology offers a community committed to being changed but struggles to demonstrate real difference; anthropology effortlessly shows real difference but struggles to find a community that might be changed. Anthropology has the tools of inquiry but no community; theology has the community but lacks the tools of inquiry. The reason for theology's struggle to demonstrate real difference is, I suppose, not a problem with its willingness to assert such difference, but its reluctance to undertake the detailed descriptions that would render these accounts plausible to a tough crowd. Robbins casts anthropologists as the tough crowd, with himself acting as their spokesperson.

There are at least three more immediate reasons why Milbank's *Theology and Social Theory* might claim the attention of a social anthropologist such as Robbins. First, Milbank thinks historically and offers his critique of social

---

[18] Ibid., 286–7.   [19] Ibid., 289.   [20] Ibid., 288.   [21] Ibid.
[22] Robbins, "Anthropology and Theology," 287.   [23] Ibid., 288.   [24] Ibid.

theory as a contribution to the history of ideas. Robbins has consistently shown a deep interest in the history of his discipline and tends to understand its contemporary questions as the outcomes of previous shifts in perspective and inquiry. Second, Milbank engages directly with social anthropology and concerns himself with its fundamental categories and shapes of thinking. This was rare at the time of publication and, in some ways, arguably remains so. Although many theologians today often engage anthropological literature, especially particular ethnographies and approaches, it is still unusual to find investigations of fundamental anthropological categories. Third, and over-lapping with the second, Milbank accuses anthropology of resting on an "ontology of violence" and insists that *only* (a favorite term for Milbank) theology, with its ontology of peaceful difference rooted in the doctrine of the Trinity, can offer a social theory that changes lives for the better. Milbank's claim is vague: it is not clear whether the accusation touches all anthropolo-gists all the way, certain tendencies in all anthropologists, or some tendencies in some anthropologists. One can nonetheless see why an anthropologist such as Robbins, who is sensitive to history, to suffering, and to the need to change lives, might be appropriately anxious about whether the charge sticks or at least is virtuously envious of an account that promises not only to diagnose a violent sickness but also to cure it.

There is a less obvious fourth reason: *Theology and Social Theory* is, itself, a retelling of Hegel's "struggle of Enlightenment against superstition."[25] Mil-bank, who knows Hegel's account well, perhaps via Gillian Rose, even if he does not acknowledge it, argues that secular social theory is, in fact, a devel-opment of theological tendencies that extend back into an earlier period. That is exactly what Hegel says about the Enlightenment's secularizing tendencies. Just as Hegel diagnoses the pure insight of the Enlightenment as a product of early Reformation anti-institutionalism, so Milbank diagnoses secular social theory as a product of heretical theologies. Milbank is not the first late-twentieth-century thinker to retell Hegel's thesis in this manner. He has rival contemporary versions of this retelling in Michael Buckley's *At the Origins of Modern Atheism* and Amos Funkenstein's *Theology and the Scien-tific Imagination.*[26]

Robbins' "An Awkward Relationship" and Milbank's *Theology and Social Theory* thus have a shared root in Hegel's work and further back in Hume's *Essays Moral, Political, and Literary*. To anthropologists who read Robbins,

[25] J. Milbank, *Theology and Social Theory: Beyond Secular Reason* (Oxford: Blackwell Pub-lishing, 1990).
[26] M. Buckley, *At the Origins of Modern Atheism* (New Haven: Yale University Press, 1987); A. Funkenstein, *Theology and the Scientific Imagination from the Middle Ages to the Seventeenth Century* (Princeton: Princeton University Press, 1986). Buckley wrote a PhD thesis with a substantial component on Hegel; Funkenstein, like many Jewish intellectuals of his generation, was thoroughly versed in Hegel.

judging from the many lively responses to it, his account looks like a remarkable development where two opposed ways of thinking are brought into fruitful dialogue. To theologians who read Hegel, it rather resembles two rival developments of a Hegelian thesis about Enlightenment: Robbins via Marilyn Strathern; Milbank via Gillian Rose.[27]

I wonder if Robbins' envy of theology is, however, not so much misplaced as exaggerated. I also wonder if there are more suitable objects of a properly mitigated envy. I propose to build a case with two prongs. The first is a proposal that a bit of history is good but more history is better. This is because more uncertainties, contingencies, and hesitations are introduced. The second is a suggestion that important questions of scale are in play. I offer two essays by Timothy Jenkins as expert witnesses in this second prong: "Anglicanism: The Only Answer to Modernity" and *The Life of Property*.[28]

First, the matter of history. Robbins shows great appreciation for Milbank's contribution to what he calls "alternative social ontologies."[29] It is indeed a powerful and persuasive vision. It is, however, worth drawing attention to a feature of the prose in which such alternatives are described. Milbank displays an embattled stance: medieval theology against modernity; Christianity against Islam; Aquinas against Scotus. This plays out conceptually in strong binary oppositions. It leaves little room for diagnosing rival tendencies in texts and thinkers and obscures overlapping influences, such as his own strongly Enlightenment (as Hegel narrates it) tendency to pursue pure insight, rescued from emptiness at or even after the last minute by invocations of Augustine, or his profoundly Nietzschean tendency to fight to the death, almost tempered by appeals to Aquinas's privileging of love. The alternatives are sharply posed for effect. This is achieved largely by staging gladiatorial combat with and between texts rather than narrating historical change and interpreting texts as symptoms of that change.

For Milbank the Platonist, ideas shape life. Ideas and texts are saturated with hope and danger. There is no cause to argue with this view as it stands. Clearly ideas do shape life. This insight is not errant so much as incomplete. Ideas shape life, in part, because they are, again in part, the conscious expressions of often unconscious forces, and it is those forces we must guess at. There are reasons why Scotus's ideas were ascendant in Paris in the 1600s, just as there are reasons why Aquinas's ideas were ascendant in Rome in the 1900s. Both are fundamental developments for Milbank. It is surely a matter of historical inquiry to discover, or at least to test hypotheses about, those reasons. As Collingwood, another student of Hegel, persuasively insists, texts

---

[27] Tracing this genealogy with more precision would be interesting. Perhaps an anthropologist with an interest in the history of ideas would be well placed to undertake this task.
[28] See note 2.   [29] Robbins, "Theology and Anthropology," 292.

are answers to questions, and questions are posed in response to changing circumstances.[30] Milbank tends to be interested in the answers to questions more than in naming the questions themselves, and certainly more than in the changing circumstances to which questions are responses. This is curious and unsatisfactory if the aim is to change circumstances. I shall try, without degenerating into exaggerated and fruitless critique of Milbank, to diagnose this unsatisfactoriness more precisely later.

In Milbank's defense, it must be said that there is a reluctance among many historians to see it as their business to change circumstances, and many historians wear that reluctance as a badge of honor. There is quite an "awkward relationship" between history and theology to be explored, and I would anticipate that Milbank would rightly feature, and prominently, in that exploration, too. Nonetheless, if changing circumstances is our business, as it is for Robbins, and if ideas are our tools, it is reasonable to suppose that a more energetic historical interest is required. There are generative models of this in such figures as Hume, Hegel, and Collingwood who very noticeably devote time to discussing the circumstances in which ideas arise and mutate, alongside the practical social action that they propose to their readers.

Second, the matter of scale. Much is at stake here, and I turn to the work of Timothy Jenkins to illuminate it. To get a sense of the intellectual engine that drives Jenkins' notoriously understated work, it is advisable to read his second and third books: *An Experiment in Providence* and *The Life of Property*.[31] Jenkins has a well-developed readership for each, but almost none for both. There is good reason to consider them together.

An Experiment in Providence is a miscellany of short think pieces and sermons. There are eighteen of them over 140 pages; many are *ristretto* short. They are written primarily for a readership concerned with how to articulate faith in the light of contemporary questions but in a style intended to permit other interested parties to listen in. The ancient genre they most resemble is perhaps the pastoral epistle: written for a community so that it might repent of its evil and deepen its faith. It is, thus, a good candidate for addressing those whom Robbins calls "readers [who might] . . . let these differences transform their lives."[32] It is also extremely funny in parts, punctuated by grim humor and wry observations on human idiocy. In the essay "Anglicanism: The Only Answer to Modernity," which I shall discuss shortly, Jenkins vigorously interrogates the prevalent idea that religious faith in Europe is a thing of the past, or at least on the point of being abolished under the pressure of modernity.[33]

---

[30] R. G. Collingwood, *An Autobiography* (Oxford: Oxford University Press, 1982), 29–43.
[31] T. Jenkins, *An Experiment in Providence* (London: SPCK, 2006); *The Life of Property*.
[32] Robbins, "Theology and Anthropology," 288.   [33] Jenkins, "Anglicanism."

The Life of Property is an ethnography of part of the Pyrenees, with a focus on family structures and transmission of goods across generations. Its thesis is that while it is difficult to identify the causes of change in these structures and modes of transmission, a good case can be made that they are, in part, the outcomes of intersecting legal codes whose relations alter over time. Shifts in the meaning of fundamental concepts—most centrally *the house*—express but also bring about such change. Jenkins notes a curious feature of his anthropological predecessors' accounts of life in this region of France: observers repeatedly claim it is about to disappear because of pressures by modernity on traditional habits of thought and action. "Being about to disappear" is, it seems, an almost permanent hazard for the Pyrenean house. Jenkins demurs. It does better justice to the reported phenomena, he proposes, to see the house as a (perhaps surprisingly) mobile expression of different forces: national and local laws, urban and rural life, newcomers and established families. Constantly adapting, rarely transparent, it forces its ethnographers to guess at the forces of whose passing resolutions it is the effect. Echoing Hegel's insight from *Philosophy of Right* that ethical clarity is achieved only at the moment when what is taken for granted starts to break down, Jenkins suggests that the moments of "maximal definitional intensity" of local values are the large farming families whose children prefer city life and whose marriages throw the transmission of property into doubt.[34] It is when the city comes to town that one truly sees the town.

In two contrasting genres—the pastoral epistle and the ethnography—a similar errant tendency is identified and challenged: the narrative of decline. Various actors, including religious folk, have a tendency to claim that religion is in decline. Various observers, including anthropologists, have a tendency to claim that the old life in the Pyrenees is in decline. Jenkins observes that narratives of decline are themselves surprisingly durable. In the case of Béarn, he offers the reader the comic spectacle of generation after generation of intellectuals visiting the place to taste its delights for the last time and to pronounce its imminent demise: a sort of restaurant at the end of the universe. Likewise, everyone knows or fears that religion is on the point of collapse, yet here it is, unto this day, sufficiently audacious as to think that even anthropology should be theologically engaged.

Jenkins offers an alternative. Developing a metaphor from Darwinian biology, he proposes that we think in terms of adaptation rather than decline. Developing a metaphor from Newtonian physics, he proposes that we consider adaptation in terms of forces. And borrowing a central theme from Collingwood's *Essay on Philosophical Method*, he proposes that we consider the scale at which concepts and categories operate.

---

[34] Jenkins, *The Life of Property*, 1970.

Jenkins' "Anglicanism: The Only Answer to Modernity" provides the answer to two questions: first, what is distinctive about Anglicanism; and second, does it deserve to be taken seriously? It opens with a discussion of the narrative of religion's decline and characteristically moves immediately to differentiate scales of perspective within which this narrative might play out. They are three.

The first is small-scale everyday life. It is a local scale. From the perspective of the churchgoer, life goes on in broadly good order: "Aspects of life make sense, the local church makes a difference, individuals come to faith, people try to live decent lives, and so forth."[35] The second is a broader scale: "The world appears to be full of forces that are indifferent to faith. . . . There is an unfocused anxiety about what we might call the plausibility of faith, even for believers (or especially for believers)."[36] The third is a vast scale: "There seems to be, against the second view, a belief in the ultimate goodness of the universe . . . [even among] people who appear indifferent to the specific claims of the Christian faith."[37] If one takes seriously the different outcomes to the question of decline, depending on the scale at which the question operates, one quickly produces a complex picture. This is typical of Jenkins' reasoning in both books. We have, then, three scales: the everyday, the broader, and the vast. I propose to name these the *local*, the *middle distance*, and the *cosmic*.

This complex picture is then immediately reduced, while preserving the complexity, to contrasting theological terms: people see the world as a theater of potential for good and evil with the promise or threat of salvation or damnation. As a rhetorical strategy (in Robbins' terms, "to point to wholly different ways of living"[38]), this is striking. The purpose is to wean the reader from doom and move him or her on to complexity, but in terms that can be readily digested.

This complex picture then invites a historical question: whence this complex view? Jenkins offers a historical account whose contours and basic categories have a good deal in common with Hume's essay "Of Superstition and Enthusiasm," already mentioned.[39] Jenkins briefly tells the story of the seventeenth-century wars of religion with his characteristic persistent reduction to primordial terms, again with the aim of preserving complexity in digestible form. For Jenkins, following George Duby, the fundamental categories in play are order, freedom, and flourishing. Order is expressed primarily in institutions and laws; freedom is expressed primarily in actors' capacity to act in ways not determined by such institutions and laws; and flourishing is expressed in lives well led. The birth of the modern world is, for Jenkins, a change from one settlement in which order, freedom, and

---

[35] Jenkins, "Anglicanism," 103.   [36] Ibid., 104.   [37] Ibid.
[38] Robbins, "Theology and Anthropology," 288.
[39] Hume, "Of Superstition and Enthusiasm."

flourishing were relatively stable—namely, feudalism—through a period of bloody and exhausting transition, during which this stability broke down, to a new Westphalian settlement of stability. In this account, the freedom and the flourishing are not the major objects of change. It is rather the institutions and laws that undergo significant mutation. With Hume, according to the second of his three succinct points rehearsed previously, Jenkins sees the breakdown of the feudal system as a failure of religion: the hopelessly violent attempt by one institution—the church—to assert its order over and against others' freedoms.[40]

Running through Jenkins' account is a question of hierarchy in relation to order, freedom, and flourishing. Times are hard when these three forces jostle for supremacy, especially when either order or freedom wins out; life is good when order and freedom contend with one another under the aegis of flourishing. And in Jenkins' typically conservative vision, life is especially good when there is an absolute commitment to flourishing, an abundance of order, and just enough freedom.

Jenkins displays a point of view that contrasts strongly with Milbank's. The Peace of Westphalia was not negotiated via a competition between "alternative social ontologies" but was the outcome of what Jenkins calls pragmatism: "See what will work, rather than being guided by tradition or by 'ultimate questions.'"[41] I wish here to draw attention to the contrast in approach to ultimate questions (Jenkins) and alternative social ontologies (Milbank). I take ultimate questions and social ontologies to be roughly equivalent, at least in terms of their scale: they lie at the cosmic end. For Jenkins, human flourishing was achieved in that period precisely because alternative social ontologies were not the deciding factor. The battle of ideas is never won, and the body count piles up. Modernity was born, Jenkins suggests, when actors decided together to suspend the battle of ideas and to agree on a settlement based on "what will work." In other words, this settlement was achieved when the scale at which thinking and action played out moved from the cosmic to the middle distance, in terms of theology, and from the middle distance to the local, in terms of what accommodations were made on the ground in particular communities. It is worth noticing that for Milbank the theatre of conflict is and should be shifted back towards the cosmic scale.

Anglicanism, for Jenkins, is the most pragmatic expression of this spirit of pragmatism. Or, it is the paradigm for introducing multiple scales as a repair of tendencies to operate solely at the cosmic end of the scale. Anglicanism is not guided primarily by ideas, and it is not the victory of one fundamental ontology over its rivals. It is a settlement in which competing ideas, and incompatible ontologies, can go on together. But it is not a bare pragmatism.

---

[40] Jenkins, "Anglicanism," 104.   [41] Ibid., 105.

It also labors under a confession of idolatry: what will work is not the highest good. Only God knows what that is, and if our pragmatic vision displaces this acknowledgement, corruption and suffering once again gain the upper hand.[42]

I offer here a brief note for Anglicans and their observers. Jenkins' proposals for understanding Anglicanism as a settlement more than a theology have some important implications for understanding his (and my) tradition. It aligns more closely with Diarmaid MacCulloch's *The Later Reformation in England 1547–1603* and *Thomas Cranmer: A Life* and with Mark Chapman's *Anglican Theology* than with attempts to identify what makes Anglican theology distinctive, such as Stephen Sykes' *Unashamed Anglicanism* or Samuel Wells' *What Anglicans Believe*, or those which seek to articulate its coherence, such as Sykes' *Integrity of Anglicanism* or Rowan Williams' *Anglican Identities* (these two written thirty years apart, and the latter in 2006, in the middle of the breakdown of a common Anglican vision).[43] Put differently, it privileges the categories used by historians more than those used by theologians. This betrays a dual concern <with historical settlements as well as historical doctrines—but it significantly mitigates the latter's dominance in many conceptions of what Anglicanism might be. Moreover, it can also be thought of as a stress upon intellectual work at the local scale, alongside the cosmic but again strongly mitigating its intellectual hegemony in theology.

Jenkins' view is unfashionable in theology today, so for good measure he makes it thoroughly explicit. In the spirit of Nicholas Lash, but also showing the influence of Daniel Hardy, he insists that theological confidence cannot be the basis of political settlement. To spell this out, as he does not, concerns on the cosmic scale do not straightforwardly shape concerns at the middle distance or on the local scale. It is, on the contrary, a willingness to face up to theological uncertainty that must underpin a commitment to others' flourishing. This is a matter of the appropriate scale for action and knowledge. The human scale, as contrasted with the divine scale, is limited, temporary, and provisional. This is accompanied by Jenkins' clear-eyed acknowledgement of the unpopularity of his proposal: "More 'principled' Christian churches tend to regard this pragmatism with suspicion, and sometimes disdain."[44] That is putting it mildly.

The rest of Jenkins' essay develops further proposals for considering the scale of action and knowledge and for understanding the relation among

---

[42] Ibid.

[43] D. MacCulloch, *The Later Reformation in England 1547–1603* (London: Palgrave, 1990); *Thomas Cranmer: A Life* (New Haven: Yale University Press, 1998); M. Chapman, *Anglican Theology* (London: Bloomsbury, 2012); S. Sykes, *Unashamed Anglicanism* (Nashville: Abingdon Press, 1995); S. Wells, *What Anglicans Believe* (Norwich: Canterbury Press, 2011); S. Sykes, *Integrity of Anglicanism* (London: Mowbray, 1978); R. Williams, *Anglican Identities* (Plymouth, UK: Cowley Publications, 2003).

[44] Jenkins, "Anglicanism," 108.

order, freedom, and flourishing. Most of its effort is devoted to outlining the kind of order that Anglicanism promotes, and this turns out to be, in large part, a matter of daily worship at a local scale rather than a battle of ideas at a cosmic scale.

A quick ending of this discussion might be sharply to point out the difference between Milbank's advocacy of an alternative social ontology as the basis for political settlement and Jenkins' advocacy of pragmatism tempered by checks on idolatry and a suggestion that Robbins might find Jenkins' approach more conducive to a desire to change our circumstances. It seems to me worthwhile to blunt this sharp contrast, however, using Jenkins' own Collingwoodian tools and to cast this whole matter itself as a question of scale.

Jenkins offers three scales of operation of ideas: the local, the middle distance, and the cosmic. Milbank's alternative social ontology, its vision of a wholly other way of life, operates somewhere between the middle distance and the cosmic. It is large-scale stuff, and it is the feature that arguably intoxicates the young. Jenkins' proposals, by contrast, work on all three levels. Its concern with idolatry operates on a cosmic scale; its proposals for political settlement operate in the middle distance; and its concern with daily prayer operates on a local scale. This seems to me to be of great interest and to offer a more fruitful way of repairing Milbank's highly stimulating theology than the familiar, rather sterile attacks and defenses that his work often seems to invite. One can appreciate Milbank's work while drawing attention to its one-sidedness or incompleteness or its scalar drift towards the cosmic.

I return, then, to the question of Robbins' exploration of the awkward relationship between theology and anthropology. How awkward is it, really? I want to suggest that in one respect it is not awkward in the slightest and that, in another, it is far more awkward than he imagines.

When considering the chiasmus—theology has transformable community but struggles persuasively to articulate alternative social ontologies; anthropology persuasively articulates alternative social ontologies but struggles to find a community to be transformed by them—I think Hegel's original offers some useful pointers. Faith and the Enlightenment, to use Hegel's terms in the chiasmus, have a common root: Enlightenment lacks community precisely because it has exaggerated certain features of Protestantism that unleashed freedom of conscience against ecclesial order. Its pursuit of pure insight is, in other words, not simply a mistake. It is more a one-sided and, crucially, forgetful development of a tendency of which one can make sense if one knows some religious history: a Catholic Church violently imposing its order gave rise to violent bids for freedom. This unleashed not only war, which was bloody and short-term, but also a catastrophic anti-institutional impulse, which was corrosive and long-term. The repair of this situation, Hegel suggests, is to revisit the relation between community and reason or, in Jenkins' terms, order and freedom, and integrate what has been put asunder. Hegel, like Jenkins, privileges flourishing, which he typically calls love. Both Hegel and Jenkins are emphatic about the centrality of institutions. There is no great awkwardness if theology and anthropology are understood in these terms, with a common root. There will be much work to do in both disciplines, and if Robbins is right, it will presumably mean theologians becoming more competent historians in order not only to insist upon but to demonstrate the radical otherness of its own tradition. It will also mean anthropologists embracing the communities of imagination to which they are intellectually, as well as socially, the heirs and to whom they may have the confidence to speak.

When it comes to imagining the practical effects of these proposals, however, it seems to me that certain kinds of awkwardness stubbornly persist. Robbins generously imagines that anthropologists can learn from theologians' boldness of vision and the confidence with which they address their communities in the expectation of social change.

But the lesson here is that one needs to pay attention to scale. If theologians are expressing a boldness of vision at a scale somewhere between the middle distance and the cosmic, it is likely to be inspiring but will very possibly operate only at that scale. This is, in Jenkins' terms, the realm of anxiety and reassurance rather than the arena of local action and everyday virtues. To be effective, in the way that Robbins anticipates, theology would need to operate intellectually on a more local scale. And for that, one will need to look further afield than Milbank, as he himself would cheerfully admit.

In closing, let me try to recast Hegel's chiasmus in an alternative form, changing it into a hypothesis that might bear testing in various ways. Theology and anthropology stem from a common root, for us, just as faith and Enlightenment stem from a common root for Hegel, but there is a certain one-sidedness in their developments from that root. Anthropology arguably tends to operate at two scales: the local and the middle distance. It concerns itself locally with ordinary lives but also demonstrates more broadly the alternative social ontologies that these lives embody. Theology has also tended to operate at two scales, but they are not the same ones: the middle distance and the cosmic. It concerns itself with alternative social ontologies expressed doctrinally in accounts of church, mission, and ethics. But it also concerns itself more cosmically with breathtaking visions of creation, redemption, and hopeful vitality extending beyond the last things.

If anthropology mocks theology, it is for its failure to operate at the local scale. This might mean its failure to do justice to daily worship, to disciplines of prayer, to the everyday service in community that discipleship requires. Doubtless one can find a few theologians to mock in this regard. (And a few, including Jenkins, whose work resists such mockery.)

However, if theology mocks anthropology, is it for its failure to operate at the cosmic scale? This would mean anthropology's failure to do justice to the encompassing vision of the beginning and the end and the role of reconciliation in the meantime. It is a failure to inspire. This is not far off what Robbins says, but in my version, it is perhaps rather less compelling for anthropologists. For Robbins it is the identification of a community to receive a bold vision that is in view, but it is core to my account that a community whose practices operate at a local scale cannot plausibly be transformed solely by thinking, nor by thinking that operates solely on a cosmic scale. Here, by contrast, theology's distinctiveness, and therefore its place in the chiasmus, lies in the identification of claims on a cosmic scale. Perhaps there are anthropologists who might be receptive to being mocked in this way. I would be interested to meet them.

11

Anthropology and Theology

Fugues of Thought and Action

Douglas J. Davies

Projection versus revelation—how easy it would be to approach the interplay of theology and anthropology by setting up anthropology's general assumption of the social construction of ideas and their projection as forms of *religious knowing* in opposition to a classical theological notion of a divine revelation of truth. Whether in terms of direct biblical authority, Spirit-inspired hermeneutics of authority-guided churches, or a liberal alertness to the cultural contextualizing of religious tradition, entailments of revelation might soon have theologians disagreeing among themselves, let alone seeking to colonize anthropology through their historically and institutionally achieved social high ground. Anthropologists might, for their part, simply take a church as their *demos* of choice with some priests as immediate informants and with some other religious traditions for wider comparison, all set within an ethnography that not only serves as a status-defining document among anthropologists but whose description and analysis may also *tame* the piety of the devotees studied.

Instead of such a stark scheme of binary division between projection and revelation or, indeed, of colonizing and taming projects, this chapter's softer approach advocates the gentler form of conversation as interdisciplinary activity between theologians and anthropologists. However, and I stress this point for emphasis, the *conversational pattern* may not only appear as behavior between partners but also as a form of interior dialogue for a single person familiar with at least some theology and anthropology. My reason for emphasizing such an internal dialogue is, first, because of my own intellectual experience, thought processing, and life practice over many years and, second, because I use this chapter as its own form of biographical case study of the interplay of selected anthropological and theological ideas. In general terms, the phenomenon of inner dialogue is likely to be as common a human experience in daily life as within professional forms of reflection. For anthropologists it is likely to constitute one foundational experience when relating one's experience of field-work in new contexts to one's more familiar *home* cultural knowledge. In other words, theoretical concerns over narrative, autobiographical, and reflexive forms of anthropology are very likely to have interior dialogues as their generative base.

Such interior language is also vital within many religious traditions which frame theological discussion with prayer, a sense of communication with the divine, and with various forms of replaying public liturgy within one's interior sacred place.[1] Such phenomena, and it is probably better to think in the plural than in the singular, are far from being understood but should not be ignored within the context of the interplay of differing bundles of ideas, conventions, and experiences. Some will recall Malinowski's posthumously published *Diary in the Strict Sense of the Term*[2] and might note the much more recent engagement with *Emotions in the Field* to witness the complexities involved.[3]

Precisely because of such complexity, I speak of *fugues of thought and action* in this chapter's title in the hope that the musical allusion will fix attention on human creativity as it engages diverse themes while striving for satisfying resolutions of disciplinary tensions even if these are not achieved. In connection with this thought, I should also add that I have not sought to furnish references for the many topics raised in this discussion. Suffice it to say that very many are contained in the key publications that are cited. What then of the broad structure of this tripartite chapter?

The first, entitled "Intrapersonal and Interpersonal Dialogue," is heavily autobiographical, and I trust that readers will accept this as its own kind of case study of reflexivity, excusing its indulgence in biographical reflection on account of its intention to pinpoint the very particular and contextual nature of idea development. Perhaps a whole series of such case studies drawn from both anthropologists and theologians and mixed cases would go some considerable way toward illuminating what otherwise might simply fall into a more abstract mode of intellectual discussion of ideas.

The second part, headed "Further Conversation Pieces," picks up just such ideas open to anthropological–theological conversation, including a cautionary gloss on the over-easy use of *anthropology* and *theology* as discrete terms. This echoes Brian Howell's rhetorical questioning of *which anthropology and which theology* in this volume[4] and acknowledges that because these disciplines are complex in themselves we can expect conversations between them to

---

[1] Douglas J. Davies, "Inner Speech and Religious Traditions," in *Theorizing Religion*, ed. James A. Beckford and John Walliss (Aldershot, UK: Ashgate, 2006), 211–23.

[2] Bronislaw Malinowski, *A Diary in the Strict Sense of the Term* (New York: Harcourt, Brace & World, 1967).

[3] James Davies and Dimitrina Spencer, *Emotions in the Field. The Psychology and Anthropology of Fieldwork Experience* (Stanford: Stanford University Press, 2010).

[4] Brian M. Howell, Chapter 2, 29–49.

be challenging. Moreover, to speak of *disciplines* is itself to create an abstract plane of discourse that is, potentially, far removed from the individuals who pursue and embody them and who may well be transformed by them while also creatively transforming them in the process.

The third and final part, described as "Disciplinary Quandaries," takes some of these formal classifications of disciplines further and also brings together some personal and institutional factors surrounding both anthropological and theological practice. It ends by leaving open many issues, by leaving potential conversations in the air, and by not seeking the mental pleasure of a conclusion.

INTRAPERSONAL AND INTERPERSONAL DIALOGUE

The intrapersonal aspect of the disciplinary interplay just alluded to is significant for me, having first studied social and physical anthropology at Durham, then social anthropology and the sociology of religion at Oxford before training, again at Durham, in traditional academic theology as well as in more pastoral theology. I then became a university teacher charged with initiating courses in the study of religion within fairly traditional departments of theology first at Nottingham University and twenty or so years later at Durham University. Concurrently, I was ordained as an Anglican clergyman and served extensively in diverse parishes and other ecclesial activities while being a full-time university teacher.

My pathway to ordination had, doubtless, gained a foothold in infancy and childhood as someone born into an ordinary kind of Anglican life in the Church in Wales with its frequent liturgical experience of the Eucharist and, certainly as important, of Evensong. All these events helped generate a ritual sense and performative competence. Furthermore, daily chapel services throughout the entirety of school, university, and theological life amounted roughly to twenty years of public ritual accompanied by that inner-world dialogue framed by religious and secular academic work. Other experience involved Christian organizations, denominations, and influential individuals of liberal, evangelical, and Anglo-Catholic persuasions. Formal ecclesial ministry has, so far, encompassed forty years of activity, all aligned with academic research and teaching and driven by a largely anthropological perspective and complex theological metamorphoses. Together this experience makes for a considerable ritual–emotional–theological pool of potential orientations to the world and to the interplay of anthropology and theology. It would take a volume of its own to detail all its entailments.

More specifically, from 1969 I began academic work on Mormon life and culture, which has continued in various ways ever since. I also worked briefly with

Sikhs and in a couple of formal research projects on Anglicans, along with major projects on the ritual symbolism of modern cremation, traditional and woodland burial rites, and the theology of death. Some considerable anthropological–theological interplay has undergirded these endeavors, with each being sometimes less and sometimes more evident. Interplay has also influenced many postgraduate dissertations by individuals of many and no religious persuasion.

All this experience has involved a complex flux of feedback processes that have engendered a cumulative perspective that sometimes makes distinguishing the conceptual and emotive forces at work difficult. One is reminded of Dan Sperber's earlier anthropological framing of the distinction between symbolic and encyclopedic knowledge and especially of how symbolic knowledge is ever changed by new experience, just as new experience ever changes preexisting symbolic domains.[5] Such internal transformations, in themselves, have helped forge my identity as I assume they do in many anthropologists and theologians and in those with complex blends of worldviews. In some ways, this makes certain kinds of discussion of discrete academic disciplines potentially unconvincing, or at least somewhat difficult once abstractly distinctive theories pass into lived identity. Moreover, as we see again in the following paragraphs, both theologians (as opposed to theology) and anthropologists (as opposed to anthropology) are familiar with the experience of being formed through their respective ways of life: The beloved notion of *habitus* has, after all, deep roots in religious traditions as in social scientific discussions. This experiential domain drives what I allude to as a parallel between worship and fieldwork as creative arenas of identity formation.

Formation as both an academic and Anglican priest draws me, in terms of this volume, to comment on Howell's typology of theology, which is, as he rightly observes, "infinitely contestable."[6] I simply pinpoint two aspects of his scheme that have, for me, become especially creatively combined—that is, theology as phenomenology and as correlation. For nearly twenty years, I jointly taught a course formally entitled "Philosophy and Phenomenology of Religion" with my former teacher and friend John Heywood Thomas. The *phenomenology* element increasingly became a descriptive cultural anthropology while the philosophy featured an engagement between systematics and philosophical theology. The key point here is that its source, Heywood Thomas, is an extremely competent scholar not only as a member of the Kierkegaard Academy but also as a former graduate student of Paul Tillich at Union Theological Seminary. My many years of integrated and very companionable seminar-style work with him led to a slow and almost imperceptible appropriation of a Tillich *cum* Thomas approach to a theology of culture with its own commitment to the notion of theology as correlation. While this was

---

[5] Dan Sperber, *Rethinking Symbolism* (Cambridge: Cambridge University Press, 1975).
[6] Howell, Chapter 2, 34.

most explicit in my own *Theology of Death*,[7] it underlay a great deal of earlier thought and publication. It also made Rappaport's magisterial account of *Ritual in the Making of Humanity* a useful text when bringing theological students into the anthropological arena given the use he made of Tillich.[8]

Similarly, the theological interest in existential issues definitely ensured the appeal of Stanner's Australian anthropology with its powerful philosophical, or even theological-like, accounts of human existence and the trials of life, and pervaded my original doctoral work and its ensuing publication.[9] This gives me a considerable affinity with the theme of *blessing* as explored in Don Seeman's reflections in this volume. I explored *blessing* in my own work under the anthropological influence of Rodney Needham's use of the dual sovereignty model of human social processing of authority.[10] I also found that model very valuable when analyzing Mormon social organization, and it bears strongly on the kind of issues of leadership and emotional dissonance Fenella Cannell describes in this volume.[11] Needham's insights have also proved significant for me when depicting contemporary British aspects of justice and the cultural remembrance of the war dead.[12] Again, I agree with Seeman on Michael Jackson's work and its approach to everyday life and would add to it Alfred Schutz's earlier phenomenology of the everyday life world that added its own descriptive dimension to my anthropological concern with pragmatic human behavior.[13] To this list I would certainly add Dan Miller's contemporary descriptive anthropology, especially when he places theoretical analyses rather after the event, a practice of considerable illustrative value for ecclesial initiates into church-related ethnography.[14]

* * *

To give further shape to these biographical comments, theoretical issues, and disciplinary interplay let me pinpoint the practice-related volume *Studies in Pastoral Theology and Social Anthropology*, first published in 1986.[15] The title

[7] Douglas J. Davies, *Theology of Death* (London: T&T Clark/Continuum, 2008).

[8] Roy Rappaport, *Ritual in the Making of Humanity* (Cambridge: Cambridge University Press, 1999).

[9] Douglas J. Davies, "The Notion of Meaning and Salvation in Religious Studies," PhD dissertation (University of Nottingham, 1979).

[10] Douglas J. Davies, *Emotion, Identity and Religion: Hope, Reciprocity, and Otherness* (Oxford: Oxford University Press, 2011), 198, 225, 246.

[11] Douglas J. Davies, *The Mormon Culture of Salvation* (Aldershot, UK: Ashgate, 2000); Fenella Cannell, Chapter 14, 244–65.

[12] Douglas J. Davies, *Mors Britannica: Lifestyle and Death-Style in Britain Today* (Oxford: Oxford University Press, 2015), 46–52, 272–5.

[13] Douglas J. Davies, *Meaning and Salvation in Religious Studies* (Leiden: Brill, 1984), 22–4, 163–4.

[14] For example, see Daniel Miller, *The Comfort of Things* (Cambridge: Polity Press, 2008).

[15] Douglas J. Davies, *Studies in Pastoral Theology and Social Anthropology*, 2nd edn (1986; Birmingham: University of Birmingham Institute for the Study of Worship and Religious Architecture, 1990).

marked the fact that it was produced to aid courses taught for people in the UK's East Midlands who were then training for the Anglican and Methodist ministries through a part-time, nonresidential program at Nottingham University. It would hardly have been feasible, however, without my ongoing work with Heywood Thomas that constantly prompted anthropological engagement with a subtle theological mind. This small book also reflected its own kind of interpersonal dialogue with class members outside of our Theology Department at Nottingham, many of whom brought with them numerous professional, academic, and life skills and experience commensurate with their mature adult and often middle-aged experience. Though published by Birmingham University's once influential Institute for the Study of Worship and Religious Architecture, under the wise leadership of Gordon Davies (1919–90), Birmingham's Cadbury Professor of Theology, it was not widely circulated.

Notably, these editions included three chapters by Nottingham Theology Department postgraduates. Laurence Oliver, writing on "Liminality and the Hospital Ward,"[16] produced what was probably one of the earliest UK accounts of theology related to ethnography. Graham Keyes considered his parochial and pastoral experience of talking to older people in a chapter entitled "Prayer in the Second Half of Life: Expectation and Reality," focused on a small set of six case studies. Deeply informed by the sociological–psychological literature of the day on the phenomenon of loneliness, he did not find those interviewed to be lonely. What he did find was personal worlds of "conversation and communication" with God, often learned early in life from the mother and "with little expectation that intercessory prayer would be effective, beyond changing the disposition of the person praying."[17] Both Oliver and Keyes revealed an open-endedness to what, decades later, would be called *lived religion* and how it might or might not reflect formal theology.

Then, David Walker, an ordinand in training for the Anglican priesthood, took his disciplinary expertise in systematic theology into a discussion of "Pastoral Theology and the Suffering God."[18] Sadly, this young colleague was killed in a motor accident in the very early years of his first pastoral appointment. His concern with hospital wards peopled with folk asking why they were there led him to discuss the notion of the wounded healer and to explore the work of the once-renowned Anglican priest Geoffrey Studdert Kennedy, a famed wartime chaplain exercised by the wounded soldier at Amiens asking him, "What is God like?" These diverse authors were more than happy to see their work published in a book entitled *Studies in Pastoral Theology and Social Anthropology*.[19] That book's conclusion—"Prospective Reconnoitres"—itemized the need for "stimulated imaginations" in pastors

---

[16] Ibid., 70–8.   [17] Ibid., 97.   [18] Ibid., 102–13.   [19] Ibid., the volume's title.

and saw anthropology as one potential source of stimulation.[20] It pinpointed group fellowship as a mode of power and highlighted ideas of embodiment; as a caution over any excessive sociological reductionism, it affirmed "the individual as the irreducible centre of mystery."[21]

Over a decade later, that volume, but without the additional three authored chapters, developed into the more widely circulated monograph *Anthropology and Theology*.[22] This explicitly described itself in terms of a conversation between these domains and focused on topics that seemed to bear an affinity with each other across disciplines. A stronger emphasis on anthropological rather than theological ideas was based on the assumption that theological readers, reckoned the majority readership, would be less familiar with anthropological notions than vice versa. Still, I doubt whether many anthropologists ever read it. The chapter titles pinpoint the potentially interrogative affinities between theology and anthropology:

Embodiment and Incarnation,
Merit-Making and Salvation,
Ritual and Experience,
From Meaning to Salvation,
Symbolism and Sacrament,
Gift and Charismata, and
Sacrifice, Body and Spirit.

Each pair aligned selected elements of systematic theology and social anthropology in a conversation between disciplines. Moreover, the book explicitly described its chapters as unsystematic, rather in imitation of creative conversations, and it clearly stated, "There is no priority of speaker.... Theology is not assumed to be queen of the sciences, using anthropology in a servile fashion, any more than anthropology is taken to be the foundational source of truthfulness concerning humanity."[23] The profound difficulties inherent in these partner positions were highlighted, both in terms of the comparative method itself assumed to be integral to social anthropology and of the confessional nature of theology as a stance assuming belief in God portrayed through the distinctive theological lens of each church tradition and appropriating that belief through liturgical and devotional experiences within an ethical frame of life. I cannot spell out the detailed content of each of these chapters.

However, one of those chapter titles, "From Meaning to Salvation,"[24] had interested me for some time and had been the topic of my doctorate, published as the monograph, *Meaning and Salvation in Religious Studies*.[25] It had taken

---

[20] Ibid., 114–16.   [21] Ibid., 116.
[22] Douglas J. Davies, *Anthropology and Theology* (Oxford: Berg Publishers, 2002).
[23] Ibid., 3.   [24] Ibid., 145–72.   [25] Davies, *Meaning and Salvation*.

the theological idea of salvation and considered or reconsidered it in terms of the sociology of knowledge rather than in terms of any confessional theology. The goal was to provide a nontheological grammar of discourse for the widespread human phenomenon of the transcendence of life's problems. Its underlying question of why and how the drive for meaning might become the need for salvation remains with me and, perhaps, constitutes one point that theology in its varied ecclesial versions can address to anthropology.[26] In the 1970s I had disliked the way that those discussing salvation religions seemed to assume that salvation was a higher-order phenomenon, and, rightly or wrongly, I wanted to counter that division and approach salvation as a phenomenon encountered in many cultural domains. This was its own kind of argument against primitive religious mentalities. Tangentially, it has been interesting to see the notion of salvation largely drop from religious studies and its various professional associations in Britain from somewhere around the 1980s with perhaps a slight resurgence in the present decade.[27] Perhaps British theology and mainstream churches have also seemed less interested in salvation as such over a similar period.

Even from what I have said so far, I obviously give some precedence to the issue of a person's identity as raised both by theology and anthropology as academic disciplines, not least to the scholar's identity as its own key influence upon what is studied and how it is studied. One entailment of this process concerns the theme of vocational modes of life, an issue prompted by the fact that both theology and anthropology can be construed as involving a kind of calling—an orientation to the world as familiar to ecclesial spirituality as to Weberian sociology. To do some small justice to the emotional complexities of both theology and anthropology, I sought, in *Anthropology and Theology*, to compare confessional theology with fieldwork anthropology. One reason for doing so was because the ordinands taught through its antecedent, *Studies in Pastoral Theology and Social Anthropology*, were mature adults whose own professional and domestic lives were alert to life-changing events.

While cautious over comparing "worship for the theologian with fieldwork for the anthropologist," I nevertheless alluded to "a certain family resemblance rooted in experience"[28] that often typifies exponents of these hermeneutical bases of life. These resemblances lie in their respective arenas of practice that foster emotional outlooks to a considerable extent, for, arguably, the repetitive nature of personal and liturgical prayer within the overall domain of worship generates its own implicit power over a person's worldview. In the language of

---

[26] Douglas J. Davies, "Salvation, Death and Nature as Grace," in *Alternative Salvations: Engaging the Sacred and the Secular*, ed. Hannah Bacon, Wendy Dossett, and Steve Knowles (London: Bloomsbury, 2015), 85–96.

[27] Hannah Bacon, Wendy Dossett, and Steve Knowles (eds), *Alternative Salvations: Engaging the Sacred and the Secular* (London: Bloomsbury, 2015).

[28] Davies, *Anthropology and Theology*, 7.

traditional Christian spirituality, a person is formed; indeed, spiritual formation or priestly formation are explicit terms fully understood within ecclesial worlds, especially in terms of church leadership. Cannell's consideration of *registers* of modes of talk in her Latter-Day Saint studies in this volume offers one clear theoretical expression of formation and identity and of how devotees may deploy it when seeking to achieve a goal within a community that senses what is going on even if at a more implicit level of cultural knowing.[29]

Similarly, those within professional anthropological circles often both explicitly and implicitly reference the transformative power of fieldwork. Despite discussions about doing anthropology at home and the like, it is not uncommon to detect a kind of disciplinary guilt in some anthropologists if they seem to lack fieldwork of an appropriate duration in some acceptably distant or exotic community. Similarly, there is often considerable pride and self-assurance among those possessing just such experience. Perhaps, few other academic disciplines have such experiential and contextual markers even though many disciplines host something akin to status markers, albeit rooted in the scholar's research supervisor or high-status university department.

In other words, experience counts, whether religious experience or fieldwork experience. But because experience of this nature is also, implicitly and often explicitly, transformative, it can easily engender a kind of competition of experiences that quite likely manifests itself when anthropology and theology come together. It will take one form in meetings of anthropologists and theologians and another within a single person engaged in both theological–worshipful life and anthropological–fieldwork life. Such issues raise delightful complexity, and I have, for many years, been mindful to speak of *brain pain* when beginning to introduce theology students to the study of religion from an essentially anthropological perspective but always wanting to comment on brain pain's more fully embodied form of *heart pain*, too. This factor might itself trigger an interesting conversation between theology and anthropology in terms of both identity defense and the desire to explore new ideas in students of many ages. Novel experiences, whether within theological or anthropological endeavors, can be eye-opening and furnish their own form of growing pains intrinsic to education itself.

Just how each of us comes to some accommodation with life experience will long evade full analysis, but issues of fear and uncertainty, as well as of compassion and moments of oceanic rapture crystallizing total insight, are but part of our identity's ever-developing complexity. Moreover, individuals often experience their own life crises and family traumas as their anthropological or theological work is pursued. Here, perhaps, anthropologist Daniel Miller's sense of there being "no evidence of people being 'fully formed' at

---

[29] Cannell, Chapter 14, 244–65.

some point in their lives" is also wisely instructive.[30] That thought reflects our opening gambit on just how the hermeneutical models of revelation—beloved of the theologian—and of projection—beloved of the social scientist—may be handled by an individual.

FURTHER CONVERSATION PIECES

From these personal and theoretical themes, this next part of the chapter pinpoints further theologically framed ideas that might be of ongoing interest to anthropology. I simply cite these as discrete topics for potential discussion without imposing any formal connection between them. Here, perhaps, as in many expressions of a mind and meetings of minds, one idea emerges and passes to another as potential points in the conversational model that I favor as the medium for interplaying theology and anthropology.

Celebration

Reiterating yet extending the conversational model, I recall theologian Rowan Williams' suggestion that theology's venture sometimes drew on "celebratory, communicative and critical styles,"[31] a reflection that leads me to wonder what anthropology's equivalents might be. Certainly anthropology has possessed much in terms of critical styles, sometimes to the point of near paralysis, and certainly its communicative capacity is considerable, especially when deploying the comparative method to reveal the many splendored thing of human unity and diversity. What, I wonder, about anthropology's celebratory mode? Perhaps conferences, ethnographic films, seminars, or the like spark such pleasure. Though some would doubt this remark concerning certain conferences! Nevertheless, I am reminded of the 1994 centenary celebration at Aberdeen, marking William Robertson Smith's death, when anthropologists, theologians, Arabic specialists, and biblical scholars joined to celebrate that man's remarkable contribution to late Victorian culture and, as Mary Douglas had it, to the germination of social anthropology itself.[32] Perhaps it is to the celebration of humanity itself that theology prompts anthropology with its store of data, theories, and the capacity of comparison.

---

[30] Miller, *The Comfort of Things*, 291.
[31] Rowan Williams, *On Christian Theology* (Oxford: Blackwell Publishers, 2000), xiii, as quoted in Davies, *Anthropology and Theology*, 17.
[32] W. Johnstone (ed.), *William Robertson Smith: Essays in Reassessment* (Sheffield: Sheffield Academic Press, 1995).

Ethnography

Robertson Smith was, of course, far from being a stay-at-home scholar, and much of his technical work sometimes echoes his Middle Eastern travels. This reference gives us one opportunity to raise the theme of ethnography, of the comparative method within anthropology, and, in particular, of the rise of ethnography as a perspective of choice in a variety of pastoral domains and clergy-training contexts. This ecclesial increase of interest in the notion of ethnography takes me back to my *Anthropology and Theology*, produced as it was for some UK clergy in training and some time before *ethnography* was a word that might be heard alongside systematics, patristics, or hermeneutics on a theological agenda. Now, however, increasing numbers of theologians and ecclesial educationists are asking anthropologists about ethnography, becoming an almost methodological industry with journals and conferences and, at Durham at least, involving postgraduate degree modules.

Mercy

From another direction we might identify various outcomes of theological analysis that might prompt some anthropologists to activate their comparative method and choose some theoretical driver to study—for example, theological ideas of covenant, justice, and mercy. Historically speaking, it is well-known that, for example, Durkheim's study of religion in *The Elementary Forms of the Religious Life,* especially its sense of the "moral community" and of the empowerment gained from corporate, sacrificial ritual, as probably also his study of *Suicide,* was deeply influenced by William Robertson Smith's work, not least his *Religion of the Semites*—a volume that was, it might be argued, significantly influenced by Smith's theological presuppositions.[33]

The idea of mercy might especially be pinpointed as a theological idea prompting anthropological analyses. Interestingly, and from the theological direction, I was recently approached to comment from both an anthropological and Anglican perspective—an interesting conjunction—on this idea of mercy for a French Catholic journal published in this year declared by Pope Francis as a year of mercy.[34] This invitation was probably due to having engaged with the notion of mercy some years ago when asked by Mormon

---

[33] Emile Durkheim, *The Elementary Forms of the Religious Life*, trans. Joseph Ward Swain (London: George Allen and Unwin, 1915); Emile Durkheim, *Suicide*, trans. J. A. Spalding and G. Simpson (London: Routledge and Kegan Paul, 1952); William Robertson Smith, *Religion of the Semites* (London: Adam and Charles Black, 1889).

[34] Douglas J. Davies, "La miséricorde: mot, doctrine et appropriation," *Unité des Chrétiens* 182 (April 2016): 11–15.

scholars to give an account of salvation in Anglicanism, when it seemed to me that *mercy* dominated the *Book of Common Prayer*.[35] I mention this to reiterate something of the networked complexity of disciplines within an individual's life and in relation to other people and groups. Along any research path of mercy, we would find historical value in, for example, Robert Hertz (1881–1915) and his interest in sin and expiation or David Parkin's edited volume on *The Anthropology of Evil*.[36]

Grace

Somewhat connected with mercy in a theoretical way, another cluster of theological ideas that might challenge anthropology's theoretical and comparative resources lies in the notion of grace, or even more specifically, in the love–grace union of devotee with deity that plays an enormous role in a variety of Christian, Jewish, Hindu, Sikh, and wider sacred texts and practices. Here the biocultural nature of emotions and the complex dynamics of relationship between individual and society would emerge in the anthropology of embodiment and social organization. Or, again, the bond between devotee and deity as might be conceived by theology offers an intriguing test of social theory, not least in the contestation of ideas of "the individual" and "the dividual" as developed from Marriott's anthropology of India into the New Melanesian anthropology.[37]

Driven by notions of complex and partible personhood, this approach offers interesting scope for systematic theology in Christology and its theological anthropology of the believer as a member in the body of Christ. This realistic approach to personhood is certainly something that has engaged me in terms of grief and death.[38] Models of personhood are determinative within analyses of such themes as grace, mercy, and certainly the love–grace union, and would enhance anthropology's considerable theoretical apparatus of reciprocity

[35] Douglas J. Davies, "Anglican Soteriology: Incarnation, Worship and the Property of Mercy," in *Salvation in Christ: Comparative Christian Views*, ed. Roger Keller and Robert L. Millett (Provo, UT: Religious Studies Center, Brigham Young University, 2005), 53–68.

[36] Robert Parkin, *The Dark Side of Humanity: The World of Robert Hertz and Its Legacies* (London: Harwood Academic Publishers, 1996); David Parkin (ed.), *The Anthropology of Evil* (New York: Wiley-Blackwell, 1987).

[37] McKim Marriott, "Hindu Transactions: Diversity without Dualism," in *Transactions and Meaning: Directions in the Anthropology of Exchange and Symbolic Behaviour*, ed. Bruce Kapferer (Philadelphia: Institute for the Study of Human Issues, 1976), 109–42; Marylin Strathern, *The Gender of the Gift* (Berkeley: University of California Press, 1988); Benjamin R. Smith, "Sorcery and the Dividual in Australia," *Journal of the Royal Anthropological Institute* 22/3 (September 2016): 670–87.

[38] Douglas J. Davies, *Death, Ritual and Belief: The Rhetoric of Funerary Rites*, 3rd edn (London: Continuum, forthcoming).

theory derived from Marcel Mauss and many later critics, including Maurice Godelier.[39] Still, there doubtless remains a great deal more to be said on this front as the love–grace dynamic contends with reciprocity's ready creation of merit. Here Mauss's work, as notably enhanced, for example, by Godelier and others, has much to offer in the complex worlds of practical religion where ideal theological types of grace and works commingle. The use of such theoretical approaches reflects the issue of obedience as a key theme in the Mormon Church and cultural life as depicted by Cannell in this volume. Wider still, biblical scholar John Barclay's recent study of *Paul and the Gift* offers one valuable volume that draws heavily on gift theory in anthropology for considering the foundational import of Paul for Christian cultures.[40]

Prayer

One other domain in which individual and dividual notions of personhood have yet to be connected in any extensive way between anthropology and theology is in the domain of prayer. Both the liturgically explicit and devotionally interior dialogue present ongoing challenges to the ongoing anthropology of embodiment, language, and communication. Prayer could contribute to anthropological ideas of the self, transformation of the self, and notions of otherness, not forgetting how theology once engaged with anthropology through the mediating field of the history and phenomenology of religion in such matters as Rudolph Otto's famed *Idea of the Holy* or Friedrich Heiler's *Prayer: A Study in the History and Psychology of Religion.*[41] Prayer inevitably raises issues of speech, silence, ritual practice, and the framing tonality of each, not to mention the life experience and aptitudes of scholars. Here I am reminded of Oxford's Institute of Social Anthropology in the early seventies when, today, one listened to Evans-Pritchard on Islamic mysticism[42] and tomorrow to Needham's Wittgensteinian-influenced lectures on religious experience[43] with perhaps the only linking features being place of delivery and the lecturers wearing gowns. This memory alerts us to the diversity of anthropological attitude to religious experiences.

[39] Maurice Godelier, *The Enigma of the Gift* (Oxford: Blackwell Publishers, 1999); Marcel Mauss, *The Gift, Forms and Functions of Exchange in Archaic Societies*, trans. Ian Cunnison (London: Routledge and Kegan Paul, 1970).

[40] John Barclay, *Paul and the Gift* (Cambridge: William B. Eerdmans Publishing Co., 2015).

[41] Rudoph Otto, *The Idea of the Holy*, trans. John W. Harvey (Oxford: Oxford University Press, 1924); Friedrich Heiler, *Prayer: A Study in the History and Psychology of Religion*, trans. Samuel McComb (Oxford: Oxford University Press, 1932).

[42] E. E. Evans-Pritchard, "Some Reflections on Mysticism," *DYN, Journal of the Durham University Anthropological Society* 1 (1970): 99–116.

[43] Rodney Needham, *Belief, Language and Experience* (Oxford: Basil Blackwell, 1972).

Sects, Betrayal, etc.

The tonality framing diverse patterns of management of experience is especially evident when accounting for both subtle and not so subtle divergence of theological opinion in sectarian groups, as Cannell has exemplified for Mormonism in this volume.[44] Indeed, sectarianism is a telling phenomenon that theology might still offer anthropology as an avenue of research. One of Professor Carol Harrison's (now of Christ Church, Oxford) recent doctoral students, Adam Powell, has begun valuable work in this area by looking at the theme of the sociology of heresy, focusing on Irenaeus and, across a millennium and more, on Joseph Smith.[45] The very notion of truth, integral to theology, is raised through sectarianism, as it was throughout patristic debates over creeds, and is an issue that theology can, rightly, pose to anthropology: What are differences about? A key related topic inherent in early Christianity's contribution to theological consideration, and which anthropology might develop to illuminating effect, is that of betrayal. An anthropology of betrayal would doubtless yield interesting cultural dynamics associated with the interplay of embodiment theory and the sociology of knowledge. Earliest Christian issues of self-identity and of the relationship between Christ and his Apostles cannot be understood apart from betrayal motifs. In medieval Durham, for example, a ritual of betrayal was developed and has been restored in very recent years, enacted on Maundy Thursday after the Eucharist of the Last Supper. Such liturgical revivals also offer anthropology fertile ground for the analysis of ritual within changing social circumstances.

Death

While betrayal as estrangement and loss is its own form of relational death, the fact of biological death and its many theological and ethical interpretations have long offered anthropology scope for analysis, and this continues today. Theological ideas of divine eternal being, the interplay of life, death, and resurrected, or samsaric existences still offer material for anthropological approaches to mortality, vitality, and the regeneration of communal life. Despite many ethnographic and theoretical studies in most of these fields, the wide scope of human experience still hints at the potential for anthropology to expand its existing insight.

---

[44] Cannell, Chapter 14, 244–65.
[45] Adam Powell, *Irenaeus, Joseph Smith and God-Making Heresy* (Cranbury: Fairleigh Dickinson University Press, 2016).

DISCIPLINARY QUANDARIES

Despite the themes already listed, and as I draw to something of a conclusion, I am confronted with a trembling paradox underlying the apparently secure idea that theology does actually possess questions for anthropological work. Echoing my earlier autobiographical notes, this paradox comes from having taught the anthropology of religion in various ways in two theology departments, and from many engagements with theologically educated students, with ecclesial contexts, and with society at large. As for speaking of the *apparently secure question* concerning both anthropology and theology as discrete academic disciplines, I reiterate Howell's comments in this volume on the diversity alluded to in phrasing *which anthropology* and *which theology*. There are so many schools within each.

To take theology first, apparent security is tenuous given the way the institutional academic–political nature of theology varies tremendously from society to society, usually in terms of the cultural influence of religious or other institutions. In many European countries, *theology* is frequently embedded in Catholic, Protestant, or Orthodox faculties whose academics may or may not speak to each other and where interpretations can easily become guarded and defended territories. In the USA, theology is most frequently embedded in colleges and universities founded and funded by discrete denominations, while state universities usually ignore such theology while pursuing religious studies. Scotland for a long time had its theology situated in its *state* universities where ministers of the Kirk were trained. England, the land of the *via media*, of the English Reformation, and of a slow acceptance of Catholicism, notably defined as *Roman* Catholicism, partly to accommodate the Anglo-Catholicism of an influential party within the state church, developed its own complex framing of theology within the academy largely because of the relative independence of Oxbridge colleges and of the place of clergy in relation to the British establishment. Durham, too, has had and has even recently increased its number of canon professors with chairs in the university and stalls in the cathedral. Though much could be said about such things, not least at a time of apparent secularization, I desist as far as this chapter is concerned.

The rise of UK religious studies, largely from the later 1960s, brought potential and some actual ripples to theological–academic lakes as notions of neutral study of religion rather than confessional study of theology emerged. Over the last fifty years, there have been an ongoing dynamic interplay and occasional face-offs between churches and university departments that involve the politics of churches and their financial support for university departments of theology. Most of these departments now include *religion*, the *study of religion*, or *religious studies* in their titles, often with much debate behind their nomenclature. Underlying names and name changes is the crucial question of recruiting both undergraduate and graduate students and the funding this raises.

This complex scene should not, however, only be considered in terms of institutions and their hereditary and contemporary funding and attraction of students but also in terms of the life commitments of teachers. As I have already alluded to when aligning worship and fieldwork, the affection people feel for particular doctrinal or theoretical perspectives can often be appropriated, even embodied, as its own habitus. Priests have, for example, been known to dress according to their espousal of distinctive theological and liturgical schemes, and holy dress often plays a significant role when personnel of different traditions meet. Perhaps one conversation between disciplines might ask how theoretical or methodological issues are, for example, signaled in anthropology. This would be interesting in terms of anthropology that has, within my academic career, embraced, rejected, and partially re-embraced theoretical emphases on function, the mental generation of cultural phenomena, the ritual–symbolic nature of behavior, the power of narrative, autobiographical tension of critical awareness, gender, power, and postcolonial sensitivity, and the role of genetic and cognitive factors in human survival, meaning making, and flourishing. These diverse schools, let alone allied issues of method and practice, make anthropology as a singular noun deeply problematic, much as in theology with its broad Protestant, Catholic, and Orthodox outlooks and their own forms of fine-tuning. From the later nineteenth century, the Church of England, for example, created theological colleges in which to train leaders; even terms such as *priest* or *minister* reflected stark differences of worldview as did the diverse naming of the ritual, with theological commitments speaking of the Mass, the Holy Communion, Holy Eucharist, or Lord's Supper. When theology pervaded ecclesial organization, the word *priest* became even more problematic when some considered that status impossible for a woman. While anthropology has not, perhaps, experienced that ontological issue in such a fashion over its theory, practice, and gender issue in relation to fieldwork, questions of access to gendered forms of social life might certainly cultivate a valuable discussion.

My point is made. There is a great deal of difference of opinion, theological format, and occasional ferment within Christianity, as in most other religious traditions. There are many bands, tribes, and nations here. This situation lays down the challenge for our task of considering what this grandly diverse entity known as *theology* has to bring to a fairly diverse entity, *anthropology*, all as part of a creative challenge of humanity's self-knowing. Perhaps only certain tribes or sects within anthropology and theology are interested in meeting, and where might be their preferred meeting-place, and what of its ethos and tonality? One answer invokes the British via media, notably, a kind of establishment stage of polite engagement, one that invites its own cultural analysis in terms of power, status, and the respectability, prestige, and worldviews of partners and their institutions. Is it the same in the USA, for example, or are there distinctive interests that motivate the desire for discussion? Who has what to gain? What of cognitive and emotional competition for status among participants? Why should anyone, especially in anthropology, ask *if* theology has a question for anthropology? This raises the distinction between the relatively easy pursuit of an anthropology of Christianity, of the more doctrinally driven self-identity and sensitivity of Christian anthropology, and of the conversational nature of participants interested in each other's issues highlighted in this chapter. While it is obvious that, in all of these pursuits, talk is not cheap, their potential for engaged conversation to generate valuable understanding makes the venture a capital endeavor. Perhaps trembling paradox is, in itself, highly valuable as a state resembling Ernesto de Martino's "crisis of presence," which typifies so much of human existence.[46]

---

[46] Fabrizio M. Ferrari, *Ernesto de Martino: The Crisis and the Presence* (Sheffield: Equinox, 2012).

12

Athens Engaging Jerusalem

Michael A. Rynkiewich

"What has Athens to do with Jerusalem?"[1] the theologian Tertullian (*c*.155–*c*.240) famously queried. Of course, Tertullian was asking whether or not the methods of philosophical inquiry were appropriate for biblical studies. He concluded not. A contemporary version might read, "What has anthropology to do with theology?" However, this time the question is slanted in the opposite direction, wondering why anthropology should pay any attention to theology.[2]

I have spent most of my academic life compartmentalized, and I have no regrets. At first, I taught anthropology through the week,[3] and I taught Sunday school on the weekends.[4] Toward the end of my career, I spend a lot of time teaching anthropology to seminary students, trying to help them shape or refine their vision for ministry and mission.[5] Along the way, I have always been curious about the fact that, along with such subtopics as Christology, harmatology, and eschatology, theological studies also have a branch called anthropology. A brief survey conducted years ago led me to conclude that, although the name was the same, this area was a completely different subject. In other words, while a theology of mission and ministry would benefit from the insights of anthropology, I was not clear on why anthropology should pay any attention to theology.

I would like to thank Steve Ybarrola, Ruth Tipton, Timothy Pawl, and particularly Khaled Furani for their comments on earlier drafts of this chapter.

[1] Tertullian, *De praescriptione haereticorum* [On the prescription of heretics], ch. 7, <www.tertullian.org/works/de_praescriptione_haereticorum.htm>.

[2] An issue that Wolfhart Pannenberg addresses in "Theological Questions to Scientists," *Zygon* 16/1 (1981): 65–76, which reappears as chapter 1 of his *Toward a Theology of Nature: Essays on Science and Faith* (Louisville, KY: Westminster John Knox Press, 1993), 15–28.

[3] At Macalester College from 1971–81, along with James Spradley and David McCurdy.

[4] At Central Evangelical Free Church in downtown Minneapolis.

[5] At Asbury Theological Seminary from 2002 to present, now retired but continuing part-time.

It is not that I thought anthropology was perfect or without blind spots. In fact, I resigned my position as chair of the Department of Anthropology at Macalester College in 1981 in part because I was disappointed that the promise of anthropology was not being fulfilled. Like many others in graduate school, I had believed that education would solve problems. I pictured my vocation as teaching anthropology, exposing ethnocentrism and racism, and sending off reconstructed students to build a just society. My experience in the decade of the 1970s was that about one-third of my students understood it, about one-third just needed a grade in a required class but did not care about the course content, and about one-third took their new understanding of culture as a tool they could use to compete better in the business world.

Now, with the postmodern turn, anthropology has undergone its own self-critique that reveals other blind spots or obstacles to understanding. Perhaps anthropology could learn something from theology—not least, as Furani notes in this work, to recognize the theology already inherent in anthropology.[6]

I try to avoid treating the Other—theology in this case—in generic terms,[7] although at times one may find it necessary to characterize a theological tradition. Thus, I choose a specific issue and name theologians who might be of interest to anthropologists. While a number of issues beckon (e.g., rationalism, dualism, the concept of progress), I want to turn to a fundamental concept: personhood. Wolfhart Pannenberg (1928–2014), among others, claims, "Hegel and more recently Adolf von Harnack were right therefore in considering the assertion of the infinite value of the individual to be a central idea in Christianity."[8] This claim corresponds to the understanding in anthropology. For example, Marcel Mauss claimed as well, "It is Christians who have made a metaphysical entity of the 'moral person' (*personne morale*) after they become aware of its religious power. Our own notion of the human person is still basically the Christian one."[9] The modern/Western *person* (in its most individualist mode) does have a genealogical link to St Thomas Aquinas (1225–74), or back to St Augustine (354–430), and, others say, back to the Greeks.[10] Augustine's work established the *one person* as reflecting the image of the *one God* (*imago Dei*), thus dignifying the person as an agent with a

---

[6] Khaled Furani, Chapter 4, 66–82.

[7] Philip Fountain and Sin Wen Lau, "Anthropological Theologies: Engagements and Encounters," *Australian Journal of Anthropology* 24/3 (2013): 231.

[8] Wolfhart Pannenberg, *Anthropology in Theological Perspective* (Philadelphia: Westminster Press, 1985), 167.

[9] Marcel Mauss, "A Category of the Human Mind: The Notion of Person, the Notion of Self," in *The Category of the Person: Anthropology, Philosophy, History*, ed. Michael Carrithers, Steven Collins, and Steven Lukes (Cambridge: Cambridge University Press, 1985), 19. See also Louis Dumont, "A Modified View of Our Origins: The Christian Beginnings of Modern Individualism," in the same volume, 94–6.

[10] Kenelm Burridge, *Someone, No One: An Essay on Individuality* (Princeton: Princeton University Press, 1979), 11.

reasonable spirit that is lightly and temporarily connected to an earthly body.[11] The Trinitarian nature of God, however, was revealed only in the interior character of the soul: in spirit, knowledge, and love; that is, in substance and not in relationship.[12] After Augustine, Boethius produced the classic account of the person.

It was Boethius who established the essential Western definition of the person:

> Boethius' definition of person as rational individuality became normative for the subsequent philosophical tradition. It suppressed the older meaning of the word "person" as role, mask, face, and held its own against medieval attempts, suggested by the doctrine of the Trinity, at a relational understanding of the person. Given the Boethian interpretation of person as rational individuality, it is understandable that the idealist philosophies of the modern age should think of the person as constituted by self-consciousness. Then, since self-consciousness was understood in terms of the ego, ego, subject, and person could become interchangeable concepts.[13]

Depending on one's perspective, Boethius's work was either a great achievement for Western philosophy or a misstep for our understanding of persons: "Boethius (487–524) provided us with an idea which was to prove a most lasting concept. He defined a person as an 'individual substance in a rational nature.' The key elements of that definition of individuality—distinctiveness, substantiveness, and rationality—travelled safely from the fifth century, through early humanism, into the Enlightenment and on to the very end of the twentieth century where it is now being savaged."[14] And not without reason.

Aquinas extended the rational part by conceiving of the person as one with *natura intellectualis*.[15] In the imagined monarchical model of the Trinity, Aquinas allowed that from the "rational creature" came "a word procession as regards the intelligence and a love procession as regards the will."[16] The person, by definition, is complete and separate from all else. Aquinas does talk about participation, *methexis*, in the sense that a human being shares in the being of God as a creature shares in the existence of a creator. That is, the

---

[11] Augustine, *De Trinitate (On the Trinity)*, Book V, in *The Essential Augustine*, ed. Vernon J. Bourke (New York: New American Library, 1964), 138–9.

[12] Jürgen Moltmann, *God in Creation: A New Theology of Creation and the Spirit of God*, *The Gifford Lectures 1984–1985* (Minneapolis, MN: Fortress Press, 1993), 236–7.

[13] Pannenberg, *Anthropology in Theological Perspective*, 235–6.

[14] Elaine Storkey, "Modernity and Anthropology," in *Faith and Modernity*, ed. Philip Sampson, Vinay Samuel, and Chris Sugden (Oxford: Regnum Books International, 1994), 139.

[15] Thomas Aquinas, *Summa Theologica*, I, q 79, Article 1, in Anton C. Pegis, *Introduction to Saint Thomas Aquinas* (New York: The Modern Library, 1948), 337.

[16] Thomas Aquinas, *Summa Theologica*, I, q 93, Article 6. See also Moltmann, *God in Creation*, 238.

creature is permitted to share in existence, which is the sole property of the creator. Down through time, Aquinas's nuanced view of participation has been eclipsed by the notion of a separate rational person.[17]

Louis Dumont argues that the final twist on the concept of the individual in the West is attributable to John Calvin: "My thesis is simple: with Calvin the hierarchical dichotomy that characterized our field of consideration comes to an end: the antagonistic worldly element that individualism had hitherto accommodated disappears entirely in Calvin's theocracy. The field is absolutely unified. *The individual is now in the world, and the individualist values rules without restriction or limitation.* The inworldly individual is before us."[18] With Calvin, the individual identified with the sovereign will of God becomes the rational lord and master of his own fate while love, emotion, and mystery fade into the background. Milbank claims that this strand of Western theology, "by abandoning participation in divine Being and Unity for a 'covenantal bond' between God and men,... provided a model for human interrelationships as 'contractual' ones."[19] In the process, the notion of participation in the Other was diminished.

Thus, with respect to personhood, as conceived in this genealogy of knowledge, the person is a unified being, just as God is, independent but capable of making contractual relations.[20] With respect to the dynamics of the person, the person is plural internally because God is Trinitarian. As the Father is the monarch of the Trinity, so rationality or reason is the monarch of the person. From this intellectual genealogy, Descartes, reflecting Augustine,[21] could proclaim, "I think, therefore I am," or Freud could imagine an ego and id dominated by a superego, and both could think that there was something inside that managed the exterior presentation of a person. And so the modern person was born, whole at birth with body, soul/mind, and spirit, ready to negotiate his or her way into society or change the world by his or her intelligence and independence.

---

[17] Joseph W. Koterski, "The Doctrine of Participation in Thomistic Metaphysics," in *The Future of Thomism*, ed. Deal W. Hudson and Dennis W. Moran (Notre Dame, IN: University of Notre Dame Press, 1992), 185–96.

[18] Louis Dumont, "A Modified View of Our Origins: The Christian Beginnings of Modern Individualism," in *The Category of the Person: Anthropology, Philosophy, History*, ed. Michael Carrithers, Steven Collins, and Steven Lukes (Cambridge: Cambridge University Press, 1985), 113–14.

[19] John Milbank, *Theology and Social Theory: Beyond Secular Reason*, 2nd edn (Malden, MA: Blackwell Publishing, 2006), 16.

[20] Marcel Mauss made this same argument, as Bailecki and Daswani point out. Jon Bialecki and Girish Daswani, "What Is an Individual? The View from Christianity," *HAU: Journal of Ethnographic Theory* 5/1 (2015): 286.

[21] *City of God*, XI, 26, in *The Essential Augustine*, ed. Vernon J. Bourke (New York: New American Library, 1964), 33.

Philosopher Elaine Storkey concludes:

Thus, the fundamental doctrine of the person changed from dependence on God to independence from any higher authority. It also changed from being relational to being avowedly individual. Because the dependent relationship with God had been severed, there was now no ontological basis for community. Autonomous human individuals do not readily give up their self-sufficiency to care for others in society. The contest between the twin giants of rational individualism and imposed collectivism began, fought out on the platform of the world stage.[22]

This conception of the individual is foundational not only for Western culture but also for the social sciences.

Western social sciences are based on the assumption that this kind of person not only exists but is the norm. Anthropologist Alan Page Fiske claims, "The prevailing assumption in Western psychology has been that humans are by nature asocial individualists. Psychologists (and most other social scientists) usually explain social relationships as instrumental means to extrinsic, nonsocial ends, or as constraints on the satisfaction of individual desires."[23] Thus, the dominant issue for the Western social sciences has been, as Meyer Fortes says, "The perennial problem of how individual and society are interconnected"[24]: (1) how an already existing person learns to live in society, (2) what happens if he or she fails to adjust and mature, and (3) how a person negotiates relationships yet remains an individual person.

As Howell and Clooney argue in their chapters, theology is not monistic; there are different kinds of theology, even different kinds of Christian theology.[25] My claim, which in some ways moves in the opposite direction from Larsen and King, is that a critique of the unified "sovereign individual"[26] notion of personhood might have emerged earlier if anthropologists had paid attention to other theological traditions, both Christian and otherwise. I will provide examples from three eras where alternate conceptions of the person might be found. First, the early Church Fathers in the Eastern Orthodox tradition have provided an alternate view of the person. Second, in the twentieth century, missionary anthropologists operating at the boundary of the disciplines of theology and anthropology explored indigenous alternate views of the person. Finally, contemporary theologians have emerged in the

---

[22] Storkey, "Modernity and Anthropology," 139.

[23] Alan Page Fiske, "The Four Elementary Forms of Sociality: Frameworks for a Unified Theory of Social Relations," *Psychological Review* 99/4 (1992): 689.

[24] Meyer Fortes, "On the Concept of the Person among the Tallensi," in *La Notion de la Personne en Afrique Noire*, ed. G. Dieterlen (Paris: Éditions du Centre National de la Recherche Scientifique, 1973), 288. Cited in J. S. LaFontaine, "Person and Individual: Some Anthropological Reflections," in *The Category of the Person: Anthropology, Philosophy, History* (Cambridge: Cambridge University Press, 1985), 125.

[25] Brian M. Howell, Chapter 2, 29–49; Francis X. Clooney, Chapter 16, 280–95.

[26] My thanks to Khaled Furani for this term.

West who now critique the traditional view of the person. Anthropologists missed these opportunities, delaying the critique of the conception of person until the 1980s and 1990s.

* * *

The story told by many, from Augustine through Aquinas, from Calvin and Luther through Dumont and Burridge, is only one of the histories of Christianity.[27] As the anthropology of Christianity ethnographers have affirmed, many "Christianities" exist.[28] Eastern Orthodox theology did not follow the path that led to the enthronement of the rational individual connected only by contract or covenant to God and others. Joel Robbins' claim that anthropologists might learn something about *otherness* from theologians[29] can be further nuanced by the question "which theologians?"

The emergence of the Eastern Church's concept of person is traced, as in the West, to theological disputes concerning the Incarnation (i.e., Christ as God and man, two in one and one in two) and the Trinity (i.e., three in one and one in three). Gregory of Nazianzus (*c.*329–390) both precedes and overlaps with Augustine here, and therein lies the fork in the road.

Gregory contributes a *person* who is deeply connected to the Other. As Scalise notes, "The first use of the verb *perichōréō* (from which *perichōrēsis* is derived) appears in Gregory of Nazianzus' works."[30] Gregory worked out a theology that developed the concept of *perichōrēsis* variously translated as *interpenetration, exchange,* or *coinherence.* Gregory argues that Christ is the "heavenly man," with "the names being mingled like the natures, . . . flowing [*perichōréō*] into one another, according to the law of their intimate union."[31] Neither Gregory nor other theologians of his time were yet concerned with how coinherence happened;[32] however, Gregory was certain that *perichōrēsis* did not involve a simple exchange nor end in the disappearance of the person. Scalise concludes, "Whatever semantic boundaries and resulting connotations for *perichōréō* result from this study, it may be said that the meaning is not 'to be contained in so as to be dissolved.'"[33] Thus, the emerging understanding of personhood was both relational and fluid—that is, not based on persistent substance but rather on movement.

---

[27] Mark Mosko, "Partible Penitents: Dividual Personhood and Christian Practice in Melanesia and the West," *Journal of the Royal Anthropological Institute* 16/2 (2010): 220.

[28] Fenella Cannell, "Introduction," in *The Anthropology of Christianity*, ed. Fenella Cannell (Durham, NC: Duke University Press, 2006), 4, 7.

[29] Joel Robbins, "Anthropology and Theology: An Awkward Relationship?" *Anthropological Quarterly* 79/2 (2006): 287.

[30] Brian T. Scalise, "Perichoresis in Gregory Nazianzen and Maximus the Confessor," *Eleutheria* 2/1 (2012): 58, <http://digitalcommons.liberty.edu/eleu/vol2/iss1/5>.

[31] Gregory of Nazianzus, Epistle CI, par. 4. Cited in Scalise, "Perichoresis," 59.

[32] Scalise, "Perichoresis," 61.   [33] Ibid., 62.

Maximus the Confessor (580–662) extended Gregory's ideas:

The term *perichōrēsis* continues to develop significantly through Maximus. The conjoining of "ever-active" with "repose" constructs the paradoxical "rest in movement" or "rest with movement." With this paradox, the distinction between the *coinherence* and *interpenetration* is manifest. *Perichōrēsis* can be translated as either because of the semantic elasticity of the word. On the one hand, *coinherence* emphasizes the static, that is, repose. On the other hand, *interpenetration* highlights movement, that is, the "ever-active."[34]

Relationship within the Trinity, if we may speak this way, is both like and unlike the relationship between God and man or woman. Concerned about an *interpenetration* that might imply too much about humanity's contribution to the person of God, Maximus consistently maintained a limit by distancing God such that humanity's movement was always toward God but never actually arriving in a place of equal exchange with God.

Maximus the Confessor contributed conceptually to a related notion. He taught an epistemology in which the rational knowledge of God and creation was held in balance with, and held in check by, *metousia,* which can be translated as *participation, experience,* or *communion.* The kind of knowledge generated by participation was not always rational and sometimes had a feeling of *mystica* (mystery).[35] Thus, one could know by contemplation, know through experience, or know through mystical insight. This collective nature of *knowing* is intertwined with *ousia* or *being* but is not *being* itself, which is attributed only to God. *Metousia* thus means to participate in God's being. In Maximus's theology, the journey is an ontological one, towards *theosis* or union with God, but always towards.

Thus, the person (*prosôpon*) exists (or subsists) only in relationship, not in being (*ousia*). "Whatever we share with others, we are: it belongs to our nature. But what it is to be a person is not some thing, some quality, that we do *not* share with others—as if there were an irreducible somewhat within each one of us that makes us the unique persons we are. What is unique about us is what we have made of the nature that we have: our own unique mode of existence. . . . "[36] This view, of course, is counter to the dominant Western view of persons.

In the combined system of Gregory and Maximus, even the persons of God exist, not so much in and of themselves but in relationship with each other. Likewise, the human person does not exist either prior to or outside of

---

[34] Ibid., 66.

[35] Paul M. Blowers and Robert Louis Wilken (ed. and trans.), *On the Cosmic Mystery of Jesus Christ* (Crestwood, NY: St Vladimir's Seminary Press, 2003), 126–7. See also Peter Bellini, *Participation: Epistemology and Mission Theology* (Lexington, KY: Emeth Press, 2010), 101–3.

[36] Andrew Louth, *Maximus the Confessor,* The Early Church Fathers, gen. ed. Carol Harrison (London: Routledge, 1996), 59.

relationship with God and with others. No rational individual stands alone in this genealogy of theology. No static, nonchanging person stands at the base of it all; rather the person moves and flows with the relationship.

This conception of the person stands as a critique of Western theology. Storkey claims, "Of course, Boethius was wrong, or was wrongly angled. To locate our human identity in some essential distinctiveness rather than in our relationality (especially our relationship to God), got anthropology off to a very bad start."[37] Anthropology does not escape from the same critique.

From Maximus the Confessor one can trace a genealogy of ideas leading to contemporary theologian John Zizoulas, Metropolitan of Pergamon (1931–). Zizoulas locates the differences between Western and Eastern theology in the starting point: substance versus relationships. Among the Eastern Greek Fathers what is critical about defining God, the Trinity, is not substance but relations. Ontologically, Zizoulas positions "being as communion," which is the title of his most influential book.[38] Both with the Trinity and with humanity "the substance never exists in a 'naked' state, that is, without hypostasis, without a 'mode of existence . . . .' Love as God's mode of existence 'hypostasizes' God, *constitutes* His being."[39] This conception of the person is significant for Eastern Orthodox soteriology because if God's personhood were based on substance, then humans could never attain to it, but if God's personhood is based on hypostasis, mode of being, or relationship, then humans have hope.

This other long genealogy of theology is mostly outside the gaze of Western theology and Western anthropology. As Morton summarizes, "The emergent discipline of anthropology founded itself by tending largely to ignore long-standing aspects of theological discourse that have been open to otherness and genuine discovery."[40] Eastern Orthodox theology, overlooked by both Western anthropology and the Western church, might have given us a more relational understanding of person.

*   *   *

Enlightenment-era missionaries were also seduced by the Western Christian theory of the person. As I claimed elsewhere, "We have had to move to other languages (*missio Dei, imago Dei, hypostasis*) and to other cultures (Greek Orthodox) and to other times (early Church Fathers) to get a handle on a biblical construction of persons that differs from the Western view that has

[37] Storkey, "Modernity and Anthropology," 139.

[38] John D. Zizoulas, *Being as Communion: Studies in Personhood and the Church* (Crestwood, NY: St Vladimir's Seminary Press, 1985).

[39] Zizoulas, *Being as Communion*, 41, 46.

[40] John Morton, "Durkheim, Freud and I in Aboriginal Australia, or Should Anthropology Contain Theology?" *Australian Journal of Anthropology* 24/3 (2013): 236. Morton is summarizing Mark L. Taylor, *Beyond Explanation: Religious Dimensions in Cultural Anthropology* (Macon, GA: Mercer University Press, 1986), 17–66.

coalesced in the last two hundred years."[41] However, some missionaries were able to break out of the Western theological tradition in their perception of persons precisely because they were open to the indigenous Other. In his chapter, Clooney is an example of a theologian who has opened up to the possibility of a relational, even multiple, personhood through engagement with other traditions.[42]

Maurice Leenhardt (1878–1954) was a missionary of the Paris Evangelical Mission Society in its work in New Caledonia (1902–27). Leenhardt returned to France in 1927 to transition into an academic career, eventually succeeding Marcel Mauss at the École Pratique des Hautes Études, where he was himself succeeded by Claude Lévi-Strauss. Though his training was surely in Western theology, Leenhardt in the field evinced an Eastern Orthodox modality; he learned through his experience with the Other. His style of research and writing "may all be seen as strategies designed to frustrate theoretical foreclosure and too easy appropriation of the Other."[43] The world that the Canaque lived in, theorized Leenhardt, was not human-centered (anthropomorphic) but rather centered outside the self (cosmomorphic): "In cosmomorphic experience the substances of nature actually live in the person. There is no clear cut separation between self and the world; the same flux of life circulates in the body, in the sap of a plant, in the colors of a stone.... There is no felt distance between subject and object, no mediation of similarity in difference."[44]

This identification with nature Leenhardt calls *participation*, echoing Maximus the Confessor but more likely derived directly from Lucien Levy-Bruhl. Levy-Bruhl used participation to represent the relationship between persons and/or things such that the person identified with the Other and thought that he or she was of the same substance with the Other.[45] The person did not disappear, but "in accordance with the principle of mystical participation, society is as much merged in the individual as the individual is merged with society."[46] Levy-Bruhl had in mind more than exchange or even exchange of parts of the person. Rather, he and Leenhardt envisioned the emergence of the mystical in the flow between subjects. His concept of participation was little appreciated during his lifetime and was soon eclipsed by the overly optimistic certainty of structuralism.

---

[41] Michael A. Rynkiewich, "What about the Dust? Missiological Musings on Anthropology," in *What about the Soul? Neuroscience and Christian Anthropology*, ed. Joel B. Green (Nashville, TN: Abingdon Press, 2004), 140.

[42] Clooney, Chapter 16, 280–95.

[43] James Clifford, *Person and Myth: Maurice Leenhardt in the Melanesian World* (Durham, NC: Duke University Press, 1982), 172.

[44] Clifford, *Person and Myth*, 173.

[45] Stanley Jeyaraja Tambiah, *Magic, Science and Religion and the Scope of Rationality* (Cambridge: Cambridge University Press, 1990), 86.

[46] Ibid.

One who, not surprisingly, lamented the sidelining of Levy-Bruhl was E. E. Evans-Pritchard:

> In France and Germany Levy-Bruhl's views have been extensively examined and criticised and it is difficult to understand why they were met with so great neglect and derision among English anthropologists. Their reception is perhaps partly due to the key expressions used by Levy-Bruhl in his writings, such as "prologique," "representations collectives," "mystique," "participations," and so forth. Doubtless it is also due in part to the uncritical manner in which Levy-Bruhl handled his material which was often of a poor quality in any case. But responsibility must be shared by his critics who made little effort to grasp the ideas which lay behind the cumbersome terminology in which they were frequently expressed.[47]

Perhaps participation and mystique came too close to belief in the supernatural and thus paled by comparison to a safe reductionist, mechanical, and aseptic structuralism.

While other anthropologists might have been, Leenhardt was not averse to religion. Participation, according to Leenhardt, involves "two coexisting modes of apprehension: 'mythic knowledge' and 'rational knowledge.'"[48] Thus, this person lives outside of his or her body by participating in Nature and the Other, guided by a mythic hermeneutic. Leenhardt argues that some things could not be known rationally but only through experience outside of oneself in another time and in another space. Leenhardt sometimes referred to participation and communion together, implying that they were different in that communion occurs between more distinct persons than the boundary-less participation:[49]

> Leenhardt saw Melanesian life as a dynamic totalistic weaving of nature, society, myth and technology, and he saw the Melanesian village as the centre of a surrounding mythic landscape, where mountains, rocks, trees and animals were seen as familiar, and as endowed with the power of its ancestor-god and with totemic life. Such natural entities and phenomena were regarded as discrete presences in which the living were implicated. The landscape was a mediator between the invisible and the visible worlds, an area of "lived myth," and the life of each group was guarded by its totems and ancestors immanent in the landscape. The concept of participation conveyed to Leenhardt this felt relation between the self and person, and the phenomena of the mythic landscape.[50]

The exchange with others engaged many levels.

Clifford agrees with Evans-Pritchard, lamenting that Leenhardt's thinking, whether theory or theology, was eclipsed by structuralism where seemingly clear concepts such as kinship structure, language, and myth blew away the mist of an entangled mythic and rational knowledge and dissolved the

---

[47] E. E. Evans-Pritchard, "Levy-Bruhl's Theory of Primitive Mentality," *Journal of the Anthropological Society of Oxford* 1/2 (1970): 39.
[48] Clifford, *Person and Myth*, 174.   [49] Ibid., 184–7.
[50] Tambiah, *Magic, Science and Religion*, 106.

difference between a person and a person-in-relationship. Leenhardt was much more cautious and provisional in his understanding. Leenhardt was sidelined until the emergence of post-structuralism when the person-in-relationship, or *sociality* as Marilyn Strathern calls it, reappears in anthropology.[51]

I, too, lament that both anthropologists and missionaries did not take up Leenhardt's thinking and some, but not all, of Levy-Bruhl's thinking, particularly with reference to land and land tenure. The relationship between person and ownership has long been the labor of Western law and the burden of colonized peoples. Western law narrows to the question of who owns the land, but indigenous groups more than own the land. They participate with each other in the land and the land in them. I led researchers at the Melanesian Institute in a four-year research project on land and churches in Melanesia.[52] The vast gulf between Western legal concepts and Melanesian notions of land use continued to contribute to conflict over land. Melanesians struggled to convey the sense of identity and consubstantiation[53] with one's ancestors and ancestral group and the whole environment, including the land.[54] If anthropologists address the matter, they do so from the perspective either of human rights, in which case it is based on the Western notion of an individual person under the law, or from a concern for indigenous peoples, which tends toward an essentialist view of the human person. The matter of personhood is not just a theoretical issue but one of practical concern, one of ownership and agency, especially for people who are forced into the cast of someone else's making. Howell's chapter shows how a Christian contribution to personhood is also complicit in a people's reshaping and repositioning of their own identity and personhood as a form of resistance to perceived inequality.[55]

* * *

The concept of participation of a person-in-relationship proves significant for understanding the nature of sociality as well as property law. This line of reasoning is being recovered in Western theology by the two most prominent Protestant theologians of the second half of the twentieth century: Jürgen Moltmann and Wolfhart Pannenberg.

Jürgen Moltmann (1926–) recognizes "the one-sidedness of Western anthropology."[56] Moltmann links "the tendency toward monotheism in the concept of God" with "a trend towards individualism in anthropology."[57] This pairing

---

[51] Marilyn Strathern, *The Gender of the Gift: Problems with Women and Problems with Society in Melanesia* (Berkeley: University of California Press, 1988), 12; see also 29, 269.

[52] This work resulted in two edited volumes: Michael A. Rynkiewich (ed.), *Land and Churches in Melanesia: Issues and Contexts, Point No. 25* (Goroka: The Melanesian Institute, 2001); *Land and Churches in Melanesia: Cases and Procedures, Point No. 27* (Goroka: The Melanesian Institute, 2004).

[53] Tambiah's terms.

[54] See articles by Bernard Narokobi and Henry Paroi in Rynkiewich, *Land and Churches, Point No. 25.*

[55] Howell, Chapter 2, 29–49.   [56] Moltmann, *God in Creation*, 235.   [57] Ibid., 234.

was accomplished by internalizing the plurality of the Trinity within the one soul as spirit, knowledge, and love, and Moltmann finds this move problematic in its dependence on the monarchical Trinity, the body/soul dualism, and its inherent patriarchy. What Moltmann proposes is a reconsideration of "the concept of the social image of God developed by the Greek Fathers of the church."[58] Thus, "The inner fellowship of the Father, the Son and the Holy Spirit is represented in the fundamental human communities, and is manifested in them through creation and redemption."[59] The sense of fluidity, movement, and openness is preserved in this model: "Instead of starting with a closed and self-contained Trinity which manifests itself outwardly without differentiation, we have taken as our premise an open Trinity which manifests itself outwardly in differentiated form . . . . That is to say that through the Son the divine Trinity throws itself open for human beings."[60] Moltmann argues then that the goal of this process is the *embodiment* of the person rather than creating a dualism of body and soul. He imagines "a *perichoretic* relationship of mutual interpenetration and differentiated unity; but we shall not introduce one-sided structures of domination into it."[61] Thus Moltmann draws on the long history of theology reaching back before the East–West schism.

Wolfhart Pannenberg agrees, in some respects, with the notion of an *open Trinity*, and sees the implications for anthropology: "In Scheler and Gehlen this place is described by the concept of 'openness to the world.' Plessner, for his part, prefers the expression 'exocentricity'; he intends to express the same content, however, and the new term points only to a critical limitation of that content and represents an effort to define it more precisely."[62] Anthropology could pair exocentricity with the concept of ethnocentricity.

This concept resonates with Damasio's "extended consciousness."[63] The realization of self comes from a distancing from oneself and an extension into the world of other selves. Pannenberg recognizes a tension between what he calls *animal centrality* or egocentricity and exocentricity.[64] Exocentricity involves the alienation of the self while recognizing the *Other* as engaged with self: "Therefore, the question raised at the beginning of this section must be faced: Is human exocentricity perhaps to be defined as sociality? Do human beings perhaps live outside themselves, *extra se*, to the extent that they live by participating in the enveloping context of their social and cultural world with its traditions?"[65] This perspective takes us beyond Western individualism.

The claim that human beings live outside themselves is not unlike the claim that, while the brain is in the cranium, the mind is not. With a faint echo of

[58] Ibid., 240.   [59] Ibid., 241.   [60] Ibid., 242–3.   [61] Ibid., 259.

[62] Pannenberg, *Anthropology in Theological Perspective*, 35.

[63] Antonio Damasio, *The Feeling of What Happens: Body and Emotion in the Making of Consciousness* (New York: Harcourt, 1999), 195–233.

[64] Pannenberg, *Anthropology in Theological Perspective*, 80–1.   [65] Ibid., 164.

Jesus's claim, "For those who want to save their life will lose it, and those who lose their life for my sake will save it,"[66] Pannenberg notes, "The idea, voiced by Wilhelm von Humboldt as early as 1793 and subsequently developed by Hegel, that human beings must go out of themselves in order to gain themselves, is most likely connected with 'alienation' in Rousseau's sense of the term."[67] The ability to see the world through another's eyes has long been linked to the capacity for ethical living.

As Milbank, Storkey, and Bellini have pointed out, the practice of the person as substance, as an individual standing alone, gives rise to self-creation, then self-promotion, and then self-aggrandizement.[68] As Cannell, following Weber and Dumont, claims, the result of this genealogy of ideas and practice is "the creation of the capitalist individual."[69]

In a word, such a conception of a person eases the way to violence. Because the liberation of the individual from community necessarily *others the Other* and opens the way to power differentials. By contrast, the claim of Eastern Orthodox theology as well as Canaque theology is that the Other is already part of the participatory person and thus should not be separated for violence. The solution, Milbank claims, is "to try to put forward an alternative *mythos*, equally unfounded [by modernist standards], but nonetheless embodying an 'ontology of peace', which conceives differences as analogically related, rather than equivocally at variance."[70] Difference is what makes the Other like us.

Robbins takes up this claim for an ontology of peace built on the "value of salvation," which includes the "practices of charity and reconciliation," but does not go far enough. It is not just a value but a matter of being, *metousia*, being with, participation, in which one does not just value the other but identifies with the other, beyond value and beyond relationship.[71] This ontology gives a real basis for hope.[72]

This ontology of peace does not distance the Other with the risk of objectifying the subject[73] but is open to knowing the Other, not in a rational sense but as a mysterious part of Oneself. The danger is that anthropology fails to engage the Other as self because of its "contemplative stance" that disbelieves

---

[66] Luke 9:24, NRSV.   [67] Pannenberg, *Anthropology in Theological Perspective*, 269–70.

[68] Milbank, *Theology and Social Theory*, 278–9; Storkey, "Modernity and Anthropology," 145–6; Bellini, *Participation*, 85.

[69] Cannell, "Introduction," 20. We have ethnographies that already question the simplistic line of causation among Westernization, secularization, and the capitalistic individual. See, for example, Lisa Hoffman, *Patriotic Professonalism in Urban China: Fostering Talent* (Philadelphia: Temple University Press, 2010).

[70] Milbank, *Theology and Social Theory*, 279.

[71] Robbins, "Anthropology and Theology," 291.   [72] Ibid., 292.

[73] Once in Papua New Guinea, I was talking with a doctoral student who was badly shaken by an incident in his village where two old widows had been beaten and burned, accused of practicing witchcraft. He told me that he called his supervisor seeking emotional support, and the supervisor only asked, "Did you take good notes?"

and distances.[74] Godfrey Lienhardt writing about personhood in parts of Africa concludes the following about the limitations of anthropology: "But here, in the acceptance of the interpenetration from time to time of the human and divine (and of the divine as defined, of course, by their tradition), there appears an experience into which foreigners cannot really enter, for while living in the same political and social world, they do not belong to it by descent, and descent itself has profound religious value."[75] Perhaps it is mainly Western anthropologists who are unable to enter into a reality where the person exists by relationship.

* * *

Anthropology, as Western theology, has suffered from inheriting too narrow a conception of personhood. Anthropology is only now finding its way out of the cul-de-sac, and Eastern Orthodox theology and Canaque theology, as well as critical contemporary Western theologians, may offer help in this matter. The myth of the *rational individual* has dominated Western theology as well as the social sciences for centuries. In contrast, there stands the relational person, a communal-minded person engaged in the exchange of goods as part of the definition of self.[76]

In recent years, ethnographers, aided by their subjects, have imagined the dividual person, permeable and partible,[77] as one in an exchange relationship with other persons, dividual or individual, but where the things exchanged are parts of the self. This discussion has been useful, helping to explain, for example, the difference between a Melanesian "big man" and a "*rabisman*,"[78] or the relationship between naming, personhood, and cargo cult leaders.[79]

I want to suggest, with little sense of originality, that there is more. Levy-Bruhl and especially Maurice Leenhardt were working in this direction when the winds of theory changed and left them adrift. They were developing the concept of the participatory person, who exists only in *perichoretic* ("rest with movement") relationship with the Other, to whom the participatory person is open because the participatory person is, by nature, exocentric. That is, his

[74] Keith Dwyer and F. Muhammad, *Moroccan Dialogues: Anthropology in Question* (Baltimore, MD: Johns Hopkins University Press, 1982), 269, as cited in Rachel Morgain, "The Alchemy of Life: Magic, Anthropology and Human Nature," *Australian Journal of Anthropology* 24 (2013): 292–3.

[75] Godfrey Lienhardt, "Self: Public, Private. Some African Representations," in *The Category of the Person: Anthropology, Philosophy, History*, ed. Michael Carrithers, Steven Collins, and Steven Lukes (Cambridge: Cambridge University Press, 1985), 141–55 (here 154).

[76] Thus, along with Furani in his chapter, I question both the integrity (monolithic) as well as the autonomy (nonrelational) nature of the person considered in a broad range of cultures and theologies.

[77] I recognize that Mosko, at least, does not equate *dividual* and *partible*. Mosko, "Partible Penitents," 216.

[78] A "rubbish man" in Tok Pisin; the opposite of a "big man."

[79] Michael A. Rynkiewich, "Person in Mission: Social Theory and Sociality in Melanesia," *Missiology: An International Review* 31/2 (2003): 155–68.

openness defines his person and the Other as part of his same family. This person subsists, participates, *metousia*, in the being of the Other, thus opening the way for *koinonia*, fellowship, identification, and empathy with the Other. In this sense, something "emerges"[80] from the relationship that did not exist at the other levels of understanding of the person, something such as a mystical union (*hypostasis*) of persons in community and in nature.

If anthropologists had, from the beginning, read more broadly in theology, then they might have overcome the Enlightenment (i.e., Western European, Catholic, and Protestant) bias against individuals with the Eastern Orthodox (e.g., Gregory of Nazianzus to John Zizoulas) emphasis on relationship and community as foundational assumptions for personhood.

If anthropologists had, in the heyday of missionary anthropologists, such as Maurice Leenhardt, read their theology as well as their anthropology, then they might have engaged in the postmodern critique even earlier than they did while appreciating the meaning of participation for emerging person-hood rather than settle for individualism, suspicion, and violence.[81] If anthropologists had continued to engage theology into present decades and through the postmodern turn, then they might have encountered thinkers such as Moltmann and Pannenberg, who would have helped them challenge assumptions about fractured and whole selves, and about the relationship between the self and the Other that plays on tensions between exocentrism and ethnocentrism.

---

[80] I would like to pursue the notion of emergence theory here to oppose reductionist notions of the person but do not have space. See Philip Clayton and Paul Davies (eds), *The Re-Emergence of Emergence: The Emergentist Hypothesis from Science to Religion* (New York: Oxford University Press, 2006). See also Mark S. Mosko and Frederick H. Damon (eds), *On the Order of Chaos: Social Anthropology and the Science of Chaos* (New York: Berghahn, 2005).

[81] Robbins, "Anthropology and Theology," 290. See also Milbank, *Theology and Social Theory*, 6.

13

World Christianity and the Reorganization of Disciplines

On the Emerging Dialogue between Anthropology and Theology

Joel Robbins

The stress on dialogue is important when looking at the prospects for a dialogue between anthropology and theology. Surely many theologians have read anthropological works and put them to use for their own purposes, and in recent years a few anthropologists have begun, at least tentatively, to do the same with theology. However, this practice is not what I mean by dialogue in the present context. What we mostly have now is more a matter of scholars finding some new means to help them reach ends they have long held. I have, for example, sometimes found myself disappointed when reading works in which theologians enthusiastically take up ethnography as a method for studying their own home communities, often enough their own churches, and count that work as an engagement with my discipline. Too often, they want to use ethnography to document things they already knew were present in the situations they studied, such as the fact that the voices of some community members are not routinely heard by others or that religious practice is fundamental to religious life and thought. Granted, these are important findings, but they just are not the kind of findings that theologians particularly need anthropology to produce. In addition, they are not the kind of findings that anthropologists have generally, at least until recently, wanted fieldwork to produce—the kinds of findings one had not even guessed were in the world when one started one's research.[1] For example, in many societies of

---

[1] John Borneman and Abdellah Hammoudi, "The Fieldwork Encounter, Experience, and the Making of Truth: An Introduction," in *Being There: The Fieldwork Encounter and the Making of Truth*, ed. J. Borneman and A. Hammoudi (Berkeley: University of California Press, 2009), 1–24.

the South Pacific, people insist that they cannot ever have any idea what other people are thinking, and they consistently act accordingly,[2] or that a group of people are very attached to and deeply moved by a ceremony in which dancers sing all night to their hosts about relatives of the hosts who have recently died and do not stop until the hosts burn them severely and repeatedly with resin soaked torches, forcing them to give up the dance,[3] or that some women who take up sex work in Papua New Guinea do so not for the small amounts of cash they sometimes earn but to protest the fact that their fathers and brothers have given up pursuing traditional bridewealth payments from the men they marry.[4] Without the motive of finding out surprising things such as these about ways of living one never imagined, ethnography may retain some of its strengths as a method but not as a specifically anthropological one. As a result, when theologians tell me that what they love about anthropology is ethnography, I am often inclined to point out that they might as well tell me they love us for our money—for the means we can provide to reach ends we have no part in defining. I am sure that some anthropological uses of theological ideas look this way to theologians as well. In personal terms, this instrumentally defined love is not the kind people seek, and in intellectual terms, it is not the right starting point for the kind of dialogue I am hopeful might grow between theology and anthropology.

The kind of dialogue I am looking for is one that would in some ways, perhaps surprising ways, transform each discipline, that would make some contribution to expanding each discipline's sense of its ends rather than merely augmenting its means of attaining them. This type of interdisciplinary encounter has happened for anthropology before. The dialogue with linguistics that produced anthropological structuralism, for example, fundamentally redefined the kinds of meaningful orders anthropologists aimed to discover in social life. A more recent encounter with the discipline of history upended our sense of the basic temporal nature of the things we study. Notably, anthropology has rung some changes on some branches of linguistic and historical research as well, so the dialogue has been two-way. Even with my as-yet rudimentary state of knowledge, I can safely say that theology has over the centuries had a number of these kinds of goalpost-moving encounters with philosophy, where both disciplines have been deeply shaped by the other. I would like to hope that we have a chance to develop this kind of conversation between anthropology and theology now.

---

[2] Joel Robbins and Alan Rumsey, "Introduction: Cultural and Linguistic Anthropology and the Opacity of Other Minds," *Anthropological Quarterly* 81/2 (2008): 407–20.

[3] Edward L. Schieffelin, *The Sorrow of the Lonely and the Burning of the Dancers* (New York: St Martin's Press, 1976).

[4] Holly Wardlow, *Wayward Women: Sexuality and Agency in a New Guinea Society* (Berkeley: University of California Press, 2006).

In exploring possible means for accomplishing this task, I am going to pursue two avenues of investigation. The first briefly reviews recent changes in both disciplines and suggests that these changes bring them to a point where, in fact, their paths are ready to cross. The change in anthropology I want to consider is the unexpectedly rapid rise of what is called the anthropology of Christianity. The change in theology and religious studies is the recent advent and rapid mainstreaming of the notion of global or world Christianity. I want to review why these changes occurred, what new kinds of thinking they have afforded, and, crucially for my concerns in this work, how they might open theology and anthropology to new kinds of encounters with one another.

The second avenue I want to go down looks at one kind of Christianity that I think anthropologists and theologians alike find difficult to address—this is the prosperity gospel, in which believers are convinced that God wants health and wealth for them in this world and they overwhelmingly stress these themes in their worship. Scholars in the Western academy, at least, tend to find this kind of Christianity hard to assimilate to their more general understandings of the faith, or at least to their favorite understandings. I believe a closer look at how this kind of Christianity trips up both theologians and anthropologists may reveal places where both disciplines would be open to help from each other, the provision of which might lay the basis for the kind of transformative dialogue I am seeking. With this outline in place, I will begin by looking at how anthropologists came to study the Christian faith and theologians began to think about something they have come to call world Christianity.

*   *   *

Both the rise of the anthropology of Christianity and the advent of the notion of world Christianity happened around the same time—starting from the second half of the 1990s. They were, as far as I can tell, independent developments, but I think both were responses to some of the same changes in the world. For this reason, the basis for claiming they might be relevant to one another has been present from the start. I will first offer brief accounts of how the anthropology of Christianity and the idea of world Christianity came about, and then I will return to the issue of their shared origins in our changing world.

The vast amount of literature that anthropologists had produced about Christianity by 2016, found by consulting the excellent bibliography blog *anthrocybib* that in May 2016 listed almost nine hundred entries for books and articles published in this field just in the last five years, might make one think that anthropologists had been avidly studying Christian groups for a long time. However, in looking a little more closely, one would discover that this first impression is misleading. A search only up to the mid-1990s would find the discipline looking radically different. Up to that time, some excellent ethnographic studies of Christianity did exist, particularly from the hands of scholars working in Africa, and even two or so edited volumes on the subject published in hard-to-find editions, but there was nothing like the outpouring of work one finds today, and more importantly, the work that did exist had no sense of a shared anthropological project to which research on Christians around the world could contribute. Africanists wrote about Christianity assuming they spoke to their Africanist colleagues; Mediterraneanists wrote for Mediterraneanists, and so on.

In conscious opposition to this status quo, a group of younger scholars began, near the turn of the millennium, to argue that given how many Christians there are in the world, anthropologists really ought to be studying Christianity more regularly, and, as importantly, they ought to do so in conversation with one another, working to develop a distinctively anthropological approach to Christianity and turning their findings to use in helping to make novel theoretical claims of relevance to the whole discipline. Some theoretically generative themes quickly fell into place, turning around questions such as those of the extent to which Christian conversion among previously non-Christian populations tends to foster unusually radical cultural change, the frequency with which Christianity leads people to explore new forms of individualism that move them in modernizing directions, the possibility that one of Christianity's most profound effects brings about a fundamental transformation of people's notions of language, and the idea that Christianity is invariably a religion focused on transcendence.[5] All of these topics and more have been at the center of vigorous debates, and anthropologists have quickly joined them on the basis of studies from all over the world—from Eastern Europe to Latin America, from the South Pacific to Asia, from North America to Africa. By now, the anthropology of Christianity is well established as one of the major trends in the twenty-first-century discipline.

A natural first question to ask, given how quickly the anthropology of Christianity has grown, is why it was so late to get off the ground.[6] Many answers have been proposed to this question, of which I will only mention one. From the outset anthropology defined itself as the study of other cultures, and Christianity was, for many anthropologists, at the very center of the cultures from which they came. In addition, many anthropologists initially turn to the study of other cultures because they are at least gently alienated from their own, or deeply reflexive about it, and we can imagine that this would lead them to feel that Christianity is not the kind of thing they want to study. As a result, then, Christianity became a somewhat taboo topic for the discipline, what Susan Harding memorably called a "repugnant cultural other"

---

[5] Joel Robbins, "Transcendence and the Anthropology of Christianity: Language, Change, and Individualism," Edward Westermarck Memorial Lecture, October 2011, *Journal of the Finnish Anthropological Society* 37/2 (2012): 5–23.

[6] Joel Robbins, "The Anthropology of Christianity: Unity, Diversity, New Directions," introduction to supplement, *Current Anthropology* 55/S10 (2014): S157–S171.

for a crowd that otherwise prided itself on its radical openness to different ways of life.[7]

Given this and other strong impediments to the development of an anthropology of Christianity, a second question to ask is why it took off when it did. There are many approaches to this question, too, but most of them turn around the issue of whether changes in anthropology as a discipline made the rise of the anthropology of Christianity possible or whether changes in the world that anthropologists study made the difference.[8] In this case, saying both were important is not a cop-out. On the side of changes internal to anthropology, one has to note that the advent of the anthropology of Christianity came right on the heels of a period of intense disciplinary questioning about the epistemological, political, and ethical difficulties that attend studying "the other". In the wake of decolonization and the wave of postcolonial thought that followed, along with the rapid turn to identity politics throughout the West, by the 1980s "speaking for" others or even "about" them became deeply problematic, and anthropologists quickly began critically to scrutinize and dismantle their self-understanding as practitioners of a discipline that defined itself primarily as a science of otherness. The anthropological turn to the study of Christianity thus arose just as the otherness test for suitability as an anthropological object—the very test that Christianity had always failed to pass—had been discarded.

So anthropology had been changing from within for a while by the mid-1990s, but at the same time that this internal ferment was taking place, many of the paradigmatically *other* places in the world that anthropologists had in the past tended to study were also changing in ways that helped push for the development of an anthropology of Christianity. One key development at this time was the explosive growth of Pentecostal and charismatic Christianity. What I will henceforth simply call Pentecostal Christianity for ease of expression is that strand of the faith in which believers hold that the gifts of the Holy Spirit, such as speaking in tongues, healing, prophesying, and delivering the afflicted from spiritual bondage, are potentially available to everyone to be used in ways that affect earthly life. Having come into existence only in the early 1900s, by the first decade of the current century credible estimates suggest Pentecostalism has 500 million adherents, representing one-quarter of the world's total Christian population.[9] From the 1960s onward, much of this growth has occurred in the traditional anthropological stomping grounds of Asia, Africa,

---

[7] Susan F. Harding, "Representing Fundamentalism: The Problem of the Repugnant Cultural Other," *Social Research* 58/2 (1991): 373–93.

[8] Bronwen Douglas, "From Invisible Christians to Gothic Theatre: The Romance of the Millennial in Melanesian Anthropology," *Current Anthropology* 42/1 (2001): 615–50.

[9] Katherine Attanasi, "The Plurality of Prosperity Theologies and Pentecostalism," in *Pentecostalism and Prosperity: The Socio-Economics of the Global Charismatic Movement*, ed. K. Attanasi and A. Yong (New York: Palgrave Macmillan, 2012), 1–12 (here 2).

Latin America, and the South Pacific. Suddenly, anthropologists were finding Pentecostals everywhere they went, and as a form of the faith with a very active public ritual presence, and one that insists on the relevance of religion for all aspects of life, anthropologists who encountered Pentecostalism in the course of their research were unable easily to ignore it. It is little surprise then that much of the early work in the anthropology of Christianity took up Pentecostalism, insisting that ethnography had to reflect its centrality in the lives of those who converted to it. Indeed, the early anthropology of Christianity was often criticized for being too heavily focused on Pentecostalism.[10] That problem has abated now with large and growing anthropological literatures on most kinds of Christianity, but it is fair to say that the global growth of Pentecostalism had a lot to do with the initial anthropological turn to studying Christianity more generally by forcing the issue on many anthropologists who, like myself, might have gone to the field imagining they were going to study something else.

Having brought up Pentecostalism's dramatic growth throughout the second half of the twentieth century, I will now turn to the second scholarly development I want to chart, for the construction of the notion of "world" or "global" Christianity is also, in part, a response to this phenomenon. The terms *world Christianity* and *global Christianity* trip so easily off the tongue today, and their use has so much institutional support in the form of courses, named chairs, conferences, and publications of all sorts that deploy them, that one might forget that as features of common parlance they are no older than the anthropology of Christianity.[11] And of course, they are not mere terminological innovations, for they index the development of what Mark Shaw calls "both a perspective and a discipline."[12]

In his contribution to a new Baker Academic book series entitled "Turning South: Christian Scholars in an Age of World Christianity," the historian of Christianity, Mark Noll, elegantly narrates how he grew up during the 1950s and early 1960s in a Baptist household in the Midwest of the United States that featured a world map in the dining room dotted with pins marking the locations in which missionaries that their church supported were working. At the time, this choice of household decoration did not, he goes on to note, lead him to consider "how important the world as a whole actually was for the history of Christianity."[13] Only during the 1990s did he make a shift to recognizing the

---

[10] Brian M. Howell, "Practical Belief and the Localization of Christianity: Pentecostal and Denominational Christianity in Global/Local Perspective," *Religion* 33/3 (2003): 233–48.

[11] See Robert Wuthnow, *Boundless Faith: The Global Outreach of American Churches* (Berkeley: University of California Press, 2009).

[12] Mark Shaw, "Robert Wuthnow and World Christianity: A Response to *Boundless Faith*," *International Bulletin of Mission Research* 36/4 (2012): 179–84 (here 179).

[13] Mark A. Noll, *From Every Tribe and Nation: A Historian's Discovery of the Global Christian Story* (Grand Rapids, MI: Baker Academic, 2014), 2.

existence of a world Christianity that was not an exclusive product of the West and its traditions, and only in 2000 did he begin regularly teaching courses in this subject.[14] He then goes on to note, "Changes even in the short span of years since 2000 indicate how very rapidly 'world Christianity' has become...an extraordinarily active venue for research, interpretation, controversy, and discussion."[15] Like many others, Noll credits a few scholars, all theologians and/or historians of mission such as Andrew Walls, Lamin Sannah, and Dana Robert, with being out ahead of himself and others in recognizing that something novel enough to deserve a new coinage such as *world Christianity* had come into being at increasing speed over the course of the latter part of the twentieth century. Nonetheless, as a genuine academic trend, he confirms that the wide scholarly embrace and development of this notion is only about twenty years old, its first great breakthrough into wider consciousness marked by the great academic and popular success of Philip Jenkins' highly accessible book *The Next Christendom: The Coming of Global Christianity* and the widely read digest of it featured in the popular US magazine *The Atlantic*.[16]

For the many scholars who have come to embrace the idea of world Christianity, the resulting change in their view of things amounts to something like a Kuhnian paradigm shift. When one sees the world through the lens of what the sociologist Robert Wuthnow in fact calls the "Global Christianity paradigm,"[17] several phenomena and claims move from the periphery to the center of one's concerns. First, in statistical terms, the greatest recent growth of Christianity, driven in important respects by the same growth of Pentecostalism that has captured anthropological attention, has not been in its traditional strongholds of Europe, North America, and their settler colonies but in what adherents call the global South. Dana L. Robert summarizes this point in terms that have been oft repeated: "The typical late twentieth-century Christian was no longer a white man, but a Latin American or African woman."[18] Second, patterns of missionization are changing, with more and more missionaries moving from the South to the South and from the South to the North, sometimes with the kind of spectacular results the Nigerian Sunday Adelaja has had in founding the largest church in Eastern Europe or the Brazilian Universal Church of the Kingdom of God has had in spreading throughout the world since its founding in 1977.[19] Finally, there is the key claim that the influence of "Southern" Christian theology and practice will more and more come to shape the future of

---

[14] Ibid., 110.   [15] Ibid., 113.

[16] Philip Jenkins, *The Next Christendom: The Coming of Global Christianity* (Oxford: Oxford University Press, 2002); Philip Jenkins, "The Next Christianity," *The Atlantic* (October 2002), 53–68.

[17] Wuthnow, *Boundless Faith*, 32–61.

[18] Dana L. Robert, "Shifting Southward: Global Christianity Since 1945," *International Bulletin of Mission Research* 24/2 (2000): 50–8 (here 50).

[19] Nimi Wariboko, "Pentecostal Paradigms of National Economic Prosperity in Africa," in *Pentecostalism and Prosperity: The Socio-Economics of the Global Charismatic Movement*, ed.

Christianity, with Western traditions having to accept their less dominant role. Recent struggles over sexuality in the Anglican communion are often taken as indicative of the kinds of global interactions likely to shape Christianity in the future, and another sign is the impressive Pentecostalization that has led worship at many northern churches to at least sometimes come to resemble the kind of worship that is so prevalent in other parts of the world. To speak of world or global Christianity, then, has come to mean seeing the trends I mention as crucial to the contemporary faith—a view of the faith that sees it as global not just in its reach but also in the factors driving its development.

Whenever a major new paradigm or research program emerges, disciplinary space gets rearranged. Students find themselves interested in new topics, funding and hiring priorities shift, new journals take off. What I have wanted to suggest to this point in my remarks is that theology and the broader study of Christianity have lately undergone a space-shifting change of this kind to accommodate the phenomenon that has come to be known as world Christianity during just the period that anthropology has undergone a similar one as it reckoned with the growing disciplinary interest in Christianity. Both fields are, thus, in some transition. I now want to consider how the upheavals both disciplines have experienced might bring them to the kind of transformative dialogue I called for at the outset of this chapter.

* * *

In this second part of my remarks, my tone will shift. I feel confident about the histories of recent disciplinary transformation I have just recounted, but the anthropology–theology dialogue itself is so new that I can report no settled conclusions. Instead of reviewing firm findings or proven approaches to putting anthropology and theology productively to work together, I will turn to examining an expression of Christianity which I think scholars in both camps struggle to understand. By gathering around a version of the faith about which neither discipline is given to confident pronouncements, I hope we might discover some ways we can be relevant to one another.

The expression of Christianity that I have in mind is the prosperity, health and wealth, or word–faith gospel. Preachers in this tradition exhort their congregants to recognize that God has promised them, indeed through Christ's atonement he has contractually obligated himself to provide them with, material plenty and good health on earth. All they need do to claim what is rightfully theirs is believe strongly, tithe regularly, and claim from God, or as movement jargon has it, positively confess to Him, what it is they want and need. Notably, the prosperity gospel developed, in part, out of the same Pentecostal movement

K. Attanasi and A. Yong (New York: Palgrave Macmillan, 2012), 35–59 (here 51); Eloy H. Nolivos, "Capitalism and Pentecostalism in Latin America: Trajectories of Prosperity and Development," in *Pentecostalism and Prosperity: The Socio-Economics of the Global Charismatic Movement*, ed. K. Attanasi and A. Yong (New York: Palgrave, 2012), 87–106 (here 98).

that has done so much to bring both the anthropology of Christianity and the notion of world Christianity into being. Its spectacular growth in many of the same places in which Pentecostalism is expanding has made it a force that scholars working in both fields cannot ignore. At the same time, however, these scholars have had difficulty welcoming the prosperity gospel into their visions of the faith, no matter how broad such visions have recently become.

Many responses to the prosperity gospel from both quarters have been flatly negative in their evaluations of what many take to be a form of Christianity that preys on the poor and needy, taking what little believers have in tithes extracted through the cultivation of false hopes of a spectacular return. Pentecostal theologian Robert Bowman, for example, called the prosperity gospel "Pentecostalism at its (near) worst,"[20] and Rob Starner, another Pentecostal theologian, defines it as "a sword of division within the ranks of Christendom."[21] Martyn Percy, sociologist and theologian, suggests that the prosperity gospel is more prone than many other strands of Christianity to becoming "abusive religion."[22] In anthropology, too, with the brave exception of Simon Coleman's work on a well-known Swedish prosperity church,[23] most of those willing to risk joining the new move to studying Christianity still seemed to find prosperity gospel churches to be a repugnant other, and most have managed to steer clear of them. Of those anthropologists who have taken notice of the prosperity gospel's increasing influence, many follow the Comaroffs in lumping the prosperity gospel in with what they call, following Evans-Pritchard, forms of "new magic," such as witchcraft beliefs that hold that witches kill in order to create zombie workforces under their own control. Folded in with such magical trends, the prosperity gospel figures as a component of what the Comaroffs call "occult economies," phantasmagoric cultural formations that they argue represent people's failed attempts to understand the complex new neoliberal, global economy they have been forced to join, or try to join, but cannot really comprehend.[24] This approach makes no attempt to reckon with the specificities of the prosperity gospel as an outgrowth of the Christian tradition and as a faith that both leaders and followers are highly committed to seeing as still within its borders.

Even as such frankly negative responses to the prosperity gospel have been influential in both anthropology and theology, more sober assessments

---

[20] As cited in Glyn J. Ackerley, *Importing Faith: The Effect of American "Word of Faith" Culture on Contemporary English Evangelical Revivalism* (Eugene, OR: Pickwick Publications, 2015), 20.

[21] Rob Starner, "Prosperity Theology," in *Encyclopedia of Pentecostal and Charismatic Christianity*, ed. S. M. Burgess (New York: Routledge, 2006), 392–7 (here 392).

[22] Martyn Percy, foreword to *Importing Faith: The Effect of American "Word of Faith" Culture on Contemporary English Evangelical Revivalism*, ed. G. J. Ackerley (Eugene, OR: Pickwick Publications, 2015), vii–xi (here vii).

[23] Simon Coleman, *The Globalisation of Charismatic Christianity: Spreading the Gospel of Prosperity* (Cambridge: Cambridge University Press, 2000).

[24] Jean Comaroff and John L. Comaroff, "Occult Economies and the Violence of Abstraction: Notes from the South African Postcolony," *American Ethnologist* 26/2 (1999): 279–303.

of this form of the faith have recently appeared. What is of interest here is the different shapes these reconsiderations have taken in each discipline, for these differences reveal some unexpected common ground between the two fields even as they also highlight what is one of the most profound differences.

I will start with anthropology. Among themselves, anthropologists often joke that one reason they have trouble capturing the attention of a wide public, even on issues about which they clearly have something to say, is that their answer to every question tends to be, "Well, it's complicated."[25] The serious point buried in this self-deprecatory observation is that anthropology at its best looks at how the different parts of a cultural formation are tied together in knots that often are, in fact, quite intricate, and anthropologists insist that when one does so none of the parts will appear to be freakish or bluntly irrational, nor will they evidence the simple ignorance of those who live in light of them. Even the prosperity gospel turns out to be susceptible to this treatment. On careful analysis, it usually turns out to be more than merely a confused attempt to construe the neoliberal world or a sop to people's worst selfish tendencies, standing instead as a cultural phenomenon that fosters meaningful links between the various values by which believers aim to live their lives.

One of the best examples of this approach to the prosperity gospel is anthropologist Naomi Haynes' work on the Zambian Copperbelt. By the time Haynes began her fieldwork in 2006, the economic boom times that once characterized Copperbelt life were long over. If not destitute, the people she studied were certainly not well off, and they were much poorer than they or the generation of their parents had expected they would be. The economic ground having shifted underneath their feet, one might see these Zambians' turn to the hundreds of prosperity churches in the town Haynes studied as representing just the kind of desperate grab at a simplistic and faulty framework for understanding the harsh new world they inhabit that some anthropologist would expect them to make. However, Haynes' analysis does not follow this line. Instead, she focuses on one of the features of these churches that scholars often find discomfiting—their strongly hierarchical structure that elevates pastors as models of God-given success and conduits of divine power high above their flocks—in order to explore their fit with core Zambian concerns. Through careful cultural and historical analysis, Haynes shows that Zambians have always favored the creation of patron–client relationships that connect people across differences in power and resources. To participate in such links is, as they told her, to realize the value of "moving" ahead socially, the value that they find most important to pursue. In their churches, when they pray for blessings and breakthroughs, they hope to produce this kind of movement. And often they do produce this value in their Christian lives, for the

---

[25] See Webb Keane, "Self-Interpretation, Agency, and the Objects of Anthropology: Reflections on a Genealogy," *Comparative Studies in Society and History* 45 (2003): 222–48.

fostering of relations with powerful pastors, and through them with the Holy Spirit and God, constitutes success in this endeavor. Prosperity in this setting is not the fulfillment of selfish, neoliberally informed individual desires for material goods for their own sake, but, as Haynes notes, a relationally expansive kind of advancement that puts Copperbelt prosperity churches at the center of people's efforts to build community during materially difficult times.[26]

Haynes is not the only anthropologist who has found that life in prosperity churches is more complex than one might expect at first glance. One thing common to such work is that the anthropologists who produce it strive to adopt the generally nonjudgmental stance that has, at least until recently, been a hallmark of anthropological writing. They do not pronounce on the value of prosperity churches in relation to some fixed standard, even as they are concerned, as anthropologists always are, to show that church members do not live less than human lives, devoid of intelligence or of social and moral concern. They follow the old relativist saw that everyone makes sense in their own terms and show that this is as true of prosperity gospel followers as it is of anyone else. This stance has produced wonderful and, as I noted previously, surprising ethnography, but the disciplinary centrality of this goal of rendering those we study in complicated, fully human terms can leave anthropologists tongue-tied in cases where they worry they cannot reach it. In my experience, this happens very rarely, perhaps because when it does anthropologists abandon the project at hand and news of their failure never reaches the literature. Still, at least one anthropologist has found herself in this position vis-à-vis her fieldwork in a prosperity gospel church and has had the courage to write a major anthropological study in spite of the difficulties her situation presents.

Ilana van Wyk carried out ethnographic fieldwork in the Universal Church of the Kingdom of God in Durban, South Africa. I mentioned the Universal Church earlier. It is widely known as one of the paradigm cases of successful cultural/religious globalization from the South to the South and the North. Since its founding in Rio de Janeiro, Brazil, in 1977, the Universal Church has spread to at least sixty countries, and in 2005 it was opening a new church every week in South Africa alone.[27] The Universal Church is solidly in the prosperity tradition, promising followers that their strong faith and generous tithes will result in their substantial enrichment. Like many other prosperity churches, it adds to this promise a core emphasis on the claim that one reason churchgoers sometimes fail to prosper is that they are blocked by demons who hold them down. Much of church practice therefore

---

[26] Naomi Haynes, "Pentecostalism and the Morality of Money: Prosperity, Inequality, and Religious Sociality on the Zambian Copperbelt," *Journal of the Royal Anthropological Institute* 18 (2012): 123–39.

[27] Nolivos, "Capitalism and Pentecostalism," 98–9; Illana van Wyk, *The Universal Church of the Kingdom of God in South Africa: A Church of Strangers* (Cambridge: Cambridge University Press, 2014), 13.

takes the form of spiritual warfare aimed at *binding* and vanquishing such demons so that members will be free to achieve success.

The book van Wyk wrote on the basis of her fieldwork is entitled *The Universal Church of the Kingdom of God in South Africa: A Church of Strangers*. For our purposes the subtitle of the book reveals its core argument. The church in Durban, she shows in great detail, does nothing to build community among its members. It has no small groups, does little by way of development projects or charitable good works, and the leadership moves pastors regularly to prevent them from becoming too close with those who attend services. In addition, sermons regularly focus on the claim that demons set to block believers' access to God's bounty can deceitfully take the form of people they might find appealing, such as those sitting next to them in the pews. It is not surprising, then, that church members mostly keep to themselves, and even the relatively small number of them who attend the church year after year tend to have few relationships with other members. Alongside the isolating talk of demonic omnipresence, demands for tithes and other gifts to the church are constant and sometimes accompanied by threat; one pastor even insisted that "old women who hid money in their bras for the taxi fare home would be killed or maimed en route, while parents who paid school fees instead of tithes would see their children fail or die."[28] Such tactics are deployed in a context where the gifts many of the very poor congregants give serve to estrange them from their families, who are enraged by the diversion of what little funds are available from pressing household needs. It is difficult to escape the suspicion that we are here in the presence of Percy's "abusive religion"—a hard case for the anthropological impulse to dwell on complication and strive to make sense of people's lives in the round.

To van Wyk's credit, she acknowledges the difficulty this church presents to her as an anthropologist. In her book, she is open in her dislike of the church, and she has written a searching article in which she counters the often implicit anthropological assumption that liking those whom we study is a crucial part of our method.[29] But it is also telling that in the end van Wyk's anthropological teaching leaves her with few tools for elaborating her unhappiness with the church into a firmly grounded judgment upon it. Instead, that training leads her to conclusions very close to those of Haynes:

> While "unbelievers" [to whom she presented her work] were shocked by the meanness, selfishness and violence that the ... [Universal Church] apparently inspired, "strong" members insisted that this was part of their warrior ethic. I chose to write about this ethic, not to confirm secular suspicions about the ... [Church's] depravity, but to illustrate the depth of their belief and the

---

[28] Van Wyk, *The Universal Church*, 31.
[29] Illana van Wyk, "Beyond Ethical Imperatives in South African Anthropology: Morally Repugnant and Unlikeable Subjects," *Anthropology Southern Africa* 36/1–2 (2013): 68–79.

fundamentally positive social goals to which their behaviour was ultimately directed. Indeed, [Church] members believed that through sacrifices, "strong" behaviour and steadfastness they could reinstate God's blessings in the lives of their families; theirs was not a "selfish" faith.[30]

In the end, van Wyk, too, argues that those who attend the Universal Church she studied in Durban are not less than full human beings, possessed of intelligence, moral impulses, and social concern. I applaud her for this conclusion, and as an anthropologist I would not have wanted her to come to any different conclusions. However, her work shows us clearly that when it comes to making critical judgments, the anthropological spade is often turned, and this is true even when we manage, as van Wyk has, to convey material that seems to cry out for it. This is, I think, an important point of contrast with theologians who deal with world Christianity.

In fact, I have already quoted some of the harsher judgments theologians have made about the prosperity gospel. What interests me now is the theological reasoning processes that lead them to these judgments, reasoning processes in which anthropologists tend not to engage. I want to ask in anthropological fashion how theologians can fit such practices of judgment into their own scholarly lives, lives that make sense, I presume, on their own terms.

An initial observation to make is that in the sources I have searched to this point, I am impressed with what I take to be a stance of humility that theologians tend to maintain in the judgment process. Even the scholars who made the harsh pronouncements I quoted previously had done a lot of work to reach their conclusions. In most texts I have encountered, the authors are careful to refer to their own limits when rendering judgment on forms of the Christian faith they do not practice. Several are also keenly aware of the caution theologians living relatively comfortable lives in the global North need to exercise when approaching churches that appeal so strongly to those living far more precarious lives.[31] But theological humility does not go so far as suspending judgment altogether, as one can argue anthropological humility does as a matter of method and sometimes of theory. In the end, theologians are charged with making what Kathryn Tanner refers to as "normative theological judgments—judgments about what is authentically Christian,"[32] and it is from this vantage point they ultimately approach the prosperity gospel.

---

[30] Ibid., 75.

[31] Amos Yong, "A Typology of Prosperity Theology: A Religious Economy of Global Renewal or a Renewal Economics," in *Pentecostalism and Prosperity: The Socio-Economics of the Global Charismatic Movement*, ed. K. Attanasi and A. Yong (New York: Palgrave Macmillan, 2012), 15–34 (here 20–1); see Mika Vähäkangas, "The Prosperity Gospel in the African Diaspora: Unethical Theory or Gospel in Context," *Exchange* 44 (2015): 353–80.

[32] Kathryn Tanner, "Theology and Cultural Contest in the University," in *Religious Studies, Theology, and the University: Conflicting Maps, Changing Terrain*, ed. L. E. Cady and D. Brown (Albany: State University of New York Press, 2002), 199–212 (here 203).

Within the texts I have consulted, the process of reaching such judgments tends to proceed along one of two lines. Some check the accuracy of the biblical pronouncements of prosperity preachers against other, more widely academically acceptable ways of interpreting the text. The well-known Pentecostal biblical scholar Gordon Fee takes this approach, finding prosperity interpretations to be "purely subjective and arbitrary."[33] He offers as a case in point a common prosperity understanding of 3 John 2. In the King James Version, this passage reads, "Beloved, I wish above all things that thou mayest prosper and be in health, even as thy soul prospereth." If one returns to the Greek and explores the way the language was used at the time it was written, Fee points out, this verse is merely a standard formal greeting, such as, "I hope all is well with you," and not an assertion that we *should* or *have a right* to prosper.[34]

An expanded form of such critiques based in biblical scholarship and hermeneutic criticism checks the prosperity gospel against traditional Christian teachings more broadly and finds them wanting.[35] In this form of critique, one finds that the roots of the prosperity gospel are not solely Christian, for new thought and gnostic ideas were also in the mix from the origins of the movement in the United States.[36] Likewise, the prosperity tendency to assert that the Bible is, in effect, a contract with believers and that those who pray strongly and tithe regularly obligate God to deliver them blessings, is often classed as a magical practice that does not recognize the traditionally normative Christian notions of God's sovereign freedom.[37] This point is tied to another, to which I will return, which is that the prosperity gospel may well have a theological anthropology that is too high, defining human beings as capable of too much and God, correlatively, of too little.[38]

A second line of critical investigation does not set the prosperity gospel against the measuring stick of the Bible or the Christian tradition but instead looks more closely at the situations in which followers of the prosperity gospel live their lives and asks in correlational or contextual terms whether it succeeds in rendering the Christian message meaningful for them in their own circumstances. This work can sometimes make use of anthropological methods and even findings as it aims to capture the complicated lives that prosperity

---

[33] Gordon D. Fee, *The Disease of the Health and Wealth Gospel* (Vancouver, BC: Regent College Publishing, 2006), 9; see also Starner, "Prosperity Theology," 396.

[34] Fee, *The Disease*, 10.

[35] Wolfgang Vondey, *Pentecostalism: A Guide for the Perplexed* (London: Bloomsbury, 2013), 103.

[36] Ackerley, *Importing Faith*; Kate Bowler, *Blessed: A History of the American Prosperity Gospel* (Oxford: Oxford University Press, 2013); Ogbu Kalu, *African Pentecostalism: An Introduction* (New York: Oxford University Press, 2008).

[37] Milmon F. Harrison, *Righteous Riches: The Word of Faith Movement in Contemporary African American Religion* (New York: Oxford University Press, 2005), 9.

[38] Bowler, *Blessed*, 31; Vondey, *Pentecostalism*, 101.

believers live. Mika Vähäkangas draws on Haynes' work in this way to point out that African migrants in Finland define prosperity in social–relational terms in the course of making an argument that traditional African concerns, as much as or even more than neoliberal ones, are part of the foundations of their faith.[39] However, in theological hands, embedding the prosperity gospel in the wider social contexts of which it forms a part is not a substitute for judgment but a prelude to it. For there is always the possibility for contextualization to go too far, becoming in the cases under consideration what the Pentecostal theologian Frank Macchia calls "a heretical accommodation of the gospel to the larger cult of personal prosperity" that "lacks faithfulness to vital elements of the gospel that might challenge the priorities of capitalist economics"[40] or that similarly takes too accommodating an approach to indigenous cultural concerns it may have come to address. In this spirit, Vähäkangas ends his largely positive contextual account of the migrant churches he studied in Helsinki by acknowledging that "the unanswered question that we are left with is whether a church whose message is aimed almost exclusively at the successful and socially attractive (and those en route) can really be a church for all."[41] Thus, even when theologians tack closest to anthropologists in their approach to the prosperity gospel, the call to judgment remains to prevent any collapse of disciplinary identities.

*   *   *

Having arranged a meeting between anthropology and theology on the globally expansive grounds of the prosperity gospel, I want to bring my discussion to a conclusion by considering what this encounter may tell us about the prospects for a mutually transformative dialogue between the two disciplines. I will focus on two issues around which I think such a dialogue can be productive. One—that of judgment—I have already extensively introduced. The other—having to do with what were for me at least some unforeseen similarities in both disciplines' fundamental views of humanity—I will turn to in closing out my discussion.

The finding that one thing that renders anthropology and theology different from each other is that certain practices of critical judgment are central to theology and almost forbidden in anthropology may seem a bit too obvious to bear even the attention I have already given it. Those who have been through the battles that beset the relationship between religious studies and theology must feel that they have heard some version of this kind of observation before, but the framework of those discussions tends to be set by the notion of normativity, the

---

[39] Vähäkangas, "The Prosperity Gospel."
[40] Frank D. Macchia, "A Call for Careful Discernment: A Theological Response to Prosperity Preaching," in *Pentecostalism and Prosperity: The Socio-Economics of the Global Charismatic Movement*, ed. K. Attanasi and A. Yong (New York: Palgrave Macmillan, 2012), 225–38 (here 232).
[41] Vähäkangas, "The Prosperity Gospel," 379.

key question being how disciplines that are normative and those that are not sit side by side. I have very deliberately avoided that framework by choosing judgment as the axis around which my argument has turned. Granted, normativity and judgment are closely related, but they are not the same. If it is common now, and not only for postmodernists, to acknowledge that all disciplines are inescapably normative whether they admit it or not, it is an observable feature of academic life that not all disciplines aim at rendering explicit judgments on the objects they study. It is in this respect that theology and anthropology clearly differ.[42]

More than that, to understand anthropology, I think it is important to realize that its suspension of judgment does not just follow from worries about how normative commitments can compromise objectivity but also from the role the positive doctrine of relativism, itself once normative in the discipline, has in rendering the withholding of judgment a virtuous act. Remember, anthropology is the discipline that once registered an official dissent during the comment period for the 1948 United Nations Declaration of Human Rights, expressing concern that its focus on the claims of individuals might be culture-bound. It should come as no surprise, then, that for generations anthropologists have been carefully, if often implicitly, trained in how to withhold judgment, lead to test themselves against all kinds of ethnographic reports that challenge their own normative sensibilities, and taught to bracket those sensibilities in order to work toward figuring out how all groups of people make sense in their own terms. This educational tradition has a lot to do with the discipline's unique place in the intellectual universe, but the emphasis on it has also meant that anthropologists are not well trained in making judgments when they might want to. In this respect, they have a lot to learn from theology about how to judge with humility on the basis of explicit standards that have been hammered out over long periods of scholarly effort. For reasons I cannot go into here, I think that anthropological relativism is in quite a bit of disarray these days. Personally, I hope it will survive in some form, but whether it does or does not, its current difficulties suggest the time is right for anthropologists, more and more interested in rendering frank judgments, to come into dialogue with theologians about the role of judgment in their tradition and the ways its practice is best cultivated and carried out.

Since I am not a theologian, I find pronouncing on what theologians might learn from anthropologists about matters of judgment more awkward. Nonetheless, perhaps inverting the argument I just made could indicate one angle of approach. In a sense, I have so far suggested that even if anthropologists do not

---

[42] I was first led to thinking about judgment as a key topic by means of which to consider the differences between anthropology and theology by discussions with Patrick McKearney and readings of early versions of his 2016 article. I thank him for setting me on this track. Patrick McKearney, "The Genre of Judgment," *Journal of Religious Ethics* 44 (2016): 544–73.

seek in theology to discover what specific judgments about the world they should make, they can learn from theology about responsible ways of making any kind of judgments at all. Turning this observation around, theologians might also learn from anthropologists about the depth and complexity of the kinds of cultural expressions they are often called upon to judge. Anthropologists of Christianity have, by now, learned a lot about the very wide range of things Christians around the world value and the grounds for the judgments these Christians have themselves made. Theologians might take from anthropologists some lessons about how keeping this kind of variation constantly in mind might inform their own ways of judgment.

I could have made this argument about the potential benefits of a discussion between anthropology and theology about judgment even without a discussion of the two parties' divergent approaches to the prosperity gospel, but given the challenges this kind of Christianity presents to those in both disciplines, I think that discussion helped to focus some of the issues in play. The other topic I want to suggest is ripe for consideration between the two fields is one that might not have stood out so clearly without the provocations the prosperity gospel provides. I have already noted that some theologians worry about the very high theological anthropology that underwrites prosperity doctrine. It holds that believers have great power and that they can assure their own salvation through the cultivation of strong faith. In this scheme, God has little to do beyond meeting his obligations when believers meet theirs. The power accorded to human action in this scheme, I think, leads some theologians and anthropologists alike to class it as very nearly a form of magic.

Working at the edges of my knowledge for a moment, I am going to guess that relatively few academic theologians subscribe to a vision of humanity that gives individuals quite so much power of their own and expects that by themselves human beings can wholly control their own spiritual and material destinies. Put in just this very general way, one that sets God and salvation aside, I can say with more confidence that anthropologists are with theologians on this point. The philosophical anthropology that underwrites anthropology emphasizes, as Clifford Geertz famously put it, that human beings are incomplete animals. All of them require, as his theoretical framework has it, upbringing in a culture to allow them to make anything of their lives.[43] Other anthropological theorists would stress human dependence on social relations and society more generally where Geertz stresses culture, but all of them come together in the broad belief that individuals are never on their own able to create truly human lives. Anthropology, then, is a discipline founded on a notion of the human lack of self-sufficiency. What human beings on their own lack in various theological traditions is, of course, not quite culture or society, or not only those things, but still, the sense that individuals on their own are

---

[43] Clifford Geertz, *The Interpretation of Cultures* (New York: Basic Books, 1973), 46–7, 218.

not able to reach their greatest potential seems to me a key assumption of theological anthropology as well. It is little wonder, then, that we both tend to recoil from what one theologian calls the "triumphalism," or I might call the individualist triumphalism, of the prosperity gospel. We share a kindred sense that along with whatever else this kind of faith might get wrong, it misses the ways in which human individuals need more than themselves and their own ambitions and drives to reach their highest development.[44]

So this matter of human incompleteness is another topic around which anthropologists and theologians might start a mutually transformative conversation. I cannot yet really predict how such a conversation might go, and I have not left space to explore how this theme of human incompleteness and that of judgment might relate to each other. But I hope that taken together they indicate some of the promise of the dialogue these two disciplines, recently shaken out of some longstanding routines and thrown together out of their need to come to grips with a larger world than they formerly reckoned with, might begin to undertake.

---

[44] Vondey, *Pentecostalism*, ch. 5.

14

Latter-Day Saints and the Problem
of Theology

Fenella Cannell

"'I'll freely admit that I'm not a theologian,' Bishop Hammond said."

In April 2014, the Church of Jesus Christ of Latter-Day Saints (LDS) excommunicated one of its rank-and-file members, a woman named Kate Kelly. Kelly was declared apostate for advocating for her church's recognition of women as members of the lay priesthood, which is currently reserved to adult men. In October 2013, representatives of the LDS group Ordain Women, to which Kelly belonged, made news in Utah and other Mormon stronghold states by requesting tickets to attend the "priesthood sessions"—that is, men-only sessions—of the semi-annual conference of the LDS church. These are held in the Conference Center in Salt Lake City, but are livestreamed to various satellite locations where "priesthood holders" (i.e., men) are invited and expected to go to watch them collectively. Footage posted online that year and the following year showed examples of what happened in some locations. For instance, Brigham Young University (BYU) graduate Abbey Hansen and others gained entrance to watch the broadcasts with the men at BYU's Marriott Center in October 2015. The video shows a very Mormon encounter, in which polite and modestly dressed members of Ordain Women awkwardly ask to be allowed to enter the meeting, and are eventually, though very reluctantly, admitted by an equally polite and respectably dressed lady on the door (Karen Roberts). The encounter takes place in a register of determined propriety, which does not, however, conceal the sense of extreme risk on the part of those requesting, or the painfully shocked and resentful way in which admission is conceded; Roberts says something like "I'm not going to stop you!"; which suggests an unspoken portion of the sentence, as in, "I'm not going to stop you [putting your head in that noose]."[1]

---

[1] Kristen Moulton, "Some Women Get into Mormon Priesthood Session," *The Salt Lake Tribune*, last modified April 18, 2015, <www.sltrib.com/entertainment/1668099-155/women-priesthood-session-ordain-meeting-church>, accessed May 5, 2015.

The church leadership had issued instructions that women should be admitted if to refuse them entrance would cause significant disruption. Disruption is not beloved of the present-day LDS church, which has a commitment to corporate-style public relations management. However, once the conference was over, the church disciplined Kelly, excommunicating her through the usual LDS system of local courts and eventually turning down her final appeal to the First Presidency of the Church in Salt Lake City. Also in 2014 the church excommunicated another member of intellectual inclinations, a psychologist named John Dehlin. Dehlin was expelled from his church for running the website, podcast series, and blog "Mormon Stories" (www. mormonstories.org), which had included among its features a series of in-depth discussions on the views of Ordain Women. Dehlin's podcasts are sympathetic and receptive to Kelly's position but also represent a range of different informed responses, including discussion from well-known LDS women scholars and feminists in good standing with the church, who take a different approach from Kelly. They do not include interviews with the church authorities who disciplined her.

Members of Ordain Women were not seeking to provoke the LDS leadership for provocation's sake but were aware that their views were unlikely to be popular in those circles. There is nothing secret about the *content* of the conference priesthood meetings, which are available to members of both genders as live broadcasts and then as online recordings;[2] however, the male-only priesthood meetings are a reflection of the central but contentious gendered division of authority within the LDS church, according to which adult men and not adult women will hold all the major positions of leadership within their church, up to and including eligibility for succession to the role of Prophet and President, the male leader of the worldwide church. LDS women have their own meetings at conference, which correspond to the regular local meetings of the women's organization known as the Relief Society, but although this is an important body, it cannot be a stepping stone to the role of General Authority, Apostle, or Prophet, even for the President of the Relief Society. John Dehlin's excommunication came as more of a shock to many LDS observers and commentators than Kelly's and was read by some as a worrying sign that Salt Lake was moving towards a closed and punitive attitude towards debate within the church.

The members of Ordain Women would certainly like Mormon women to be given LDS priesthood powers; however, its primary aim is simply to open a discussion on these matters within the church.[3] What was at issue was not just a particular decision (i.e., whether or not LDS women can be part of the priesthood) but the whole space of possibility of debate within the LDS church

---

[2] See, for instance, the online access to the conference talks from October 2015 at <www.lds.org/general-conference/sessions/2015/10?lang=eng>.

[3] "Mission Statement," *Ordain Women*, <http://ordainwomen.org/mission/>, accessed June 12, 2015.

and the question of how LDS leaders could be persuaded to acknowledge such debate as legitimate rather than to close it down.

All Christian churches at present consider themselves as confronting the problem of a mainstream culture that is, or at least thinks itself to be, secular. Anthropologists tend to consider objectified *secularism* and *religion* as linked artefacts of the modern imagination[4] and have traced the consequences of their polarization in a number of ethnographies.[5] Some theologians and some philosophers have mounted sustained critiques of the claims of the secular to encompass all human reality and to supersede religious ways of being and knowing.[6] A different response has been for some church leaders and theologians to take an increasingly narrow definition of what is acceptable in religion and an increasingly anxious stance towards members who wish to open new topics of debate. Whether by accident or intention, such debate may result in the undermining of religious values by mainstream secularism. Situations that seem to threaten such secular invasions may be particularly likely to trigger the shutting down of debate. The problem is to hold open a space for faithful discussion and questioning. In some situations of this kind in the Roman Catholic Church, the space of debate has been held open by (some) Catholic theologians who can draw on the long history that recognizes their expertise (under the authority of the Pope) on the church's own teachings, processes, and protocols. Thus, the Cambridge professor of divinity Nicholas Lash published a highly controversial article "On Not Inventing Doctrine" in *The Tablet*,[7] which challenged the then-Pope's claim that the ban on Catholic women priests had been made infallibly. Lash argued that the refusal to discuss the admissibility of women priests could not be justified on scriptural grounds and that the claim of infallibility was faulty.[8] Although Lash came under serious pressure over this statement from his superiors in the church, his scholarship on what constituted the proper basis for declaring infallible doctrine could not be disproved. Some Mormon intellectuals and campaigners seek something like this role of holding the church leadership accountable according to its own criteria. This chapter describes some aspects of these efforts as an attempt to establish a Mormon theology.

---

[4] Fenella Cannell, "The Anthropology of Secularism," *Annual Review of Anthropology* 39 (October 2010): 85–100; Susan McKinnon and Fenella Cannell (eds), *Vital Relations: Modernity and the Persistent Life of Kinship* (Santa Fe: SAR Press, 2013).

[5] For example, Susan F. Harding, *The Book of Jerry Falwell: Fundamentalist Language and Politics* (Princeton: Princeton University Press, 2001).

[6] P. Henri de Lubac, *Surnaturel: Études historiques* (1946; Paris: Desclée de Brouwer, 1991); John Milbank, *Theology and Social Theory; Beyond Secular Reason* (Oxford: Blackwell Publishing, 1990); Charles Taylor, *A Secular Age* (Harvard: Harvard University Press, 2007).

[7] Nicholas Lash, "On Not Inventing Doctrine," *The Tablet* (December 2, 1995): 1544, <www.womenpriests.org/teaching/lash.asp>, accessed March 2, 2016.

[8] I am indebted to co-participant Nicholas Adams for drawing my attention to this parallel and for many illuminating comments and questions.

The excommunications of 2014 created a sense of anxiety among church members, in part because they appeared to reprise previous traumatic events that many had hoped were firmly in the past. The year 2013 marked the twentieth anniversary of the excommunication of a number of very well respected and distinguished Mormon writers, speakers, and scholars known in media coverage as the "September Six."[9] These six members were expelled at the same time as each other and stood in a metonymic relation to a wider group of other historians, feminists, writers, and speakers who advocated for broader discussion and tolerance in the church and among whom further excommunications followed.

The distinguishing feature of the excommunications of 1993 was their anti-intellectualism. The September Six were all committed, church-going, believing members of the Church of Jesus Christ of Latter-Day Saints, and none of them wished to leave their church or to challenge the reality of the prophetic revelations on which it is based. Rather, all the excommunicates asserted their right to open and engage in debate on issues that most people would recognize as matters of theology. In particular, the excommunications of 1993 were bound up with the flowering of Mormon feminism and Mormon feminist scholarship, which occurred somewhat later than in main-stream American culture. This flowering took distinctively theological forms rather than being presented in terms of legal entitlements or rights to equal status under the law.[10]

The status of LDS women relative to their non-LDS contemporaries both now and in the past is complex and can be interpreted in a variety of different ways. Mormon culture and religious charisma are heavily patriarchal in several respects,[11] but Mormon women's religious roles also obtained for them the support of their church for both the right to divorce and the right to suffrage in Utah at a date earlier than that of many other American states.[12] Marriage (defined as exclusively heterosexual) is essential for Latter-Day

[9] Peggy Fletcher Stack, "Where Mormonism's 'September Six' Are Now," *The Salt Lake Tribune*, June 16, 2014, <http://archive.sltrib.com/story.php?ref=/sltrib/news/58060420-78/mormon-church-lds-excommunicated.html.csp>, accessed May 25, 2016. The September Six are Avraham Gileadi, Michael Quinn, Maxine Hanks, Lynne Kanavel Whitesides, Paul Toscano, and Lavina Fielding Anderson.

[10] Bialecki observes that Mormon universal priesthood "waters down the division of labor necessary for the production of a formal theology" (Bialecki, Chapter 9, 173–4). The present chapter instead focuses on Mormon theology as emergent from the exclusion of women from Mormon priesthood.

[11] I do not directly discuss here the issue of nineteenth-century LDS religious polygamy, the implications of which in terms of women's status and experience are one of the most intensely contested topics in a contentious field. It is important to be clear that the official LDS church ended polygamy in 1890, although its cultural legacy remains important.

[12] The right to divorce was important where women joined the church as converts in the nineteenth century but their husbands did not; converted women could free themselves from one marriage and marry again a faithful member of the church.

Saints to enter into the highest state of resurrected life, and current teaching within the church suggests that righteous souls who are unfortunate enough not to find a spouse in this life may hope to be assigned one post-mortally and so enter into the state of Exaltation. The bearing and rearing of children is also an essential part of the work of Christ for Mormons; since it is necessary for every human person to pass through mortality before the end of the world and the return of the Savior, all married couples have a duty to raise children so that the waiting spirits may be housed in earthly bodies.[13] Men and women are, therefore, interdependent in terms of the Mormon economy of salvation, and women are highly valued within their church as wives, mothers, teachers, daughters, and sisters.

The official teachings and hierarchy of the LDS church currently promote and enforce a socially conservative view of gender roles within the family and claim that gender complementarity of the *equal but different* school is the only view compatible with Mormon doctrine and also the right path to human happiness and eternal salvation. For some within the church, however, these tendencies bear the hallmark of a too-close accommodation to the forms of life typical of American conservative Protestants who have been a political and social power worth allying with especially since the 1980s but whose theologies are in several ways profoundly different from and, in fact, contradictory to those of the Latter-Day Saints.[14] LDS church leaders during and after the Reagan years could see the benefits of emphasizing what was shared with evangelical Protestants rather than what was not, and these benefits included the potential softening of the exclusionary and critical attitudes to which Mormons had often been subjected within mainstream America. These shifts in attitude towards Protestants came, in addition to earlier and continuing profound efforts within the LDS church, towards centralization of institutional power and processes and the standardization of practice and doctrine in every locality. These changes took shape beginning under President Harold B. Lee in the early 1960s[15] and were known as Correlation. They were consciously motivated by the church leadership's concerns about maintaining its own identity and orthodoxy in a time of vastly increasing worldwide membership.[16] While Mormonism has always

---

[13] Children will also continue to be born to exalted couples in the Celestial Kingdom after death. See Fenella Cannell, "The Christianity of Anthropology," *Journal of the Royal Anthropological Society* 11 (2005): 335–56 and Cannell, "Book of Remembrance: Mormon Sacred Kinship in Secular America" (in preparation).

[14] See O. Kendall White, "Mormon Neo-Orthodoxy: A Crisis Theology" (Salt Lake City, UT: Signature Books, 1987).

[15] Correlation was built on a range of changes that took place at intervals in the church, often in response to generational crises about perceived distance from the life of the first Prophet.

[16] "Chapter Forty-Three: An Era of Correlation and Consolidation," *Church History in the Fulness of Times Student Manual* (Salt Lake City, UT: Church of Jesus Christ of Latter-Day

been a hierarchical church in which the authority of the present-day Prophets is centrally important, Utah Mormons of the nineteenth and earlier twentieth centuries viewed that authority as paradigmatically personal, homespun, and accessible through face-to-face encounters between the members and their Prophet and Apostles. Even if it was, in fact, unlikely that an ordinary member would flag down an Apostle on the streets of Salt Lake City to ask his advice, the idea that this could happen remained a powerful element in the Mormon imaginary. The legendary obedience that Latter-Day Saints have volunteered to their leaders rested on a sense of personal trust in genuine religious charisma. Obedience to leaders is ultimately a form of obedience to God (Heavenly Father), and given Mormon emphasis on the centrality of human free agency, it is fundamentally considered as a gift. The gift may be, and often is, felt as a sacrifice. It may be (is) a moral obligation but should not be an automatic process of exaction.

Correlation dealt with the problem of a church expanding beyond the conceivable limits of personal authority by creating bureaucratic structures and mass systems for the maintenance of orthodoxy. The creation of standardized student and teacher guides from which all members would be taught about their religion during regular weekly Gospel Doctrine classes; the specification of clear roles for different groups within the church, including for men's and women's organizations; the institution of visiting teaching in 1964, under which lay members are assigned people within their local church congregations (known as wards) to visit once a month and with whom to read Scripture; the creation of a synchronized program of Gospel readings such that every ward in the church studies the same Scriptures each week all over the world all created a sense of coordination, gratitude to the church's leaders, and pride in the powerful organizational capacities of the church. They also, however, created experiential anomalies for many ordinary members for whom religious dedication had been locally grounded in small ways of doing things they knew as authentic and orthodox Mormonism but which now came under restraint, if not actually under question, within the centralized and homogenized system.

Latter-Day Saints continue to place a very high value on the idea of their Prophets and Apostles as holders of religious charisma and of the relationship between leaders and followers in the church as ultimately a personal one, at least in the sense that it is not supposed to be an *impersonal* relationship. LDS leaders may not be able to know every member individually, but they are still vehicles for the Holy Spirit and conduits for radical present-day revelation; therefore, their actions should not contradict the longed-for capacities of God to be concerned with the irreducible value and non-interchangeability

Saints, 2003), 562–78, <www.lds.org/manual/church-history-in-the-fulness-of-times-student-manual/chapter-forty-three?lang=eng>, accessed February 11, 2018.

of every human being, however pressingly numerous human beings become. The increasing corporatism of the Church of Jesus Christ of Latter-Day Saints, on which many commentators and critics have remarked, therefore seems to set up structural tensions and instabilities.[17] On the one hand, it can appear as the natural outgrowth of the practical capacities and diligence that Mormons regard as characteristic of their church and desired by God; on the other hand, the gulf between prophets and systems can sometimes open unexpectedly beneath an individual's feet. Hierarchical power transmitted top-down through a rationalized and partly depersonalized system has a different effect on those who encounter it than hierarchical power transmitted from a living prophet directly to a known follower.

During the early 1990s, these tensions may have been troubling numbers of members in large or small ways but were particularly keenly felt, and particularly clearly expressed, by Mormon scholars and intellectuals, including those employed at Brigham Young University in Provo, Utah.[18] Mormon historians, writers, and feminist speakers had presented work that demonstrated the existence of more variable positions available within Mormon doctrine than were acknowledged or encouraged by the church's leaders. In particular, this work demonstrated the complexity of the unfolding of Mormon teaching during the lifetime of the first Prophet, Joseph Smith, Jr, and beyond, so that it became clear that it was difficult or impossible to assert a single, narrow statement of that doctrine, which would encompass the historical truth. This work of scholarship was important because from the time of its inception, Mormonism has understood itself both as a religion of authoritative revelation through present-day prophets and also as a religion compatible with the reality of historical events and with empirical evidence about past events, whether documentary, archaeological, linguistic, or biogenetic.[19] In addition to this general issue of historical complexity, LDS feminists were especially attentive to nineteenth-century Mormon practices and teachings regarding the religious status of women compared to that of men. Elements that absorbed their attention included in particular the teaching on God the Mother, which acknowledges that God (like every other resurrected and divine being in Mormon understanding) has a spouse in heaven whose reality was

[17] See Daymon Smith, "The Book of Mammon: A Book about a Book about the Corporation that Owns the Mormons" (Create Space Independent Publishing Platform, 2010). Givens describes Latter-Day Saints as a "people of paradox," including the tension between authority and freedom in Mormon culture. Terryl Givens, *By the Hand of Mormon: The American Scripture That Launched a New World* (Oxford: Oxford University Press, 2002).

[18] Standards of conduct at Brigham Young University (BYU) conform to a special code designed to be compatible with church values, including modest dress and the avoidance of sex before marriage. Academic standards at BYU are very high. It is the university of first choice for many young Latter-Day Saints, and it is said to be more difficult to secure admission at BYU than at Harvard. BYU is also, notoriously, a socially intense marriage market for LDS students.

[19] See Givens, *By the Hand*, 89–155.

recognized by nineteenth-century prophets, as well as a reconsideration of the relationship between male and female access to priesthood power and the relative standing of the priesthood (adult male) and Relief Society (adult female) organizations intended by the first Prophet, Joseph Smith, Jr.[20] It was argued, and evidence was presented to show, that the women of the Relief Society had been endowed by Smith with the power and responsibility to act as priesthood holders in their own right in certain contexts.

Mormonism frames priesthood power as the restoration via Joseph Smith of capacities of blessing, healing, and the authority to enact rituals necessary for salvation and resurrection on persons both living and dead, and to connect (i.e., seal) persons to one another so that kinship relations can endure beyond death. Mormon feminist scholars in the 1990s did not claim that Joseph Smith, Jr had endowed men and women with priesthood roles that were identical to each other but did argue that the Relief Society was always intended to share in these powers. It also became clear that nineteenth-century and early twentieth-century Mormon women had themselves explored and debated aspects of women's relationships to priesthood power without reprimand from the leaders of the church. Further historical research demonstrated that nineteenth-century Mormon women understood themselves to be entitled and required to use priesthood powers in various contexts, and particularly in the care of children, healing from sickness, the blessing of other women, and in midwifery.[21]

Although the social script encouraged by the church leadership at this time was that "men have the priesthood; women have motherhood," a formula that could be heard as a variation on Protestant ideas about gender complementarity under male headship,[22] Mormon feminism was taking some of its energy from contrary strains in the central rituals of Mormonism, conducted in LDS temples.[23] These rituals are necessary for salvation, and the LDS leadership has expressly encouraged all its members to attend the temples frequently in recent decades[24] as a means to experience the absolute reality of Mormon

---

[20] The present-day Church of Jesus Christ of Latter-Day Saints grew out of the multiple religious revivals of the early nineteenth century in the Eastern states of the US, often known as the burned-over district. Its first Prophet, Joseph Smith, Jr, experienced a theophany in which Christ and God the Father, recognized as two separate resurrected divine persons, instructed him to restore the full meaning of Christianity lost for many centuries, including additional scriptures and additional ritual components.

[21] For example, Maxine Hanks, *Mormon Women and Authority: Re-Emerging Mormon Feminism* (Salt Lake City, UT: Signature Books, 1992).

[22] Readers will be familiar with conservative Protestant arguments that because Christ was male, God intended headship within both church and family to be held by men; women's roles were complementary, and in many interpretations included holding men to righteous standards.

[23] LDS temples are not to be confused with the local congregation (ward) meeting houses where Saints regularly meet each Sunday for Eucharist and Scripture study.

[24] An emphasis on temple attendance and a program of building numerous smaller and more local temples is especially associated with the presidency of Gordon B. Hinckley (1995–2008).

revelation. LDS leaders often write guides to the correct attitude to the temple and the correct emotions to experience in the temple but also universally emphasize that the details of its liturgy should not be discussed, as this would encroach on its sacredness, understood as a separateness or setting apart from ordinary life. As I have argued elsewhere, however, the unspeakability of the details of temple ritual opens a space in which Latter-Day Saints may experience *unpredictable* and *unscripted* emotions and understandings of their religion, rather than simply those considered correct by the church authorities.[25] This occurs despite the fact that Mormons are generally quite anxious (with an anxiety apparently related to the Protestant side of the Mormon legacy) about ritual itself and often monitor their own reactions to temple ritual with a high degree of concern about whether they are feeling the right thing. The affective power of temple ritual, or the discordant absence of affect for some people, can work either to enhance a person's sense of the overall rightness of the church hierarchy or to disturb that sense, but it does not appear to create a fully predictable or straightforward increase in approved models of experience, as church leadership logic would suppose.

Some elements of the symbolism and practice of temple ritual are widely apprehended by Latter-Day Saints as suggesting that women, as well as men, are holders of priesthood power; indeed, the logic of requiring women as well as men to pass through temple ritual would imply this in itself. For many people, the lacuna between this apprehension and the *women have motherhood* message was one that they did not find troublesome or need to probe to its conclusion. For many others, however, Mormon feminist writing and scholarship spoke into forms of embodied experience that had already been felt as real, even if they had not been put into words. Thus, works such as Margaret and Paul Toscano's *Strangers in Paradox*, which explored the potential of Mormon ritual in relation to gender complementarity, had a resonance for Mormon audiences not confined to academic circles.[26]

In the circumstances I have sketched, therefore, Mormon feminism appeared not as a single-issue movement focused on gender politics or gender rights but as an instance or emergence of fundamental questions of the sayable, the grounds of experience, and the proper understanding of the character of God

At other periods in the history of the church, Latter-Day Saints normally attend temple ritual rarely, either because of the difficulty of traveling to a temple in some parts of the world or, for Utah Mormons, because of lack of motivation. Many Latter-Day Saints still prefer the practical side of Mormonism embodied in the regular Sunday services at the ward meeting houses to the ceremony of the temple.

[25] Fenella Cannell, "How Does Ritual Matter?" in *Questions of Anthropology*, ed. R. Astuti, J. Parry, and C. Stafford, London School of Economics Monographs on Social Anthropology (London: Berg Publishers, 2007), 105–36.

[26] Margaret Toscano and Paul Toscano, *Strangers in Paradox: Explorations in Mormon Theology* (Salt Lake City, UT: Signature Books, 1990).

and religious authority within the LDS church. This reaching for the right to articulate what many people believed was a direct experience of the power of Mormon religious reality found itself in conflict with certain figures among the then LDS central leadership. Among these, one of the most uncompromising was the Apostle Boyd K. Packer, who gave an address in 1993 in which he defined the three main enemies of the LDS church as feminists, homosexuals, and intellectuals.[27]

> The dangers I speak of come from the gay-lesbian movement, the feminist movement (both of which are relatively new), and the ever-present challenge from the so-called scholars or intellectuals. Our local leaders must deal with all three of them with ever-increasing frequency. In each case, the members who are hurting have the conviction that the Church somehow is doing something wrong to members or that the Church is not doing enough for them.[28]

Apostle Packer's argument was that the reality of human suffering was not sufficient grounds for altering or wishing away revealed truth:

> When members are hurting, it is so easy to convince ourselves that we are justified, even duty bound, to use the influence of our appointment or our calling to somehow represent them. We then become their advocates—sympathize with their complaints against the Church, and perhaps even soften the command-ments to comfort them. Unwittingly we may turn about and face the wrong way. Then the channels of revelation are reversed. Let me say that again. Then the channels of revelation are reversed. In our efforts to comfort them, we lose our bearings and leave that segment of the line to which we are assigned unprotected. The question is not whether they need help and comfort. That goes without saying. The question is "How?" The Prophet Joseph Smith, when he organized the Relief Society said, "There is the need for decisions of character aside from sympathy."[29]

For Elder Packer, faith requires the ability to carry on in obedience to the church despite the inequalities of mortal life, trusting that the reasons for these inequities will be revealed in the life to come: "Only when they have some knowledge of the plan of redemption will they understand the supposed inequities of life. Only then will they understand the commandments God has given us. If we do not teach the plan of redemption, whatever else we do by way of programs and activities and instructions will not be enough."[30] In other words, the trials on earth through which we pass are designed by God for our ultimate good, to allow us to grow to our full potential as human beings and, therefore, to inherit the resurrected glory of the Mormon Celestial Kingdom.

---

[27] Boyd K. Packer, "Devotional Address," address presented to the All-Church Coordinating Council, May 18, 1993, <www.lightplanet.com/mormons/priesthood/prophets/packer_coordin ating.html>.
[28] Ibid.   [29] Ibid.   [30] Ibid.

From that vantage point, all earthly suffering will either seem trivial or will be understandable within the larger framing in which ultimate achievement makes suffering purposeful, not senseless, and productive, not destructive of the true self.

Boyd K. Packer was not arguing that no comfort should be offered to those suffering in the here and now, but he did argue that there was an unanswerable requirement from God to keep the commandments revealed through his church.

Many Latter-Day Saints who heard Elder Packer's speech at the time remember it with great pain. His perspective had a deep and emotional appeal, which was felt powerfully even by those members who disagreed with his social views because all faithful Latter-Day Saints wish, with Elder Packer, to defend the principle that their church is based on present-day revelation and that its leaders continue to receive special gifts of prophecy from God. Members understand, also, that their leaders are consciously charting a course that upholds the legitimacy of religious authority and the value of church unity in a context in which many kinds of *secular* values have become mainstream and integral to the state.

While some members acknowledged that Boyd K. Packer was trying to do good by his own lights, they felt anguished that their church leaders would give so little legitimacy to any interpretations of LDS revelation other than their own. Mormon scholars often thought that Elder Packer had wrongly labeled them as opponents of their own church. They braced themselves against what they experienced as the overbearing authoritarianism of the leadership in Packer's generation by a sustained consideration of the inspired authorities of their church's past, whose fit with Packer's views was only partial and incomplete.

Janice Merrill Allred was one of the feminist thinkers and writers excommunicated following the exclusion of the September Six, several of whom were her colleagues, friends, and family members. Allred's sister's husband, Paul Toscano, had been one of the original excommunicates, and her sister, Paul's wife Margaret Toscano, was later also excluded from the church. Allred was excommunicated by a church court in 1995 and later published a full account of the proceedings of that court in the journal *Case Reports of the Mormon Alliance*, edited by Lavina Fielding Anderson. The details of this court, which make for excruciating reading, circled repeatedly around the question of who had the right to discern or declare where authority resides in the Mormon church:

> I pointed out that [the facts] showed that I had not disobeyed him. "In any case,"
> I argued, "I am not under any obligation to follow your counsel. Since there is no
> Church law against speaking publicly or publishing articles about God the
> Mother, it is unfair to punish me for disobeying something which is neither a
> law of the Church nor a Commandment of God."

President Bacon told me, . . . "What difference does that make? I'm your leader
and you should do what I say. I represent Jesus Christ to you." He told me.
   I replied, "I am also a servant of Jesus Christ."[31]

In another passage of the deliberations, Bishop Hammond said,

> "I'll freely admit I'm not a theologian. I don't know the scriptures that well. In any
> doctrinal discussion you could run rings around me and beat me under the table.
> But I don't see that we need to discuss the doctrinal issues at all in either of your
> papers because it's so obvious that what you're saying goes against Church
> doctrine."
>   "It's not obvious at all," I replied. "That's your opinion. I've told you a number
> of times that my interpretation of the Godhead is based on the scriptures and it
> does not contradict what Jesus says the doctrine of his Church is, so how does it
> go against Church doctrine? You tell me that 'Him Shall Ye Hear'[32] contains false
> doctrine, but I don't think it does. You won't even say what you think the false
> doctrine *is* other than the main idea. I think that the idea that the prophet will
> never lead the Church astray is false doctrine. There is no scriptural basis for this
> idea. There is no revelation supporting it. It is antithetical to the gospel of Jesus
> Christ, and it contradicts my principle of free agency. There is no historical
> precedent for it. There's no reason at all for claiming that Church leaders can't
> or won't lead the Church astray except that some leaders said so."
>   "That's good enough for me," Bishop Hammond said.[33]

In accounts written by these excommunicates, the outcome of the court
deliberations is felt by those who pass through them already to have been
decided before they began. Although Allred's husband, friends, and children
paced the corridors or hovered by the telephone as they waited anxiously for
the outcome of her trial, the protagonist herself seemed already reluctantly
resigned to what was to come:

> I continued my final plea for exoneration. "Believing what you do about what it
> would mean to excommunicate me—that it would invalidate my baptismal
> covenant, that it would take away the sealing with my husband and children,
> that it would mean that I couldn't participate or serve in the Church or be with
> my children at important times in their lives—believing all this, how could you do
> this to me? You know of my belief in God and my desire and efforts to do what is
> right. How can you punish me in this way just because you think I have broken
> these rules, these rules which are not from God but which you made up?"
>   Bishop Hammond was obviously angry with me. Up to this point he had
> usually spoken quietly and slowly. Now he spoke quickly, with more energy, and
> there was a hard edge to his voice. "You have to take some of the responsibility.

---

[31] Janice M. Allred, "White Bird Flying," in *Case Reports of the Mormon Alliance*, vol. 2, ed.
Lavina Fielding Anderson and Janice Merrill Allred (Salt Lake City, UT: Mormon Alliance,
1996), 137.
[32] A talk written by Janice Allred.   [33] Allred, "White Bird Flying," 137.

You can't lay it all on us. You knew you were going over the line. You knew you were doing what we didn't want you to do. We told you what the consequences would be."

I didn't respond. It seemed so hopeless. I just didn't have the energy to point out one more time that they had drawn the line, that it could be drawn in another way, or that, better yet, it didn't have to be drawn at all.[34]

Janice Allred's account of her disciplinary hearing seems, in fact, to stand in a long tradition of religious writing about persecution, faith, and dissent. The labors of the accused to maintain a tone of reason under extreme duress, the painstaking detail, the forensic reconstruction of just what was said and how it was said, the sudden, momentary outbursts of brutality on the part of those who held power all claim for Allred's experience affinity with Christians over the centuries who have suffered for their faith and whose trials have been recorded in spiritual autobiography, biography, and martyrology. Latter-Day Saints do not usually make explicit claims on historical Protestant traditions, although they are aware that many nineteenth-century converts to their church were drawn from dissenting groups such as the Methodists. Still less do they like to claim comparison with Roman Catholics, since the Catholic Church is associated with a historical epoch of European apostasy for Mormons. The most immediate referent for a Latter-Day Saint under trial is the suffering of the first Prophet Joseph Smith, Jr and the first generation of Mormons. The difficulty for Latter-Day Saints in contention with their leaders is that those leaders will always emphasize obedience to the Prophet and to the church hierarchy that developed after Joseph Smith's death. In Allred's account, therefore, we hear a direct appeal to the authority of the Savior above even the authority of the Prophet: "I am also a servant of Jesus Christ," says Allred.[35]

Behind every Christian life narrative is the model of Christ's own life narrative.[36] Christ submitted himself to the justice of the Roman Empire. Punishment and injustice was dealt to him, and he transcended through the power of God. Every Christian martyr, saint, and reformer since has depended on that fact to sustain them when they felt obliged to defend their faith against the unrighteous power of either state or church. Implicitly, Allred, too, reaches for this tradition, but her critics and judges cannot share or acknowledge it. Yet as Allred presents her story, throughout the trial her accusers constantly made visible the contradictions in their own position: "We think you're a good neighbor, a good person. We don't think you're a bad person. You have a lot of integrity. We recognize your desire to do what is right and

---

[34] Ibid., 223–4.   [35] Ibid.
[36] In this volume, McGrath suggests the usefulness of comparing theological and anthropological approaches to narrative (Chapter 7, 123–39).

follow your principles. We want you to know that we love you and welcome you to come to church and we'll help you in any way we can."[37]

At the moment of her excommunication, Allred received a direct assurance that she was not abandoned by God:

> They were all sitting in the same chairs they had been in during the court. Every one of them looked devastated. Their faces were averted and downcast. No one looked at me. Bishop Hammond read a statement. "It is the decision of this disciplinary council that you be excommunicated from the Church of Jesus Christ of Latter-Day Saints."
>
> The words pierced my heart, but then a warm sensation, beginning in my breast, suffused my entire body, filling me and surrounding me with a perfect spirit of peace and love. God had comforted me and granted me my desire. Through the power of his spirit, I was able to forgive and love the men who had unrighteously judged me and whose judgment would cause many others to similarly judge me. I saw them as lost sheep who had been led astray; I wanted to gather them into the fold of God's love where they could be healed of their blindness and soothed of their fear.[38]

This *warm sensation* is instantly recognizable by all Latter-Day Saints as the unmistakable action of the Holy Spirit creating the "burning in the bosom"[39] by which Joseph Smith, Jr and all who follow him have identified the truth of God and of their religion. As Allred explicitly points out, Mormons are given the gift of having the Holy Spirit always with them when they are baptized. Through the guiding presence of the Spirit, they may avail themselves of the gift of personal revelation. All Latter-Day Saints have this gift, through which the Spirit will assist them to know what the Heavenly Father wishes them to do in their lives, either when they pray or sometimes through unlooked-for gifts of minor revelation. The gift is only dimmed or lost if a person commits serious sins.

The church leadership is very careful to define the relationship of personal revelation to the great gift of revelation for the whole church, which is given to the Prophet alone. In theory, the two never can nor should conflict. But people can believe this yet draw different conclusions when conflict does, in fact, occur. The members of the LDS disciplinary court had become convinced that the leaders of the church could never commit an error. They believed that because the appointment of church officers is considered to be inspired by the Holy Spirit, they must have the advantage in any case of doubt. For this reason, as Properzi points out, many Latter-Day Saints prefer to delegate the interpretation of doctrine to those who have the mantle of church authority. Janice Allred was convinced, on the contrary, that this was not the case. Her case was based partly on the pitting of past, undoubted authorities against

---

[37] Allred, "White Bird Flying," 225.   [38] Ibid.   [39] Ibid.

present leaders, Scripture as the word of God against the statements of her accusers. The intimate assurance that the Holy Spirit was with her even when the court had removed her church membership underlined this belief. If the excommunication had been a just one, Allred should have been deprived of the presence of the Spirit and of the gift of personal revelation. However, since Allred's experience of the Spirit is necessarily subjective, she could only convey its truth and the claims she based on it performatively, through her Christlike conduct and words.

Other excommunicates took slightly different narrative and performative paths in their encounters with and responses to LDS authorities. Maxine Hanks, for example, who was punished as one of the September Six, has since become famous as the only member of that group to have since rejoined the church. Interestingly, she did so in 2012, just before Ordain Women began mounting demonstrations to petition for the admission of women to priesthood meetings. Maxine has spoken on a number of occasions about her decisions and has also given interviews for John Dehlin's *Mormon Stories* podcast series. For some former members of the church, her decision to rejoin came as a shock and suggested either that she had been deceived by church leaders who persuaded her to rejoin for the sake of a public relations victory or that she was insincere. Maxine's own account of what happened, however, which is on record in a number of locations, is quite truthful to the best of my knowledge and explicitly excludes the idea of deception by the church.[40]

Maxine Hanks had been a pivotal member of the Mormon feminist group in the 1990s and had published a now classic book, *Mormon Women and Authority*, which discusses a range of topics on LDS women's roles and includes essays on God the Mother by Janice Allred and others.[41] She was disciplined and excommunicated by the church because she declined to promise to stop speaking or writing on these topics. Maxine then spent nearly twenty years outside the church. During this time, she trained in the Gnostic church and acted as minister in an interfaith chapel for many years, often writing her own liturgy. Within Gnosticism, she passed through the Deaconate and a number of other orders short of final ordination. She also studied at Harvard Divinity School and worked with women Episcopalian ministers and considered joining them as a priest. From 2002, she participated in roundtable interfaith discussions that included leaders of the LDS church, and in 2011 she decided to rejoin the church. Maxine has described how a lifelong LDS friend wrote to the First Presidency on her behalf in 2011 while she herself

---

[40] See Maxine Hanks, "Pillars of My Faith 2012," audio session, August 4, 2012, <www.sunstonemagazine.com/pillars-of-my-faith-2012/>.

[41] Maxine Hanks (ed.), *Mormon Women and Authority: Re-Emerging Mormon Feminism* (Salt Lake City, UT: Signature Books, 1992).

was still wondering how to make an approach to the church. The church then invited her to return.

One important aspect of Maxine Hanks' rebaptism into the church[42] is that she was not asked to undergo a repentance process. Normally, an excommunicate is required to pass through a formal and quite testing process of demonstration of repentance and conformity of life to church standards, which involves a number of stages of discussion with bishops (that is, local lay ministers) or other officers of the church. The fact that Maxine was not required to do this is central to her story, since from her point of view it is a clear demonstration that the church leadership had changed its attitude since her excommunication and no longer viewed her as an apostate. This shift in her view constituted a central concession, since it was, in effect, an admission that she was not an obdurate sinner against the revealed truth of her faith. By extension, it was a tacit admission that she, too, had not been deprived of the presence and guidance of the Holy Spirit during the years of her exclusion from the church.

In her statements and interviews, Maxine Hanks is not primarily concerned, as Allred's account that I have quoted here is, to detail the process of her excommunication. Allred's texts and Hanks' texts are, therefore, not exactly of the same kind. Both, however, are episodes in spiritual autobiography, and both evidence the processes and resources with which their authors claimed the competence to debate the nature of God, to speak theologically. Maxine Hanks, if my ear is correctly attuned, often moves into liturgical intonations and reaches intuitively for liturgical phrasing when she speaks about her excommunication and return to the church. For example, she gave an address to the liberal and enquiring Mormon forum Sunstone, where many among the audience had been her supporters after she was exiled from the church, to explain why she had agreed to be rebaptized. This talk has become well-known in LDS circles. Near the start of the talk, Maxine says:

> It felt as though the excommunications happened to *all* of us; we were all excommunicated. Um, . . . so many people suffered with this; it changed them and their lives. I'll never forget [names two church members who are not excommunicates] who would stand speechless with tears running down their faces, that all they could do was hug us and say how sorry they were. J. B. Williams had this whole page in the Tribune[43] with hundreds of signatures supporting us. There was a great conflict . . . that affected both sides, the liberals and progressives, and the church. It affected *both* sides.

---

[42] Non-LDS readers may be surprised by the mention of rebaptism, given the contrast with non-LDS understandings of baptism as an irreversible sacrament. I am indebted to Nicholas Adams for drawing my attention to this example of the shift of religious terms across different forms of Christianity.

[43] *The Salt Lake Tribune*, one of the most widely read newspapers in Utah.

It was a conflict within the larger personality of Mormonism, yet I have a feeling now that it was meant to happen. We all play our parts in getting to know ourselves and the church better.

We were all tested together, so perhaps healing happens together as well.

We are gathered together on a path of light, to manifest the power of Christ, within.

And to participate in a great mystery that was, and is, and is yet to come.[44]

Again, after a speech of some power, complexity and length, she closes the same talk by saying,

It's the Spirit . . . that's democratic, not the Church, but the working of the Spirit is democratic. . . . I see Joseph Smith as a prophet in the true sense of the word, a real prophet, a seer, a revelator, a visionary, and I have for many years. . . . Comprehending the complexity, the depth and genius of his role, he was a wounded healer, with a gift greater than his wounds and a personality greater than either of them. . . . He was on a hero's journey, too, when he said, "No man knows my history." He could have said, "No one knows my journey. . . ." He entered the infinite dimensions of himself every day, and he constantly brought the spiritual into the material world in text, theology, and organization. . . . I think his work on Mormonism *was* complete, but we just haven't fully seen it yet. I think the answers are, . . . I think we're just now starting to . . . excavate them more fully. I see Mormons as a powerful lay Christian church, not just Christian but meta-Christian. Mormonism revives [many traditions in Christianity, including Gnosticism]. . . . I see all of those elements represented in specific ways in Mormonism. I am amazed that JS facilitated all the revival of all those elements of early Christianity. . . . It's also a Pan-Christianity. . . . It has elements from . . . a synthesis of multiple traditions, far more sophisticated, deep and rich than we've I think realized.

One last thought here: Anyone who thinks that Mormonism is a conservative religion doesn't know its history, theology, doctrine. Mormonism was a radical restorationist faith with prophets and prophetesses and seers and visionaries aflame with the Spirit of God like a fire. Joseph Smith facilitated something so grand and complex that it's up to us to complete it, to excavate it, until as the Gnostics say the mystery is completed in us.

I'll leave you with the blessing I said at the end of every service at Holy Cross chapel: There is a Power that makes all things new, within us and within those who know us, as one with God. May that peace live over you, and may that Power lift you into light, now and forever, Amen.[45] [Applause]

Even to non-Mormon readers, it may be clear from this extract that Maxine Hanks can speak authentically and with conviction from within what we might identify as a priestly register. The liturgy she has used and written

---

[44] Hanks, "Pillars of My Faith 2012." My transcription. The set lines on these paragraphs approximate the pacing and pauses of Maxine Hanks's delivery.
[45] Ibid.

comes naturally to her; so do forms of action and engagement that we could think of as sacramental. She mediates meaning; she offers a blessing for others. Earlier in her talk, she tells the audience that part of her service within the Gnostic church involved the practice of consecrating others, and that she has officiated with permission at many kinds of office and liturgy. However, she stopped just short of accepting a permanent priestly role in another church and returned to the church of her upbringing. Unlike Kate Kelly, Maxine Hanks does not feel the need to campaign for the immediate admission of women to all the formal functions of the male Mormon priesthood. She seems presently to be seeking to work from within a position of reconciliation with the church and not from a continuation of direct conflict. It also seems clear from what she says that she feels that she has acquired her own inalienable sense of priesthood and means of expressing it, which she is taking back into the LDS church, with what results it remains to be seen.

One of the original grounds on which Hanks replied explicitly to her critics prior to her excommunication was to refer to her own family pedigree in the church. She is descended from multiple lines of first-generation Mormons who knew the Prophet and is also descended from Joseph Smith himself. This claim requires some explanation in an LDS context beyond the obvious implication that Hanks had a solid grounding in the principles of the church. Mormons believe that salvation (and apotheosis) is available to everyone, by the exercise of their free agency. Therefore, they strongly reject formal doctrines of Election or Predestination. However, Mormons also understand that individuals can be foreordained for certain roles on earth, although they may succeed or fail in carrying out these obligations and must make a conscious effort to succeed. This idea rests on the LDS understanding of time, in which there is a pre-mortal existence as well as a mortal and post-mortal one. Our actions in this world may relate to promises made in our pre-mortal existence, although on earth we have little memory of that time. Further, many Mormons think that God asked particular groups of people to take on special tasks in historical earthly time for the good of all. Although one cannot literally "inherit" prophetic power in any automatic sense, therefore, many people would assume that those descended from the first Prophet and his followers might have been part of a group of special souls to whom some important divine purpose had been entrusted.

Given the relationship between pre-mortal, mortal, and post-mortal time, Mormons are particularly attuned to what I would term typological (or perhaps hyper-typological) resonances in life narratives.[46] One of the characteristics of Joseph Smith's gifts of prophecy was his capacity to make connections between apparently disconnected texts, events, and persons, a capacity

---

[46] Fenella Cannell, "Book of Remembrance: Mormon Kinship in Secular America" (unpublished manuscript).

that Samuel Morris Brown has insightfully commented was identified by Joseph Smith with practices of "translation."[47]

To me it appears that Maxine Hanks' instantiation of Mormonism draws in part on her sense that she is herself in some way a Prophetess and a possessor of the priesthood in a church that is, after all, as she says, composed of saints who have been given the Spirit of God. The connection with Joseph Smith is also suggested, including in the extracts already quoted, by her recourse to the idea of the hero's journey, a phrase taken from the writer Joseph Campbell and from his interest in the idea of human religious and mythic universals. Hanks has often replied to questions about what her return to the LDS church means to others who have been excommunicated by explaining that she does not intend to impose her own journey on anyone else. She speaks in terms (familiar to any anthropologist raised on Van Gennep, Victor Turner, and other theorists of initiation and ritual) of a three-stage process of expulsion, exile, and return. In the extracts quoted, she links these models of mythic passage to the life of Joseph Smith: "He was on a hero's journey, too." Her trials outside the Mormon church are what have enabled her to return to the church, stronger than when she left it.

In making these references, Maxine Hanks is speaking in ways that connect very profoundly to Mormon concepts and assumptions, and not just to a general audience with a taste for mythic universals. Mormons are restorationists. In parallel to their "typological" approach to personal narratives, they tend to think of the LDS church as the fulfillment of all (good) things from the past, so that all historical wisdom and virtue is seen as foreshadowing the greater truths of Mormon revelation. What Maxine Hanks is doing, therefore, is inhabiting a very resonant Mormon position; she places her present-day self as the fulfillment of truths and purposes for the church earlier only imperfectly glimpsed by her former critics. Like a prophet, she reveals in retrospect the underlying pattern of a godly plan hidden to others around her.[48]

*   *   *

Sarah Coakley in this volume has urged anthropologists to remember that their interlocutors may be animated by profound theological understandings and motivations not reducible to other factors and encouraged theologians to take from anthropology the insight that theologies are always socially

---

[47] Samuel Morris Brown, *In Heaven as It Is on Earth: Joseph Smith and the Early Mormon Conquest of Death* (Oxford: Oxford University Press, 2012). One corollary of this practice is that ordinary LDS kinship is a lived and narrated means of translating experience in prophetic registers through a form of intensified typology. See Cannell, "Book of Remembrance."

[48] I note convergences with Douglas Davies' interests in implicit theology in this volume and am indebted to him for many helpful comments on this material (Chapter 11, 194–210. For Davies' explication of the LDS Plan of Salvation as a correlate to Trinitarian theology, see Douglas J. Davies, *Joseph Smith, Jesus and Satanic Opposition: Atonement, Evil and the Mormon Vision* (Farnham, UK: Ashgate, 2010).

situated.[49] I agree with both these suggestions, and both are relevant to the present chapter.

Allred, Fielding Anderson, and other members of the Mormon Alliance based their program of critical engagement with their church's leadership on impeccably scriptural grounds. Identifying the problem within their church as one of authoritarianism,[50] they advanced to challenge this tendency a famous statement from the founding prophet Joseph Smith on unrighteous dominion. Writing from jail during the persecution of the church in Missouri on the advent of his martyrdom, he wrote, "Almost all men, as soon as they get a little authority, as they suppose, will begin to exercise unrighteous dominion." Further,

> 6 That the rights of the priesthood are inseparably connected with the powers of heaven, and that the powers of heaven cannot be controlled nor handled only upon the principles of righteousness.
>
> 37 That they may be conferred upon us, it is true; but when we undertake to cover our sins, or to gratify our pride, our vain ambition, or to exercise control or dominion or compulsion upon the souls of the children of men, in any degree of unrighteousness, behold, the heavens withdraw themselves; the Spirit of the Lord is grieved; and when it is withdrawn, Amen to the priesthood or the authority of that man.[51]

In other words, Mormon priesthood authority is self-cancelling if it is used to oppress others. No Latter-Day Saint disputes that this statement is the inspired word of Joseph Smith. It is difficult to imagine any LDS Prophet and President wishing to set aside the claim of righteousness in governing the church, since this would be a self-invalidating act. The gift of continuing inspiration given to LDS Prophets and Presidents for the leadership of their church has taken Mormonism through some controversial and notorious changes in doctrine, of which perhaps the most famous was the revelation in 1890 that plural marriage should be ended, so that the church could survive persecution by the federal government. The preference for religious polygyny was a revelation given to Smith, and the later revelation set it aside. Seismic as were the changes this brought about, they were possible, not least because Mormonism existed before polygamy. But a leadership claim that contested the identification of Mormon priesthood with the powers of heaven would not be conceivable either to progressives or conservatives. *Unrighteous dominion*, therefore, constituted a powerful grounding from which to try to open debate on Mormon principles.

---

[49] Sarah Coakley and Joel Robbins, Chapter 20, 335–76.

[50] This term and many others used in Mormon dissent are clearly derived from contexts outside the LDS scriptures; my argument here is simply that their endeavors are not reducible to or founded on external, secular agendas.

[51] *Doctrine and Covenants*, 121; 33–44.

Previously, I noted the forensic level of detail and precision with which Janice Allred's account of her excommunication process is offered to the reader. The same is true of many of the cases published by the Mormon Alliance, and this is intentional. Having established the scriptural basis for a claim to consideration, the Alliance writers then put forward their evidence. By implication the readers (perhaps guided by the Holy Spirit) are to weigh their claims justly where Bishop Hammond and his colleagues have failed to do so. The many Bishop Hammonds of the world are, it seems to be hoped, to have their consciences stirred and brought to life. The legalistic framing is not, however, just a "secular" borrowing; it addresses the LDS church's processes of excommunication, since these operate through its own religious "courts." It details lapses of procedure where these occur, and identifies lacunae in the reasoning of those presiding. The same evidential intent is also present in some of the material recorded by John Dehlin for his *Mormon Stories* podcasts. The underlying hope is that, as E. P. Thompson argued in a very different context, law and legal process are never purely ideological.[52] Even where those in power, according to this view, control its operations by the existence of a legal system that contains the potential for those involved to be persuaded to make a decision against their own entrenched interests.

I have suggested that one further way in which anthropology might contribute to a dialogue with theology is to consider the local meanings of theology itself in particular times and places. In the Mormon context, this question is intimately linked to the effort to bring a Mormon theology into being. The theology here considered is the category neither of anthropologists nor of professional theologians, but of a lived category, put into play in a specific unequal encounter. For some Mormons, as Bishop Hammond intimated, the word itself can be suspect, suggesting a possible attack on prophecy or, alternatively, associations with the theological tradition of the Roman Catholic church, which Mormons regard as flawed and incomplete.[53] For other Mormons, the practice of theology, whether or not they explicitly insist on that term, is a space of potential for the longed-for future flourishing of their church. Janice Allred does not insist on the term *theology*, but neither does she use it as a term of disparagement. For Allred, the practices of Scripture reading, praying, and reasoning about the Mormon faith and the history of the church to which she and all Latter-Day Saints are enjoined are the beginnings of a process that, given sufficient time and properly scholarly study, becomes a Mormon theology. For Bishop Hammond, any point at which Allred's work brings her into tension with the interpretations of her

---

[52] E. P. Thompson, *Whigs and Hunters: The Origin of the Black Act* (New York: Pantheon Books, 1975), 263.

[53] See also Mauro Properzi, *Mormonism and the Emotions* (Madison, NJ: Farleigh Dickenson University Press, 2015).

church leaders is the point at which she should defer because church leaders must, by definition, be those who know best what present-day revelation can tell us. For him, presumably, any future development of a Mormon theology could only be safely led from the top.

Within an LDS hierarchy that was skeptical of, and sometimes hostile to, the legitimacy of theological discourse, theological debate (e.g., on God the Mother) could not simply be engaged. Before that could happen, it first had to come to be recognized as a possible Mormon form. It was not sufficient to cite a text from Joseph Smith. Mormon dissenters did not just talk back to authority; they talked back using certain elements of the existing Mormon repertoire in slightly new ways, so as to talk with authority. I have suggested that both Janice Allred and Maxine Hanks, in addition to many other Mormon men and women, had to create a space for Mormon theology performatively, as well as scripturally or legally. What they had to achieve was to enact an inhabitation of their own position that would communicate authenticity to other Latter-Day Saints and would be recognized by them as indicating the presence of a person guided by the Holy Spirit and gifted with forms of prophetic authority. As certain historical studies in the development of early Christianity have argued,[54] changes in discourse depend on the change being in some way meaningful and comprehensible to those to whom it is proposed; that is, the new has to speak in part through forms that are already familiar. Or as anthropologists, following Max Weber, have sometimes described, some people become capable of changing things because they are able to join previously disengaged worlds of meaning in ways that persuade others.[55] As Weber originally suggested, therefore, many forms of charismatic leadership have affinities with prophecy. In this chapter, I have suggested that for Latter-Day Saints, at least, prophetic modes of action with special affinities with the seership of Joseph Smith seem to be necessary for the localized grounding of theology.

---

[54] Averil Cameron, *Christianity and the Rhetoric of Empire: The Development of Christian Discourse* (Berkeley: University of California Press, 1991).

[55] Luke Freeman, "Why Are Some People Powerful?" in *Questions of Anthropology*, ed. R. Astuti, J. Parry, and C. Stafford, London School of Economics Monographs on Social Anthropology (London: Berg Publishers, 2007), 281–307.

15

Theology on the Ground

Naomi Haynes

Any exploration of theologically engaged anthropology ought to begin with a clear definition of what is meant by *theology*. Most simply, we could say that theology is a system or set of ideas about the divine; theology is what people think about God and how they ought to relate to him. This definition is quite broad, and one might want to qualify it with a connection, if not to the academic discipline of theology, then at least to the work of religious specialists. In order for theology to be different from something more general such as cosmology, it seems to require a certain kind of expertise or access to a particular intellectual tradition. While I see the reasoning behind such claims, I want to argue against such a narrowing impulse by providing a broad view of Christian theology "on the ground." This democratizing approach enables me to treat theology as an ethnographic object and, by extension, as the basis for anthropological analysis. This, in turn, allows me to address one of the most vexing problems in the anthropology of Christianity—namely, how to write about divine action in a way that preserves the integrity of both our informants' experiences and that of anthropological frameworks.[1]

In the discussion that follows, I approach theology as a particular kind of reflexive action aimed at understanding who God is, how he works in the world, how people ought to relate to God, and what they can expect from him. This reflexive work is, as I have already suggested, as ably done by church leaders and scholars as it is by ordinary laypeople, although in this chapter I focus more on the efforts of pastors than I do on the members of their congregations. In the Protestant tradition, theology so defined has historically meant engagement with the biblical text, and in the Pentecostal case that I examine here, we will see that this type of textual engagement takes on a very

---

[1] Timothy Jenkins, Chapter 6, 102–22; Jon Bialecki, "Does God Exist in Methodological Atheism? On Tanya Luhrmann's *When God Talks Back* and Bruno Latour," *Anthropology of Consciousness* 25/1 (2014): 32–52.

particular form. To wit, Pentecostal theology involves creating analogies with the narratives of scripture, reaching forward and backward across history in a process of infinite recursion that collapses Pentecostal time into an expansive, magical present. Analogy, and metaphor more generally, have been a central concern in both theology and anthropology and, as such, represent a helpful point of cross-pollination between the two disciplines.

My definition of theology as a wide-reaching, democratic project has been forged in a particular ethnographic context. The Zambian Copperbelt, where I have worked since 2003, is a collection of mining towns that has long been central to anthropological analyses of urbanization, social change, and religion. I have carried out most of my fieldwork on the Copperbelt in a township that I call Nsofu, a middle-class community with a population of roughly 25,000 people, located on the outskirts of the city of Kitwe. A great deal of my time in this neighborhood has been spent in small, locally initiated Pentecostal churches, as well as in informal prayer groups and in the homes of Pentecostal believers. Pentecostalism is one of the most democratic forms of Christianity, structured by the biblical promise that the Spirit will be poured out on "all flesh."[2] While believers on the Copperbelt place a good deal of stock in the teachings of their leaders, we will see that these are by no means taken as binding. Indeed, there is a great deal of debate in Pentecostal churches, and the work of theology—of understanding how God works in the world and how people ought to relate to him—is shared out among all Pentecostals. This egalitarian impulse has unquestionably shaped my commitment to a democratic definition of theology, though in the conclusion I will show that there are significant intellectual reasons for this definition as well.

Having clarified what I mean by *theology*, I can now address what it means to study theology "on the ground," as I have put it—that is, what it means to study theology ethnographically. I propose that we begin with a distinction between theology as something people have and theology as something people do—or, building on discussions of value that I have developed elsewhere, between theology as a noun and theology as a verb.[3] While both of these aspects of theology lend themselves to ethnography, in this chapter I have chosen to focus on theology as a verb for two reasons. First is the simple fact that I find this emphasis more satisfying; it is far more interesting to examine those spaces in which people are actively engaged in theological work than it is to ask them to give their particular take on a theological problem. Second, and more importantly, my ultimate aim in this chapter, as in similar contributions in this volume,[4] is to think with theology as an ethnographic category so as to

---

[2] Joel 2:28.

[3] Naomi Haynes, *Moving by the Spirit: Pentecostal Social Life on the Zambian Copperbelt* (Berkeley: University of California Press, 2017).

[4] For example, Fenella Cannell, Chapter 14, 244–65; Joseph Webster, Chapter 18, 315–35.

better use it analytically. Doing so requires us first to explore the practice of Pentecostal theology on the Copperbelt in greater detail.

* * *

The central practice through which Pentecostals on the Copperbelt do theology is the sermon. Paradigmatically, preaching is the task of church leaders, but Pentecostal laypeople do a lot of preaching too, not just in formal settings such as church services, where they offer testimonies or words of encouragement, but informally as well. Copperbelt Pentecostals preach to each other in the course of conversation, perhaps prompted by a Christian television program, reflection on a recent church service, or a friend's description of his or her problems.[5] The work of theology as demonstrated in preaching, then, is shared among the majority of Pentecostals, both leaders and laypeople alike.

When I arrived in Nsofu for the first time in February 2008, the members of Higher Calling, a Pentecostal prayer-gathering-turned-church, were meeting in a small chapel they had constructed from wooden offcuts over a foundation of poured cement. Narrow benches were lined up on either side of the room facing a raised dais, which had been decorated with large plastic buckets full of wildflowers. Half a dozen mismatched curtain panels hung over the rough wooden walls. When I initially began to attend meetings at Higher Calling, the chapel was bursting at the seams, thanks primarily to the popularity of the group's founder, a young mother whom I call Bana Mfuwe.[6] In April 2008 Bana Mfuwe moved with her family to South Africa where her husband had been offered a job. Before her departure Bana Mfuwe appointed Bana Chilomba, a middle-aged widow who lived in a small house in an adjacent township, to take her place. Bana Chilomba lacked the charisma of her predecessor, and in the wake of Bana Mfuwe's departure, attendance at Higher Calling declined rapidly. As the church wrestled with the difficulties brought on by a drop in membership, the Copperbelt was also feeling the worst effects of the 2008 global financial crisis. As the price of copper plummeted and the value of the Zambian currency fell, workers were laid off in droves and small-scale trading ground to a halt.

One rainy Wednesday in January 2009, Bana Chilomba stood up in front of Higher Calling's remaining members to preach. The group had assembled in the sitting room of a lay believer on account of the chapel's leaky roof, and I was wedged into the corner of an overstuffed, but surprisingly hard, green sofa. Bana Chilomba began her message by reading the story of Jesus and his disciples crossing the Sea of Galilee in a boat. Like Jesus and his first followers, she said, it was time for the members of Higher Calling to cross over from

---

[5] Cf. Joel Robbins, "Pentecostal Networks and the Spirit of Globalization: On the Social Productivity of Ritual Forms," *Social Analysis* 53/1 (2009): 55–66.

[6] The feminine prefix *Bana* can be used to indicate a teknonym or as a Bemba analogue to *Mrs*, as in this case. The names of all people and congregations used here are pseudonyms.

where they were to the other side. Building on this initial observation, Bana Chilomba went on to make a number of related points, drawn from a series of biblical texts. She first turned to the Old Testament account of the budding of Aaron's staff, which had signaled the election of the tribe of Levi for the priesthood. What this passage demonstrated, Bana Chilomba explained, was that God made a distinction among people; therefore, the way that crossing over happened in one person's life may be different from the way it happened in another's. Believers should therefore not allow themselves to be distracted by their friends, particularly those who did not show a serious commitment to Pentecostal practice. Bana Chilomba's next point was that sin could keep people from crossing over. Here she drew on the example of the Israelites, some of whom were not permitted to enter the Promised Land.

As Bana Chilomba went on, she continued to employ the Exodus account, reading out loud the passage in which Pharaoh offered to allow the Hebrew slaves to go out to the desert to worship if they would only leave their possessions behind. Moses rejected this offer, saying that they needed their animals and belongings with them to use in worship. Building on this story, Bana Chilomba observed that some believers tried to cross over without their possessions—that is, they thought they could have a *breakthrough*, as Pentecostals describe it, without giving to the work of the church. Like Moses, Bana Chilomba rejected this approach, highlighting the prosperity gospel principle that through giving believers produced an obligation in God to pour out a return blessing. To illustrate this point, she recalled the example of Abraham's generosity and the blessing that followed. Bana Chilomba concluded her message by reading a passage that was very popular in Copperbelt Pentecostal groups around that time: Moses's promise to the Israelites that they would never again see the Egyptians who had them trapped against the Red Sea. In the same way, proclaimed Bana Chilomba, those who stood strong in their faith would never again see the problems they were facing at that moment.

Before analyzing Bana Chilomba's message, I want to provide a brief example of a sermon offered by a layperson in order to demonstrate that the theological method employed by church leaders such as Bana Chilomba is common among all Copperbelt believers.[7] One evening, just as it was getting dark, I stopped in to see my neighbor, a sometime Pentecostal woman named Bana Veronica, who lived with her two young children in the back room of a local private school. Bana Veronica acted as the building's caretaker in exchange for her lodging, matriculation of her children in the school, and,

---

[7] A quick caveat—in Nsofu, the line between laypeople and church leaders can be blurry. There is a general expectation that prominent and devout church members are on their way to the pastorate, and the democratic thrust of Pentecostal theology means that church leadership structures are always potentially subject to reorganization. Naomi Haynes, "Egalitarianism and Hierarchy in Copperbelt Religious Practice: On the Social Work of Pentecostal Ritual," *Religion* 45/2 (January 14, 2015): 273–92, doi:10.1080/0048721X.2014.992106.

I assumed, some small wages. Her husband lived and worked on a farm outside the city. Bana Veronica had been having trouble fulfilling her work duties as an injury to her arm made sweeping and polishing the floors difficult. I knew that she had gone to see a doctor and had dropped by to ask what the results of the visit had been. I could see that her arm was very swollen, and a quick glance at the X-ray film Bana Veronica had carried back from the hospital revealed that her shoulder was dislocated. Rather than realign the joint, the doctor had merely given her a prescription for painkillers, and Bana Veronica was trying to cope as best she could. While we were visiting, Bana Veronica and I were joined by two young Pentecostal women, Esther and Mavis, who were on their way to an overnight prayer meeting. Upon seeing the X-rays, Esther delivered a short sermon to Bana Veronica. The prophet Ezekiel had spoken to a valley full of dry bones, Esther began, and when he did so they had come together to form an army. In the same way, she concluded, Bana Veronica should pray for herself, lay her hand on her own shoulder, and speak to her bones so that they would come together.

In the sermons delivered by Bana Chilomba and by Esther, we have the core of Copperbelt Pentecostal theology as a verb. Although, as we will see, the way that these women approached and used scripture reflects patterns found among Pentecostals in other parts of the world, I want to argue that something particular is going on in the Zambian case. Through their engagement with the biblical text, my informants are seeking to expand their present by mapping their experience onto the experience of biblical history. This requires a bit of explanation.

*   *   *

While there are many similarities in how Pentecostal believers and other conservative Protestants engage the Bible, there are also important points of contrast. These differences are helpfully demonstrated by James Bielo's analysis of a Lutheran Bible study group with one Pentecostal member, a "non-denom brother" who took it upon himself to challenge the interpretive strategies of the rest of the group. For this lone Pentecostal participant, the Bible was "a book of promises," guaranteeing such things as prosperity and healing. In contrast, Bielo writes that the remaining members of the group were more cautious in claiming specific biblical promises for themselves. As a result, while the Pentecostal in the group had no problem inserting himself directly into the text, other readers were mindful of the distance between their lives and the biblical narrative. In Bielo's treatment, the difference in how Pentecostals and other Protestants use scripture therefore boils down to a difference in the perceived continuity of experience with the characters presented in the Bible.[8]

---

[8] James S. Bielo, "How Much of This Is Promise? God as Sincere Speaker in Evangelical Bible Reading," *Anthropological Quarterly* 84/3 (2011): 631–53.

Pentecostal theologian Amos Yong takes up a similar line of analysis in situating Pentecostals alongside other readers of scripture. Because the experience of contemporary Pentecostal believers is defined by the in-breaking of the Holy Spirit through signs and wonders, he argues, they are easily able to identify with the experiences of the early church. The result is what Yong calls a "'this is that!' hermeneutic which sees the 'this' of the present connecting with the 'that' of [especially] the apostolic life...and vice versa."[9] Elsewhere, Yong has highlighted the particular importance of Luke–Acts for Pentecostals, arguing that the narrative of Jesus and the Apostles has "served somewhat as a template allowing readers to enter into the world of the early church."[10]

Writing about Nigerian Pentecostalism, Ruth Marshall calls this way of doing theology "the history of the present." In her words, the experiential proximity of the biblical narrative brings the Bible's "principal protagonists into the everyday lives of converts, such that an imaginary dialogue may be established with these figures from a distant time and place."[11] This tendency to bring the Bible close is, I would argue, at the heart of the classic Pentecostal preference for narrative over didactic portions of scripture.[12] Because Pentecostals connect to the Bible on the basis of common experience, it is no surprise that those portions of the text that relate human experience in narrative form would be those in which believers would take the most interest.

Building on these discussions, we can now begin to explore in more detail how Pentecostals such as Bana Chilomba do theology. As Marshall describes it, this task involves tacking back and forth across the arc of history, bringing the principal protagonists of scripture into daily life so that believers speak as familiarly of St Peter or King David as they do of their relatives or neighbors.[13] As Yong points out, this process also works in the opposite direction; just as the common experience of the Holy Spirit can usher characters out of the Bible and into the present, it can also insert believers into the biblical narrative.[14] It is a particular version of this move to locate one's experience in scripture that I want to emphasize in my discussion of Copperbelt Pentecostal theology.

An example from Key of David, another Pentecostal church in Nsofu, neatly demonstrates the process I am after here. Each January the leaders of

---

[9] Amos Yong, *In the Days of Caesar: Pentecostalism and Political Theology* (Grand Rapids, MI: W. B. Eerdmans, 2010), 89.

[10] Amos Yong, *The Spirit Poured Out on All Flesh: Pentecostalism and the Possibility of Global Theology* (Grand Rapids, MI: Baker Academic, 2005), 27; Allan Heaton Anderson, "'Stretching Out Hands to God': Origins and Development of Pentecostalism in Africa," in *Pentecostalism in Africa: Presence and Impact of Pneumatic Christianity in Postcolonial Societies*, ed. M. Lindhardt (Leiden: Brill, 2015), 248–69.

[11] Ruth Marshall, *Political Spiritualities: The Pentecostal Revolution in Nigeria* (Chicago: University of Chicago Press, 2009), 89.

[12] Donald W. Dayton, *Theological Roots of Pentecostalism* (Grand Rapids, MI: Francis Asbury, 1987), 23.

[13] Marshall, *Political Spiritualities*, 89.   [14] Yong, *The Spirit Poured Out*, 27.

Figure 15.1 Annual theme verse displayed over the dais at Key of David. Photo by the Author.

this congregation choose a theme for the New Year, which is grounded in a key text. This theme is printed out on a colorful banner and hung at the front of the sanctuary (see Figure 15.1). Banners from previous years are also displayed. Each banner is phrased in the form of a proclamation—for example, "2014, My Season of Blessing and Enlargement, 1 Chronicles 4:9"[15] and "2012, My Season of Distinction and Rest, Exodus 33:14–16."[16] These verses give accounts of Jabez and Moses respectively, but in mobilizing these narratives in their annual theme, members of Key of David have framed them in the first person; 2012 is *my* season of distinction and rest, not Moses's. Through this process of identification with biblical characters, believers come to stand for those characters in their recorded biographies. In effect, believers become these biblical figures by taking their places in the narratives of their lives—that is, in the experiences that give them a particular identity.[17]

[15] "Jabez was more honorable than his brothers. His mother had named him Jabez, saying, 'I gave birth to him in pain.'"

[16] "The Lord replied, 'My Presence will go with you, and I will give you rest.' Then Moses said to him, 'If your Presence does not go with us, do not send us up from here. How will anyone know that you are pleased with me and with your people unless you go with us? What else will distinguish me and your people from all the other people on the face of the earth?'"

[17] Cf. Naomi Haynes, "Standing in the Gap: Mediation in Ethnographic, Theoretical, and Methodological Perspective," *Swedish Missiological Themes* 101/3–4 (2013): 251–66.

Pentecostal theology therefore short-circuits history by expanding the present. There is a subtle but important difference in the way that my informants on the Copperbelt make this happen. Yong is clear in his description of the "This is that!" hermeneutic that what connects believers across space and time is the actual experience of the Holy Spirit. In his treatment, what has already happened to Pentecostals brings them to a point of personal identification with the narrative of scripture, especially that of Luke–Acts.[18] In contrast to this retrospective recognition, when Copperbelt believers seek to locate themselves in the narrative of scripture, they do so prospectively. Their aim in situating themselves in the stories of the Bible, in taking the place of Moses or Jabez or Ezekiel or Abraham, is to obtain the same results that these people did. Pentecostals on the Copperbelt are therefore not so much recognizing their experience in the biblical text as they are trying to transform their experience into that which is recorded in the Bible. Rather than a "This is that!" hermeneutic, then, we might say that for my informants theology is a matter of "Let this be that!"[19]

As a side note, I should point out here that the "Let this be that!" hermeneutic may explain why my informants are so focused on the Old Testament narrative, rather than the Luke–Acts account that is so central to the lives of Western Pentecostals. In the Old Testament, God relates to his people through a series of covenantal promises in which blessing is guaranteed to follow obedience. The framework of covenant is central to the teachings of the prosperity gospel,[20] and is a key component of my informants' religious lives.[21] Many, though not all, believers on the Copperbelt are concerned with finding ways to relate to God that will compel him to act on their behalf, which explains the emphasis on covenantal language.

Pentecostal theology can therefore be said to work by analogy, by the assimilation of one "complex of objects" to another.[22] Here we find a definition of theology that echoes one put forward by David Tracy: "[an attempt] to correlate certain specified meanings and truths in our common human experience and language with the interpreted meanings and truths of a specific

---

[18] Here a few examples from my own charismatic upbringing illustrate the point quite nicely. My parents, Jesus Movement converts to Christianity, listened to music by a group called the "Second Chapter of Acts," attended a congregation called "New Testament Church," and put me to bed at night with a cassette recording of the book of Acts.

[19] Cf. James T. Siegel, "The Truth of Sorcery," *Cultural Anthropology* 18/2 (2003): 135–55 (here 149).

[20] See Nimi Wariboko, "Pentecostal Paradigms of National Economic Prosperity in Africa," in *Pentecostalism and Prosperity: The Socio-Economics of the Global Charismatic Movement*, ed. A. Yong and K. Attanasi (New York: Palgrave Macmillan, 2012), 37–44.

[21] Naomi Haynes, "Zambia Shall Be Saved! Prosperity Gospel Politics in a Self-Proclaimed Christian Nation," *Nova Religio* 19/1 (2015): 5–24.

[22] G. E. R. Lloyd, *Polarity and Analogy: Two Types of Argumentation in Early Greek Thought* (Cambridge: Cambridge University Press, 1966), 175.

religious tradition."[23] From an anthropological perspective, there is a clear parallel between theology thus defined and magic,[24] including divination[25] and sorcery.[26] In all of these cases, analogy (or metaphor, of which analogy is an example) is described as the key to ritual efficacy.[27] Through analogy, "two objects are seen as having resemblances and differences, and an attempt is made to transfer the desirable quality of one to the other which is in a defective state."[28] In the Copperbelt Pentecostal case, believers' lives are thought to be in a defective state: Their finances need a dose of prosperity; their bones need healing. By teasing apart the causal relationships presented in the biblical narrative—prayer leads to healing, giving leads to blessing—Copperbelt Pentecostals seek to (re)produce the results obtained by people in scripture by aligning the elements of their lives according to the same chain of events. One puts oneself in Ezekiel's position to get what Ezekiel got. This theological process, like Pentecostal speech more generally,[29] is performative, "[calling] those things which do not exist as though they did," as St Paul writes.[30]

The theological work of analogy has important social effects. "Imaginative flights of reference" that cast a woman with an injured shoulder as the prophet Ezekiel or a mine foreman as Jabez "[form] and [transform] their understandings and experiences of the domains they [inhabit],... changing their world fundamentally and irrevocably."[31] The primary way that this is accomplished is by moving "inchoate subjects into an optimum position in quality space" through metaphors of "adornment or disparagement."[32] The theological analogies through which believers engage the biblical text position them on the side of victory and cast others as their enemies. In other words, through analogy, different members of the Copperbelt community are positioned inside, outside, or on the wrong side of the biblical narrative.[33] A final ethnographic example will demonstrate this process more fully.

*   *   *

---

[23] David Tracy, "Metaphor and Religion: The Test Case of Christian Texts," *Critical Inquiry* 5/1 (1978): 91–106 (here 93).

[24] Stanley J. Tambiah, "The Magical Power of Words," *Man* 3/2 (1968): 175–208; "Form and Meaning of Magical Acts: A Point of View," in *Modes of Thought: Essays on Thinking in Western and Non-Western Societies*, ed. R. Horton and R. H. Finnegan (London: Faber & Faber, 1973), 199–229.

[25] Allan Young, "Order, Analogy, and Efficacy in Ethiopian Medical Divination," *Culture, Medicine and Psychiatry* 1/2 (1977): 183–99.

[26] Siegel, "The Truth of Sorcery"; Harry G. West, *Ethnographic Sorcery* (Chicago: University of Chicago Press, 2007).

[27] Lloyd, *Polarity and Analogy*, 178–9.   [28] Tambiah, "Form and Meaning," 222–3.

[29] See Simon Coleman, "The Charismatic Gift," *The Journal of the Royal Anthropological Institute* 10/2 (2004): 421–42.

[30] Romans 4:17.   [31] West, *Ethnographic Sorcery*, 63.

[32] James Fernandez, "The Mission of Metaphor in Expressive Culture," *Current Anthropology* 15/2 (1974): 119–45 (here 124).

[33] Cf. Bambi B. Schieffelin, "Christianizing Language and the Dis-placement of Culture in Bosavi, Papua New Guinea," supplement, *Current Anthropology* 55/S10 (2014): S226–S237.

Pastor Kangwa was a young preacher appointed to oversee a tiny congregation that church leaders from Nsofu had "planted" just outside the city of Kitwe. In July of that year, under a thick curtain of dry-season dust, members of Pastor Kangwa's infant church traveled to Nsofu in the back of an open-topped Canter truck to spend three days with the "mother" congregation for a conference. They carried bedrolls and mattresses so that they could sleep in the church, a temporary structure similar to the one used by Higher Calling, with wooden benches and a few bare light bulbs swinging precariously from the rafters.

The final day of the conference was a Sunday, and during the morning service Pastor Kangwa took the pulpit, clad in a khaki-colored suit, orange dress shirt, and tie. His message was entitled "A Mixed Multitude," a phrase he took from Exodus 12. Pastor Kangwa began his sermon by reading from this chapter: "Then the children of Israel journeyed from Rameses to Succoth, about six hundred thousand men on foot, besides children. A mixed multitude went up with them also, and flocks and herds—a great deal of livestock. And they baked unleavened cakes of the dough which they had brought out of Egypt; for it was not leavened, because they were driven out of Egypt and could not wait, nor had they prepared provisions for themselves."[34] The "mixed multitude" that went out from slavery in Egypt, Pastor Kangwa began, referred to the presence of ethnically mixed people among the Israelites. After 430 years in slavery, the Israelites and the surrounding people would have intermarried, he explained, and as a result Egyptians would have made their homes in the midst of Israel. These "unstable, double-minded" individuals, Pastor Kangwa said, drawing on James 1:8, caused problems for Moses—the opposition to his leadership at the Red Sea, for instance, and the construction of the golden calf while he was on top of Mount Sinai. Such people, he added, had ungodly appetites. Here Pastor Kangwa asked the congregation to turn to Numbers 11:5, which records complaints about the manna God had provided and a desire instead for the foods of Egypt: fish, leeks, cucumbers, garlic, and melons. Pastor Kangwa described such complaints this way:

> These people had a real problem. God has provided them with bread from heaven, which had a very wonderful taste, which had all the nutrients. And whenever they ate manna, these people would seem to become more healthy. But they got to a place where they began to say, "We are tired of this menu because we remember the fish in Egypt, we remember the cucumbers, we remember the leeks, we remember the onions." Can you look at this kind of menu? What can come out of this diet? The onion, the garlic, the watermelons, the cucumbers, plus the fish, eaten together. Can you imagine how you would feel

---

[34] Exodus 12:37–9.

in the stomach? These people had a weird appetite. God has given them fresh
bread, but they still long for the very bad appetite.

The climax of Pastor Kangwa's sermon came with the declaration that those
present were also a mixed multitude and that among them were people with
strange, even perverse appetites, including those who would sleep with married men. The church's Moses had grown tired of what Pastor Kangwa
referred to as murmuring, and it was time to repent and be faithful or else
suffer the diseases of Egypt. As Pastor Kangwa preached, the back of his suit
jacket grew damp with sweat while the huge loudspeakers brought in for the
conference sent his voice reverberating across the township. At one point a
woman marched from the back of the church and slipped some money into
his pocket, a mark of appreciation used on the Copperbelt for skilled dancers
and powerful preachers alike. She was not the only one who approved of
Pastor Kangwa's message. After the service I walked home with Bana Mercy, a
long-time member of Freedom Bible Church and an important informant in
my later fieldwork. As we walked across an unpaved road drifted over with
fine red dust, Bana Mercy told me that in her estimation the congregation had
people who fit the description of the double-minded individuals that Pastor
Kangwa offered. For instance, one woman had attended the Sunday service
despite the fact that, as Bana Mercy put it, she was still "living in the world."
    In this example, Pastor Kangwa employed the familiar Pentecostal theo-
logical process of analogy in order to position himself and his listeners in
quality space. On the surface church members appeared to be one body. They
had all come to worship that morning, just as they had all sung and danced
enthusiastically during the praise and worship time. Nevertheless, the analogical work of Pastor Kangwa's sermon made this apparently united group
into a "mixed multitude." As the congregation was brought into the Exodus
story, the preacher and his fellow church leaders became Moses, the faithful
became the children of Israel, and those who caused problems became
Egyptians, people of strange appetites who murmured against those in
charge. Through this process, Pastor Kangwa effectively issued a warning to
those who found themselves on the wrong side of the story. The Exodus
account is already written, and the fate of those who murmur is sealed:
Egyptians would get the diseases Egyptians got, while the true Israelites
would enter the Promised Land. In this way, Pastor Kangwa's sermon mobilized the familiar paradigm of expected blessing and, by extension, expected
curse—"Let this be that!"—as he positioned himself and the members of his
church on different sides of a biblical story in the expansive Pentecostal
present.
    Although Bana Mercy's response to this sermon suggests that the signifi-
cance of Pastor Kangwa's analogical work was clear in the minds of those
who heard it, the narrative he created nevertheless presented some ambiguity,

and therefore some flexibility. While Pastor Kangwa had plainly positioned himself and the other members of the church leadership in the role of Moses, and while he had said in no uncertain terms that the congregation contained both Israelites and Egyptians, just who fell into which group was never specified. This ambiguity is always, albeit to varying degrees, a feature of Pentecostal theology as I have defined it here. Although some aspects of the Pentecostal expansive present are fixed—namely, the causal and logical relationships revealed in the biblical narrative—what happens on the other side of the analogical equation, so to speak, is a matter of debate. One person's Egyptian is another person's Israelite.

As noted in the introduction, the particular characteristics of Copperbelt Pentecostalism make it an especially fertile ground for this sort of theological contestation. To return to a point made previously, because the inspiration of the Holy Spirit is, by definition, available to anyone, all believers, whether leaders or laypeople, have the capacity to do theology, to find in the narrative of scripture read at home or discussed with friends analogies between their experience and those of people in the Bible. These analogic relationships do not need to be established by pastors and might even be different from the analogies created by a particular church leader. A second factor is the number of pastors, prophets, and preachers vying for attention on the Copperbelt. This crowded religious playing field opens space for interpretive variation. Although the process of doing theology by analogy is consistent among the dozens of Copperbelt Pentecostal groups I have visited over the years, the particular analogical relationships—who and what fit where in a given story— are subject to a wide range of variation even among religious specialists.[35]

It is easy to interpret this contested analogical work as a kind of group politics, as believers jockey for positions within Pentecostal groups and draw boundaries within and around their congregations. An argument along these lines would be in very good company. As Courtney Handman has recently pointed out, there is a tendency in the social scientific study of Christianity to view conflicts such as schism (Handman's particular topic of interest) as nothing more than the sort of political struggle one might find in any social setting. According to Handman, this approach is mistaken. Relational fractures in churches are not like relational fractures in other social groups, she argues, because churches are not like other social groups. The reason for this difference is that churches are sites of religious mediation, mechanisms that help Christians connect with God.[36] This is certainly true in the Copperbelt

---

[35] I should also acknowledge the particular open-endedness of the sermon as a communicative genre, since this further contributes to the contested nature of analogic theology. To borrow a truism from media studies, the reception of a message will be as diverse as its audience, and the performative work of Pentecostal sermons will necessarily meet with a range of responses.

[36] Courtney Handman, *Critical Christianity: Translation and Denominational Conflict in Papua New Guinea* (Berkeley: University of California Press, 2014). See also Courtney

case. For Pentecostals in Nsofu, theology provides a conduit for divine action, channeling the power of God to intervene in the world and bring about the transformations for which they are hoping. This last point returns us to the broader aims of a theologically engaged anthropology.

*   *   *

In Chapter 1 of this volume, J. Derrick Lemons argues that "anthropologists must engage with theology to deepen and expand the scholarship of the anthropology of religion."[37] This charge is important. Broadly speaking, while theologians have had little trouble in adopting the tools and insights of anthropology,[38] anthropologists have had more difficulty incorporating theology into their work. One of the main reasons is that, as Timothy Jenkins points out in his chapter of this volume,[39] anthropology struggles to create space for the divine agency that is implicit in theological models. It is frankly difficult for anthropologists, whose methodological atheism is effectively axiomatic, to write God into the equation, and when confronted with this problem, most anthropologists simply "[conjure] away" the divine.[40]

There are several reasons why the inability to write God into anthropological analysis is a bad thing. To focus exclusively on Christianity for a moment, an atheistic model of religious life does not accurately represent the experiences of our informants. In the words of a South African Zionist, "There is one enormous omission throughout the whole history that has been written by outsiders. The work of the Holy Spirit through our history has simply been left out."[41] Similar critiques have come from within the framework of anthropology. As Jon Bialecki has recently noted, "To ignore God as an agent in the world is not just to ignore or belittle the beliefs of many of our informants, but to overlook an often vital mode of their engagement with the world."[42] This omission often leads to reductivism, the very erasure of religion that the anthropology of Christianity initially set out to address.[43] Still, the problem remains how anthropologists can write about the experience of

---

Handman, "Becoming the Body of Christ: Sacrificing the Speaking Subject in the Making of the Colonial Lutheran Church in New Guinea," supplement, *Current Anthropology* 55/S10 (2014): S205–S215.

[37] J. Derrick Lemons, Chapter 1, 19.

[38] For an excellent, recent example, see Michael Banner, *The Ethics of Everyday Life: Moral Theology, Social Anthropology, and the Imagination of the Human* (Oxford: Oxford University Press, 2014).

[39] Jenkins, Chapter 6, 102–22.   [40] Ibid., 119.

[41] Ndumiso Harry Ngada, *Speaking for Ourselves: Members of African Independent Churches Report on their Pilot Study of the History and Theology of their Churches* (Braamfontein, South Africa: Institute for Contextual Theology, 1985), 21.

[42] Bialecki, "Does God Exist in Methodological Atheism?" 33.

[43] Joel Robbins, "Continuity Thinking and the Problem of Christian Culture: Belief, Time, and the Anthropology of Christianity," *Current Anthropology* 48/1 (2007): 5–38; "What Is a Christian? Notes toward an Anthropology of Christianity," *Religion* 33/3 (2003): 191–9.

Christians without destabilizing their own experiences. How, in other words, can they "find sense in the worldviews of others without rendering their own views of the world nonsensical?"[44]

Here is where theology on the ground becomes especially important. In the framework I have developed, God's action in the world figures not as part of an a priori theistic commitment on the part of the ethnographer, but rather as the result of the analogical efforts of my informants. God's agency, in other words, is part of the theological process under study and is therefore accessible to anthropological analysis in a way that academic theological concepts may not be. When theology is understood as a result of the critical work of people who are trying to understand God and, at least in the Pentecostal case, to make him act, we are able to write about God anthropologically because we can write about him ethnographically. True, in this framework we cannot treat God as more than an element of the theological process, but importantly, we cannot treat him as less than that either.[45] Theology on the ground therefore gives us a way to include divine action in anthropological analysis by grounding it in ethnography.

In this chapter, I have argued for a definition of theology that is democratic and far-reaching, situated in the reflexive work of, in this case, all Pentecostals as they explore and debate how God is working in the world and, by extension, who God is and what he is like. In so doing, my aim has been to develop an ethnographic view of theology that allows us to represent more fully the worlds of our religious informants by including God in the anthropological models developed through engagement with those worlds. While this is not the only way to develop a theologically engaged anthropology, it is of vital importance to this overall project, a crucial step in opening up anthropological discussion to theological categories, most importantly the category of the divine. By treating theology as an ethnographic object in these terms, we are better able to apply it to anthropological analysis.

---

[44] West, *Ethnographic Sorcery*, 22.
[45] Cf. Bialecki, "Does God Exist in Methodological Atheism?"

16

Comparative Theology

Writing between Worlds of Meaning

Francis X. Clooney, SJ

The current conversation on the ways in which anthropologists can learn from theologians and from theological teachings about the world and humanity seems to presume, on the anthropologist's side, that theology is normatively grounded in a single tradition and that its intellectual work is thought through, taught, and explained within the scope of that tradition's resources. Similarly, theological anthropology is seen as a discipline and set of doctrines developed within some specific tradition. All of these points make sense, but in the following pages I will complicate matters by highlighting how theologians can also consider the boundaries of religions to be permeable.

Conversely, when the theologian seeks to contribute to the conversation with anthropologists, he or she generally does so by way of indicating the complementarity between what is learned from the sources of theology (e.g., in Scripture and tradition, by reason and through experience) as textual and doctrinal matters, and what is learned from lived religion and popular religiosity. Text and lived religion are complementary. The theologian, if not becoming an anthropologist, is in our era increasingly ready to learn from anthropology and the social sciences and imitate the best practices of anthropologists who likewise care about living communities and lived religion. All of this, too, is very good, and we are all better off because of our interdisciplinary commitments.

Most writings on the interrelationship of theology and anthropology seem, reasonably enough, also to take Christian theology as the paradigmatic form of theology. We naturally think of theology as a Christian discipline and thus limit the exchange with anthropologists as to what is meant by theology in the modern, Christian West. Even so, we must still distinguish varieties of Christian theology, taking seriously the particularity of theologies and resisting the notion of an abstract, generalized theology or of a theology that is simply an academic discipline. It will be worthwhile to reflect for a moment on what is basic to

Christian theologizing as an intellectual practice, and what is at stake when we stop identifying *theology* with (modern Western) *Christian theology*.

I have found useful thinking of theology as a rich and diverse practice that proceeds in accord with certain rules or habits: *leges credendi, orandi, quaerendi, legendi*, the rules of believing, praying, seeking, reading. The first two rules are not expendable; the third gives theology its intellectual dimensions; and, while the fourth is not sufficient by itself, it is the most common practice by which one does the work of seeking. Theology in its richer sense remains the work of individuals, yet the individual who would be a Catholic theologian must in some real sense, even if not submissively or without tension, be in conversation with a wider guild of theologians and in union with the hierarchy, the bishops of the Church, including the Pope. Thus are balanced authority, tradition, and the voice of the people. Before and after Catholic theology turns its attention to a wider world, it is a family matter.

Theology is a discipline of faith yet intellectually ever borrowing from a much wider body of knowing and experiencing; it is grounded in community, yet always reaching beyond the immediate boundaries of that community's self-understanding and interests. It balances critical understanding and empathetic connectedness. Faith provides answers; theology happens only when that faith is also productive of openness to new questions. These new questions very often arise in academic settings where the free exploration of ideas is favored.

While Christian theology does, in fact, function as an academic discipline within university settings, we need to note that as an academic discipline it may or may not retain distinctive features—faith, community, practice, and openness to the Transcendent Reality. When it does retain them, this kind of theology is different from theology as a mode of study within the academic study of religion that, while indebted for its origins to living theology, is primarily a reduced discipline, not possessing the strong features just mentioned. The latter is theology as an academic discipline that too often is still somewhat Christian, but only by habit or with respect to old habits.

Doctrinally, of course, the Catholic tradition affirms the Nicene Creed and holds together also a large body of doctrine and rules regarding moral behavior. It honors intellectual work, though its intellectual traditions, with their emphasis on philosophical issues and refined reasoning, stand alongside deep commitment to practices and respect for sacramentality, materiality, and indeed religion dependent on its material forms. Most Catholics, theologians included, would agree with the claim that Catholicism is a way of life, not merely a religious organization one joins (or leaves). The Catholic tradition is also catholic—global, inclusive of many cultural and local instantiations of Catholic faith and behavior. Being a Catholic is, or can be, constitutive of a life. As we shall see later, the religions we study, too, are not mere objects of study but likewise form those within their fold and shape their lives.

So there are many ways to think about theology, inside and outside religious communities and the academic, and with reference to ideas, practices, and ways of life. There are, however, three other factors that further complicate matters. First, theology, whether named as such or not, is an intellectual practice that flourishes in other religious traditions. Other chapters in this volume, such as those by Paul Kollman and Michael A. Rynkiewich, work with rich, nuanced understandings of theology but do not advert to the phenomenon of equating *theology* with *Christian theology*.[1] However, too close an identification of theology with Christian theology needlessly narrows and mars the conversation. Recognizing the fact of theology across religious traditions both expands the significance of theology as a discipline and puts firmly in context the claims made by any particular Christian theology to universal normativity. Recognizing theology outside Christianity, therefore, both enhances the importance of theology and, by pluralizing it, reduces the difference between theology and a humane anthropology. Elsewhere, I have argued for the fact and importance of Hindu theology.[2]

Second, when we assert that certain theologies are Christian, Hindu, or belonging to any particular tradition, this does not mean that those instances of theology are entirely self-sufficient within the traditions in which they are embedded. Intellectually, in practice, and experientially religious intellectuals interact with people in other traditions, benefiting from the religious resources found in those traditions. Even *ordinary* Catholic theology now works with an awareness of those other traditions; just as theology has drawn on other areas such as philosophy, physical science, and social sciences, theology now draws regularly on resources either directly from other religious traditions or from the sometimes mediating study of religious discipline.

Third, this chapter is about a particular, to some even peculiar, mode of Catholic Christian theology, a *Catholic comparative theology* with great indebtedness to Hindu theologies. This instance of Catholic theology, I will suggest, bears certain analogies to anthropological learning. I myself am a Catholic theologian. Being a comparativist who studies Hinduism in depth does not, in my view, diminish or counter my primary professional and vocational identity as a Catholic theologian, even if my work takes on a personal tone that is different from much of what counts as academic and ecclesial theology today.

I must advert here to the parallelism and contrast of my own path with that of another Catholic contributor to this volume. In his autobiographical account, Kollman traces the path of his theological training, experience in Kenya, and studies in the history of religions at the University of Chicago, and

---

[1] Paul Kollman, Chapter 5, 83–101; Michael A. Rynkiewich, Chapter 12, 211–25.

[2] Francis X. Clooney, "Restoring 'Hindu Theology' as a Category in Indian Intellectual Discourse," in *The Blackwell Companion to Hinduism*, ed. Gavin Flood (Oxford: Blackwell Publishing, 2003), 447–77.

shows how theology and anthropology came together for him in a particularly fruitful manner: "Instead of anthropology being at the service of theology as in stage one," he writes, "now theology was generally in the service of anthropology, especially in the service of an anthropological understanding of distinct historical processes like those I studied."[3] With a similar seminary training and my own early experience teaching in a school in Kathmandu, I, too, went to the University of Chicago, not to Swift Hall but to Foster Hall, home to the Department of South Asian Languages and Civilizations. There, in a heavily philological and text-grounded program, I invested much of my time and energy in learning Sanskrit and Tamil, so that in Chicago and with teachers in Madras (now Chennai) I could extend my classical Christian theological dispositions into the study of classical Hindu texts, which I read and took to heart in an analogous fashion to the way I read and took to heart the Christian theological tradition. Fashioning my own version of comparative theology, about which I will say more, was my response to this complex education. In those days, my only sense of anthropology had to do with the traditional theological category, theological anthropology, the study of the human as it opens into the mystery of God. The force of my studies was rather to expand my understanding of theology beyond any ordinary sense of the term into the relatively uncharted, risky space between traditions.

* * *

At this point, the questions about theology across religious borders come alive, and herein lies the rationale for the work of comparative theology, itself a grand balancing act. The learning operative in comparative theology is similar to anthropological learning and, perhaps, theological practices of interest to the anthropologist. To be a comparative theologian entails, a crossing over and, too, a returning home. One loses one's familiar home yet finds a way back to it again.

If the theological sensitivities of the home tradition are to remain in place, such that the learning from the other is theological, then the comparative theologian needs to be able to keep, adjust, and stretch his or her theological sensitivities, so as to learn from the other without either reducing the other simply to objects of theological judgment, or to the natural (as opposed to that which is graced, already transformed by the transcendent/revealed), or to possessors merely of a reduced natural wisdom. This complication of theology is analogous to the work of anthropology. The act of crossing over and the skills and benefits and risks it entails are, I suggest, of particular interest in the current conversation about the mutual enrichment of theology and anthropology. I therefore put aside the otherwise very important topic of how theologians draw on fieldwork and, in simpler terms familiar to the theologian, from the

---

[3] Kollman, Chapter 5, 88.

lived experience of the community that remains ever a primary source of theological knowledge.

* * *

Given the interdisciplinary nature of this project, to clarify matters I now put forward some remarks on the nature of comparative theology and the skills it entails, even when it is and remains a determinedly textual discipline, and even when we do not focus on the relation between the intellectual/academic discipline of theology and popular, lived religion.[4] In our religiously diverse context, a vital theology has to resist too tight a binding by tradition, but it must also resist the notion that religious diversity renders strong claims about truth and value impossible. Comparative theology is a manner of learning that is both free and disciplined by specific faith commitments. It takes seriously diversity and tradition, openness and truth, allowing neither to decide the meaning of a religious situation without recourse to the other. Countering a cultural tendency to retreat into private spirituality or into a defensive assertion of truth, this comparative theology is hopeful about the value of learning. Indeed, the theological confidence that we can respect diversity and tradition, that we can study traditions in their particularity and receive truth in this way in order to know God better, is at the core of comparative theology.

Since there are other ways to think about and respond to diversity that are appropriate but not comparative theology, I now draw on my 2010 work, *Comparative Theology*, to put forward a few preliminary distinctions regarding various modes of interreligious reflection, so that we can proceed with greater clarity though still without entirely fixed categories, in understanding comparative theology. *Comparative religion*, along with the possibly distinct fields of the *history of religions* and social scientific approaches to religion, "entails the study of religion—in ideas, words, images and acts, historical developments—as found in two or more traditions or strands of tradition."[5] Here the ideal is scholarly detachment, neutrality with respect to what is compared and where the comparison might lead.

When I use the term *theology*, I mean "a mode of inquiry that engages a wide range of issues with full intellectual force, but ordinarily does so within the constraints of a commitment to a religious community, respect for its scriptures, traditions, and practices, and a willingness to affirm the truths and values of that tradition."[6] This theology is, in accord with a traditional way of speaking, faith seeking understanding, "a practice in which all three words— the faith, the search, the intellectual goal—have their full force and remain in fruitful tension with one another."[7] The *theology of religions* is a theological discipline "that discerns and evaluates the religious significance of other

---

[4] The following paragraphs are taken, with some adaptation, from Chapter 1 of my *Comparative Theology: Deep Learning across Religious Borders* (Malden, MA: Wiley-Blackwell, 2010), 9–12.
[5] Ibid., 9.   [6] Ibid.   [7] Ibid.

religious traditions in accord with the truths and goals defining one's own religion. It may be greatly detailed with respect to the nuances of the home tradition, but most often remains broadly general regarding the traditions that are being talked about":[8] it is about religions rather than an engagement in learning from them. If interreligious dialogue is the direct conversation among people of different faiths, then *dialogical theology* seeks to identify and maximize what can be learned from the dialogues, with openness to how the dialogue changes how we think about and talk about the religions involved.

In distinction from the preceding ventures, *comparative theology*, comparative and theological beginning to end, "marks acts of faith seeking understanding which are rooted in a particular faith tradition but which, from that foundation, venture into learning from one or more other faith traditions. This learning is sought for the sake of fresh theological insights that are indebted to the newly encountered tradition/s as well as the home tradition."[9] Comparative theology thus combines tradition-rooted theological concerns with actual study of another tradition. It is not an exercise in the study of religion or religions for the sake of clarifying the phenomenon. It is not a theology about religions, nor is it the practice of dialogue.

Comparative theology is *comparative* because it is interreligious and complex in its appropriation of one's own and another tradition in relation to one another; and it is theological because, even as comparative and interreligious, it is still the work of faith seeking understanding. In some instances, this comparison may involve evaluation, but ordinarily the priority is more simply the dynamics of a back and forth learning. It is a theological discipline confident about the possibility of being intelligently faithful to tradition even while seeking fresh understanding outside that tradition. It remains an intellectual and most often academic practice even if, like other forms of theology, it can occur in popular forms as well. As I have already stated, while I write from a Christian perspective, comparative theology is not essentially Christian as I describe it. But even when comparative theology is grounded in other traditions, and even in particular personal pathways, *faith seeking understanding* will still be the operative principle.[10]

*   *   *

Comparative theology requires a mature or ever-maturing interiority to balance rootedness in one tradition and deep openness to another. Even heavily textual work—translations, the study of scholastic systems, the tracing of lines of thought in commentaries, the decipherment of ritual and moral codes—requires the ability to learn from the other, crossing over to it. While scholarly expertise is indispensable—linguistic skills, historical awareness, the ability to

---

[8] Ibid., 10.   [9] Ibid.

[10] Here ends the set of paragraphs drawn largely from *Comparative Theology*.

read critically—interreligious theological learning must be transformative, indebted to the religious Other that allows one to see inside that other tradition, even while the learning remains grounded at beginning and end in a home tradition—in my case, a steadfastly Roman Catholic comparative theology deeply informed by Hinduism.

This serious interreligious study may helpfully be thought to include the essential virtues Catherine Cornille has proposed: humility, commitment, interconnection, empathy, and hospitality.[11]

- *Doctrinal or epistemic humility*—"recognition of one's own fallibility and imperfection . . . a certain degree of admission of the finite and limited ways in which the ultimate truth has been grasped and expressed within one's own religious teachings, practices, and/or institutional forms";[12]

- *Commitment* to a particular religious tradition—remaining "rooted in the particular religious community from which and for which [we] speak";[13]

- *Interconnection*—"the belief that the teachings and practices of the other religion are in some way related to or relevant for one's own religious tradition; . . . the belief that the teachings and practices of other religions may in some way derive from or point to one's own conception of ultimate reality";[14]

- *Empathy*—"not only an intellectual but also an experiential understanding of the other; . . . a fuller understanding of the religious other must include some grasp of the religious meaning of particular teachings and their impact on the life of believers . . . [such that] they may have an impact on one's own religious tradition";[15] and

- *Hospitality*—"the recognition of other religions as potential sources of genuine and distinctive truth; . . . a belief in the possibility of discovering distinctive truth in the other religion, . . . [such as] renders dialogue not only possible, but also necessary."[16]

For the purposes of our conversation, I add four related virtues, posited in my own words:

- *Risk-taking*—experimenting, allowing the possibility of mistakes and the possibility of becoming more entangled than one would wish in the other religious tradition;

- *Patience with ambiguity*—because of the experimentation and because of the multiple complexities to be negotiated without hope of a single, governing method or system by which to simplify the complications;

---

[11] Catherine Cornille, *The Im-Possibility of Interreligious Dialogue* (New York: Crossroad Publishing, 2008).
[12] Ibid., 4.   [13] Ibid.   [14] Ibid., 5.   [15] Ibid.   [16] Ibid., 6.

- *New dwelling*—the ability to become only imperfectly and analogously yet still deeply an insider in the other community; and

- *Marginality*—we are what we learn and read and write, and so too is required the ability to live on the margins of one's own community, wherein most have not engaged in similar, border-crossing experiments.

These virtues—and surely others, since the list is not exhaustive—facilitate the intellectual and affective conversion necessary for entering upon the other, for the sake of understanding, and writing from within that other tradition. I admit that this comparative theological learning is not synonymous with Catholic theology as ordinarily conceived, but there is no reason to deny that it can also still be Catholic, or Protestant or Orthodox or Jewish or Hindu, theology. It resides interestingly in the liminal space between traditions, between home and the other. And yet, the comparative theologian intends to return home, and so his or her writing and teaching in the end *become* once more signally of the home tradition. I also propose, for our discussion, that this comparative theology enacts key practices and values operative in anthropological research, simply by its empathetic dwelling in and with the Other.

* * *

For a moment now and with some hesitation, I wish to reverse directions in order to state my curiosity regarding how anthropologists deal with the values and challenges of crossing over to the other. I am curious about the balance required to become and remain a recognized member of one's academic guild, researching and writing with critical awareness and attention appropriate to the academy, while yet adapting to and learning from the community of the other that one visits and to which one is indebted. I will also be interested to hear whether the nine virtues I have proposed will be recognized as virtues incumbent upon the anthropologist, too.

As a placeholder for this conversation, I present with minimal comment some passages from the preface of *Between One and One Another*, a recent work by the Harvard anthropologist Michael Jackson.[17] I find his insights to be remarkably attuned to the delicate balancing that I have highlighted as central to comparative theological work.

First, Jackson sees his work as engaging the world, immersed in a great experiment:

I have never believed that standing back from the world is the best way to see it for what it is, and I have always felt an affinity for thinkers who sought to understand the world through active engagement with it, even at the risk of

[17] Michael Jackson, *Between One and One Another* (Berkeley: University of California Press, 2012). See also Veena Das, Michael Jackson, Arthur Kleinman, and Bhrigupati Singh (eds), *The Ground Between: Anthropologists Engage Philosophy* (Durham, NC: Duke University Press, 2014) for analogous reflections on how anthropologists relate to philosophical systems.

appearing ridiculous, ... My real interest, I discovered, was in neither making the world an object of contemplation nor changing it for the better, but in making myself the subject of an experiment, allowing the world to work on me, reshaping my thinking and guiding my actions.[18]

Second, Jackson's manner of anthropological inquiry is a thinking that occurs between home and world:

I am always mindful of the irony that, having escaped the confines of the academy and cast myself adrift in the world, I find myself, within a few weeks or months of labor-intensive fieldwork, longing to get back to the sheltered precincts from which I so elatedly sallied forth. John Dewey argued that this dialectical movement between home and the world is the natural rhythm of human life, for we are constantly forced to rethink our lives in light of new experiences that unsettle what we once took for granted or regarded as tried and true.[19]

Third, this situated thinking balances presence and absence:

There are, of course, many ways in which one can absent oneself from the world, and many reasons for doing so, including disenchantment, dread, disablement, or a desire for intellectual or spiritual illumination. And there are just as many ways in which one can be actively present in the world, gregarious and engaged. But the task of balancing these modes of thinking and of being—rather than ranking them or emphasizing one at the expense of the other—is difficult.[20]

Fourth, Jackson aims for an immanence, declining transcendence, that is open, by an openness that eschews the distancing of grand theory:

As an anthropologist, I have never sought the kind of knowledge of others that purports to transcend the world of their experience, reducing human lives to cultural representations, innate imperatives, social rules, traditional values, or global processes; my interest is in the knowledge that may contribute to tolerant coexistence in a world of entrenched divisions and ineradicable differences. To this end one needs an ability *both* to think for oneself *and* to be open to the thinking of others, and a capacity for both self-analysis and social critique.[21]

Fifth, an anthropologist of this kind is an "outside insider":

Even though one's initial separateness becomes, in time, transmuted into a nominal kinship or genuine feeling for the world into which one has ventured, one never ceases to stand out in that world—by one's appearance, accent, idiosyncratic interests, and transience. What gives anthropological writing its unique character is its interweaving of these very different modes of being-with others—relating to the other as a fellow subject (a friend) and relation to the other as an object of intellectual interest (a stranger).[22]

---

[18] Jackson, *Between One and One Another*, 5.   [19] Ibid., 6.   [20] Ibid., 7.
[21] Ibid., 7–8.   [22] Ibid., 9–10.

Sixth, this anthropologist lives on the edge and resists self-protection:

> There is always a risk, in making comparisons, of not finding in the other anything that bears comparison with what one can find in oneself. Confronted by what appears to be the unthinkable alterity of the other, or the uninhabitability of his or her lifeworld, one may retreat into one's own world and make it the measure of all things. This is the danger of the non-empirical philosophy against which Dewey rails. It suggests a loss of balance between the need to distance ourselves from a situation that proves too overwhelming to manage and the need to engage with a situation in order to test our assumptions about it.[23]

These tensions and balances can perhaps unexpectedly be recast as virtues necessary to the comparative theologian as well: experimental vulnerability, liminal dwelling, owning up to absence and presence, immanent openness, homelessness even at home, and profound risk. While I cannot comment on Jackson's proposals from the professional anthropologist's perspective, we have a habitus shared by some anthropologists and some theologians; however the two do or do not converge or communicate as disciplines, in practice, in certain lives, theology and anthropology already overlap. My books are theological and reflect a search for truth, Truth, and God in ways from which an anthropologist such as Jackson would surely keep his distance, yet the personal virtues of comparative theological learning are not dissimilar from those of anthropologists. Perhaps I should not be surprised, since it is good Christian theology to hold that the truth of God and the truth of the human, and the methods of knowing them, cannot be entirely dissimilar; as we know and are human, we prepare to know and become the divine.

* * *

But it is time to get concrete. I now turn to some examples from my own work—comparative theological experiments on the edge between traditions that seem to live up to the demands imposed on both the comparative theologian and the anthropologist.[24]

First, I point to *Divine Mother, Blessed Mother: Hindu Goddesses and the Virgin Mary*.[25] In this book I argue first that Christian theologians and feminist scholars, who debate the nature of the divine, the divine person, God, in relation to the feminine, have unnaturally constrained their work by

---

[23] Ibid., 11.

[24] I hope my readers will indulge my decision to quote extensively from myself. By such quotes I hope to show that the kind of textual work I have done, enriched by some fifteen trips to India over the years, succeeds in putting me, as reader, in this difficult space between traditions and, in quoting myself, accentuating the reflexive nature of comparative theology. It is this eventuality, however challenging, that has made me interested in the work of anthropologists and, possibly, made the work of comparative theology potentially of interest to anthropologists.

[25] Francis X. Clooney, *Divine Mother, Blessed Mother: Hindu Goddesses and the Virgin Mary* (Oxford: Oxford University Press, 2005).

not paying attention to the Hindu goddess traditions—well over two thousand years of goddess worship documented in art and ritual and in an abundance of texts. To make concrete the possibilities, I chose three goddess hymns—great hymns, respectively of 61, 100, and 100 verses in length. I chose hymns in order to make the encounter more intense, since such texts, addressed directly to the goddess and inviting the reader to become a participant in recitation, dare the theologian who begins to understand them to appropriate the words as her or his own. In turn, pairing them to the study of the three goddess hymns, I chose three Marian hymns, by which to engage the problems of receiving the goddesses into Christian tradition, by reading back and forth. I sought intensity in the reading and the encounter across the margins of the two sets of hymns. The book ends dwelling in the liminal space between traditions—a Catholic notice of the goddesses yet without either confessing belief in them or denying it.

All of this works if the Catholic theologian, presumably able to feel deep affinity with the traditions of Marian piety, is also able to go beyond the status of a distant observer with respect to the goddess traditions. Were the theologian to relate deeply to the Marian tradition but not to the goddess traditions, he or she would deflate and subvert the work to be done by reducing what is learned to pre-theological or less than theological wisdom.

I sought a difficult balance in finishing the book. In the last chapter, I wrote, regarding the study of the Hindu goddess hymns: "The hymns invite us more urgently to participation, and if we do not want to participate, we may first have to protect ourselves by refusing to engage in the reading, thinking, and understanding that open the way to participation."[26] In response, I suggested, some readers may become worshippers of the goddesses named; others may choose to focus on the hymns to Mary, now read in a new way by readers mindful of the goddess hymns; and still others may simply read back and forth without making a choice. Where the reader ends up is a possibility and burden to be borne by that reader. If she or he is a theologian, the stakes and opportunities are all the more abundant, important, and difficult.

Second, in a different vein, I have pushed further the same questions of belonging and identity in *Beyond Compare* and in *His Hiding Place Is Darkness*. These books focus further on the passionate engagement that is required, and play at the borderland.[27] Both books are, by my intention, intended to be evident to the reader as deeply Catholic works, by a Catholic theologian, just as *Divine Mother, Blessed Mother* was. In both, at issue is how far one can go in the learning of the other without becoming a member of that tradition and

---

[26] Ibid., 234.

[27] Francis X. Clooney, *Beyond Compare: St. Francis de Sales and Sri Vedanta Desika on Loving Surrender to God* (Washington, DC: Georgetown University Press, 2008), 81–2; *His Hiding Place Is Darkness* (Stanford: Stanford University Press, 2013).

how hesitant one can be with so timidly holding back that the purpose of the learning is frustrated. It is a matter of going as far as one can, becoming one with the other, without abandoning one's starting point.

In *Beyond Compare*, I examine the spiritual and theological virtue of surrender to God, as it is described and inculcated in two great theological works: the seventeenth-century *Treatise on the Love of God* by the Catholic theologian Francis de Sales and the fourteenth-century *Essence of the Three Mysteries* by the Hindu theologian Vedanta Deshika. Both are about love in its many forms; both hold to the ideal of radical surrender into God's hands as the ultimate love; and both authors intend, by their books, to move the reader, intellectually and affectively, toward that surrender.

I describe three interlocking ways of reading. Each unsettles, constructively, what precedes it: "First, there is the bedrock value of a reading practiced within one's own religious tradition, as occurs when I read the *Treatise* and learn from Francis de Sales more of the truth and spirit of my Catholic tradition. Even if readers learn something about their own tradition, this learning has to do with one's own community and its history, and what is learned will most often appear consonant with established and practiced dispositions."[28] This necessary reading in one's own tradition is followed by "a reading practiced across religious boundaries,"[29] as when I, a Roman Catholic, read the *Essence*, a Hindu text, and learn it in accord with the reading traditions of Srivaishnavism. In this case, the reader is approaching a hitherto unfamiliar text in another tradition and reads his or her way into that tradition. In this instance, reading is still a learning process but by a different dynamic. The reader is drawn into this other tradition, understanding it and discovering attractive, affective bonds to it. Dependent on the two preceding ways of reading, the third is the practice of reading back and forth between the two traditions. This learning, I suggest, "further unsettles the reader who, once sufficiently educated by the texts, will be neither here nor there or, perhaps, both here and there."[30] This reading may throw both communities off balance as their prized texts are studied, but alongside hitherto unfamiliar texts from an alien tradition. It is hard to adhere to this manner of reading instead of retreating to a theory or reasoned objectivity that leaves the reader outside both traditions, deeply committed to neither of them. If the reader stays immersed in the two traditions by the process of reading back and forth, this reader "is rendered vulnerable to intellectual, imaginative, and affective transformation; she gains the capacity to engage and respond to these traditions in a fuller way, with honesty regarding their potentially radical impact on how she lives."[31] As a result, new ways of reading, and of theologizing, come to the fore, indebted to two traditions rather than one, and these

---

[28] Clooney, *Beyond Compare*, 81. [29] Ibid., 81. [30] Ibid., 82. [31] Ibid., 208.

adventuresome readers "become part of a limited (self-selecting, but not necessarily elitist) audience."[32]

The comparative theologian is one who writes in this in-between, liminal space, now as a religious intellectual who can reaffirm the power of these texts, reinvigorated in light of one another. This theologian is in a position to reject oversimplifications of the tradition other than his or her own, even while also rejecting simplistic methodologies that reduce the texts studied to mere information or mere instances of a larger theology about religious or human experience. To read de Sales and Deshika is to be persuaded, motivated, challenged by the author, and one must either go along or resist; mere neutrality, as of a detached historian of spirituality, is a less interesting option. But to belong to one of the traditions and read in the other—my reading the *Essence*—is to be subjected to the persuasions of a Hindu author with a response analogous to but necessarily different from how I read the *Treatise*. To read both books together is to some extent to do damage, reducing them to comparable examples or, as I think, to intensify both books by reading them together. The result of this double reading is both more powerful and more bewildering. This new situation may mark a loss of theological grounding, or it may inaugurate the fashioning of a richer, broader base whereby two traditions have a certain normativity even while losing absolute control.

My book *His Hiding Place is Darkness* is another experiment in comparative reading, my most recent completed project. I drew first on the biblical Song of Songs, read with the medieval Cistercian sermon writers, Bernard of Clairvaux (chapters 1–2), Gilbert of Hoyland (chapters 3–4), and John of Ford (chapters 4–8). I read with it the ninth-century Tamil Hindu classic, *Holy Word of Mouth*, read with medieval Hindu teachers Nanjiyar and Nampillai,[33] in particular. If in *Beyond Compare* I focused on the challenging issue of surrender to God, here I focused on what is a major strand in both works—the divine Beloved who withdraws, hides from the human lover. I proposed, in the course of this reading, that the effect of the double reading can be to confuse and isolate the reader who might find the Beloved in either tradition, acutely feel divine absence in either tradition, but now finds the same dynamics at work in both at the same time. Here too, the classic texts, though from my perspective harmonious, do not anticipate one another, and indeed do not welcome rivals at all. Yet by violating their privacy, as it were, and reading them together, I strove to take them very seriously. I chose to read them out of context, as a reader for a time liminal to both worlds. As a Catholic theologian, however,

---

[32] Ibid.
[33] Clooney, *His Hiding Place*; *Holy Word of Mouth* (*Tiruvaymoli*). Since none of the existing translations does justice to this spiritual and theological classical, I have used the richly commented Tamil original, *Bhagavat Vishayam*, ed. S. Krishnaswami Ayyangar (Trichy: Sri Nivasam Accukkutam, 1975–87).

I still intended a homecoming of sorts. At the end of *His Hiding Place Is Darkness*, I wrote that this set of exercises sought "a delicate balance between a most intense and particular truth, Jesus the beloved, and the unending drama of aesthetic, dramatic, and true apprehensions that draw us perilously near to other such loves—Krishna the beloved."[34] Here, too, I have sought a difficult balance; while making no secret of my own Catholic faith, "with a certain theological confidence chastened by the discipline of the theopoetic and the theodramatic, I have managed not to forget that other woman's love and her hiding, hidden beloved, Krishna."[35]

Quite different again is my current book project, tentatively and awkwardly entitled, *Slow Learning in Fast Times: On Reading of Six Difficult Hindu and Christian Classics and Why It Matters*. In the part I have already begun in a number of essays, I have thus far been reading Madhavacharya's *Garland of Jaimini's Reasons*, a text of Hindu ritual analysis from the fourteenth century. It treats in a very succinct form some nine hundred important cases of ambiguity in the interpretation of ritual texts and performance.[36]

Dealing with this ritual reasoning and argument is a very different instance. It first of all requires a very acute commitment to reasoning and focus on sparely stated arguments. It requires also willingness to suffer the discomfort arising from having to think through unfamiliar categories, working with material details very foreign and hardly of immediate interest (perhaps even in the fourteenth century), all without any discernible payoff in generalizations that would noticeably reward the hard work. Indeed, the point of the Mimamsa analysis is to resist and exclude worthwhile generalizations and to keep the focus on the actual specificities of ritual, even while attending to the problems arising. Madhava—the author—is resistant to theory and never backs away from the details, though reasoning with extreme precision amidst those details.

Scholars such as Madhava are, in a sense, like us, seeking to refine ways of reasoning, to state complicated matters as simply as possible, and to clarify what is at stake in certain texts for the sake of conversations among intellectuals at a remove from the actual practices originally generative of the texts of analysis.

What is particularly tantalizing, or frustrating, in reading this ritual material as distilled and thought through to a most economical perfection is that we are faced here with a text all about ritual that does not help much with the performance of rituals. *Garland* is ostensibly about an ancient world unfamiliar to us, yet in its utter lucidity it also opens up for us a rich world of reasoning regarding the ancient rites and the social world around them. If in a sense we are introduced to the world of ancient Vedic rituals and ritual

---

[34] Clooney, *His Hiding Place*, 140.   [35] Ibid.

[36] This work has never been translated, and I have used a standard Sanskrit edition: the *Jaiminīyanyāyamālāvistara*, ed. Pandit Sivadatta (Pune: Anandasrama Press, 1892).

texts, we are also and more directly being introduced to a certain strand of fourteenth-century interest in those rituals, refinements undertaken for certain fourteenth-century purposes. Because of the necessary focus on reasoning about practice, the text is rich likewise in ethical implications, again regarding both the older world of the sacrificers and the newer world of the analysts of ritual. If my prior examples—*Divine Mother, Blessed Mother, Beyond Compare*, and *His Hiding Place Is Darkness*—explore the limits to affective engagement in the other while maintaining original loyalties, *Slow Learning* explores, probes, and expands how we think in and after the study of an ancient ritual tradition.

The path back from this close analysis of difficult texts of summary and case reasoning to Catholic theology is, admittedly, a long one. At this writing, and for the next year or two, I am out in the field, so to speak, visiting in a land almost entirely unknown to my Catholic theological peers. When and how I return, to what reception, remain open matters.

These cases, examples from my own work, illustrate the actual complexity of textual study and its multidimensionality, and the demand on the comparative theologian to be able to learn from the other deeply yet without losing grounding in his or her own tradition.

*   *   *

In the preceding section, I turned to detailed cases of my own work in comparative theology that, while very much textual problems, open up issues that by their content and the methods required to pursue them may catch the attention of the anthropologist open to learning from theology. Throughout the entire essay, indeed, I have adhered rather closely to what I do as a scholar, rather than exploring the more expected topic: how textwork and fieldwork need one another. It remains true that, although located on the textual side of the text/living religion distinction, these instances leave room for actual fieldwork and need movement in that direction. There is no reason for the theologian of texts not to welcome insights from religion as practiced, popular religion, or even elite and learned religion as practiced. The worship of goddesses is abundantly alive in popular Hinduism, and even the use of the texts I have discussed might be tracked in terms of popularity, use in domestic and public worship. The Vedic rituals are not in common, ordinary practice, to be sure, but the destiny of Vedic worship can fairly be studied, along with the allied issues of Brahminical learning, the possibility of expertise, the use of such materials in teaching in traditional schools. I leave it to my readers to consider how much more thick description is required to make the materials come to life for those unfamiliar with the ideas, actions, and sentiments discussed.

In this manner of writing, I have intended to highlight certain intellectual demands on the theologian that nevertheless also require empathy. I have sought to show how even for a theologian rooted in a tradition, in this case Roman Catholic, this learning extends with some exertion and difficulty across religious boundaries, yet in a meaningful way that allows the scholar to begin to understand and, in a sense, inhabit the second tradition without converting to it. My overall proposal then remains simple: the work of the comparative theologian models many of the same insider–outside tensions that face the anthropologist, and we do well to be in conversation with one another, balanced as we are, between worlds.

17

Passionate Coolness

Exploring Mood and Character in Ecclesial Polity

Martyn Percy

Every denomination is, to some extent—to borrow a phrase from John Caputo—an attempt to express the "mood of God."[1] Ecclesial life is, inevitably, the social reification of any group's theological priorities and spiritual procliv-ities. Class, ethnicity, gender, and various contextual factors all have a bearing on the shaping of denominational life, of course. But the mood of a denom-ination of congregation essentially captures and communicates what it thinks is the heart, mind, and nature of God. Emotions are an underappreciated dynamic in ecclesiology, and in what follows I want to outline why an anthropology of emotions and moods might be a helpful lens through which to refract a different kind of theological reflection. This one takes the *ideal emotional temperature* of a denomination or congregation seriously and understands its potential for perceiving new ways of configuring the theo-logical repertoires of ecclesial communities.

A very short excursion into my own intellectual autobiography might help explain one starting point for this essay. A book that I often muse on penning, but am equally sure I will never write, would be entitled *Weather Reports: Towards a Climatology of Denominations and Congregations*. The emotional rep-ertoire and optimum temperature of ecclesial communities has interested me from the outset of my doctoral work, more than twenty-five years ago. I studied

---

[1] See Gary Gutting, "Deconstructing God," *The New York Times*, March 9, 2014, <http://opinionator.blogs.nytimes.com/2014/03/09/deconstructing-god/?_r=0>, in an interview with John Caputo discussing his book, *The Prayers and Tears of Jacques Derrida: Religion without Religion* (Bloomington: Indiana University Press, 1997).

revivalism and specifically the theme of power in contemporary charismatic renewal.[2] The groups I studied were within the *romantic negotiation*—a term coined by James Hopewell in his groundbreaking and, it has to be said, rather eclectic *Congregation: Stories and Structures*.[3] Hopewell's work drew on two key interlocutors. First, that of Clifford Geertz, and most especially his observation that religion is "a system of symbols which acts to establish powerful, pervasive and long-lasting moods and motivations in men by formulating conceptions of a general order of existence and clothing these conceptions with such an aura of factuality that the moods and motivations seem uniquely realistic."[4] The mention of *moods* here intrigues. It takes us directly back to the question posed by the theologian–philosopher John Caputo: How do churches, church leaders, and congregations convey "the mood of God"? One must look at the meaning of *mood* in this situation. The term is not precise, by any means. A mood is not merely an emotional state, since moods differ from emotions, feelings, or affects in that they are less specific, less intense, and less likely to be triggered by a particular stimulus or event.

Moods are more like dispositions or outlooks. People usually speak of being in a good mood or a bad mood. Mood also differs from temperaments or personality traits, both of which are longer lasting. Moods can change over time. Thus, one can have a national mood (e.g., gloom or optimism) just as much as a prevailing ecclesial mood (e.g., pessimism or hopefulness), but moods are not necessarily fixed. Congregations and denominations will clearly have many moods. However, they will also have a prevailing bandwidth of moods, often found in their favored *a*scriptions of God (i.e., their worship) that they, of course, identify as *de*scriptions. The favored conceptualizations of God acquire an aura of factuality and become sacralized. The ethos and worldview of an ecclesial community, therefore, combine to form an environment, which we might describe as a microclimate of mood that is specific to a congregation or denomination.

In some respects, ecclesial differences are partly about understanding why and how the apparent mood of God has been reified and expressed in different churches. Some moods are light; others heavy. Some are warm; others decidedly cool or even cold. Some are passionate; others cerebral. Of course, anthropologists cannot tell us what God's mood is, only that some churches will often try to *reflect* what they think God's mood is. A mood is the emotional condition and

---

[2] See M. Percy, *Words, Wonders and Powers: Understanding Contemporary Christian Fundamentalism and Revivalism* (London: SPCK, 1995); "The Morphology of Pilgrimage in the Toronto Blessing," *Religion* 28/3 (July 1998): 281–9; "Adventure and Atrophy in a Charismatic Movement," in *Practicing Faith: The Ritual Life of Pentecostal-Charismatic Christians*, ed. Martin Lindhardt (New York: Berghahn Books, 2011), 152–78.

[3] James Hopewell, *Congregation: Stories and Structures* (London: SCM, 1987).

[4] Clifford Geertz, *The Interpretation of Cultures* (New York: Basic Books, 1973), 90.

frame of mind of an individual or body. One might call it the inner weather of a culture.

The second interlocutor on which Hopewell drew was Northrop Frye and specifically his *Anatomy of Criticism*,[5] with Hopewell adapting and proposing Frye's typology of drama and literature—comedy, tragedy, irony, and romance. Hopewell superimposed ecclesial and theological worldviews onto Frye's fourfold typology, equating canonic with tragedy, empiric with irony, gnostic with comedy, and charismatic with romantic. This chapter is not the place or space to extrapolate these typologies further, but suffice to say, Hopewell held that each congregation and church (and, by implication, denomination, as well as individual members) was formed through a negotiation of worldview and ethos among the canonic, empiric, gnostic, and charismatic. Each congregation, church, or denomination, therefore, reified moods and dispositions that they held to as, firstly, normative, and, secondly, sacral. That is to say, their own beliefs, practices, and behaviors somehow reflected (or captured?) the mood or disposition of God.

I have tended to refer to this endeavor as the unpacking of implicit theology. In paying attention to gestures, moods, stories, testimonies—or the casual-habitual use of anything from phrases to furniture, or humor to hospitality—churches are complex fields of negotiation in which the life of God as experienced or desired meets the life of the world, and then forms a highly distinctive culture. A distinctive microclimate, if you will, of ecclesial life. Much like the air around us, or the weather for that matter, members of churches and congregations take their environments mostly for granted, including those social constructions of reality and plausibility structures that they partially build, and by which they themselves are constructed and subsequently inhabit.

* * *

The word *implicit* is suggestive. Normally used as an antonym with *explicit*, the term has a complex etymological history. *Implicit* is derived from the Latin *implicitus*, meaning to implicate, a term, in turn, that suggests involvement, interweaving, and entanglement. The Latin word *implicatus* expresses this idea with *plicare* conveying the notion of folding in the sense of mixing and combining, rather as one might expect to fold an ingredient into a recipe. Thus, *implicit* means the meaningful folding together and close connecting of a variety of strands. Correspondingly, making something *explicit* is an unfolding, unraveling, or explaining of knotty miscibility bringing order from apparent chaos and clarity from complexity.

I will illustrate this point with one simple comparative example: seating. In the revivalist churches that I studied in my doctoral work, the seats at the

---

[5] Northrop Frye, *Anatomy of Criticism: Four Essays* (Princeton: Princeton University Press, 1957).

front tended to be filled. People sat close together, or at least in clusters, and rarely did I see someone sitting on their own. Seats at the back of the church or auditorium were often empty and reserved for latecomers. The proxemics of this situation have significant theological and spiritual resonance. The *intensity* of fellowship—being *close* to one another in prayer and worship—is held to be one way of God's presence being reified in the collective lives of the worshippers. It was a kind of informally structured spiritual intimacy.

People sit together because doing so amplifies the sense of God's intense presence and his engaged immediacy. They tune into one another's extemporary prayer language and grammar, as they huddle together in small hubs of informal intercession. As a result, in hushed, intense tones, one might hear phrases such as "Father, we really just want to . . . "; "Lord, we just uphold . . . "; "Holy Spirit, we just ask you to bless . . . "; and so forth. In other words, having meaningful fellowship with someone sitting on his or her own, several pews back, is difficult. The constant use of the word *just* conveys the immediacy of the moment and the sense of God being present in the here and now. In terms of spiritual climatology, the mood is decidedly warm. Indeed, these are hearts strangely warmed, as Wesley described: God meets us in intense spiritual experiences that are often reified in and through intense fellowship.

My experience of ordinary English rural parish churches and their worship is, in contrast, quite different. I lived for ten years in the village of Cuddesdon, a few miles outside the city of Oxford. I was Principal of the Anglican theological college (Ripon College) in the village, which had around 150 students training for ordination in the Church of England. The village had a population of around 350 souls. I was a regular attender at the 8 a.m. *Book of Common Prayer* Eucharist.

Intense is not really a word one would normally associate with this service. True, anyone could concentrate intensely and contemplatively; the service takes about half an hour and contains exquisite and highly symbolic liturgical tropes and actions. The mood is not in any sense ardent. It is reverent, to be sure, but also measured, mellow, serious, sober; yet also with an inclination to mildness. The temperature of the liturgy is, therefore, essentially temperate, perhaps even bordering on the cool. It is a reflective and contemplative service in which the epiphanies permeate through aesthetics, language, and the complex culture we normally refer to as liturgy. It is a collective gathering of individuals, and few words are exchanged between them except, perhaps, on departure.

Rarely, in the small congregation that gathered each Sunday, usually around a dozen or so, did anyone share a pew. But not because the villagers were unfriendly towards one another, or to me. The proxemics here carried an implicit theology: God meets us in space; moreover, God respects our space as individuals. God does not crowd us. Indeed, being more alone in a larger sacred space has some spiritual value and does something physical closeness cannot convey and reify. To have sat right next to a parishioner at one of these services would have the potential to cause mild alarm. Not that anyone would vocalize such a concern, mind you. Their eyes would do all the talking: "Why are you sitting next to me? We are not married or otherwise related. We know each other but not intimately. There are many other spare pews here, which you can surely see, enough for each person to have one of their own." Their eyes would then involuntarily cast around the church at the available empty pews, confirming this prognosis, before settling back on the person who was now sitting next to them. Again the eyes would say, "So why are you sitting *this close* to me?"

In the first charismatic church I described, if it were the same size as the Sunday 8 a.m. congregation, they would congregate as this kind of fellowship normally does: Twelve of them would fill two pews at the front. The second congregation would most likely take one pew each, nearer the back of church. All of this action is unplanned and unscripted, with the decisions on seating entirely determined by a spiritual subconscious. Yet as Jim Nieman perceptively observes, these congregations, in acting in this way, "implicitly assert a view of God."[6] Hopewell goes further and argues:

> As slight and predictable as the language of a congregation might seem on casual inspection, it actually reflects a complex process of human imagination. Each is a negotiation of metaphors, a field of tales and histories and meanings that identify its life, its world, and God. Word, gesture, and artefact form local language—a system of construable signs that Clifford Geertz, following Weber, calls a "web of significance." Even a plain church on a pale day catches one in a deep current of narrative interpretation and representation by which people give sense and order to their lives. Most of this creative stream is unconscious and involuntary, drawing in part upon images lodged long ago in the human struggle for meaning. Thus, a congregation is held together by much more than creeds, governing structures and programs. At a deeper level, it is implicated in the symbols and signals of the world, gathering and surrounding them in the congregation's own idiom.[7]

In what follows, I will explore the terrain of a typical rural Church of England parish church, and seek to offer an outline sketch of rural English ecclesial life, rooted in an enterprise that some might call ethnographic theology. Others might simply refer to it as congregational studies, and still others might describe it as anthropologically attuned theological reflection. One can never claim that such an enterprise is anything more than an interpretative impression; a sketch, if you will; a thick description. Englishness (whatever that might mean) matters in this equation, too, just as much. Kate Fox has described our national fondness for "Eeyorishness," her word for mild

---

[6] James Nieman, "Attending Locally: Theologies in Congregations," *International Journal of Practical Theology* 6 (2002): 198–225 (here 199).

[7] Hopewell, *Congregation*, 5.

moaning and an unerring capacity for understatement. Expressions such as "Mustn't grumble"; "OK, I suppose"; "Could do worse"; "Curate's egg"; and "All things in moderation" are part of the national canon of our most cherished casual phrases as though passion and excess were some kind of nasty continental disease that you might get on vacation and treat as a rash with antiseptic.[8]

This kind of exercise, however, has to be grounded in an appropriate humility, for such a study cannot claim to be more than an impression from ground level. In interpretively sketching Anglican polity in this kind of way, and more specifically in the Church of England, I do not presume to have an elevated view of the field I survey. There is no bird's-eye or, for that matter, God's-eye view of the church. Indeed, even thick descriptions tend to be inherently impressionistic. One can only write and interpret what one sees on the ground of which I and any interpreter are inescapably part and parcel.

At the same time, I am aware of the dangers of over-characterization—a trap into which anthropology can easily fall. To some extent, so can any scholar working in the field of ecclesiology, and I will confess that this essay might be particularly fallible on these grounds, for in the narrations preceding and following, I am more than aware that I am offering something of an ideal ecclesial vision: a gentle, irenic, mild, grounded Anglicanism that strolls along in its own way, trusting in God and not being overly dominated by the mission-minded managerialism that often shapes ecclesial horizons these days. This essay may be, to some extent, an elegy for Anglicanism—a vision of what once might have been, is currently lost, but may yet return.

Anthropologists possess many skills, but arguably their primary gift is *noticing*—seeing things that other eyes usually pass over, noticing the ordinary and just how *distinctive* it actually is and excavating the taken-for-granted. In other words, reflecting and interpreting back to a community what it communicated, but could not hear, see, smell, taste, or sense until it was pointed out. Anthropologists pay attention to detail, especially the tiny details that seem, on the surface, insignificant at first sight. Yet as we have already seen with the example and brief discursive mediation on seating, even the very mundane can have meaning and significance that is not immediately explicit. As *implicit* theological material, however, it has serious currency for comprehension.

Much of my work in ecclesiology, drawing on anthropological frames of reference, has tended to imagine Anglicanism in spatial terms and as a series of complex relations between church and world.[9] That said, more is attempted

---

[8] Kate Fox, *Watching the English: The Hidden Rules of English Behaviour* (London: Hodder & Stoughton, 2004). The word *Eeyorish* implies always looking on the dark side of life and comes from Eeyore, the name of a donkey characterized by his gloomy outlook on life in A. A. Milne's *The Complete Tales of Winnie-the-Pooh* (Boston: Dutton Children's Books, 1996).

[9] See Simon Coleman, "Locating the Church: On Corridors and Shadows in the Study of Anglicanism," in *Contemporary Issues in the Worldwide Anglican Communion: Powers and*

here than mere sketching. As Natalie Wigg-Stevenson suggests, and drawing on the reflexive sociology work of Pierre Bourdieu and the cultural theology of Katherine Tanner,[10] theologians dig and excavate; they look for meanings below the obvious surfaces they encounter. They look for hidden linkages and the underlying body of rules or patterned order that may exist.

This might, in part, explain why theology and anthropology are not pure empirical disciplines. Both disciplines involve tactics, guesswork, hunches, and preliminary findings, all of which are gradually refined as more material is unearthed, discerned, and interpreted. Theology, like anthropology, is not a matter of locating singular agreement but of finding meaningful interpretations that are faithful to their subject. Both anthropology and theology practice engagement: They are inherently relational discourses and practices, born of hybridity, not purity.[11] As noted previously, some would see this enterprise as theological reflection or ethnographic theology; some might call it congregational studies—more in the qualitative–interpretative tradition of Hopewell, I think, rather than the quantitative–descriptive tradition favored by others. To some extent, I am happy to own some of these nomenclatures, provided one understands that the heart of this labor is deeply infused with anthropological approaches. As such, it has to be modest and circumspect in order to construct meaningful accounts of ordinary ecclesial life rather than to proscribe the church or denomination through the use of theological or social science metanarratives.

Considering Nicholas Adams' and James S. Bielo's insights in this volume,[12] my approach is inherently theological and anthropological. My early academic training, as mentioned, though arrived at inductively, has begun to crystallize at a point when the very arrival of ethnographic theology as a field (and, therefore, my implicit theology) is informed by fusions of theology and interpretative social science. For instance, Adams notes:

> Anthropology arguably tends to operate at two scales: the local and the middle distance. It concerns itself locally with ordinary lives but also demonstrates more broadly the alternative social ontologies that these lives embody. Theology has also tended to operate at two scales, but they are not the same ones: the middle distance and the cosmic. It concerns itself with alternative social ontologies expressed doctrinally in accounts of church, mission, and ethics. But it also concerns itself more cosmically with breathtaking visions of creation, redemption, and hopeful vitality extending beyond the last things.[13]

Pieties, ed. Abby Day (Farnham, UK: Ashgate, 2015), 213–26. Coleman discusses my spatial approach to Anglican identity and the field of ecclesiology.

[10] See Natalie Wigg-Stevenson, *Ethnographic Theology* (London: Palgrave Macmillan, 2014), 11.

[11] Cf. Wigg-Stevenson, *Ethnographic Theology*, 24.

[12] Nicholas Adams, Chapter 10, 179–93; James S. Bielo, Chapter 8, 140–55.

[13] Adams, Chapter 10, 192

This chapter, then, operates on all three scales of perspective—the local, middle, and cosmic distance, offering some theological insights implied by ethnographic observations.

Bielo's work is arguably more appropriate to my approach, as his offering is pointed directly towards scholars already operating in the field of ethnographic theology. He suggests that ethnographic theologians: (1) "write with more transparency about their process and decision making with respect to research design, methodology, and analysis"; and (2) consider other ethnographic modes, beyond the classic model of fieldwork, as "they promise to open new opportunities regarding the central goal of producing critical theological reflection."[14] To this end, I admit to taking an approach closer to a classic model of fieldwork. Although evident in these two sections thus far, I hope that I am being as transparent about the interpretative framework as possible. Without further ado, I begin the enterprise of implicit theology in this next section, introducing my approach within some general observations that I have made of Christian life to which I believe many may relate.

∗   ∗   ∗

Garrison Keillor's *A Prairie Home Companion* was a live radio variety show.[15] The show was normally broadcast from Saint Paul, Minnesota. The program is noted for its musical guests, especially folk and traditional musicians, and its distinctive ironic and tongue-in-cheek radio drama, particularly Keillor's own storytelling segment, "The News from Lake Wobegon." Keillor is a storyteller and not an anthropologist, but his observations about Lutherans, the Brethren, and, more distantly, Catholics, are deliciously wry, deeply incisive, and highly nuanced. His careful attention to detail is an object lesson in interpretative ethnography. Moreover, Keillor has a deep sense of how the mood of ecclesial life emerges. He embeds his reflections on local ecclesial polity and proclivities in the wider culture of the humorously dour, reflective culture in which the various congregations reside.

The program was aired on noncommercial radio, so did not carry real advertisements. However, the show features imaginary sponsors along with fictitious advertisements for fictional products, which are performed in the style of live, old-time radio commercials. For example, the show is "sponsored" by the fictitious "Powdermilk Biscuits," with the slogan: "Made from whole-wheat raised in the rich bottomlands of the Lake Wobegon river valley by Norwegian bachelor farmers, so you know they're not only good for you, but also pure, mostly," which "give shy persons the strength to get up and do what needs to be done. Heavens, they're tasty and expeditious." Other fictional advertisers include Mournful Oatmeal ("Calvinism in a Box": a parody of

---

[14] Bielo, Chapter 8, 144.
[15] The final episode was broadcast in July 2016, after over forty years of programing.

Quaker Oats), the Fearmonger's Shop (a rather peculiar yet comforting purveyor of security devices for the permanently paranoid), and Bob's Bank (with slogans including "Save at the sign of the Sock": "Neither a Borrower nor a Lender Be"). Keillor's creations perfectly capture a wary, slightly pessimistic folk spurred on by the Protestant work ethic and dollops of residual guilt built into the DNA of individuals, families, church, and community, being fiscally prudent and suspicious of excess in all things—be it wealth, religion, or personal outbursts and emotional displays.

In "The Secret Lutherans,"[16] aired in 2014, Keillor takes a handful of seemingly ordinary happenstances to reflect on what the program does so successfully, week by week—namely, to use the weather of Lake Wobegon as a means of excavating the mood that forms the primary identity of the community. Thus, a few beautiful, enjoyable days of summer are regarded as "almost intolerable" because they cannot be relied upon as a constant. They are, by implication, fleeting and probably fickle—a mirage that tempts the wary away from realism to the realms of individual indulgence in opulent warmth. Winter is "solid," something which you can rely on; it is predictable in its coldness and is utterly dependable.

The episode discusses Cindy Headland, a solid Lutheran wife and mother, married to a Lutheran farmer, Roger. However, Cindy begins to realize something is missing from her life; she has a "vague sense of dissatisfaction." In effect, she is having a midlife crisis after her grown-up children have left home. She knows this must be so because she contemplated buying a Chevrolet car, not a Ford. As Keillor points out, Lutherans drive Fords, not Chevrolets. Fords are solid and reliable. You know where you are with a Ford. They are not flashy. But she is tempted by a Chevrolet Caprice, which has many features and extras her Ford does not have: dozens of different positions for the driver's seat, adjusting heights and angles, for example. She wonders to herself how many options a person can really ever need. Deep down, she knows this is "a car of the wrong faith."

The Ford dealership is owned by Lutherans. Cindy mulls over that some of the profits will go from the owners to feed the poor and preach the gospel, a good, wholesome prospect. In contrast, the Chevrolet dealership is owned by Roman Catholics. She imagines the profits going to buy more opulent and unnecessary statues for their church and diamond-studded shoelaces for the Pope: in a word, excess. The car dealer does a good job of selling the Caprice. He offers some slack on the price and tells her it handles better than a Ford. It does, too, and it has many more options and extras and greater speed. She is enticed, and almost takes a test drive but draws back, musing to herself that this kind of temptation (i.e., try before you buy) "is what adultery must be

---

[16] "The Secret Lutherans," broadcast on January 20, 2014, <www.youtube.com/watch?v=4L6uXvpSC4A>.

like." She does not buy the car. Guilt, her own "inner spiritual weather," and dispositional mood make contemplating something that she knows, rationally, she might really enjoy difficult. Because she also knows, spiritually, that to enjoy something might be just a bit wrong.

As the episode progresses, we learn that she has encountered a new church—a group of charismatic Lutherans. At those church meetings, members of the congregation laugh and weep; they sob, hug, and dance. The emotional contrast is beautifully played up between the congregation of which she is normally a part and that of the charismatic Lutherans. This difference is refracted through weather-related motifs. In a similar vein, in Keillor's novel *Lake Wobegon Days*,[17] one of several he has penned that features the community, the Lutheran and Brethren congregations are consistently associated with dour, plain weather. These are cold, cerebral, even chilly forms of ecclesial polity and proclivity, and they are frequently contrasted with the unpredictable Pentecostal or charismatic congregations and experiences, which are treated, in effect, as unreliable sunny weather. Even more problematic for the Lutherans and the Brethren are the Roman Catholics, who are consistently sunny in outlook and regarded with some degree of alterity. Keillor's novels and broadcasts about Lake Wobegon consistently contrast the riot of colors and vibrancy of Roman Catholic feasts, festivals, and processions, which are seen as excessive and overly tempting, and the solid reliability of monochrome Lutheran and Brethren expressions of faith.

In one sense, we could say that religion is a regulative framework for moods and emotions. Emotion is not a thing, of course; it is embedded in situations, contexts, people, and encounters—the world at large. Emotions relate us to cultural symbols, society, and to ourselves. When we enter into social settings, we instinctively read the atmosphere of a place or time and, in a barely conscious way, adjust our emotional selves to the mood of the place, thereby creating a complementarity.[18]

Another brief spatial example might illustrate this phenomenon. As Dean of Christ Church, I live in the middle of Oxford's largest college but also right next door to its cathedral. Tourists and visitors from all over the world come in droves and marvel at the dining hall, Tom Quad, and many other architectural and historical features. They chatter away busily and animatedly in their tour groups as they move around the place, taking pictures, posing for others, and taking selfies. However, when they take their first step inside the cathedral, they change. They become stiller and quieter. Their behavior changes. Now, the cathedral door has no sign to announce itself, no notice that says, "Please

---

[17] Garrison Keillor, *Lake Wobegon Days* (New York: Viking Penguin, 1985).

[18] For a discussion of the place of emotion in religion in the Victorian era, see John Corrigan, *Business of the Heart: Religion and Emotion in the Nineteenth Century* (Berkeley: University of California Press, 2002).

be quiet: you are on holy ground and entering scared space." There is, in fact, no obvious demarcation between the college and the cathedral. But somehow, at some subconscious level, the quite different atmosphere of the cathedral causes individuals and groups to behave in quite different ways the moment they enter it. Reverence and respect replace excitable chatter. Their mood changes, and this behavior is probably a dynamic that emerges as a result of the interaction *between* individuals (or groups) and contexts.[19]

The mood and atmosphere of a church, with or without its congregation, is often striking at subconscious levels. Personally, I find the smell of old prayer books in a completely empty rural parish church—slightly musty leather covers and India paper—heavenly, spiritual nectar. It moves me. The fragrance of incense left over from a service the day before, with the distant scent of some spring flowers near the altar, tells me that this church is prayed in and holy. A slight whiff of polish on the pews and brass will trigger the same. Care for these aesthetics means God is cherished here, and Christian memory and presence flourishes in this place.

Other Christians of quite different persuasions, and with quite different olfactory imaginations, would find this stimulation of the senses strange. They would find the smell of freshly vacuumed carpet tiles in an extensive auditorium an indication of populous, vivid, anticipative congregational life and of an imminent service of celebration. This scent association for me is resonant with a hotel or conference center. I smell nothing sensually sacred in these places, only a secular odor.

Christianity is a faith of the senses with things of beauty to see and texts to read, sounds and words to hear, artifacts and objects to touch, and sacraments to taste and savor. We rarely think of our faith in terms of its sense of smell, but that is rather surprising when one considers just how important the olfactory imagination was in the ancient world: "the scent of salvation," to borrow a phrase from one theologian.[20] In the scents and odors of Scripture, tradition, and church, we have intimations of the divine. As Geertz says, "religious symbols *reek* of meaning."[21] Sometimes they literally do reek; the message is in the smell. Our faith is formed through emotional responses to moods and atmospheres that are locked and lodged, long ago, in the psyche of our spiritual proclivities and preferred ecclesial polity.

If the nasal senses are so attuned to mood and atmosphere, then this may be even more true in our aural sensibilities. The theology that ultimately shapes and informs faith is both implicit and explicit. The explicit is, perhaps,

---

[19] See L. Woodhead and Ole Riis, *A Sociology of Religious Emotion* (Oxford: Oxford University Press, 2010).

[20] Susan Ashbrook Harvey, *Scenting Salvation: Ancient Christianity and the Olfactory Imagination* (Berkeley: University of California Press, 2006).

[21] Geertz, *The Interpretation of Cultures*, 87.

obvious: the creeds, the articles, and the tradition. Nevertheless, we can gain considerably richer understandings of faith traditions when we attend to the implicit—the apparently background material of music, for example—that not only supports the tradition but actually contributes to its shape and eventual reception. "Amazing Grace," sung to an old hymn tune, is deeply reassuring. Sung to the tune of "The House of the Rising Sun," it gains a new (folksy?) place and relevance in a believer's composition of faith. Music moves our mood; it is not merely an accompaniment to faith but an actual expression of it.

I recall a visit to an American Episcopalian Church in Hartford, Connecticut, some years ago. I preached in my usual English style: a mixture of humor, reason, reflection, and passion. The congregation, almost entirely African-American, sang old spirituals with reserved and restrained Pentecostal fervor. The liturgy came from the 1928 *Prayer Book*, and there were clouds of incense. It was spine-tingling.

A focus on micro-ecclesial ecologies and climates is invariably revealing. We have already drawn attention to some of the spatial and spiritual connections in local churches, which shape our ecclesial experience. In the case of rural Anglicanism, and once again drawing on Cuddesdon, I was often struck by the careful calibration of moods and emotions at meetings, in services, and at festivals. The Annual Parish Fête, held in the grounds of the theological college, attracted around two thousand people every year. It was a remarkably traditional village fête, making little, if any, attempt at modernization. The Haddenham Hoofers would dance to folk music; the Silverdale Brass Band played their music. They might have a dog show, and a minor celebrity might open the proceedings, too. The genius of the fête was its sense of timing—no more than three hours and set somewhere in the 1950s. An afternoon of reassurance, accompanied by a cup of tea and a scone, were guaranteed. The prevailing mood was one of cheerful resilience and was perfectly complemented in the ethos of parish meetings throughout the year: intense where needed, more usually poised and restrained, invariably good-humored, and more or less always good-natured. Serious but light.[22]

The mood of the fête reflects an underlying dimension of the congregation's polity and its deeper identity as a body within the village, composed of villagers.

---

[22] Indeed, this is resonant with the characterization from Kate Fox in her *Watching the English*, which discusses "reflexes . . . our deeply ingrained impulses. Our automatic, unthinking ways of being/ways of doing things. Our knee-jerk responses. Our 'default modes'. Cultural equivalents to the laws of gravity . . ." (401ff.). She then identifies three basic reflexes that characterize the English: (1) humor, (2) moderation, and (3) hypocrisy. She links these to "outlooks" (empiricism, class-consciousness, and Eeyorishness) and "values" (fair play, courtesy, and modesty), all of which are designed to combat and address social dis-ease. Fox speculates on the cause of this complex potage that comprises the English character, and suggests that climate, island identity, and history may be factors—but no reductionist or determinist account is ultimately offered.

Hopewell's prescient work argued that attention should be paid not just to what is apparent and observable in the church but also to what is not evident or immediately visible. So, Hopewell might have been intrigued by my recent visit to Cuddesdon on an August bank holiday. It was a soggy wet day, but the coffee morning was in full swing, the sole purpose being to raise money for the twelfth-century Norman parish church.

Cake stall and plant stands mixed easily with tables selling secondhand books. Parishioners and pensioners shuffled around in damp coats, whilst children and dogs weaved in and out around them, gaining momentary affirming pats, strokes, and greetings by the adults. A raffle that recycled the unwanted Christmas bottles and boxes of biscuits did a roaring trade. Most of the people who donated books, cakes, and plants looked on approvingly as their near neighbors browse and buy. They would take their turn to buy soon, for this virtuous cycle is one in which all must participate. They cannot just give something away; they have to take something back, too. Your fulfilment of the offering–receiving relationship makes the entire event sacramentally valid. A huge tea urn steamed away in the corner, that reassuring secular thurible so beloved of the Women's Institute. The room may be damp (it was very wet outside), but the mood was not.

Out of a population of four hundred, there were around eighty attendees, a 20 percent turnout. The eighty attendees could be subdivided into four roughly equal groups: (1) those who came to church frequently, (2) those who came regularly (e.g., Christmas, Easter, harvest), (3) those who came very occasionally (e.g., funerals), and (4) those who never come to church but nonetheless care enough to help sustain it. Unless someone knew these individuals personally, they could not tell them apart.

The striking fact about village churches is that they are remarkably resilient and, despite their limited resources, continue to persist and flourish. A village church is a support-based institution to which many subscribe. It is not a member-based organization in which everyone knows who belongs and who does not. Indeed, those who habitually attend would be resistant to such demarcations. The church is a body with a soul—a mystery, and more than the sum of its parts. It is a social–transcendent reality, occupied with God, virtue, and values. Many in the community pull together to support it, irrespective of their faith.

The field of theology and religious studies has been thoroughly exposed to conversations with social sciences—such as anthropology and sociology—for more than a century. A focus on implicit theology seeks to pay attention to the normally neglected and often overlooked dimensions of ecclesial life that are constitutive for belief and practice. The realization of a relationship between the gentle framing of faith and belief through structures and practices allows us to ponder the significance of many things we might take for granted, and their theological weight. The type of music a congregation chooses, the way in which the music does or does not move them, dress codes, manners, the moderation of the collective emotional temperature—all have a bearing on the emerging vision of God within each congregation and denomination.

One does not cause the other. The task for any implicit theology is not to distinguish between God and the world but to realize that within these apparently innocuous and innocent beliefs and practices are, in fact, texts that demand interpretation. Because the shape of the church is partly brought about by the subliminal as much as by the liminal, by the subconscious as much as the conscious, and by the implicit as much as by the explicit.

Naturally, there can be no doubt that faith communities, churches, and congregations do look to formal theological propositions, creeds, articles of faith, to order their inner life, establish their identity, and maintain their distinctiveness in the world. Nonetheless, music, moods and manners, informal beliefs and learned, valued behavior, apparently innocuous and innocent practices and patterns of polity, along with performance, dance and dramaturgy, together with aesthetics and applied theological thinking each of these are no less constitutive for the shaping of the church. Attention to the role and vitality of the implicit is vital if one wishes to comprehend the depth, density, identity, and shaping of faith communities.

Having said that, all differences are not rooted in proclivity or context. All that can be said here is that such factors, while significant and worthy of theological evaluation, are not necessarily determinative. Although variable ecclesial inflections (e.g., Baptist, Anglican, Methodist) sometimes accentuate differences, ecclesial communities cannot evade their intrinsic and extrinsic unity. As Tanner observes, "Religious beliefs are a form of culture, inextricably implicated in the material practices of daily social living on the part of those who hold them . . . in the concrete circumstances in which beliefs are lived . . . actions, attitudes, and interests are likely to be as much infiltrated and informed by the beliefs one holds as beliefs are to be influenced by actions, attitudes and interests."[23] Contextual theology therefore pays careful attention to such detail.

*   *   *

Robert Runcie once described Anglican polity as a matter of passionate coolness. In fact, Runcie used the phrase quite often to refer to ideal English Anglican polity, as well as for the Blessed Virgin Mary at the Annunciation; or of the deceased and much-mourned Anglican contextual theologian and Dean of Sewanee seminary, Urban Terry Holmes.[24] The phrase is as striking as it is

---

[23] Kathryn Tanner, *The Politics of God: Christian Theologies and Social Justice* (Augsburg: Fortress Publishers, 1992), 9.

[24] At the fifth meeting of the Anglican Consultative Council in Newcastle, England, and on the occasion of a Eucharist at the Feast of the Nativity of the Blessed Virgin Mary. See <http://episcopalarchives.org/cgi-bin/ENS/ENSpress_release.pl?pr_number=81249>.

oxymoronic. Runcie believed that Anglican polity was essentially gentle, mild, and cool by which he meant temperamentally measured and reflective, even rational. Just the same, it was passionate about this coolness and passionate in its aesthetics expressed in the measured intensity of its dramatic liturgy; the beauty of its architecture, music, poetry; and its spiritual piety, whether high, low, or broad. This passionate coolness, crucially, *gathered people*—but did not force or corral. Much like a great work of art, passionate coolness draws people in, and draws them together but still leaves space for God to be present in deep experiences of the numinous and for themselves to be individuals while still providing ample space to be together.

One can be mildly humorous about the modest and temperate proclivities of Anglicanism. Rather like the climate of the nation that gave birth to its national church, it is often overcast with light drizzle but also sunny and raining with warm spells. As a nation, we over-narrate our weather, but our climate is, in reality, temperate. As Bill Bryson wryly observed in his *Notes from a Small Island*,[25] the rest of the world sniggers when English newspapers carry headlines such as "Phew, What a Scorcher!" or perhaps more risibly "Britain Sizzles in the 70s." In many parts of the world, this temperature is not even warm, let alone hot.

Caught between extremes, critics of Anglican polity have often ruminated that Anglicanism cannot escape its Laodicean identity: neither hot nor cold— just tepid; the classic *via media*—room temperature. Because Anglicanism is born of England, and just like its climate, the polity often struggles to cope with extremities. Anglicanism is mostly a temperate ecclesial polity: cloudy, with occasional sunny spells and the odd shower. The outlook, in a word, is mild. The English love mildness. Anglicanism, at least in its English forms, has almost apotheosized mildness as the ideal spiritual temperature to set the necessary tone and mood.

The climatology of a denomination or church, together with its optimum emotional temperature, is an important interpretive key in comprehending ecclesial life. In terms of mood, refracted through a climatological motif, we can instantly see, for example, how mild or cold fronts, when encountering hot winds, create storms. Indeed, in intra-ecclesial disputes, such as the Global South Anglican Provinces versus those of the North on the issue of human sexuality, we might be witnessing a clash of moods and temperaments as much as we are also seeing explicit theological differences emerge.

Indeed, the emerging ecclesiastical climatology witnessed at the beginning of the twenty-first century, like the rest of the planet, now finds itself exposed to extremities. Normal and temperate weather configurations seem to have given way to immoderate and excessive patterns of behavior that are driving a

---

[25] Bill Bryson, *Notes from a Small Island* (London: HarperCollins, 1995).

new agenda. The sense of furious religion has returned. Cool, calm religion—that beloved export of Europe for so many centuries—is giving way to hot and sultry expressions of faith that despise moderation and temperateness. Anglicans of all hues are caught up in the new extremes of spiritual weather. Ecclesiastical global warming has arrived.[26]

Some churches, of course, thrive on intensity and heat. They are signs of vibrant life and feisty faith. Others who are of a more temperate hue find such ecclesial expressiveness disturbing: heated exchanges, anger, and passions seem to dismay more than they console. Anglicanism, then, as a *via media* expression of faith, finds the soul of its polity profoundly troubled by excess.

Passionate coolness, then, is a typically (English) Anglican phrase, framing ecclesial identity within an apparent paradox. Anglicanism is, then, a kind of practical and mystical idea that embodies how people might be together. Anglicanism is a social vision before it is an ecclesiology, and not a confessional church in which membership is conditional upon precise agreement with articles or statements. In spite of the internal difficulties that global Anglicanism encounters, its strength may still lie in its apparent paradoxes: its unity in its diversity, its coherence in its difference, its shape in its diffusiveness, its hope in a degree of faithful doubt, its energy in passionate coolness. As a polity, it embodies faint conviction; it practices truthful duplicity; it is Protestant and Catholic; it is synodical and episcopal; it allows for troubled commitment; or, as one commentator notes, it can hardly ever resist the pairing of two three-letter words: yes, but.[27]

*   *   *

As a side note here, I think it is highly important to point out that with every social scientific work, there will be always some sort of implicit, if not explicit, agenda. One concern of Anglicans in most of the English-speaking world is the undeniable trend of the decline in church attendance.

As a response, the administrative bodies of the Anglican Communion have assumed that empty churches mean dead churches, and have been focusing their energies and resources on building expressions of Christianity that can fill church pews with more physical bodies. This assumption has thus favored the more charismatic and evangelical forms of churchmanship and neglected, if not abandoned, more traditional forms, such as those in the rural parish sketched in this chapter.

As I intimated earlier, by highlighting the implicit theology of one rural Anglican church, I seek to present an expression of Christianity that is rapidly

---

[26] See Martyn Percy, *Anglicanism: Confidence, Commitment and Communion* (Farnham, UK: Ashgate, 2013).

[27] Urban T. Holmes, *What Is Anglicanism?* (Harrisburg, PA: Morehouse, 1982), 5. In a typically irenic way, Holmes suggests that Anglicans are at their best when they "acknowledge the penultimate nature of [our] answers to the character of God," which he claims as an appropriate modesty.

disappearing, partly with the help of the church. Perhaps I am guilty of some nostalgia here, and about a process that is perhaps inevitable. But within social scientific scholarship, the assumption that "an empty church means a dead church" (arguably a common trope in more membership-based evangelical congregations) is far from being unanimously accepted.

The most notable work that addresses this issue is Grace Davie's observation of what she calls "vicarious religion."[28] In short, she observes that despite the decline in church attendance and membership in the United Kingdom, the public role of institutional religion remains an important part of British society. She highlights four observable ways in which British society continues to live vicariously in the church:

1. "Churches and church leaders perform ritual on behalf of others";
2. "Church leaders and churchgoers believe on behalf of others";
3. "Church leaders and churchgoers embody moral codes on behalf of others";
4. "Churches can offer space for the vicarious debate of unresolved issues in modern societies."[29]

A church, in other words, is a public entity and not a private affair.

Thus, though the pews may *seem* to be close to empty in some rural Anglican churches on Sundays, they may still be holding an important role in the church's mere visibility within a community and parish. Shutting them down completely may only be exacerbating the situation of the decline of church attendance and membership, not to mention exterminating a form of churchmanship that is very near to the heart of English culture.

As for the aforementioned agenda of juggling the disciplines of theology and the social sciences, which both Adams and Bielo address in their chapters, this particular example is no more than an explicit demonstration of how theology can benefit through judicious insights gleaned from social sciences.

*   *   *

Returning to the subject of mood, within the prevailing emotional ethos of a distinctive ecclesial environmental culture such as English Anglicanism (especially its rural contexts), this somewhat discursive essay has sought to reflect on the potential significance of implicit theology—that is to say, how the medium might be as important as the message. To pay attention to the mood, emotional weather, or optimum spiritual temperature of a church, congregation, or denomination might be as significant as its explicit

---

[28] Grace Davie, "Vicarious Religion: A Methodological Challenge," in *Everyday Religion: Observing Modern Religious Lives*, ed. N. Ammerman (Oxford: Oxford University Press, 2007), 21–36.
[29] Davie, "Vicarious Religion," 23.

theological claims. Indeed, they are most likely already fused within a compacted alloy. The coldness of cerebral conservative evangelical Calvinism in the Anglican tradition, and its antipathy towards the emotions as any kind of reliable register for experiencing God, contrasts sharply with the manifestations of warm mood and climes of contemporary charismatic renewal.

The antipathy between these two ecclesial expressions, which share a common heritage of evangelicalism, is striking. Differences frequently emerge on matters of temperament that are intricately fused to theologies or doctrine. Communities of faith (unavoidably) convey their sense of the mood of God. For conservative evangelicals, God is a rather distant, cold father figure; but one with an almost insatiable anger and wrath against sin that requires a sacrifice (i.e., Jesus). The response from believers must be unquestioning obedience. Like a disciplined child, good behavior from now on is mandatory. Conservative evangelicals *instruct*, with an emphasis on being kept in line. For charismatically orientated Christians, spirituality and ecclesial value-laden behavior tend to be rather different. The charismatic–romantic nego-tiation that Hopewell identifies, and previously mentioned, stresses the value placed on the motif of adventure but with the virtual assurance of happily resolved endings and emotional bliss. The immediacy of God's love is encoun-tered through warm, radiant, and largely affirming, even ecstatic, religious experiences.[30]

Much more could be said on the nature of English emotions and their place in society. Two recent studies suggest further possible avenues of exploration. Thomas Dixon's recent *Weeping Britannia* examines the generational shifts in expression of emotions. Oliver Cromwell used to burst into tears at the slightest opportunity; the traditional stiff upper lip belongs to another era. As a nation, the English have only recently learned to re-engage with public displays of emotions (e.g., Princess Diana's death). In *Spaces for Feeling*, Susan Broomhall comments on the role of religion in both containing and amplifying emotions from the seventeenth to nineteenth centuries.[31]

More recent theologically attuned work from Abby Day, Nigel Rooms, and Ian Bradley has drawn attention to how moods and emotions can be treated as significant theological, ecclesiological, and spiritual material.[32] Indeed,

---

[30] See Peter Herriot, *Warfare and Waves: Calvinists and Charismatics in the Church of England* (Eugene, OR: Pickwick Publications, 2016); see also Hopewell, *Congregation*, and his discussion of the tragic–canonic and romantic–charismatic negotiations.

[31] Thomas Dixon, *Weeping Britannia: Portrait of a Nation in Tears* (Oxford: Oxford University Press, 2015); Susan Broomhall, *Spaces for Feeling: Emotions and Sensibilities in Britain, 1650–1850* (London: Routledge, 2015).

[32] Abby Day, *Contemporary Issues in the Worldwide Anglican Communion: Powers and Pieties* (Farnham, UK: Ashgate, 2015); Nigel Rooms, *The Faith of the English: Integrating Christ and Culture* (London: SPCK, 2011); "Deep Listening: A Call for Missionary Anthropology," *Theology* 115/2 (2012): 88–108; Ian Bradley, *Believing in Britain: The Spiritual Identity of the British* (London: I. B. Tauris, 2007).

theologies of the church would be helped by developing anthropologies that enable greater ecclesial emotional intelligence. In ending, we simply renew our invitation to theology to take seriously the role of mood, atmosphere, and emotional disposition in relation to the shaping of ecclesial life. As Emily Carr (1871–1945), the Canadian artist, once remarked, "There is something bigger than fact: the underlying spirit, all it stands for, the mood, the vastness, the wildness. . . . "[33] Those untidy wild terrains of emotion and temperament await further investigation to discover how the faithful convey the mood of God.

[33] Emily Carr, *Hundreds and Thousands: The Journals of Emily Carr* (Toronto: Douglas & McIntyre, 1966), 5

18

The Exclusive Brethren "Doctrine of Separation"

An Anthropology of Theology

Joseph Webster

Attending a service at a Plymouth Brethren Christian Church (PBCC), the UK's largest Exclusive Brethren (EB) denomination, is quite an undertaking. I discovered this for myself about three years ago when trying to organize just such a visit to the PBCC on the outskirts of north Belfast. Having located the church's central UK website, I eventually found the relevant contact information for Belfast, which gave an address but no phone number. This posed a problem because previous research among different Brethren groupings in northeast Scotland had taught me that it would be essential to telephone in advance to make a formal request to attend a gospel service—the only meeting of ten weekly services that members of the public are customarily able to attend. After hunting in vain for a Belfast telephone number, I gave up and opted to call the only UK number on the website, which was listed alongside an address in Surrey. The man who answered listened to my request in what felt like suspicious silence, surely heightened by my open, if rather short, admission that I was an anthropologist wanting to learn more about the Plymouth Brethren in Northern Ireland. He took my email address and said someone would be in touch.

To my surprise, someone did email me—a man whom I later learned was widely recognized to be a UK leader of the PBCC. After an email exchange in which I again explained my planned research, he arranged to speak with me on the phone, allowing me to give further details of my work and background and, interestingly, allowing him to share his thoughts on the eminent sociologist of religion Bryan Wilson. This somewhat disorientating conversation ended with him providing me with a telephone number for David Adler,[1] a man

---

[1] All names are pseudonyms.

attached to the PBCC congregation in Belfast. The next day I duly phoned Mr Adler, and although I was aware he had probably already been thoroughly briefed, once again explained who I was and what my research would entail—a project that, in the first instance at least, would involve nothing more than regularly attending their Sunday evening gospel service. Mr Adler's manner, while hesitant, was warm and kind. In addition, he seemed genuinely intrigued by the work I was proposing. To discuss the matter further, he arranged for me to visit his home the following Saturday afternoon.

Upon arrival I was greeted by Mr Adler and Simon Cunnie, a man in his early thirties, whom I was told would also be present for our discussion. The Adlers' house was an average middle-class home—a detached bungalow, scrupulously clean and tidy, with plenty of comfortable seating. Ushered into the living room, I was very briefly introduced to Mr Adler's wife and daughter who were working in the kitchen, but moments later, the kitchen door was shut, and after some small talk about my journey and the weather, Mr Adler and Mr Cunnie sat me down ready to talk business. As I expected, in contrast to typical Northern Irish etiquette when meeting with strangers, neither man took tea or biscuits, and none was offered to me.

As we talked, I tried to explain in clear and unpretentious terms what anthropology was and why I wanted to study the PBCC. I explained that I had previously studied Brethrenism in Scotland and now wanted to do so in Northern Ireland. I also noted that the Exclusive Brethren had been maligned in the press in recent years and explained that my aims were entirely different: I wanted to learn about the beliefs and practices of the PBCC from members themselves and would do so by listening, rather than by rushing to judgment. Then, in a possibly somewhat misguided attempt to establish my academic credentials and to make the conversation more concrete, I produced a copy of my book and offered it to them as a way to understand better what my research entailed. Mr Cunnie took the book and asked to pay for it, a request I politely declined. Finally, in a probably even more misguided attempt to establish some kind of shared Christian values and to explain better my personal motivation for the proposed study, I described how a long and difficult period of research among the Orange Order, involving being witness to seemingly endless binge drinking and swearing, had left me ready to return to earlier, and quieter, fieldwork among Brethren communities. Mr Adler and Mr Cunnie both listened carefully but gave very little away. The meeting ended as it began, with smiles and handshakes on Mr Adler's porch but with the addition of a confirmed invitation to attend an evening gospel service the following night. With address and directions in hand, I thanked them both and left.

Roughly twenty-four hours later I was driving north in search of the PBCC. Despite good written directions and a satnav, I drove straight past the hall, not seeing a small sign inside and to the right of the main gate stating that what lay behind the fences was a "Brethren's meeting room place of public religious worship." While the meeting room itself was certainly large, it was well set back from the road and entirely surrounded by fences and high hedges, making it nearly impossible to see. Indeed, the building was so well hidden that I found it only after seeing a family in distinctive Brethren dress turn off the main road, go through a steel gate, and enter a parking lot. The surrounding area was a nondescript industrial estate, home to a waste water firm, an independent Land Rover specialist, a company producing pumping equipment, and, interestingly, a nondenominational charismatic church. Driving through the gates, I quickly realized I was early, noticing few cars and even fewer people. Once inside the main parking lot, I could see the full effect of the fencing, which obscured nearly all views beyond the church property. A few people looked to be entering the main doors at the front, but I had been instructed to drive around the back of the hall, where I would be met.

As promised, Mr Adler and Mr Cunnie were waiting. We greeted each other and I was ushered into a small anteroom attached to the main hall. This room contained several racks of tracts and other Brethren leaflets, as well as a bookcase lined with new Darby Bibles—the only translation the PBCC use. I was handed a Darby Bible and a *Little Flock* hymn book and led into the main hall—an impressive amphitheater-style space, with rings of seating descending downwards toward a central standing area used for preaching. This large room, which looked to be able to seat about eight hundred, had no windows. The pew in which I was seated was marked out for visitors, was roped off, and was set away from the main sections of ringed seating by being placed against the back wall, immediately beside the anteroom door. Mr Adler sat to my left and Mr Cunnie to my right; we were the only three in the pew. The effect of being flanked in this way by the two men, who had clearly been designated as my handlers, was both disconcerting and somehow comforting. I was certainly hemmed in, but unlike previous experiences of attending services at other Exclusive Brethren denominations, I was not left to sit entirely by myself.

I watched carefully as people began to arrive and take their seats. Members came in through the main doors at the front of the hall into a spacious foyer. Men and women generally did so through opposite doors (although not universally so) with many of the women pausing at small mirrors on the wall to adjust their head coverings before they entered the main auditorium. Here, seating was gender-segregated, with men and boys occupying the rings of pews closest to the preaching area, and women and girls sitting behind the males but in front of visitors. The dress code was also strongly gendered; men wore smart shoes, suit trousers, shirts, and sweaters but no jackets or ties; women wore modest dresses, or skirts and blouses, and a scarf tied around the back as a head covering. To my surprise, many of these scarves looked to be made from expensive silk, displayed designer logos, such as Calvin Klein and Louis Vuitton, and were brightly patterned. Perhaps unsurprisingly, my careful observations appeared to be being reciprocated, and the quick, inquisitive glances I received clearly indicated that visitors to the church were probably unusual.

The service itself, despite the very distinctive architecture, felt familiar. The meeting lasted about an hour, and, as among the Gamrie Closed Brethren, contained a mixture of hymns and prayers, as well as three short gospel addresses given by different men. Each preaching began with three Bible readings, with the message itself generally focusing on thankfulness for one's salvation and exhortations to continue to live a godly life. The details are scant here because, in an attempt to make my presence as normal as possible, I neither took notes nor used a recording device. At the end of the service, as I was chatting to Mr Adler and Mr Cunnie, two or three of those whom I took to be leading men—that is, informally recognized in positions of authority over the assembly—came over to say hello and shake my hand. While Mr Adler introduced me, these men seemed already to know precisely who I was. Their manner was friendly but formal and, as with the others, eminently cautious. After a few brief words of welcome, they made their way back down to the center of the hall and then toward the main doors to exit. Once again I was left sitting in the back pew of the nearly empty hall flanked by Mr Adler and Mr Cunnie. Moving back to the anteroom, I was told the Bible I had been given was mine to keep and was also given a few tracts and other booklets. As I was leaving, I must have been anxious to appear friendly because after offering my thanks for Bible and tracts, I blurted out, "And thanks for your *friendship*." "Oh, well," Mr Adler said, chuckling awkwardly, "not at all." Realizing I had made the situation more difficult than it needed to be, I simply smiled, thanked them both again, got in my car, and left.

*   *   *

What are we to make of the ethnography above? Why did it take so long to arrange to attend a service? Once I had permission, why was the church building so hard to find? Why the tiny sign, large metal gates, high fences, and obscuring hedges? Why build a main church sanctuary with no windows? Why have a separate back entrance for visitors? Why have a separate visitors' pew set away from the main seating, roped off, and behind the female congregants? Why have visitors flanked and handled or, perhaps more generously, seated in-between and chaperoned by church members for the entirety of their visit? Knowing a little more about the material and symbolic culture of the Exclusive Brethren prompts further related questions. Why, for example, do the PBCC shun, or *withdraw from*, excommunicated members, including immediate family? Why do they temporarily withdraw all contact from, or *shut up*, those members under church discipline? Why, as far as possible, do they educate their children in PBCC schools? Why do they refuse to eat, drink, or socialize with non-members? Why do they only live in detached houses? Why will they employ outsiders in their businesses, but never be employed by them? Why do they reject TV and radio? Why do they refuse to vote while simultaneously making public statements or donations to individual politicians?

My answer, simply put, is theology. The PBCC do what they do—and do not do what they do not do—because of a strong, near totalizing, and ever-expanding commitment to theology and, specifically, to one particular doctrine—namely, the doctrine of separation. In this sense, this chapter is not just about theology but is also about *doctrine*—"a body of instruction or teaching" forming a "system of principles or tenets" that are collectively "laid down as true."[2] Furthermore, my focus remains on *religious* doctrine of a particular and dogmatic kind. Here, PBCC teaching takes the form of transcribed weekly discussions between church leaders about various biblical texts. Transcriptions from these Bible readings or ministry meetings are then published as members-only multivolume book series, for which all PBCC households must pay a subscription, and which, because such teaching is held to have prophetic authority, all adult members are required to study. Taken within this context, my anthropological focus on the lived experience of this kind of dogmatic doctrine acts, I think, to distinguish (partially) the category of *theology* from related categories anthropology is more accustomed to deploying, such as *cosmology* and *ideology*, which are not commonly thought to be so rigorously codified and so carefully disseminated. Before I begin to explain how a complex religious culture can be seen as reducible to a single theological doctrine, some brief historical context is needed.

*   *   *

The Brethren formed in Dublin during the mid-1820s when a small group of men began to question the validity of Anglican theology, worship, and church governance. Under the leadership of John Nelson Darby, the grouping emerged as a distinct ecclesiastical entity in Ireland as early as 1827, and "by 1832, Brethren assemblies had been established in Bristol, Bournemouth, Exeter and Plymouth."[3] Crucially, under the leadership of Darby, "separation from ecclesiastical error of any kind was a prerequisite for establishing Christian unity."[4] As Darby further developed his separatist agenda, disagreements arose about, among other things, with whom Brethren followers could share the Lord's Supper. This conflict caused a major schism by 1848, leading to the formation of the strongly centralized or *connectional* Exclusive Brethren led by

---

[2] *Oxford English Dictionary*, s.v. "doctrine."
[3] M. Tonts, "The Exclusive Brethren and an Australian Rural Community," *Journal of Rural Studies* 17 (2001): 309–22 (here 312).
[4] Ibid.

Darby and the more decentralized or *independent* Open Brethren led by various regional leaders across Britain. Among the Exclusive Brethren, this connectional pattern, according to Shuff, was characterized by "a high degree of inter-dependence within a network of assemblies," achieved via "strong and often centrally regulated" forms of leadership that "had the propensity to spawn an increasingly ridged separatism."[5] Crucially, connectionalism sought to create "a universal structure of... church government"[6] that "insist[ed] that the receiving or rejection of a person by one assembly was binding upon all assemblies."[7] What did such a structure mean for the development of Exclusive Brethren theology in the past, and what bearing might it have in the present and future?

First, the connectional Exclusive Brethrenism of the PBCC stakes its (not undisputed) claim to being the only *original* and *true* form of Brethrenism on the basis of its tracing an unbroken line of leadership—a *lineage*, in a literal sense—from J. N. Darby, to J. B. Stoney, to F. E. Raven, to James Taylor, Sr, to James Taylor, Jr, to James Symington, to John Hales, and finally to its current leader, Bruce Hales.[8] Importantly, as this lineage has developed and become elongated, so has the terminology used to describe the role and status of the leader. When James Taylor, Jr took over after the death of his father in 1953, he added to the already established title "man of God" by proclaiming himself the "elect vessel," finding scriptural warrant for this "on the basis of Acts 9:15–16 and Isaiah 42:1."[9] More importantly still, such titles and the authority they bestowed had a very real impact on the leader's ability to impose new theology and doctrinal practices on members. One such example was Taylor, Jr's "separate tables" edict, which extended the principle of a closed table for the Lord's Supper by applying it to *all* forms of eating and drinking. The edict meant that Exclusive Brethren were no longer permitted to eat with non-members under any circumstances, including spouses and immediate family.

Crucially, however, those leaders who imposed such new theology and doctrine did not regard them as new. Indeed, far from having anything to do with innovation or novelty, these developments in Exclusive Brethren belief and practice were regarded as a return to the earliest days of the New Testament church. Thus, Exclusive Brethrenism was, from its earliest days under Darby's leadership, a restorationist movement that sought (again, *literally*) to rediscover and restore God's divine plan and pattern for the church. Nonetheless, regardless of the divine or human authorship of such restorations/innovations, Exclusive Brethren terminology and theology continued

---

[5] R. Shuff, *Searching for the True Church: Brethren and Evangelicals in Mid-Twentieth-Century England* (Carlisle, UK: Paternoster, 2005), 3.

[6] Ibid., 5.   [7] Ibid., 31.

[8] This lineage has led to the common shorthand name the Raven–Taylor–Hales Brethren to distinguish it from other strands of Exclusive Brethrenism and Plymouth Brethrenism.

[9] Tonts, "The Exclusive Brethren," 312.

to develop. One such development came about in response to the Aberdeen Incident of July 1970, where an ageing Taylor, Jr was found, apparently drunk, in bed with a married woman.[10] The ensuing scandal, which received gleeful coverage in the tabloids, split the Exclusive movement. In the spiritual and institutional turmoil that followed, those who remained loyal to Taylor, Jr found themselves in possession of a new term with which to refer to their leader: "Minister of the Lord in the Recovery." The PBCC explanation of this term is insightful:

> The term Minister of the Lord in the Recovery was a descriptive phrase suggested by eminent lawyers when the church was renewing their trust documents after a division in the 1970s. The term was suggested as a means of allowing the church to identify those who remained with the original fellowship and in particular provided a reference point as to who were subscribing to the faith in the unlikely event of a division. It describes the person the Brethren look to for universal leadership, following the unbroken line from Mr John Nelson Darby to the present.[11]

This is crucial because it shows that as well as being a restorationist movement, the PBCC is also a prophetic movement, which, similar to the Church of Jesus Christ of Latter-Day Saints, holds to a model of theological epistemology (and ontology) that may be described as being built around "continuing revelation,"[12] whereby true religion is progressively recovered. The title Minister of

---

[10] The official account given by the PBCC on this scandal seems to have changed in recent years. During my fieldwork in NE Scotland in 2008–10, I was informed by a PBCC street preacher that Taylor, Jr *intentionally orchestrated* the Aberdeen Incident by placing himself in a situation that *appeared* compromising but was, in fact, a morally faultless ruse as a way of exposing who was (and was not) loyal to him, decided on the basis of who would (and would not) give him the benefit of the doubt. Correspondingly, a letter written in 1988 by Taylor loyalists for circulation among the Exclusive Brethren referred to Taylor's actions as "the extension of the strategy of ambush *in the events that he initiated and controlled* in the house that weekend" (see Shuff, *Searching for the True Church*, 268; emphasis added). More recently, however, in response to a critical article about the PBCC printed in the *Winnipeg Free Press* that discussed the Aberdeen Incident, the church released this statement: "ALLEGATION: Mr. Taylor was caught in bed with a married woman half his age in Aberdeen, Scotland. RESPONSE: This is a false allegation that originated at a time when a Brother and his wife were providing much needed care for Mr. Taylor when he wasn't well, and very very weak physically, 3 months before he was taken from this earthly scene by our Lord Jesus Christ on October 14, 1970." Bill Redekop, "The Closed-Door Church," *Winnipeg Free Press*, May 10, 2014, <www.winnipegfreepress.com/local/The-closed-door-church-258336281.html>. PBCC response here: <www.plymouthbrethrenchristianchurch.org/winnipeg-free-press-plymouth-brethren-response/>, accessed January 15, 2016.
[11] This quote was published on their old website Theexclusivebrethren.com but does not appear on their new website Plymouth Brethren Christian Church, <plymouthbrethrenchristianchurch.org> (to which the old web address redirects). Original quote archived at <http://definiteanswers.com/q/What-does-the-term-Minister-Of-The-Lord-in-The-Recovery-mean-4c1219f49a591>.
[12] D. Holland, *Sacred Borders: Continuing Revelation and Canonical Restraint in Early America* (Oxford: Oxford University Press, 2011).

the Lord in the Recovery shows that while the PBCC *canon* is closed, including only the Old and New Testaments, as translated by Darby, PBCC *theology* is certainly not. Thus, PBCC theological developments—insofar as they are regarded as part of a recovery only achievable by *the man of God* who, being the *elect vessel*, provides universal leadership—become their own kind of *apokálypsis*. Indeed, newly received PBCC theology may be regarded as not only a divine *recovery* of the pattern and truth of early New Testament Christianity but also a divine *uncovering* of further truths, whereby the impoverished condition of seeing through a glass darkly is slowly relieved, allowing more and more to be seen. Indeed, for the PBCC, "the expectation [was] that the truth would be progressively 'opened up.' ... The succession of leading Brethren, travelling the world and holding 'readings' implied that the truth—already received in a higher degree of completeness than Christendom had known it since New Testament times—would be expounded. Increasingly it came to mean that new light was expected."[13] In essence, then, as Minister of the Lord in the Recovery, the elect vessel of the PBCC has direct *access to* and thereby *produces* (extra-canonical) divine revelation, allowing old truths to be recovered and new truths to be uncovered. Like the President of the Latter-Day Saints church, the universal leader of the PBCC fulfills the role of prophet, seer, and revelator. Such is the PBCC theology of God's ongoing special revelation.

*   *   *

But how do we get from a theology of special revelation to an ethnography of the Plymouth Brethren Christian Church, and how do we get from these ethnographic specifics to a more general anthropology of detachment? For the purposes of this chapter, we do so, I suggest, via the PBCC doctrine of separation. My argument is that from this theology of special revelation—a theology of the restoration of past truth via prophetic access to newly revealed truth in the present and future—the way of life of the PBCC, as centrally defined by their exclusivism, takes shape.

Indeed, the doctrine of separation is subject to special revelation as channeled through the Minister of the Lord in the Recovery, who is receiving progressively more insight about how God's chosen remnant is to live apart from the world. Thus, Darby was able to recover the truth that the biblical call, "Let every one who names the name of [the] Lord withdraw from iniquity" (2 Tim. 2:19) meant separation from apostate churches. This revelation required him and his companions to leave the Anglican Church and, eventually, establish a grouping that became known as the Plymouth Brethren. Later, Darby recovered further truth regarding the doctrine of separation, coming to

---

[13] Bryan R. Wilson, *Patterns of Sectarianism: Organisation and Ideology in Social and Religious Movements* (London: Heinemann, 1967), 316.

understand that having a closed table required eating the Lord's Supper only with members of the Plymouth Brethren, prompting the Exclusive/Open split.[14] Later still, Darby was able to recover the truth that preserving total purity of ecclesiastical separation also required being separate from those who fellowshipped with anyone with whom you did not fellowship.[15]

A century on, Taylor, Jr recovered the truth that Darby's closed table doctrine needed to be applied beyond the Lord's Supper to all forms of eating and drinking. The same was true of Darby's model of total ecclesiastical separation, which Taylor, Jr recovered as properly applying beyond institutional relations between churches to encompass personal relations within families. These latter developments, which came about during Taylor, Jr's leadership, made the Plymouth Brethren Christian Church infamous regarding its separatist practices. During my fieldwork in Gamrie (where none of the Brethren fellowships in the village had stayed within the Taylorite strand of the movement beyond 1970), many of my informants told me stories of fishing crews that had to be dissolved when the separate tables edict was brought in due to the impossibility of finding sufficient space on board the boats for EB and non-EB crew to eat separately. Families, too, I was told, were divided, with non-EB spouses and children having to eat at a separate table from their immediate EB family. Village and family religious events were also deeply problematic, I was told, with stories of EB uncles not attending the weddings of their non-EB nieces or, more shockingly to my informants, EB daughters refusing to attend the funeral of their non-EB mother.[16]

Thus, from the time of Taylor, Jr's leadership, the extension of Darby's teaching on ecclesiastical separation by applying it to relations within the home has led to allegations that the PBCC is an extremist cult that breaks up families. The allegation emerges from the fact that if a person leaves the PBCC, his or her family is generally required to sever contact with the individual concerned or face excommunication themselves. The practice has, in some cases, led to acrimonious custody battles, as well as to the formation of online support groups for ex-members, such as WikiPeebia. com, a staunchly critical anti-PBCC website that actively campaigns against the church. So common is the accusation that the PBCC breaks up families that the church has published a partial response to it as part of their online FAQs.[17] In addition to excommunication, referred to by the church as being

---

[14] See Schuff, *Searching for the True Church*, 3.

[15] So, if EB group 1 separates themselves from EB group 2, then EB group 3 will only be permitted to have continued fellowship with EB group 1 if they also separate from EB group 2.

[16] J. Webster, *The Anthropology of Protestantism: Faith and Crisis among Scottish Fishermen* (New York: Palgrave Macmillan, 2013).

[17] "No. The incidence of marriage break-up amongst the Plymouth Brethren Christian Church is fortunately very rare and well below societal norms. Any breakdown of relationships within a family is always tragic and every effort is expended to prevent this occurring or to try

withdrawn from, the PBCC have an intermediate form of church discipline called *shutting up*, whereby errant members are placed into seclusion for a period of time and are visited only by community elders who counsel them to repent. Those who fail to do so are withdrawn from—a process that can entail not only losing contact with family and friends but also losing one's house and job, since many PBCC are employed by other members and also receive financial support from the church in finding suitable detached housing. Clearly, such costs act as a real and effective disincentive to leave. Wilson summarizes the situation:

> Brethren have no friends and no near-acquaintances outside the movement, but within it intense mutual reliance and affection. To break away or to be expelled is a more profound thing than simply losing the right to participate in worship; it is intellectually the loss of a whole context of discourse, emotionally the destruction of every assurance, and socially the loss of everyone who is near and dear and whose existence has any meaning.[18]

Yet the doctrine of separation extends well beyond ecclesiastical exclusivism, the refusal to eat with outsiders, and the practice of withdrawing from those who leave or are excommunicated from the church. Beyond the intellectual, emotional, and social aspects, as Wilson demarcates them, another obvious sphere in which the doctrine of separation is enacted is through the material culture of church architecture. As mentioned in my opening description, PBCC churches are surrounded by high fences with large gates, and visitors to the church enter and exit through a different door at the back of the building and are seated apart from members in a separate roped-off pew located at the back behind the women, who are themselves seated behind the men. This layout, which has become standardized for all newly built PBCC halls in line with truth recovered under the leadership of current elect vessel Bruce Hales, echoes the spatial separation of Jews and Gentiles under Second Temple architecture. The result is that interaction between members and visitors is prevented unless specifically initiated by leading elders who choose to greet visitors formally after worship. Additionally, while older nineteenth-century Exclusive Brethren halls do have windows into the sanctuary, the new design of PBCC halls contains no windows in the main auditorium, a fact that physically and symbolically shuts out the world from the church.

In addition to material culture, other things make attending a PBCC service difficult and *casually* attending such a service largely impossible. Unlike most churches of which I am aware, any visitor is strongly expected if not required

---

and bring in reconciliation if it does." "Do the Plymouth Brethren Break-Up Families?" Plymouth Brethren Christian Church, <www.plymouthbrethrenchristianchurch.org/faqs/family-communitydo-the-plymouth-brethren-break-up-families/>.

[18] Wilson, *Patterns of Sectarianism*, as cited in Tonts, "The Exclusive Brethren," 313.

to telephone in advance a request to attend a PBCC service. Indeed, the casual visitor would have no way of knowing at what times PBCC services are held, for no such times are advertised on their website or on the signage attached to the entry gates of church buildings. The solution is to telephone a central UK number, which, in my case, initiated a complex and involved string of emails, telephone calls, and a house visit in order to be permitted to attend, and only then while being carefully chaperoned for the duration of my visit, albeit in a warm and friendly manner. While I am certainly aware that my being upfront about my occupation and research plans made this process more heightened than it might otherwise have been, my sense is that all visitors, what few there are, receive similarly cautious treatment.

One possible explanation is that PBCC members have become cautious only after having been maligned by the media and interrogated by politicians. To be sure, such critique has arisen both in the UK and Australia, not only as a result of their practice of withdrawing from ex-members but also because of allegations of strict gender segregation in their schools, because of accusations of misdemeanors in their tax affairs, and because of suggestions of inappropriate lobbying of right-wing political parties despite their refusal to vote in elections. None of these circumstances has endeared the group to the press or to policymakers. Most recently, the PBCC in the UK attracted the attention of the Charity Commission, when in 2012 the Commission refused to grant a PBCC congregation in England charitable status because it was deemed not to have had sufficient beneficial impact on the wider community—the consequence of which was that the PBCC no longer qualified for tax breaks under charity legislation. The church responded robustly by launching a new website to explain their beliefs and by lobbying two hundred Members of Parliament to protest the ruling. Additionally, the PBCC set up a voluntary not-for-profit organization called the Rapid Relief Team to provide catering to emergency services personnel among other community-based relief works. Lastly, in what critics regard as a cynical public relations exercise, but which members regard as simply a return to their original identity marker, the church changed its name from Exclusive Brethren to Plymouth Brethren Christian Church, which, for legal purposes, was incorporated under the title Plymouth Brethren (Exclusive Brethren) Christian Church Ltd. The result was that, after extensive debate and enquiry in the House of Lords, charitable status was reinstated in 2014 after new PBCC commitments to extend its religious and social engagement.[19] It seems, then, that the PBCC had (and possibly *have*) good reason to be cautious.

Yet, all of the above seems to elide the more salient point, at least for the *anthropological* purposes of this chapter, that the PBCC are cautious of

---

[19] *Charity Commission for England and Wales Preston Down Trust*, January 3, 2014, <www. gov.uk/government/uploads/system/uploads/attachment_data/file/336112/preston_down_trust_ full_decision.pdf>.

outsiders and have been so since their formation in 1827, not primarily because of how outsiders might *react to* the strictures of the doctrine of separation but, simply put, because outsider are outsiders—that is, because they are *not* Plymouth Brethren. By this I mean that the intrinsic (i.e., deontological) strictures of the doctrine of separation need to be placed at the center of any explanation of the ethnographic observations with which I opened this chapter, rather than how that deontology is reacted to by those who do not commit their lives to it. To be Plymouth Brethren, I suggest, is to live out the doctrine of separation, regardless of any censure such a life may or may not attract. Why remove the world from the church by constructing a sanctuary without windows in a building surrounded by high fences? Why differentiate visitors from members by having separate entrances and segregated pews? Why decline all accommodation except detached housing? Why refuse to eat with non-members? Why abstain from voting? Why shun TV and radio? Why withdraw from excommunicated members? The answer, which seems patently circular, is that to do so—to remove, to differentiate, to decline, to refuse, to abstain, to shun, to withdraw from—is to be Plymouth Brethren, to live a life of separation. More than this, for the Plymouth Brethren, to live a life of separation is to live a life worth living; it is to live a life that is good. Such a view contrasts strongly, if only partially, with some of the chapters presented in this volume, most notably by Bielo and his analysis of the craft of both anthropologists and ethnographic theologians:

> Ethnographic theologians also prize the power of intimate human relationships. Through relationships the spiritual goals of Christianity are to be sought and realized. Relationships redeem, restore, reconcile, and heal. Relationships are generative and primary, not resultant and secondary. Relationships are not a means to an end, not merely a useful strategy or helpful way to cope. They are what we ought to pursue. They are, very simply, good.[20]

As a *social anthropologist*, my instinct here is to agree with Bielo, for anthropologists are trained to consider social relations as primary, yet as an *ethnographer*, as an observer of Brethren life, my observations push me toward a very different conclusion. Indeed, in an important sense, the relations-centric anthropological impulses that I share with Bielo are, I think, at risk of producing a back-to-front understanding of the Exclusive Brethren who, in many respects, would want to affirm precisely the opposite of what Bielo states. Indeed, the PBCC prize the power of intimate human separation because through separation the spiritual goals of Christianity are sought and realized. Separation redeems the Brethren soul from an evil world; separation restores, reconciles, and heals their relationship with God and with fellow Brethren. Thus, while relations *do* persist, without such *prior relational*

---

[20] James S. Bielo, Chapter 8, 144.

separation from the world, the Brethren could not know God, nor could they know each other. Separation, then, is not a means to an end, or a helpful coping strategy, but is something to pursue in and of itself. For the Brethren, separation is simply good.

It is in this sense that the Exclusive Brethren are *exclusive*, yet, of course, to live a life of exclusivity and separation is also to live a life *alongside* those with whom you share this separateness, both within the immediate family and within the wider church community. Indeed, PBCC separation from the world fosters enormously close relationships within the group. Individuals must marry within the group, and daily religious activities, all socializing, and any sharing of food and drink are likewise only done with other members. Indeed, all prohibitions that delimit contact with non-members have the positive effect of folding the activities of the membership back onto itself, religiously, socially, and economically. My own lack of ethnographic data on PBCC family life, to take only one example, speaks to the ethnographic challenges of becoming part of the life of a community devoted to keeping outsiders out of the community.

Similarly, Wilson's account offers little by way of ethnographic specifics, sticking to more formal statements the kind of which can today be gleaned from the PBCC's formal account of themselves on their own website. On Exclusive Brethren family life, Wilson comments:

> The social practices of the Brethren ramify into the minute details of their daily lives. There is very little in which an adherent can be engaged that is not under the complete regulation of sectarian principles. The family is the dominant emphasis in contemporary Brethrenism. The assembly and the household are seen as standing in an especially intimate relationship. Prayers and hymn-singing are a rule every morning and evening in an Exclusive household, which should faithfully reflect the tone of the assembly itself. The household is a sanctified place, and the Brethren do not now eat with those who are not in fellowship—the daily meal thus becomes a reflection of the breaking of bread, which is, of course, exclusively for the fellowship. The family is rooted in the assembly, which provides it with a spiritual hygiene (of which physical hygiene is a reflection), confirms sanctity and promotes its expression in the regulation of the daily life of members.[21]

It is in this sense that the Exclusive Brethren are *brethren*, connected one to another in bonds of family and faith and fellowship. Nevertheless, while not wanting to ignore the real and enduring attachments members of the PBCC feel for each other, Wilson also argues that "dissociation has become the paramount concern of the Exclusive Brethren"[22] because to *be* part of the Plymouth Brethren (Exclusive Brethren) Christian Church Ltd is, first and foremost, to *not* be worldly, to *not* be part of the world and its people. It is in

---

[21] Wilson, *Patterns of Sectarianism*, 326–7.   [22] Ibid., 295.

this sense that the Exclusive Brethren are *exclusive*, severed from all others in acts of dissociation and detachment.

The theological, as opposed to sociological, claim the PBCC makes is radical. They are not part of the world because they are already part of the heavenlies:

> Since the Church is properly now in Him [Christ] in heavenly places, it is *apart from the world*. The saints [living Christians] are themselves in some sense now in heavenly places, and thus *have no more concern with those in the world....* [By inhabiting] "heavenly exclusiveness," they were to recognise doctrinally their apartness from the world. Thus the faithful believer is required to *withdraw from those who are evil*. Separation becomes a firm injunction. Nor is this merely an exhortation to the individual;... the act of withdrawal becomes collective in effect.[23]

Wilson's analysis is notable not only in its careful sociological attentiveness to Exclusive Brethren theology but also in its closely matching the church's current understanding of its own doctrine, almost fifty years on:

> The Lord Jesus said as to His disciples "they are not of the world, even as I am not of the world" John 17 v14. *The world in this sense refers to the system of sin and lawlessness under the domination of Satan. As a Church, we wholeheartedly seek to dedicate our lives to this principle.* We choose to follow the teachings of Jesus as set out in the Gospels and taught in the Epistles of the New Testament. Refer passages such as Matthew 16 v24–26, Mark 10 v28–30, 2 Timothy 2 v19 and 2 Corinthians 6v14–18. *Separation represents a moral distinction between what is right and what is wrong, what is righteous and what is unrighteous.* Christians as believers on the Lord Jesus Christ are exhorted to "refuse the evil and to choose the good" Isaiah 7 v15. We make a commitment to eat and drink only with those with whom we would celebrate the Lord's Supper—that is the basis of our fellowship.[24]

PBCC followers, then, even while they live on earth, already inhabit heaven, precisely because they are *apart from the world*. This apartness, understood as a kind of active, ongoing withdrawal, becomes a totalizing, life-defining effort. "As a Church, we wholeheartedly seek to dedicate our lives to this principle"— a separation that for the PBCC continually enacts a refusal of evil and a choosing of the good. These PBCC attachments are simultaneously a negation and a positive embrace—a negation of "the system of sin and lawlessness under the domination of Satan," that is, the world, and a positive embrace of a Christian community, which, while appearing to be located within this world,

---

[23] Ibid., 293–4, 296, 310–11, emphasis added.
[24] "What Is Involved in the Doctrine of Separation?" *Plymouth Brethren Christian Church*, emphasis added, <www.plymouthbrethrenchristianchurch.org/faqs/faith-and-beliefswhat-is-involved-in-the-doctrine-of-separation/>.

is also presently part of the Kingdom of Heaven and thus outside of the world and its evil system.

Yet, it is necessary, here, to return to the thrust of the second question I asked earlier—namely, how do we get from (a) an ethnographic analysis of theologies of *special revelation* and *heavenly exclusiveness* as they relate to windowless sanctuaries, detached houses, and separate tables, to (b) a more general anthropology of *detachment*?[25] My argument is that we do so by calling into question or, perhaps better said, by *inverting* the near universal tenet of anthropology that "society is a thing of connections"[26] and that humans are, broadly speaking, made of and defined by social relations.

What, then, if this were not always the case? What if PBCC theology, for example, tells us something different? What if it tells us instead that human beings are, or at least should be, made of disconnections and separations? In order to try to explore this more, I want to turn to consider new anthropological writing on the theme of detachment.

*   *   *

Much of *Detachment: Essays on the Limits of Relational Thinking* analyzes ideas about the kinds of epistemological detachment generally associated with nineteenth-century projects of modernist science—namely, "the desirability of distanced perspectives" and "a singular epistemic ideal of objectivity."[27] While this is not the kind of detachment in which I am primarily interested, the authors also discuss the distinction between *engagement* and *detachment*—a topic more directly relevant to the core focus of this chapter. Thus, where engagement "abuts with a number of seductive cultural tropes, such as participation, democracy, voice, equality, diversity and empowerment... detachment has come to symbolise a range of social harms: authoritarianism and hierarchy, being out of touch, bureaucratic coldness and unresponsiveness, a lack of empathy, and passivity and inaction."[28] This framing certainly seems more relevant, although the *equality* and *diversity* connotations of engagement do not find their binary opposites in that of detachment. Toward the end of the introduction, however, no less than sixty alternative meanings of detachment are provided, nine of which seem directly applicable to this topic:

15. Detachment as the closing off of/turning away from something in pursuit of an end,
22. Detachment as distancing,
26. Detachment as untouchability,

---

[25] Matei Candea et al. (eds), *Detachment: Essays on the Limits of Relational Thinking* (Manchester: Manchester University Press, 2015).
[26] J. Robbins, "Engaged Disbelief: Communities of Detachment in Christianity and in the Anthropology of Christianity," in *Detachment: Essays on the Limits of Relational Thinking*, ed. M. Candea et al. (Manchester: Manchester University Press, 2015), 115–29 (here 115).
[27] Candea et al., *Detachment*, 5.   [28] Ibid., 1.

30. Detachment as exclusion/expulsion,
32. Detachment as removal from public view,
34. Detachment as separation,
37. Detachment as a sign of the sacred,
41. Detachment as safe distance, and
49. Detachment as spiritual renunciation.[29]

I want, first, simply to affirm, along with the authors, that detachment is "a real phenomenon" and worthy of being "taken seriously."[30] Returning to Keane's suggestion that "we shouldn't decide in advance what ethics looks like,"[31] it strikes me that taking detachment seriously means not deciding in advance that detachment is a bad thing to be placed in negative relationship with the imagined opposites of equality and diversity—a point I want to develop more. However, before I do so, I first want to go further than simply affirming that detachment is a real phenomenon. I also want to suggest that, very frequently, detachment is a religious and particularly a *theological* phenomenon. Robbins' chapter in the same volume, entitled "Engaged Disbelief: Communities of Detachment in Christianity and in the Anthropology of Christianity" provides a helpful starting point.[32]

Robbins opens by noting that, in the Protestant imagination, "to believe *in* some being, to have faith in that being, is to tie yourself to it in a highly committed way. If religion is a matter of belief, then it is nothing if not a matter of connection."[33] Nevertheless, as Robbins correctly goes on to note, within some strands of the Protestant tradition, most especially within Pentecostal and charismatic Christianity, achieving a proper connection to good requires one to detach oneself dramatically from evil and particularly from the evil spirits that populated one's pre-Christian life, as seen in rituals of spiritual warfare and deliverance from demons.[34] In my own work among Brethren fisher families in Gamrie, northeast Scotland, this required not only diligent prayer and Bible reading but also the destruction of ungodly material objects (e.g., videocassettes, Harry Potter merchandise) that, if not physically detached from in this way, would threaten to bring unknown spiritual attack upon one's household.[35]

Such observations, which Robbins aptly calls "an elaborate theatre of detachment,"[36] may help us question whether some basic anthropological

---

[29] Ibid., 17–18.   [30] Ibid., 16.

[31] W. Keane, "Freedom, Reflexivity, and the Sheer Everydayness of Ethics," *HAU: Journal of Ethnographic Theory* 4/1 (2014): 443–57 (here 444).

[32] Joel Robbins, "Engaged Disbelief: Communities of Detachment in Christianity and in the Anthropology of Christianity," in Candea et al., *Detachment*, 115–29.

[33] Ibid., 116.   [34] Ibid., 117.

[35] J. Webster, "The Immanence of Transcendence: God and the Devil on the Aberdeenshire Coast," *Ethnos: Journal of Anthropology* 78/3 (2013): 380–402.

[36] Robbins, "Engaged Disbelief," 117.

assumptions about religion and belief as *connection* need to be rethought. Might we need to rethink the suggestion that "if religion is a matter of beliefs, then it is nothing if not a matter of connection,"[37] by, for example, turning our analysis to beliefs about *dis*connection? And might theology be one route to doing so? My analysis of the PBCC doctrine of separation, I think, points us in this direction, suggesting that a theology of disconnection or separation is flatly unavoidable in any ethnographic description of the Brethren but also, I contend, epistemologically central to any anthropological theory that seeks to account for and make sense of that description. For the PBCC, if religion is a matter of theology, then it is nothing if not a matter of separation. The result is that, for the Brethren, disconnection and detachment are the only secure basis for connection and attachment. Hence, Darby required not only that Exclusive assemblies split from all those he regarded as having abandoned the Brethren recovery but also that they split from all those who, while themselves being in good standing, continued to share fellowship with those not in good standing. Put another way, if the friend of my friend is my theological enemy, then my friend, too, must become my enemy.

On one level, then, the PBCC represent a strong version of a "solidarity through detachment"[38] model of group formation. This same process of producing a "unity in rejection"[39] has, of course, other strong expressions as described, for example, by Ayala Fader[40] in her work among Hasidic Jews in Brooklyn or what I found in my encounter with the Scottish Orange Order.[41] Yet, so strong is the PBCC version of this process whereby the Christian community is not "*in part* formed out of their shared detachments"[42] but is formed *almost entirely* from them that I am inclined to suggest that its outcomes are different from those that emerge from the other cases mentioned. My point is that if, for the PBCC, society really is, in essence, a thing of disconnections, and if these disconnections are conceptualized primarily in theological terms, then this has profound effects on the manner in which one goes about making sense of how to address questions about identification and personhood.

Thus, instead of anthropologists imagining that the groups they study make sense of their collective identity primarily by asking and answering the question "Who *are* we?" perhaps, in some contexts, a better way of imaginatively entering into the natives' point of view would be to suppose that those same natives are instead asking, "Who are we *not*?" Crucially, in posing such a question, I want to argue that its formulation in the negative actually produces

---

[37] Ibid., 116.   [38] Ibid., 121.   [39] Ibid.

[40] A. Fader, *Mitzvah Girls: Bringing Up the Next Generation of Hasidic Jews in Brooklyn* (Princeton: Princeton University Press, 2009).

[41] J. Webster, "Objects of Transcendence: Scots Protestantism and an Anthropology of Things," in *Material Religion in Modern Britain: The Spirit of Things*, ed. T. W. Jones and L. Matthews-Jones (New York: Palgrave Macmillan, 2015), 17–35.

[42] Robbins, "Engaged Disbelief," 121, emphasis added.

a highly specific and comprehensive collective identity but always primarily with reference to that which it is *not*. To explain what I mean here better, let me take the example of veganism. Veganism is defined by abstention from animal products primarily in relation to diet. Vegans do not eat meat, fish, eggs, dairy, or any other kind of animal products, such as honey. Some vegans will choose not to wear clothing that contains animal products, such as leather, wool, or silk. Some vegans will avoid certain vaccines that are grown in hens' eggs. My point is merely that veganism is defined in the negative, by a series of abstentions. Put another way, a vegan *is* what a vegan *does not do*; a vegan does not eat meat, does not drink milk, does not wear leather, and so on. Note also that a key ethical claim of veganism—that animals are not commodities— defines animals in negative terms.

This framing of veganism in the negative mirrors, I argue, how the PBCC have come to understand themselves and their Christian community theologically through the doctrine of separation. A Brethren believer *is* what a Brethren believer *separates from*—that is, from the world, its people, its entertainments, its politics, its architecture, its commensality. To push this point a bit further, consider the contrast between formulating what one *is not* (in the negative), with what one *is* (in the positive), a contrast I have represented in Figure 18.1.

Expressing identity in the negative, as the diagram on the left does, manages to make an explicit statement about fifty-nine out of a possible sixty squares. In contrast, expressing identity in the positive, as the diagram on the right does, only manages to make an explicit statement about one square. Of course, I am well aware that anthropology deals with human realities that often operate at the level of the implied and that such realities are much more complex, diverse, and jumbled than a neat grid of squares on a page. In addition, as previously argued, this is not to deny that the PBCC also expresses positive attachments to fellow Brethren, in both their families and assemblies. But this is to miss the point—namely, that negative statements about what one *is not* are actually highly elaborated and worked-out statements of non-belonging, often much more so than are positive statements of belonging.

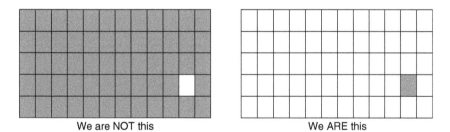

We are NOT this   We ARE this

Figure 18.1 We are NOT this; We ARE this

Being able to observe and analyze such sociological statements, whether in church architecture, in seating arrangements, in eating arrangements, or in housing requirements, only makes sense, in the PBCC case at least, in and through *an anthropology of theology*, and, in emic terms, only where such theology has been divinely recovered by the elect vessel, inscribed in multi-volume Brethren ministry books, and then reinscribed upon high fences, windowless sanctuaries, separate pews, separate dinner tables, and detached housing—all of which become objects of theology in the process.

*   *   *

I want to finish by briefly suggesting where we might be able to find such theologies of detachment outside the fences that surround Plymouth Brethren halls. Detachment and disconnection, as well as the negative statements of non-belonging that accompany them, can be found, I suggest, in spheres of thought and practice not normally regarded as religious. Note here the immediate reappearance of statements formulated in the negative—*not normally regarded as religious*—my use of which seems to echo other negative definitional framings of the same, such as secular and atheist, which, within the anthropology of religion, have begun to form their own sub-subdiscipline, framed as the study of non-religion. Consider, for example, certain strong formulations of pluralism, which function in remarkably similar ways to the doctrine of separation. I contend that pluralism of this kind may be definable as *a rejection of everything that rejects anything*. In more specific terms, pluralism, in this framing, takes shape around a series of denunciations—of homophobia, sexism, racism, sectarianism, ageism, disability discrimination, class prejudice, and so on. To be pluralist is to exclude all such exclusions; it is to separate from those who separate; it is, in the words of David Cameron, a call to be "more intolerant of intolerance."[43] Importantly, the past Prime Minister is not alone in making such a call. The political theorist William Connolly, for example, in his analysis of "deep pluralism," states:

> Tolerance of negotiation, mutual adjustment, reciprocal folding in, and relational modesty are, up to a point, cardinal virtues of deep pluralism. The limit point is reached when pluralism itself is threatened by powerful unitarian forces that demand the end of pluralism in the name of defeating "relativism," "nihilism," or "rootlessness." At a certain point of danger—which cannot be specified with precision in advance—a militant assemblage of pluralists, with each party drawing on modes of inspiration that do not coincide with the others, must coalesce to resist such an onslaught.[44]

---

[43] David Cameron, "David Cameron: We Must Be Intolerant of Isil Intolerance," *Telegraph*, June 28, 2015, <www.telegraph.co.uk/news/politics/david-cameron/11704576/David-Cameron-We-must-be-intolerant-of-Isil-intolerance.html>.

[44] W. E. Connolly, *Pluralism* (Durham, NC: Duke University Press, 2005), 67.

Connolly imagines the only mode of inspiration (note here the religious language) that this militant assemblage shares is a total commitment to defeat unitarian forces that threaten the "cardinal virtues of deep pluralism."[45] They have a common enemy—exclusionary non-pluralism—that must be excluded on that basis. Yet, pointing to the deep irony of Connolly's position is not my intended purpose. Rather, my purpose here is to indicate that such views, or clarion calls, extend well beyond the normative arguments of political theory. Anthropology, too, is capable of exhibiting this same insistence upon upholding its own cardinal virtues, which, in doing so, become functionally equivalent to Christian theology. Indeed, beyond the discipline's written code of ethics, anthropology, perhaps especially in the United States, also seems to exhibit a dogmatic (i.e., theological) tendency toward excluding, rejecting, and separating from those deemed to be insufficiently pluralist as indicated by American Anthropological Association resolutions prohibiting the signing of contracts for annual meetings in states with anti-sodomy laws, or denouncing the government of Honduras, or proposing a boycott of Israeli academic institutions. To be clear, my comments here should not be read as a critique of these prohibitions, denunciations, or proposed boycotts. Rather, they should be read as a comment that such prohibitions, denunciations, and boycotts exist within anthropology, which indicates that the kind of strong pluralism for which Connolly is calling is at work within, to echo Sahlins in part,[46] the native cosmology of Western anthropology.

I am convinced that these observations are uncontroversial. Khaled Furani, in this volume, makes a related point when he argues not only that anthropological fieldwork can be seen, in part, as "mimicking redemption and divinity" but also calls for anthropologists to "retain the possibility that cultural diversity represents only a certain kind of diversity and with it a certain vision of the world."[47] Indeed, it would not be hard to argue that anthropology has, at least for many decades now, self-consciously sided with whomever or whatever the discipline regards as the underdog. This certain vision of the world is also, very probably, connected to the now established and utterly orthodox reflexive turn within anthropology, which was itself birthed by an anti-imperialist critique of anthropology's ugly colonial past. Thus, while not wanting to return to the pre-reflexive bad old days, I am left wondering what kind of native cosmology, or theology, anthropology might rearticulate to better fulfill its arguably more primary ethnographic and theoretical quest for cross-cultural understanding— a quest where the worldview of the informant, and not the anthropologist, is permitted to take center stage.

---

[45] Ibid.

[46] M. Sahlins, "The Sadness of Sweetness: The Native Anthropology of Western Cosmology," *Current Anthropology* 37/3 (1996): 395–428.

[47] Khaled Furani, Chapter 4, 77.

My argument seems to suggest that a version of pluralism even more radically relativist than that for which Connolly is calling might be of some help, but only if by relativism we mean an ethnographic willingness to *listen to* and *be taught by* our informants. This kind of radical listening would, hopefully, be willing to learn from non-pluralist voices, rather than rising up in a militant assemblage to defeat the non-pluralist in our midst. The implications here for my own study of PBCC theology are obvious—namely, to allow my informants to teach me how society is primarily a thing of disconnections and teach me why such separation is simply good. The alternative seems less helpful—namely, my ethnographically assuming, and theoretically insisting, that society is a thing of connections and that separation is less valuable than relationality, thereby rendering PBCC cosmology null in the process. More than this, by drawing inspiration from Keane's suggestions that "we shouldn't decide in advance what ethics will look like,"[48] such an anthropology of theology might then be able to go further by looking at the native cosmology of the PBCC or any non-pluralist, non-liberal worldview and conclude that it is good. Put another way, such an anthropology might conclude that the PBCC are just as capable of outlining convincing models of the good rather than assume that good morality, like good culture, must, by definition, enact a strong version of pluralism by dogmatically separating from those who separate.

---

[48] Keane, "Freedom," 444.

19

Divinity Inhabits the Social

Ethnography in a Phenomenological Key

Don Seeman

The recent explosion of interest in ethnography among a certain class of Christian theologians has engendered a more tepid response from professional anthropology. This is not entirely surprising; anthropology arguably came of age over the past century precisely by endeavoring, unevenly and imperfectly, to divest itself of the missionary and colonial interests that had contributed to its disciplinary genesis. For some anthropologists, almost any serious engagement with theology seems to be at odds with anthropology's implicitly secularizing, relativizing project. While theologians may, with some justification, come to believe that anthropologists who appropriate theological categories risk denuding them of their irreducibly sacred content, anthropologists may worry, in turn, that engaging with theology on its own ground will only serve to impose (or reinforce) a Christian conceptual bias in anthropological practice.[1] Nevertheless, I want to argue that anthropologists and theologians have good reasons to see themselves as natural conversation partners, not just because of their overlapping and sometimes conflictual disciplinary genealogies but more fundamentally because almost everywhere we look, divinity inhabits and helps to constitute the social world.

Divinity inhabits the social. On the most basic level, this means that revered ancestors, village goddesses, and possessing spirits are all encountered as actors, moral agents, and participants—sometimes overwhelmingly important

---

[1] See Fenella Cannell, "The Christianity of Anthropology," *Journal of the Royal Anthropological Institute* 11/2 (2005): 335–56; Don Seeman, "Kinship as Ethical Relation: An Alternative to the Spiritual Kinship Paradigm," in *New Directions in Spiritual Kinship: Sacred Ties across the Abrahamic Religions*, ed. Todne Thomas, Asiya Malik, and Rose Wellman (New York: Palgrave Macmillan), 85–108.

participants—in the social order that anthropologists study,[2] as is the biblical God who haggled over the fate of Sodom with Abraham and the amiable Jesus that some American evangelicals say they chat with over coffee.[3] Yet even the difficulties faced by philosophically minded critics of anthropomorphism such as Ibn Rushd or Maimonides, who each subjected the *personhood* of divinity to sustained conceptual critique, ultimately testify to the challenge of thinking about divinity in any other terms.[4] These medieval iconoclasts were also deeply *political* thinkers, trying mightily—through their very iconoclasm—to shape the course of the societies in which they lived. Nor do Buddhist renunciation and enlightenment make much sense except against the backdrop of a recalcitrant social, cosmic, and political order which the Buddhist program seeks to respond or, in some sense, overcome. My point is not just that religions have social contexts, which should be obvious, but that the basic phenomena of religious life manifest in social fields and that despite any handwringing about disciplinary boundaries and objectives, this means that neither anthropology nor theology can afford to avoid the phenomenology of social life where divinity (for lack of a better term) *happens*. I should admit that my view of the potential collaboration between these two disciplines requires each of them to reconfigure, to some degree, around phenomenological concerns. The approach I want to advocate here insists, inter alia, that confrontation with the plenitude of situated human experiences will bear more significant fruit for our purposes than any degree of abstract theorizing about cultural systems or theological constructs.

Let me put this another way. Theologians have sometimes appropriated ethnographic methodology shorn of the specifically *anthropological* concerns that motivated its parent discipline, which can generate admiration and anxiety among anthropologists who read this material.[5] But the converse may also be true: Theology may prove most useful to anthropologists when it is appropriated in ways that feel unfamiliar to many theologians but that help to further what we anthropologists take to be the core of the ethnographic project—namely, that it yields more adequate descriptions and analyses of the situated contexts in which human life transpires. This begs the question,

---

[2] See, for instance, Joyce Flueckiger, "When the Goddess Speaks Her Mind: Possession, Presence, and Narrative Theology in the Gangamma Tradition of Tirupati (South India)," *International Journal of Hindu Studies* 21/2 (2017), np; LeRhonda S. Manigault-Bryant, *Talking to the Dead: Religion, Music and Lived Memory among Gullah/Geechee Women* (Durham, NC: Duke University Press, 2014).

[3] T. M. Luhrmann, *When God Talks Back: Understanding the American Evangelical Relationship with God* (New York: Alfred A. Knopf, 2012).

[4] See Don Seeman, "Divine Honor as Virtue and Practice in Maimonides," *Journal of Jewish Thought and Philosophy* 16/2 (2008): 195–251; Don Seeman, "Violence, Ethics and Divine Honor in Modern Jewish Thought," *Journal of the American Academy of Religion* 73/4 (2005): 1015–48.

[5] See James S. Bielo, Chapter 8, 140–55.

however, of what makes any description or analysis seem more adequate. The question, as Brian M. Howell perceptively asks in this volume, is not whether theology and anthropology can contribute to one another but rather *which* anthropologies and *which* theologies might most usefully be juxtaposed.[6] Writing in this chapter primarily from an anthropological perspective, my own commitment is to an existential or broadly phenomenological anthropology that takes human life and lived experience rather than the "interpretation of cultures" as its central descriptive goal.[7] This is an anthropology that attends to the life projects and circumstances of informants and to the intersubjective horizons of the life-worlds they inhabit, where culture is an important but never simply determinative feature; and it is from this position, which I have described and defended elsewhere, that I have come to appreciate the way theological language can help to illuminate facets of human experience that standard social scientific tools may falter to describe.

I cannot say whether this news will necessarily be welcome to all of my interlocutors, but I would suggest two primary ways in which theology—both academic and vernacular—can contribute to the ethnographic project. First, theologies serve as important repositories of differentiated cultural knowledge that needs to be taken as seriously as any other data we collect in fieldwork on societies in which they have played an influential role. Theological ways of thinking about or interacting with the world are, on this level, "social facts" like any other. But theologies may also point to theoretical or analytic insights that contribute in their own right to the generation of better and more adequate accounts of human affairs, and this is the relatively neglected project that captures my attention. I want to use theology not just as a data field to be mined, in other words, but as a prism that can help me to see things I might otherwise have been blind to.

*   *   *

Several years ago, I supervised the ethnographic component of an interdisciplinary research project involving medical anthropologists, public health experts, and religious studies scholars seeking to understand the religious factors that might be contributing to unintended pregnancy among homeless and very poor women of color in the American Southeast.[8] Our ethnography was carried out over the course of eighteen months at a nonsectarian (but

---

[6] Brian M. Howell, Chapter 2, 29–49.

[7] Sarah Willen and Don Seeman (eds), "Introduction: Experience and Inquiétude," *Horizons of Experience: Reinvigorating Dialogue between Phenomenological and Psychoanalytic Anthropologies*, Special Issue of *Ethos: Journal of Psychological Anthropology* 40/1 (2012): 1–23; Don Seeman, "Coffee and the Moral Order: Ethiopian Jews and Pentecostals against Culture," *American Ethnologist* 42/4 (2015): 734–48; Michael Jackson and Albert Piette (eds), *What is Existential Anthropology?* (New York: Berghahn Books, 2015).

[8] Don Seeman, Iman Roushdy-Hammady, Annie Hardison-Moody, Winnifred W. Thompson, Laura M. Gaydos, and Carol J. Rowland Hogue, "Blessing Unintended Pregnancy: Religion and the

mostly church-sponsored) homeless shelter we called Naomi's House, dedicated primarily to women with children. The fieldwork team conducted participant observation, life history interviews, and a focus group with women between the ages of 18 and 37, all of whom were African-American. Researchers also attended some local church services that some Naomi's House residents attended, and participated in some of the classes and focus groups that were organized for house residents. Though public health literature had primed us to view unintended pregnancies by homeless women as a disaster (reducing unintended pregnancy, especially among poor women, is a key goal of public health research), we were surprised to find that many of the women with whom we had spoken actually described their unplanned motherhood as a *blessing*, even when they also identified it as the proximate cause of their homelessness. We began to believe, we wrote, that "a more basic consideration of concepts related to planning, control, and reproductive agency was needed" and that consideration of women's experience of blessing might be an important prism through which to begin that process.[9]

Naomi's House residents did not romanticize their circumstances or the complex factors that had led them to seek shelter there. As we outlined in much greater detail in our published paper, they spoke about failed contraceptives and fear of side effects from some of the contraceptives that were most commonly available to them, such as Norplant. They also described encounters with racism or demeaning treatment by healthcare professionals that led them to mistrust the medical system as a whole. Some women spoke critically about their own weakness in having unprotected sex, and almost all spoke about the failure of men in their lives to take responsibility for the consequences of fatherhood. In most cases, becoming a mother was described as something unplanned or even unplannable and beyond their control. Yet despite these matter-of-fact assessments, almost all of the women we interviewed also portrayed pregnancy and motherhood as blessings that helped change the trajectory of their lives for the better. A woman whom we called Tiffany told us, "I could have ... stayed with family and with friends, but I didn't want to. ... I needed to start over; I needed to better myself for my children. I needed to stop and break the pattern, so I went there [to Naomi's House]."[10] Eva's friends similarly told her that "nobody knows but God what he had planned for you. ... Just because you was on the birth control you probably got pregnant for a reason. You don't know that reason right now because it's just a learned process you're going through."[11]

These women's responses resonated with findings by other researchers who have shown that motherhood can serve as a catalyst for positive change in the

---

Discourse of Women's Agency in Public Health," *Medicine Anthropology Theory* 3/1 (2016): 29–54. Roushdy-Hammady and Hardison-Moody were the lead ethnographers.

[9] Ibid., 30.   [10] Ibid., 33.   [11] Ibid., 35.

lives of poor women,[12] but many of our informants also used heavily religious language that has been poorly documented in public health and medical anthropology literature. A woman we called Janine told us:

> I believe that children are a blessing. I believe He [God] blessed me, you know, with three babies, you know. It's an honor to be a mom, you know, a mother, it is. And it's an honor to be a father. It's an honor to procreate period and I feel like I was selected as a chosen, you know, there's people right now that can't even have babies. You know, my, one of my best friends, you know, she had some intestinal issues, so I think for her to become pregnant will be hard, hard for her.[13]

Twenty-seven-year-old Demetria, similarly, told us that she was eager to have or foster more children before the age of thirty-five (she was currently a foster parent, had given birth to one child, and undergone two abortions while a teenager): "People are like, 'You already [had] a boy and a girl, why do you want more,' but I'm like, 'Maybe it's because I'm blessed enough to have them.' Some people can't have kids—I'm like, 'A child is a blessing to all, so I want that blessing over and over again, as many as I can have.'"[14] Demetria, we learned, was seeking to set right what had been ruined through her own mistreatment by a foster parent when she was a child, and, in general, we found that "religious and spiritual themes relating to pregnancy or motherhood were most powerful when they were related to specific events in the mother's own life, against which they achieved resonance and meaning."[15]

Interpreting women's stories requires some care, however, because Naomi's House residents used a number of different tropes for starting over, receiving blessing, or triumphing over adversity. Lisa's assertion that she would "do it all over again" because otherwise she "wouldn't be... able to tell my testimony and help others" clearly seems to resonate with Christian tropes of redemptive testimony about suffering, but we should be cautious about assigning too explicit a theological backdrop where Lisa did not offer one.[16] A term like blessing itself is complicated because it might participate in several different registers of meaning that have to be ethnographically disarticulated. Is a woman who says that she feels blessed (even blessed by God) necessarily reflecting some well-established theological trope that corresponds to the way these terms might be invoked by an academic theologian? I will argue that anthropologists and theologians both need to do better at parsing the implications of vernacular theologies that frequently go unrecognized or

---

[12] See Judith W. Herman, "The Voices of Teen Mothers: The Experience of Repeat Pregnancy," *MCN: The American Journal of Maternal Child Nursing* 31/4 (2006): 243–9; Kathryn Edlin and Maria Kefalas, *Promises I Can Keep: Why Poor Women Put Motherhood before Marriage* (Berkeley: University of California Press, 2005).

[13] Seeman et al., "Blessing Unintended Pregnancy," 37.   [14] Ibid., 38.   [15] Ibid.

[16] Ibid., 37.

under-theorized, but it is important to remember that there are no interpretive shortcuts for choosing the best frame to make sense of people's lives.

Nearly all of the women in our group, for example, described themselves as "spiritual but not religious," seeming to confirm a whole spate of recent studies that have established *spirituality* as an unprecedented new category in the study of modern life.[17] Yet quite a few of those spiritual but not religious women attend church regularly, pray to Jesus Christ, and, in focus groups, talk about him as their ideal husband. Bridgette told us that while spirituality is about having a "relationship with God," religion is about ritual repetition and disdain for sinners.[18] The pastor of Bridgette's apostolic Pentecostal church gave a Sunday sermon in which she, too, identified *religion* with "mere Hollywood Christianity, . . . putting the word of the pastor before the word of God," and pledged to "do things outside of the box, . . . following the spirit of the Lord and never going back to what I left [mere institutional religion]."[19] In this context, the popular dichotomy between religion and spirituality seems more like one element of an *internal* Christian discourse that does not so much challenge the Christian frame as confirm a particular partisan view of where Christian authenticity lies. The ethnographer trying to make sense of all this needs to be sure not to assume that he or she knows the meaning of words or concepts that span different discursive regimes.

Cambridge theologian Andrew Davison has described the contested place that blessing has held in Christian practice and theology.[20] One reason to which he points for that contestation is the argument by some modern theologians that the immanence of blessing in everyday life creates a conceptual opposition (welcome or unwelcome, depending on their individual perspective) to the Church's focus on salvation, which can be conceived as a kind of rupture with the world as currently constituted. This is an important dispute for anthropologists to understand, inasmuch as *rupture* (with family, ancestral religion or even the idea of culture as a whole) has been identified as a leading trope in the anthropology of Christianity, while *blessing* has been relatively ignored.[21] Davison does not clearly relate the contested immanence of divine blessing with other factors that he says have also contributed to controversy, such as the identification of blessing in some quarters with *magic* or the distaste among many professional theologians for the way blessing is

---

[17] See, for example, Boaz Huss, "Spirituality: The Emergence of a New Cultural Category and its Challenge to the Religious and the Secular," *Journal of Contemporary Religion* 29/4 (2014): 47–60.

[18] Seeman et al., "Blessing Unintended Pregnancy," 40.   [19] Ibid., 41.

[20] Andrew Davison, *Blessing* (London: Canterbury Press, 2014).

[21] Joel Robbins, "Continuity Thinking and the Problem of Christian Culture," *Current Anthropology* 48/1 (2007): 5–17; Joel Robbins, "Between Reproduction and Freedom: Morality, Value and Radical Cultural Change," *Ethnos* 72/3 (2007): 293–314; Seeman, "Coffee and the Moral Order," 735–44.

invoked in prosperity gospel circles, though it seems to me these are all clearly linked. For one thing, they each invoke the problem of intentionality that Davison raises in another context.[22] Must I simply hope for blessing or may I seek it out or even demand it? Does it depend upon my actions? What is the role of human activity in the conveyance of divine blessing to others? These are not questions about which all Christians agree, and they involve blessing in a set of complex debates about the nature and efficacy of human agency.

To the extent that divine blessing is conceived as a kind of gift or abundance that transcends human intention and planning, it may seem further removed from magic, but this view also places limits on rational-actor style theories of planning that reign in fields such as economics and public health. That is certainly how the women in our study invoked blessing, as a kind of thankfulness for a plenitude they could not have planned or achieved on their own and through which the lack of control they experienced as inimical in other contexts might suddenly come to seem like evidence of transcendent care. This belief is a far cry from the way theologian and Christian ethicist Amy Laura Hall argues that mainline Protestant denominations during the last century acted in tandem with public health officials in support of a "meticulously planned procreation"—a "delineated, racially encoded domesticity"—that she does not shrink from identifying with eugenics.[23] What both these approaches have in common is the use of Christian language to delineate what are considered reasonable—though conflicting—expectations for reproductive planning and contingency. There is no single Christian position on these matters from an anthropological point of view but rather a set of oppositions that reveal over time what anxieties may be at stake in different ways of thinking about human reproduction.

Modern public health continues to identify unplanned pregnancy with a variety of negative health outcomes, though the term *unplanned* itself has been used loosely enough to encompass almost half of all American pregnancies.[24] At the same time, researchers have begun to realize that "binary taxonomies of intended and unintended pregnancy may elide important distinctions between unplanned, unwanted, or merely mistimed pregnancies, and that alternative descriptive frameworks must be found to accommodate the mixed intentions and ambivalence, contingency and sociocultural or religious constraints that characterize many women's reproductive experiences."[25] Jennifer Johnson-Hanks, an anthropologist working on these issues in Cameroon, has argued

---

[22] Davison, *Blessing*, 119–21.

[23] Amy Laura Hall, *Conceiving Parenthood: American Protestantism and the Spirit of Reproduction* (Grand Rapids, MI: W. B. Eerdmans Publishing, 2008), 10, cited in Seeman et al., "Blessing Unintended Pregnancy," 42.

[24] US Department of Health and Human Services, *Healthy People 2020*, <www.healthypeople.gov/2020/topics-objectives/topic/family-planning>, accessed December 10, 2014.

[25] Seeman et al., "Blessing Unintended Pregnancy," 30, and sources cited there.

succinctly that "reproduction offers a particularly appropriate locus for the study of intentionality and its limits, because 'planning,' 'intending' and 'trying' are at once indispensable and insufficient modes of understanding social action around childbearing."[26] Given the range of meanings and controversies attendant to blessing in the Christian tradition, this would seem a natural point of contact for anthropological concern. Yet while the importance of *blessing* to women's discourse on pregnancy and motherhood in a wide variety of Christian, Muslim, and Jewish contexts has been documented by ethnographers, there has been little direct theoretical attention given as to how this might further complicate the understanding of women's reproductive intentionality in these settings.[27] Our argument was that attention to blessing as a feature of vernacular religious life offered one more way to "disrupt or lend nuance to the binary distinction between intended and unintended pregnancy."[28] Our Naomi's House ethnography pointed to "a view of reproductive contingency that is often beyond planning, as well as to fields of agency that transcend individuals."[29]

My hope is that this very brief summary will suffice to illustrate some of the benefits and challenges of theologically engaged anthropology. For one thing, the fact that some of the individuals in our research group had religious studies and theological training as well as public health and medical anthropology expertise made us infinitely more sensitive to the connotations of language about blessing than we might otherwise have been. My own previous work on the contingency of motherhood as an organizing theme in the Book of Genesis certainly encouraged me to think carefully about what it meant when women at Naomi's House attributed their unplanned and frequently difficult motherhood to divine blessing. But rather than reduce this to a comment about the cultural or religious backgrounds of women at Naomi's House as we might have done, we tried to use this insight to probe much larger questions about the contingency of all reproductive planning and the inadequacy of public health models to the experience of the very women whose unplanned pregnancies have been a source of concern to public health professionals. For at least some of them, blessing is not just a way of asserting the positive valence of

---

[26] Jennifer Johnson-Hanks, "When the Future Decides: Uncertainty and Intentional Action in Contemporary Cameroon," *Current Anthropology* 46/3 (2005): 363, as cited in Seeman et al., "Blessing Unintended Pregnancy," 30.

[27] See, for example, Caroline H. Bledsoe, *Contingent Lives: Fertility, Time and Aging in West Africa* (Chicago: University of Chicago Press, 2002), 253–5; Susan Martha Kahn, *Reproducing Jews: A Cultural Account of Assisted Reproduction in Israel* (Durham, NC: Duke University Press, 2000); Jennifer Johnson-Hanks, "On the Politics and Practice of Muslim Fertility: Comparative Evidence from West Africa," *Medical Anthropology Quarterly* 20/1 (2006): 12–20; Faye Ginsburg, *Contested Lives: The Abortion Debate within an American Community* (Berkeley: University of California Press, 1989).

[28] Seeman et al., "Blessing Unintended Pregnancy," 31.   [29] Ibid.

children, planned or unplanned, but also an expression of the way divine agency and personality condition the everyday phenomenal world.

Framing the problem this way, rather than focusing narrowly on the culture of the homeless shelter or on local forms of Christianity allowed us to explore suggestive juxtapositions with research in other settings. Women in our study did not just invoke divinity to call attention to their own inability to plan or control reproductive outcomes but, in some cases, also to assert that it was wrong even to attempt such control. Whitney expressed her sadness and regret on having undergone a tubal ligation in precisely these terms: "I believe in God you know. And that's one thing that made me depressed when I made the decision to get my tubes tied. I wanted to wait on menopause, but because I don't [think] man has the right to decide what's best. You know what I'm saying? In some aspects, medical decisions, you know, I don't think, you know, you should, I just didn't believe in getting my tubes tied because it wasn't based in the Bible."[30] But this is a very broad feature of the conversation about reproduction in America, not at all limited to poor African-American women. Research conducted during the 1980s among mostly white, middle-class women who opposed abortion showed that they too were more likely to embrace legitimate contingency over narratives about reproductive control and expediency.[31] The kind of vernacular anxiety about openness to divine blessing we encountered at Naomi's House is at any rate quite distinct from more abstract debates about when precisely life begins or how we might balance the rights of women and fetuses that have characterized the American abortion debate on a public political level.

Methodologically, I cannot emphasize enough that we took our first analytic cues not from any religious canon or theological formulation but as much as possible from women's stories and our own observations regarding shelter life. Religious studies and theological literature were certainly in the background as we began to think these notions through, and some theologians—particularly those, such as Monica Coleman, who themselves begin from the analysis of lived religion—did figure explicitly in our argument (my co-author Annie Hardison-Moody, who brought a background in Christian theological materials to bear, was invaluable to the team in that regard).[32] However, for the most part, we had to bracket the kinds of systematic concerns that motivate most theological writing. A work such as Davison's *Blessing* provides useful historical and conceptual background, but Davison works too hard to domesticate blessing under the rubric of discursive theology—to force it into consistency

---

[30] Ibid., 34.
[31] Faye Ginsburg, *Contested Lives*, as cited in Seeman et al., "Blessing Unintended Pregnancy," 45.
[32] Monica A. Coleman, *Making a Way Out of No Way: A Womanist Theology* (Minneapolis, MN: Fortress Press, 2008).

with accepted scriptural understandings and to reconcile it with scientific notions of causality—to be of much direct use in understanding women's narratives. As with any body of highly theoretical literature such as medicine or public health, there is a real danger in ethnographic engagement with theology that we might come to treat those expert discourses as somehow more authoritative than what we can learn from our informants.

Paying too much attention, or the wrong kinds of attention, to theological literature might be as harmful as too little when working deductively to describe some otherwise neglected facet of the local moral world. So the first and, in some ways, most basic level of analysis always involves hugging the shoreline of lived experience, both because that is our empirical ground and also because it is part of the fundamental moral compact we make with those who give us access to their lives and travails in fieldwork. "You goddamn better tell the truth," one survivor of childhood clergy sexual abuse challengingly told Robert Orsi.[33] This is, of course, particularly true where we are dealing with people who have been relatively disempowered or subject to structural violence of one kind or another.

A second dilemma revolves around seeking the right analytic depth for subsequent stages of analysis. It is one thing to notice women's privileging of blessing as an unplanned gift or plenitude over the kinds of regularized intentionality presumed by rational-actor theory in a field such as public health. We also need to ask what this means concretely in the life of a person like Lisa, whose great-grandmother (a nondenominational preacher) helped her come to terms with her own unintended pregnancy:

> When my great-grandmother, she was—she put, like, that stamp of approval [on it]. You know—even though that happened—it was out of wedlock. [But, she told me] "It's not the end of the world and you won't have an abortion because of it, you won't be ashamed of her because of it." You know, "It's not a mistake. Nothing's by chance." So she really, you know, let me know that it's OK and "you will survive and you're going to make it with this baby." You know, Rebekah was a very joy, you know, she was.[34]

There is more in this statement to define the deep existential texture of divine blessing than I have found in many learned academic tomes, but at some point the researcher also needs to make a decision about how far to push his or her analysis. Does this data suggest additional comparisons with other settings in which human reproductive contingency is at stake? How might blessing in this

---

[33] Robert A. Orsi, "Doing Religious Studies with your Whole Body," *Practical Matters Journal* 6 (March 1, 2013), <https://wp.me/p6QAmj-eE>, accessed September 7, 2016; see also my response, which was part of a roundtable devoted to ethnography and theology. Don Seeman, "Ethnography of the Hard Edge," *Practical Matters Journal* 6 (March 1, 2013), <http://wp.me/p6QAmj-kL>.

[34] Seeman et al., "Blessing Unintended Pregnancy," 35.

context, moreover, be compared with other quite different ways of framing contingency that are more pronounced in other settings such as appeals to fate, destiny, or moral luck? At this secondary level of analysis, anthropologists need to choose among a variety of analytic options based on their ability to make a compelling argument about the way this particular case opens onto questions of broader human or theoretical concern.

A different research group might have chosen to explore in detail the continuities and discontinuities between the way blessing emerged from our fieldwork and its biblical or post-biblical Christian sources; another, with equal justification, might have chosen African-American women's religion as their primary frame. Our own, phenomenologically inflected decision was to treat blessing in this context as just one structural variation among others in a set of recognizable responses to a shared human dilemma—the tension between planning and irreducible contingency in at least some women's reproductive experience, for which we also found other evidence in the ethnographic literature. There is nothing in this approach that seeks to deny or debunk the powerful theological resonances of blessing in the lives of Naomi's House women, but exploring those resonances was actually only part of our goal. Unlike the cultural-interpretive approach, which tends to revel in the very incommensurability of symbol systems, the existential tack we adopted often finds in human diversity a set of different approaches to common human problems. The goal is not primarily to show how cleverly culture creates its own symbolic coherency across multiple fields of human endeavor but to show how culture as one among many other factors—such as regimes of power and the many imponderables of individual life experience—shapes distinctive ways of human being-in-the-world through which we navigate our shared human condition. Conceptual vocabularies derived from theology can play an important role in helping anthropologists become more attentive to social phenomena they might otherwise miss or misrecognize, but chances are good that categories that some theologians treat as foundational—for example, blessing, grace, or salvation—will be treated by sympathetic anthropologists as exemplars of something else, more foundational to our own concerns. The challenge, as always, is how to do so in ways that are both illuminating and fair.

* * *

It should be clear by now that I am describing the engagement between anthropology and theology in two rather different but interdependent registers. On the one hand, anthropology's engagement with the academic discipline of theology may, in principle, be compared to its productive (and sometimes agonistic) engagement with other disciplines that make strong analytic and prescriptive claims, such as medicine, psychology, or public health. Some anthropologists have adopted a relatively cooperative attitude towards those disciplines while others have focused on the deconstruction of their categories and assumptions, but anthropology itself has also been changed and enriched by the need to confront social suffering, sickness, and other issues that engagement with these disciplines requires. Today, medical, psychological, and public health anthropology are among the most generative subfields in the discipline precisely because of the friction that sometimes emerges from thinking through and across disciplinary or subject content boundaries. The areas in which I think engagement with theology might play a similarly powerful role include forcing us to confront different ways of thinking about otherness and intersubjectivity as well as moral experience, given theology's rich history of thinking through ethical issues in light of its confrontation with a divine other (or others).

In my view, social science boasts a relatively impoverished vocabulary for the analysis and description of alterity or transcendence of self, which is one of the reasons it consistently overplays the symbolic meaning of ritual activity at the expense of its role in creating avenues for getting outside of oneself in forging relationships or in the "ethical gesture" I have written about elsewhere.[35] Theological work on blessing, for example, emphasizes not just its semiotic dimensions but also the problem of efficacy in relation to a divine that is not just framed as a symbolic backdrop for social drama. Blessing might be thought of as a kind of gift exchange between social actors in the Maussian sense but without the hard emphasis on reciprocal exchange that somehow differentiates the Melanesian *kula*, for example, from the Abrahamic or specifically Christian notion of grace.[36] Anthropologists who engage theology should no more jettison their own theoretical concerns and analytical strictures than anthropologists who engage biomedicine or psychoanalysis, but like medical or psychoanalytic anthropologists, they also should mine those other disciplines for specialized conceptual language that might help them make sense of what they encounter in the field.

The analogy between academic theology and biomedicine I am building on here is crucial because both are fields that, from an anthropological point of view, subject the evidence of lived experience—suffering and loss, ethical impulses, the sense of transcendence—to highly theorized forms of understanding for particular purposes.[37] This is one way of understanding what has become an old bromide of theology as "faith seeking understanding," where understanding refers to certain kinds of theorized and philosophically

---

[35] Don Seeman, "Otherwise than Meaning: On the Generosity of Ritual," *Social Analysis* 48/2 (2004): 55–71; Talal Asad, *Genealogies of Religion: Discipline and Reasons of Power in Christianity and Islam* (Baltimore, MD: Johns Hopkins University Press, 1993).

[36] See J. G. Perisitany and Julian Pitt-Rivers (eds), *Honor and Grace in Anthropology* (Cambridge: Cambridge University Press, 2005).

[37] See also Jon Bialecki, Chapter 9, 156–78.

inflected knowledge.[38] Nevertheless, the incredible power and efficacy brought to bear by this process, certainly in the case of biomedicine, also alienates basic elements of the human condition from their experiential contexts—*suffering*, for better and worse, becomes *disease*.[39] Medical anthropology proved its value over the last half-century through a set of interlocking projects whose analogues might prove useful in the theological realm. Medical anthropologists learned, for instance, to treat biomedicine (not always unsympathetically) as a cultural and political system deserving anthropological analysis in its own right, breaking down some of its claims to unique objectivity and institutional power in the process. They also showed, over several decades, how engagement with and better understanding of vernacular idioms of distress—often stubbornly inseparable into discrete biophysical, psychological, and social dimensions—could enhance biomedical practice by renewing its conceptual matrix. Not only are there *culture-bound syndromes* to borrow an unfortunate term from contemporary psychiatry, but even allegedly universal pathologies such as depression or schizophrenia turn out to manifest in culturally and sociopolitically distinctive ways.[40] Finally, medical anthropologists demonstrated the dynamic and sometimes powerful tension between local moral categories, which include vernacular religious categories, and their biomedical derivatives or analogues (e.g., *sorrow* becomes *depression*). While these are all projects that beckon a future theological anthropology analogous to today's medical anthropology, it is the last of these projects that primarily interests me here because of the way it contributes to possibilities for describing lived experience.

Our ethnography at Naomi's House made use of published theological material in a fairly limited way to help set the stage for thinking about what women in our study told us about their struggles to get by, their awareness of blessing, and the sensed fragility of their attainments. None of these are entirely surprising themes in this religious setting: "Ever since the Hebrew Bible," notes theologian Thierry Maertens, "the womb has been the organ that 'shall be the privileged locus of divine benedictions.'"[41] However, the specificity with which such ideas are invoked in particular settings makes them worthy of anthropological consideration. In the Hebrew Bible, I have shown elsewhere, divine blessing is frequently associated with women's activism in their quest to become

---

[38] See Thomas William, "Saint Anselm," in *Stanford Encyclopedia of Philosophy*, ed. Edward N. Zalta (Stanford: Stanford University Press, 2014), <plato.stanford.edu/entries/anselm/>, accessed September 9, 2016.

[39] See, for example, Arthur Kleinman, *The Illness Narratives: Suffering, Healing and the Human Condition* (New York: Basic Books, 1988).

[40] There is by now a rich literature on this question. For just one influential early work, see Arthur Kleinman, *Patients and Healers in the Context of Culture: An Exploration of the Borderland between Anthropology, Medicine and Psychiatry* (Berkeley: University of California Press, 1980).

[41] Cited in Andre LaCocque and Paul Ricoeur, *Thinking Biblically: Exegetical and Hermeneutic Strategies* (Chicago: University of Chicago Press, 1998), 24.

mothers.[42] Such blessing is also frequently framed by an agonistic context of reproductive competition between or within patrilineal kin groups (i.e., houses) and between the women who are married into them. This kind of kin-based activism did not emerge at all in our American ethnography, yet the crucial continuity between ideas about blessing in the Hebrew Bible and at Naomi's House was their shared invocation of reproductive contingency that exceeds women's own ability to plan or achieve outcomes of their choosing and the confidence that what does transpire can, at least sometimes, be attributed to a benevolent divine agency more powerful than their own.

The corollary of this recognition, however, is that it would be a fundamental mistake to believe that biblical theologies of blessing are simply finding expression at Naomi's House or that the biblical notion of blessing in any of its variations could be treated as somehow foundational to human experience. Any approach that starts with theological categories and then searches out their expressions in the social world—looking for analogues to blessing, for example, in culture after culture—would strike me as misguided. Not just because discontinuities in the way those categories appear from time to time and place to place abound but more fundamentally because theology, like any highly theorized professional field, is sometimes tempted to treat its own taxonomies as foundational and to elide their relatedness to other ways of organizing or experiencing the world. Blessing, for example, can best be compared with moral luck or any of the other ways contingency is framed in different social settings when it is first understood as a response to basic human dilemmas *for which there are almost certain to be other possible responses.* This view is inevitably corrosive to certain kinds of universalizing theological projects, but that result cannot be helped. One of the primary goals of anthropological engagement with theology should be helping researchers find additional ways to break out of their own cultural or ideological strait-jackets, making them better listeners to a wider variety of human conversations and better observers of a wide variety of human conditions. To impose a category such as blessing on a field from which it did not naturally emerge would risk doing violence to the experience of one's informants in exactly the same way that public health researchers do when they impose a prism of rational-choice theory or when anthropologists of any theoretical stripe fail to attend with sufficient seriousness to what is at stake in local terms for the people about whose lives they write.[43]

---

[42] Don Seeman, "'Where Is Sarah Your Wife?' The Cultural Poetics of Gender and Nation-hood in the Hebrew Bible," *Harvard Theological Review* 91/2 (1998): 103–25; Don Seeman, "The Watcher at the Window: Cultural Poetics of a Biblical Motif," *Prooftexts* 24 (2004): 1–50.

[43] My thinking is centrally influenced here by the seminal work of Arthur Kleinman and Joan Kleinman, "Suffering and its Professional Transformation: Toward an Ethnography of Interpersonal Experience," *Culture, Medicine and Psychiatry* 15/3 (1991): 275–301; Unni Wikan, "Toward an Experience-Near Anthropology," *Current Anthropology* 6 (1991): 285–305.

That is why vernacular religion (or vernacular theology if you prefer) is so important to the approach I am trying to describe here: as Jon Bialecki, in this volume, also suggests, it is a link between lived experience and more formal kinds of theological reflection that include those of the academy.[44] Some theologian colleagues with whom I have discussed this view have been as enthusiastic about the idea of vernacular theologies as I am, but others have been guarded or even dismissive. Some of their hesitancy, if I understand it correctly, proceeds from the idea that it would discredit formal theology to be confused, as it were, with the unsystematic and frequently unschooled religious instincts of non-theologians. It has also been suggested, conversely, that it would be demeaning to our informants to suggest that *their* theology is merely vernacular and not up to par with that of the experts. Suffice it to say that neither of these suppositions conforms to my intent. I do not seek to devalue academic theology or to demean vernacular religion in any way but to place them along a continuum somewhat analogous to the one that links vernacular illness or idioms of distress with the meticulously defined categories of biomedical disorder. This is slightly different from Martyn Percy's evocative use of "implicit theology" in this volume[45] because vernacular theologies as I conceive them may (or may not) be quite explicitly articulated by the people who hold them. What matters is that they emerge from and remain close to everyday experience in a way that professionalized taxonomies like those constructed by academic theologians frequently do not. One paradoxical benefit of this way of looking at things, which still requires some clarification, is that this phenomenological view of the engagement between theology and anthropology frees that encounter from enthrallment to the anthropology of religion.

Joel Robbins is undoubtedly correct that one of the most important ways in which engagement with theology can be of benefit to anthropology is in helping anthropologists track changes in religious cultures that can be mapped by shifting theological discourse. Anthropologists of Christianity, including Robbins and others represented in this volume, have been especially adept at doing so.[46] But while this may be the most natural *starting point* for any engagement with theological materials in anthropology, it is not where I envision the most important theoretical contributions being made. If one accepts my claim that theological resources can be used to open up new

---

[44] Bialecki, Chapter 9, 156–78.   [45] Martyn Percy, Chapter 17, 298.

[46] Joel Robbins, "Anthropology and Theology: An Awkward Relationship?" *Anthropological Quarterly* 79/2 (2006): 285–94. I also have in mind here gifted anthropologists such as Matthew Engelke and Webb Keane who have made such productive use of theological materials as backgrounds to their ethnography. See, for example, Matthew Engelke, *A Problem of Presence: Beyond Scripture in an African Church* (Berkeley: University of California Press, 2007); Webb Keane, *Christian Moderns: Freedom and Fetish in the Missionary Encounter* (Berkeley: University of California Press, 2007).

horizons in the understanding of lived experience (the contingency of women's reproductive experience, for example), it follows that the insights gleaned from this kind of engagement may take us far afield from what are typically treated as *anthropology of religion* contexts. If blessing is, among other things, a way of coming to grips with or even celebrating contingency and limits on planning, for example, then we might look for footprints of similar expressions in other contexts, such as the reproductive experience of women who identify as secular or in the modern ecological movement or in the hesitations and resistance that broadly accompany our economic, biomedical, and technological attempts to eliminate uncertainty. The American abortion debate might look very different if, instead of assuming that the warring moieties of American public life are primarily divided by articulate religious or doctrinal commitments we recognized that they might also be divided by diffuse, vernacular intuitions regarding the *rightness* of asserting determinative human control in these areas. The phenomenological register I envision helps to break down received taxonomies that tend to ghettoize the anthropology of religion rather than treating it as a prism through which to examine the broadest range of problems with which social science has been concerned. Theologically engaged anthropology should contribute not just to the anthropology of religion but also to the anthropology of science, to medical and psychological anthropology, the anthropology of the state, and every other important subfield.

* * *

One final dilemma needs to be named in the context of this chapter, which is how the current conversation about anthropological engagement with theology might move beyond its initial, quite natural preoccupation with Christian theology and the anthropology of Christianity. There are a few reasons I hope it does so. First, because I doubt that the broader discipline of anthropology will ever embrace a conversation that seems, fairly or not, to privilege one set of faith commitments or heritage above any other (or none at all). No one, I hasten to add, has so far suggested that the project represented by this volume should be limited in this way, but the fact remains that all of the theologians who have participated in the handful of publications devoted to this conversation have been Christian theologians (from a variety of different backgrounds), while most of the anthropologists, whether or not they identify personally as Christians, have certainly been best known as anthropologists of Christianity. Khaled Furani and I may be the only anthropologists contributing to this volume whose primary research has *not* been conducted in Christian contexts. I am glad that Furani chose to explore a set of Islamic resonances in his chapter, but I did not do the same with Jewish ones here because my arguments would have been unduly complicated by first having to translate the kinds of Jewish materials I frequently work with into terms that resonate with overwhelmingly Christian academic theology. The very term *theology* remains a contested one in Jewish lay and academic circles, and though some of my own scholarship touches on normative themes in Jewish intellectual history that could easily have been glossed as theological, that is not a term I would naturally have used before I began conversing with Christian scholars for whom that term holds important cultural and institutional references. I note that my title for this chapter, "divinity inhabits the social," recalls the notion of *dirah ba-tachtonim*—the idea that infinite divinity desires a habitation "down below" in the phenomenal world—popularized by the Chabad Hasidim who have contributed to my current fieldwork. For them this is more of a ritual and exegetical matrix than an abstract discursive construct, enacting their denial of any firm distinction between immanence and transcendence.[47] They would call the formulation of these ideas *hasidus*, not theology.

This is not a trivial matter. Anselm's "faith in search of understanding" may well resonate beyond the Christian context, but it may also be that this way of formulating the matter, with its strong, though not uncontested, residue of distinctively Christian concerns about the reconciliation of faith and discursive reason also unwittingly excludes many forms of religious life, including some Christian ones, from its purview. There are certainly robust exemplars of theological discourse in the history of Judaism or Islam, for example, but would anyone deny that the real center of gravity in these traditions has been occupied by different forms of legal and casuistic practice that have their own critical lens for examining and ordering a sacred tradition? Would Kabbalah as a formative mode of systematic practical and intellectual engagement with revealed tradition also constitute "faith seeking understanding" in a manner that could serve as a viable conversation partner for social science?[48] What about the practical rationality and articulation of values embodied by Jewish *halakhah* or Muslim *shariah*, each undoubtedly among the most important ways that religious and intellectual experts in these communities have bridged their own gaps between expert and vernacular knowledge of what religious life entails?[49]

My own view is that such gaps should be explored using all of the tools at our disposal. I am sympathetic to the insight of those scholars who have followed Talal Asad in emphasizing habitual practice and virtue formation as important loci of contemporary Islamic discourse and used that insight to push back

---

[47] Elliot R. Wolfson, *Open Secret: Postmessianic Messianism and the Mystical Revision of Menahem Mendel Scheerson* (New York: Columbia University Press, 2009).

[48] This is part of a question raised by sociologist Philip Wexler in his *Mystical Sociology: Toward Cosmic Social Theory* (London: Peter Lang, 2013).

[49] See Don Seeman, "Ethnography, Exegesis and Ethical Reflection: The New Reproductive Technologies in Israel," in *Kin, Gene Community: Reproductive Technologies among Jewish Israelis*, ed. Daphna Birenbaum Carmelli and Yoram S. Carmelli (New York: Berghahn Books, 2010), 343–61.

against the frequent post-Reformation emphasis on "semiotic systems" and "symbolic meaning" of ritual practice in anthropology.[50] Asad's lucid account of the link between developments in Christian theology and anthropological theory should certainly give pause to anthropologists who think they can understand their own discipline without recourse to knowledge of theology as an intellectual field. But I also note that this productive trend in the anthropology of Islam has been accompanied by a tendency to describe Islam as a coherent discursive tradition at the expense of engagement with the specific legal and theological schools whose struggles for power and influence have helped to define the stakes of contemporary Muslim life.[51] Anthropology very often needs theology to help it make sense of lived religion, but it also needs to embrace a broader understanding of what theology might entail in different religious and ethnographic contexts.

For me, at any rate, theology is not only an academic discipline situated in mostly Christian schools of divinity but a family of different kinds of expert discourse about religion, each differently situated with respect to the vernacular discourses that exist alongside them.

If this is true even with respect to the religious traditions most closely related to Christianity, furthermore, it should give us pause when considering quite different traditions, like the sprawling shastric discourse of moral and ritual regulation described by anthropologist of India Leela Prasad.[52] My point is not just that engagement between anthropology and theology needs to include and be open to non-Christian theologies but that this can only happen when we are willing to evince a methodological openness to the question of what counts as theology in the first place. The productive tension I have tried to generate in this essay by analogizing theology to biomedicine and then distinguishing both from the vernacular knowledge of everyday life should apply to all sorts of expert knowledge that are recognized or authorized by different communities in relation to the divine. These are languages, institutional practices, and sources of authority we need to think through carefully and sometimes skeptically as ethnographers who are devoted to understanding the human world as lived.

---

[50] See Asad, *Genealogies of Religion*; Charles Hirschkind, *The Ethical Soundscape: Cassette Sermons and Islamic Counterpublics* (New York: Columbia University Press, 2009); Saba Mahmood, *Politics of Piety: The Islamic Revival and the Feminist Subject* (Princeton: Princeton University Press, 2011).

[51] This critique should be read in tandem with that offered from a different direction by Samuli Schielke, "Second Thoughts about the Anthropology of Islam, or How to Make Sense of Grand Schemes in Everyday Life," *ZOM Working Papers*, no. 2 (2010), <www.zmo.de/publikationen/WorkingPapers/schielke_2010.pdf>.

[52] Leela Prasad, *Poetics of Conduct: Oral Narrative and Moral Being in a South Indian Town* (New York: Columbia University Press, 2006).

Despite my otherwise deep indebtedness to his existential approach, this is one area in which I take issue with my colleague Michael Jackson, who has called on anthropologists to "approach religiosity without a theological vocabulary, repudiate the notion of religion as *sui generis* phenomenon, and distance ourselves from the assumption of a necessary relationship between espoused belief and subjective experience."[53] In fairness to Jackson, these are all crucial methodological cautions that I try to teach my own students. But by elevating the rejection of theological language to an unwavering analytic principle, I fear that this approach may also blind us to facets of lived experience to which theological language might at least on occasion bear better witness than the constructs of theorists favored by contemporary anthropologists like Heidegger and Merleau-Ponty, whose views of the human condition have sometimes been adopted by anthropologists with insufficient care. At the end of the day, it is the analytic movement back and forth between these expert and vernacular landscapes that can help to generate understanding by highlighting what may be missing from each. The conceptual (and existential) plenitude of blessing is hardly exhausted by the idea of reproductive contingency, for example, but thinking through contingency in local and comparative contexts is what makes blessing into a window on human life beyond the anthropology of Christianity or even the anthropology of religion. As always (and here I agree with Jackson), the test must be empirical. Engaged judiciously and without preconceptions, who knows? Theological languages (I use that term advisedly in the plural) might even prove a blessing to anthropology.

---

[53] Michael Jackson, *The Palm at the End of the Mind: Relatedness, Religiosity and the Real* (Durham, NC: Duke University Press, 2009), 99.

20

Anthropological and Theological Responses
to Theologically Engaged Anthropology

Sarah Coakley and Joel Robbins

AN ANTHROPOLOGICAL RESPONSE BY JOEL ROBBINS

There is a tension between the general framing of this fine volume and the combined contents of its chapters. As the general framing would have it, the core topic at hand is "theologically engaged anthropology." The key question from this point of view is the one of how greater knowledge of theology can improve the work of anthropologists. But many of the contributors seem to hope that the engagement between the disciplines can be two-way, with theology enriching anthropology as expected by the main framing, but with theology also emerging a little changed by the encounter, and hopefully for the better. I have been involved with this project from its inception, and my own relation to it has come into gentle tension with its framing in just these ways all along. Reading all of the chapters in final form at the end of the process, I'm happy to see that I am not the only one to feel the need to contextualize theologically informed anthropology by placing it alongside anthropologically informed theology. Maybe in my own case this feeling is just the anthropological impulse to see a foundational role for relations of reciprocity in social life (one of our few robust findings) coming to the surface, but I cannot help but think that it is the ability to sustain movement in both directions that will keep the parties to this dialogue at the table in the future.

Since my response here is paired with one from the theology side by Sarah Coakley, I will take the liberty of reading these chapters mostly for some of their contributions to the development of anthropology. These contributions work at several levels. Relying on a quite banal classification that nonetheless can do some work in this case, we might think of these as the ethnographic, the theoretical, and the disciplinary. I will organize my remarks in these terms.

* * *

Many of these chapters demonstrate beyond a shadow of a doubt that the ethnographic study of Christian populations can be improved by greater engagement with theology. We might call such work theologically informed ethnography. In this volume, it comes in at least two flavors: cases in which ethnographic accounts are rendered deeper and more compelling by researchers' knowledge of what we might call the formal or elite theological background of ideas in play in the situations they study; and other instances in which researchers direct attention to the "folk" theologizing that those they study carry out in the course of living lives not devoted professionally, primarily, or explicitly to theological reflection. The relative desirability of studying elite versus folk theologies is a matter of discussion within and between these chapters. Paul Kollman, for example, would have us not focus on theological elites, or not only on such elites, while James Bielo calls for us to "study up" precisely so we can reach them. Don Seeman, writing from a phenomeno-logical perspective, notes how complex the relations between points on what he sees as a vernacular–elite continuum of degrees of theological formalism and abstraction can be in practice. Debates about where on such a continuum to focus attention have at once normative, theoretical, and methodological shadings. I will simply note their existence for the moment, and return to them after tracking some of the impressive work these chapters have accomplished by way of bringing attention to various kinds of theology to bear on ethno-graphic research and analysis.

Derrick Lemons, Joseph Webster, and Naomi Haynes all provide accounts in which comprehending theological ideas elaborated by elites is necessary for understanding the lived religion of specific Christian populations that contain many members who are not themselves producers of elite theological systems. Lemons traces the rise of the set of ideas that went into the making of missional theology and then explores how this theological movement led to a major shift in the lives of members of the Wesleyan Church, as they began to reach out to the world rather than pull away from it. In his chapter, Webster looks at how the Exclusive Brethren doctrine of separation, which exists in systematically articulated form in the writings of church elites, shapes a wide range of the behaviors of the church's members, including not only their social practices but also the kinds of physical structures they build and inhabit. Haynes looks at how the widespread and sometimes academically articulated Pentecostal "this is that" hermeneutic, a method of interpretation that ties together biblical texts and current circumstances to create an "expanded present" in which believers can live their lives, shapes formal and informal sermonizing on the Zambian Copperbelt. In all of these cases, and several others documented in the volume (e.g., in the chapters by Bialecki, Howell, and Kollman), ethnographic accounts and analyses would be much poorer, if not downright uncomprehending, if their authors were not aware of elite theological framings that inform the social lives of those they study.

It is worthy of note, however, that Haynes represents the "this is that" interpretive work Zambian Christians carry out not just as the expression of a wider and sometimes elite strand of Pentecostal theology, but as a feature of local theological creation as well. Brian Howell is similarly interested in the local production of theology "in a confessing community, from that community and for that community" in his study of a group in the Northern Luzon region of the Philippines. Fennella Cannell's study of the innovative ways several Mormon women claim a theological voice in the face of official opposition both to their message and to their claim to possess the authority to theologize at all also belongs in this group, as does Seeman's consideration of the use of the notion of "blessing" as a framework of understanding by pregnant single women. And though quite different in the kinds of materials examined, perhaps Martyn Percy's subtle account of the creation of a specifically Anglican "mood" as a matter of implicit theology in a rural English church also qualifies as a study of local theological production informed by wider theological currents but very much made in situ.

For anthropologists, both sets of chapters—those that look at how the theological productions of elites come to play an important role in the lives of Christians who did not themselves produce them, and those that look at local theology making—have some precursors, such as Susan Harding's influential work on Jerry Falwell's church,[1] Simon Coleman's on the Swedish Word of Life church,[2] Matthew Engelke's on Masowe apostolics in Zambia,[3] and my own markedly more minor work on the elite theological origins and later very wide global spread and folk elaboration of Spiritual Warfare as a set of linked doctrines and practices.[4] What is new in the chapters in this volume is a clear and sustained focus on the fact that what is being investigated is theology, rather than simply people's Christian understandings, utterances, or practices more generally. As accounts of theology qua theology, they raise a host of interesting questions about the relations between thought and social life. By thought here, I do not primarily mean mental categories or collective representations or the like—the study of the relations of this aspect of "thought," what we might call its scaffolding, to social life already has a long and notably successful history in anthropology. Rather, I mean specifically intellectual

---

[1] Susan F. Harding, *The Book of Jerry Falwell: Fundamentalist Language and Politics* (Princeton: Princeton University Press, 2001).

[2] Simon Coleman, *The Globalisation of Charismatic Christianity: Spreading the Gospel of Prosperity* (Cambridge: Cambridge University Press, 2000).

[3] Matthew Engelke, *A Problem of Presence: Beyond Scripture in an African Church* (Berkeley: University of California Press, 2007).

[4] Joel Robbins, "On Enchanting Science and Disenchanting Nature: Spiritual Warfare in North America and Papua New Guinea," in *Nature, Science, and Religion: Intersections Shaping Society and the Environment*, ed. C. M. Tucker (Santa Fe: School for Advanced Research Press, 2012), 45–64.

productions, more or less self-conscious attempts to articulate explicitly sets of ideas and work them into coherent statements of one kind or another about how things are and/or should be. It is the relation of such intellectual productions to how people live together that these chapters help bring into focus. Lemons, Webster, Haynes, and Cannell all have things to tell us about how the social vitality of such intellectual productions draws from, and often enough depends upon, the authority of those who articulate them. At the same time, all of these chapters inform us about the ways ideas can saturate social formations and find lives within them that move beyond those imagined by the persons, whether or not possessed of authority, who first articulated them. Anthropology has to this point focused too little on the intellectual life of Christians, and this work begins to address this gap. Furthermore, for the anthropology of Christianity, the glimpses of the complex circulation of theological ideas through social formations that we see in these chapters point to the further development of an emerging emphasis on the study of religious divisions of labor, such as between the clergy and the laity, so that it can comprehend divisions of intellectual labor alongside others.[5]

My talk of religious divisions of labor and structures of intellectual authority within religious groups and traditions leads us back to the issue I passed over quickly above concerning whether theologically informed ethnography should focus on the intellectual productions of elites, the theological probing of "ordinary people," or the implicit theological understandings embodied in the ways of life that anthropologists study. For the purposes of ethnography in particular, choosing to focus on any one of these phenomena over the others as a matter of general principle has to be a mistake. It is much more useful, recalling Seeman's framing, to see these categories as forming points along a continuum and to ask why kinds of theology situated at one place along it seem most prominent in some situations and those that rest at another location are more to the fore in others. When and where do elite theologies matter? When and where do implicit theologies carry a heavier load? In what circumstances do theologies made on the spot by religious leaders or others who do not conceptualize themselves as theologians dominate the scene in terms of Christian self-understandings? Questions like these are grist for the mill of a theologically engaged ethnography that should probably never decide in advance or in the abstract the question of which kind of theology to attend to. Albeit staying largely within theology, Francis Clooney demonstrates the technique of such open exploration of comparative possibilities across kinds of

---

[5] Andreas Bandak and Tom Boylston, "The 'Orthodoxy' of Orthodoxy: On Moral Imperfection, Correctness, and Deferral in Religious Worlds," *Religion and Society: Advances in Research* 5/1 (2014): 25–46; Maya Mayblin, "The Lapsed and the Laity: Discipline and Lenience in the Study of Religion," *Journal of the Royal Anthropological Institute* 5/3 (2017): 1–20.

theological expression, and some of the fruits it can produce, in his account of the nature of his work in comparative theology.

*   *   *

Theologically engaged anthropological theory is also an important topic in this volume. Timothy Jenkins' careful reading of T. M. Luhrmann's *When God Talks Back* (2012) argues that Denys Turner's (1995) theological work on the mutual dependence of apophatic and cataphatic prayer can enrich her treatment of religious experience among members of the Vineyard Church in the United States.[6] But Jenkins' argument is after more than ethnographic improvement, for he also has a theoretical point to make about the complexity of shaping up "experience," as opposed to prospective and retrospective accounts of experience, as a concept fit for ethnographic study. It is certainly possible that Jenkins could have made his point by using other tools—and I would wager that philosophical discussions of the nature of "experience" and its relationship to time are already lurking in the background of his argument— but it remains the case that the force of his argument as presented here relies on counterposing Turner's theological account of prayer to Luhrmann's use of other theological work and her own ethnographic materials to explore the experience of the divine among members of the Vineyard. This is a straightforward case, then, of a particular theological engagement enriching a particular strand of anthropological theorizing. Michael Rynkiewich takes a kindred approach to bringing theology to bear on anthropological theory in his chapter, exploring the ways an encounter with some theological works can contribute to anthropological debates about the nature of personhood, and an ambitious recent article by Meneses et al. also fits this mold, looking at ways Christian theological anthropology might expand existing anthropological approaches to the study of violence.[7]

A number of other chapters in this volume, particularly when read together, inject new impetus into very general debates that get at crucial underlying assumptions of anthropology as a field. The chapter by Timothy Larsen and Daniel King, for example, opens up issues that go well beyond the already important points they make by way of their elegant institutional-cum-intellectual historical narrative. The heart of their chapter is an account of the signal contribution theological defenses of the monogenetic position on human origins made to the development of the anthropological understanding of the psychic unity of humankind during the nineteenth century. As they

---

[6] T. M. Luhrmann, *When God Talks Back: Understanding the American Evangelical Relationship with God* (New York: Alfred A. Knopf, 2012); Denys Turner, *The Darkness of God: Negativity in Christian Mysticism* (Cambridge: Cambridge University Press, 1995).

[7] Eloise Meneses, Lindy Backues, David Bronkema, Eric Flett, and Benjamin L. Hartley, "Engaging the Religiously Committed Other: Anthropologists and Theologians in Dialogue," *Current Anthropology* 55/1 (2014): 82–104.

rightly note, the notion of psychic unity is so fundamental to anthropology as to be a matter of "doctrine" more than theory. The aspect of this doctrine Larsen and King focus upon, and that they show has distinctively Christian roots, is the claim that all persons are born with the same mental equipment and basic mental capabilities. But as anthropologists deploy this doctrine, it has another facet that is not to the fore in the story that Larsen and King tell—a facet that makes it in practice very complex. This facet, a specifically anthropological twist on the original theological assertion that human beings are in crucially important respects all alike, is that one of the key psychic capabilities all humans share is that of being able to, and indeed needing to, acquire a culture in order to flourish. And in anthropological understanding, even as the capacity that supports the acquisition of culture is universal, the cultures that people acquire are hugely variable, promoting a wide range of understandings of the world and values relevant to living in it (Geertz's text is important for Larsen and King and is an excellent presentation of this position).[8] In anthropological hands, then, psychic unity becomes a claim about human similarity or commonality that supports an equally strong claim about the importance of human difference.

With this claim about the centrality of culture and cultural variation to the making of human life, the anthropological doctrine of psychic unity outruns the original theological theory of human monogenesis that helped launch it and strays onto the terrain of profound human cultural difference—a terrain that has proven challenging for theology even as it has become the home ground from which anthropology is nourished. This becomes clear when one turns to Kollman's chapter in this volume, where he makes the brilliant move of setting side by side the largely ignored but deeply sensitive study of missionaries by the otherwise influential anthropologist Kenelm Burridge and Andrew Walls' essay "The Gospel as Prisoner and Liberator of Culture," a piece that has had a huge influence on the development of the field of world or global Christianity that I track in my own chapter in this volume (and that I know anecdotally has helped inspire a number of young scholars to take up the anthropology of Christianity).[9] Burridge and Walls, as Kollman shows, both meditate profoundly on tensions between opposed valuations of commonality/universality and difference as they have found expression within the Christian tradition. Burridge shapes up this tension as a clash between Christian missionary approaches to culture that are "affirmative," based on the biblically enjoined love and acceptance of others, and those that are "devotional," dedicated to the conviction that the cultures of non-Christians should

---

[8] Clifford Geertz, *The Interpretation of Cultures* (New York: Basic Books, 1973).

[9] Kenelm Burridge, *In the Way: A Study of Christian Missionary Endeavours* (Vancouver: UBC Press, 1991); Andrew F. Walls, *The Missionary Movement in Christian History: Studies in the Transmission of Faith* (Maryknoll, NY: Orbis Books, 1996).

be improved by means of the Christian faith. For Walls, a similar tension arises in the course of the historical spread of Christianity between what he calls an "indigenizing principle" rooted in the idea that God accepts people as they are, and a "pilgrim principle" that assumes that God seeks to transform people so that they can come to embody normatively universal aspects of the Christian faith. These two scholars grapple with issues of the existence and value of elements of universality and particularity in the Christian under-standing of human life that at least echo, if they do not in part reproduce, the opposing elements that make the anthropological doctrine of psychic unity complex and tension-laden enough to provide the ongoing foundation for a thriving discipline that is open to change.[10]

Against the background of Kollman's discussion of Burridge and Walls, it should perhaps not come as a surprise that anthropologists of Christianity have found themselves contending with questions of the universal and the particular in relation to the nature of Christianity in their own ways. For them, core debates have turned around whether Christianity has enough consistency as a cultural formation, or as a complex of ideas and practices, to count as a single object of comparative study, or if we should not speak of "Christianities" instead, dwelling far more on the particularities of religious expression in each of the settings anthropologists study, and much less on the way studies carried out in different settings might inform comparative reflections on features of a "Christianity" that exist beyond its local expressions.[11] In some respects, this discussion reflects wider debates about the viability of cross-cultural compari-son as a project that have flourished in anthropology since the passing of the late twentieth-century heyday of postmodernism,[12] but when set beside the theological considerations Kollman explores, and that others have taken up in discussions around issues like inculturation and contextual theology,[13] it becomes clear that anthropological discussions of this kind stand to benefit from dialogue with theology, and that theology might likewise find it useful to

---

[10] Jon Bialecki, Naomi Haynes, and Joel Robbins, "The Anthropology of Christianity," *Religion Compass* 2/6 (2008): 1143. Kenelm Burridge, *Encountering Aborigines: A Case Study: Anthropology and the Australian Aboriginal* (New York: Pergamon, 1973).

[11] Jon Bialecki, "Virtual Christianity in an Age of Nominalist Anthropology," *Anthropological Theory* 12/3 (2012): 295–319; William Garriott and Kevin Lewis O'Neill, "What is a Christian? Toward a Dialogic Approach in the Anthropology of Christianity," *Anthropological Theory* 8/4 (2008): 381–98; Joel Robbins, "What is a Christian? Notes Toward an Anthropology of Chris-tianity," *Religion* 33/3 (2003): 191–9.

[12] Webb Keane, "Self-Interpretation, Agency, and the Objects of Anthropology: Reflections on a Genealogy," *Comparative Studies in Society and History* 45/2 (2003): 222–48; Joel Robbins, Bambi B. Schieffelin, and Aparecida Vilaça, "Evangelical Conversion and the Transformation of the Self in Amazonia and Melanesia: Christianity and the Revival of Anthropological Compari-son," *Comparative Studies in Society and History* 56/3 (2014): 559–90.

[13] Stephen B. Bevans, *Models of Contextual Theology* (Maryknoll, NY: Orbis Books, 2002).

engage what has become of the notion of psychic unity and its intellectual sequels in anthropology since it first took root in theological soil.

As it happens, Kollman's discussion of Burridge and Walls also provides an excellent route into another issue that shows up across a number of chapters and that warrants discussion in this section on theologically engaged anthropological theorizing. Having established the similarities between Burridge's devotional–affirmative pairing and Walls' indigenizing–pilgrimage principles, Kollman goes on to note that where the two most obviously differ is in their accounts of the "agency that allows the two [sides of each pair] to operate in a productive tension."[14] For Walls, "[t]he agent at work in enacting the principles...is primarily God, acting in Jesus and the Holy Spirit."[15] Burridge, by contrast, "places the agency squarely on missionaries themselves" as "human agents."[16] It is this difference between Walls and Burridge, Kollman avers, that "locates their disciplinary orientation within theology and anthropology."[17] One cannot really call this finding surprising, but often, surely in part because of secular and liberal notions of privacy and politeness as they apply to academic discussion, it has not been as central to nascent discussions between anthropology and theology as one might have expected. But it does receive some notice in this volume. Not only does Kollman's account bring it out with rare force and clarity, many other contributors here take at least passing note of the gulf that opens between the two fields in light of their different approaches to the role of divine action in the world. Thus, Alister McGrath points out that anthropologists are wary of "non-empirical methods and outcomes,"[18] Larsen and King cite Edmund Leach's insistence that when it comes to analyzing the biblical book of Genesis, and more generally when considering any phenomenon they study, anthropologists reject "the idea of a supernatural sender,"[19] and Francis Clooney notes that one of the distinctive features of theology, at least in some cases, is its openness to "the Transcendent Reality."[20] If theological and anthropological traditions of thought about topics like the nature of experience and the complexities of maintaining both the universal and the particular as foci of a single field cause the disciplines to mirror one another in potentially productive ways, when it comes to the question of divine action in the world, members of neither field can easily recognize their concerns in the work of the other, at least not in their usual disciplinary terms.

There is little chance that this difference around the issue of divine efficacy in the world is going to disappear soon. The question that thus arises is one of

---

[14] Paul Kollman, Chapter 5, 98.   [15] Ibid., 98.   [16] Ibid., 98.   [17] Ibid., 98.

[18] Alister E. McGrath, Chapter 7, 126.

[19] Timothy Larsen and Daniel J. King, Chapter 3, 53, citing Edmund Leach, *Genesis as Myth and Other Essays* (London: Grossman, 1969).

[20] Francis X. Clooney, Chapter 16, 281.

how to avoid treating lack of agreement on this point as a "conversation-stopper" that would set severe limits on the range and depth of interaction between the two fields.[21] Haynes offers an ethnographic framing of this problem from the anthropological side, noting that "how to write about divine action in a way that preserves the integrity of both our informants' experiences and of anthropological frameworks" is "one of the most vexing problems in the anthropology of Christianity."[22] Her proposed solution is also ethnographic, suggesting that we study local notions of the efficacy of the divine as part of studying local theological productions. Bialecki (2014), in another close reading of Luhrmann's book, has recently taken a similar approach to settling the ethnographic problem of divine agency by encompassing it within widely influential attempts by actor–network theory to define agency down, such that inanimate things, ideas, and other formerly poor candidates for scholarly treatment as agents are now seen to have agency in quite full form and can be treated as agents in ethnographic discussions.[23]

Both Haynes and Bialecki demonstrate that it is possible for anthropologists to work with notions of divine agency that they encounter in the field without troubling the background assumptions of their own wider discipline. I have no doubt that this is a valuable way forward for anthropologists as ethnographers; we surely stand to learn more about how those we study conceive of divine action by taking (or continuing to take) their claims about it seriously and examining them thoroughly. Moreover, we should remember Jenkins' claim, made at the very end of his piece, that in learning to reckon in our accounts of Christian communities with what the people who inhabit them take to be the task of grasping "effects that cannot be readily controlled by human categories," we may well be learning about a "unique feature" of Christian ways of engaging the world.[24] Put otherwise, in dwelling on the issue of divine action in the world as Christians conceptualize it, we might have identified one of Christianity's distinctive features, a kind of human understanding best grasped by studying Christians. The extent to which influential early anthropological reflections on Christianity, such as those by Asad (1993) and Ruel (1997), have troubled the formerly taken-for-granted use of "belief" as straightforward descriptive category is one foreshadowing of the broader disciplinary impact ethnography around the topic of divine efficacy might eventually have.[25]

[21] Richard Rorty, *Philosophy and Social Hope* (London: Penguin 1999).

[22] Naomi Haynes, Chapter 15, 266.

[23] Jon Bialecki, "Does God Exist in Methodological Atheism? On Tanya Luhrmann's *When God Talks Back* and Bruno Latour," *Anthropology of Consciousness* 25/1 (2014): 32–52.

[24] Timothy Jenkins, Chapter 6, 121.

[25] Talal Asad, *Genealogies of Religion: Discipline and Reasons of Power in Christianity and Islam* (Baltimore, MD: Johns Hopkins University Press, 1993); Malcolm Ruel, *Belief, Ritual and the Securing of Life: Reflexive Essays on a Bantu Religion* (Leiden: E. J. Brill, 1997).

But the fact remains that theological and anthropological divergence over issues of divine efficacy are relevant well beyond the ethnographic issues Christian understandings of the divine sometimes raise for anthropologists in the field. How might scholars like Walls and Burridge have productive theoretical, rather than ethnographic, conversations across differences of explanatory approach as significant as the one Kollman identifies? Khaled Furani's chapter comes closest of those in this volume to approaching this kind of question head-on, albeit only from the anthropological side. His searching consideration of the ways encounters with theology can help to reveal anthropology's secular constitution as a discipline, and the limits this constitution has placed on its understandings of the kinds of otherness and difference that are worthy of study, gets us to the very edges of anthropological thought about itself as a discipline—a place we rarely let ethnography alone take us.[26] But even as Furani takes anthropology to its limits, and at least implies that the otherness of the divine is one kind of otherness the secularism of anthropology leads us to recoil from, he does not tell us in his chapter what we might do if we break beyond those limits. I have to confess I have no suggestions here myself at the moment. But it is clear that figuring out what lies beyond anthropology's secular constitution is one task anthropologists might hope to take up in further dialogue with theology about issues of divine agency.

*   *   *

With Furani's discussion of anthropology's secular constitution, we are clearly nudging beyond the issues of theological engagement with anthropological theory that were the focus of the last section and into those I want to take up in this final section, where I consider whether conversations between anthropology and theology can lead anthropologists, and maybe theologians as well, to think in new ways about the nature of their own disciplines more generally. Alister McGrath, Douglas Davies, and Jon Bialecki, in their chapters here, each lay out some productive ground-rules for interdisciplinary relationships. They all converge on the desirability or even necessity of each discipline preserving its own distinctive sense of self. I am not sure if Furani is calling for an encounter of an entirely different kind than these three contributors suggest—one in which anthropology would more radically set concerns for disciplinary integrity and distinctiveness aside—or simply for one that would render changes in anthropology short of those that would undo its specificity as a field. Nor am I interested in deciding at the moment on the desirability of one or the other approach to this problem. But it is important not to lose sight of the issues McGrath, Davies, and Bialecki raise so well, and the ways Furani's approach might trouble their positions, as

---

[26] The valiant efforts of the recent ontological turn notwithstanding. See Martin Holbraad and Morten Axel Pedersen, *The Ontological Turn: An Anthropological Exposition* (Cambridge: Cambridge University Press, 2017).

such issues will clearly shadow any really robust development of the project this volume inaugurates.

Nicholas Adams' bracing chapter belongs with McGrath's, Davies', and Bialecki's as a serious meditation on the nature of interdisciplinary relationships, though it comes at these relationships from a very different direction. We might say, in fact, that Adams builds the categories of his argument in almost ethnographic fashion, by way of close readings of particular works, rather than on the basis of a theoretical position that on its own renders the relations between things like disciplines ripe for analytic discussion. The categories he ends up relying on most heavily are ones he borrows from several of Jenkins' previous works,[27] but finds applicable to my own work and also to that of John Milbank among others. These are categories of scale: the local (that of "everyday life"), "the middle distance" (that of broader forces that impinge on the local but do not arise only out of it), and the cosmic or the "vast" (the scale that takes into account what the universe is really like). Each of these categories picks up further content as Adams' argument develops, so my glosses are just rough approximations, not suggestions of exhaustive definitions for them that Adams or anyone else should adopt. I pick up these categories of scale in the first place to point out that they might have, without too much fiddling, replaced the ethnographic, the theoretical, and the disciplinary as the ones I have used for organizing my contribution to this afterword. And in the second place, I turn to them because I want to note that Adams' concern in laying out these categories, as he tells us has been Jenkins' own in developing them, is in figuring out what the right relationship between them should be in any given theoretical, descriptive, or practical endeavor. For Jenkins, Adams suggests, the correct relationship results in a formation in which the local and middle distance figure most centrally, and where one (analyst or other kind of social actor) is careful about mixing too much of the cosmic into the encounter between them. This is the recipe, Adams and Jenkins tell us, for a kind of Anglican "pragmatism" that one suspects is a key constituent of what Percy calls the "passionate coolness" that represents Anglicanism's "ideal emotional temperature," and it is a protocol for forging relations between these scales that Adams seems to endorse. Putting my first and second observations on Adams' work together, I want to suggest that we could also use his categories and the ways different academic fields tend to coordinate relations between them to think about some of the meaningful differences between, and even perhaps the comparative strengths and weaknesses of, anthropology and theology as disciplines.

Even if I had the space to work out such a project fully here, I would not have the competence, especially when it comes to thinking about theology in

---

[27] Timothy Jenkins, *An Experiment in Providence* (London: SPCK, 2006); *The Life of Property: Family and Inheritance in Béarn, South-West France* (London: Berghahn Books, 2010).

these ways. But let me close with a few thoughts about how thinking along such lines could further contribute to the growth of a theologically engaged anthropology. One of these thoughts picks up the issue of coordinating scales between any bodies of work from the two disciplines we might choose to bring together. Efforts at such coordination, I want to suggest, are crucial when we attempt to set up dialogues around topics or problems of shared concern, a technique Bialecki, Davies, and McGrath all recommend. For example, the treatment of divine efficacy as a local-scale ethnographic issue mentioned in the last section is not likely to serve as a satisfying focus of comparison with theological discussions of this topic pitched at the cosmic level. If one were comparing cosmic concerns between the two disciplines, one might rather set divine efficacy in theology against something like culture or difference or the social constitution of human life as they figure in anthropological thought. What is crucial in setting up objects of comparative discussion in this scheme is not similarities in their concrete features, but rather those in the places they occupy within each discipline's hierarchies of concern.[28] With this in mind, we might consider McGrath's argument about narrative—a topic of enduring but only very rarely truly fundamental or cosmic interest in anthropology—to ask if narrative works on different levels in the two fields (a topic I think he comes close to opening up when he asks, in what I take to be an anthropologically inflected voice, how it is that some narratives come to be treated as sacred, an approach that makes narrative an object of study for anthropology, rather than one of its theoretical foundations). Of course, as Jenkins' argument about Anglican pragmatism reminds us, different theologies will organize the scales at which they work differently and will apportion objects to them in different ways, as will different versions of anthropology. And even if one imagines with Furani that the range of variation in this regard, at least within anthropology but perhaps within theology as well, may in practice have limits, it remains the case that this way of approaching our dialogue will not remove the challenge Howell sets us of choosing which anthropologies and which theologies to bring together. It could, however, provide one principled way of making such choices in any given case.

I will close with a second set of observations spurred by thinking about Adams' deployment of scales as a way of thinking about the comparative strengths of anthropology and theology. In his conclusion, Adams observes that anthropology has tended to be most interested in two of his three scales: the local and the middle distance. For its part, theology has also dwelled on only two of them: the middle distance and the cosmic. I find this observation suggestive, but I would not want us to take this to mean that either field has in

---

[28] This point is informed by Louis Dumont's approach to comparison, see Cecile Barraud, Daniel de Coppet, Andre Iteanu, and Raymond Jamou, *Of Relations and the Dead: Four Societies Viewed from the Angle of their Exchanges*, trans. S. J. Suffern (Oxford: Berg Publishers, 1994).

the past or should as a matter of principle ignore in the future the scale it tends explicitly to focus on least. The authors of several of these chapters quote a passage in an earlier article of mine in which I suggested that one thing anthropologists might gain from an engagement with theology is a deeper understanding of what it might mean to carry out their work in the hope that it could lead to "real change" in the lives of its readers and perhaps the societies in which they dwell.[29] Kollman takes strong issue with this claim, arguing that in "studying believers and their communities" (and presumably in studying any other group of people) anthropologists should aim only to "understand them better," not to try to learn how to contribute to any kind of change in the worlds of those for whom they write.[30] He is undoubtedly right that understanding groups of people is what anthropologists do most fluently and with the best rate of success, but anthropology has never functioned, and likely never could, without some ambitions that are a bit more cosmic in scope than this. These ambitions can change, but the space they occupy never remains empty (e.g., Robbins 2004, 2013).[31] In light of this reading of Kollman's claim through Adams' categories, I'm inclined to see the observations I make in my own chapter about how anthropologists might learn from theologians about how to train scholars in practices of judgment as precisely an attempt to use some skills theologians have developed for relating the cosmic to other scales to inform how anthropologists might become more aware of and better able to carry out their own similar attempts. But regardless of any success that specific project might have, I have my doubts about the viability of any effort to police one or other discipline away from engagement with any of the levels Adams delineates for us. On the contrary, I think the fact that all of them are significantly in play in both disciplines is one reason that the prospect of working between them holds such promise.

A THEOLOGICAL RESPONSE BY SARAH COAKLEY

Joel Robbins' insightful comments on the contents of this volume from his anthropological perspective have rightly focused primarily on the issue of how theological perspectives might best inform, and even enhance or improve, the projects of anthropologists. This is in itself controversial territory, of course, given the "secular" history of late-modern anthropology. But Robbins also

---

[29] Joel Robbins, "Anthropology and Theology: An Awkward Relationship?" *Anthropological Quarterly* 79/2 (2006): 285–94.

[30] Kollman, Chapter 5, 101.

[31] Joel Robbins, "On the Critique in Cargo and the Cargo in Critique: Towards a Comparative Anthropology of Critical Practice," in *Cargo, Cult and Culture Critique*, ed. H. Jebens (Honolulu: University of Hawaii Press, 2004), 243–59. "Beyond the Suffering Subject: Toward an Anthropology of the Good," *Journal of the Royal Anthropological Institute* 19/3 (2013): 447–62.

sagely remarks that it is unlikely that these proposed enrichments to anthropology will prosper and endure unless the conversation is "two-way"; and in these concluding remarks to this volume I hope to contribute some further thoughts on how, conversely, theology can and should be enriched by engagements with anthropology.

*   *   *

But first there is a crucial semantic issue to clear up, and it is not a simple matter. Indeed, it will take a good deal of reflection. The discerning reader may have already noticed that there is no agreed definition of "theology" in this volume, although several contributors, including the editor, have a stab at providing one. This is a potentially confusing scenario for our interchange. Unless we can generate *some* clarity in this area, there are likely to be continuing misunderstandings and tensions between the parties in these two contiguous (and, as we shall see, sometimes overlapping) fields of theology and anthropology. Not least is this the case because the semantic issue is implicitly entangled with the worrisome matter of whether "theology" is necessarily *prescriptive* or *normative*, and if so in what sense; it is often along this line that the boundary between the two disciplines is supposed to reside.

Derrick Lemons suggests in his Introduction that we may start working with a generic (Anselmian) definition of "theology" as "faith seeking understanding."[32] At first blush this appears innocuous enough as a starting point. But as this volume unfolds and other contributors add their own definitions and perspectives, we find that it comes with at least three immediate problems in its train. First, it assumes that "theology" always and everywhere *assumes* "faith," whereas the basic etymological meaning of the word ("talking about God") does not necessarily imply that: many an atheist or agnostic "talks about God" (sometimes ad nauseam!), and so engages in *some* sense in the "theological" task; and, conversely, many academic "theologians" spend their lives largely commenting on, or criticizing, what other theologians have said (in terms of coherence, philosophical or textual acuity, historical accuracy, etc.), without necessarily declaring any personal "faith" perspective at all: indeed, in some contexts of academia it is regarded as suspect or naive so to do.[33] So it is not intrinsically obvious that theology presumes faith. Secondly, the Anselmian tag tells us, *in se*, nothing about the *boundaries* of such an endeavor—that is, about its (inter)disciplinary range, scope, and varied forms of validation. Does "theology" on this definition include, for instance, philosophical analysis, historical investigation, textual exegesis, political/ecclesiological

---

[32] J. Derrick Lemons, "Introduction," 3–4.

[33] This point is rarely commented upon in academic discussion. But it should be. One might more readily call theology of this sort "theologology" ("talking about talking about God") than directly "talking about God," but it is a well-established genre of "theology" in the academy, and can thus neatly evade potential charges of "fideism."

reflection, observation of (or engagement in) worship, prayer, or ritual practice, appreciation of aesthetic religious artifacts, etc.? The wider the range of "theological" undertakings, the more it seems they may overlap, or even encompass and swallow up, those of "anthropology"; for theology is indeed a "field-encompassing" field. The third problem, however (and it is inverse to the first), is the one that most often bothers anthropologists when they rub up against theologians; and that is that the Anselmian definition, in presuming "faith" as its starting point, seemingly front-loads a particular sort of religious *normativity* which the modern anthropologist is meant to distrust and eschew. Joel Robbins has already commented at length on this problem,[34] and I shall come back to it again at the end of this short response. To anticipate my conclusions here: if "theology" assumes certain (varied) sorts of normative judgment, then anthropology undeniably does too; and depending on the version of "theology" that one is espousing, the forms of judgment—along a range of different possible options—may not *all* be as different in the two disciplines as is commonly assumed.

Perhaps then we need to try again with our definitional task, since the Anselmian approach appears to give too many hostages to fortune. It is worth briefly comparing other approaches which are found in this volume, and which precisely intersect with the three issues already raised here. Here are some examples.

Some of the contributors to this volume do indeed presume that theology's special characteristic resides in its particular forms of normative religious judgment (problem 3, above, in riposte to problem 1); but they do not agree about what the *content* or quality of such judgment will be. Timothy Jenkins sees theology as not just describing religious phenomena but as seeking to "repair" or "rectify" some element of a religious tradition: on this view the "theological" is always at the service of the critical redirection of a religious impulse or "specific form of practical life."[35] Joseph Webster's study of Plymouth Brethren makes that suggestion considerably more specific, as his subject matter dictates. He sees "theology" as a "separatist" form of what used to be called by anthropologists a "cosmology": "detachment" or "separation" are key to such theology, and are exhibited in "dogmatic" form.[36] A somewhat different focus is found in Naomi Haynes' definition of theology as "a particular kind of reflexive action, aimed at understanding who God is, *how he works in the world*, how people ought to relate to God, and what they can expect from him."[37] And this focus on "acts of God" as key to theology finds some support in *en passant* remarks made at the end of Timothy Jenkins' essay on Luhrmann too, when Jenkins comments on the importance of the

---

[34] See Joel Robbins, Chapter 13, 35, 36, 37; 240–1, and this chapter, 361.
[35] See Jenkins, Chapter 6, 119.   [36] See Joseph Webster, Chapter 18, 319.
[37] See Haynes, Chapter 15, 267, my emphasis.

"recognition of non-human agency" as precisely that which is problematic to anthropological accounts of religious practices (but usually endemic to theological ones).[38] What we learn from these scattered definitional attempts in this volume is this: if theology *is* essentially normative or prescriptive, it is not a priori obvious *in what way.* We shall come back to this issue.

A rather different approach is taken in this volume by those who assume from the outset that no *one* definition of theology is likely to catch everything that the term bespeaks: what we need, instead, is some sort of typology or range of systematic alternatives that can be brought into play (this instinct speaks to problem 2, above). This approach, though more complicated, seems inherently promising, and more likely to rise to the challenge of the diversity of views about theology's meanings already noted; yet still there are hazards.

One such, explicitly acknowledged by Brian Howell, is that typologies can often be covertly normative themselves, as indeed is the one utilized by Howell himself and taken from Hans Frei.[39] In this particular typology, five different expressions of the "theological" task are ranged along a line from being very committed to a correlation with existing secular philosophical norms, to being very committed to expressing an intra-Christian form of life with no concern for such philosophical "foundations." Even when Frei first expounded this typology, however (at a time when a particular combination of Barthianism and Wittgensteinianism had become regnant at Yale, partly under his influence, and anti-"foundationalism" was coming into vogue), Frei's own sympathies were clearly at the latter end of the alternatives outlined; and some have suggested that the types (1–3) that he disfavored were not delineated with as much depth or care as the others. "Normative" typologies such as these, therefore, are somewhat blind guides for our particular comparative purpose. Rather than adopting a framework already leaning to one theological side, we may well do better to consider some sort of "ideal typology" in a more strictly Weberian sense, with "mixed types" as additional possibilities.

A second problem that arises with the laudable attempt to provide a malleable set of definitions for "theology" is pointed out by Nicholas Adams, in conversation with others in the volume (especially Robbins and Kollman). It is not just that "theologies" may have different sorts of relationship with secular philosophy and culture (so Frei, following his own teacher Richard Niebuhr), but that their general "scope" (Adams) may be of different sorts: "local," "middle distance," or "cosmic."[40] Adams goes on to draw attention to the fact that Robbins (2006) has in the past overestimated the centrality of the "cosmic" scope for "theology," when in fact that is a comparatively rare

    [38] See Jenkins, Chapter 6, 121.
    [39] See Bryan M. Howell, Chapter 2, 29–49, citing Hans W. Frei, *Types of Christian Theology,* ed. George Hunsinger and William C. Placher (New Haven, CT: Yale University Press, 1992).
    [40] See Nicholas Adams, Chapter 10, 179–93.

phenomenon in contemporary theological work in general.[41] Thus Robbins' earlier focus on the work of John Milbank, with his sweeping genealogical vision of theology's exposure of the "social scientific" as pseudo-liberal theology in disguise,[42] neglected other forms of theological analysis from theologians whose interest focuses more on the "local" or the "middle distance." But when one gives *them* due attention, the contrasts with certain brands of anthropology seem less marked. A similar point is made by Paul Kollmann, who also chides Robbins (2006) for overemphasis on Milbank as a representative "theologian," to the effect that "theology" then seems to be merely "the written practice of elites."[43] But surely, Kollmann ripostes, *any* "reflection upon religious faith more generally" deserves the title of "theology";[44] and if so, we are again much closer to certain forms of anthropological discourse than we might have expected.

What then do we learn from these object lessons and disagreements about the nature of "theology," even within the contributions to this volume?

My own modest suggestion here is that it is fruitless to attempt a generic, essentializing definition of "theology" (beyond the bland etymological one: "talk about God"), since there are so many competing historic and contemporary accounts of what it is or should be, often fuelled by combative and political forces understood only in context. We should settle here, therefore, for an acknowledgement of a set of "family resemblance" alternatives for the meanings of "theology." But it is possible to make some schematic sense of these by weaving a typological warp and woof across the theological landscapes. On the one hand, Adams has usefully provided a set of alternatives which move one way and delineate the "scope" involved in different sorts of theological work (the warp); on the other hand, distinctions need to be made between theologies which variously represent different "genres" of expression (the woof), for instance: 1. Exegetical or homiletic accounts of the meaning of Scriptures; 2. Historic creedal definitions of faith; 3. Magisterial and authoritative directives from official ecclesial bodies; 4. "Systematic" accounts of the coherence of core beliefs; 5. Visionary or revelatory messages vouchsafed to individuals; 6. Prophetic or reformatory calls to ecclesiastical change; 7. Unofficial commentaries on local, or "implicit," religious practices; 8. Academic debates on "a-theology" *versus* rational belief in God. This list could doubtless be extended; but the point is that the different genres and intents of varying forms of "theological" discourse, both within and without "faith" and/

---

[41] Joel Robbins, "Anthropology and Theology: An Awkward Relationship?" *Anthropological Quarterly* 79/2 (2006): 285–94.

[42] John Milbank, *Theology and Social Theory: Beyond Secular Reason* (Oxford: Blackwell Publishing, 1990).

[43] See Kollmann, Chapter 5, 92; Joel Robbins, "Anthropology and Theology: An Awkward Relationship?" *Anthropological Quarterly* 79/2 (2006): 285–94.

[44] Ibid.

or ecclesiastical mandate, render any simplistic or generalized account of the relation of "theology" and "anthropology" suspicious or even void. In contrast, the warp and woof of "scope" and "genre" make the presentation of "ideal types" in theological expression particularly rich and varied. And if this is so, so much the more is it so where the delineation of "prescriptive" or "norma- tive" judgments herein are concerned. Depending on the "ideal type" of theology involved, different kinds of such assessment will be made: some from the apparently unassailable bulwarks of magisterial "faith," some from the matrix of charismatic or fundamentalist preaching, some from the philo- sophical and scientific appeals of academic debate about the existence of God, some from the linguistic expertise of textual exegetes, some from the cautious "theologologists" in academia who prefer to hide any suggestion of personal "faith," some from the critical observers of such "faith" as practiced ritually and liturgically—and so on. It would take a much longer analysis to explicate how many *different* kinds of normative "judgment" are being made in each of these cases. But it will surely be clear that they are not all of the same ilk: it is not a simple, unified matter of "faith seeking understanding." But nor is it a morass of relativism: truth (of one sort or another) is ever at stake here, and infinitely contestable. Some types of "theology," indeed, will involve observa- tion and critical assessment not very different from those applied in anthropo- logical "fieldwork," especially when the "scope" involved is what Adams calls "local." But others will go far beyond that.

But does not this same complexity—we may ask—apply too, *mutatis mutandis*, to contemporary forms of anthropology in all its diversity? Much of the interest in this volume resides in the breaking down of false disjunctions between the two disciplines of theology and anthropology, precisely to indi- cate such areas of overlap, mutual concern, and complementary interest, as well as to highlight conflicting opinions on the very "methods" of defensible anthropological endeavor. That does not mean that most theological forms of expression are not, in contrast, still engaged in somewhat different *goals* and *purposes* from most anthropological investigations. But the prospect of a clear-cut disjunction between universalizable "faith" statements ("theology"), on the one hand, and dispassionate, contextualized descriptive analyses ("anthropology"), on the other, is surely by now open to serious question. It smacks of a classic (but feigned) *modern* "binary" which Milbank, amongst others, has caused us to reconsider.

*   *   *

I have taken this amount of time and space on the problematic definitional question of what theology *is* because it has direct bearing on what I wish to say about the potential importance for contemporary theology of anthropology in its various forms. In outlining three reasons here why I see anthropology as richly significant for theology, I shall make no bones about the fact that I am already speaking from a particular normative position *within* our "scale"/ "genre" typological grid. That is, I am an exponent of "systematic theology" (one of the genres mentioned above) who gives particular attention to the "local" without neglecting the "middle distance" or the "vast"; and I do so with a special focus on certain kinds of prophetic and feminist critique of institutional theology, and with an equal insistence that "lay" (non-elite) voices and insights may be especially important for redirecting and "repairing" (Jenkins' word) contemporary theological thinking. Thus, it may be obvious by now that the degree to which one thinks anthropology is important for theology will depend vitally on where one positions oneself on the typological grid I have just outlined; and my own position represents one very specific placement on that grid.[45] What I go on to say here, then, is inevitably open to controversy and discussion.

With that crucial point clarified, now let me briefly outline three special *promises* that anthropology holds for contemporary theological thinking, as I see it.

First, the new anthropology of Christianity is capable of probing the parts of the ecclesial consciousness that its institutional leadership characteristically neglects, indeed sometimes downgrades and ignores. These include practitioners' everyday embodied practices (in personal prayer, ritual enactment, acts of charity), their often "heterodox" narratives of belief or half-belief, and their superstitions, fears, and doubts. These aspects of contemporary religiosity are particularly important within the so-called "secularized" cultures of Northern Europe, where the "sacred canopy" appears to have evaporated, yet leaving many forms of "spirituality" in its wake as unofficial replacements for more robustly institutional and creedal "faith." However, even within the realms of the "faithful" in these same climes, close attention to the views of the people in the pews is, as Martyn Percy observes in this volume, a relatively rare phenomenon in the realm of official or academic theological pronouncements. Anthropological techniques are here potentially of vital significance for the informing of clerical and academic elites about contemporary religiosity— in all its richness and strangeness. If clergy are unable even to recognize the forms of imaginative, diverse, practiced belief and "half-belief" that characterize their charges' spiritual lives, and still less that of those who hover at the edges of the life of the church (yet constantly intersect with it at moments of transition and crisis), then formal, official, or academic theology is impoverished indeed.

---

[45] What follows draws on the exposition of the new "systematic" theological method that I outline and defend in my *God, Sexuality and the Self: An Essay "On the Trinity"* (Cambridge: Cambridge University Press, 2013), esp. ch. 1. I should add that the interest in putting "contextual" anthropological investigation at the heart of this method does not, in my view, suggest any necessary drift to "relativism" or to reductive "liberal" theological conclusions. To presume that is merely to reiterate some shibboleths that this volume has been concerned to question.

But secondly, however (and even more critically for ecclesiastical reflection on controversial contemporary issues such as sexuality, gender, race, and ethnicity), anthropological investigation is in principle capable of charting the *distortions* or manipulations of doctrinal or ethical teaching which occur "in the field" under the guise of theological rectitude. It is not uncommon, that is, for a veneer of orthodox theological observance amongst the clergy to hide a "multitude of sins" in terms of behaviors, practices, and prejudices: anything from child abuse to rampant sexism and racism are in principle compatible with "high" commitments to ritual and theological observance of the most demanding sort. Who is then to chart, or expose, the paradoxicality of these combined factors? Sometimes this is left to the press, when scandal finally threatens exposure. But that is in extreme cases. More generally, it is anthropology that holds in its hands the tools of observation and *reportage* that are capable of engendering sustained reflection on the difference between "faith" professed and "faith" as lived. In the area of the "hermeneutics of suspicion," therefore, anthropology potentially offers unique assistance to the task of theological thinking for those who care about the oppressed, abused, and underrepresented.

But thirdly, and finally, anthropology is not restricted in its potential significance for theology to the task of "suspicion" here, nor even to the uncovering of the "embarrassments" of half- or heterodox belief. For in attending in detail to the "lived religion" of ordinary religious practitioners, anthropology offers to theology the possibility of unexpected *riches* of insight and wisdom for her sustained reflection. Out of the mouths of the practitioner (orthodox, heterodox, or otherwise) come perceptions from "left field" that would never be garnered simply from the classic sources of Scripture, reason, and tradition (important as all these are). Here are insights that often demand the most searing new reflection on those classic sources, since almost always they creatively entangle *with* them. In short, when doctrine and theological ethics are "earthed" in "lived religion," one has the opportunity to realign the kaleidoscope vision of "systematic" theology in ever-creative and novel ways. Anthropology may supply the means of gathering these insights; but finally it is the theologian who must "judge" what they mean and signify; for (as Jenkins puts it) "repairing" the theological tradition and going forward with it in a new context is essential to the very task of theology, considered thus "systematically."

Of necessity, then, a "systematic" theologian will be aware of the crucial moment when a specifically *theological* assessment is being brought to bear on ethnographic evidences—that is, when those evidences are deemed to tell us something specific about *God* and God's ways with humans. And that is clearly a moment that will go beyond, and be distinct from, what anthropologists set out to undertake. But the overall "judgments" of theology in various different forms on the "scale"/"genre" grid may well be of different and varied forms from these "systematic" ones, as already discussed; and some will be not too far removed from those made by anthropologists if they remain at the level of sorting and analyzing for the sake of assessing coherence and cultural significance. There will also, however, be occasional "vast" methodological judgments from theologians (Milbank's project is a notable case in point) on some forms of anthropology that are deemed problematically *reductive* from a theological perspective: that is, that they are explaining away irreducibly theological claims in some other, secular explanatory terms. It follows that the range of judgments exercised on anthropology by theologians are not themselves uniform, any more than those of anthropologists on theology are. And Robbins' hopes that anthropologists might learn from theologians in this matter may well have to be tempered by an equal insistence that the opposite could also be the case. What both sides may agree upon in the light of this volume, however, is that there is no such thing as a non-normative anthropology, any more than there is a non-normative theology: that chimera has been finally exposed.

If, as Don Seeman rightly puts it, "almost everywhere we look, divinity inhabits and helps to constitute the social world,"[46] our two disciplines are going to have to continue both to contest, and to collaborate in, any reckoning on the significance of that undeniable fact. In short, we have more business, much more business, to do with one another. This volume is just a start.

---

[46] See Seeman, Chapter 19, 337.

Bibliography

Anthropology

Ammerman, Nancy, *Baptist Battles: Social Change and Religious Conflict in the Southern Baptist Convention* (New Brunswick: Rutgers University Press, 1990).

Asad, Talal, *Genealogies of Religion: Discipline and Reasons of Power in Christianity and Islam* (Baltimore, MD: Johns Hopkins University Press, 1993).

Asad, Talal, *Formations of the Secular: Christianity, Islam, Modernity* (Palo Alto, CA: Stanford University Press, 2003).

Bender, Courtney, *The New Metaphysicals* (Chicago: University of Chicago Press, 2010).

Bialecki, Jon, *A Diagram for Fire: Miracles and Variation in an American Charismatic Movement* (Berkeley: University of California Press, 2017).

Bielo, James S., *Words upon the Word: An Ethnography of Evangelical Group Bible Study* (New York: New York University Press, 2009).

Bielo, James S., *Emerging Evangelicals: Faith, Modernity, and the Desire for Authenticity* (New York: New York University Press, 2011).

Brown, Karen McCarthy, *Mama Lola: A Vodou Priestess in Brooklyn* (Berkeley: University of California Press, 1991).

Cannell, Fenella, "The Christianity of Anthropology," *Journal of the Royal Anthropological Institute* 11/2 (2005): 335–56.

Cannell, Fenella (ed.), *The Anthropology of Christianity* (Durham, NC: Duke University Press, 2006).

Cannell, Fenella, "The Anthropology of Secularism," *Annual Review of Anthropology* 39 (October 2010): 85–100.

Coleman, Simon, *The Globalisation of Charismatic Christianity: Spreading the Gospel of Prosperity* (Cambridge: Cambridge University Press, 2000).

Douglas, Mary, *Natural Symbols* (London: Barrie & Rockliff, 1970).

Durkheim, Emile, *The Elementary Forms of the Religious Life*, trans. Joseph Ward Swain (London: George Allen and Unwin, 1915).

El-Zein, Abdul Hamid, "Beyond Ideology and Theology: The Search for the Anthropology of Islam," *Annual Review of Anthropology* 6/1 (1977): 227–54.

Elisha, Omri, *Moral Ambition: Mobilization and Social Outreach in Evangelical Megachurches* (Berkeley: University of California Press, 2011).

Engelke, Matthew, *A Problem of Presence: Beyond Scripture in an African Church* (Berkeley: University of California Press, 2007).

Evans-Pritchard, E. E., *Nuer Religion* (Oxford: Clarendon Press, 1956).

Fader, Ayala, *Mitzvah Girls: Bringing Up the Next Generation of Hasidic Jews in Brooklyn* (Princeton: Princeton University Press, 2009).

Furani, Khaled, "Is There a Postsecular?" *Journal of the American Academy of Religion* 83/1 (2015): 1–26.

Geertz, Clifford, "Religion as a Cultural System," in *The Interpretation of Cultures: Selected Essays* (New York: Basic Books, 1973), 87–125.

Handman, Courtney, *Critical Christianity: Translation and Denominational Conflict in Papua New Guinea* (Berkeley: University of California Press, 2014).

Harding, Susan F., *The Book of Jerry Falwell: Fundamentalist Language and Politics* (Princeton: Princeton University Press, 2001).

Haynes, Naomi, *Moving by the Spirit: Pentecostal Social Life on the Zambian Copperbelt* (Berkeley: University of California Press, 2017).

Hirschkind, Charles, *The Ethical Soundscape: Cassette Sermons and Islamic Counterpublics* (New York: Columbia University Press, 2009).

Howell, Brian M., *Christianity in the Local Context: Southern Baptists in the Philippines* (New York: Palgrave Macmillan, 2008).

Howell, Brian M., *Short-Term Mission: An Ethnography of Christian Travel Narrative and Experience* (Westmont, IL: InterVarsity Press, 2012).

Jackson, Michael, *Between One and One Another* (Berkeley: University of California Press, 2012).

Jenkins, Timothy, *Religion in English Everyday Life: An Ethnographic Study* (Oxford: Berghahn Books, 1999).

Jenkins, Timothy, "The Anthropology of Christianity: Situation and Critique," *Ethnos: Journal of Anthropology* 77/4 (2012): 459–76.

Keane, Webb, *Christian Moderns: Freedom and Fetish in the Mission Encounter* (Berkeley: University of California Press, 2007).

Klassen, Pamela, "Christianity as a Polemical Concept," in *A Companion to the Anthropology of Religion*, ed. Janice Boddy and Michael Lambek (New York: John Wiley & Sons, 2013).

Kollman, Paul, "Classifying African Christianities, Part One: Past, Present, and Future," *Journal of Religion in Africa* 40/1 (2010): 3–32.

Kollman, Paul, "Classifying African Christianities, Part Two: The Anthropology of Christianity and Generations of African Christians," *Journal of Religion in Africa* 40/2 (2010): 118–48.

Leach, Edmund, *Genesis as Myth* (London: Jonathan Cape, 1969).

Lienhardt, Godfrey, *Divinity and Experience: The Religion of the Dinka* (Oxford: Clarendon Press, 1961).

Lindhardt, Martin (ed.), *Pentecostalism in Africa: Presence and Impact of Pneumatic Christianity in Postcolonial Societies* (Leiden: Brill, 2015).

Luhrmann, T. M., *When God Talks Back. Understanding the American Evangelical Relationship with God* (New York: Alfred A. Knopf, 2012).

Mahmood, Saba, *Politics of Piety: The Islamic Revival and the Feminist Subject* (Princeton: Princeton University Press, 2011).

Marshall, Ruth, *Political Spiritualities: The Pentecostal Revolution in Nigeria* (Chicago: University of Chicago Press, 2009).

McIntosh, Janet, *The Edge of Islam: Power, Personhood, and Ethnoreligious Boundaries on the Kenya Coast* (Durham, NC: Duke University Press, 2009).

Mittermaier, Amira, *Dreams that Matter: Egyptian Landscapes of the Imagination* (Berkeley: University of California Press, 2010).

Needham, Rodney, *Belief, Language, and Experience* (Oxford: Basil Blackwell, 1972).

Palmié, Stephan, *The Cooking of History: How Not to Study Afro-Cuban Religion* (Chicago: University of Chicago Press, 2013).

Ramberg, Lucinda, *Given to the Goddess: South Indian Devadasis and the Sexuality of Religion* (Durham, NC: Duke University Press, 2014).

Rappaport, Roy A., *Ritual and Religion in the Making of Humanity* (New York: Cambridge University Press, 1999).

Robbins, Joel, *Becoming Sinners: Christianity and Moral Torment in a Papua New Guinea Society* (Berkeley: University of California Press, 2004).

Robbins, Joel, "Continuity Thinking and the Problem of Christian Culture: Belief, Time, and the Anthropology of Christianity," *Current Anthropology* 48/1 (2007): 5–38.

Robbins, Joel, and Naomi Haynes (eds), *The Anthropology of Christianity: Unity, Diversity, New Directions*, Special Issue of *Current Anthropology* 55/S10 (2014): S155–S366.

Roberts, Nathaniel, *To Be Cared For: The Power of Conversion and Foreignness of Belonging in an Indian Slum* (Berkeley: University of California Press, 2016).

Ruel, Malcolm, "Christians as Believers," in *Religious Organization and Religious Experience*, ed. John Davis (London: Academic Press, 1982), 9–31.

Seeman, Don, "Violence, Ethics and Divine Honor in Modern Jewish Thought," *Journal of the American Academy of Religion* 73/4 (2005): 1015–48.

Seeman, Don, "Coffee and the Moral Order: Ethiopian Jews and Pentecostals against Culture," *American Ethnologist* 42/4 (2015): 734–48.

Tambiah, Stanley J., *Magic, Science and Religion and the Scope of Rationality* (Cambridge: Cambridge University Press, 1990).

Tomlinson, Matt, *Ritual Textuality: Pattern and Motion in Performance* (New York: Oxford University Press, 2014).

Weber, Max, *The Protestant Ethic and the Spirit of Capitalism and Other Writings* (London: Penguin, 2002).

Webster, Joseph, *The Anthropology of Protestantism: Faith and Crisis among Scottish Fishermen* (New York: Palgrave Macmillan, 2013).

Theology

Adams, Nicholas, George Pattison, and Graham Ward (eds), *The Oxford Handbook of Theology and Modern European Thought* (Oxford: Oxford University Press, 2013).

Barth, Karl, *Church Dogmatics*, 31 vols (1936–77; London: T&T Clark, 2009).

Battle, Michael, *Reconciliation: The Ubuntu Theology of Desmond Tutu* (Cleveland: Pilgrim Press, 1997).

Bevans, Stephen B., *Models of Contextual Theology* (New York: Orbis Books, 1992).

Bevans, Stephen B. and Roger P. Schroeder, *Constants in Context: A Theology of Mission for Today* (New York: Orbis Books, 2004).

Bonhoeffer, Dietrich, *Letters and Papers from Prison* (1951; Minneapolis, MN: Fortress Press, 2010).

Bosch, David J., *Transforming Mission: Paradigm Shifts in Theology of Mission* (New York: Orbis Books, 1991).

Browning, Don, *A Fundamental Practical Theology: Descriptive and Strategic Proposals* (Minneapolis, MN: Fortress Press, 1991).

Bultmann, Rudolf, *Theology of the New Testament* (Waco, TX: Baylor University Press, 1951).

Clooney, Francis X., *Divine Mother, Blessed Mother: Hindu Goddesses and the Virgin Mary* (Oxford: Oxford University Press, 2005).

Clooney, Francis X., *Beyond Compare: St. Francis de Sales and Sri Vedanta Desika on Loving Surrender to God* (Washington, DC: Georgetown University Press, 2008).

Clooney, Francis X., *Comparative Theology: Deep Learning across Religious Borders* (Chichester, UK and Malden, MA: Wiley-Blackwell, 2010).

Coakley, Sarah (ed.), *Religion and the Body* (Cambridge: Cambridge University Press, 2000).

Coakley, Sarah, *God, Sexuality, and the Self* (Cambridge: Cambridge University Press, 2013).

Coleman, Monica A., *Making a Way Out of No Way: A Womanist Theology* (Minneapolis, MN: Fortress Press, 2008).

Dayton, Donald W., *Theological Roots of Pentecostalism* (Grand Rapids, MI: Francis Asbury, 1987).

Frei, Hans W., *Types of Christian Theology* (New Haven, CT: Yale University Press, 1992).

Fulkerson, Mary McClintock, *Places of Redemption: Theology for a Worldly Church* (Oxford: Oxford University Press, 2007).

Funkenstein, Amos, *Theology and the Scientific Imagination from the Middle Ages to the Seventeenth Century* (Princeton: Princeton University Press, 1986).

Grenz, Stanley and John Franke, *Beyond Foundationalism: Shaping Theology in a Postmodern Context* (Louisville, KY: Westminster John Knox Press, 2001).

Gutiérrez, Gustavo, *A Theology of Liberation: History, Politics, and Salvation*, ed. and trans. Sister Caridad Inda and John Eagleson (New York: Orbis Books, 1973).

Isasi-Diaz, Ada Maria, *En La Lucha/In the Struggle: A Hispanic Women's Liberation Theology* (New York: Orbis Books, 2004).

Kalu, Ogbu, *African Pentecostalism: An Introduction* (New York: Oxford University Press, 2008).

Kollman, Paul, "Understanding the World-Christian Turn in the History of Christianity and Theology," *Theology Today* 71/2 (2014): 164–77.

Lindbeck, George, *The Nature of Doctrine: Religion and Theology in a Postliberal Age* (Louisville, KY: Westminster John Knox Press, 1984).

Mbiti, John S., *Bible and Theology in African Christianity* (Oxford: Oxford University Press, 1986).

McFague, Sally, *The Body of God: An Ecological Theology* (Minneapolis, MN: Fortress Press, 1993).

McGrath, Alister E., *A Scientific Theology*, vol. 1: *Nature* (London: T&T Clark, 2001).

McGrath, Alister E., *A Scientific Theology*, vol. 2: *Reality* (London: T&T Clark, 2002).

McGrath, Alister E., *A Scientific Theology*, vol. 3: *Theory* (London: T&T Clark, 2003).

McGrath, Alister E., *Christian Theology: An Introduction*, 5th edn (Oxford: Wiley-Blackwell, 2011).

Migliore, Daniel L., *Faith Seeking Understanding: An Introduction to Christian Theology*, 3rd edn (Grand Rapids, MI: William B. Eerdmans, 2014).

Moltmann, Jürgen, *God in Creation: A New Theology of Creation and the Spirit of God*, The Gifford Lectures 1984–1985 (Minneapolis, MN: Fortress Press, 1993).

Newbigin, Lesslie, *The Gospel in a Pluralist Society* (Grand Rapids, MI: William B. Eerdmans, 1989).

Ngada, Ndumiso Harry, *Speaking for Ourselves: Members of African Independent Churches Report on their Pilot Study of the History and Theology of their Churches* (Braamfontein, South Africa: Institute for Contextual Theology, 1985).

Niebuhr, H. Richard, *Christ and Culture* (New York: Harper & Row, 1956).

Niebuhr, Reinhold, *Moral Man and Immoral Society: A Study in Ethics and Politics* (1932; Louisville, KY: Westminster John Knox Press, 2013).

Pannenberg, Wolfhart, *Anthropology in Theological Perspective* (Philadelphia: Westminster Press, 1985).

Pannenberg, Wolfhart, *Toward a Theology of Nature: Essays on Science and Faith* (Louisville, KY: Westminster John Knox Press, 1993).

Percy, Martyn, *Shaping the Church: The Promise of Implicit Theology* (Farnham, UK: Ashgate, 2010).

Percy, Martyn, *Engaging with Contemporary Culture: Christianity, Theology and the Concrete Church* (London: Routledge, 2016).

Pobee, John S., *Toward an African Theology* (Nashville, TN: Abingdon Press, 1979).

Reinders, Hans S., *Receiving the Gift of Friendship: Profound Disability, Theological Anthropology, and Ethics* (Grand Rapids, MI: William B. Eerdmans, 2008).

Rubenstein, Richard L., *After Auschwitz: History, Theology and Contemporary Judaism* (1966; Baltimore, MD: Johns Hopkins University Press, 1992).

Ruether, Rosemary R., *Gaia and God: An Ecofeminist Theology of Earth Healing* (New York: HarperCollins, 1992).

Ruether, Rosemary R., *Sexism and God-Talk: Toward a Feminist Theology* (Boston, MA: Beacon Press, 1993).

Schleiermacher, Friedrich, *A Brief Outline of Theology as a Field of Study*, trans. Terrence N. Tice (1811; Louisville, KY: Westminster John Knox Press, 2011).

Schmitt, Karl, *Political Theology: Four Chapters on the Concept of Sovereignty* (Cambridge, MA: MIT Press, 1985).

Stroup, George W., *The Promise of Narrative Theology: Recovering the Gospel in the Church* (Atlanta, GA: John Knox Press, 1981).

Tillich, Paul, *Dynamics of Faith* (New York: Harper & Row, 1958).

Tillich, Paul, *Theology of Culture* (Oxford: Oxford University Press, 1964).

Torrance, Thomas F., *Reality and Scientific Theology* (Eugene, OR: Wipf and Stock, 1985).

Volf, Miroslav, *Exclusion and Embrace: A Theological Exploration of Identity, Otherness, and Reconciliation* (Nashville, TN: Abingdon Press, 2010).

Williams, Delores S., "Womanist Theology: Black Women's Voices," in *The Womanist Reader*, ed. Layli Phillips (New York: Routledge, 2006).

Williams, Rowan, *On Christian Theology* (Oxford: Blackwell Publishers, 2000).

Williams, Rowan, *Anglican Identities* (Plymouth: Cowley Publications, 2003).

Yong, Amos, *The Spirit Poured Out on All Flesh: Pentecostalism and the Possibility of Global Theology* (Grand Rapids, MI: Baker Academic, 2005).

Yong, Amos, *In the Days of Caesar: Pentecostalism and Political Theology* (Grand Rapids, MI: William B. Eerdmans, 2010).

Zizioulas, John, *Being as Communion: Studies in Personhood and the Church* (Yonkers, NY: SVS Press, 1985).

Theologically Engaged Anthropology

Adams, Nicholas and Charles Elliott, "Ethnography is Dogmatics: Making Description Central to Systematic Theology," *Scottish Journal of Theology* 53/3 (2000): 339–64.

Baker, Coleman A., "Early Christian Identity Formation: From Ethnicity and Theology to Socio-Narrative Criticism," *Currents in Biblical Research* 9/2 (2011): 228–37.

Banner, Michael C., *The Ethics of Everyday Life: Moral Theology, Social Anthropology, and the Imagination of the Human* (Oxford: Oxford University Press, 2014).

Brown, Delwin, Sheila Greeve Davaney, and Kathryn Tanner (eds), *Converging on Culture: Theologians in Dialogue with Cultural Analysis and Criticism* (New York: Oxford University Press, 2001).

Burridge, Kenelm, *In the Way: A Study of Christian Missionary Endeavours* (Vancouver: UBC Press, 1991).

Coleman, Simon, "An Anthropological Apologetics," *South Atlantic Quarterly* 109/4 (2010): 791–810.

Comaroff, Jean and David Kyuman Kim, "Anthropology, Theology, Critical Pedagogy: A Conversation with Jean Comaroff and David Kyuman Kim," *Cultural Anthropology* 26/2 (2011): 158–78.

Das, Veena, "For a Folk-Theology and Theological Anthropology of Islam," *Contributions to Indian Sociology* 18/2 (1984): 293–300.

Davies, Douglas J., *Studies in Pastoral Theology and Social Anthropology*, 2nd edn (1986; Birmingham: University of Birmingham Institute for the Study of Worship and Religious Architecture, 1990).

Davies, Douglas J., *Anthropology and Theology* (Oxford: Berg Publishers, 2002).

Engelke, Matthew, "The Problem of Belief: Evans-Pritchard and Victor Turner on the Inner Life," *Anthropology Today* 18/6 (2002): 3–8.

Flueckiger, Joyce, "When the Goddess Speaks her Mind: Possession, Presence, and Narrative Theology in the Gangamma Tradition of Tirupati, South India," *International Journal of Hindu Studies* 21/2 (2017): 165–85.

Fountain, Philip, "Toward a Post-Secular Anthropology," *Australian Journal of Anthropology* 24/3 (2013): 310–28.

Fountain, Philip and Sin Wen Lau, "Anthropological Theologies: Engagements and Encounters," *Australian Journal of Anthropology* 24/3 (2013): 227–34.

Goldstone, Brian and Stanley Hauerwas, "Disciplined Seeing: Forms of Christianity and Forms of Life," *South Atlantic Quarterly* 109/4 (2010): 765–90.

Haynes, Naomi, "Standing in the Gap: Mediation in Ethnographic, Theoretical, and Methodological Perspective," *Swedish Missiological Themes* 101/3–4 (2013): 251–66.

Hiebert, Paul G., *Anthropological Insights for Missionaries* (Grand Rapids, MI: Baker Academic, 1986).

Hiebert, Paul G., *Anthropological Reflections on Missiological Issues* (Grand Rapids, MI: Baker Academic, 1994).

Hiebert, Paul G., *Transforming Worldviews: An Anthropological Understanding of How People Change* (Grand Rapids, MI: Baker Academic, 2008).

Howell, Brian M., "The Repugnant Cultural Other Speaks Back: Christian Identity as Ethnographic 'Standpoint,'" *Anthropological Theory* 7/4 (2007): 371–91.

Howell, Brian M. and Jenell Williams Paris, *Introducing Cultural Anthropology: A Christian Perspective* (Grand Rapids, MI: Baker Academic, 2010).

Kidd, Susannah L. and Rebecca Spurrier (eds), *Engaging Religious Experience: A Return to Ethnography and Theology*, Practical Matters: A Journal of Religious Practices and Practical Theology 6 (March 2013), <http://practicalmattersjournal. org/category/issue-6/>.

Larsen, Timothy, *The Slain God: Anthropologists and the Christian Faith* (Oxford: Oxford University Press, 2014).

Lemons, J. Derrick, *The Pastor as Missional Church Architect* (Ann Arbor: ProQuest Information and Learning, 2009).

Marshall, Ruth, "The Sovereignty of Miracles: Pentecostal Political Theology in Nigeria," *Constellations* 17/2 (2010): 197–223.

Martin, Lerone and Luke Whitmore (eds), *Ethnography and Theology*, Practical Matters: A Journal of Religious Practices and Practical Theology 3 (March 2010), <http://practicalmattersjournal.org/category/issue-3/>.

Meneses, Eloise, Lindy Backues, David Bronkema, Eric Flett, and Benjamin L. Hartley, "Engaging the Religiously Committed Other: Anthropologists and Theologians in Dialogue," *Current Anthropology* 55/1 (2014): 82–104.

Merz, Johannes and Sharon Merz, "Occupying the Ontological Penumbra: Towards a Postsecular and Theologically Minded Anthropology," *Religions* 8/5 (2017), <www.mdpi.com/2077-1444/8/5/80/htm>.

Milbank, John, *Theology and Social Theory: Beyond Secular Reason* (1990; Oxford: Blackwell Publishing, 2006).

Phillips, Elizabeth, "Charting the 'Ethnographic Turn': Theologians and the Study of Christian Congregations," in *Perspectives on Ecclesiology and Ethnography*, ed. Pete Ward (Grand Rapids, MI: William B. Eerdmans, 2012), 95–106.

Priest, Robert J. et al., "Missionary Positions: Christian, Modernist, Postmodernist," *Current Anthropology* 42/1 (2001): 29–68.

Robbins, Joel, "Anthropology and Theology: An Awkward Relationship?" *Anthropological Quarterly* 79/2 (2006): 285–94.

Robbins, Joel, "Afterword: Let's Keep It Awkward: Anthropology, Theology, and Otherness," *Australian Journal of Anthropology* 24/3 (2013): 329–37.

Roberts, Richard H., *Religion, Theology and the Human Sciences* (Cambridge: Cambridge University Press, 2002).

Rooms, Nigel, "Deep Listening: A Call for Missionary Anthropology," *Theology* 115/2 (2012): 88–108.

Rynkiewich, Michael, *Soul, Self, and Society: A Postmodern Anthropology for Mission in a Postcolonial World* (Eugene, OR: Wipf and Stock, 2011).

Scharen, Christian B., *Fieldwork in Theology: Exploring the Social Context of God's Work in the World* (Grand Rapids, MI: Baker Academic, 2015).

Scharen, Christian B. and Aana Marie Vigen (eds), *Ethnography as Christian Theology and Ethics* (London and New York: Continuum, 2011).

Stipe, Claude E. et al., "Anthropologists Versus Missionaries: The Influence of Presuppositions," *Current Anthropology* 21/2 (1980): 165–79.

Swinton, John and Harriett Mowat, *Practical Theology and Qualitative Research* (Suffolk, UK: SCM Press, 2006).

Tanner, Kathryn, *Theories of Culture: A New Agenda for Theology* (Minneapolis, MN: Fortress Press, 1997).

Tomlinson, Matt, "Christian Difference: A Review Essay," *Comparative Studies in Society and History* 59/3 (2017): 1–11.

Walls, Andrew F., "The Gospel as Prisoner and Liberator of Culture," in *The Missionary Movement in Christian History: Studies in the Transmission of Faith* (Maryknoll, NY: Orbis Books, 1996), 3–15.

Ward, Pete (ed.), *Perspectives on Ecclesiology and Ethnography* (Grand Rapids, MI: William B. Eerdmans, 2012).

Whitmore, Todd, "Crossing the Road: The Role of Ethnographic Fieldwork in Christian Ethics," *Journal of the Society of Christian Ethics* 27/2 (2007): 273–94.

Wigg-Stevenson, Natalie, *Ethnographic Theology: An Inquiry into the Production of Theological Knowledge* (New York: Palgrave, 2014).

Index

Milton Keynes UK
Ingram Content Group UK Ltd.
UKHW051232030823
426168UK00008B/78